Amazonian Linguistics
Studies in Lowland South American Languages

Edited by
Doris L. Payne

UNIVERSITY OF TEXAS PRESS, AUSTIN

First Edition, 1990

Requests for permission to reproduce material from this work
should be sent to Permissions, University of Texas Press, Box
7819, Austin, Texas 78713-7819.

⊗The paper used in this publication meets the minimum re-
quirements of American National Standard for Information
Sciences—Permanence of Paper for Printed Library Materials,
ANSI Z39.48-1984.

For reasons of economy and speed this volume has been printed
from camera-ready copy furnished by the editor, who assumes full
responsibility for its contents.

Library of Congress Cataloging-in-Publication Data
Amazonian linguistics : studies in lowland South American
    languages / edited by Doris L. Payne. — 1st ed.
        p.   cm. — (Texas linguistics series)
    "Selected papers from the Working Conference on Amazonian
Languages held at the University of Oregon in August 1987"—
CIP pref.
    Includes bibliographical references.
    ISBN 0-292-70414-3 (alk. paper)
    1. Indians of South America—Languages—Congresses.   2.
Indians of South America—Amazon River Valley—Languages—
Congresses.
I. Payne, Doris L., 1952–   .   II. Working Conference on
Amazonian Languages (1987 : University of Oregon)   III. Series.
PM5002.A43   1990
498—dc20   89-37601
                                                      CIP

TABLE OF CONTENTS

IV. Transitivity and Grammatical Relations

V. Morphosyntax in Its Wider Context

PREFACE

This volume contains selected papers from the Working Conference on Amazonian Languages held at the University of Oregon in August 1987. In addition to the participants represented by these papers, conferees included Ellen Basso, Neusa Carson, Colette Craig, Daniel Everett, T. Givón, Maurizio Gnerre, Allen Jensen, Harriet Klein, Laurence Krute, Yonne Leite, Eugene Loos, Marie-Claude Mattéi-Muller, Ernest Migliazza, Geoffrey Pullum, Daniele Rodrigues, Andrés Romero, and Greg Urban. The research represented in this volume, as well as other research pursued at the conference, was partially supported by the National Endowment for the Humanities (grant RX-20870-87), the National Science Foundation (grant BNS-8617854), the University of Oregon Foundation, and the Department of Linguistics at the University of Oregon. In addition, we thank the home institutions of several participants for individual support which made it possible for them to attend.

No work such as this could be accomplished without the help, if not downright altruism, of people like Betty Valentine, Judy Wilson, Richard Heinzkill and the staff of the University of Oregon Library, the staff of the South American Indian Languages Documentation project in Berkeley, Donna Fisher, Pam Gaderlund, Brett Matthews, Tanka Sunuwar, Spike Gildea, Larry Hayashi, Kathy Howard, and Audra Phillips. We thank them all sincerely — with special appreciation to Lucy Seki and Spike Gildea for good music. To Win Lehmann, director of the Linguistics Research Center, University of Texas at Austin, and Frankie Westbrook of the University of Texas Press go our sincere thanks for helping this research see the light of day.

We offer this volume to Bill, Hugo, and Nelson Carson. Bill's wife, Neusa Carson, was our friend and fellow fieldworder, dedicated to researching aspects of the Macuxi language (Carib of Brazil) and to establishing an archive for the native languages of Brazil. Neusa had planned to contribute a paper on Macuxi to this volume. Her participation in discussing the research represented here was warmly welcomed by all of us. In December 1987 Neusa died from cancer. We thank Bill, Hugo, and Nelson for sharing her with us in the weeks prior to the end of that year.

LIST OF CONTRIBUTORS

JANET BARNES, *Summer Institute of Linguistics, Colombia*

DESMOND C. DERBYSHIRE, *Summer Institute of Linguistics, Brazil*

WOLF DIETRICH, *Universtät Münster*

ROBERT A. DOOLEY, *Summer Institute of Linguistics, Brazil*

BRUNA FRANCHETTO, *Museu Nacional, Universidade Federal do Rio de Janeiro*

BEREND J. HOFF, *Rijksuniversiteit te Leiden*

CHERYL JENSEN, *Summer Institute of Linguistics, Brazil*

TERRENCE KAUFMAN, *University of Pittsburgh*

IVAN LOWE, *Summer Institute of Linguistics, Brazil*

DAVID L. PAYNE, *Summer Institute of Linguistics, Peru*

DORIS L. PAYNE, *University of Oregon*

JUDITH PAYNE, *Summer Institute of Linguistics, Peru*

THOMAS E. PAYNE, *University of Oregon*

ARYON RODRIGUES, *Universidade Estadual de Campinas*

LUCY SEKI, *Universidade Estadual de Campinas*

E. M. HELEN WEIR, *Summer Institute of Linguistics, Brazil*

MARY RUTH WISE, *Summer Institute of Linguistics, Peru*

AMAZONIAN LINGUISTICS

STUDIES IN LOWLAND SOUTH AMERICAN LANGUAGES

Introduction

Doris L. Payne

The ostensible purpose of an introduction like this is to say how significant each paper is, to let the scholarly public believe that there was some carefully-orchestrated plan as to why the following papers are here and not others. However, I now know the truth: the purpose of an introduction is to disguise the amount of cajolling that really accounts for why any papers at all happen to see a reasonable degree of polish in a reasonable amount of time. But just in case it should prove impolitic to raise such things in a public forum, I shall proceed as if there was no such stick and carrot process and instead attempt to convince you that you should, after all, bother to go further through these pages.

This volume exists for three reasons.

FIRST, this volume exists because nearly all the contributors have known the experience of spending far too much time in relative isolation, pondering the apparent idiosyncracies of some little-known language with little opportunity to read about or discuss similar problems in genetically and areally related languages. To speak from personal experience, Tom Payne and I once sat in a small Peruvian village, wondering what was transpiring with Yagua nominal and verbal morphology, why a verb-initial language should also have a number of OV features including far too many postpositions and no prepositions, and other such oddities. After some time of sitting by ourselves we gained access to manuscripts on other lowland Peruvian languages. That research material made it apparent that Yagua was not the only language in Peru which displayed these various features. For example, SOV, SVO, VSO and VOS orders are all found in different Peruvian Arawakan languages, but all additionally have a number of OV features in other aspects of their grammar. Nominal morphology similar to that found in Yagua turned up in Sabela (or Waorani, an Ecuadorian isolate), Tucanoan, Saliban, Huitotoan, Zaparoan, Cahuapanan, and to some extent Maipurean Arawakan and Harakmbet families as well — languages which are at best distantly related to each other (if at all). Intriguing morphological similarities surfaced in Zaparoan and Yaguan verbal morphology and in the forms of several nominalizers — yet few lexical correspondences have yet been demonstrated. Significant language contact increasingly raised its head as a possible explanation for the number of shared similarities. Both during our time of sitting in Peruvian villages and subsequent to that, we have not had easy access to data from nearby language families in these other countries, simply because of political boundaries and the travel costs involved. Such isolation has been a common problem to South Americanists.

The Yaguas happen to live in the northeast corner of Peru along major rivers of the region such as the Napo, Amazon, Putumayo, and Yavarí. These water highways easily connect this area with Ecuador, Colombia, and Brazil, as well as with southern Peru. Obviously, knowledge of languages from these contiguous areas is imperative in ferreting out whether the shared features are likely to be independent developments or due to language contact. If they are independent developments, what could be the pathways whereby particular word order correlations kept surfacing in this area of the world — correlations which are apparently rare or nonexistent in other areas of the world?

Shortly after our time of wondering, we discovered in 1983 that the University of Oregon was hosting a conference on noun classification, including representation of languages from Mesoamerica, Africa, Southeast Asia, China, American Sign Language, and even including various types of classification systems in Indo-European languages. However, no South American languages were represented at that conference. This absence was indicative of the fact that anthropologists and linguists generally were unaware of the extent of noun classification systems in South America, and — more tellingly — reflected the general unawareness of South Americanists themselves at that time about the elaborate noun classification systems right under their feet. A notable exception is represented by Gómez-Imbert's 1982 work on Tatuyo (Tucanoan). A few other South Americanists had previously noted the relevant morphology involved in a few languages (e.g. Peeke 1973 on Waorani; Powlison and Powlison 1958 on Yagua), but investigation of the systems — qua systems — and their areal extent remained unstudied.

As papers from the Oregon noun classification conference leaked out (Craig 1986), they shed increasing light on the fact that the nominal morphology we were contemplating formed bona fide noun classification systems on a par with Southeast Asian systems in terms of their complexity, but with certain uniquenesses of their own (Doris Payne 1987). In the process, the value of collegiate discussion etched itself forcefully on our minds as a means of intensifying not only the quantity, but also the quality of research results that South Americanists might be able to achieve.

The University of Oregon more than rectified the omission of South American languages by hosting lowland South Americanists en masse at a Working Conference on Amazonian Languages in the summer of 1987. The working conference addressed a broad range of issues in the study of lowland

South American languages, extending far beyond nominal morphology. The studies contained in this volume were improved considerably by communal discussion and constitute a significant instance of sharing new data from a few of the roughly 400 language of lowland South America.

What can we now conclude about language contact in the Amazon region? The term 'Amazonia' denotes a geographical region which includes the Guyanas, most of the Amazon basin of Brazil, and some eastern portions of Bolivia, Colombia, and Peru (Derbyshire and Pullum 1986; Meggers and Evans 1983). Current linguistic studies, including the studies in this volume, fail to suggest that there is an 'Amazonian' linguistic area in the technical sense (cf. Campbell, Kaufman and Smith-Stark 1986), as distinct from the rest of South America, or even from Mesoamerica plus South America. A search for areal features at this point should either include all of South America, or else focus on regions smaller than Amazonia proper. To take one example, in many Amazonian languages order of constituents depends (mildly to strongly) on discourse context; subject and object are usually expressed just by verb affixes or bound pronouns; there is a consequent lack of subject and object phrases in most of the clauses that occur in any kind of discourse. One might initially suppose, therefore, that 'flexible' surface order is at least a South American, if not a strictly Amazonian, feature. However, these word order characteristics are widely found THROUGHOUT the Americas including the Andes highlands and many regions of Mesoamerica and North America - not just in the Amazonian region.

Constituent order is just one issue, however. Derbyshire 1987 lists other morpho-syntactic characteristics which have been observed in a number of Amazonian languages, but which he notes need further investigation in a greater number of languages: nonfinite clauses as the dominant form of subordinate clause; absence of passive constructions; extensive use of right-dislocated constructions that modify the main clausal predication or some constituent thereof; frequent occurrence of particles that syntactically are constituents of a phrase but have discourse or evidential functions that extend beyond the phrase; absence of coordinating particles and conjunctions; heavy use of direct quotation with a corresponding lack of indirect forms; and relatively complex verbal morphology.

Two of these characteristics are dealt with in some of the papers which follow. First, Derbyshire suggested that inter-sentential coordinating particles and conjunctions which overtly signal interpropositional relations are not widely found; such relations are instead largely implicit. In a number of languages, however, we should note that postpositions on nominalized clauses serve to signal interpropositional relations. **Ivan Lowe's** culturally sensitive study shows that in Nambiquara, at least, cause and reason relations are overtly signalled. The relevant morphemes do not operate exclusively to relate clauses to each other, as some also occur on nouns. The relevant morphemes signal more than just 'cause' and 'reason' according to a Western viewpoint.

Second, Derbyshire noted the frequent occurrence of 'particles'. **Robert Dooley** shows that non-pronominal clitics or 'particles' do appear to be a widespread feature and details discourse-pragmatic factors, as well as syntactic ones, which affect their placement. **Berend Hoff** discusses the complex system of Suriname Carib non-modal particles (or non-inflecting words) and their influence on constituent order. In and of itself, however, the widespread presence of clitics and 'particles' does not constitute evidence of a linguistic area; these are found around the world and certainly in other parts of the Americas as well.

In actual fact, however, tremendous diversity is found throughout lowland South America. The morphological survey by **Doris Payne** shows that the languages in the western Amazonian region are highly polysynthetic. In contrast, language families centered towards the eastern portion of lowland South America tend towards an isolating morphological type (Tupí-Guaraní, Je, Carib). A few languages from smaller families sandwiched between the eastern and western areas are also quite highly isolating (Hupda Makú, Nadëb). Nevertheless, **Wolf Deitrich's** comparative study of Chiriguano and Guarayo (Tupí-Guaranian) makes it plain that even some of the more isolating families of lowland South America evidence a fair amount of derivational morphology. **Helen Weir's** data illustrates the strongly isolating nature of Nadëb, despite the fact that there are definite incorporation processes of a lexical nature which change grammatical relations.

The paper by **Desmond Derbyshire** and **Doris Payne** explores the types of noun classification systems throughout the entire lowland South American region. The variety of noun classification systems found and the absence of any such systems in some families — plus the fact that not-disimilar noun classification phenomena are found in North America and Mesoamerica — show that noun classification is not a mark of any coherent 'Amazonian' linguistic area.

There is also extreme diversity in systems of grammatical rrelations: nominative/accusative, stative/active, rather strongly ergative/absolutive grammatical systems, and many types of split systems, are all found (cf. Camp 1985, Urban 1985, Derbyshire 1987 inter alia). **Bruna Franchetto** discusses both case marking and verb agreement in Kuikúro (Carib of Brazil) and compares the system there with that of several other Cariban languages. Kuikúro is strongly ergative in its case marking, while many other Carib languages are not; verb agreement patterns vary subtly from one language to another. **Thomas Payne** discusses ergativity in Panare (Carib of Venezuela). Panare has a construction which at first glance is ambiguous as to whether it is an ergative or a passive. T. Payne explores its morphosyntax and discourse function and concludes that it is most insightfully regarded as a passive construction. This construction is important to Carib studies generally, as cognate morphology in other Carib languages may have different functions.

Aryon Rodrigues, Lucy Seki and **Cheryl Jensen** all address the intricate problem of grammatical relations in the Tupí-Guaraní family. These studies show that at least some Tupí-Guaraní languages are NOT primarily ergative, but instead display complex stative-active systems with different 'splits' in different subparts of the grammar. The system of grammatical relations used in any particular instance depends both on the type of syntactic construction and on a person hierarchy; the range of constructions displaying a given system varies from one language to another. Jensen provides a historical perspective, arguing that a move away from an old ergative system is proceeding in a definite direction across a number of syntactic constructions. Transitive clauses, for instance, are affected later than intransitive clauses in a move towards stative-active and eventually nominative systems.

Despite the assertion that there is no 'Amazonian' linguistic area per se, there are likely to be some subareal phenomena. In particular, there are initial indications that the WESTERN Amazon may form a linguistic area in the technical sense. Geographically this region extends along the eastern base of the Andes mountains from Bolivia up through Peru, parts of Ecuador, Colombia, and into Venezuela. However, the linguistic area should include languages whose speakers may have migrated from that region — e.g. Pirahã in Brazil. The studies by **Judith Payne** and **David Payne** are indicative of the fairly complex stress and pitch accent systems found in many of the highly polysynthetic languages of the western Amazon. The liklihood that these are areal features is indicated by the number of studies dealing with them from a variety of language families (cf. Key 1961, Levin 1985, Matteson 1965, Everett and Everett 1984a, b; several articles in Brend 1985; inter alia).

We alluded above to a particular type of western Amazonian noun classification system found in at least Yagua, Waorani, Tucanoan, Saliban, Huitotoan, Zaparoan, and Cahuapanan languages. **Janet Barnes** provides an in-depth study of both the semantics and morphosyntax of the Tuyuca (Tucanoan) system; this research provides comparative data complementing Gómez-Imbert's extensive 1982 study of Tatuyo and allowing for future investigation of the morphosyntactic variability found among these 'western Amazonian classification' systems.

The complexity of the stress/accent systems and the suffixal/nominalizing nature of noun classification morphology in the western Amazon no doubt arise at least partially from the highly polysynthetic nature of languages in the western Amazon. The morphological survey by **Doris Payne** shows that verbal morphology in the western Amazon is particularly compex. Directional, locational, and positional verbal morphemes are common. Several languages allow variable positioning of morphemes within the verb (i.e. both XY and YX orders of morphemes may occur). Both this paper and the Aguaruna paper by **David Payne** raise the possiblity of complicated morpho-semantic layers or 'planes' of morphemes.

A SECOND REASON THIS VOLUME EXISTS is because South Americanists have of late complained that "their" language area has been ignored by scholars who have attempted to develop and refine theoretical claims and uncover universals of language — of course to the sad detriment of theory construction and typological universals. Part of the reason this area has been ignored is simply the relative paucity of published works that are readily accessible to broad-scale typologists and theoreticians. There are roughly 400 languages in lowland South America. In preparation for the Working Conference on Amazonian languages we began developing a bibliographical data base covering these 400-some languages. Although this data base is not yet definitive, it provisionally indicates that there is a ratio of about 1 grammar for every 4 languages. These grammars are, of course, of widely varying comprehensiveness, theoretical perspective, and quality. There are even fewer substantive dictionaries than there are grammars. If the languages of this region were typologically and genetically homogenous, these statistics might not seem particularly sparse. However, the available published work stretches very thinly over tremendous diversity, leaving substantive areas essentially undocumented (especially for many of the smaller families of the region).

Against this backdrop, ten of the studies which follow are particularly welcome in that they present new data on twelve languages, representing seven language families: Asheninca (Maipuran Arawakan, **J. Payne**), Aguaruna (Jivaroan, **David Payne**), Tuyuca (Tucanoan, **Barnes**), Chiriguano and Guarayo (Tupí-Guaraní, **Deitrich**), Kamaiurá (Tupí-Guaraní, **Seki**), Nadëb (Maku, **Weir**), Kuikúro (Carib, **Franchetto**), Panare (Carib, **T. Payne**), Suriname Carib (**Hoff**), and Nambiquara (Nambiquaran, **Lowe**). **Rodrigues'** paper on Tupinambá (Tupí-Guaraní) presents a new analysis of previously recalcitrant data.

Although nearly all the papers in this volume are 'descriptive' (and we make no apologies for sticking to our data), some of the contributions are obviously relevant to recent developments in phonological and morphological theory construction. The pitch-accent and stress studies by **David Payne** and **Judith Payne** contribute more complex data to the development of non-linear theories of phonology than has heretofore been available. The Asheninca data also provide evidence that syllable onsets are relevant to weight considerations.

Helen Weir's study of noun and postposition incorporation in Nadëb (Maku, Brazil) not only presents fascinating data in its own right, but also shows how this bears on Mithun's (1984) and Mardirussian's (1975) proposed universals of incorporation, and convincingly shows that Mark Baker's theory of incorporation and grammatical relation changing processes should be revised (Baker 1985, 1986); some noun and postposition incorporation combinations which Baker predicts should not occur, do in fact occur in Nadëb.

A THIRD REASON THIS VOLUME EXISTS stems from the fact that lowland South American languages are too rapidly becoming extinct. For instance, there are no Zaparoan languages (Peru, Ecuador) which today have more than 150 speakers. Migliazza 1985 tells us that in the Orinoco-Amazon region there were about fifty languages a century ago; today there are only twenty-three and some of these are almost extinct. Rodrigues 1985a refers to 'the precarious conditions of survival for many languages' in Brazil, pleading for the 'intensification and speeding up of research'.

As languages and cultures disappear, the historical and language contact picture will become increasingly obscure; hence solid studies of genetic relationships and migratory patterns will become more difficult. Greenberg 1987 makes the strong claim that all languages in lowland South America (as well as the languages of Mesoamerica and most in North America) are genetically related and proposes a number of specific groupings. **Terrence Kaufman** argues strongly that Greenberg's hypotheses need to be substantiated on the basis of much more detailed study. In light of the current South American situation, detailed descriptive studies of a number of languages must be undertaken now if they are to be undertaken at all. In the meantime, Kaufman presents a conservative retrenchment of the classification situation, based on overall agreements in the classifications of Loukotka 1968, Greenberg 1987, Suárez 1974, Swadesh 1959, and on examination of the evidence in many other studies of language classification in South America. He concludes that there are 118 known genetic units in all of South America (defining South America to include everything south of Mesoamerica).

David Payne's study of forms found widely spread across a number of distinct South American families is intriguing in the face of Greenberg's hypothesis — is the widespread presence of such forms due to common genetic inheritance, or to contact? Payne argues specifically that there must be a relationship between Tupí-Guaraní and Arawakan, either via contact of early ancestor languages, or some early but now-distant genetic relationship. However, it is clear that Arawakan is typologically quite distinct from Tupí-Guaraní, while Tupí-Guaraní, Carib and Je are much more similar typologically. The latter are all more towards the isolating end of the morphological spectrum while Arawakan is highly polysynthetic; the latter lack any real noun classification systems while Arawakan has some. Carib and Tupí-Guaraní display person hierarchies with some ergativity and do not make gender distinctions, while Arawakan languages have fairly straightforward gender distinctions and are largely nominative-accusative. Some Tupí-Guaraní and Je languages have stative-active systems, while Arawakan languages are not noted for this. In fact, Rodrigues 1985b has argued that Carib, Tupí-Guaraní and Je must have a fairly close genetic relationship to each other.

Descriptive work in some of the larger language families of South America is sufficiently advanced so that aspects of historical grammar and morphology can be profitably reconstructed, eventually leading toward refinement of subclassifications. Two of the first South American studies of grammatical and morphological reconstruction are included here. **Mary Ruth Wise** examines data from twenty-six Maipuran Arawakan languages and makes tentative reconstructions of valence-changing and related affixes. She finds that there are both prefixal and suffixal cognates of certain morphemes and relates this to processes of word order change in the family. **Cheryl Jensen** presents reconstructed forms for Tupí-Guaraní pronominal cross-referencing forms and traces the diachronic changes in systems of grammatical relations that have occurred in eight subgroups of the family. She demonstrates the step-wise manner in which a move towards greater accusativity has spread across eleven morphosyntactic categories, noting that changes in intransitive constructions are generally a step ahead of changes in their transitive counterparts.

That there is still room for substantial basic research in South America is evident. We offer this volume in the hopes that it will entice others to explore at least the three issues addressed above: (1) What are the languages of South America individually like? (2) What genetic units can be established beyond what is currently known? (3) To what extent are certain apparently widespread features due to language contact, versus to genetic relationship? Finally, as an increasing number of languages are individually described, the evident diversity of morphological and syntactic phenomena even within single families will provide rich ground for study of historical grammatical change.

REFERENCES

Baker, Mark. 1985. *Incorporation. A theory of grammatical function changing.* MIT doctoral dissertation.

Baker, Mark. 1986. Incorporation and the syntax of applicative constructions. MS.

Brend, Ruth (ed.) 1985. *From phonology to discourse. (Language Data Amerindian Series 9.)* Dallas: Summer Institute of Linguistics.

Camp, Elizabeth. 1985. Split ergativity in Cavineña. *International Journal of American Linguistics* 51.38-58.

Campbell, Lyle, Terrence Kaufman, and Thomas Smith-Stark. 1986. Meso-America as a linguistic area. *Language* 62.530-570.

Craig, Colette (ed.). 1986. *Noun classes and categorization.* Amsterdam: J. Benjamins.

Derbyshire, Desmond. 1987. Morphosyntactic areal characteristics of Amazonian languages. *International Journal of American Linguistics* 53.311-326.

Derbyshire, Desmond and Geoffrey Pullum (eds.). 1986. *Handbook of Amazonian Languages, 1.* Berlin: Mouton de Gruyter.

Everett, Daniel and Keren Everett. 1984a. On the relevance of syllable onsets to stress placement. *Linguistic Inquiry* 15.705-711.

Everett, Daniel and Keren Everett. 1984b. Stress placement and syllable onsets in Pirahã. *West Coast Conference on Formal Linguistics* 3.105-117.

Gómez-Imbert, Elsa. 1982. De la forme et du sens dans la classification nominal en Tatuyo. Universite Sorbonne doctoral thesis.

Greenberg, Joseph. 1987. *Language in the Americas.* Stanford: Stanford University Press.

Key, Harold. 1961. Phonotactics of Cayuvava. *International Journal of American Linguistics* 27.143-150.

Levin, J. 1985. Generating ternary feet. University of Texas at Austin. MS.

Loukotka, Cestmir. 1968. *Classification of South American Indian languages.* (Edited by Johannes Wilbert.) Los Angeles: Latin American Center, University of California.

Mardirussian, Galut. 1975. Noun incorporation in universal grammar. *Papers from the eleventh regional meeting of the Chicago Linguistics Society*, 383-389. Chicago: University of Chicago Press.

Matteson, Esther. 1965. *The Piro (Arawakan) Language. (University of California Publications in Linguistics 42.)* Berkeley: University of California Press.

Meggers, B. J. and C. Evans. 1983. Lowland South America and the Antilles. *Ancient South Americans.* Ed. by J. D. Jennings, 287-385. San Francisco: W. H. Freeman.

Migliazza, Ernest. 1985. Languages of the Orinoco-Amazon region: current status. *South American Indian languages: retrospect and prospect.* Ed. by Harriet Klein and Louisa Stark, 17-139. Austin: University of Texas Press.

Mithun, Marianne. 1984. The evolution of noun incorporation. *Language* 60.847-894.

Payne, Doris. 1987. Noun classification in the western Amazon. *Language Sciences (special issue), Comparative linguistics of South American Indian languages.* Ed. by Mary Ritchie Key, 9.21-44.

Peeke, Catherine. 1973. *Preliminary grammar of Auca.* Norman, OK: Summer Institute of Linguistics and University of Oklahoma.

Powlison, Esther and Paul Powlison. 1958. El sistema numérico del yagua (pebano). *Tradición: Revista Peruana de Cultura* 8.69-74. Cuzco, Peru.

Rodrigues, Aryon. 1985a. The present state of the study of Brazilian Indian languages. *South American Indian languages: retrospect and prospect.* Ed. by Harriet Klein and Louisa Stark, 405-439. Austin: University of Texas Press.

Rodrigues, Aryon. 1985b. Evidence for Tupi-Carib relationships. *South American Indian languages: retrospect and prospect.* Ed. by Harriet Klein and Louisa Stark, 371-404. Austin: University of Texas Press.

Suárez, Jorge A. 1974. South American Indian languages. *Encyclopedia Brittanica Macropedia* (15th ed.) 17.105-112.

Swadesh, Maurice. 1959. *Mapas de clasificación lingüística de México y las Américas. (Cuadernos del Instituto del Historia, Serie Antropológica No. 8).* Mexico: Universidad Nacional Autonoma de México.

Urban, Greg. 1985. Ergativity and accusativity in Shokleng (Ge). *International Journal of American Linguistics* 51.164-187.

I. Historical and Comparative Studies

Language History in South America:
What We Know and How to Know More

Terrence Kaufman

WHAT THIS PAPER IS ABOUT. This paper will deal systematically with two topics: (a) what are the truly known genetic groups of languages in South America (SA), and (b) what must be done to accurately and thoroughly understand the linguistic history of South America. A further topic will be covered more superficially: (c) what proposals for connexions across known genetic groups have been made by continent-wide classifiers and how these proposals conflict and/or can be harmonized with one another. All the language families and isolates of South America will be named. A systematic set of principles for naming languages and families is proposed and used; a systematic spelling system for international usage is outlined and used. (When I cite names of families, stocks, and languages from other writers, I cite them using the spellings those writers use. I use my own spellings when I refer directly to a language or genetic group.)*

THE SCOPE OF SOUTH AMERICA. This paper treats the language families and isolates of South America, the methods of reconstructing linguistic history and the results of their application in South America. South America is defined as continental South America, lower Central America, and the Antilles: i.e., Latin America without MesoAmerica. The boundary between MesoAmerica and South America assigns Xinka [Shinka] (Sp Xinca), Chilanga, Lenka (Sp Lenca), and Jikake [Hikake] (Sp Jicaque) to MesoAmerica and Garífuna, Mískitu, Paya, Sumu, Ulwa, Kakaopera (Sp Cacaopera), Matagalpa, and Rama to South America. Pipil, Chorotega-Mange (Sp -Mangue) and Sutiaba-Maribio are MesoAmerican outliers in lower Central America. (Names of MesoAmerican languages are spelled according to the conventions adopted by various academies of indigenous Guatemalan languages and supported by presidential decree in November of 1987. The spelling conventions I use for South American languages follow in square brackets when they differ. Sp = the name is spelled this way in Spanish, when it differs from the spelling I use; AKA [also known as] = in English, the name is also/usually spelled X).

PART I

DIACHRONIC LINGUISTIC RESEARCH AND THE COMPARATIVE METHOD. I want to outline what I think is a proper set of goals for diachronic linguistic research in SA and the means for reaching those goals; I also want to provide an evaluation of work that has been done in this area up till now. I would like to stress at the outset that we should strive to carry out historical and comparative work that will stand the test of time. This is important in all aspects of linguistics. One should approach questions with a view to the long haul and try to find answers that are not dependent on ephemeral viewpoints that will almost certainly be rejected by our successors. South America has been the scene of numerous, mostly ill-starred, attempts to work out far-reaching reductions in the number of families and isolates. These attempts have largely been inopportune owing to the scarcity of reliable and useful data. It is appropriate to rehearse here what I consider to be the necessary approaches to historical linguistic research in SA, since beginners in the study of SA languages may not be familiar with historical linguistic research in other parts of the world.

My remarks in the first part of this paper are methodological rather than defining the state of the art. The 'art' of diachronic linguistics is the method, in any case: the comparative method. This method is fairly well developed at this point, and what is really needed is to apply it rather than to figure out how it could be better, or worse yet, try to short-cut it.

All historical linguistic research depends crucially on accurate and extensive documentation of languages still spoken. Consequently, the primary focus for linguistic research must remain descriptive. The descriptive materials collected must not be limited by the theoretical questions that are considered to be interesting or answerable by the investigator and his colleagues or superiors. They must be as ample as is possible given the necessity for an orderly set of procedures for data collection. Phonology should be studied before syntax, lexicon should be collected before sentences, and syntax without morphology is also sterile. Text material must be collected, and it should reflect indigenous themes, concerns, and interests. Phonology, Lexicon, Morphology, Texts, Syntax. This is the meat. The rest can come later: dialects, speech styles, men's and women's speech, language acquisition, theory testing. To repeat: we need lots of accurate and well understood data from each language.

Given the small group size and political weakness of most of the surviving Indian ethnic groups, due to the rapacity of the elements in Latin America who are determined to gobble up the resources of the area no matter what the long-term cost, most of the languages still spoken in SA will be dead in fifty years. The concerns of historical linguistic study can help to pinpoint languages that will be most useful in reconstructing the linguistic and cultural history of SA, as will be pointed out later.

The central job of comparative-historical linguistics is the identification of groups of genetically related languages, the reconstruction of their ancestors, and the tracing of the historical development of each of the member languages. This central process has several antecedent or preparatory stages and several spin-offs and subsequent applications.

To develop hypotheses of genetic relatedness, we need data that can be compared. Having developed hypotheses, they must be tested by the comparative method. The comparative method allows the reconstruction of phonological systems, lexical items and semantic fields, morphological systems and syntactic patterns. Tracing the step-wise development of daughter languages from the mother language via non-trivial common innovations and through any necessary intermediate states that are in turn the ancestors of later languages provides the evidence for a classification (an **established classification**). The normal way of presenting a classification is in a table or on a tree diagram. It is a simplified recapitulation of a model of the diversification of a family. A set of guesses made before reconstruction is carried out about how a set of languages believed to be related are to be classified is a **hypothesized** or **probabilistic classification**.

As characterized in Thomason & Kaufman 1988 (201-202):

> The Comparative Method is... a means by which a hypothesis of genetic relationship is demonstrated through the following kinds of evidence: not only (1) the establishment of phonological correspondences in words of same or related meaning, including much basic vocabulary, but also (2) the reconstruction of phonological systems, (3) the establishment of grammatical correspondences, and (4) the reconstruction of grammatical systems, to whatever extent is possible. Where more than two languages are involved, a thorough exploitation of the Comparative Method also includes (5) construction of a subgrouping model for the languages and (6) the elaboration of a diversification model.
>
> Implicit in the term 'reconstruction' is the notion of regularity in the correspondences that are posited, because it is regularity that permits the formulation of a specific set of diachronic rules for each language which will derive the phonological shapes of attested morphemes from reconstructed morphemes and attested grammatical rules from reconstructed ones. For historical phonology, of course, this is possible only under the constraint that sound change is regular unless interfered with.
>
> When one or more of points (1)-(4) cannot be attained, some doubt, ranging from minor to serious, can be cast on a hypothesis of genetic relationship....Our position is...that a hypothesis which is supported only by regular sound correspondences in basic vocabulary can be considered no more than 'promising'.

HYPOTHESIS GENERATION AND GREENBERG'S METHODS. How do we develop the hypotheses? Hypotheses abound in SA, yet individual scholars keep coming up with new ones. Joseph Greenberg (see especially Greenberg 1987) has expounded a very good method for forming hypotheses about genetic relatedness, but has included some practices and excluded some others that have the overall effect of hampering its effectiveness. Greenberg's method is to compare a sizeable amount of basic vocabulary and grammatical morphemes from all the languages of a particular part of the world, all at the same time. His method is hampered because of his unwillingness to hold back on the task until accurate and extensive data are available. His list of linguistic elements to be compared is on the order of 400 lexical items and 50 grammatical elements. Greenberg has applied his method to the languages of the New World (Greenberg 1987), and come up with a 'classification'. Greenberg uses any data at all, no matter how inaccurate or scanty. Though it is naturally impossible for him to become proficient in very many of the more than 500 living languages of the New World, he does not shrink from comparing words whose morphemic make-up he does not understand. He rejects demands that reconstruction be carried out, though the effects of borrowing, both from related and unrelated languages cannot be controlled for without performing phonological reconstruction on a set of related languages. He often includes in postulated etymologies from particular language families morphemes that specialists in those families know are not mutually cognate. He does not always recognize lexical borrowings from Spanish and Portuguese. He allows a fair amount of latitude in semantic similarity. In fact, he argues that a reasonable number of sets of items that are similar in sound and meaning — and where said similarity is not likely to be the result of borrowing, sound symbolism, or chance — are not only grounds for hypothesizing a genetic relationship, but are tantamount to a demonstration of genetic relationship. He does not want to leave any language unclassified. These limitations, along with several other flaws in Greenberg's method, make his effort at classifying the languages of the New World at best a set of hypotheses to be tested. Greenberg quite clearly does not intend to argue in detail for any of the particular genetic connexions he advances; in effect, he simply demands acceptance. In any case, the 'classification' that Greenberg offers is a **probabilistic classification.**

Greenberg compares his work to the work of the early IndoEuropeanists, claiming they established valid etymologies without establishing sound correspondences and without reconstructing; but, unlike the situation in South America, they were comparing a relatively small number of languages which were well-known and which they knew well (e.g. Greek, Latin, Sanskrit). While it is true that the majority of the etymologies proposed by the early IndoEuropeanists have turned out to be valid, there are various ways in which many of them are not valid. Some include non-cognate material, and some fail to include cognate material that was overlooked because the sound changes operating in particular cases rendered the true cognates hard to recognize. Many supposed etymologies were totally false, seemingly plausible but due to borrowing or accident. Large numbers of valid etymologies were not suspected, though our predecessors had much the same data we do (Anatolian and Tocharian excepted). The work of the IndoEuropeanists of the first half of the 19th century was good and has proved largely adequate; but it was not complete nor was it refined. In fact, only the comparative method with its central axiom of the regularity of sound change and the necessity for reconstruction was able to provide the necessary refinement. Greenberg implies that we should accept him as a scholar of the same rank as these early IndoEuropeanists, in spite of the fact that his knowledge of Spanish, Portugese, and the Amerindian languages themselves is cursory. Because he does not know these languages, the linguistic forms that he cites in his proposed etymologies are very often not correctly analyzed into their constituent morphemes.[1]

Greenberg's central idea is, however, worthwhile. With the carelessness and false claims removed, it is as follows: Compare a rather large standard set of basic vocabulary and grammatical morphemes in all the languages of a particular area in order to catalog similarities in sound and meaning and **generate hypotheses** about genetic relatedness.

GETTING THE DATA READY. Data to be used in linguistic comparisons must be accurate. It must first be analyzed phonologically so as to reveal the regular patterns of alternation in both the inflexional and derivational systems. A thorough knowledge of the phonotactic patterning of the language is required. The analysis should be as abstract as the analyst is capable of. Two tendencies in phonological analysis are subversive to the goals of historical phonology: one is the tendency to view the phonology of the language in terms of how it can be matched with the built-in orthographical prejudices of Spanish or Portuguese orthography, or how the system should be analyzed in terms of autonomous phonemes, given the presence of numerous lexical borrowings and perhaps phonetic traits and phonemic contrasts borrowed from Spanish or Portuguese. Another damaging tendency is the preference for relating the underlying forms of morphemes and lexical items only to rules that can be shown to be cognitively active with modern speakers, along with the prejudice **against** absolute neutralization and for believing that the basic shape of any morpheme will occur in at least some, even many, of its surface phonemic realizations. The job of the historical phonologist is to discover regularities and subregularities that relate not only to the current state of the language, but also to past states — states when Spanish and Portuguese were not on the scene, when orthographies were not being devised, and when different allophonic rules were in effect.

Second, unless you know the morphemic constituency of lexical items to be compared, you might compare things that are not comparable. Therefore the lexical material of the language must be completely analyzed morphologically. Not only must lexical items be stripped of inflexional affixes, but the derivational patterns of the language must be known, both the productive ones and also the patterns that are now represented in only a few lexemes each.

Third, internal reconstruction should be carried out and morphemes and lexical items rewritten accordingly. This does not mean that internally reconstructed morpheme shapes should be used **instead** of attested shapes: they should be used **alongside** them, since the effects of analogy/levelling may lead to an internal reconstruction that is historically wrong.

It is necessary to use extensive amounts of data. Lists of 200-300 items from each language are **not** adequate, except in a term-paper-level exercise. I believe that between 500 and 600 items of basic vocabulary are necessary. 700 items is about the maximum size of basic vocabulary without names of local flora, fauna, tools, and social categories. About 100 points of grammar of the type represented by affixes and particles should also be among the items compared.

Do not imagine you are doing serious comparative work if you do not conform to these principles.

APPLYING THE COMPARATIVE METHOD. Let us assume we have a hypothesis that a set of languages are related. What procedure do we follow to test the hypothesis? First, we compare the languages that seem to be more closely related. Once such languages have been chosen, the first step in the comparative method is to postulate etymologies: each potential etymology is a set of morphemes from the languages being compared that we hypothesize are descended from a single form or set of forms in the protolanguage. An etymology is a set of cognates. Morphemes are cognate because they have always been in each of the languages containing them since before their ancestor began to diversify. There is no other meaning for **cognate**. Similarities between morphemes that are due to borrowing are by definition not cognate. At least 300 potential etymologies are necessary if all of the phonological entities of the protolanguage are to be illustrated often enough for traces of them to be found in the daughter languages. In the end, knowing what the set of true etymologies is that unites a linguistic family is the **result** of applying the comparative method. You start the process with a hypothesized set of etymologies and refine them as needed.

PHONOLOGICAL RECONSTRUCTION. Phonological reconstruction is the next step. This is a complex step with three parts: (1) postulate a proto-phonemic system; (2) postulate a proto-morpheme (string) for each etymology; (3) postulate a set of diachronic phonological rules for each language that, applying essentially without exception, will derive the forms associated with the etymologies. The work of reconstruction is a combination of bookkeeping and imagination. The more experience the practitioner has, the more usefully the imagination can be applied.

Since sound change is regular unless interfered with by analogy, the cognates in a cognate set (= etymology) will show regular correspondences between the phonological elements that represent them. Regular phonological correspondences are normally recurrent throughout all the valid etymologies belonging to a particular genetic group (= language family). However, the relative frequency of particular phonemes in the protolanguage, combined with the particular diachronic phonological changes that each language has undergone, may combine to produce the effect of correspondences that are of low frequency or even non-recurrent. Thus, the requirement that sound correspondences be recurrent is a heuristic device designed to keep you from wasting your time. It has no theoretical status. The real requirement is that all the phonemes and morphemes of an etymology be accounted for.

The proto-phonemic system must be established by playing off the regular correspondences against a knowledge of what real-life phonological systems can be like, what the phonemic systems of the languages being compared are like, and what kinds of sound change are more likely than what others.

Since the diachronic phonological rules for each language did in fact occur in a particular order, the unpacking of the effects of postulated diachronic phonological rules will most naturally be statable in a particular order; however, not all diachronic changes relate to enough of the phonemes for them to produce enough effects for their absolute order to be recoverable.

Phonological reconstruction, when successful, establishes a historical connexion between the lexical components of a set of languages. However, since creoles, jargons, and mixed languages occur, the demonstration of a historical connexion in the lexicons of a set of languages is not proof of genetic relationship (Thomason & Kaufman 201-206). It is also necessary to demonstrate grammatical agreements. This is more easily done in languages that have a moderate to heavy amount of affixaton; but all languages probably have some affixes, and even what seem to be totally isolating languages probably had them in the past in such a way that their vestiges are still embedded in the lexicon. They will probably have some in the future, as well.

HOW MANY LEXICAL RECONSTRUCTIONS? In families whose member languages are known via vocabularies of between 1000 and 2000 items, and whose time depth is under 5000 years, it should be easy to find at least 500 valid etymologies that go back to the ultimate protolanguage. I have seen this to be the case in Mije-Soke [Mihe-Soke] (Sp Mixe-Zoque) (Wonderly, Nordell, mainly Kaufman: 3500 years, 500 sets), Yutonawa (AKA UtoAztecan: Sapir, Whorf, Voegelins & Hale, mainly Miller: 4500 years, 500 sets), Siuan (AKA Siouan: Dorsey, Wolff, mainly Mathews: 4000 years, 500 sets), Panoan (Shell: 500 sets), Takanan (Key, Girard: 500 sets), and Otomange (Sp Otomangue) (Swadesh, Kaufman, mainly Rensch: 6000 years, 450 sets). Where the data are more extensive, as in Mayan, more etymologies can be identified (4000 years, 800 sets).

GRAMMATICAL RECONSTRUCTION. In language families of up to three thousand years' time depth, there should be a great deal of grammatical detail wherein the languages mostly agree, and a great number of traits peculiar to that group of languages, including grammatical irregularities in closed classes of morphemes. As time depth increases, grammatical changes can have the long-term effect of changing the typological profiles of some or all the daughters of a given protolanguage, and more reliance will have to be placed on irregularities and suppletions, especially in minor morphemes. Even after 6000 or even 7000 years, however, it is reasonable to expect the possibility of reconstructing large parts of most of the grammatical subsystems of a protolanguage, **as long as it has enough descendants**.

If we can demonstrate that many of the similarities in the grammars of a set of languages are specific to that set of languages and if the facts allow the reconstruction of large chunks of grammar of the postulated ancestor, then we have proof of genetic relationship, provided that the phonologies and lexicons also show a historical connection of the type outlined above. Lack of lexical cognates in languages largely similar in grammar could also be due to creolization, jargonization, or language mixture (Thomason & Kaufman 48-50, 205).

A reconstruction allows you to recover the facts of the languages it is based on. A protolanguage can be as realistic as any attested language (or due to gaps in the family tree the reconstruction that is possible may be a highly truncated version of the real protolanguage). Just because a protolanguage is inferred, and hypothetical, does not mean that a reconstruction has a necessarily relatively lower degree of reliability than data from attested languages.

EVALUATING RECONSTRUCTIONS. How do we evaluate reconstructions? An adequate reconstruction is realistic and accounts for the data it is based on. A reconstruction that is based on more data than another is likely to be more reliable. If a reconstruction accounts for the facts of languages that were not used in formulation of the reconstruction, then the reconstruction is validated and the language in question is demonstrated to be a member of the same linguistic family.

Even though based on the best possible extant data, and even though the data is thoroughly analyzed for the purpose of comparison, a reconstruction is only as good as the data distribution it is based on. Some ancestors go back a few hundred years; other ancestors go back several thousand years. In the process of diversification a language family may branch many times at many time depths; others may branch only a few times at very remote time depths. There may be major extinctions in various segments of the language family, or there may be few such events. If there is much time depth (say 5000-7000 years) and few languages, then the reconstruction will be less ample and have more uncertainties and gaps. If there is little time depth and many languages, the reconstruction will be ample and repeatedly confirmed by additional data and additional languages. There are also cases of various types in between these extremes. In any case, every language family presents a different problem. It is not the case therefore that a reconstruction for one family, no matter how carefully the data has been analyzed and prepared, is as reliable as a reconstruction for any other family. Every case is different; it is the job of the reconstructor to make clear the nature of the hypothesized construct he is offering for examination.

RECONSTRUCTION OF CULTURE AND ENVIRONMENT. The fact that a set of languages can be shown to be genetically related entails that there was a real protolanguage, spoken by a particular group of people, in a particular region, at a particular time period. The social organization, natural environment, and cognitive systems of the protolanguage's speakers will all be reflected in the reconstructed protolanguage's lexicon (and grammatical system, to a minor degree). However, if all or most of the daughter languages are spoken by groups who have undergone a great deal of geographical displacement and sociocultural change, the traces of the homeland and ancestral culture may be faint. All feasible efforts to determine the culture and homeland of the speakers of particular protolanguages should be made.

DIVERSIFICATION MODELS AND CLASSIFICATION. The known distributions of the languages of a genetic group, combined with determination of the sources of borrowing from other languages, is very useful for determining a probable homeland for a protolanguage; this is especially true if an analysis of the reconstructed lexicon is unambiguous in pointing to a particular type of natural environment.

Even without a specific set of hypotheses about the geographical diversification of a language family, the purely linguistic evidence of phonological, morphological, syntactic, lexical, and semantic change, particularly when filtered through the test of non-trivial common innovation, will yield a stepwise model of how the language family diversified. Splits need not be binary, but they often are.

LINGUISTIC DIFFUSION AND OTHER HISTORICAL FACTORS. The comparative method and reconstruction identify a **genetic component** for each language with known relatives. Languages have other components as well: elements borrowed from other languages, often several different ones at different horizons; items produced via, or influenced by, sound symbolism, and morphemes that have been created out of nothing (though usually through lexical association and/or sound symbolism). The study of linguistic diffusion is the complement to genetic study, but the former can only be approached without ambiguity and uncertainty after genetic studies have been carried out which establish for obvious similarities what is or can be cognate; in doing so they define by exclusion what cannot be cognate and what must thus be due to other factors. The effects of language contact can be very rich and elaborate, providing detailed information about contact between non-cognate languages, as well as between cognate languages which no longer form dialect networks. The effects of linguistic diffusion in SA have not been effectively studied because gross similarities between unrelated languages have usually been taken as prima facie evidence for distant genetic relationship, rather than for language contact. There is much to be done here, once we can distinguish between similarity due to common origin and similarity due to contact.

UNCLASSIFIABLE LANGUAGES. Some languages are dead and poorly documented. Others are so distant from their nearest relatives that these latter will never be known. Though a pair or set of particular languages may have a common origin, it may not be possible to prove this in particular cases. It is pointless to waste time trying to classify unclassifiable languages. The time could be better spent on other pursuits.

THE GENETIC MODEL VS. OTHER MODELS. In their diversification, some languages may change more than others. Some languages may undergo more foreign influence than others. Nevertheless, no language can change its genetic affiliation. Creole languages have no ancestors. Mixed languages exist and have no genetic affiliation. Jargons are special vocabularies, sometimes remarkably complete, inserted into the mechanism of an entirely different language (Thomason & Kaufman 2-3, 9-12, 100-104).

As time depth becomes greater there is more uncertainty because there is less evidence. This does not mean that a model different from the genetic model is applicable.[2] The 'wave-theory' model of linguistic diversification, while partly based on the observed phenomena of dialect geography, is unintelligible without the postulate of regular linguistic change; if pushed very far it becomes absurd. Shared similarities between languages can be due to common origin, common innovation, dialect borrowing, cross-linguistic borrowing, sound symbolism, or chance. If languages share similarities due to diffusion (whether after they are no longer dialects of the same language, or whether they were never dialects of the same language), it does not follow that the languages are therefore genetically related. If languages are shown or known to be related, it will be on the basis of the comparative method.

PRIORITIES FOR DESCRIPTION. If we have been successful in establishing that a group of languages is genetically related, and have further been able to make an initial formulation of the protophonology and diachronic rules necessary to derive the daughters, then we can usually see that the daughters sort out into three types:

a. those that have changed a great deal, with sound changes yielding morph shapes whose relationships to their true cognates are often opaque;

b. those that have changed relatively little;

c. those somewhere in between.

Given that not all the languages of SA will ever be described, we should assign a higher priority to those languages we know to be conservative in sense (b) above. Of course, languages belonging to no known family, or distantly related to the remaining languages of their family, should receive higher priority. And languages in immediate danger of extinction should receive the highest priority of all. Languages that are not very different from well-known languages or that will not easily yield diachronically useful information should simply receive a low priority when it is being decided what language to work on next.

To illustrate my claim about conservative languages, the following living Indo-European languages would be on my list: Balochi, Sindhi, Romani, Icelandic, Westfalian, Greek, Sardinian, Lithuanian, and SerboCroatian. I would place the following Mayan languages on the list: Yukateko (Sp Yucateco), Tzutujil [Tsutuhil], Kekchí, Tektiteko (Sp Tectiteco), Mochó, and Wasteko (Sp Huasteco). Of Otomange (Sp Otomangue) languages I would include: Sapoteko (Sp Zapoteco), Tlapaneko (Sp Tlapaneco), Iskateko (Sp Ixcateco), Pame, and Amusgo (Sp Amuzgo). Of Yutonawa (AKA UtoAztecan) languages I would include Shoshoni, Hopi, Luisenyo, Káhita (Sp Cáhita), Wichol (Sp Huichol), and Nawa (Sp Nahua). Of Siuan (AKA Siouan) languages I would choose Dakota, Mandan, Hidatsa, and Dhégiha. The above languages are conservative: this does **not** mean, however, that one could reconstruct the protolanguage for each of these families based only on the languages listed here. The claim is rather that these are languages that **should not be done without**.

ACCESSIBLE TIME DEPTH. A temporal ceiling of 7000 to 8000 years is inherent in the methods of comparative linguistic reconstruction. We can recover genetic relationships that are that old, but probably no earlier than that. The methods possibly will be expanded, but for the moment we have to operate within that limit in drawing inferences. I have a personal preference for doing historical linguistic work that can provide a **detailed**, rather than highly fragmentary, picture of past linguistic and cultural states. I am interested in what people have said, thought, and done, and where they have been in the last 10,000 years. I think it is possible to know a good deal about this, even without a time machine.

LONG RANGE COMPARISON. Long range comparison is a notion that refers to three kinds of study: (a) it attempts to uncover likely genetic connexions between known families and/or isolates that have not already been recognized; (b) it attempts to show that hypotheses of genetic connexions between certain established groups and isolates are better than any alternate hypotheses for explaining the observed similarities; (c) it works towards demonstrating the validity of a postulated but still unproven cross-family genetic connexion by means of the comparative method. In category (a) we may put the work of Greenberg 1987. In category (b) we may put the work of Sapir (Sapir 1917) on Yana within Hoka (AKA Hokan). In category (c) I would place the work of Calvin Rensch 1976 and Kaufman 1983ms, 1988msa on Otomange (Sp Otomangue), and of Kaufman 1988msb on Hoka (AKA Hokan). Endeavors of category (c), if successful, become part of the set of demonstrated genetic relationships and can probably be fit into a time frame within the last 7000 years. As of 1920, Otomange (Sp Otomangue) was a hypothesis like that for Hoka (AKA Hokan). Now it is demonstrated. Hoka (AKA Hokan) itself could achieve that status if the comparative method is successfully applied to it. It is not obvious, but nevertheless true, that a good deal of the uncertainty about the reliability of many cross-family hypotheses is due to the lack of sustained research effort directed towards solving particular problems. Linguistic comparison has many subparts; individual scholars often do not have the time or energy (quite apart from insight and imagination) to carry out all the analytical and comparative steps for a large set of languages that are ostensibly not very closely related to one another. Hard-to-prove hypotheses will never be proved by their opponents: only their proponents can be expected to have the will to do so; if after considerable effort their case remains weak, they must acknowledge it.

I have already discussed Greenberg's method for generating hypotheses of genetic relatedness not suspected earlier. Nevertheless, category (a) long range comparison should operate within the following constraints:

A. PREPARING THE DATA:
1. Data should be accurate.
2. Data should be analyzed phonologically.
3. Data should be analyzed morphologically.
4. Outlines of the grammar of all languages should be known.
5. A standard set of at least 500 basic lexical items and 50 points of core grammar should be compared.
6. Known loans should be eliminated.
7. Items subject to sound symbolism should be tagged and eliminated unless they show sound correspondences established on other grounds.
8. When families are being compared, reconstructed forms should be used whenever possible.
9. When families are being compared, evidence that items are native to each family should be established through their occurrence in valid cognate sets for each family.

B. COMPARING THE DATA:
10. Except in languages with monosyllabic roots of shape CV, possible lexical cognates should show CVC matching.
11. Only the most pedestrian of semantic discrepancies (for lexical items) or functional discrepancies (for affixes) should be allowed in counting compared elements as possibly cognate.

12. Pan-Americanisms need not be eliminated except as evidence for sub-grouping.

13. Recurrent phonological correspondences should be found; the proposed cognate sets should be distributed in separate sets by ad hoc or empirically-based criteria, according to reliability.

14. Grammatical correspondences involving agreements in sound, function, and distribution should be found.

C. EVALUATING THE COMPARISONS:

15. Families and/or isolates must be evaluated by pairs — even if the comparison is a mass comparison.

16. If at least 50 lexical and 10 grammatical comparisons seem promising, further research may be undertaken. With less than this, further effort might well be wasted.

I would like now to focus on type (b) long range comparison: What do we need to see to convince us that genetic relationship is the only reasonable hypothesis?

17. We need to expand the set of basic items being compared and find further similarities not likely to be the result of chance, borrowing, or sound symbolism. If this added effort is not rewarded with new material, the effort is probably in vain.

18. We need to find grammatical peculiarities so unusual they could not imaginably have been borrowed or be the result of chance.

19. We need to find tentative or solid phonological correspondences that account for all of the phonemes of the languages being compared that are not known to be the result of borrowing or sound symbolism.

If 17, 18, and 19 can be successfully carried off, there is a prima facie case for genetic relationship; in the absence of successful application of the comparative method, such a case would remain unproven. All prima facie cases are subject to revision and possible rejection via a more adequate explanation for the observed similarities. A relationship demonstrated via the comparative method as defined here is subject only to clarification — never to disconfirmation.[3]

IS AMERIND REAL AND DEMONSTRABLE? Greenberg and Swadesh have said in print and in public that all the indigenous languages of the New World (except Na-Dené and Eskimo-Aleut) are genetically related to each other. Other scholars (Mary Haas, Victor Golla, myself) have opined that this may well be true, allowing for a reasonable number of languages unclassifiable for various reasons. I do not, however, think that this can be proven by the comparative method and I do not intend to try. Humans have certainly been in

the New World for a minimum of 20,000 years. It may be the case that more
than one Old World linguistic family sent colonists to the Western Hemisphere,
and at several successive time periods. It may be that the known Amerindian
languages do not descend from the speech of any of the groups that arrived as
far back as 18,000 BC. My opinion about possible genetic relationship is not
based on these considerations. My opinion is based on the extremely informal
observation that there is a good deal of similarity among American Indian
languages overall, and that the similarities I have in mind are not usually due to
borrowing. These similarities are often referred to as 'pan-Americanisms'.
The main interest inhering in pan-Americanisms is that they cannot be used as
evidence for a **special** relationship between any two New World families. I do
not believe that all the known languages of the New World, even if having a
common origin, could have a common origin as late as 10,000 years ago, given
that people began arriving in the New World at least 20,000 years ago.
Therefore, the proof of a common origin for the indigenous languages of this
hemisphere is not accessible to the comparative method as we know it. In
Greenberg 1987 there is data that appears to tend to support the hypothesis of
a common origin for the New World's languages (called 'Amerind' by
Greenberg, and defined so as to exclude Na-Dené and Eskimo-Aleut); but this
data will have to be very carefully sifted and will elicit much cursing from those
selfless individuals who undertake the task of cleaning out the Greenbergian
stables. In fact, it might be preferable to attack the problem of applying mass
comparison in the New World from scratch.

ESTIMATING TIME DEPTH: GLOTTOCHRONOLOGY. There are two ways of
estimating time depth in the branching of sets of languages known to have a
common origin: by intuition, and by glottochronology. Intuition involves
comparing the degree of diversity in question with cases where reasonably
good approximate dates are known, such as Romance, Germanic, Slavic, and
IndoAryan. Glottochronology is a method of time depth calibration that
assumes that in the basic vocabulary of a language there is a certain subset of
items that as a whole have a standard likelihood (in percentage points) of
replacement or loss over a fixed period of time. Over a period of years Morris
Swadesh established a list of 100 glosses that (a) are the names of concepts all
languages have ways of expressing lexically, and that (b) over 1000 years will
keep approximately 86% of the concepts associated with the original
morphemes or morpheme strings; in approximately 14% of cases these
concepts will change the morphemes or morpheme strings that represent them.
The calculation was based on thirteen languages having a recorded history of at
least 1000 years. In order for the method of glottochronology to be applied it
is necessary to fill out the list with the equivalents for all the languages to be
compared. The lists must be complete and the glosses supplied must be the
most commonly used everyday words for expressing the concept; furthermore,
when comparing lists from related languages it is necessary to know whether

each item compared is cognate or not. Guessing is not allowed. If the above constraints are not met, the method is not reliable. There has been considerable controversy over the method and theory of glottochronology, leading to widespread doubt as to its validity over the past 20 years. This doubt is fed by two streams of thought. The first is that many linguists believe it does not make sense that a small subset of **lexical** material should change at a constant rate and thus provide a means of calibrating time depth. They observe that (a) all the linguistic subsystems undergo change and different ones can be observed to change at different rates; (b) some languages seem to change less through time overall than others. This objection is mainly theoretical, however. Whether there is or is not a set of lexical material in every language that has a statable rate of resistance to replacement through time is an **empirical** question; theoretically based doubts are irrelevant. Theoretically-minded linguists should direct their attention to trying to explain empirical correlations, not try to deny them because they can't figure out why they should work or because they can imagine circumstances that might vitiate the method's validity. In my view our job is to determine the facts; if the facts cannot currently be explained, that job should be left to a later and wiser generation. The part of the objection that says different subsystems can change at observably different rates is countered by the proviso of glottochronology that it is applicable only at time depths of at least 500 years. The part of the objection that is based on the claim that some languages in fact do not change as rapidly as others relates to how the claims of glottochronology should be stated; this objection does not imply that glottochronology should be denied. The claims of glottochronology should be stated something like this: 'If the method is applied properly, the glotto-chronological rate of retention on the 100-word list is 86% +/- 3% over 1000 years and is applicable to 95% of all languages'. My own experience in applying glottochronology to the Mayan and Mije-Soke [Mihe-Soke] (Sp Mixe-Zoque) languages leads me to the belief that whenever external evidence for dating is plausibly associable with linguistic inferences, the calibration provided by glottochronology is impressively robust (see Justeson et al. 1985.57-62). The widespread discounting of glottochronology by linguists is almost totally a knee-jerk response typically offered by people who never tried to apply glottochronology because they were warned off before they could get their feet wet.

MISUSES OF GLOTTOCHRONOLOGY. Part of the widespread aversion to glottochronology is due to two kinds of misapplication that involve using it for something it can't do. One is the inspection of 100-word lists from large numbers of languages to see if evidence for previously unrecognized genetic connexions might be visible. This is not reliable because the only kind of re-lationship that would be visible in such a list would be so obvious that it would have already been noticed. 100 words is not enough material to look at either to see distant genetic relationships or to find evidence to prove them. It may, of course, be used for generating hypotheses which would have to be supported by the successful application of the comparative method. Another misuse of glottochronology is to use it to calibrate time depth when one merely assumes that the languages are related and counts look-alikes as cognate. A variant of this misuse is to apply glottochronology to languages known to be related but where a reliable means of distinguishing true cognates from look-alikes is not yet part of the lore of the language family. Every one of these abuses was perpetrated by Swadesh himself; this may help account for much of the bad press that glottochronology suffers from. The fact remains that when applied as it should be applied, glottochronology seems to agree remarkably well with linguistic inferences arrived at by other means, such as branching models based on shared non-trivial innovations or absolute chronology derived from dated monuments.

IMPROVEMENTS IN GLOTTOCHRONOLOGY. Glottochronology could be better than it is. It could be based on more documented cases. There are about fifty languages in the world that have (or had, in cases like Akkadian or Egyptian) recorded histories of at least 1000 years. The basic vocabulary list could be much larger, say up to 500 items. Swadesh used a 100-item list because it was easier to do calculations that way. With computers we could just as easily have a list of 237 items, or a customized list of any size, within limits. If we had a study of the lexical replacements in basic vocabulary of thirty or forty languages, for each item we could establish a rate of retention. For each two-way comparison of basic vocabulary, we could then establish a percentage of retention for the list as a whole, no matter what subset of the full list we were able to compare. Some constraints would have to apply, such as requiring that a minimum number of items be compared, and perhaps that a minimum number be taken from each of a number of subsections of the list (to be empirically determined through experimentation). I hope that an effort will be made to develop an improved glottochronology because I know it that in its current form it works (reasonably well) even though I do not have a theory that will explain why.

SAILDP, A DATABASE FOR SOUTH AMERICAN INDIAN LANGUAGES. The South American Indian Languages Documentation Project (SAILDP; under the direction of Brent Berlin, Terrence Kaufman, and Aryon Rodrigues, and headquartered in the Department of Anthropology, University of California, Berkeley) is assembling in a computerized database a standard set of lexical data for each SA language. This database includes about 800 items of universal and stable basic vocabulary and about 1000 items of regional and cultural core vocabulary. A somewhat open-ended amount of structural (phonological, morphological, syntactic) data is being collected for each language, using a 33-page list of rubrics and specific questions. The database is being compiled by reference to published and public sources and with the collaboration of scholars currently doing research in SA. This database, which will be available to all interested parties at cost, can be put to a variety of uses. The ones most relevant to the topics of this article are:

1. It will be possible to find the data for reconstructing phonology and basic vocabulary in the families of SA. To the extent that the grammatical questionnaires are completed, it will be possible to do grammatical reconstruction. For each family, languages crucial for the further development of the reconstruction can be identified for documentation in greater depth.

2. It will be possible to do a mass comparison by computer and generate hypotheses of remote genetic relationship. (Close genetic relationships have already been identified, and many — sometimes it seems like too many — proposals for remote relationship have been made as well.) When investigating hypotheses of remote genetic relationship, what will be compared are isolates and families. The **reconstructed ancestors of the families**, rather than individual descendants of the protolanguages, should enter into the comparison at the initial stages.

3. The distribution of linguistic traits can be displayed on a continent-wide scale using SAPIR (South American Prehistoric Inference Resource; a software package for mapping developed by David Miller in the Department of History at Carnegie-Mellon University), in consultation with SAILDP. Diffusion zones will then be identifiable; unsuspected correlations are expected to fall out of a systematic survey of the distribution of linguistic features (see Newsletter VI:4 of the Society for the Study of the Indigenous Languages of the Americas).

The SAILDP lexical questionnaire's basic vocabulary component was determined in 1968 by computerizing and collating the glosses on cognate sets from thirty-five comparative linguistic studies involving reconstruction around the globe. These studies contained between 200 and 800 cognate sets: the upper limit of 800 was set in order to avoid the enormous number of etymologies known from Indo-European, Uralic, Semitic, Austronesian, and Bantu. The lower limit was set so that a reasonable amount of truly basic vocabulary could be assured from these small-scale studies. The total set of distinct glosses that occurred in these 35 comparative studies was approximately 2100. The 700 items that occurred with greatest frequency — ranging between 35 and 6 times — in these 35 studies are the universal basic vocabulary of the SAILDP lexical questionnaire. These items are known to range in stability between **reasonably stable** and **extremely stable**; I am confident that this list (Kaufman 1973ms), if applied to a set of related languages, will yield more true cognates than any other list of its size. For example, in Mayan, with a time depth of about 4000 years, around 250 cognates would be found between the two most diverse languages, namely Wasteko (Sp Huasteco) and any other language; this is enough to begin serious reconstruction. Naturally, amplification by reference to more extensive sources is possible and desirable once a preliminary reconstruction has been made.

COORDINATING THE RESULTS OF DIFFERENT DIACHRONIC DISCIPLINES. I consider the purpose of diachronic linguistic research to be part of the larger goal of reconstructing the culture history of a genetic group and an area of the world.   In general, this requires coordinating the facts of linguistics, ethnography, history, archeology, and physical anthropology.

History depends on documents. These we have for South America since 1492 only. Inevitably, we use the written record for as far as it will take us.

Archeology is very thin in Lowland South America. Former living things rot, rather than dry out. What is left are pots and few other kinds of artifacts. Highland and desert SA preserve the kind of archeological remains that can be parlayed into moderately elaborate pictures of past cultural patterns. This is a relatively small part of the land surface of SA. In parts of the world where archeology can find traces of Man's artifacts sufficient to work up an elaborated picture of the mode of subsistence, technology, and art of a past culture, the correlation of archeological and diachronic linguistic data has been quite fruitful, even when rather speculative. Not much scope for this kind of correlation is present in Lowland SA.

Physical anthropology: The mutability of gene distributions is at best an imponderable, and at worst notorious. As is well-known, they do not in general correlate with obvious and low-level linguistic groupings. Their possible connexion with linguistic groupings that are too old to be demonstrated by the comparative method are simply an independent set of data which may be subject to a variety of explanations. Occasionally they may mesh nicely with linguistic **knowledge**, but their correlation with linguistic **guesswork** is to be avoided.

Cross-cultural diachronic models: The comparative method of linguistics allows us to reach back behind the domestication of plants, which is the major cultural revolution in any part of the world. Thus, linguistics offers at least as much time depth as comparative ethnography. Cultural patterns seem clearly to change more readily than linguistic ones. The distribution of cultural patterns, while due primarily to diffusion, does not readily distinguish between originally related and originally unrelated groups. Ethnography that deals with semantics and cognition as reflected in linguistic behavior is the kind of ethnography that can most readily be correlated with the diachronic linguistic study of phonology, morphology, syntax, and lexicon, and with typological and diffusional studies.

Methods of historical inference based on unproven hypotheses about linguistic relatedness and the distributions of genetic traits such as tooth shape and blood factors can tell us little in fact, and practically nothing in detail, about the history of a region unless we are willing to operate within a 'wouldn't it be neat if we could draw reliable inferences from this kind of data?' model. Enthusiasts for this kind of inference game do not realize how short is the list of solid inferences that result from it.

Thus it should be clear that while archeology, genetics, and comparative ethnology will help flesh out and provide some shading in the picture of precolumbian South American Man, it is comparative linguistic study, combined with some of the results of cross-cultural study, that will supply the bones, sinews, muscles, and mind of our reconstructed model of earlier folk and their ways in this part of the world.

PART II

THE KNOWN LANGUAGE FAMILIES, GENETIC UNITS, AND ISOLATES OF SOUTH AMERICA. The following classification was prepared in 1985 as an internal document of the SAILDP (an earlier attempt at this was made in 1966). It is based on the overall agreements in the classifications of Loukotka 1968, Greenberg 1987, Suárez 1974, and Swadesh 1959 as to what genetic groups and isolates are found in SA. It is also based on an examination of the evidence found in Loukotka as well as many other (but by no means all) studies of language classification in SA. The data of Greenberg 1987 still await careful examination, though it does not so much bear on the validity of the groups recognized here as on possible genetic connexions across them. All the languages of SA are grouped into 118 stocks, families, language complexes, language areas (see Appendix for the meaning of these two terms), and isolates; I call these **genetic units**. Of these, 70 are isolates and 48 are groups of at least two languages. Each of these latter groups contains only languages of undoubted genetic relationship (i.e., of common origin). There are certainly genetic relationships across/among many of these 118 isolates and groups. In a few cases only, some initial evidence that roughly conforms to the demands of the comparative method has been offered in support of cross-unit genetic connexions. (These will be mentioned later.) Genetic connexions across non-controversial genetic units are in general not accepted herein unless there is widespread agreement as to their validity **and** some reason for me to believe them beyond mere assertion by authorities. Such postulated connexions are referred to in the classification proper by linking numbers for genetic units with plusses (+) and labelling them GOOD, PROBABLE, PROMISING, or MAYBE. In order to devise a manageable way to list the genetic units, SA has been broken up into geolinguistic regions; cross-unit proposals have been taken account of in setting up these regions, as well as in the ordering of genetic units within them, and in the external ordering of the geolinguistic regions with respect to one another. I have tried, to the extent possible, to make sense of and harmonize the classifications referred to above. When different classification schemes are in disagreement, where Swadesh gives a glottochronological figure under 50mc (22%) I tend to prefer Swadesh; where Greenberg has a lower case letter under an Arabic numeral, e.g. 1e, I tend to prefer Greenberg. When these criteria are not met, geography prevails; that is, a genetic group is listed under the geolinguistic area within which it falls, but after all clusterings that are supported by either Greenberg or Swadesh as qualified above. Note that Swadesh and Greenberg's groupings are used not for making the classification but for ordering the genetic units with respect to each other. This is in order to place near each other in the list entities that may later be shown to be genetically related. The internal classification of genetic groups containing more than two languages is not given in the current listing, although reference will be made to the number of languages, amount of internal diversification, and glottochronological time depth as calculated by Swadesh in his quick and dirty way. In fact, for most of the genetic groups a reliable classification is not yet possible because reconstruction and the tracing of common innovations has not yet been carried out.

Abbreviations used to refer to earlier classifications of the languages of SA are: Gr = Greenberg 1956 (1960), 1987; Sw = Swadesh 1959; L = Loukotka 1968; JS = Suárez 1974; AT = Tovar and Tovar 1984 [not a classification]; AR = Rodrigues 1986 [Brazil only]. Language **family** names are spelled with accents in the main listing of genetic groups; elsewhere they are spelled without accents. **Language** and **language area** names, however, are always spelled with accents, as needed.

GEOLINGUISTIC REGIONS OF SOUTH AMERICA. I have sought a way to list the stocks, families, language complexes, language areas, and isolates of SA in manageable chunks. I have tried to establish linguistic regions for SA based on genetic linguistic, typological linguistic, cultural, and geographical features. SA has been divided into twelve **geolinguistic regions**; these are zones showing a high degree of geographical and cultural-ecological coherence wherein, in general, languages of one of the larger SA families predominate. Some of these regions, however, do not contain one of the larger SA families, e.g., Northern Foothills, The Cone, the Andes, or Northeast Brazil. The closest thing to a large family in the Chaco is Waikuruan (8 languages).

CHARACTERIZATION OF THE GEOLINGUISTIC REGIONS

I. NORTHWEST (a) contains the Chibchan stock and all languages of this part of SA generally believed to be related to Chibchan; (b) it also contains the remaining languages of the region defined by (a): Yurimangi, Timotean, Hiraharan, and Chokó; (c) and it contains Ezmeralda, an outlier from Northern Foothills. Note that this region includes all of lower Central America.

AMAZONIA. Amazonia is the home of three large stocks (Arawakan, Kariban, and Tupian) and of one mid-sized one (Tukanoan). Amazonia can be defined as the outlined area that contains any language of the above families, apart from obvious outliers. A large number of other languages and small groupings are found in Amazonia. The eastern slopes of the Andes, which are called *montaña* in Spanish, are here called FOOTHILLS; these are excluded from Amazonia.

Three of Greenberg's SA phyla account for most of Amazonia and are largely limited to Amazonia, though they have outliers: macro-Cariban (including my Kariban), Equatorial (including my Arawakan and Tupian), and macro-Tucanoan (including my Tukanoan). Amazonia is hard to break down into smaller geolinguistic regions for two reasons: (a) the linguistic families of Amazonia are to a significant exent interspersed (although basic divisions are clear: Kariban north of the Amazon, Tukanoan westerly along the Amazon, Tupian south of the Amazon in Eastern/Central Amazonia, Arawakan in Western Amazonia); (b) except for Greenberg, most classifiers of SA languages have not assigned the languages of Amazonia to a small number of genetic groups; thus, there is no concensus to refer to: if we want to break Amazonia down we may use Greenberg as a starting point, or do nothing at all. I have divided the languages of Amazonia into four batches:

1. Arawakan and its postulated relatives: **Western Amazonia I** (WA I);
2. Tukanoan and its postulated relatives in Western Amazonia: **Western Amazonia II** (WA II);
3. Tupian south of the Amazon and other languages of the region so defined: **Central Amazonia;**
4. Kariban north of the Amazon and other languages of the region so defined: **Northern Amazonia.**

Thus, for example, Northern Amazonia includes the area where the Kariban languages constitute a solid block; any unaffiliated languages that fall within the zone so defined are listed in that zone. The same is true respectively of the other zones. In this classification the two Western Amazonia regions are listed together, and the Central and Northern Amazonia regions are listed together, but elsewhere. Thus, Amazonia as a whole is not ordered as a solid block, even though the external ordering of geolinguistic groups is basically geographical. This is because proposed genetic connexions across geolinguistic groups are more straightforwardly displayed using the order employed here.

II. WESTERN AMAZONIA I contains (a) the Arawakan stock and languages generally believed to be related to it; Chapakuran is one of these latter found as an 'outlier' in Central Amazonia; (b) the other languages of Greenberg's macro-Arawakan, except Katembrí; (c) Jaruro, an outlier from Northern Foothills; and (d) several Panoan subgroups, outliers from Southern Foothills. Western Amazonia I consists of two discontinuous zones, a smaller northern one, and a larger southern one.

III. WESTERN AMAZONIA II contains (a) the Puinavean stock and other languages not in the spheres of Tupian and Kariban; and (b) the other languages of Greenberg's macro-Tucanoan that are not in the spheres of Tupian or Kariban.

IV. NORTHERN FOOTHILLS (a) contains Hívaro and all languages of the Northern Montaña believed by Greenberg, Swadesh, or Suárez to be related to Hívaro. Jaruro (found in WA I) is listed here because it seems to form a family with Ezmeralda (found in NW). (b) It also contains Witotoan and all languages of the Northern Montaña believed by Greenberg or Swadesh to be related to Witotoan. These languages are probably too closely related to be considered as constituting a superstock.

V. SOUTHERN FOOTHILLS contains the Pano-Takana stock and other languages of the Bolivian Montaña considered by Greenberg or Suárez to be related to it. Chon is an 'outlier' of this extended grouping found in the Cone. Southern Foothills consists of two discontinuous areas, a southern one, and a northern one. The northern one is a solid block of Panoan languages in WA I territory.

VII. THE CONE contains Mapudungu and all other languages of the region considered by either Greenberg or Suárez to be related to it.

VIII. THE CHACO contains (a) Waikuruan and all other languages of the region classified with it by Greenberg (2A-D); and (b) the remaining languages of the region defined by (a): Samukoan and Gorgotoki.

IX. EASTERN BRAZIL contains (a) the Je stock and all the languages considered by Greenberg, Suárez, or Rodrigues to be related to it; (b) the other languages of the region classified by Greenberg in his macro-Ge; one of Greenberg's macro-Ge families, Jabutian, is found (and listed) in Central Amazonia; and (c) Kukurá, which Greenberg classifies in his macro-Cariban.

X. NORTHEASTERN BRAZIL is a region containing 'outliers' of Greenberg's Equatorial and macro-Tucanoan phyla. Generally speaking, other scholars have not proposed genetic relationships either among these languages or with languages elsewhere in SA. All these languages seem to be dead. A few of them are reasonably well documented.

XI. CENTRAL AMAZONIA contains (a) languages of the Tupian stock spoken south of the Amazon outside the Chaco, the Southern Foothills, and Eastern Brazil; (b) other languages of the area defined by (a) that belong to Greenberg's Equatorial Phylum; (c) other languages of the area defined by (a) that belong to Greenberg's macro-Tucanoan Phylum; (d) other languages of the area defined by (a) that are widely considered to be related to Chibchan; this includes Kunsa, which appears to be related to Kapishaná; (e) Jabutian, which Greenberg assigns to macro-Ge; (f) Chapakuran, widely thought to be related to Arawakan; and (g) Rikbaktsá, considered to be related to Je.

XII. NORTHERN AMAZONIA contains (a) those Kariban languages found to the north of the Amazon ouside the Northwest region; (b) languages thought to be related to Puinavean lying outside WA II; these are classified by Greenberg within his Macro-Tucanoan; (c) other languages of the region defined by (a) belonging to Greenberg's Equatorial Phylum; (d) the Yanomaman family and Warao, both widely thought to be related to Chibchan; and (e) Hotí, a recently discovered and as yet unclassified language.

INVASION ZONES (or SUMPS). There are five regions in SA that are occupied almost entirely by languages whose closest relatives are concentrated elsewhere. These are:

I. The mouth of the Amazon, where both Maipurean (Palikur, Aruã) and Tupian (Wayampí) languages are found far from home.

II. The Upper Xingú, where along with unaffiliated Trumai are found Kariban (Bakairí group), Maipurean (Paresí), 'macro-Je' (Rikbaktsá), and Tupian (Awetí, Kamayurá) languages. The latter two are not all that far from home, but they are disjunct with respect to their congeners.

III. The Upper Amazon, where Tupian (Kokama, Omawa) and one Maipurean (Morike) language find themselves far from home.

IV. The Paraná valley, where Tupian (Tupí-Guaraní, Guajakí) and Maipurean (Terena) languages find themselves far from home.

V. The Northwest Chaco, occupied by Chiriguano, a Tupí-Guaraní language.

It is well understood that Eastern Brazil had been invaded by speakers of Tupí not long before the beginning of the historical period. Eastern Brazil does not constitute an invasion zone in the above sense. There are a few Kariban outliers in the Northwest. This is not necessarily an invasion zone, either.

NOMENCLATURE

NAMES FOR FAMILIES. All family and stock names, except those that refer to the group only and none of its constituent members (such as Je or Chon), and also excepting those family or stock names made by combining two names such as Pano-Takana, contain the suffix -an; this conforms with the usage of linguists writing in English. It is considered unnecessary to append -an to names formed by combining two or more names. The systematic application of the principles referred to will inevitably produce some deviation from 'standard usage', if such exists. In SA usage is in flux; virtually all of my specific choices have already been favored by one or more previous writer. In Spanish also, the suffix -ano, -ana is used to form language family names. This has been the case at least in Mexico since at least the turn of the century (athough it has not been customary in the Spanish-speaking world generally). The Mexican practice should be emulated in the interest of explicitness. I have devised Spanish names for the genetic groups recognized in this classification.[4]

LANGUAGE NAMES. The native name (autonym) is preferred when available exonyms (names used in a local colonial language) are (a) not standardized in vernacular usage; (b) pejorative; (c) ambiguous; (d) items of Spanish or Portuguese lexicon; or (e) obsolete in current usage. Otherwise an established exonym is preferred.

SPELLING OF NAMES. A single orthographical system has been used for the spelling of all names and a single spelling has been adopted for each name. This system must be able to represent the sounds of both Spanish and Portuguese and does not fully follow the principles of either.[5] Each symbol and digraph has only one value. The symbols in this system (hereafter known as TKSA) have the values assigned by the IPA or Americanist phonetic tradition unless otherwise noted. The symbols **p t m n l r i u a y** are pronounced as in Spanish and Portuguese. The following equivalences and principles of pronunciation hold:

TKSA	Spanish	Portuguese	Brazilian Indianist	English
sh [š]	sh	x,ch	x	sh
ch [č]	ch	tx	tx	ch
j [ž]	>y	j	j	zh
y	y,i	i	y	y
v	b,v	v	v	v
b	b,v	b	b	b
h	j,h	rr,h	h	h,kh
s	s,z/c	s(s),ç	s	s
w	gu/gü,hu	u	w	w
ly	ll	lh	lh	ly
ny	ñ	nh	nh	ny
k	c/qu	c/qu	k	k
g	g/gu	g/gu	g	g
CuV [CwV]	CuV	CuV	CwV,CuV	CwV
CiV [CyV]	CiV	CiV	CyV,CiV	CyV
Ṽ#	Vn	Ṽ,Vm	Ṽ	Vn
e	e	é,ê	é	e
o	o	ó,ô	ó	o

NON-EUROPEAN SOUNDS

TKSA	Spanish	Portuguese	Brazilian Indianist	International
q				[q]
lh				'barred l'
ü				'barred i'
ö				'schwa'
'				'glottal stop'

STRESS RULE. Stress any vowel marked with an accent. Otherwise, stress the vowel preceding the rightmost consonant of the word, unless that consonant is word-final <n> or <s>. Any VV# cluster where the second member is a high or mid vowel counts as VC#.

THE CLASSIFICATION. The classification given here is meant to be radically **conservative**. Every genetic group recognized here is either obvious on inspection or has been demonstrated by standard procedures. This classification can be simplified by the merging of separately numbered groups once cross-group genetic connexions are established by the comparative method. The numbers left unused will remain idle until a totally new classification is put together about twenty years down the line. If any new genetic groups, including unclassified individual languages, need to be added to the list, they will be assigned numbers from 119 on. It is conceivable that several new languages will be discovered over the next twenty years. It is believed that there is little likelihood that any of the groups recognized here will be broken apart. Having sifted the data, I feel obliged to point out and stress that Loukotka's 1968 classification is practically error-free as far as genetic groups are concerned. The mistakes in Loukotka are easily summarized. He includes names of languages for which no data exists; these can simply be disregarded, since he tells us when there is no data. An occasional language has been assigned to the wrong genetic group, but these instances are few. The subgrouping claimed for the recognized groups is often faulty; since subgrouping must depend on reconstruction, we can disregard those mistakes and simply forgo the explicit subgrouping. There are two glaring instances of groupings that are simply not supported by the facts as we know them: following Rivet, Loukotka includes in Chibchan [8] the following genetic

groups which are related to Chibchan at the phylum level (see Appendix for
definition), if at all: Ezmeralda [27], Jaruro [28], Paesan [6], Barbakoan [7],
Betoi [5], and Kamsá [10]. He also includes Wahivoan [15] within Arawakan
[16], though this postulated relationship has never been demonstrated.
(Numbers in square brackets are the ones used in my classification).

KINDS OF INFORMATION GIVEN. Each entry in the following classification
contains the following informations:

Spanish and Portuguese versions of the names

glottochronological time depth as estimated in Swadesh 1959

number of languages in the group

number of living languages in the group (or 'all dead')

where spoken

other names used for the group or language [not exhaustive]

[population figures and coordinates are not given]

Loukotka's group number [L]

Greenberg's group number [Gr]

Sáurez's group number [JS]

Swadesh's group number [Sw]

location in Tovar [AT]

affiliation given by Migliazza 1980ms [EM]

Portuguese names for isolates and families follow the spellings found in Rodrigues 1986. Spanish names for isolates and families follow the spellings
found in Tovar 1984 except where there are known errors, and except for the
fact that every family name is formed by combining two or three names or ends
in -ano, -ana.

ABBREVIATIONS FOR NAMES OF COUNTRIES AND GEOLINGUISTIC AREAS.
The following abbreviations are used in the classification: AMA Amazonia,
ARG Argentina, BEL Belize = British Honduras, BOL Bolivia, BRA Brazil,
CHI Chile, COL Colombia, CR Costa Rica, CUB Cuba, DOM Dominica, ECU
Ecuador, EBr Eastern Brazil, ES El Salvador, FLO Florida, FG French Guiana,
GA Greater Antilles, GUA Guatemala, GUY Guyana = British Guiana, HON
Honduras, LA Lesser Antilles, MEX Mexico, MG Mato Grosso, NIC
Nicaragua, NEBr Northeast Brazil, PAR Paraguay, PAT Patagonia, PER Peru,
PR Puerto Rico, SD Santo Domingo = Dominican Republic + Haiti, SUR
Surinam = Dutch Guiana, SBr Southern Brazil, URU Uruguay, VEN
Venezuela.

I. NORTHWESTERN REGION

1. **Yurimangi language <Sp Yurimangui>.** dead. COL. L-99; Gr-IC5 [Hokan!]; JS-80; Sw-2.5 [macro-Zamuco]. AT 22.4.

2. **Timótean family <Sp Timoteano, familia Timoteana>.** 15mc. 2 lgs, both dead. VEN. L-95; Gr-VB8 [Equatorial]; JS-80; Sw-C5. AT 19.14.

3. **Hiraháran family <Jirajarano, familia Jirajarana>.** 19mc. 3 lgs, all dead. VEN. L-96; Gr-IIIB6 [Paezan]; JS-66; Sw-S6.6 [macro-Caribe]. AT 19.5. EM unclassified.

4. **Chokó language area <Sp Chocó>.** 7mc. 5 lgs, 2 dead. PAN, COL. L-97; Gr-IIIB8c [Paezan:Nuclear Paezan]; JS-12B [with Kariban]; Sw-SE10 [macro-Leco: with Sechura and Leko]. AT 18.4. EM: ?macro-Chibchan 17.

5. **Betoi language.** dead. COL. L-94k [Chibchan]; Gr-IIIB3 [Paezan]; JS-41A5 [macro-Chibchan]; no Sw. AT 21.5. EM: macro-Chibchan 15.

6. **Páesan (sub)stock <Sp (subtronco) Paezano>.** 54mc. 7 lgs, 5 dead. COL. L-94n,o,p [Chibchan]; Gr-IIIB8a,d [Paezan:Nuclear Paezan]; JS-41A2,11,15 [macro-Chibchan]; Sw-W11.1 [macro-Páez]. Andakí is to be included in Paesan. AT 21.3-21.4. EM: macro-Chibchan 10-11,16.

7. **Barbakóan family <Sp Barbacoano, familia Barbacoana>.** 33mc. 6 lgs, 3 dead. COL,ECU. L-94q [Chibchan]; Gr-IIIB8b [Paezan:Nuclear Paezan]; JS-41A6 [macro-Chibchan]; Sw-W11.2 [macro-Páez]. AT 21.2. EM: macro-Chibchan 13.

6+7. **Páes-Barbakóa stock <Sp tronco Páez-Barbacoa>.** ??mc. = GOOD Gr-IIIB8a,b,d. There is universal agreement that these two families form a larger grouping. There are clear lexical similarities.

8. **Chíbchan (sub)stock <Sp (subtronco) Chibchano>.** 56mc. 24 lgs, 6 dead. HON, NIC, CR, PAN, COL, VEN. L-94b,c,e,f,g,(h,)i,j,l,m,u [Chibchan]; Gr-IIIA3-4 [Chibchan:Nuclear Chibchan+Paya]; JS-41A1,3,4,8,9,10,12,13,14,16 [macro-Chibchan]; Sw-C3.4-3.6 [macro-Chibcha]. Paya is a Chibchan lg. AT 21.1; 21.6.2-21.6.5; 23.4. This is a large stock, with a considerable amount of branching. EM: macro-Chibchan 1-5,7-9,14.

9. **Misumalpa family <(familia) Misumalpa>.** 43mc. 4 lgs, 2 dead. ES, HON, NIC. L-94s,t [Chibchan]; Gr-IIIA3g [Chibchan: Nuclear Chibchan]; JS-41E [macro-Chibchan]; Sw-C3.1-3.3 [macro-Chibcha]. AT 23.5-23.7. EM: ?macro-Chibchan 19.

8+9. **Chibcha-Misumalpa stock <Sp (tronco) Chibcha-Misumalpa>.** GOOD ??mc. = Gr-IIIA3-4. There is general agreement that these two groups are genetically related. Holt has assembled some evidence for this.

10. **Kamsá language** <Sp Camsá>. COL. L-94r [Chibchan]; Gr-VB3 [Equatorial]; JS-41A17 [macro-Chibchan]; Sw-E6. SYN Koche [Gr].AT 22.7. EM: macro-Chibchan 6.

II. WESTERN AMAZONIA I

11. **Tiníwan family** <Sp Tiniguano, familia Tiniguana>. 23mc. 2 lgs, both dead. COL. L-51; Gr-VB1d [Equatorial:macro-Arawakan]; JS-67; Sw-E5. AT 22.11.

12. **Otomákoan family** <Sp Otomacoano, familia Otomacoana>. 16mc. 2 lgs, both dead. VEN. L-47; Gr-VB1c [Equatorial:macro-Arawakan]; JS-54; Sw-S8 [macro-Mac]. AT 19.7.

13. **Wamo language** <Sp Guamo>. dead. VEN. L-48; Gr-VB1e(4) [Equatorial:macro-Arawakan:Arawakan]; JS-28; Sw-S7 [macro-Caribe]. AT 19.8. EM: ?macro-Arawakan.

14. **Chapakúran family** <Sp Chapacurano, familia Chapacurana; Pg família Txapakúra>. 37mc. 8 lgs, 5 dead. BRA, BOL. L-65; Gr-VB1e(3) [Equatorial:macro-Arawakan:Arawakan]; JS-18; Sw-SE12.1 [macro-Siriana:with Yanomaman 50mc!]. AT 12.2. EM: ?macro-Arawakan.

13+14. **Wamo-Chapakúra stock** <Sp (tronco) Guamo-Chapacura; Pg
GOOD   tronco Guámo-Txapakúra>. ??mc. These are placed in the same low-level group by Gr (VB1e(3,4)); there are lexical similarities.

15. **Wahívoan family** <Guajiboano, familia Guajiboana>. 23mc. 4 lgs, one dead. COL, VEN. L-46 [Arawakan]; Gr-VB1a [macro-Arawakan]; JS-26 [with Arawakan]; Sw-C4.1 [macro-Aruaco]. AT Guahibo 19.6.

16. **Maipúrean (sub)stock** <Sp (subtronco) Maipureano; Pg tronco Maipúre>. 45mc. 65 lgs, 31 dead. Spoken in every country but ES, CR, PAN, URU, CHI. L-46; Gr-VB1(e)2 [Equatorial:macro-Arawakan: Arawakan]; JS-4A,B,D,E,F,G [Arawakan: with macro-Panoan and Mayan]; Sw-C4.2-4.4+C6 [macro-Aruaco]. AT 10.2; 10.4; 16-16.4; 16.6-7. This is a large stock — the biggest in the whole New World — and it has considerable internal branching. EM: macro-Arawakan 1-6,8-10, 12-47.

Arawakan stock <Sp (tronco) Arahuacano; Pg tronco Aruák>. This name is the one normally applied to what here is called Maipurean. Maipurean used to be thought to be a major subgroup of Arawakan, but all the **living** Arawakan languages, at least, seem to need to be subgrouped with languages already found within Maipurean as commonly defined. The sorting out of the labels Maipurean and Arawakan will have to await a more sophisticated classification of the languages in question than is possible at the present state of comparative studies.

17. **Arawán family <Sp Arahuano, familia Arahuana; Pg família Arawá>.**
    32mc. 5 lgs, one dead. PER, BRA. L-88; Gr-VB1e(1) [Equatorial: macro-
    Arawakan:Arawakan]; JS-4C [Arawakan]; Sw-S13.1 [with Kukurá 54mc].
    Gr and JS link this family to Arawakan; Sw disagrees. AT 16.5. EM:
    macro-Arawakan 7.

18. **Harákmbut language area <Sp ???>.** 7mc. 2 lgs. PER. L-88(part)+77;
    Gr-VB1e(2) [Equatorial:macro-Arawakan:Arawakan]; JS-72; Sw-S11
    [macro-Macú]. Classifiers have been confused by the names given these
    languages. SYN Tuyoneri. PEJ Mashko. AT 10.8. EM: macro-Arawakan
    11.

III. WESTERN AMAZONIA II

19. **Puinávean stock <Sp (tronco) Puinaveano; Pg tronco Makú>.** 57+mc.
    6 lgs, 2 dead. BRA, COL, VEN. L-86; Gr-VA15 [macro-Tucanoan]; JS-
    56; Sw-S9.1-9.2 [macro-Macú: with Trumai 64mc]. PEJ Makú. AT 19.4.

20. **Katukínan family <Sp Catuquinano, familia Catuquinana; Pg família
    Katukína>.** ??mc. 5 lgs, 3 dead. BRA. L-87; Gr-VA4 [macro-Tucanoan];
    JS-16: Sw-S10 [macro-Macú]. AT 15.8.

21. **Tekiraka language <Sp Tequiraca>.** dead. PER. L-60; Gr-VA1 [macro-
    Tucanoan; JS-7; Sw-SW2.1 [macro-Zamuco]. This language is also
    known as Avishiri, but the term is ambiguous and should be avoided. AT
    18.8.

22. **Kanichana language <Sp Canichana>.** BOL. L-74; Gr-VA2 [macro-
    Tucanoan]; JS-10; Sw-SW1 [macro-Zamuco]. AT 11.7.

23. **Tukánoan stock <(tronco) Tucanoano; Pg tronco Tukáno>.** 45+mc. 14
    lgs, 2 dead. COL, ECU, PER, BRA. L-81; Gr-VA18 [macro-Tucanoan];
    JS-69AB; Sw-C3.7-3.8 [macro-Chibcha]. AT 19.3. This is a large stock,
    with two major branches.

24. **Tikuna language <Sp Ticuna, Tucuna; Pg Tikúna, Tukúna>.** COL,
    PER, BRA. L-53; Gr-VA17a [macro-Tucanoan:Ticuna-Yuri]; JS-65; Sw-
    SE4(part) [macro-Ye]. AT 19.1.

25. **Jurí language <Sp Yurí; Pg Jurí>.** dead. COL, BRA. L-85; Gr-VA17b
    [macro-Tucanoan:Ticuna-Yuri]; JS-79; Sw-SE4(part) [macro-Ye]. AT
    19.2.

24+25. **Jurí-Tikuna stock <Sp (tronco) Yurí-Ticuna; Pg tronco Jurí-
GOOD Tikúna>.** 46mc. Gr-VA17; Sw-SE4. Both Gr and Sw group these and
    there is lexical evidence in support.

26. **Munichi language.** PER. L-56; Gr-VA11 [macro-Tucanoan]; JS-49; Sw-
    x26. AT 22.9.

IV. Northern Foothills Region

27. **Ezmeralda language <Sp Esmeralda>.** dead. ECU. L-94a [Chibchan];
    Gr-VB4b [Equatorial:Jibaro-Candoshi]; JS-41B1; Sw-C2 [macro-Cayuvava:
    with Kayuvava 45mc!]. AT 22.5. EM unclassified.

28. **Jaruro language <Sp Yaruro>.** VEN. L-94a [Chibchan]; Gr-VB4e
    [Equatorial:Jibaro-Candoshi]; JS-41B2 [macro-Chibchan]; Sw-W10 [macro-
    Páez]. AT 21.7. EM unclassified.

27+28. **Ezmeralda-Jaruro stock <Sp tronco Esmeralda-Yaruro>.** All but
GOOD   Sw group these together. There are lexical similarities.

29. **Kofán language <Sp Cofán>.** COL, ECU. L-100; Gr-VB4a [Equatorial:
    Jibaro-Candoshi]; JS-21; Sw-SE5. AT 22.6. EM: macro-Chibchan 12.

30. **Kandoshi language <Sp Candoshi>.** PER. L-59; Gr-VB4d [Equatorial:
    Jibaro-Candoshi]; JS-51; Sw-C7. AT 10.5.

31. **Hívaro language area <Sp Jívaro>.** ??mc. 2 emergent languages. ECU,
    PER. L-62; Gr-VB4c [Equatorial:Jibaro-Candoshi]; JS-37B [Jívaro-
    Cahuapana]; Sw-S15.1,3 [macro-Jíbaro; with Kawapanan, Urarina,
    Puelche, and Warpe]. AT 22.1.

32. **Kawapánan family <Sp Cahuapanano, familia Cahuapanana>.** ??mc.
    2 languages. PER. L-55; Gr-IVC1 [Andean:Kahuapana-Zaparo]; JS-37A
    [Jvaro-Cahuapana]; Sw-S15.1 [macro-Jívaro: with Hívaro, Urarina,
    Puelche, and Warpe]. AT 22.8.

31+32.   **Hívaro-Kawapana stock <Sp tronco Jívaro-Cahuapana>.** 19mc.
MAYBE   JS-37 [with Warpe and Mapudungu]; Sw-S15 [with Urarina,
          Puelche, and Warpe]. This proposed grouping is in direct conflict
          with Gr's classification, but seems supported by some lexical data.
          Gr's Jibaro-Candoshi group is very poorly supported by the data he
          cites in LIA. EM: Jebero-Jivaroan.

33. **Sáparoan family <Sp Zaparoano, familia Zaparoana>.** 41mc. 6 lgs,
    one dead. ECU, PER. L-64; Gr-IVC2 [Andean:Kahuapana-Zaparo]; JS-
    82; Sw-S2 [Záparo-Peba: with Yawan 60mc]. AT 18.6. Taushiro is
    included here, perhaps wrongly.

34. **Yáwan family <Sp Yaguano, familia Yaguana>.** ??mc. 3 lgs, 2 dead.
    PER. L-54; Gr-VIA5 [macro-Carib]; JS-76; Sw-S2 [Záparo-Peba: with
    Saparoan 60mc]. AT 18.3.

33+34   **Sáparo-Yawa stock <Sp tronco Záparo-Yagua>.** 60mc. Sw-S2.
MAYBE   Doris Payne independently discovered this connexion, which how-
          ever is in direct conflict with Gr's classification. Needs further
          investigation.

35. **Omurano language.** dead. PER. L-58; Gr-IVB2 [Andean:Itucale-Sabela];
    JS-53; Sw-E1. SYN Maina (ambiguous) [Gr]. AT 18.7.

36. **Sabela language.** PER. L-63; Gr-IVB3 [Andean:Itucale-Sabela]; JS-59; Sw-W9. AUT Wao. PEJ Auka. AT 10.6.

37. **Urarina language.** PER. L-61; Gr-IVB1 [Andean:Itucale-Sabela]; JS-62; Sw-S15.2 [macro-Jibaro:with Hívaro-Kawapana]. SYN Shimaku [Sw]; Itukale [Gr]. AT 10.1.

38. **Bóran family <Sp Borano, familia Borana; Pg família Bora>.** 18mc. 2 lgs. COL, PER. L-83; Gr-VIA2a [macro-Carib:Bora-Uitoto]; JS-9A [Bora-Witotoan]; Sw-S5 [macro-Huitoto]. AT 18.2.

39. **Witótoan family <Sp Huitotoano, familia Huitotoana; Pg família Witóto>.** ??mc. 7 lgs, 4 dead. COL, PER, BRA. L-84; Gr-VIA2b [macro-Carib:Bora-Uitoto]; JS-9B [Bora-Witotoan]; Sw-S4 [with Andoke]. AT 18.1.

40. **Andoke language <Sp Andoque>.** COL, PER. L-82; Gr-VIA1 [macro-Carib]; JS-2; Sw-S4 [macro-Huitoto]. AT 18.5.

38+39+40. **Bora-Witoto stock <Sp (tronco) Bora-Huitoto; Pg tronco Bóra-**
MAYBE   Witóto>. 54mc. Both Gr and Sw group 38-39-40 together; L gives them all consecutive numbers; JS groups 38 and 39. Because of the general consensus and low glottochronological figure I have tentatively recognized this group. EM: macro-Arawakan 48.

V. ANDES REGION

41. **Chimúan family <Sp Chimuano, familia Chimuana>.** 21+mc. 3 lgs, all dead. ECU, PER. L-106; Gr-IIIB4 [Paezan]; JS-78; Sw-SE2+x10,x11. AT Yunga, Puruhá, Cañari 20.1-20.2. EM unclassified or ?macro-Arawakan.

42. **Cholónan family <Sp Cholonano, familia Cholonana>.** 22mc. 2 lgs, both dead. PER. L-57; Gr-IVD2 [Andean:Northern Andean]; JS-20; Sw-W11.3 macro-Pez]. AT 22.2.

43. **Kulyi language <Sp Culli>.** dead. PER. L-103; Gr-IVD3 [Andean: Northern Andean]; JS-22; Sw-W11.5 [macro-Páez]. AT 22.10.

44. **Sechura language.** dead. PER. L-101; Gr-IVD5 [Andean:Northern Andean]; JS-61; Sw-SE10 [macro-Leco; with Leko and Chokó]. SYN Sek, Talyán. AT 20.3.

45. **Katakáoan family <Sp Catacaoano, familia Catacaoana>.** ??mc. 2 lgs, both dead. L-102; Gr-IVD1 [Andean:Northern Andean]; JS-14; no Sw. AT 20.3.

44+45. **Sechura-Katakao stock <Sp (tronco) Sechura-Catacao>.** ??mc. Gr
GOOD   groups these and L places them side by side. There is supporting lexical evidence.

46. **Leko language <Sp Leco>.** dead. BOL. L-112; Gr-IVD4 [Andean: Northern Andean]; JS-39; Sw-SE10 [macro-Leco: with Sechura and Chokó]. SYN Lapalapa. AT 11.2.

47. **Kechua language complex <Sp Quechua>.** ??mc. 7 virtual lgs. COL, ECU, PER, BOL, ARG. L-107; Gr-IVE [Andean]; JS-58B [Quechumaran]; Sw-W7.1(part) [macro-Quechuachón: with Haki]. AT 8.
48. **Haki language complex <Sp Jaqui>.** 13mc. 2 lgs. PER, BOL, CHI, ARG. L-108; Gr-IVA [Andean]; JS-58A [Quechumaran]; Sw-W7.1 [macro-Quechuachón: with Kechua]. SYN Aimara [Gr]. AT 7; 10.7.

47+48. **Kechumara stock <Sp (tronco) Quechumara>.** 45mc. There is
GOOD? general agreement among the authorities used here that these two groups are genetically related. There is a good deal of argumentation to the contrary, however. EM: Quechua-Aymara.

49. **Chipaya language area.** 2 emergent lgs. BOL. L-110; Gr-VB1e(5) [Equatorial:macro-Arawakan:Arawakan: with Pukina]; JS-43; Sw-W7.2 [macro-Quechuachón: with Pukina]. Gr connects Chipaya to Arawakan. Olson tried to connect it to Mayan. JS accepts both these connexions. Sw has different ideas. The evidence for connecting Chipaya with anything else is extremely weak. AT 6.1. EM: ?macro-Arawakan.
50. **Pukina language <Sp Puquina>.** dead. BOL. L-109; Gr-VB1e(5) [Equatorial:macro-Arawakan:Arawakan: with Chipaya]; JS-57; Sw-W7.2 [macro-Quechuachón: with Chipaya]. The grouping by Gr and Sw of Pukina with Chipaya seems to be based on taking someone's incorrect assertion that they are the same language at face value. In fact, they are quite dissimilar. AT 6.1. EM: ?macro-Arawakan.
51. **Kolyawaya jargon <Sp Collahuaya, Callahuaya>.** BOL. L-109; Gr-VB1e(5) [Equatorial:Mecro-Arawakan:Arawakan]; no JS; no Sw. This is a jargon used by Kechua speakers who (apparently) used to speak Pukina, in any event a language related to Pukina. SYN Pohena. Since it is not known where all its components come from, it is preferable to give it a separate number. Since its elements are basically indigenous, it seems appropiate to list it here. Both Gr and L apparently believe this is the same as Pukina.

50+51. **Pukina-Kolyawaya family?** Such a group would be recognized if
MAYBE Kolyawaya were shown to descend from a sister of Pukina rather than Pukina itself.

VI. SOUTHERN FOOTHILLS REGION

52. **Yurakare language <Sp Yuracare>.** BOL. L-78; Gr-VB11 [Equatorial]; JS-44D [macro-Panoan: with Pano-Takana, Mosetén, and Chon]; Sw-C1. AT Yuracar 11.4. EM: macro-Panoan 5.
53. **Pánoan family <Sp Panoano, familia Panoana; Pg família Páno>.** ??mc. 28 lgs, 13 dead. BRA, PER, BOL. L-75; Gr-VIB6a [macro-Panoan: with Takanan]; JS-44C [with Takanan]; Sw-W7.3 [with Takanan]. AT 9. This is a large family with a considerable amount of branching. EM: macro-Panoan 1.

54. **Takánan family <Sp Tacanano, familia Tacanana>.** ??mc. 5 lgs. BOL, PER. L-76; Gr-VIB6b [macro-Panoan: with Panoan]; JS-44C [with Panoan]; Sw-W7.3 [with Panoan]. AT 11.1. EM: macro-Panoan 2.

53+54. **Pano-Takana stock <Sp (tronco) Pano-Tacana; Pg tronco Páno-**
GOOD **Takána>.** 47mc. Gr-VIB6 [macro-Panoan:Pano-Tacana]; JS -44C [macro-Panoan]; Sw-W7.3 [macro-Quechuachón]. There is universal agreement that these two families constitute a unique node. Mary Key, Victor Girard, and Eugene Loos have all assembled evidence to support this.

55. **Mosetén language area.** 2 emergent languages. BOL. L-79; Gr-VIB5 [macro-Panoan]; JS-44B [macro-Panoan: with Chon, Pano-Takana, and Yurakare]; Sw-W7.4 [macro-Kechuachón: with Chon]. AT 11.3. EM: macro-Panoan 4.

56. **Chon family.** 24mc. ARG, CHI. 3 lgs, 2 dead. L-4; Gr-IVF4 [Andean:Southern Andean]; JS-44A [macro-Panoan]; Sw-W7.5 [macro-Kechuachón: with Mosetén]. SYN Patagón [Gr]. AT 1.3 Tehuelche-Ona. EM: macro-Panoan 6.

55+56. **Mosetén-Chon stock <Sp (tronco) Mosetén-Chon>.** 51mc. JS
GOOD? and Sw agree on grouping these together; JS has presented evidence for it. Gr, on the other hand, links Mosetén to Pano-Takana, but Chon to other languages of the Cone.

VII. THE CONE

57. **Yámana language.** dead. CHI. L-1; Gr-IVF5 [Andean:Southern Andean]; JS-77 [with macro-Chibchan]; Sw-SW10. SYN Yagán. AT 1.1.

58. **Kawéskar language (area).** 2 emergent lgs, one dead. CHI. L-2+3; Gr-IVF1 [Andean:Southern Andean]; JS-1 [with Matakoan and Tupian]; Sw-SW9. PEJ Alakaluf. AT 1.2 Alacaluf; 1.7 Aksana o Kaueskar. EM: macro-Panoan 7.

59. **Mapudungu language (area).** CHI, ARG. L-113; Gr-IVF2 [Andean: Southern Andean]; JS-3 [with Warpe and Hívaro-Kawapana]; Sw-SW3 [macro-Mapundunguan]. SYN Araukano [Gr]. AT 2.1 Araucano. EM: macro-Panoan 8.

60. **Puelche language.** dead. ARG. L-5; Gr-IVF3 [Andean:Southern Andean];JS-30; Sw-S15.5 [macro-Jíbaro: with Warpe, Hívaro-Kawapana, and Urarina]. SYN Gennaken (ambig) [Gr]. AT 2.2.

61. **Warpe language area <Sp Huarpe>.** 11mc. 2 emergent lgs, both dead. ARG. L-117; Gr-IIIB1 [Paezan]; JS-32 [with Mapudungu]; Sw-S15.4 [macro-Jíbaro: with Puelche, Hívaro-Kawapana, and Urarina]. Both Sw and JS agree that Warpe is related to Hívaro-Kawapana. The matter should be looked into. AT 3.1.

VIII. CHACO REGION

62. **Matákoan family <Sp Matacoano, familia Matacoana>**. 17mc. 4 lgs.
ARG, PAR, BOL. L-10; Gr-VIB4b [macro-Panoan:Mataco-Guaicuru];
JS-47 [with Kawéskar and Tupian]; Sw-SW4+7 [macro-Mapuche]. AT
5.1.1-5.1.3. EM: macro-Guaycuru 2.

63. **Waikurúan family <Sp Guaycuruano, family Guaycuruana; Pg
familia Guaikurú>**. 35mc. 8 lgs, 4 dead. PAR, BRA, ARG, BOL. L-8; Gr-
VIB4a [macro-Panoan:Mataco-Guaicuru]; JS-27B [with Charruan]; Sw-
SW6 [macro-Mapuche]. Wachí is a member of this family. AT 5.4. EM:
macro-Guaycuru 1.

64. **Charrúan family <Sp Charruano, familia Charruana>**. 2 lgs, both
dead. URU. L-15; Gr-VIB1 [macro-Panoan]; JS-27A [with Waikuruan];
Sw-SW2.3 [macro-Zamuco]. AT 3.4.

65. **Lule language**. dead. ARG. L-9; Gr-VIB3a [Lule-Vilela]; JS-40A [with
Vilela]; Sw-SW8(part) [with Vilela]. AT 4.4.

66. **Vilela language**. ARG. L-116; GR-VIB3b [Lule-Vilela]; JS-40B [with
Lule]; Sw-SW8(part) [with Lule]. AT 4.5.

65+66. **Lule-Vilela stock <Sp (tronco) Lule-Vilela>**. 58mc. Gr-VIB3
GOOD [macro-Panoan]; JS-40 [with Movima]; Sw-SW8. There is general
agreement, apart from L, that this is a genetic group. There is lexical
evidence to support it. EM: Lule-Vilela.

67. **Maskóian family <Sp Mascoyano, familia Mascoyana>**. ??mc. 4 lgs,
one dead. PAR. L-11; Gr-VIB2 [macro-Panoan]; JS-46; Sw-SW5 [macro-
Mapuche]. SYN Lengua [Gr]. AT 5.2-5.3.

68. **Samúkoan family <Sp Zamucoano, familia Zamucoana>**. 28mc. 2 lgs.
PAR, BOL. L-12; Gr-VB12 [Equatorial]; JS-81 [with Tupian]; Sw-SW2.2
[macro-Zamuco]. AT 5.5.

69. **Gorgotoki language <Sp Gorgotoqui>**. dead. BOL. L-14; no Gr; JS-25;
Sw-x17. This language should be perhaps not listed here because it may be
completely undocumented. AT 12.4.

IX. EASTERN BRAZIL

70. **Chikitano language <Sp Chiquitano>**. BOL. L-13; Gr-VIC4 [macro-
Ge]; JS-19; Sw-SE 11.2 [macro-Tupí: with Bororoan]. AT 12.3.

71. **Boróroan family <Sp Bororoano, familia Bororoana; Pg família
Boróro>**. ??mc. 3 lgs, one dead. BRA. L-27; Gr-VIC1 [macro-Ge]; JS-
42A [macro-Ge]; Sw-SE11.1 [macro-Tupí: with Chikitano]. AT 15.1.

72. **Aimoré language complex <Pg família Botocudo>**. 16mc. 3 emergent
lgs, 2 dead. BRA. L-20; Gr-VIC2 [macro-Ge]; JS-42B [macro-Ge]; Sw-
SE6 [macro-Ye]. SYN Botocudo (Pg word) [Gr]. AT 14.9. EM: macro-
Ge 3.

73. **Rikbaktsá language.** BRA. L-41; Gr-VIC5 [macro-Ge]; JS-23; no Sw. AT 14.10.

74. **Je stock <Sp (tronco) Ye; Pg tronco Je>.** 54mc. 13 lgs, 6 dead. BRA. L-16+24; Gr-VIB7 [macro-Ge]; JS-42D [macro-Ge]; Sw-SE8.1-2 [macro-Ye]. AT 14.1-14.2. EM: macro-Ge 8.

75. **Jeikó language.** dead. BRA. L-24; Gr-VIC7b [macro-Ge:Ge-Kaingan]; JS-42E [macro-Ge]; Sw-SE8.2 [macro-Ye]. AT 14.2. EM: macro-Ge 5.

76. **Kamakánan family <Pg família Kamakã>.** 32mc. 4 lgs, all dead. BRA. L-22; Gr-VIC9 [macro-Ge]; JS-42F [macro-Ge]; Sw-SE7 [macro-Ye]. AT 14.3. EM: macro-Ge 7.

77. **Mashakalían family <Pg família Maxakalí>.** 38mc. 3 lgs, 2 dead. BRA. L-19; Gr-VIC10 [macro-Ge]; JS-42H [macro-Ge]; Sw-S1.3+x20 [macro-Ye: with Purian and Fulnió]. Includes Patashó. AT 14.4. EM: macro-Ge 1.

78. **Purían family <Pg família Purí>.** 32mc. 2 lgs, both dead. BRA. L-18; Gr-VIC13 [macro-Ge]; JS-42J [macro-Ge]; Sw-S1.1 [macro-Ye: with Mashakalian and Fulnió]. AT 14.5. EM: macro-Ge 4.

79. **Fulnió language.** BRA. L-23; Gr-VIC6 [macro-Ge]; JS-42C [macro-Ge]; Sw-S1.2 [macro-Ye: with Mashakalian and Purian]. SYN Yaté, Karnijó. AT 14.12.1.

80. **Karajá language area.** 2 emergent lgs. BRA. L-28; Gr-VIC3 [macro-Ge]; JS-42G [macro-Ge]; Sw-E3. AT 15.7. EM: macro-Ge 2.

81. **Ofayé language.** BRA. L-17; Gr-VIC11 [macro-Ge]; JS-42I [macro-Ge]; Sw-SW2.4 [macro-Zamuco]. AT 14.7. EM: macro-Ge 6.

82. **Guató language.** BRA. L-80; Gr-VIC8 [macro-Ge]; JS-29; Sw-S6.5 [macro-Caribe]. AT 5.6.

70-82. **macro-Je.** Davis presents evidence that 72 and 74-81 are
PROBABLE related. Loukotka also presented evidence relating 72, 74-78, and 81. Rodrigues presents evidence that 71-82 are related. Gr and Sw both agree that 70 and 71 are related. There is good reason for believing all these to be related and detailed comparative work should be carried out. The time depth may not be as great as Sw's estimates might suggest. Davis also points to connexions with Tupian.

83. **Otí language.** dead. BRA. L-26; Gr-VIC12 [macro-Ge]; no JS; Sw-x19. Only Gr dares to link this lg to anything else. AT 14.6.

84. **Baenã language.** dead. BRA. L-21; no Gr; JS-8; no Sw. This lg is too poorly known for even Gr to dare classifying it. Not in AT.

85. **Kukurá language.** dead. BRA. L-25; Gr-VIA4 [macro-Carib]; JS-38; Sw-S13.2 [with Arawan 54mc!]. AT 14.8.

X. NORTHEASTERN BRAZIL

86. **Katembrí language.** dead. BRA. L-29; Gr-VB1b [Equatorial:macro-Arawakan]; JS-15; Sw-S6.3 [macro-Caribe]. SYN Mirandela. AT 14.16.

87. **Karirí language (area).** 5mc. dead. BRA. L-36; Gr-VB5a [Equatorial: with Tupian]; JS-13; Sw-S6.2 [macro-Caribe]. AT 14.13.

88. **Tushá language <Pg Tuxá>.** dead. BRA. L-30; Gr-VB10 [Equatorial]; JS-71; Sw-x14. AT 14.12.4.

89. **Pankararú language.** dead. BRA. l-31; Gr-VA14 [macro-Tucanoan]; JS-55; Sw-x28. AT 14.12.2.

90. **Natú language.** dead. BRA. L-34; Gr-VA13 [macro-Tucanoan]; no JS; Sw-x27. Only Gr dares to classify this lg. AT 14.12.4.

91. **Shukurú language <Pg Xukurú>.** dead. BRA. L-35; Gr-VA16 [macro-Tucanoan]; JS-74; Sw-x16. SYN Ichikile. Only Gr dares to classify this lg. AT 14.12.3.

92. **Gamela language.** dead. BRA. L-38; Gr-VA5 [macro-Tucanoan]; JS-74; Sw-x13. Only Gr dares to classify this lg. AT 14.15.

93. **Wamoé language.** dead. BRA. L-33; Gr-VA19 [macro-Tucanoan]; JS-73; no Sw. SYN Um. Only Gr dares to classify this lg. AT 14.12.4.

94. **Tairairiú language.** dead. BRA. L-37; no Gr; JS-63; Sw-x15. Not even Gr dares classify this lg. AT 14.12.4.

95. **Shokó language <Pg Xokó>.** dead. BRA. L-32; no Gr; no JS; no Sw. Not even Gr will classify this lg. AT 14.12.4.

XI. CENTRAL AMAZONIA

96. **Múran family <Pg família Múra>.** ??mc. 2 lgs, one dead. BRA. L-39; Gr-IIIB7(part); JS-41C(part); Sw-S14(part). AT 15.5.

97. **Matanawí language.** dead. BRA. L-40; Gr-IIIB7(part); JS-41C(part); Sw-S14(part). AT 15.4.

96+97. **Mura-Matanawí family <Pg família Múra-Matanawí>.**
PROBABLE 30mc. L-39+40; Gr-IIIB7 [Paezan]; JS-41 [macro-Chibchan]; Sw-S14 [macro-Jíbaro]. Except for L, there is general agreement that these lgs all form a family. EM unclassified.

98. **Itonama language.** BOL. L-73; Gr-IIIB5 [Paezan]; JS-41C [macro-Chibchan]; Sw-W11.4 [macro-Páez]. AT 11.8. EM unclassified.

99. **Kunsa language <Sp Cunza>.** dead. CHI,BOL. L-111; Gr-IIIB2 [Paezan]; JS-5; Sw-W8.3 [macro-Páez]. SYN Atakama [Gr]. AT 4.3. EM unclassified.

100. **Kapishaná language <Pg Kapixaná>.** BRA. L-67; Gr-VA3 [macro-Tucanoan]; JS-11; Sw-W8.2 [macro-Páez]. SYN Kanoé. Price 1978 thinks this might be related to Nambikuara [104]. AT 12.1.2.

99+100.   **Kunsa-Kapishaná stock.** <49mc.>, Sw groups these together
MAYBE   with a fairly low time depth and the lexical evidence it looks
          promising. Gr does not agree.

101. **Jabutían family <Pg família Jabutí>.** ??mc. 3 lgs. BRA. L-44; Gr-
     VIC14 [macro-Ge]; JS-75; Sw-W8.1 [macro-Páez]. Sw groups this with
     Kunsa-Kapishaná, with only 49mc of time depth; the available lexical
     material does not look promising. AT 12.5.

102. **Koayá language <Pg Koaiá>.** dead. BRA. L-68; Gr-VA9 [macro-
     Tucanoan]; JS-36; no Sw. AT 12.6.

103. **Aikaná language.** BRA. L-66; Gr-VA6 [macro-Tucanoan]; JS-31; Sw-
     S7. SYN Warí [Gr]. AT 12.1.1.

104. **Nambikuara family <Pg família Nambikwára>.** ??mc. 4 lgs. BRA. L-
     42; Gr-VA12 [macro-Tucanoan]; JS-52; Sw-E2. Includes Kabishí,
     perhaps wrongly. AT 15.2-15.3.

105. **Iranshe language <Pg Irantxe>.** BRA. L-43; Gr-VA7 [macro-
     Tucanoan]; JS-33 [with Arawakan]; no Sw. SYN Münkü. AT 16.8.

106. **Trumai language.** BRA. L-70; Gr-VB9 [Equatorial]; JS-68; Sw-S9.3
     [macro-Macú: with Puinavean 64mc]. AT 15.6.

107. **Movima language.** BOL. L-72; Gr-VA10 [macro-Tucanoan]; JS-48
     [with Waikuruan]; Sw-SE9.2 [macro-Tupian: with Tupian 70mc]. AT
     11.5.

108. **Kayuvava language <Sp Cayuvava>.** BOL. L-71; Gr-VB2
     [Equatorial]; S-17 [with Tupian]; Sw-W12 [with Ezmeralda 42mc]. Gr
     and JS both support a connexion with Tupian. AT 11.6.

109. **Tupían stock <Sp (tronco) Tupiano; Pg tronco Tupí>.** 55-60mc. 37
     lgs, 12 dead. VEN, COL, BRA, BOL, ARG, PAR. L-45+69; Gr-VB5b
     [Kariri-Tupi]; JS-70A-H [with Kariban]; Sw-SE9.1 [macro-Tupí: with
     Movima]. AT 13. This is a large stock with a good deal of branching.
     The majority of the languages belong to a single branch, the Tupí-
     Guaraní family.

XII. NORTHERN AMAZONIA

110. **Káriban family <Sp Caribano, familia Caribana; Pg família Karíb>.**
     37mc. 43 lgs, 19 dead. COL, VEN, SUR, GUY, FG, TRI, BRA. L-89; Gr-
     VIA3 [macro-Carib]; JS-12A [with Chokó; related to Tupian]; SwS6.1
     [macro-Caribe]. AT 14.14. AT 17. This is a large family with a large
     number of subgroups that do not seem to group together into major
     divisions. Future work will clarify whether this impression is correct.

111. **Yanomáman family <Sp Yanomamano, familia Yanomamana; Pg família Yamomámi>**. 21mc. 4 lgs. VEN, BRA. L-90; Gr-IIIA7 [Chibchan]; JS-41F [macro-Chibchan; a Chibchan-Kariban link]; Sw-SE12.2 [macro-Siriana: with Chapakuran 50mc]. AT 19.9. EM: macro-Panoan 3.

112. **Warao language**. GUY, SUR, VEN. L-91; Gr-IIIB10 [Paezan]; JS-41G [macro-Chibchan; a Chibchan-Kariban link]; Sw-S3. AT 19.13. EM: ?macro-Chibchan 18.

113. **Taruma language**. dead. BRA, GUY. L-49; Gr-VB9 [Equatorial]; JS-64; Sw-S6.4 [macro-Caribe]. AT 15.9.

114. **Sálivan family <Sp Salivano, familia Salivana>**. 20mc. 2 lgs. COL, VEN. L-50; Gr-VB6 [Equatorial]; JS-60; Sw-SE3 [macro-Ye]. SYN Piaroan [Gr]. AT 19.5.

115. **Awaké language <Sp Ahuaqué>**. BRA, VEN. L-92; Gr-VA8a [macro-Tucanoan:Kaliana-Maku]; JS-6; Sw-SE1(part) [with Kaliana]. SYN Arutani, Uruak. AT 19.12.

116. **Kaliana language <Sp Caliana; Pg Kaliána>**. VEN, BRA. L-93; Gr-VA8b [macro-Tucanoan:Kaliana-Maku]; JS-35; Sw-SE1(part). SYN Sapé.

115+116. **Awaké-Kaliana family <Sp (familia) Ahuaqué-Caliana; Pg**
GOOD   **família Awaké-Kaliána>**. 47mc. Both Gr and Sw group these and there is lexical evidence to support this. L lists them side by side.

117. **Maku language <Sp Macu; Pg Máku>**. dead. BRA, VEN. L-52; Gr-VA8c [macro-Tucanoan:Kaliana-Maku]; JS-45; Sw-S12 [macro-Macú]. AT 19.10.

115+116+117.   **Kaliánan stock <Sp (tronco) Calianano>**. ??mc. Gr links
PROMISING   all three of these groups and the proposal looks promising.

118. **Hotí language**. VEN. Not found in any of the classifications referred to, but definitely alive. SYN Waruwaru. Not in AT.

PART III

COMPARATIVE WORK: RECONSTRUCTION AND CLASSIFICATION. We can divide up the genetic groups of SA in terms of the number of languages and internal diversification. The following categories seem convenient. Family/ stock name is preceded by the number in my listing and followed by the number of languages in the group, followed by glottochronological time depth in minimum centuries when given by Swadesh.

Category A: ten or more languages
[8] Chibchan 24 56mc
[16] Maipurean 65 45mc
[23] Tukanoan 14 >45mc
[38-39-40] Bora-Witoto 10 54mc
[53] Panoan 28 <47mc
[53-54] Pano-Takana 33 47mc
[109] Tupian 37 55-60mc
[110] Kariban 43 37mc

Category B: four to eight languages
[4] Chokó 5 7mc
[6] Paesan 7 54mc
[7] Barbakoan 6 33mc
[9] Misumalpa 4 43mc
[14] Chapakuran 8 37mc
[15] Wahivoan 4 23mc
[17] Arawan 5 32mc
[19] Puinavean 6 >57mc
[20] Katukinan 5
[33] Saparoan 6 41mc
[33-34] Sáparo-Yawa 9 60mc
[39] Witotoan 7 <54mc
[47] Kechua 7
[54] Takanan 5 <47mc
[62] Matakoan 4 17mc
[63] Waikuruan 8 35mc
[67] Maskoian 4
[74] Je 6 54mc
[76] Kamakanan 4 (all dead) 32mc
[104] Nambikuara 4
[111] Yanomaman 4 21mc

Category C: three languages
[3] Hiraharan (all dead) 19mc
[34] Yawan
[41] Chimuan (all dead)
[56] Chon (all dead) 24mc
[71] Bororoan
[72] Aimoré 16mc
[77] Mashakalian (all dead) 38mc
[101] Jabutian

There are approximately 20 families consisting of just two languages. There are approximately 60 isolated languages.

The eight category-A families and stocks are the most challenging. They have internal diversity ranging from that of Mije-Soke [Mihe-Soke] (Sp Mixe-Zoque), Mistekan (Sp Mixtecano), and Otopame, through that of Mayan, to that of Otomange (Sp Otomangue) and IndoEuropean.

The combined work of several scholars will be required to bring order and understanding to the histories of these language families. All of them, of course, have been the object of considerable study already, but most work before the middle fifties was hampered by the absence of accurate data.

The twenty category B families and stocks are the most manageable and rewarding in the short run. On the high end, they can have as much internal time depth as families and stocks of class A. Less manpower will be needed to achieve a fairly good understanding of the history of these families, but each family should have the full attention of at least one scholar over a professional lifetime.

Category C families are inherently less rewarding because most of the languages are dead; inevitably they have been documented to a less than desirable degree.

The families and stocks of categories A and B are where the comparative efforts of South Americanist linguists should be concentrated over the next twenty or so years. As the protolanguages for these groups take shape, we will have on hand the entities to which the numerically abundant isolates should be compared.

I urge comparativists in SA to carry out detailed reconstructions of protolanguages for those families with meaningful amounts of diversification; only in that way will we have the means of comparing one family with another and with the numerous isolates of SA. All languages to be compared, whether isolates or members of diversified families, should have their structures subjected to a thorough phonological and morphophonological analysis and their lexicons should also be analyzed to the hilt.

The level of cross-family comparison in SA is still quite primitive. Many valid connexions remain to be demonstrated; although many have been noticed, others await discovery. Many proposed connexions have proved illusory, being due to borrowing, or even chance. The efforts in this direction of Girard, Holt, Migliazza, and others who have compared protolanguages to each other are to be applauded.

I also urge all interested scholars to carefully scrutinize Greenberg's data so that the valid and questionable parts can be distinguished from each other and the bugaboo effect can be neutralized. (Greenberg 1987 treats the whole set of Americanist comparativists as a bugaboo, and the converse process is already developing apace.) Until then, concern with the sociopolitical effects of Greenberg's 'classification' will plague comparative Amerindian studies. The only ways to neutralize any bad effects of Greenberg's work on the uninformed public are to (a) do the comparative job right where it can be done; (b) point out the cases where it can't be done; (c) learn a few things about popularizing science.

PART IV

LARGER GROUPINGS: CLUSTERS AND NETWORKS. I have considered the proposals to link various sets of the genetic groups listed here that have been made by serious scholars since 1955, including Girard 1971, Greenberg 1987, Holt 1986, Loukotka 1968, Key n.d., Migliazza 1980ms, 1987ms, Rodrigues 1985, Suárez 1969, 1973, 1974, and Swadesh 1959. I started working on this problem in 1966. It must for the moment be viewed as a puzzle that involves juggling opinions rather than resolving questions, but I think it can serve to identify the hypotheses that most need testing. I have not had a chance to evaluate Gr's data; even if he turns out to have data that is convincing in some or even many cases, hypotheses offered by others also using reasonably extensive data are often in conflict with those of Gr and equally deserve to be checked out. The proposals can be treated at two levels. First there are several sets of proposed genetic groups that form what I call **clusters** (rather than the customary **phyla** or **superstocks**). I prefix the name of a member family with **macro-** in order to name them. Second, all these proposals taken together include all the languages of South America and many of MesoAmerica and North America as well. They form two vast networks, which I call Western and Eastern.

The clusters I set up here do not all just simply fall out of a straightforward comparison of existing classification schemes. When any two of the four classifiers agree on associating two genetic groups, I assign them to the nucleus of the same cluster. There are no known cases of an evenly split opinion. The cluster is augmented by attaching to it any genetic groups that at least one classifier thinks is especially close to one of the members of a nucleus, and where others have not located it in the other network. Clusters and nuclei are in boldface.

The clusters and networks are:

Western Network
   macro-Chibchan cluster [most of Gr's Chibchan]
   macro-Tukanoan cluster [part of Gr's macro-Tucanoan]
   macro-Paesan cluster [most of Gr's Paezan]
   Andean cluster [part of Gr's Andean]
   macro-Waikuruan cluster [part of Gr's macro-Panoan]
   macro-Panoan cluster [part of Gr's macro-Panoan]

Eastern Network
   macro-Kariban cluster [most of Gr's macro-Carib]
   macro-Arawakan cluster [part of Gr's Equatorial]
   macro-Puinavean cluster [part of Gr's macro-Tucanoan]
   macro-Tupian cluster [part of Gr's Equatorial]
   macro-Je [most of Gr's macro-Ge]

We now turn to discussion of specific clusters within the WESTERN NETWORK. For each cluster the classifications of Greenberg, Swadesh, Suárez, and Loukotka are given (in that order).

macro-Chibchan cluster

Tano	IIA	C8	[absent]	[absent]
Yutonawa	IIC	C9.1	[absent]	[absent]
Kuitlateko	IIIA1	C9.2	[absent]	[absent]
Chibchan [8]	IIIA3-4	C:C3.4-3.6	41A	94
Misumalpa [9]	IIIA3g	C:C3.1-3.3	41E	94
Tukanoan [23]	VA18 C:	C3.7-8	69AB	81

The nucleus of macro-Chibchan is the intersection of Gr's Chibchan (IIIA), Sw's macro-Chibcha (C3,C:), JS's macro-Chibchan (41), and L's Chibchan (94), or agreement between any two. (Swadesh and Holt have both compared Yutonawa to Chibchan. Girard has compared Pano-Takana to Tukanoan. Thus both Sw and Girard support separating Tukanoan from the Eastern Network, where Gr puts it.)

macro-Paesan cluster

Kunsa [99]	IIIB2	P:W8.3	5	111
Betoi [5]	IIIB3	[absent]	41A	94
Paes-Barbakoan [6+7]	IIIB8a,b,d	P:W11.2	41A	94
Itonama [100]	IIIB5	P:W11.4	41C	5
Warao [112]	IIIB10	S3	41G	91
Kamsá [10]	VB3	E6	41A	94
Timukua	IIIB9	E4	[absent]	[absent]

The nucleus of macro-Paesan is the intersection of Gr's Paezan (IIIB), Sw's macro-Páez [P], JS' macro-Chibchan (41), and L's Chibchan (94), or agreement between any two. Migliazza excludes Itonama from macro-Chibchan or macro-Paesan.

macro-Chibchan for some, macro-Paesan for others				
Jabutian [101]	VIC14	P:W8.1	75	44
Kapishaná [100]	VA3	P:W8.2	11	67
Nambikuara [104]	VA12	E2	52	42
Tarasko	IIIA5	W6	[absent]	[absent]

Nambikuara is included here because Gr's VA macro-Tucanoan includes Tukanoan, which has been placed here in the Western Network, and because many of Sw's E[astern] groups are placed in the Western Network on other grounds. Kapishana likewise is in Gr's macro-Tucanoan, and Sw's macro-Páez. Jabutian, which Gr puts in macro-Ge, is put by Sw with Kunsa and Kapishaná with only 49mc of time depth. The case needs to be examined carefully.

Andean cluster				
Hívaro [31]	VB4c	H:S15.1,3	H:37B(+32+3)	62
Kawapanan [32]	IVC1	H:S15.1	H:37A(+32+3)	55
Puelche [60]	IVF3	H:S15.4	30	5
Urarina [37]	IVB1	H:S15.2	62	61
Sabela [36]	IVB3	W9	59	63
Omurano [35]	IVB2	E1	53	58

The nucleus of Andean is the intersection of Gr's Andean (IV), Sw's macro-Jíbaro [H], and JS's Hívaro-Kawapana [H], or agreement between any two.

macro-Paesan for some, Andean for others				
Ezmeralda [27]	VB4b	C2	41B1	94
Jaruro [28]	VB4e	P:W10	41B2	94
Kulyi [43]	IVD3	P:W11.5	22	103
Cholonan [42]	IVD2	P:W11.3	20	57
Leko [46]	IVD4	L:SE10	39	112
Sechura [44]	IVD5	L:SE10	61	101
Katakaoan [45]	IVD1	[absent]	14	102
Chokó [4]	IIIB8c	L:SE10	66	96
Warpe [61]	IIIB1	H:S15.4	H:32(+37+3)	117
Mura-Matanawí [96+97]	IIIB7	H:S14	41C	39+40

JS puts Chokó [4] and Kariban [110] in the same stock. Kariban belongs to the Eastern Network. Migliazza thinks Chokó might be macro-Chibchan or macro-Paesan, and thinks that Jaruro-Ezmeralda are **not** macro-Chibchan or macro-Paesan.

macro-Waikuruan cluster				
Matakoan [62]	VIB4b	M:SW4,7	47(+1)	10
Waikuruan [63]	VIB4a	M:SW6	27B	8
Charruan [64]	VIB1	M:SW2.3	27A	15
Maskoian [67]	VIB2	M:SW5	46	11
Lule-Vilela [65+66]	VIB3	SW8	40	9+116

The nucleus of macro-Waikuruan is the intersection of Gr's macro- Panoan (VIB), Sw's macro-Mapuche [M], and JS's Waikuru-Charrúa, or agreement between any two. JS sees a connexion between Matakoan [62] and Tupian [109].

macro-Panoan cluster				
Pano-Takana [53+54]	VIB6	K:W7.3	44C	75+76
Mosetén [55]	VIB5	K:W7.4	44B	79
Chon [56]	IVB5	K:W7.5	44A	4

The nucleus of macro-Panoan is the intersection of Gr's macro- Panoan, Sw's Quechuachón [K], and JS's macro-Panoan (44), or agreement between any two. Migliazza places all of these in macro- Panoan.

Andean for some, macro-Panoan for others				
Kechua [47]	IVE	K:W7.1	58B	107
Haki [48]	IVA	K:W7.1	58A	108

Andean for some, macro-Panoan for others, macro-Waikuruan for still others				
Kawéskar [58]	IVF1	SW9	1(+47)	2,3
Mapudungu [59]	IVF2	M:SW3	H:3(+32+37)	59
Yámana [57]	IVF5	SW10	77(+41)	1

Migliazza places Kawéskar and Mapudungu in macro-Panoan. JS sees a connexion between Kawéskar [58] and Tupian [109].

macro-Panoan for some, macro-Chibchan for others				
Yanomaman [111]	IIIA7	SE12.2	41F	90
?Yurakare [52]	VB11	C1	44D	78

It is not clear whether Sw considered Yurakare to be more closely related to macro-Chibcha (C3) or to macro-Aruaco (C4). If the former, he agrees with JS. If the latter, he agrees with Gr. Migliazza places Yanomaman and Yurakare in macro-Panoan. (Girard compared Pano-Takana to Tukanoan, transitively to macro-Chibchan, if Sw is followed. Migliazza compared Panoan to Yanomaman, transitively to macro-Chibchan if Gr is followed. Holt compared Takanan to Chibchan and Yutonawa. Key compared Yutonawa, Kechumara, Mapudungu, Mosetén, Pano-Takana, Chon, and Kawéskar.)

Note that Gr and Swadesh have linked the following to SA groups: Tarasko, Kuitlateko, and Timukua.

We now turn to discussion of specific clusters within the EASTERN NETWORK. Again, the classifications of Greenberg, Swadesh, Suárez, and Loukotka are given (in that order).

macro-Kariban cluster				
Kariban [110]	VIA3	K:S6.1	12A	89
Andoke [40]	VIA1	W:S4	2	82
Witotoan [39]	VIA2b	W:S4	9B	84
Boran [38]	VIA2a	W:S5	9A	83
Yawan [34]	VIA5	S2	76	54
Saparoan [33]	IVC2	S2	82	64
Hiraharan [3]	IIIB6	K:S6.6	66	96

The nucleus of macro-Kariban is the intersecton of Gr's macro-Carib (VIA), and Sw's macro-Caribe (S6;K:) and macro-Huitoto (S4-5;W:). Hiraharan [3] is located by Gr in Paezan, by Sw in macro-Caribe, but with 100mc of separation. Migliazza thinks Hiraharan is **not** macro-Chibchan or macro-Paesan. Examination of the data is needed. Sw links Yawan [37] and Saparoan [33] with 60mc of separation. Doris Payne 1984 independently suggested the connexion. Migliazza thinks Bora-Witoto-Andoke is macro-Arawakan, but that is because he thought Resígaro was Bora-Witotoan. In fact it is Arawakan (Maipurean) and **not** Bora-Witotoan. The removal of Bora-Witoto would leave very little content to macro-Kariban.

macro-Arawakan cluster

Tiniwan [11]	VB1d	E5	67	51
Arawan [17]	VB1e(1)	S13.1	4C	88
Maipurean [16]	VB1e(2)	A:C4.2-4.4+C6	4	46
Wahivoan [15]	VB1a	A:C4.1	26 (+4)	46
Timotean [2]	VB8	C5	66	96
Kandoshi [30]	VB4d	C7	51	59
?Yurakare [52]	VB11	C1	44D	78

The nucleus of macro-Arawakan is the intersection of Gr's macro-Arawakan (VB1), Sw's macro-Aruaco (C4;A:), JS's Arawakan, and L's Arawak. Note that Sw's Arawak belongs to his Central division which includes his macro-Chibcha (C3). I take his C2-C3 to go with macro-Chibchan and his and C4-C7 to go with macro-Arawakan. The rest of macro-Arawakan, apart from the nucleus, is made up of groups from Gr's Equatorial and Sw's Central division. It is not clear whether Sw considered Yurakare to be more closely related to his macro-Chibcha (C3) or to his macro-Aruaco (C4). If the former, he agrees with JS, and if the latter, he agrees with Gr. JS sees a relationship between macro-Panoan and macro-Arawakan. If accepted, this would put macro-Arawakan in the Western network. The most frequent connexions for macro-Arawakan, however, are with groups belonging to the Eastern network.

macro-Kariban for some, macro-Arawakan for others

Taruma [113]	VB9	K:S6.4	64	49
Katembrí [86]	VB1b	K:S6.3	15	29
Wamo [13]	VB1e(4)	S7	28	48
Chapakuran [14]	VB1e(3)	SE12.1	18	65
Kukurá [85]	VIA4	S13.2	38	25

Sw connects Chapakuran [14] with Yanomaman [111] with only 50mc separation. Sw connects Kukurá [85] with Arawan [17] with only 54mc separation. Migliazza thinks Wamo and Chapakuran might be macro-Arawakan.

macro-Puinavean cluster				
Puinavean [19]	VA15	M:S9.1-9.2	56	86
Katukinan [20]	VA4	M:S10	16	87
Maku [117]	VA8c	M:S12	45	52
Awaké-Kaliana [115+116]	VA8a,b	SE1	6+35	92+93

The nucleus of macro-Puinavean is the intersection of Gr's macro-Tucanoan (VA) and Sw's macro-Macú (M).

macro-Puinavean for some, macro-Kariban for others				
Aikaná [103]	VA6	S7	31	66

macro-Arawakan for some, macro-Puinavean for others				
Iranshe [105]	VA7	[absent]	33 (+4)	43
Harákmbut [18]	VB1e(2)	M:S11	72	88+77
Otomakoan [12]	VB1c	M:S8	54	47
Trumai [106]	VB7	M:S9.3	68 7	0

Migliazza includes Iranshe in Arawakan.

macro-Tupian cluster				
Samukoan [68]	VB12	Z:SW2.2	81 (+70)	12
Kayuvava [108]	VB2	W12	17 (+70)	71
Tupian [109]	VB5b	T:SE9.1	70	45+69
Salivan [114]	VB6	SE3	48	72

The nucleus of macro-Tupian is the intersection of Gr's Equatorial and the groups that JS links with Tupian, not including Kawéskar [58] and Matakoan [62]. This cluster is not very coherent and perhaps should be dismantled. Rodrigues, JS, and Migliazza all link Tupian to Kariban, and Davis links it to Je. Tupian seems comparable to everything in South America, but this may be due to the fact that Miriam Lemle's 221 proto-Tupí-Guaraní reconstructions have been around since 1971 for classifiers to examine. Sw links Kayuvava [108] with Ezmeralda [27] (Western network) with 45mc of separation.

macro-Puinavean for some, macro-Tupian for others				
Tekiraka [21]	VA1	Z:SW2.1	7	60
Kanichana [22]	VA2	Z:SW1	10	74
Movima [107]	VA10	T:SE9.2	48 7	2

Sw places both Tekiraka [21] and Kanichana [22] in macro-Zamuco. JS links Movima [107] to Waikuruan [63] and Charruan [64].

macro-Tupian for some, macro-Kariban for others			
Karirí [87]	VB5a	K:S6.2	13	36

(Rodrigues, Suárez and Migliazza have all compared Tupian to Kariban.)

macro-Je cluster				
Aimoré [72]	IC2	J:SE6	42B	J:20
Rikbaktsá [73]	VIC5	[absent]	23	41
Je [74]	VIC7	J:SE8.1-2	42D	J:16+24
Jeikó [75]	VIC7b	J:SE8.2	42E	J:24
Kamakanan [76]	VIC9	J:SE7	42F	J:22
Mashakalian [77]	VIC10	J:S1.3+x20	42H	J:19
Purian [78]	VIC13	J:S1.1	42J	J:18
Fulnió [79]	VIC6	J:S1.2	42C	23
Karajá [80]	VIC3	E3	42G	28

The macro-Je cluster is the best supported of all SA clusters: evidence has been assembled by Loukotka, Davis, and Rodrigues, among others; all continent-wide classifiers (including Migliazza) recognize its validity. Its precise bounds, however, have not yet been defined. Sw excludes Karajá from macro-Je.

macro-Je for some, macro-Kariban for others				
Guató [82]	VIC8	K:S6.5	29	80

macro-Puinavean for some, macro-Je for others				
Tikuna-Jurí [24+25]	VA17a	SE4	65+79	53+85
Kofán [29]	VB4a	SE5	21	100
Chimúan [41]	IIIB4	SE2	76	106

Migliazza thinks Kofán is macro-Chibchan or macro-Paesan, and that Chimúan is macro-Arawakan.

macro-Tupian for some, macro-Je for others				
Chikitano [70]	VIC4	T:SE11.2	19	13
Bororoan [71]	VIC1	T:SE11.1	42A	27
Ofayé [81]	VIC11	SW2.4	42I	J:28

(Davis and Rodrigues have both compared Tupian to Je.) Migliazza classifies Ofayé in macro-Je.

UNCLUSTERED AND UNNETWORKED genetic units are as follows: Munichi [26] not in Sw; Otí [83]; Baenã [84]; Tushá [88]; Pankararú [89]; Natú [90]; Shukurú [91]; Gamela [92]; Wamoé [93]; Tarairiú [94]; Shokó [95]; Koayá [102]; Hotí [118] no data: alive; Gorgotoki [69] no data: dead; Yurimangi [1]: Gr in Hoka, Sw in macro-Zamuco;

Also belonging here are Chipaya [49] and Pukina [50]: Gr lists these with macro-Arawakan, Sw with Quechuachón; Olson with Mayan (this is not a very good case). JS accepts both Arawakan and Mayan connexions. Migliazza puts them in macro-Arawakan.

How Greenberg compares to others. The following groupings
proposed by Gr show the least internal consistency if the classifications made
by others are to be given any credit:

a. Ge-Pano-Carib. There is practically no special lexical connexion for linking these in the evidence given by Gr.

b. Equatorial-Tucanoan. As for Ge-Pano-Carib, there are practically no
special lexical agreements between the two in Gr's data.

c. Equatorial. There seem to be two poles, those languages showing a
similarity to Arawakan, and those showing a similarity with Tupian.
There are quite a few which also show similarities with macro-Chibchan
and/or macro-Paesan and/or Andean in the narrower sense used here.

d. macro-Tucanoan. There seem again to be two poles, those languages
showing a similarity to Puinavean, and those showing a similarity to
Tukanoan. Tukanoan has been included in the Western network on the
strength of observations by Swadesh and Girard. Gr's macro-Tucanoan
contains a sizeable number of languages that are so poorly known that
other classifiers have been unwilling to attempt classifying them.

e. Central Amerind. This is made up of Nawa-Tano (AKA Aztec-Tanoan)
and Otomange (AKA Otomanguean). Nawa-Tano is connected to
macro-Chibchan and the Western SA network by Swadesh and Holt, and
Otomange is connected to Hoka (AKA Hokan) by Kaufman 1987ms.
Otomange is thus a part of some kind of version of Gr's Northern
Amerind. Gr's Central Amerind thus falls to pieces.[6]

Since as early as 1956 Greenberg has postulated a language group called
'Jibaro-Candoshi', made up of the following languages: Ezmeralda, Jaruro,
Kofán, Kandoshi, and Hívaro. This group is in turn supposed to be a part of
Greenberg's Equatorial group. The evidence for Greenberg's Jibaro-Candoshi
is found in Greenberg 1987 and stands as a particularly horrible example.
There are only 19 sets that provide evidence for any connexion at all between
any two of these five languages. Ezmeralda enters into 10 of them, Jaruro into
3 of them, Kofán into 9 of them, Kandoshi into 8 of them, and Hívaro into 13
(or 14) of them. These sets are: Eq 13 BLACK (2 lgs), Eq 35 EAT (1) (2 lgs),
Eq 37 EAT (3) (2 lgs), Eq 52 GRASS (2 lgs), Eq 68 LIVER (1) (3 lgs), Eq 76
MAKE (2) (2 lgs), Eq 81 MOON (2 lgs), Eq 83 MOUNTAIN (2 or 3 lgs), Eq
90 OLD (2 lgs), Eq 100 SMALL (2) (2 lgs), Am 11 Eq ASHES (3 lgs), Am 95
Eq EARTH (2) (2 lgs), Am 97 Eq UNDER (2 lgs), Am 104 Eq EYE (4 lgs), Am
155 Eq KILL (2 lgs), Am 165 Eq LEG (3 lgs), Am 200 Eq NIGHT (2 lgs), Am
217 Eq SAY (2 lgs), Am 194 Eq NAVEL (2 lgs). In 6 more sets Ezmeralda is
compared to other Eq languages; Jaruro in 3 more; Kofán in 9 more; Kandoshi
in 12 more; Hívaro in 19 more. This amount of evidence is almost pitifully
small, and the phonological similarities in the items compared are rather vague
in at least a third of the cases.

Out of just eleven words compared by Loukotka 1968 (p234) four show similarities between Ezmeralda and Jaruro, and only one comparison is the same as Greenberg's. Loukotka's glosses are HAND, FOOT (= Gr's LEG), WATER, BOAT. Ezmeralda and Jaruro may be related, and the matter should certainly be looked into, but Gr's Jibaro-Candoshi group is not supported. A few years ago David Payne (p.c.) compared Hívaro and Kandoshi and found a reasonable number of lexical similarities, but they were almost entirely in the domain of plant and animal names, and doubtless due to diffusion.

CONCLUDING REMARKS. I believe that the 118 **genetic groups** defined here are valid. In some cases we know of valid genetic connexions across some of these groups. The larger groups of Greenberg, Swadesh, Migliazza, and others are hypotheses which may be valid in part or not at all. The same is true of the **clusters** and **networks** set out here. They are meant to synthesize and partly harmonize claims made by the large-scale classifiers. I have **no stake whatsoever** in the validity or non-validity of any connexion that I have not labelled GOOD, PROMISING, or PROBABLE. I would like to know which of these hypotheses test true, but I am more interested in reconstructing the proto-languages of the valid and demonstrable groups, and in determining the correct classification/subgrouping of the valid groups by developing a model for the diversification of each family. It should also be obvious that part of the lack of clarity about what languages are mutually related must be due to the effects of linguistic diffusion muddying the waters. Thus recognition and identification of language contact phenomena will be among the steps required to unravel the tangled skein of South American linguistic relationships.

NOTES

*ACKNOWLEDGMENTS. Thanks to Lyle Campbell, Joseph Greenberg, Eric Hamp, Margaret Langdon, Sara Lickey, and Doris Payne for comments that enabled me to abbreviate, expand, or stubbornly stick to what I had written in earlier drafts. In particular, the didactic or preachy tone and rehearsal of what should be well-known principles of comparative linguistics were objected to. I feel, however, that many of Greenberg's (1987) and Ruhlen's (1987) avowed values are subversive and should be explicitly argued against. If there were two or three expositions of the comparative method and ancillary methods that covered all the principles of conceptualization and methodology that I outline in this paper and that were complementary, not contradictory, and acceptable to me, I would be glad to cite them and forego repeating what they said. But in my view they simply do not exist. It is my responsibility to promote the efforts I consider to be of greatest value in historical-comparative linguistics. Maybe all right-thinking comparativists will consider my methodological remarks to be redundant, but I strongly suspect that many who consider themselves to be right-thinking will find things here that are both new and food for thought and/ or threatening and objectionable to them. If so, my efforts will not have been wasted.

[1]   Lest the reader ask himself 'If Greenberg's classificatory innovations in Africa have been so widely accepted, how could he be so wrong in the New World?', let him keep these three points in mind: (1) much of what Gr did in Africa was to repeat the correct statements of earlier scholars, often changing labels; (2) a good deal of what he proposed involves such time depth that, even if true, it can never be demonstrated; (3) he did have some original and new ideas that were correct. Gr brought order to a field in disarray and made some useful innovations. Comparative linguistics in North America and MesoAmerica is not in disarray, though a bit more openness to the possibility of demonstrating distant genetic relationships might be in order. Admittedly, things have been moving pretty fitfully and sluggishly in South America, but this is due to scarcity of reliable data. I plan to discuss Greenberg's 'classification' of Amerindian languages in greater detail elsewhere.

[2]   One of the participants at the Working Conference on Amazonian Languages made a comment about 'Linnaean' models of relationship, as though everybody now knows that such models are not valid, and, what is worse, **outdated**. Not so.

[3]   It would be mistaken to conclude that if the principles outlined above were followed, IndoEuropean would never have been discovered. The hypothesis of an IndoEuropean family/stock arose out of the necessity of accounting for massive and recurrent similarities (within a particular set of languages) other than by borrowing. Hypotheses of relationship are not ruled out or even discouraged by my desiderata. But it is necessary to distinguish between **hypothesized** relationships based on good long-range comparative methods as outlined in the foregoing section, or on less stringent methods such as those of Greenberg, and relationships **validated** by the comparative method. I have devoted considerable effort to reconstructing aspects of proto-Otomange (1983ms, 1988msa) and validating Hoka as a stock (1988msc). Both of these entities have IE-like diversification and time depth.

[4]   Aryon Rodrigues (personal communication) objects to such a practice for forming family names being adopted in Portuguese; though I disagree with him on this matter, I will not offer Portuguese versions of the family names I propose as Spanish family names.

⁵   This spelling system is meant to be an **interface** between all representations of language and family names in all languages of the New World. It is **not an English system**, as the presence of nasalized vowels or the use of <j> for [ž] should make clear. For the languages of Latin America it provides explicit versions of Spanish and Portuguese words as well as Indian words in Spanish or Portuguese garb. For the languages of North America it provides versions of English or French words as well as Indian words in English or French garb.

⁶   The following data concerning the amount of Greenberg's evidence are provided as food for thought and not in the spirit of either sneering or praise. Further study and thought will be needed before these facts can be intelligently evaluated:

For macro-Ge Gr has 226 lexical comparisons. For macro-Panoan he has 141 lexical comparisons. For macro-Carib he has 143 lexical comparisons. For Ge-Pano-Carib he has 12 lexical and 5 grammatical comparisons. For macro-Tucanoan he has 192 lexical comparisons. For Equatorial he has 229 lexical comparisons. For Andean he has 214 lexical comparisons. He has 8 lexical and 3 grammatical comparisons linking macro-Tucanoan to Equatorial. He has 8 lexical comparisons linking Andean to Equatorial. For Chibchan-Paezan he has 324 lexical comparisons. He has 73 lexical and 8 grammatical comparisons that link all the SA groups together. He has 16 lexical sets and 3 grammatical comparisons that link his Central Amerind group to the SA groups. For Amerind as a whole there are 151 lexical sets and 24 grammatical comparisons.

REFERENCES

Davis, Irvine. 1966. Comparative Je phonology. *Estudos Lingüísticos* 1.2.10-25.

Davis, Irvine. 1968. Some Macro-Je relationships. *International Journal of American Linguistics* 34.42-47.

Girard, Victor. 1971. *Proto-Takanan phonology. (University of California Publications in Linguistics 70)* Berkeley: Univ. of California Press.

Greenberg, Joseph H. 1960. The general clasification of Central and South American Indian languages. *Men and cultures: selected papers of the 5th International Congress of Anthropological and Ethnological Sciences,* 1956. Ed. by Anthony Wallace, 791-794. Philadephia: Univ. of Pennsylvania Press.

Greenberg, Joseph H. 1987. *Language in the Americas.* Stanford: Stanford University Press.

Holt, Dennis. 1986. *History of the Paya sound system.* UCLA doctoral dissertation.

Justeson, John S., William M. Norman, Lyle Campbell, and Terrence Kaufman. 1985. *The foreign impact on lowland Mayan language and script*. New Orleans: Tulane (MARI 53).

Kaufman, Terrence. 1973ms. Kaufman's basic concept list on historical principles.

Kaufman, Terrence. 1983ms. New perspectives on comparative Otomanguean phonology.

Kaufman, Terrence. 1987ms. Tlapaneko-Sutiaba, Otomange and Hoka.

Kaufman, Terrence. 1988msa. Otomanguean tense/aspect/mood, voice, and nominalization markers.

Kaufman, Terrence. 1988msb. A research program for the reconstruction of proto-Hokan: first gropings.

Key, Mary Ritchie. 1968. *Comparative Tacanan phonology: with Cavineña phonology and notes on Pano-Tacanan relationship*. The Hague: Mouton.

Key, Mary Ritchie. ms n.d. (after 1978). Quechumaran and affinities.

Key, Mary Ritchie. ms n.d. (after 1979). North and South American linguistic connections.

Key, Mary Ritchie. ms n.d. (after 1979). South American relationships with North American Indian languages.

Lemle, Miriam. 1971. Internal classification of the Tupi-Guarani linguistic family. *Tupi studies I*. Ed. by David Bendor-Samuel, 107-129. Norman: Summer Institute of Linguistics and the University of Oklahoma.

Loos, Eugene. 1987ms. Comparative Pano[an]-Tacanan morpho-syntax.

Loukotka Čestmír. 1968. *Classification of South American Indian languages*. (Johannes Wilbert, editor.) Los Angeles: UCLA Latin American Center.

Migliazza, Ernesto. 1980ms. The languages of South America.

Migliazza, Ernesto. 1987ms. Pano-Yanomama genetic relationship.

Payne, Doris. 1984. Evidence for a Yaguan-Zaparoan connection. *SIL Work Papers (University of North Dakota Session)*. Ed. by Desmond Derbyshire, 28.131-156.

Price, David. 1978. The Nambiquara linguistic family. *Anthropological Linguistics* 20.1.14-39.

Rensch, Calvin. 1976. *Comparative Otomanguean phonology*. Bloomington: Indiana University Press.

Rodrigues, Aryon. 1985. Evidence for Tupi-Carib relationships. *South American Indian languages: retrospect and prospect*. Ed. by Harriet Klein and Louisa Stark, 371-404. Austin: Univ. of Texas Press.

Rodrigues, Aryon. 1984/1985. Relações internas na família lingüística Tupí-Guaraní. *Revista de Antropologia* 27/28.33-53.

Rodrigues, Aryon. 1986. *Línguas Brasileiras*. São Paulo: Loyola.

Ruhlen, Merritt. 1987. *A guide to the world's languages, vol. I: classification*. Stanford: Stanford University Press.

Sapir, Edward. 1917. The position of Yana in the Hokan stock. *University of California Publications in American Archaeology and Ethnology* 13.1-34.

Society for the Study of the Indigenous Languages of the Americas Newsletter VI:4.4-5,13-14. On SAPIR.

Suárez, Jorge. 1969. Moseten and Pano-Tacanan. *Anthropological Linguistics* 11.255-266.

Suárez, Jorge. 1973. Macro-Pano-Tacanan. *International Journal of American Linguistics* 39.137-154.

Suárez, Jorge. 1974. South American Indian languages. *Encyclopaedia Britannica*, 15th edition, Macropaedia 17.105-112.

Swadesh, Morris. 1959. *Mapas de clasificación lingüística de México y las Américas*. México: UNAM.

Thomason, Sarah G. and Terrence Kaufman. 1988. *Language contact, creolization, and genetic linguistics*. Los Angeles: University of California Press.

Tovar, Antonio & Consuelo Larrucea de Tovar. 1984. *Catálogo de las lenguas de América del Sur*. Nueva edición. Madrid: Gredos.

APPENDIX: LEVELS OF
RELATIONSHIP AND KINDS
OF LANGUAGES.

In the classification of languages it is customary to operate with such categories as language, dialect, variety, idiolect; phylum, stock, family, (sub)group, language. There are more kinds of phenomena that need to be accounted for in a classification than are straightforwardly named by these terms.

The problem I want to focus on is the range of phenomena between group, language, and dialect. Often the distinctions are hard to make, not because the categories are imprecise, but because we do not customarily recognize and name enough distinct categories.

It is common to find a set of two or more languages existing side by side that are closely related and where the linguistic boundaries between one language and the next are distinct and clear-cut. It is also often the case that an area of comparable linguistic diversity might lack clear-cut 'language' boundaries. The presence of this latter situation does not call the existence of the former category into question, and it would be wrongheaded and reductionist to say that is does. The different kinds of language:dialect situations that we find are the results of different patterns of linguistic change and diversification. We need to identify and label these situations in a useful/handy way.

I am intimately familiar with the language and dialect situation in Mayan languages and Xinka [Shinka] (Sp Xinca). I am quite knowledgeable about the language and dialect situation in Romani and the Germanic and Romance languages, especially English, Frisian, Low Dutch, and GalloRomance. I am well acquainted with the language and dialect situation in Yutonawa (AKA UtoAztecan), Otomange (Sp Otomangue), Mije-Soke [Mihe-Soke] (Sp Mixe-Zoque), and Slavic languages. On the basis of my familiarity with the above-named language families in Europe and the Americas, I suggest that there are the following kinds of language:dialect situations that require names. There is room for some adjustment on time depths, and particular languages that illustrate the phenomena; but I am sure that the categories are real and need names.

LANGUAGE AND DIALECT. Two sets of communities speak somewhat differently, but their natural speech is mutually intelligible without prior familiarity. All these communities speak the same language in two different dialects. Sometimes two dialects are quite well-defined, on a variety of structural traits, yet there is overall intelligibility between them. The establishment of an impassable physical barrier between two sets of communities speaking the same dialect can not lead to the loss of mutual intelligibility between them in less than 500 years.

LANGUAGE AND GENETIC GROUP. Two or more different sets of communities speak similarly to each other, but though they can be shown to be genetically related and descend from a common ancestor, they are not mutually intelligible; however, there may be a moderate degree of ability to recognize cognate words, and there is a clear boundary — sometimes an impassable one — between one set of communities and the other. The existence of an impassable boundary is not, as some would have us believe, the only situation where there can exist a clear-cut linguistic boundary between closely related languages; migration and extinction of intervening dialects are the two main causes of this kind of situation. These communities speak **separate languages** belonging to the same **genetic group**. This is the paradigm case and examples abound: (a) with no geographical separation: Kiché (Sp Quiché) vs Kakchikel (Sp Cakchiquel) (10c), GalloRomance vs IberoRomance vs ItaloRomance vs RhaetoRomance (17c), Otomí vs Masawa (Sp Mazahua) (10c), Tzeltal [Tseltal] vs Tzotzil [Tsotsil] (14c); (b) with geographical separation: English vs Frisian (15c), Irish vs Scotch Gaelic (14c), Icelandic vs Faeroese vs Continental Norse (10c), Western Romance vs Sardinian vs Balkan Romance (18c), Nawa (Sp Nahua) vs Pipil (11c), Pochuteko (Sp Pochuteco) vs General Nawa (15c), Mange (Sp Mangue) vs Chiapaneko (Sp Chiapaneco) (13c), Chikomuselteko (Sp Chicomecelteco) vs Wasteko (Sp Huasteco) (9c) [borderline case].

LANGUAGE AREA AND EMERGENT LANGUAGE. Two or more sets of communities each have a well-defined set of local linguistic traits, there are clear boundaries between one set of communities and another, yet there is a high degree of mutual intelligibility (to the untutored) across these well-defined boundaries. There is a percentage of cognates on the Swadesh 100-word list ranging between 76 and 84, which correlates with an internal time depth of between 600 and 900 years. These sets of communities constitute a **language area**; its constituent members are **emergent languages**; they themselves may have dialects or local varieties. ('Language area' is not to be confused with 'linguistic area' or **Sprachbund**.) Examples, with number of emergent languages in parentheses, include: Kanjobal-Akateko-Jakalteko [Kanhobal-Akateko-Hakalteko] (Sp Kanjobal-Acateco-Jacalteco) (3:7c), Northern Sapoteko (Sp Zapoteco) (3:9c?), Kakchikel-Tzutujil [Kakchikel-Tsutuhil] (Sp Cakchiquel-) (2:8c?), Pokom (3:10c)[borderline case], Trike (Sp Trique) (2:9c), Nawa (Sp Nahua) (4:8c?), Tlapaneko-Sutiaba (Sp Tlapaneco-) (3:8c), Matlatzinka-Okuilteko [Matlatsinka-Okuilteko] (Sp Matlatzinca- Ocuilteco) (2:8-9c), Maya (4:10c) [borderline case], Mochó-Tusanteko (Sp -Tuzanteco) (6c) [borderline case].

DIALECT CHAIN. There are several sets of communities. Each set shows a high degree of internal cohesion. Across these sets there is intelligibility with all adjacent sets, though less overall linguistic similarity throughout the whole chain than between adjacent dialects. Overall, from one end of the area to the other, there is a good deal or even a great deal of linguistic diversity; between communities at the extremes of the area intelligibility is very low or lacking altogether; yet, even though there may be well-defined dialect clusters/regions, there are not clear-cut boundaries of intelligibility and structural distinctiveness that would enable us to recognize a 'language' boundary. This is a **language** whose topological structure is that of a **dialect chain with serial intelligibility.** There is a percentage of cognates on the Swadesh 100-word list ranging from 64 percent and above, which correlates with a maximum time depth of 1500 years. Examples, with number of major dialect groups in parentheses, include: English (3:12c), Low Dutch (3:12c), Continental Norse (3:13c), Mam (3:12c).

LANGUAGE COMPLEX. In general the situation is as described for a dialect chain, but there are recognizable sets of dialects that can be postulated as constituting the functional equivalents of distinct languages within a genetic group. The distinct constituents of a language complex are **virtual languages.** Examples, with number of virtual languages in parentheses, include: Sapoteko (Sp Zapoteco) (5), Misteko (Sp Mixteco) (3:15c), GalloRomance (3:15c), IberoRomance (4:15c), ItaloRomance (3:15c), Slavic (5?:14c), Binnendeutsch (3?:16c), Xinka [Shinka] (Sp Xinca) (5+:12+c) [borderline case?].

RANKING OF CATEGORIES. Genetic groups can be made up of languages, dialect chains, and language complexes. Languages can be made up of dialects, which can occur in groups. Dialects can have varieties. Dialect chains are made up of dialects, which can occur in groups. Language complexes can be made up of virtual languages and language areas. Virtual languages are made up of dialects and dialect groups. Language areas are made up of emergent languages. Emergent languages can have dialects and dialect groups.

FAMILY AND STOCK. The unmarked genetic group is called a **family.** A set of families plus or minus whatever subparts a family can contain is called a **stock.** A set of stocks plus or minus families or whatever a family can contain is called a **phylum.** Intermediate ranks (other than language complex, language area, and dialect chain) within families can be called subfamilies, (sub)groups, branches, and divisions. Intermediate ranks (other than family) within stocks can be called substocks, branches and divisions. Intermediate ranks within phyla can be called subphyla, branches, and divisions. The typical minimum time depth for a family is 1000(-5000) years; for a stock, 4000(-8000) years; for a phylum, 7000(-10,000) years. Examples of well-known families are: Germanic (25c), Bantu (15c), Semitic (30c), Mayan (42c), Algonkian, Siuan (AKA Siouan), Selish (AKA Salish), Pomo, Yuman, Wakash, Mije-Soke [Mihe-Soke] (Sp Mixe-Zoque) (35c), Sapotekan (Sp Zapotecano) (24c), Otopame (36c), Chibchan, Kariban. Examples of well-known stocks are: IndoEuropean (55-60c), Niger-Congo, Otomange (Sp Otomangue) (60c), Yutonawa (AKA UtoAztecan), Uralic, TibetoBurman, Austronesian (70c), Algic, Maipurean, Tupian.

Phyla (also known as superstocks) are notorious, rather than well-known; the existence of not a single one has been established through reconstruction. This is primarily due to natural limitations on the applicability of the comparative method. The comparative method depends on valid etymologies. Etymologies are validated by the successful postulation of protolanguages (which are made up of protophonologies, protomorphemes, and protogrammar fragments), and plausible phonological and grammatical changes yielding a significant component of each of the languages that are claimed to be its descendants. For C. F. Voegelin, phyla were by definition of such great internal time depth that protolanguages modeling their ancestors could not be reconstructed because not enough cognate material remained such that hypotheses could be tested and proposed etymologies validated. It remains to be seen (by me) whether the 'phyla' proposed by Stefan Wurm in New Guinea conform to Voegelin's conception or whether they are subject to reconstruction after all, and if so, what time depth can be reached. SinoTibetan may be a large stock rather than a phylum. On the other hand, Nilo-Saharan in the sense of Greenberg, Bender, Ehret, Fleming, et al. is probably a phylum in Voegelin's sense. Obviously, hypotheses of long-range genetic connexion will not be demonstrated unless someone works at them. Some will pan out, others will not.

Some hypotheses of distant genetic relationship, if thoroughly studied and demonstrated through reconstruction, pass from what might have been thought to be a phylum to a stock. This may well happen in the case of Hoka (AKA Hokan) and Penuti (AKA Penutian). That is, these entities are hypothetical and subject to verification through reconstruction, which may or may not be successful, but it is not necessarily claimed that their time depth, if they are valid genetic groups, is in fact more than 7000 years. Thus, we need a distinct name for a hypothesized non-obvious genetic group of indeterminate time depth. Hoka and Penuti should not be termed phyla or superstocks.

The prepound **macro-** has been floating about for some time, with no very well defined applications. For a while superstocks/phyla were named 'macro-x'. For the most part macro- has been used to label the proposed union of two previously recognized genetic entities at least one of which was a stock. Most of the proposed macro- groupings have not panned out or have not yet been demonstrated. I propose using the element macro- to designate a set of language families and/or isolates that seem likely to be genetically related, but that have not been demonstrated to be related. The groups designated by a macro-label I would call **clusters**. As the genetic relationships within a proposed cluster are validated or debunked, the valid genetic groupings should receive names that do not include macro-. Thus, macro- would be used in an unambiguous way.

INDEX OF FAMILY AND ISOLATE NAMES
[Numerals Refer To Number Assigned To The Group]

Some Widespread Grammatical Forms in South American Languages*

David L.Payne

1. INTRODUCTION

Unraveling the tangle that characterizes our present knowledge of genetic relationships among South American languages presents us with a formidable task. A number of previous attempts at compiling cognates and positing reconstructions are fraught with problematic forms, among them those characterized as widespread forms or 'pan-americanisms' by Campbell and Kaufman 1980 and Bright 1984. These are similar forms occurring in a wide variety of American Indian languages, languages for which a large corpus of additional cognate sets is not easily found to corroborate a genetic relationship. As Campbell and Kaufman (p. 851) note: 'Though such widespread forms may suggest some common ancestry, they do not show that the languages under comparison at the moment are more closely related to one another than to any of the others containing the widespread forms which possibly are not being compared at the moment.' The best known among such widespread forms in American Indian linguistics are a first person pronoun with the phoneme /n/ plus a vowel, and a second person pronoun with the phoneme /m/ plus a vowel. Linguists engaging in comparative study need to be aware of widespread forms relevant to the area, in order to avoid the obvious pitfalls associated with them.

My purpose in the present work is to document five additional widespread grammatical forms in South American languages (Section 2) that I have encountered in researching the Maipuran Arawakan family and in perusing literature on other languages. For these five forms which occur in a number of Maipuran languages there are also similar forms in languages from several other families which are not commonly considered to have a special genetic affiliation with Maipuran. Undoubtedly there are more than just these five widespread forms in the Amazonian or South American context. Indeed the work of Matteson, et al. 1972, and more recently of Greenberg 1987, are replete with candidates (though both works purport to be compiling actual cognate sets).

In addition to these five widespread forms, in Section 3 I draw attention to a set of forms found in four language families of the Amazon basin which are not currently considered to have any special relationship. I claim that the nature of the forms is such as to imply something more intimate than the normal explanation given for the existence of widespread forms, i.e. diffusion. To be specific, the existence of a remarkably similar set of possessive devices which define noun classes in both Maipuran Arawakan and Cariban languages must have been present in the early stages of both of these language families. Since it is implausible to infer a late borrowing into all the Maipuran or Carib languages which exhibit this highly specific pattern, it appears either that there may indeed be a genetic relationship between the two language families which should be further pursued, or that there was intimate contact between the speakers of one of the remote ancestor languages and a language of the other family.

Two other Amazonian language groups, Arauán and Candoshi, show a strikingly similar pattern though with some fewer points of comparison. Some comparativists in the field of Amazonian linguistics (Aryon Rodrigues and Terrence Kaufman, personal communication) consider that the long assumed putative relationship between Arauán and Maipuran (see, for example, Noble 1965 and Matteson et al. 1972) has yet to be conclusively demonstrated. Though I am in hearty agreement with this evaluation, I suggest that the data in Section 3 showing similarity among the noun class devices for marking possession is enough to warrant keeping the option open, not just for a genetic relationship between Maipuran and Arauán, but also to include Cariban and Candoshi.

2. FIVE WIDESPREAD GRAMMATICAL FORMS

In this section, data demonstrating the existence of five widespread grammatical forms are given. In four of the five cases, the form is similar to a form given in Greenberg 1987. In each case, however, the form is attested below for a considerably wider range of languages than Greenberg's data suggest. Since unlike Greenberg, I am not asserting cognacy, I do not take the space here to indicate the source of each of the forms below, nor have I attempted to utilize a consistent phonological representation. Rather they are transcribed, for the most part, as they were in the source.

First, a widespread form for a negative morpheme, usually similar to the shape /ma/, extends outside the bounds of the usual South American context as documented in 1 below, to include Mayan. A similar form is found in several language families around the world. The form is a common one in Amazonian languages, though Greenberg (1987.315) noted it only for Macro-Panoan:

(1) NEGATIVE

*ma	Proto-Mayan
mana / ama	Quechua
mɨ	Mapudungun (Araucanian)
*ma-	Maipuran Arawakan 'privative'
*-yama	Proto-Panoan
*-ma	Proto-Tacanan
mã	Apinaye, Ge
mãñ	Tucano
*eʔĩm	Proto-Tupí
-hiaba/(-hiama)	Pirahã
ba-	Amarakaeri
mara	Madija-Culina (Arauán)
mañĩh	Nadëb
ma	Yanomama
(ta)ma	Yagua 'never' (compare -ta/tya 'negative')
-mra/-mnɨ	Hixkaryana (Carib)

The second widespread form is a causative affix most often of the shape /mV/. This form, noted by Greenberg (p. 313) for Panoan, Tupian, Arawakan and Mataco, is demonstrated for a wider range of languages in 2. Wise 1986 notes that among Maipuran Arawakan languages, this form is limited to two branches only: the Bolivian branch (Baure, Ignaciano and Trinitario), and the Pre-Andine branch (including both the Campa group, and Piro-Apurinã). It is thus quite plausible to consider that it is a loan into these languages, or into their common parent language, from one or more of the other languages that possess the widespread form.

(2) CAUSATIVE

-ɨm	Mapudungun
omi-	Campa, Arawakan
mi-	Apurinã, Arawakan
*-ma	Proto-Panoan
-me	Tacana
mo-	Tupinambá, Tupí
m-	Trumai, Tupí
mĩ-	Munduruku, Tupí
-ma	Apalaí, Carib
-ma	Hixkaryana, Carib ('benefactive')

-miti	Aguaruna, Jivaroan
ma-	Yuracare
me-	Ona
m-/-m	Tehuelche
-bo(-mo)	Pirahã
ma-	Nadɛ̈b
ma-	Yanomama

The third widespread form is another causative affix, specifically a verbal prefix consisting of a single vowel, usually a back vowel. I find nothing similar to this in Greenberg. Wise 1986 notes this form in a wide enough range of Maipuran languages to consider it to be Proto-Maipuran. By including Harakmbet and Arauán in the following list, I am not implying that I consider their putative relationship to Maipuran (cf. Matteson et al. 1972) to have been convincingly demonstrated. It has yet to be shown, in my opinion.

(3) CAUSATIVE

a-	Achagua, Guajiro, Lokono, Garífuna, Palikur, Waurá, Amuesha, Parecis (Maipuran)
i-	Terêna (Maipuran)
e-	Baure, Ignaciano (Maipuran)
o- / oi-	Campa languages (Maipuran)
V-	Aguaruna (Jivaroan)
a-	Amarakaeri (Harakmbet)
a-	Madija-Culina (Arauán)

The fourth widespread form is a directional suffix in verbal morphology meaning 'on arrival, to here or there'; this is given in 4:

(4) DIRECTIONAL (arrival, to here/there) as a verb suffix

-pu	Quechua
-pa	Mapudungun (Araucanian)
-op	Terêna (Maipuran)
-ap	Campa languages, Piro (Maipuran)
-ahp	Amuesha (Maipuran)
-pe	Waurá (Maipuran)
-nuwįį/ -nuwee	Yagua

Since this form is noted only for three language families (Quechua, Mapudungun and Maipuran) the similarity may only be accidental (though I hold that there is enough additional evidence to warrant exploring a genetic relationship between Mapudungun and Maipuran). Greenberg (p. 303) notes a locative case marker of a similar shape /-pV/, however, in Tupian, Tucanoan, and Quechua (to which could be added Nadɛ̈b /-bʉ/. I therefore suggest that both of these together, i.e. the directional and the locative forms, constitute an additional widespread form.

The final widespread grammatical form demonstrated here is an auxiliary 'have, do or be', usually containing the sequence /ka/, and often doubling in the same language as a lexical verb 'say, work'. Several lanquages unite these rather loosely related semantic concepts in the same verb, for example Maipuran languages Ignaciano and Campa in 5a, and Cariban lanquages Hixkaryana and Apalai in 5c. This shows the rationale for this degree of semantic latitude allowed for the single widespread form. This form is reflected in a limited set of forms for 'work' in Greenberg (p. 269). The more striking aspect of this widespread form is the presence in many of the same languages of a valence-changing verbal affix of the same or similar shape. In 5a I list a number of Maipuran languages which exhibit the auxiliary and/or lexical verb; 5b shows a range of valence-changing verbal affixes in Maipuran languages; and 5c shows similar forms in other South American languages:

(5) AUXILIARY 'HAVE, DO, BE', LEXICAL VERB, 'SAY, WORK' AND VALENCE-CHANGING AFFIX

    a. Maipuran (lexical and auxiliary verbs):

Ignaciano	ka-	'make, have, be'
Campa	kaNt-	'say, be, do'
	kara-	'have, be (quantity)'
Apurinã	kama	'do'
Guajiro	ka-	'be'
Resígaro	khu-	'make, do'
Waurá	ka	'have'
Lokono	aka	'tell'

    b. Valence-changing affixes in Maipuran:

        Attributive prefix: e.g. *ka-sabadu* 'shoe-ed' (i.e. having shoes)

        Garífuna; also in Taino, Guajiro, Lokono, Achagua, Piapoco, Yucuna, Waurá, Wapishana, Palikur, Terêna, Apurinã, Piro, Bauré, Ignaciano, Nomatsiguenga, Parecis

      Causative prefix: *ka-* Guajiro, Apurinã, Terêna, Ignaciano, Parecis

      Causative suffix: *-kaka* Apurinã, Campa, Waurá

      'Inchoative' suffix: fear-*kaa* + 'to become frightened' Resígaro

      Perfective suffix: *-ak* Campa

      Nominalizing suffix: I.alive-*ka* + 'my soul' Achagua

      Stem Closure suffixes (Southern Arawakan) + auxiliary verb?

c. Similar forms in other South American languages:

Quechua	ka	'copula'	-ka:	'passive'
Southern Quechua			*-s-ka	'progressive'
Central Quechua			-yka	'progressive'
Aymara	-n-ka	'locative-be'		
	-ska	'progressive'		
Jaqaru	-k	'present tense'		
Mapudungun	ka	'copulative conjunction'	-ka	'transitivizer'
Amarakaeri (Harakmbet)	kaʔ	'do'	-aʔ	'causative'
Hixkaryana (Carib)	ka	'say, do'	ka-	'causative'
Apalaí (Carib)	ka-	'say, do, be'		
Pirahã	kai	'make'		
Nadëb			ka-	'stem formative prefix'
Arauán			ka-	'transitivizer'

3. SIMILAR POSSESSIVE DEVICES WHICH DELINEATE NOUN CLASSES IN FOUR AMAZONIAN LANGUAGE GROUPS

In this section I argue that a highly specific set of devices marking possession on nouns, and which at the same time delineate noun classes (in some cases arbitrary noun classes), must have been present in both Proto-Maipuran and Proto-Cariban. This suggests either a genetic relationship or intimate contact for one of the proto languages with a language from the other family. A similar pattern for the possessive construction is documented for Arauán and Candoshi.

In Payne 1987 I posited for Proto-Maipuran five possessive devices which demarcate noun classes, and I documented their reflexes in a number of Maipuran languages. A typical manifestation of this system is found in Ashéninca (Campa) as in 6:

(6) ASHÉNINCA (MAIPURAN)

a. no-sari-ne
   1SG-macaw-POSS   'my macaw'

b. no-toniro-te
   1SG-aguaje.palm-POSS   'my aguaje palm'

c. n-aNpee-re
   1SG-cotton-POSS   'my cotton'

d. no-yanire   cf. kaniri 'manioc'
   1SG-manioc.POSS   'my manioc'

e. no-čʰarine   cf. čʰarine 'grandfather'
1SG-grandfather   'my grandfather'

The five devices in Ashéninca involve three possessive suffixes /-ne/, /-te/ and /-re/, a change of the stem final vowel to /-e/, and zero. Maipuran languages from nearly all the sub-branches of the family exhibit these noun class possessive devices, either by the entire range (Chamicuro, Campa, Piro, Waurá), or nearly the entire range (Garífuna, Resígaro, Yucuna, Palikur), or a pair of the devices, but not always the same pair from language to language (Guajiro, Parecis, Ignaciano, Amuesha). Other Maipuran languages provide data which indicate only one of the devices, though again, not always the same device or suffix from language to language (Achagua, Piapoco, Terêna, Baure). The distribution clearly shows that the five devices (i.e. the three suffixes, the final vowel change, and zero) must have been a feature of the early parent Maipuran language. In Payne 1978.66 I tentatively posit the Proto-Maipuran forms given in 7:

(7) a.   *-ni

     b.   *-te

     c.   *-re

     d.   *-V# > *-e#

     e.   ∅

Grammatical descriptions of the various Maipuran languages further suggest that the noun classes defined by these markers in early Maipuran were progressively more restricted in the order of 7a to 7d. Thus /-ni/ defined the largest, most large productive noun class, while the noun class defined by the vowel change to /-e/, for example, contained relatively few items. In some languages there does appear to be a certain amount of semantic cohesion to the noun classes. Piro, for example, is reported to use /-Vte/ for most regular nouns, /-ne/ for handcrafted household items such as flutes or feather fans, and /-le/ for another group of constructed items such as harpoons or platforms (Matteson 1965.99-100). In many Maipuran languages, either zero or the final stem vowel change is characteristic of the noun class including inalienably possessed items. These are most frequently body parts and, in some languages, kinship terms. Some terms seem to carry through most Maipuran languages with the same possessive marker. For example, 'manioc' in most languages uses the vowel change to /-e/ to mark possession. For many other nouns, however, there has been some shifting from one noun class to another, and the noun classes themselves have been redefined in some languages. In Asheninca, for example, the /-ne/ and /-te/ noun classes have been collapsed and the choice between the two suffixes is now purely phonological. Nouns with two vowels or less take /-ne/, while those with three vowels or more take /-te/. Though kinship terms predominate in the zero marked class, the other two nouns classes (i.e. those defined by /-re/ and the stem final vowel change) appear to be arbitrary. And in other languages all these noun classes have become quite arbitrary; at least they appear to be from the descriptions available. A similar set of devices is found throughout languages of the Cariban family as well (Marie-Claude Muller, personal communication). In 8 and 9 I illustrate these with data from Hixkaryana and Apalaí. According to Durbin 1985, Hixkaryana belongs to the Southern branch of Cariban, while Apalaí belongs to the Northern branch. The phenomenon is thus attested in each of the two major divisions of the Cariban family.

(8) APALAÍ (CARIBAN, from Koehn and Koehn 1986)

    a. i-tapïi-nï
       1-house-POSS   'my house' (p. 86)

    b. i-pï-tï
       3-wife-POS   'his wife' (p. 38)

    c. a-napï-rï
       2-fruit-POSS   'your fruit' (p. 86)

    d. i-pïre (zero poss. marker)
       1-gun.POS

Koehn and Koehn (p. 86) note that there is a fifth device in Apalaí, 'stem reduction'; I was unable to find an example for this.

(9) HIXKARYANA (CARIBAN, from Derbyshire 1961.134)

    a. ro-mï-nï
       1-house-POSS   'my house'

    b. o-wo-tï
       2-meat/food-POSS   'your meat/food'

    c. i-hana-rï
       3-ear-POSS   'his ear'

    d. i-kpo-ce
       3-hair-POSS   'his hair'

Other Cariban languages attest similar forms. Macuxi, from the same subgroup of Northern Carib as Apalaí, has possessive suffixes /-rï/ (also glossed 'determiner' and /-e/ glossed 'poss' (Carson 1982.107, 112). Panare, another Northern Carib language, but from a different subgroup than Apalaí and Macuxi, has suffixes /-ŋ/, /-ʔ/ and /-e/ (Muller 1974.4). The glottal stop is a likely reflex of /*t/ since constructions other than the possessives show alternations between /ʔ/ and /t/ in Panare (Tom Payne, personal communication). And Galibi (or Karina), from still another subgroup of Northern Carib, has suffixes /-rɨ/-ru/-nɨ/ and /-dɨ/, as well as zero and the change of a final vowel /-o/ to /-ɨ/ (Hoff 1968.214-220). It is also noteworthy that the three suffixes among the possessive devices in 7, i.e. /*-ni/, /*-te/, and /*-re/, are also common nominalizing and/or relativizing suffixes in both Maipuran and Cariban languages. Matteson (1972.165) posited /*-rV/ and /*-tV/ as nominalizers in her Proto-Arawakan, and I find evidence of a /-*nV/ nominalizer throughout Maipuran as well, as illustrated in 10 below:

(10) NOMINALIZING SUFFIXES IN MAIPURAN

    Garífuna: *-l* 'relator', *-ni, -ri, -li* 'nominalizer'

    Taino: *-te* 'dependent'

    Guajiro: *-in* 'tense/subordinator', *-le* 'subordinator', *-ra* 'nominalizer'

    Lokono: -(vowel nasalization) 'subordinator'

    Resígaro: *-tsi* 'nominalizer', *-ni* 'object relativizer'

    Achagua: *-ni* 'nominalizer'

    Palikur: *-atya, -tet* 'nominalizer'

    Waurá: *-re* 'nominalizer.masc'

    Amuesha: *-a:ñ* 'agent', *ehty* 'passive participle'

    Ashéninca: *-ri* 'relativizer', *-re, -ne* 'nominalizer'

    Apurinã: *-kari, -kati, -ti* 'nominalizer'

    Baure: *-ri* 'subordinator', *-ti* 'nominalizer'

    Parecis: *-tse, -la, -re* 'nominalizer'

In Cariban languages, Koehn and Koehn 1986.134 attest nominalizers /-nɨrɨ/ and /-n...-rɨ/ for Apalaí, and Derbyshire 1961.89-91 attests nominalizers /-rɨ/, /-ne/, and /-nɨ...-rɨ/ for Hixkaryana. Similar forms are also attested in the other Cariban languages cited above.

Such remarkably similar devices spread throughout both the Maipuran and Cariban families are surely not due to relatively recent diffusion. I suggest that either the two families may be genetically related, or that the possible borrowing of the system took place in the very early development of one of the language families. Cariban language divergence is thought to be more recent than Maipuran because of the greater degree of divergence in Maipuran. Therefore, the most likely direction of borrowing would have been from some Maipuran language into early Cariban.

I am not quite as ready to close the door on the possibility of a genetic relationship between Cariban and Maipuran as are, for example, Derbyshire and Pullum 1986. Mason (1950.209) suggested that Arawakan and Cariban would ultimately be shown to be related. The only evidence I have seen for this relationship is in Taylor 1953, and it is certainly not overwhelming. As Taylor (pp. 316-317) notes, the resemblances among basic vocabulary which he presents '... are perhaps more numerous than one might expect from pure chance or from borrowing in this semantic area.' The notion does bear further investigation, but only after reliable reconstructions of Maipuran and Cariban have been done.

Similar data showing devices for marking possession from two other languages, Candoshi and Madija-Culina (Arauán), are also suggestive of a possible genetic relationship, though the similarities are not as striking as those that obtain between Maipuran and Cariban. Candoshi, a language of the Northern Peruvian Amazon region, has normally been classified as Jivaroan. In an earlier work (Payne 1981), I attempted to compile the data that could demonstrate this presumed relationship. Although the reconstruction of Proto-Jivaroan (or Proto-Shuar, including Shuar, Huambisa, Achuar and Aguaruna) in that work is on solid footing, I now consider the putative evidence for the affiliation of Candoshi to that group to be deficient. A large number of the the proposed cognates that include Candoshi are names of flora and fauna, and thus potential loans. Proposed cognates from the basic vocabulary are significantly fewer, and are insufficient to conclusively demonstrate the relationship.

Instead, the devices which mark possession show enough similarity to the systems described above for Maipuran and Cariban; this, alongside some other apparent similarities between Candoshi and Maipuran languages, indicates a possibility of a genetic relationship, or at the very least some intensive contact. The data demonstrating the possessive devices which delineate noun classes in Candoshi are given in 11:

(11) CANDOSHI (from Tuggy 1966)

    a. v-ano-ri   cf. kano 'canoe'
       3-canoe-POSS   'his canoe' (p. 21)

    b. v-ašino   cf. kašini 'manioc'
       3-manioc-POSS   'his manioc' (p. 27)

    c. va-šara^{n}či   cf. šara^{n}či 'husband'
       3-husband.POSS   'her husband' (p. 113)

The suffix /-ri/ is given as the most productive of the devices, defining the largest noun class. The possessive suffix in 11a is similar to Maipuran forms such as 6c and Cariban forms such as 8c and 9c. The similarity of the Candoshi form in 11b to the Maipuran form in 6d is especially striking, both involving the same lexical item and a similar final vowel changing device marking the possession and noun class. The Candoshi form in 11c utilizes the zero possessive marking device like 6e in Maipuran and 8d in Cariban. It appears to be common among kinship terms in both Candoshi and Ashéninca that no suffix or vowel change is required to form the possessive construction, though I have not investigated this in other Maipuran languages and I do not know whether it holds true for Cariban. For the possessive constructions in Madija, as in Candoshi, there are only three noun classes delineated by the possessive construction, as opposed to the four or five in Cariban and five in Maipuran. These are, however, quite similar to forms in the other languages, as seen in 12:

(12) MADIJA (ARAUAN)

    a. bani-ri
       meat-POSS   'his meat'

    b. hai-ne
       path-NMLZR/POSS   'his trail'

    c. ene
       nose.POSS   'his nose' (an inalienably possessed form)

The suffix /-ri/ in 12a defines the most productive noun class, whereas the suffix /-ne/ delineates a more limited one. This second suffix is most apparently a nominalizer, but appears to be solely marking possession in some forms since a non-nominalized form of the possessed item is impossible to find for some of them. In any case, the two suffixes resemble the forms in Cariban and Maipuran both phonologically and in functioning as a marker of possession and nominalization.

The facts of this highly specific set of devices showing such similarity in these four language groups warrant investigating the possibility of a genetic affiliation. If it eventually proves impossible to demonstrate a genetic relationship, it may turn out to be the case that /-ri/, at least, is a widespread possessive suffix and nominalizer in Amazonian languages. Maurizio Gnerre (personal communication) has reminded me that /*-ri/ is also the possessive suffix in Jivaroan languages on regular nouns, and that no possessive suffix is required (i.e. zero) in the genitive construction for inalienable possessed nouns, which includes many kinship terms.

4. CONCLUSION

In this study I have accumulated data to document five widespread forms in South American Indian languages: a negative particle /ma/; a causative affix /mV/, a causative verbal prefix /V-/, a directional verbal suffix or locative case /-pV/, and an auxiliary /ka/ which in a number of languages coexists with a lexical verb 'say' or 'work', and/or a number of valence changing affixes of a similar phonological substance. I have also drawn attention to a pattern in Maipuran, Cariban, Arauán and Candoshi which is less likely to be accounted for by diffusion. The intricate pattern whereby a set of recurring devices for marking posession also demarcates noun classes in each of these languages or language families suggests that a genetic relationship between them should eventually be investigated.

NOTES

*   I am grateful to Des Derbyshire, Pete Landerman, Doris Payne, Mary Ruth Wise and an anonymous reviewer for commenting on an earlier version of this paper and for suggesting additional items for some of the widespread forms. I am also grateful to Patsy Adams, Rob Croese, Ernest Migliazza, Tom Payne, Joan Richards, Bob Tripp and Helen Weir for suggesting some additional items for the widespread forms which are not found in published sources. Any deficiency in the paper is my own responsibility.

REFERENCES

Bright, William. 1984. *American Indian linguistics and literature.* Berlin: Mouton.

Campbell, Lyle and Terrence Kaufman. 1980. On Mesoamerican linguistics. *American Anthropologist* 82.850-7.

Carson, Neusa. 1982. Phonology and morphosyntax of Macuxi (Carib). University of Kansas doctoral dissertation.

Derbyshire, Desmond. 1961. Hishkaryana (Carib) syntax structure, I: Word. *International Journal of American Linguistics* 27.125-142.

Derbyshire, Desmond and Geoffrey Pullum. 1986. *Handbook of Amazonian Languages, Vol. 1.* Berlin: Mouton de Gruyter.

Durbin, Marshall. 1985. A survey of the Carib language family. In Klein and Stark (eds.), 325-370.

Greenberg, Joseph. 1987. *Language in the Americas.* Stanford: Stanford University Press.

Hoff, Berend. 1968. *The Carib language. (Verhandelingen van het Koninklijk Instituut voor taal-, land- en volkenkunde, 55).* The Hague: Martinus Nijhoff.

Klein, Harriet and and Louisa Stark, eds. 1985. *South American Indian languages: retrospect and prospect.* Austin: University of Texas Press.

Koehn, Edward, and Sally Koehn. 1986. Apalai. In Derbyshire and Pullum, (eds.), 33-127.

Mason, J. Alden. 1950. The languages of South American Indians. *Handbook of South American Indians,* Ed. by Julian H. Steward. Volume 6.161-317. Bureau of American Ethnology, Bulletin 143. Washington.

Matteson, Esther. 1965. *The Piro (Arawakan) language. (University of California Publications in Linguistics, 42).* Berkeley: University of California Press.

Matteson, Esther, et al. 1972. *Comparative studies in Amerindian languages. (Janua Linguarum, Series Practica, 127).* The Hague: Mouton.

Muller, Marie-Claude. 1974. El sistema de posesión en la lengua panare. *Antropológica* 38.3-14. Caracas.

Noble, G. Kingsley. 1965. *Proto-Arawakan and its descendants.* Indiana University Research Center in Anthropology, Folkore, and Linguistics, Publication 38. (=*International Journal of American Linguistics* 31:3 Part II).

Payne, David. 1981. Bosquejo fonológico del Proto-Shuar-Candoshi: evidencia para una relación genética. *Revista del Museo Nacional* 45.323-377. Lima.

Payne, David. 1987. Some morphological elements of Maipuran Arawakan: agreement affixes and the genitive construction. *Language Sciences* 9.57-75.

Rodrigues, Aryon. 1985. Evidence for Tupi-Carib relationships. In Klein and Stark (eds.), 371-404.

Taylor, Douglas. 1953. A note on some Arawak-Carib lexical resemblances. *International Journal of American Linguistics* 19.316-317.

Wise, Mary Ruth. 1986. Causative and comitative affixes in Maipuran Arawakan languages. Paper read at the 1986 American Anthropological Association meetings, Philadelphia.

Valence-Changing Affixes in Maipuran Arawakan Languages

Mary Ruth Wise

1. INTRODUCTION

The Maipuran Arawakan family, i.e. 'mainstream' Arawakan, is one of the largest, most widely dispersed language families in Latin America. Languages of the Maipuran family at the time of the conquest of the 'New World' extended from the Bahamas and Greater Antilles in the north to the Gran Chaco in the south. In the east they were spoken at the mouth of the Amazon and along the upper Xingú River, and extended to the foothills of the Peruvian Andes in the west (Lathrap 1970.70). Perhaps because of the geographical spread and linguistic diversity of the family, comparative studies have been woefully lacking until recently (see Payne 1987 for a brief review of the literature).[1] They are still very far from being comprehensive, although a number of studies of the Maipuran Arawakan family are currently underway.

In this paper valence-changing and related affixes in twenty-five languages of the family will be examined and tentative reconstructions proposed.[2] Following Wise 1976 , 1982, and 1986 and Payne 1987 I consider Amuesha to belong to the Maipuran Arawakan family.[3]

2. VALENCE-CHANGING AFFIXES IN REPRESENTATIVE LANGUAGES

In all Maipuran Arawakan languages for which sufficient data are available there are at least two valence-changing verb affixes, causative and reflexive. In most of the Maipuran languages there are four or five such affixes.

The Campa group of languages (see the tables in section 3) is the richest in valence-changing affixes. In those languages there are several such affixes—e.g. applicative, purpose, and instrumental—which do not seem to be cognate with morphemes in other Arawakan languages and are not described in this paper.

In several of the Maipuran languages morphological causatives are marked by a prefix, or a suffix, or both. Selection, in some instances, depends on inherent transitivity of the verb; in others it is determined by whether or not the causer participates in the action; in yet others it depends on the degree of coercion exercised upon the causee. In some of the languages an affix may be glossed as both comitative (and/or reciprocal) and causative. Verbalizers, transitivizers, reflexives, attributives, thematic suffixes, epenthetic suffixes, benefactives, and passives often seem to be related in form.

The term ATTRIBUTIVE is used to gloss those prefixes which indicate 'having an attribute, belonging to a class or possessing the noun'. In most of the languages described in this paper attributives are prefixed to nouns and adjectives. In Amuesha they are prefixed to verbs also, as in 5b below.

The term THEMATIC is used to gloss affixes which have little, if any, semantic content but are required 'to mark the closure of particular strings of morphemes' (Matteson 1972.165). Like the thematic vowels of classical grammars, they are elements which are added to the root (or in Maipuran to a root or suffix) in order to constitute a theme to which inflectional affixes can be added. They are category-changing in the sense that the verb is incomplete without them. Selection usually depends upon arbitrary classes of roots.

In this section causative, comitative, reflexive, and other category-changing and valence-changing constructions of five representative languages will be described. Although verbalizers are not valence-changing, they are category-changing. The ones discussed here seem to be cognate with valence-changing suffixes, and they often function as both causative and verbalizer.

2.1 AMUESHA. In Amuesha, spoken in the Peruvian foothills of the Andes, causative constructions are formed by the addition of a causative prefix *a-/e-* to the verb root, as in 1; a causative suffix *-aht*, as in 2; both the prefix and suffix (3); or the reduplication of *-aht* (4).

(1)   a. pʸ-aʔ-bʸe.č-eʔ
           2SG-CAUS-soft-3SG
           'soften it, e.g. cook it until it is tender!'[4]

       b. aʔ-šor-e.nʸeȼ
           CAUS-to.fall-INF
           'to allow to fall' (Tripp, in preparation)

       c. Ø-e-ya-ʐ-ann-aʔt-a
           3SG-CAUS-to.cry-CHARACTERISTICALLY-RCP-TH-RF
           'they, e.g. children, characteristically make each other cry (while playing)' (Wise 1963.143)

(2)   Ø-č-aʔn-m-aht-a.n-eht
       3SG-to.go-ABL-COMP-CAUS-OBJ.FOLLOWS-3PL[5]
       'he caused them to go out'

(3) aʔ-šor-aht-e.nʸeȼ
     CAUS-to.fall-CAUS-INF
     'to cause to fall, i.e. to drop' (Tripp, in preparation)

(4) mʷeȼ-aht-aht-e.nʸeȼ
     to.kill-CAUS-CAUS-INF
     'to cause someone else to kill someone' (ibid.)

The prefix *a-/e-* is also used in attributive and passive participial constructions, as in 5. The passive participle is the only passive construction in Amuesha.

(5) a. eh-klʸay-o.r-ehtʸ-en
         ATT-money-HAB-PP-1SG
         'I am moneyed, i.e. I have money'

     b. a-kr-a.r-ehtʸ
         ATT-to.choose-HAB-PP
         'chosen'

Example 6 shows one idiomatic use of the causative suffix *-aht*.

(6) ye-ʐo.m-aht-e.n-a   ya-knʸeʔtʸ-e.r
     1PL-to.die-CAUS-PROG-RF 1PL-little-GEN
     'we cause our little ones to die, i.e. we cannot prevent our children from dying'

The semantic distinctions between the different causative constructions are not always clear-cut. However, the prefix is generally neutral with regard to intention and signals that the causer is not affected by the action. On the other hand, when the causative suffix *-aht* is used, the causer is involved in the action either directly and physically as in 'to drop' (3), or emotionally and socially, as in 6 'cause to die' where the causer is presumed to be able to prevent an action from taking place but has failed to do so. The reduplication of the suffix *-aht* (4) is mediative, i.e. it indicates 'to do by proxy or to command'. A single occurrence of *-aht*, as in 7, can also indicate 'to do by proxy' in some contexts, as yet undefined.

(7) Ø-mʷeȼ-aht-a.n   a-mʸč-aʔt-a.r-ehtʸ
     3SG-to.kill-CAUS-OBJ.FOLLOWS CAUS-to.fear-TH-HAB-PP
         šonteʔ   bʸeʐ
         much   meat
     'the chief (feared one) caused many animals to be killed (in a hunt)' (Tripp, in preparation)

A suffix which might bear only a fortuitous resemblance to -*aht* 'causative' is -*(V?)t/-V.t/-Vht* which obligatorily occurs as a 'stem closure, i.e. thematic suffix' following certain roots and suffixes. In 8 -*a?t* must occur following -*ač* 'group'. (See Wise 1963 and 1986 for detailed discussion.) It also functions as a verbalizer (9, 10, 12), and as a transitivizer. The transitivizing function can be seen by comparing 11a with b which are typical of numerous pairs differing in just this way both in form and meaning. Since it has little semantic value, I have glossed this suffix as 'thematic (TH)'. In 11b the *a?* in -*a?n* 'ablative' can be considered epenthetic, since this suffix also occurs without *a?*, as in 11c.

(8) č-ač-a?t-eht
     to.go-GROUP-TH-3PL
     'they gathered together' (Wise 1986.581)

(9) Ø-pakl^y-a?t
     3SG-house-TH
     'he built a house' (ibid.)

(10) ne-g-o?t-ahs-o?t
     1SG-fishhook-TH-LIQUID-TH
     'I fish with a hook and line at the river' (Wise 1963.134)

(11) a. Ø-čak-a?t-a.n   po-k^{y}e?
        3SG-to.break.off-TH-OBJ.FOLLOWS 3SG-arm
        'he broke off its arms, e.g. of a spider'

     b. Ø-čak-a?n-om   po-k^{y}e?
        3SG-to.break.off-ABL-COMP 3SG-arm
        'his/her/its arm broke off in passing by'

     c. Ø-ent-n-om-a.n   ače.n^y
        3SG-to.see-ABL-COMP-OBJ.FOLLOWS person
        'as he went along he saw someone'

Although historically -*(V?)t* may be related to the causative, I consider it to be a separate morpheme synchronically, since the causative use always has the form -*aht* and the epenthetic suffix includes variants -*(V?)t*, -*V.t*, and -*Vht*. The form -*Vht* occurs only in the verbalizing function (12).

(12) Ø-nont^y-eht-e.n
     3SG-canoe-TH-PROG
     'he is making a canoe'

In section 3.1 I will argue that the epenthetic suffix is historically, as well as synchronically, separate from the causative -*aht*.

The Amuesha reciprocal suffix (13a) appears to be a Panoan loan (compare 13b). The comitative suffix, illustrated in 14, does not appear to be cognate with comitative or causative affixes in any other Arawakan language for which I have data. (See section 3.6 for discussion of possible sources for *-mi* (13b), *omin-* (17) and *-imo* (26).)

(13) a. Ø-ҫo.t-a?t-ann-e.n-a
     3SG-to.hit-TH-RCP-PROG-RF
     'they are hitting each other'

    b. mïï-aná-mi-tï kï
      to.hit-RCP-CAUS-RP
      'to again cause to hit one another' (Cashibo, Shell 1957.188)

(14) pʸe-ẓ-apre.t-en
     2SG-to.eat-COM-1SG
     '(please) eat with me (an invitation to a meal)'

The Amuesha reflexive, exemplified in 6 and 13a, is *-a*. As in the Campa languages, it is required with many intransitive stems, such as *ohma.č-* 'to jump', and a few transitive ones, such as *¢e.pt-* 'to keep company with, sit and chat with'. It is also required with the reciprocal suffix.

The benefactive suffix, which can also mean 'malefactive', is *-(o)n*.

(15) o?č   Ø-w-ahp-on-apʸ-a
     FUTURE 3SG-come-arrive-BEN-2SG-RF
     'it will arrive on you (a sickness)'

The Amuesha causative suffix *-aht* and the thematic *-V?*, the causative affix *a-/-e,* and the benefactive suffix *-(o)n* are, I believe, inherited from proto-Maipuran. They are all cognate with affixes in several other geographically dispersed languages. The reciprocal suffix is not inherited, having been borrowed from Panoan. The comitative suffix does not appear to be Maipuran in origin either.[6]

2.2 NOMATSIGUENGA AND OTHER CAMPA LANGUAGES. In Nomatsiguenga, also spoken in the Peruvian foothills of the Andes, causative constructions are formed in one of the following ways: 1) by the addition of a causative prefix *(o)gi-/ga-/o-* to the verb root, as in 16; 2) infrequently by *omi(n)-*, as in 17; and 3) in some cases by voicing of the root initial stop (compare 18a and b).

(16) y-ogi-monti-ë-ri
     3M-CAUS-to.cross.river-NF-3M
     'he caused him to cross the river' (Wise 1971.104)

(17) y-omin-tsoro-k-e-ri
     3M-CAUS-to.fear-PROG-NF 3M
     'he causes him to be afraid' (Wise 1971.104)

(18) a. i-bi-ak-e-ri
        3M-CAUS+to.change.into-PF-NF-3M
        'he caused him to get lost' (ibid.)

     b. i-pi-ak-a
        3M-to.change.into-PF-NF
        'he changed (himself) into another form' (Shaver p.c.)

In these prefixal causative constructions the causer does not participate in
the action but does something which causes it. They occur only with verb roots
which are inherently intransitive; these include motion (16), stative (17) and
metamorphic (18) roots. An additional causative prefix *ti-/tiN-*, described as
forceful causation, is reported for Machiguenga (19).

(19) no-ti-sara-ak-e-ro
     1-CAUS-to.tear-PF-NF-3F
     'I made it tear' (W. Snell 1955 ms)

Inherently transitive (20), ditransitive (21), and quotative (22) verb roots
may be causativized in Nomatsiguenga by the addition of the suffix *-agant*
'mediative, proxy'; this is probably related to the verb root *kan(t)-* 'to do/say'.
In these constructions the causee is an unnamed intermediary or proxy who
performs the action at the instigation of the causer.

(20) i-hok-agant-a-i-ri
     3M-to.throw.away-MD-REGRESSIVE-NF-3M
     'he had it/him thrown away' (Wise 1971.104)

(21) i-p-agant-ĕ-ri   kireki
     3M-to.give-MD-NF-3M money
     'he sent him money' (ibid.)

(22) i-kaim-agant-ĕ-ri
     3M-to.call-MD-NF-3M
     'he sent for him' (ibid.)

There is also a causative/comitative suffix *-ag/-akak/-ak* which occurs with
all classes of verb roots except ditransitive. In these constructions the causer
usually participates in the action, as in 23, where his helping hand causes or
enables another to cross the river. (Compare 16 with 23 and 18 with 24.) In 24
the meaning may be simply comitative in some contexts.

(23) i-monti-ag-an-ë-ri
   3M-to.cross.river-COM/CAUS-ABL-NF-3M
   'he helped him to cross the river' (Wise 1971.107)

(24) i-pi-ak-ak-a-ri
   3M-to.change.into-COM-PF-NFR-3M
   'he disappeared with him' (ibid.)

In Machiguenga, a closely related language, the cognate suffix *-akag/-akak/ -ag* can indicate that the causer does not participate in the action (25). Nevertheless, in most Campa languages the causation is more indirect and the comitative meaning of *-akak/-ak/-ag* seems to be primary.

(25) no-panki-t-ag-ak-e-ri
   1-to.plant-EP-CAUS/COM-PF-NF-3M
   'I ordered him to plant/ I planted with him' (W. Snell 1955 ms)

The suffix *-(i)mo/-omo* (26) in Campa languages is usually glossed 'in the presence of'. It contrasts with the comitative in that one actor performed the action in the presence of another, rather than one actor accompanied another in performing the action. However *-(i)mo/-omo* is occasionally glossed 'comitative' or 'benefactive'.

(26) kero ni-a-t-omo-t-i-ri
   not 1-to.go-EP-PRES-EP-NF-3M
   'I don't go in his presence, i.e. to where he is (jaguar)' (Wise 1971.110)

In all of the languages of the Campa group the reciprocal is formed by the reciprocal suffix *-aw* (*-ab* in Nomatsiguenga, Machiguenga and Caquinte) obligatorily followed by *-akag/-aka* 'causative/comitative', as in the Asháninca example in 27. (See section 3.2. for a possible origin of the reciprocal construction in Campa.)

(27) i-kis-aw-aka-ak-a
   3M-to.be.angry-RCP-COM-PF-NFR
   'they are angry with each other' (Kindberg 1961.532)

The reflexive in Campa languages is fused with the tense suffix: *-a* 'nonfuture reflexive (NFR)', as in 24, 27 and 28, and *-ia* 'future reflexive'. It follows the aspectual suffix, e.g. *-ak* 'perfect' in 27, and is obligatory with the reciprocal *-aw* which precedes the aspectual suffix.

In addition to the causative, comitative, reciprocal, and reflexive morphemes, in all of the Campa languages there is an epenthetic *t* in verbs which breaks up underlying vowel clusters at morpheme boundaries. This is

illustrated in 25, 26 and 28. An epenthetic *a* is inserted between underlying
consonant clusters at morpheme boundaries, as in the Machiguenga example in
28.[7]

(28) no-kog-a-be-t-ak-a-ro
        1SG-to.want-EP-FRUSTRATIVE-EP-PF-NFR-3F
        'I wanted it in vain' (W. Snell 1955 ms)

The epenthetic *-t* is probably cognate with the thematic suffix *-V?t* in
Amuesha.

Nomatsiguenga and Machiguenga have a passive construction, formed with
the suffix *-gani/ɲani;* this is limited to third person, and the agent cannot be
named.

(29) birakoča i-p-ab-ak-e-ɲani   kireki
        whites   3M-to.give-RECEIVING-PF-NF-PAS money
        'the whites were given money' (Wise 1971.52)

There is also a passive participial or adjectival construction marked by *-ge*;
this occurs rarely (30). The *ko-* prefix is probably cognate with the *ka-*
'attributive' described for Waurá, Ignaciano, and Guajiro in sections 2.3, 2.4
and 2.5, respectively.

(30) iroro ko-p-a-ge
        it   ATT-to.eat-EP-PP
        'it is edible' (ibid. p. 55)

Benefactive suffixes include *-anont, -went/-bent* and *-nV.* Only *-nV*, as in the
Asháninca example in 31, appears to be cognate with the benefactive in other
Maipuran languages.

(31) y-owečik-i-ni-ro
        3M-to.make-NF-BEN-3F
        'he made it for her' (Kindberg 1961.537)

The perfective suffix *-ak* in Campa languages, illustrated in 18, 19, 24, 25,
27, 28, and 29 is possibly—but not certainly—cognate with the *-ka/-ha*
perfective/verbalizing/causative/thematic suffixes which occur in many other
Maipuran languages (see Table 3). If so, a causative verb root developed into a
causative suffix. Then in some languages a more general verbalizing or
thematic function developed at a later stage. In others a completive or
perfective meaning developed from 'doing' the action. It is also possible - but
not certain - that the verb root *kan(t)-* 'to do/say' (32) and the mediative suffix
-agant (20-22) are cognate with these suffixes and with the verb root *kʰu* 'to do
or make' in Resígaro (Allin 1975.207).

(32) i-kant-i-ri
    3M-to.say-NF-3M
    'he said to him' (Wise 1971.195)

The epenthetic *t*, the reciprocal *-aw*, the comitative or causative *-akag/-akak*, the passive *-gani*, and the benefactive *-nV* are clearly reflexes of proto-Maipuran affixes as seen in the tables in section 3. The status of the other causative and comitative affixes is less clear.

2.3 WAURÁ. In Waurá, spoken in the Xingú Park in Brazil, there is a causative prefix *a-/i-* (33), which is cognate with Amuesha *a-/e-*; there is also an attributive prefix *ka-* (34) which is cognate with an attributive prefix described in 2.4 for Ignaciano and also found in many Maipuran languages.

(33) a-kɨɨ
    CAUS-basket
    'to catch (fish) in a basket' (Richards MS1.5)

(34) ka-tai
    ATT-fruit
    'to have fruit' (ibid. p. 5)

Causative verbs in Waurá are also formed by the addition of the suffix *-ka* (35) to nouns, the suffix *-ta* (36) to nouns or verbs, or the prefix *a-/i-* and one of the causative suffixes (37).

(35) pɨ-ka
    onom-CAUS
    'to pour (powder)' (Richards MS1.6)

(36) n-aïtya-ta-pa-i   nu-piža   kupatɨ i-tsenu
    1-to.eat-CAUS-STAT-...   1-pet   fish   3-WITH
    'I feed my pet with fish' (Richards MS3.30)

(37) a-wakula-ta
    CAUS-stew-CAUS
    'to make stew' (Richards MS1.8)

Derbyshire (1986.513) quotes Richards as reporting that a number of suffixes end with *-ta* or *-tsa* which might be cognate with the thematic or epenthetic suffixes described above for Amuesha and Campa. A 'generated', i.e. epenthetic, vowel is also mentioned by Richards (MS4.35-36).

Comitative and reciprocal categories are often expressed in postpositional phrases, as in 38. There is also, however, a reciprocal suffix *-waka* occurring in verbs (39). Both the postposition and verb suffix are probably cognate with the

Campa comitative/causative; the reciprocal verb suffix is no doubt a fusion of the reflexive -wa and -xaka. (Compare the Campa reciprocal in 27.)

(38) nala kixekoja-pa-i   pa-pitsi-xaka
     those to.speak-STAT-... own-TO-RCP
     'they are speaking to one another' (Richards MS2.1)

(39) unupa-jõta-waka-pa-i
     to.see-INTENSE?-RCP-STAT-...
     '(they) are staring at one another' (ibid. p. 2)

The reflexive is -ua, as in 40. A nonagentive passive is formed with the suffix -kina (41).

(40) aw-á-yúku-t-uá-wi
     1PL-CAUS-urucu-CAUS-RF-PF
     'we painted ourselves with urucu' (Derbyshire 1986.511)

(41) Ø-aipiáka-kina yámukutái
     3-scarify-PAS   child
     'the child was scarified' (ibid. p. 510)

The benefactive suffix -u occurs only as a postposition in noun phrases and does not appear to be cognate with the verbal benefactive suffix in other Maipuran languages.

2.4 IGNACIANO. In Ignaciano, spoken in Bolivia, there is a causative or transitivizing prefix e-/ve- (42) and a causative prefix ími-/ím-. The prefix ími-/ím- occurs with intransitive roots only (43), while e-/ve- can occur with both transitive and intransitive roots. In the closely related Trinitario, Gill (MS) reports that im-/em- on intransitive verbs indicates an accompanying object, or action in company with the object (44), i.e. it functions as a comitative prefix. Again, the action is causative in that the initiator causes the one accompanied to perform the action by helping him do it.

(42) n-é-sina-ča
     1SG-CAUS-to.be.fat-TH
     'I fatten it' (Ott and Ott 1983.38)

(43) t-ím-ite-ka-nu
     3IMPRS-CAUS-to.come-TH-1SG
     'someone made me come' (ibid.)

(44) p-em-etereša
     2SG-CAUS-to.jump
     'jump with it' (Trinitario, Gill MS.42-43)

There is also in Ignaciano a prefix *ka-* which functions as an attributive (45) or as a causative or transitivizer (46) with intransitive and stative roots. The privative prefix *ma-* is the antonym of *ka-* 'attributive'; compare 45a with 45b.

(45) a. nu-ka-pena
     1SG-ATT-house
     'I have a house' (Ott and Ott 1983.38)

     b. má-imaru-Ø
     PRIV-husband-3
     'she doesn't have a husband' (ibid.)

(46) nu-ka-siapa
     1SG-CAUS-to.enter
     'I put it in' (ibid.)

The reciprocal suffix is *-ka(ka)* (47), cognate with the causative/comitative suffix *-akag* in Campa and the reciprocal in Waurá. In 47 the reciprocal has only one syllable following the thematic suffix *-ka*, since no more than two *ka* syllables occur in sequence in Ignaciano.

(47) ti-ni-ka-ka-na
     3IMPRS-to.bite-TH-RCP-PL
     'they bit each other' (Ott and Ott 1983.44)

The reflexive suffix *-wa* (48) can cooccur with the reciprocal *-ka(ka)* but is not obligatory (compare 47 and 49).

(48) t-éču-ka-wa
     3IMPRS-to.cut-TH-RF
     'he cut himself' (Ott and Ott 1983.44)

(49) ti-pi-ka-ka-wa-na-ri-ču
     3IMPRS-to.fear-TH-RCP-RF-PL-COMP-LIMITATIVE
     'they are afraid of each other' (ibid.)

There are also several thematic suffixes including *-ka/-ha* (illustrated in 47) and *-ča* (42). The suffix *-ča* is possibly cognate with *-V7t* of Amuesha and the epenthetic *-t* of Campa.

The passive is formed by the addition of the suffix *-kasi* to transitive verbs (50) or the prefix *ka-* and the suffix *-hi* (51).

(50) nu-kawa-kasi
     1SG-to.calm-PAS
     'I was calmed' (Ott and Ott 1983.45)

(51) nu-ka-epuči-hi
     1SG-PAS-to.club-PAS
     'I was clubbed' (ibid.)

The benefactive suffix *-ina* (52) is cognate with the benefactive in Amuesha and several other Maipuran languages (see Table 6).

(52) pi-ám-ina-nu
     2SG-to.bring-BEN-1SG
     'bring (it) to me' (Ott and Ott 1983.45)

2.5 GUAJIRO. In Guajiro there is an attributive/verbalizing prefix *k(a)-* (53) and a causative suffix *-t/-it/-ir* (54).

(53) ka-kaaʔulaa-in-waa
     ATT-goat-POSSESSIVE-INF
     'to have goats' (Mansen and Mansen 1984.402)

(54) ek-it-n-aa
     to.eat-CAUS-PAS-INF
     'to be made to eat' (ibid. p.16)

There is also a thematic suffix *-taa* (55) and an epenthetic *a(a)* (56b). The same form functions as an infinitive suffix (56a) but may be a different homophonous suffix. The prefix *a-* (55b), or occasionally another vowel, occurs in most active verbs and is probably cognate with the *a-/e-* prefix in Amuesha, Waurá, and Ignaciano.

(55) a. huru-taa
        to.be.spinning-TH
        'to be spinning around'

     b. a-hura-taa
        ACT-to.be.spinning-TH
        'to turn' (Alvarez 1985.30)

(56) a. ant-aa
        to.arrive-INF
        'to arrive' (Mansen and Mansen 1984.55)

     b. an-a-sɨ
        to.be.good-EP-N/M.GENERAL.TIME
        'it's all right' (ibid. p. 86)

There is some lack of agreement between authors, but apparently the reflexive is *-waa* (57b) or *-a* (58), and the reciprocal/comitative is *-hir(a)* (58).

However, according to Ehrman, the suffix *-hir(a)* has a causative/mediative sense also, as in 59.

(57) a. oʔotoo
　　　'to mount (tr)'

　　b. oʔoto-waa
　　　'to mount-RF' (Mansen and Mansen 1984.15)

(58) airri-a-hir-a-ši
　　　to.despise-RF-RCP-EP-M.GENERAL.TIME
　　　'we mutually despise one another' (Olza and Jusayú 1986.103)

(59) alaka-ha-hira
　　　to.cook-TH-CAUS
　　　'to order to cook' (Ehrman 1972.60)

Thematic suffixes include *-ka/-ha*. The form *-ha* is illustrated in 59.

The comitative postposition *-(a)maa* occurs in noun phrases (60) and is possibly cognate with *-imo* 'in the presence of' in Campa. There is also a postposition *-aʔaka* 'among' in noun phrases (61) which appears to be cognate with the reciprocal verb suffixes described above for Campa languages, Waurá, and Ignaciano.

(60) saašeyaain nü-maa
　　　she talks　3M-with
　　　'she talks with him' (Mansen and Mansen 1975.172)

(61) teʔitaain yaa pailuʔu s-aʔaka takorolo
　　　'I put it here among my things' (Mansen and Mansen 1984.81-82)

According to Ehrman 1972, there is a passive suffix *-hu* which can also be used when the subject is the inadvertent agent (62). Another passive suffix *-n* is illustrated in 54.

(62) ačata-hu-hee-či
　　　to.hit-PAS-FUTURE-M.SG.TIME
　　　'he will hit himself (accidentally)' (Ehrman 1972.61)

The postposition *-miin* 'toward' in noun phrases (63) may be cognate with the benefactive verb suffix in Amuesha and some of the other languages; however, it is more likely cognate with the verb suffix *-imo* 'in the presence of' in Campa.

(63) Uribia-miin
　　　Uribia-TOWARD
　　　'to Uribia' (Mansen and Mansen 1984.176)

3. TENTATIVE RECONSTRUCTIONS OF VALENCE-CHANGING AFFIXES

In the preceding section the range of causative, comitative, and related affixes in verbs and noun phrases was described and illustrated. The tables in this section summarize these affixes for twenty-five geographically representative Maipuran Arawakan languages.[8]

As shown in Table 1, in all of the languages there is at least one verbal suffix with *t* (or some alveolar or alveopalatal consonant) glossed as 'causative/ transitivizer/thematic/verbalizer/epenthetic/ detransitivizer'. For almost all of the languages there is also a verb suffix or a postposition -*ka*/-*akag*/-*kaka*/-*koko* glossed as 'causative/comitative/reciprocal' (Table 2). In most of the languages there is at least one prefix *ka*-/*ko*- glossed as 'causative/transitivizer/attributive' (Table 4) and/or a suffix -*ka*/-*ko* glossed 'verbalizer/thematic/causative/perfective' (Table 3). The antonym of *ka*- 'attributive' is *ma*- 'privative'; this prefix occurs in most of the Maipuran languages except the Campa group, as shown in Table 4.

In most of the languages which have a passive, the passive suffix is -*ka* or something similar (Table 5).

A causative/mediative suffix of the form -*kit* or some apparently cognate form occurs in several geographically dispersed languages (Table 3).

The southernmost languages have another causative/comitative prefix which includes the sequence *im*-/*mi*-, Table 6. In the Campa languages there is also a semantically related suffix with this sequence. Seven of the languages which do not have a causative/comitative prefix with the sequence *im*-/*mi*- have instead a causative/attributive/transitivizer prefix of the form *a*-/*e*-/*i*- (Table 5). In addition many verbs in some of the northern languages begin with *a*; this may be cognate with *a*-/*e*-/*i*-. In some of the languages, such as Campa, the -*t* suffix is clearly epenthetic; these languages also have an epenthetic -*a* in verbs. Epenthetic or thematic vowels also occur in Guajiro; -*a* in some of the other northern languages has been analyzed as a verbalizer (Table 4).

Of the languages for which data are available, Amuesha and Wapishana are the only ones that do not have a reciprocal or reflexive suffix which is clearly a reflex of *-*wa*/-aw* (Table 2). Instead, Amuesha shares a reflexive -*a* with Campa languages. The Wapishana reflexive is -*in*, which may be cognate with the benefactive suffixes listed in (Table 6).

On the basis of the data presented, and my suppositions about phonological correspondences, I postulate the following morphemes in the proto-set of valence-changing and related morphemes:[9] *-*tʰa* 'causative', *-*t* 'thematic/ epenthetic' , *-*kʰakʰ* postposition in noun phrase 'reciprocal' , *kʰa*- transitive verb root 'to make or do', *-*kʰitʰ* 'mediative', *ka*-/*ko*- 'attributive' , *-*ka* 'passive', *-*wa* 'refexive', *a*-/*i*- 'transitivizer/causative', *-*in* postposition in noun phrase 'benefactive' , *ma*- 'privative', *-*a* 'verbalizer/epenthetic' .

In the following sections possible sequences of development from the proto-forms are proposed.

LANGUAGE/DIALECT	*-tʰa* CAUS/VBL	*-t* TH/EP/VBL
Achagua (Colombia)	*-da* CAUS	X
Piapoco (Colombia)	*-da* CAUS	X
Curripaco (Colombia)	*-ta* CAUS	X
Yucuna (Colombia)	*-ta* CAUS/TRVR	X
Resígaro (Perú)	*-tu/-ta* CAUS	X
Guajiro (Colombia,Venezuela)	*-t/-it/-ir* CAUS	*-ta* TH
Lokono (Surinam)	*-da* VBL	*-ta/-ti/-t* TRVR/EP
Wapishana (Guyana)	*-d* TRVR/TH	*-t* TRVR/TH
Garifuna (Island Carib)	*-d/-r* TH	*-t* VBL
Garifuna (Central America)	*-d/-r* TH	*-t* VBL/STAT
Palikur (Brazil)	*-as(e)* CAUS	
Waurá (Brazil)	*-t(a)* CAUS*	*(-ta* EP?)
Amuesha (Perú)	*-aht* CAUS**	*-(VɁ)t* TH/ VBL/TRVR
Terena (Brazil)	*-ti* PROG/STAT	*-š* TH (cognate?)
Parecís (Brazil)	*-s-oa*(cognate?)DTRVR	*-ty-oa* DTRVR (cognate?)
Apurinã (Brazil)	X	*-ta* TH/VBL
Piro (Perú)	X	*-ta* TH/VBL
Baure (Bolivia)	X	*-rV* TH/*-či* VBL (cognates?)
Ignaciano (Bolivia)	X	*-ča* TH (cognate?)
Machiguenga (Perú)	X	*-t* EP
Nomatsiguenga (Perú)	X	*-t* EP
Caquinte (Perú)	X	*-t* EP
Asháninca (Perú)	X	*-t* EP
Ashéninca (Perú)	X	*-t* EP
Pajonal Ashéninca (Perú)	X	*-t* EP

*Also *a-...-ta/-ka* CAUS in Waurá.
**Also *a-...-aht* CAUS in Amuesha.

Table 1. Causatives and other morphemes with alveolar consonants

LANGUAGE	*-wa* RF	*-kʰakʰ* RCP
Achagua	*-u* RF/*-woo* RF in NP	*-yaaka* RCP V stem
Piapoco	*-wa* RF/DTRVR	*-yakaka* RCP
		-waaka RCP in NP
Curripaco	*-o* RF	*-aka* RCP
		-waka RF in VP
Yucuna	*-wa* RF in NP/*-o* RF	*-čaka* RCP/RF
		pa-...-kaka RCP/RF
Resígaro	*-pʰaa-ɓu* RF	*-kaka-ɓu* RCP
Guajiro	*-wa* RF/RCP/PAS	*-aʔaka* AMONG in NP
Lokono	*-oa*/*-n-oa* RF/PAS	*-koa(-oa)* RCP
Wapishana		*-aak* RCP/BEN
Garifuna (Island)	*-wa* RF	
Garifuna (C. Am.)	*-gua* RF/*-wa* PAS	
Palikur	*-wa* RF/*-wi* COM	*-ak*/*-ek* RCP
		-kak WITH in NP
Waurá	*-ua* RF	*-waka* RCP
		-xaka RCP in NP
Amuesha	*-a* RF	X*
Terena	*-po*/*-vu* RF	*-koko*/*-kaka* RCP
Parecís	*-wi* RF	*-kak(-oa)*
	-ty-oa/*-s-oa* DTRVR	WITH in NP
Apurinã	*-wa*/*-awa*/*-kawa* RF	*-kaka* RCP
Piro	*-wa* RF/DTRVR	*-kaka* CAUS/RCP/
		EACH in NP
Baure	*-po* RF	*-koko* RCP
Ignaciano	*-wa* RF	*-ka(ka)* RCP
Machiguenga	*-ab* RCP/*-a* RF	*-akag*/*-ag*/*-akak*
		COM/CAUS
Nomatsiguenga	*-ab*/*-ob* RCP/*-a* RF	*-ag*/*-akak*/*-ak*
		COM/CAUS
Caquinte	*-ab* RCP/*-a* RF	*-akag* COM/CAUS/
		MD
Asháninca	*-aw* RCP/*-a* RF	*-akaa* COM/CAUS
Ashéninca	*-aw* RCP/*-a* RF	*-(aw)akag* COM/
		CAUS
Pajonal Ashéninca	*-aw* RCP/*-a* RF	*-akag* COM/CAUS

*The reciprocal in Amuesha is *-ann* <Panoan.

Table 2. Reflexives and reciprocals

LANGUAGE	*-kʰitʰ* MD	*kʰa* 'to make/do' (TR.V)
Achagua	X	*-ka* COMP
Piapoco	X	*-ka* PF/TO BE
Curripaco	X	*-ka* PF
Yucuna	X	*-ka* PF
Resígaro	X	*kʰu* 'make/do' (syntactic caus)
Guajiro	*-hira* CAUS/RCP	*-ha/-ka* TH
Lokono	*-kɨt(i)*CAUS	*-ka* PF
Wapishana	*-ki?* CAUS *-kiz(i)* PERMIT	
Garifuna (Island)	*-k-it* CAUS	*-ka/-ha* VBL
Garifuna (C America)	*-gɨd/-god* CAUS	*-ka/-ha/-ga* VBL
Palikur	*-kis* CAUS	*-ha* VBL
Waurá	X	*-ka* CAUS
Amuesha	X	X
Terena		*-k/-x* TH
Parecís	*-ki* CAUS	*-ka* HAB
Apurinã	*-kĩtaka* MD	*-ka* VBL/CAUS
Piro	*-xitxa* MD	*-Vka* SEMELFAC-TIVE
Baure		*-ko* TH
Ignaciano		*-ka/-ha* TH
Machiguenga		*-ak* PF
Nomatsiguenga		*-ak* PF
Caquinte		*-ak* PF
Ashãninca		*-ak* PF
Ashéninca		*-ak* PF
Pajonal Ashéninca		*-ak* PF

Table 3. Verb 'to do/make' and mediative/causative

LANGUAGE	-a EP/VBL	ma- PRIV	ka-ATT/ CAUS/TRVR
Achagua		ma- PRIV/NEG ka- ATT	
Piapoco	-a VBL	ma- PRIV	ka- ATT
Curripaco		ma- PRIV/NEG ka- ATT	
Yucuna	-a?a VBL	ma-/me-...-ru PRIV	ka-/ke-...-ni ATT
Resígaro		ma- PRIV/NEG X -ma IRREALIS	
Guajiro	-aa INF/EP	m(a)- PRIV	k(a)- ATT k- VBL
Lokono	-a TH	ma- PRIV	ka- ATT
Wapishana	-a EP	ma-...-kan REVERSIVE	ka- MODI- FIER (ATT?)
Garifuna (Island)		ma- PRIV/NEG	g(a)- ATT
Garifuna (C. Am.)		m(a)- PRIV	g(a)-/ha- ATT
Palikur		ma- PRIV/-ma NEG	ka- ATT
Waurá	-a EP	ma- PRIV	ka- ATT
Amuesha	-a/-a? EP	ma- PRIV (rare) X	
Terena			ko-/ka- ATT/ VBL ko-/ika- CAUS/TRVR
Parecís		ma- PRIV	ka- ATT ka- CAUS/ TRVR
Apurinã		ma- PRIV	ka- ATT ka- CAUS in INTR
Piro		m- PRIV	ka- ATT ka-/ko- TRVR
Baure		mo- PRIV	ko-/ka- ATT ka- TRVR
Ignaciano		ma- PRIV	ka- ATT ka- TRVR/ CAUS
Machiguenga	-a EP	X	
Nomatsiguenga	-a EP	X	ko- ATT (in PP)
Caquinte	-a EP	X	X
Asháninca	-a EP	X	X
Ashéninca	-a EP	X	X
Pajonal Ashéninca	-a EP	X	X

Table 4. Epenthetic -a, privatives, and attributives

LANGUAGE	*a-/i-/e-* TRVR/CAUS	*-ka* PAS
Achagua	*a-* (in many words)	
Piapoco		*-kana* PP
Curripaco		
Yucuna	X	*-kana* PP
Resígaro		
Guajiro	*a-* (in most active verbs)	*-hu* PAS (cognate?)
Lokono	*a-/o-* empty V root	
Wapishana		*-kao* PAS
Garifuna (Island)	*a-/e-/i-* TH	
Garifuna (C. Am.)	*a-* VBL/TH	
Palikur	*a-/e-* TRVR	*-ka/-ki* PAS
Waurá	*a-/i-* CAUS	*-kina* PAS
Amuesha	*a-/e-* CAUS/ATT/PP	X
Terena	*i-* CAUS (with in-transitive)	*-kono/-kana* PAS
Parecís	*a-/e-* TRVR/VBL	
Apurinã		*-ka* PAS
Piro		*-ka* PAS
		-ko PAS (anticipatory)
Baure	*e-* CAUS	
Ignaciano	*e-/ve-* CAUS/TRVR	*-kasi* PAS *ka-...-hi* PAS
Machiguenga	*ogi-/og-/o-* CAUS	*-gani* PAS
Nomatsiguenga	*ga-/(o)gi-/o-* CAUS	*-ga(ni)/-ŋa(ni)* PAS
Caquinte	*ogi-/o-* CAUS	X
Asháninca	*oi-/o-* CAUS	X
Ashéninca	*oi-/ow-/o-* CAUS	X
Pajonal Ashéninca	*o-* CAUS	X

Table 5. *a-/i-* causatives and passives

LANGUAGE	-ni BEN	imo- CAUS/COM -imo COM/PRES
Achagua	-li BEN in NP	X
Piapoco	-li/-ri BEN	X
Curripaco		X
Yucuna		X
Resígaro	-nee COM in NP	X
Guajiro	-miin TOWARD in NP (cognate?) -n PAS	-(a)maa COM in NP (cognate?)
Lokono	-min BEN in NP	
Wapishana	-in RF	X
Garifuna (Island)		X
Garifuna (C. Am.)	-ni/-ū BEN in NP	X
Palikur		X
Waurá		X
Amuesha	-(o)n BEN	X
Terena	-in(o) BEN	
Parecís	-ana TO in NP	X
Apurinã		mi- COM
Piro	-(V)na MALEFACTIVE in NP	him-/hi- COM/VBL
Baure	-no BEN	i-/imo- CAUS imiri ACTION IN FRONT OF
Ignaciano	-ina BEN	imi-/im- CAUS
Machiguenga	-nV BEN	omi(n)- CAUS -imo PRES
Nomatsiguenga	-nV BEN	omi(n)- CAUS -(i)mo PRES
Caquinte	-nV 3OBJ	omi(n)- CAUS -imo PRES
Asháninca	-nV BEN	omi(n)- CAUS/COM -imo COM
Ashéninca	-nV 3OBJ	omin- CAUS -imo PRES/COM/BEN
Pajonal Ashéninca	-nV BEN	X -imo PRES

Table 6. Benefactives and imo- causatives

3.1 *-TᴴA* 'CAUSATIVE' AND *-T* 'THEMATIC/EPENTHETIC'. In all of the languages for which data are available, there is at least one suffix with *t* or some alveolar or alveopalatal consonant. However, the *-c&a* and *-rV* thematic suffixes in Ignaciano and Baure, respectively, are possibly not cognate with the *t* suffix; and the *ty* and *s* in Parecís are dubious cognates. Languages as widely scattered as Lokono in the Guianas, Garifuna (Black Carib) in Central America, and Amuesha in Peru have two apparently different valence-changing affixes with an alveolar stop (Table 1). Since there is general agreement that there were both aspirated and unaspirated stops in proto-Arawakan (e.g. Matteson 1972 and Taylor 1969), I propose that there were two proto-morphemes with an alveolar consonant in the 'causative-thematic' set. In order to account for the Amuesha causative I propose *-tʰa* as the most likely form of the causative. The proto-form for 'thematic/epenthetic/verbalizer' would then be *-t*. In its epenthetic function, *-t* was inserted to break up underlying vowel clusters, while an epenthetic *-a* (Table 4) was inserted to break up underlying consonant clusters.

The alternation between *-t/-r* is a regular morphophonemic alternation in Guajiro; *t/r* is the probable Guajiro reflex of *tʰ.* The *d* in several of the languages parallels similar correspondences in some other affixes and roots. The *-s* in Palikur may also be a regular reflex of *tʰ* (cf. *-kis* 'causative' in Table 3). A proto *tʰ* might account for the source of the aspiration in the syllable nucleus (*ah*) in Amuesha. Metathesis, a very frequent phenomenon in the language, accounts for the inversion of the *t* and *a* so that the Amuesha causative is now *-aht*.

The causative *-tʰa* is at present found only as far south as Waurá and Amuesha. If there was only one proto *-t* or *-tʰ* suffix in this set, one hypotheses is that the causative meaning was lost in the other languages and the affix became simply transitivizing, verbalizing, or epenthetic and another causative developed. However, there are enough languages with two different alveolar-consonant suffixes that it seems plausible to posit a proto-suffix *-t* 'thematic/ epenthetic/ verbalizer', as well as *-tʰa* 'causative'.

3.2 *-KᴴAKᴴ* 'RECIPROCAL', *-WA* 'REFLEXIVE', AND *KᴴA* 'TO MAKE/DO'. In almost all of the languages, there is a *-kak*, or clearly cognate, verbal suffix glossed 'reciprocal/comitative/causative' (Table 2). Some of the exceptions might be eliminated with further data, but in Amuesha a reciprocal suffix has been borrowed from Panoan; also the Amuesha comitative affix does not resemble similar affixes in other Maipuran languages, as far as I know. In Piapoco, Curripaco, Palikur, Waurá, and Piro, cognate affixes occur in postpositional phrases as well as verb phrases. In Guahiro and Parecís they occur only in postpositional phrases. In Achagua there is a reciporcal verb stem *yaaka*. The forms *-akag/-akaa/-ag* in Campa are the result of a general lenition process *k > g > ø*. The reciprocal probably developed from a postposition in noun phrases to a verb suffix in many of the languages by the process of incorporation.

Garifuna, Palikur, Waurá, Terena, Apurinã, Baure, and Ignaciano have both a reciprocal suffix with -ka/-ko and a thematic or verbalizing or causative suffix with k. In addition, many of the northern languages and the Campa group have a -ka or -ak perfective suffix which might possibly be cognate with these suffixes (Table 3). Thus, there may well have been two proto-suffixes with a velar consonant. However, Resígaro has kʰu as a verb root 'to do or make' in syntactic causatives. Therefore, I tentatively posit that the second k morpheme was a verb root *kʰa, which later became an affix in some languages.

I have glossed proto *-kʰakʰ as 'reciprocal' since that is its meaning in a wide range of languages. In others the meaning is 'comitative' which is clearly semantically related to 'reciprocal'. In the Campa languages the meaning changed from reciprocal to comitative to causative (in the sense of causing by enabling or helping). Thus, although causative and reciprocal normally are valence-changing opposites, the series of changes proposed could account for a reciprocal suffix in one language being cognate with a causative in another. Nevertheless, as indicated in section 2.2., even when -akak/-ag means 'causative' in Campa, the causer usually participates in the action, i.e. the comitative sense seems to be primary.

As David Payne has noted (p.c.) the proto-reflexive suffix was probably *-wa or *-aw (Table 2). In those languages where *-kʰakʰ now means 'comitative/causative', a new reflexive -a has developed, while *-wa/-aw has become 'reciprocal' and is obligatorily followed by -akak/-ag. (The -ɓu in Resígaro is a reflex of the proto-reflexive suffix; cf. -tu 'causative' in Table 1.)

3.3 *-KʰITʰ 'CAUSATIVE/MEDIATIVE'. The clearly cognate causatives -kiti, -gɨd, -kis, -kiʔ, -ki in Lokono, Garifuna, Wapishana, Palikur, and Parecís (Table 3) might be considered a shared innovation for a branch of Maipuran. However, -xitxa 'mandatory/mediative' in Piro appears to me to be a very likely cognate from a geographically distant branch. Accordingly, I posit *-kʰitʰ as a proto-causative or mediative suffix.

3.4 *KA- 'ATTRIBUTIVE' AND A-/E-/I- 'CAUSATIVE'. Resígaro, Amuesha, and the Campa group are the only languages discussed in this paper which do not have a prefix with ka/ga (Table 4). The absence of such a prefix in Amuesha is probably related to the loss of other kV initial syllables; compare for example kipaçi 'earth' in Nomatsiguenga with Amuesha pa.ç 'earth'.

In most languages the ka- means 'attributive, i.e. to have'. Furthermore, most Maipuran languages have a corresponding prefix ma- 'privative, i.e. not to have' which was obviously a proto-morpheme. Therefore, I consider these antonymns to have been in the proto-language and the attributive meaning to have been the original one of ka-. However, Guajiro, Terena, Parecís, Apurinã, Piro, Baure, and Ignaciano also have a ka- or ko- prefix meaning 'causative/ transitivizer'. These may be cognates of the -ka/-ko suffixes from proto *kʰa 'to do or make' which are homophonous with ka- 'attributive'; or they could possibly be extended usages of *ka- 'attributive'.

The *a-/e-/i-* 'causative/verbalizing/transitivizing/thematic' prefix occurs in most languages so that I tentatively consider it to be a proto-form. However, the fact that *y* occurs in the verb stem *yaaka* 'to do to each other' in Achagua may indicate that *y/i* was originally a verb root 'to do'.

3.5 *-KA* 'PASSIVE' AND *-NI* 'BENEFACTIVE'. In most Maipuran languages the passive is nonagentive and occurs rather infrequently. Since a form with *-kV* or a plausible reflex occurs in geographically dispersed languages, I posit *-ka* as the probable proto-form.

The proto-benefactive was probably a postposition in noun phrases; it still retains that position in Piro and the northern languages. The probable proto-form was *-ni* although the vowel may have been something other than *i*.

3.6 *IMO-/-IMO* 'CAUSATIVE/COMITATIVE'. Verb affixes of the form *omin-/imo-/ -imo* are limited to those languages which are geographically southern with respect to the rest of the Maipuran family and were probably contiguous to Panoan languages, as some of them are at present. Consequently, this affix in Maipuran languages may be a borrowing from Panoan (cf. *-mi* 'causative' in Cashibo (12b). If it is , its recent development would explain the fact that in the Campa languages the occurrence of *omi(n)-* 'causative' is relatively rare and unproductive. However, David Payne suggests (p.c.) that it is more likely a relic form, lost in the other languages. He suggests further that *mi* causatives are widespread "panamericanisms" found in Jivaroan, Tupí, Panoan, and Mapudungun, as well as southern Maipuran Arawakan languages.

In the Campa languages, which are rich in valence-changing suffixes, there is also a suffix *-imo/-omo* with the specialized meaning 'in the presence of'; in Asháninca Kindberg reports comitative and benefactive meanings also. David Payne (p.c.) suggests that this suffix and the prefix developed from a single affix. It is also possible that the suffix developed from a postposition; compare, for example, *-miin* 'toward' in Guajiro (Table 6).

4. SITUATION IN THE PROTO-LANGUAGE

At several points in the preceding sections the possibility that there are both prefixal and suffixal cognates of a single morpheme has been suggested. When the pronouns and pronominal agreement affixes are considered, we have a clear case of single morphemes with free, prefixal, and suffixal forms in almost all Maipuran Arawakan languages (see Payne 1987). Such a situation may well have arisen from a change from SOV (still found in some Maipuran languages, such as Piro) to VSO (e.g. Amuesha), SVO (e.g. Piapoco), or VOS (e.g. Baure) word order. The fact that suffixes predominate in all Arawakan languages may also be an indicator of original SOV order. I am proposing then, that as the word order changed - or is changing - from OV to VO some original suffixes have become prefixes, leaving both prefixal and suffixal reflexes of a proto-suffix.

In some instances a noun phrase postposition in one language is cognate
with a verb affix in another language, or a given cognate form may occur in both
the noun phrase and the verb phrase of a single language, e.g. -kʰakʰ 'reciprocal'. This may be indicative of their occurrence as free forms in an earlier stage
of development. Nevertheless, the evidence presented from a wide range of
languages seems to corroborate that in proto-Maipuran the following had
already become verb or verbalizing affixes: *-tʰa 'causative', *-t 'thematic/
epenthetic', *-kʰitʰ 'mediative', *ka-/ko- 'attributive', *ma- 'privative', *-ka
'passive', *-a 'epenthetic'.

In the proto-language there was probably a transitive verb root *kʰa- 'to
make or do' which must have already been in the process of becoming a prefix
or suffix in some dialects. There was probably also a verb root *a-/e-/i- 'to do/
make' which developed into a causative prefix in many languages. The
benefactive *-ni was probably a postposition in noun phrases which later was
incorporated into the verb.

NOTES

[1]   I am indebted to Doris Bartholomew, David Payne, Doris Payne, and an
anonymous reviewer for helpful suggestions in the preparation of this paper and
to Lydia Carlson and Kathy Bergman for help in the preparation of the
manuscript.

[2]   More definitive reconstructions await further work on phonological reconstructions.

[3]   Chamicuro is also clearly Maipuran Arawakan, but data on the morphemes
considered in this paper are not available.

[4]   Amuesha examples are taken from my own field notes unless otherwise
indicated. Abbreviations and symbols used in the examples and in the tables
are: ABL ablative; ACT active; ATT attributive; BEN benefactive; CAUS
causative; COM comitative; COMP completive; DTRVR detransitivizer; EP
epenthetic; F feminine; GEN genitive; HAB habitual; IMPRS impersonal; INF
infinitive; INST instrumental; LIM limitative; M masculine; MD mediative;
NEG negative; NF nonfuture; NFR nonfuture reflexive; N/M nonmasculine;
NP noun phrase; OBJ object; PAS passive; PF perfective; PL plural; PP passive
participle; PRES in the presence of; PRIV privative; PROG progressive; RCP
reciprocal; RF reflexive; RP repetitive; SG singular; STAT stative; TH
thematic; TR transitive; TRVR transitivizer; V verb/verbal, vowel; VBL verbalizer; 1 first person; 2 second person; 3 third person; X doesn't occur as far
as I can ascertain; a blank indicates that it is not found in the corpus; + in gloss
indicates gloss of two morphemes which cannot be segmented; . in gloss joins
words in a phrase used to gloss a single morpheme; ... in gloss indicates
meaning unidentified.

[5]   The suffix *-a.n*, glossed 'object follows', in the Amuesha examples indicates that there is an overt object following, either *-eht* '3PL' or the last noun phrase in the clause.

[6]   The suffix *-apiča* 'comitative (postposition in NP)' (Piapoco Klumpp 1985.122) and *-apiča* 'mediative/away from' in Asháninca are probably cognate with each other; they might be posited as rather improbable cognates of *-apre.t* in Amuesha, but no other possibilities have come to light.

[7]   See Payne 1978 and Swift 1985 for detailed descriptions of epentheses in Asháninca and Caquinte.

[8]   There was evidently a *ka-* 'attributive' prefix in Taino (Taylor and Hoff 1966.306); it is the only affix attested in the extant Taino data that is relevant to the topic of this paper.

[9]   Others have proposed some of these proto-morphemes before. Since I am not certain of the first author to propose each one, I have not mentioned them here but plan to do so in a more comprehensive reconstruction of morphosyntactic features of Maipuran languages.

[10]   David Payne, in this volume, suggests that *-ka* stem closure, i.e. thematic suffix, *ka* auxiliary verb in Quechua, and related affixes are widespread "panamericanisms". This, of course, does not preclude positing a *-ka* suffix in proto-Maipuran.

REFERENCES

Allin, Trevor R. 1975. *A grammar of Resígaro*. University of St.Andrews doctoral dissertation. (Published in three volumes. 1976. Horsleys Green, High Wycombe, England: Summer Institute of Linguistics.)

Alvarez, José. 1985. *Aspects of the phonology of Guajiro*. University of Essex doctoral dissertation.

Baptista, Priscilla and Ruth Wallin. 1967. Baure. In Matteson (ed.), 27-84.

Bendor-Samuel, John. 1961. An outline of the grammatical and phonological structure of Terena, Part I. *Arquivo Lingüístico 90*. Brasilia: Summer Institute of Linguistics.

Derbyshire, Desmond C. 1986. Comparative survey of morphology and syntax in Brazilian Arawakan. In Derbyshire and Pullum (eds.), 469-566.

Derbyshire, Desmond C. and Geoffrey K. Pullum (eds.). 1986. *Handbook of Amazonian Languages*, 1. Berlin: Mouton de Gruyter.

Eastlack, Charles. 1968. Terena (Arawakan) pronouns. *International Journal of American Linguistics* 34.1-8.

Ehrman, Susan. 1972. *Wayuunaiki: a grammar of Guajiro.* Columbia University doctoral dissertation.

Ekdahl, Muriel and Joseph E. Grimes. 1964. Terena verb inflection. *International Journal of American Linguistics* 30.261-268.

Gill, Wayne. Trinitario grammar. Cochabamba, Bolivia: New Tribes Mission. MS.

Goeje, C. H. de. 1928. *The Arawak language of Guiana.* Amsterdam: Verhandelingen der Koninklijke Akademie van Wetenschappen Afdeeling Letterkkunde, Vol. 28, No. 2.

Kindberg, Willard. 1961. Campa (Arawak) morphology. *A William Cameron Townsend en el vigésimoquinto aniversario del Instituto Lingüístico de Verano,* 519-54. Cuernavaca, México: Tipografía Indígena.

Klumpp, Delores. 1985. La oración simple en piapoco. *Artículos en Lingüística y Campos Afines* 13.113-168. Lomalinda, Meta, Colombia.

Lathrap, Donald. 1970. *The upper Amazon.* Southampton: Thames and Hudson.

Mansen, Richard and Karis Mansen. 1976. The structure of sentence and paragraph in Guajiro narrative discourse. *Discourse grammar: studies in indigenous languages of Colombia, Panama and Ecuador.* Ed. by Robert E. Longacre, 147-258. (*Summer Institute of Linguistics Publications in Linguistics and Related Fields* 52, Part 1). Dallas: Summer Institute of Linguistics.

Mansen, Karis and Richard Mansen. 1984. *Aprendamos guajiro: gramática pedagógica de guajiro.* Bogotá: Editorial Townsend.

Matteson, Esther. 1965. *The Piro (Arawakan) language.* (*University of California Publications in Linguistics* 42). Berkeley and Los Angeles: University of California Press.

Matteson, Esther (ed.). 1967. *Bolivian Indian grammars: I.* (*Summer Institute of Linguistics Publications in Linguistics and Related Fields* 16). Norman, OK: Summer Institute of Linguistics of the University of Oklahoma.

Matteson, Esther. 1972. Proto Arawakan. In Matteson, Wheeler, Jackson, Waltz and Christian, 160-242.

Matteson, Esther, Alva Wheeler, Frances L. Jackson, Nathan E. Waltz and Diana R. Christian. 1972. *Comparative studies in Amerindian languages.* (*Janua Linguarum, Series Practica* 127). The Hague: Mouton.

Olza, Jesús and Miguel Angel Jusayú. 1986. *Gramática de la lengua guajiro*. Táchira, Venezuela: Universidad Católica del Táchira.

Ott, Willis G. and Rebecca H. Ott. 1967. Ignaciano. In Matteson (ed.), 85-137.

Ott, Willis G. and Rebecca H. Ott. 1983. *Diccionario ignaciano y castellano con apuntes gramaticales*. Cochabamba, Bolivia: Instituto Lingüístico de Verano.

Payne, David L. 1981. *Phonology and morphology of Axininca Campa*. (*Summer Institute of Linguistics Publications in Linguistics* 66.) Dallas: Summer Institute of Linguistics and University of Texas at Arlington.

Payne, David L. 1987. Some morphological elements of Maipuran Arawakan: agreement affixes and the genitive construction. *Language Sciences* 9.57-75.

Pet, Willem Jan A. 1987. *Lokono dian: the Arawak language of Suriname: a sketch of its grammatical structure and lexicon*. Cornell University doctoral dissertation.

Richards, Joan. MS1. Waura verb structure.

Richards, Joan. MS2. Waura examples, 2.

Richards, Joan. MS3. Waura clauses.

Richards, Joan. MS4. Waura examples, 4.

Schauer, Stanley and Junia Schauer. 1985. Resumen del yucuna. MS.

Shell, Olive. 1957. Cashibo II: grammemic analysis of transitive and intransitive verb patterns. *International Journal of American Linguistics* 23.179-218.

Snell, Betty A. and Mary Ruth Wise. 1963. Noncontingent declarative clauses in Machiguenga (Arawakan). *Studies in Peruvian Indian languages: I* 103-44. (*Summer Institute of Linguistics Publications in Linguistics and Related Fields 9*). Norman, OK: Summer Institute of Linguistics of the University of Oklahoma.

Snell, Wayne. 1955. Machiguenga verbs. Información de Campo 113 (microfiche). Lima: Instituto Lingüístico de Verano.

Swift, Kenneth E. 1985. *Morphology of Caquinte (Preandine Arawakan)*. University of Texas at Arlington, M.A. thesis.

Taylor, Douglas. 1951a. Inflexional system of Island Carib. *International Journal of American Linguistics* 17.23-31.

Taylor, Douglas. 1951b. Morphophonemics of Island Carib (Central American dialect). *International Journal of American Linguistics* 17.224-34.

Taylor, Douglas. 1955. Phonemes of the Hopkins (British Honduras) dialect of Island Carib. *International Journal of American Linguistics* 21.233-41.

Taylor, Douglas. 1956. Island Carib II: word-classes, affixes, nouns, and verbs. *International Journal of American Linguistics* 22.1-44.

Taylor, Douglas. 1969. Consonantal correspondence and loss in Northern Arawakan with special reference to Guajiro. *Word* 25.275-88.

Taylor, Douglas. 1977. A note on Palikur and Northern Arawakan. *International Journal of American Linguistics* 43.58-60.

Taylor, Douglas and Berend Hoff. 1966. Review of *Proto-Arawakan and its descendants* by G. Kingsley Noble. *International Journal of American Linguistics* 32.303-8.

Tracy, Frances V. 1974. An introduction to Wapishana verb morphology. *International Journal of American Linguistics* 40.120-5.

Tripp, Martha. In preparation. Diccionario amuesha.

Wilson, Peter. MS. Achagua (Arawakan). To appear in *Grammar sketches of languages of Colombia*. Ed. by David Weber.

Wise, Mary Ruth. 1963. Six levels of structure in Amuesha (Arawak) verbs. *International Journal of American Linguistics* 29.132-52.

Wise, Mary Ruth. 1971. *Identification of participants in discourse: A study of aspects of form and meaning in Nomatsiguenga. (Summer Institute of Linguistics Publications in Linguistics and Related Fields 28.)* Norman, OK: Summer Institute of Linguistics of the University of Oklahoma.

Wise, Mary Ruth. 1976. Apuntes sobre la influencia inca entre los amuesha: factor que oscurece la clasificación de su idioma. *Revista del Museo Nacional* 42.355-366. Lima.

Wise, Mary Ruth. 1982. Una contribución de Julio C. Tello a la clasificación de las lenguas autóctonas. *Lexis* 6.125-9. Lima.

Wise, Mary Ruth. 1986. Grammatical characteristics of Pre-Andine Arawakan languages of Peru. In Derbyshire and Pullum (eds.), 567-642.

Cross-Referencing Changes in Some Tupí-Guaraní Languages

Cheryl Jensen

0. INTRODUCTION*

The Tupí-Guaraní language family (lowland South America) has four sets of person markers for cross-referencing on verbs. Which set of markers is employed in any given situation depends on various factors. These factors include whether a verb is transitive or intransitive; whether it is independent; whether it is preceded by an adverbial; in transitive verbs, whether the patient or the agent is superior on an agency hierarchy; and in intransitive verbs, whether the verb is agentive or nonagentive. These factors have been described in detail by Harrison 1986 for Guajajara.

To overgeneralize, most languages of the family have two basic systems for cross-referencing. The system used in independent clauses is an active-inactive system (cf. Seki, this volume, on Kamaiurá). Intransitive verbs are divided into two classes: agentive and nonagentive. Subjects (S) of agentive intransitive verbs are cross-referenced by the same set of person markers as the agent (A) of transitive verbs, while the S of a nonagentive intransitive verb is cross-referenced by the same set of person markers as is the patient (P) of a transitive verb. Cross-referencing on transitive verbs is governed by the relative position of A and P on an agency hierarchy, where 1 > 2 > 3 (i.e. first person outranks second person, which outranks third person). This arrangement may be illustrated by the following examples from Tupinambá:[1]

(1) **a-só**
    1sg-go   'I go, I went'
    S(ag)

(2) **a-i-nupã**
    1sg-3-hit   'I hit it'
    A-P

(3) **syé** nupã
    1sg hit   '(he/ she/ they/ you)
    P   hit me'

(4) **syé** katú
    1sg good   'I am good'
    S(non-ag)

In examples 1 and 2 the same prefix *a*- cross-references the first person singular S of an intransitive agentive verb (*só* 'to go') and the A of a transitive verb (*nupã* 'to hit with an instrument'). In 3 the P, not the A, of the transitive verb is cross-referenced because the P (first person) is hierarchically superior to the A (second or third person) on the agency hierarchy. The same person marker (*syé*) which cross-references the P in 3 also cross-references the S of the non-agentive verb (*katú* 'to be good') in 4.

In subordinate (temporal or conditional) clauses there is an ergative-absolutive system (cf. Harrison 1986 regarding Guajajara). In the following examples from Tupinambá subordinate clauses, we see that the first person singular S of both agentive (6) and nonagentive (7) intransitive verbs are cross-referenced by the same person marker as is the first person P of the transitive verb (5). There is no active-inactive system. The person markers on transitive verbs always reference P. The agency hierarchy is irrelevent to this construction. For this reason 9 is not acceptable; the correct way to express the same content is in 8.

(5) **syé** monó-reme-mo a-só-mo
     1sg   send-if-COND 1sg-go-COND   'If he sent me, I would go.'
     P   S(ag)

(6) **syé** só-reme
     1sg   go-if   'if/when I go'
     S(ag)

(7) **syé** katú-reme
     1sg   good-if   'if I am good'
     S(non-ag)

(8) i-nupã-reme
     3-hit-if   'if (I/ we/ you/ he/ she/ they) hit it/him'
     P

(9) *a-i-nupã-reme
     1sg-3-hit-if   'if I hit it/him'
     A-P

These two systems, along with variations which occur under other syntactic conditions, will be explained and illustrated in detail in Section 2. They have been reconstructed for Proto-Tupí-Guaraní, since they occur with little or no alternation in members of 6 of the 8 subgroups proposed for the family by Rodrigues 1984/1985. Languages considered in the present study which retain the traditional grammatical constructions are, by Rodrigues' subgrouping: Guarayu (2), Tupinambá (3), Assurini (4), Tapirape (4), Kayabi (5), Parintintin

(6), Kamaiurá (7), and, with partial modification, Guajajara (4). The geographical location of these languages is indicated in Figure 1.

Of interest to this paper are the changes that have occurred in certain members of the other two subgroups of the family: Mbya Guaraní, Kaiwa, and Chiriguano from Rodrigues' subgroup 1; Wayampi and Urubu from subgroup 8. In these languages the system which characterizes the main verbs of independent clauses in the Tupí-Guaraní family as a whole has been extended to other syntactic conditions as well. For instance, the system illustrated by 1-4 has replaced the system illustrated by 5-8. The languages in which these changes have occurred have otherwise maintained a high degree of similarity both phonologically and morphologically with the rest of the members of the family. The basic sets of A and P markers are available in all languages; what has changed in some languages is the selection of which morphemes are actually employed under certain syntactic conditions. It is the purpose of this paper to explore the extent of change in each of these languages.

Figure 1. Location of Tupí-Guaraní language groups

1. CHARACTERISTIC TUPÍ-GUARANÍ FEATURES

A number of features characteristic of the Tupí-Guaraní family are
necessary for an understanding of Tupí-Guaraní cross-referencing.

1.1 SETS OF PERSON MARKERS. Table 1 lists reconstructed Proto-Tupí-Guaraní
person markers which occur in close association with verbs.

	Set 1	Set 2	Set 3	Set 4
1s	a-	če (r-)	wi-	
1EX	oro-	ore (r-)	oro-	
1IN	ja-	jane (r-)	jere-	
2s	ere-	ne (r-)	e-	oro- (A1:P2sg)
2pl	pe-	pe (n-)	peje-	opo- (A1:P2pl)
3	o-	i-, c-	o-	

Table 1. Proto-Tupí-Guaraní person markers[2]

Set 1 prefixes refer to A and agentive S arguments in independent clauses
(section 2.1).

Set 2 person markers refer to P (sections 2.1-2.3); to nonagentive S
arguments in all syntactic constructions; to agentive S in oblique-topicalized
constructions (section 2.2.3), subordinate clauses (section 2.2.1), and nominalizations (section 2.3). These person markers also occur with nouns and
postpositions. The markers for first and second person are either identical with,
or are reductions of, a set of free pronouns.[3] They are currently analyzed by
Rodrigues (p.c.) for Tupinambá as independent words; they carry independent
stress. He reconstructs the Proto-Tupí-Guaraní forms as separate words as
well. Linguists working with some other Tupí-Guaraní languages consider
these person markers to be prefixes. In citing examples from other linguists'
work, I abide by their individual decisions regarding word division.

Set 3 prefixes occur on intransitive agentive serial verbs (section 2.2.2).[4]
The S of these verbs must always be co-referential with the S or A of the main
verb of the independent clause. In Tapirape (Leite, p.c.), Parintintin (Betts
1981), and Kayabi (Dobson 1983), these prefixes also occur as co-referentials
on nouns. The full scope of their function in Proto-Tupí-Guaraní has not been
determined.

The prefixes in Set 4, *oro-* and *opo-*, are portmanteau forms. They occur on
transitive verbs in independent clauses where A is first person (regardless of
number) and P is second person, singular and plural, respectively.

1.2 WORD CLASSES. The Tupí-Guaraní family has two arbitrary word classes into which all inflectable stems (verbs, nouns and postpositions) are divided, based on their behavior in relation to the prefixes of Set 2 of Table 1. Words of class I take the *i-* allomorph of the third person prefix and combine directly with the person markers for the first and second person. Words of class II take the *c-* allomorph and combine indirectly with the first and second person markers, requiring a linking prefix *r-*, as indicated by the parentheses in column 2 of Table 1.[5]

2. TUPI-GUARANI CROSS-REFERENCING SYSTEMS

In this section the constructions in which the person markers of Table 1 occur are described in order to later demonstrate the extent of change in those languages which have deviated from the protosystem. Representative examples are chosen from various conservative languages. Examples of non-agentive intransitive verbs will be excluded since these verbs occur exclusively with Set 2 person markers in all syntactic constructions and in all languages of the family. They are therefore outside the scope of this discussion.

2.1 CROSS REFERENCING ON INDEPENDENT VERBS. In Proto-Tupí-Guaraní, as in all of its descendents, independent intransitive agentive verbs are conjugated using Set 1 prefixes, as in the following examples from Tupinambá:

(10) a-só   'I went'
     oro-só   'we EX went'
     ja-só   'we IN went'
     ere-só   'you SG went'
     pe-só   'you PL went'
     o-só   'he/she/it/they went'

The same set of prefixes occurs with transitive verbs, referencing A, but only when P is third person. In Proto-Tupí-Guaraní the agentive prefixes are followed by a third person patient prefix from Set 2, as in Tupinambá:

(11) a-i-kutúk   'I pierced him/her/it/them.'
     oro-i-kutúk   'we EX pierced him/her/it/them'
     ja-i-kutúk   'we IN pierced him/her/it/them'
     ere-i-kutúk   'you SG pierced him/her/it/them'
     pe-i-kutúk   'you PL pierced him/her/it/them'
     o-i-kutúk   'he/she/it/they pierced him/etc.'
     a-s-ekár   'I looked for it'
     oro-s-ekár   'we EX looked for it'
     ja-s-ekár   'we IN looked for it'
     ere-s-ekár   'you SG looked for it'
     pe-s-ekár   'you PL looked for it'
     o-s-ekár   'he/she/it/they looked for it'

In 11 P is hierarchically inferior or equal to A. When, by contrast, P is superior to A, only P is referenced, using Set 2 prefixes, as in 12 from Tupinambá.

(12) syé repyák   '(he/she/it/they/you) saw me'
     oré repyák   '(he/she/it/they/you) saw us EX'
     jané repyák   '(he/she/it/they) saw us IN'
     né repyák   '(he/she/it/they) saw you SG'
     pé repyák   '(he/she/it/they) saw you PL'

There is no reference in the verbal construction to A, so 13 is not permissible:

(13) *o-pé repyák   'he/she/they saw you PL'

Example 14 is not permissible in independent clauses because a third person P cannot be hierarchically superior to A.

(14) *s-epyák   '(I/we/you/he/she/they) saw it,etc.'

The examples in 11 cover those cases where P is third person. The examples in 12 cover those where P is hierarchically superior to a third person A. Still to be accounted for are the constructions where P meets neither of the above conditions. That is, A is first person and P is second. In this situation, a set of portmanteau prefixes (Set 4) is used, as in the following examples from Tupinambá:[6]

(15) oro-epyák   'I/we saw you SG'
     opo-epyák   'I/we saw you PL'

In both these cases the A is first person, either singular or plural. The number of the patient is what determines the prefix to be used.

The cross-referencing system for independent transitive verbs is summarized in its entirety by Table 2.

Agent	Patient		
	1	2	3
1		oro- opo- SET 4	a-i-/a-c- oro-i-/oro-c- ja-i-/ja-c- ere-i-/ere-c- pe-i-/pe-c- o-i-/o-c-
2	čé (r-) oré (r-)		
3	čé (r-) oré (r-) jané (r-) SET 2	né (r-) pé (n-)	SETS 1 + 2

Table 2. Cross-referencing in P-T-G independent transitive verbs

2.2 CROSS-REFERENCING ON OTHER VERBAL CONSTRUCTIONS. Only main independent verbs employ the complicated system of cross-referencing described in section 2.1. The parameters of agentive versus nonagentive in intransitive verbs, and the relative position of A and P on the agency hierarchy, are irrelevant in subordinate (2.2.1), serial verb (2.2.2), and oblique-topicalized (2.2.3) constructions. Essentially all these constructions employ Set 2 person markers, which reference P in transitive verbs and S in intransitive verbs (both agentive and non-agentive). The exception is the intransitive serial verb construction; this takes the co-referential prefixes of Set 3.

2.2.1 SUBORDINATE VERBS. The subordinate clauses under consideration here are always temporal or conditional in nature, as illustrated in 5-8. In all cases Set 2 person markers reference S of intransitive verbs and P of transitive verbs, as in the following examples from Assurini:

(16) **i-paw-amo**   sa-ha
    3-finish-when 1IN-go   'When it finished, we went.'
    Set2   Set1

(17) i-nopo-ramo
    3-hit-when   'when (he) hit him'
    Set2

The subordinate verb in 16 is an agentive intransitive verb (*páb 'to finish') which in independent main verb constructions would take a prefix from Set 1 (*o-paw*). The verb in 17 is transitive and cross-references the P regardless of its position relative to A on the agency hierarchy. An independent clause parallel to 17 would take a prefix from Set 1 (*o-nopo*), referring to A.

In at least some languages of the family, such as Tupinambá, the Set 2 person marker does not occur if the verb stem is immediately preceded by a noun referencing S in intransitive verbs or P in transitive verbs. For example, the prefix referencing S (*i-*) in 18 is not necessary in 19 because a noun referring to S (*pajé* 'shaman') immediately precedes the subordinate verb.

(18) i-só-reme
    3-go-if   'if he goes'
    Set2

(19) pajé   só-reme
    shaman go-if   'if the shaman goes'

Likewise the prefix referencing P (*i-*) in 20 does not occur in 21 because the noun *ma'é-asý-bór-a* indicating P immediately precedes the verb.

(20) ma'é-asý-bór-a   pajé   i-subán-eme
    thing-pain-NOM-NC shaman 3-suck-if
    'if the shaman sucks (treats) the patient'

(21) pajé   ma'é-asý-bór-a   subán-eme
     shaman   thing-pain-NOM-NC   suck-if
     'if the shaman treats the patient'

2.2.2 SERIAL VERBS. By definition a serial verb in Tupí-Guaraní languages is a verb which appears together with an independent verb to express simultaneous action, purpose, or sequential action, when the subject of both verbs is identical.[7] The two verbs are perceived by the speaker as aspects of a single action. The serial verb is indicated by a suffix which in Proto-Tupí-Guaraní had three basic allomorphs: -ábo, -ta, and -a, which followed a vowel, a diphthong [Vy], and a consonant, respectively.

The transitive serial verb must be immediately preceded by the patient, in the form of a noun or a person marker from Set 2. Examples 22 and 23 from Tupinambá show P expressed by a prefix from Set 2. Example 24 is parallel to 23, but does not need the prefix because the verb stem is immediately preceded by a noun indicating P.

(22) o-úr   **s-epyák-a**
     3-come 3-see-SER   'He came to see him/her.'
     Set1   Set2

(23) o-úr   **i-kuáp-a**
     3-come 3-meet-SER   'He came to meet him.'
     Set1   Set2

(24) o-úr   kunumí **kuáp-a**
     3-come boy   meet-SER   'He came to meet the boy.'
     Set1   Obj   (Set2)

In 22-24, the A of the serial verb (epyák-a 'to see'; kuáp-a 'to know') is the same as the grammatical subject of the main verb oúr 'he came', though not expressed by any cross-referencing on the serial verb. The occurrence of third person prefixes shows that the person markers must refer to the P argument, even when P is not hierarchically superior to A.

In Tupinambá the portmanteau prefixes of Set 4, referring A and P together, are also used with transitive serial verbs.

(25) oro-epyák-a   'in order (for me/us) to see you SG'

It has not been determined whether the use of this set of prefixes with serial verbs is reconstructable for Proto-Tupí-Guaraní.

Intransitive serial verbs employ Set 3 person markers; these indicate that the subject of the serial verb is co-referential with the grammatical subject (S or A) of the main verb. In 26 from Assurini the serial verb sahok-a 'to bathe' is prefixed by sere- (1IN), which is co-referential with sa- (1IN) in the main verb (*ropyta* 'to stay with'). In 27 the serial verbs *semorai-ta* 'to play' and *sahok-a* 'to bathe' are prefixed by *oro-* (1EX), which is co-referential with *ara-* (1EX). (The prefix *ara-* is the irregular form of *oro-* which occurs with the verb *ha* 'to go'.)

(26) sa-ropyta   yhara sere-**sahok-a**   ywyri
     1IN-stayed.with boat   1IN-bathe-SER at.edge
     Set1   Set3
     'We stayed with the boat, bathing at the edge.'

(27) ara-ha   ypa'oa-pype **oro-semorai-ta** kosatyitoa-re   **oro-sahok-a**
     1EX-go island-in/on 1EX-play-SER   children-with 1EX-bathe-SER
     Set1   Set3   Set3
     'We went to the island to play with the children and bathe.'

2.2.3 OBLIQUE-TOPICALIZED VERBS. In Tupí-Guaraní languages sometimes an adverbial (adverb or postpositional phrase) is fronted to the initial position of the clause for discourse reasons. This requires a change in verb form, as in 28-29 from Guajajara. Instead of using the main independent verb form (section 2.1), the oblique-topicalized verb form is used.

(28) a'e -pe **h-eko-n**
     that-at 3-be-OBTOP   'He is there.'
           Set2

(29) ka'a-pe **ure-reraha-n**
     jungle-at 1EX-take-OBTOP   'He took us to the jungle.'
           Set2

Set 2 person markers occur on the oblique-topicalized constructions, referring to either S or P. The suffix which occurs on the verb stem varies from one language to another. The allomorph following a vowel is *-n, -w,* or *-i[y]*. The allomorph following a consonant is *-i*.

The oblique-topicalized construction occurs only with certain persons. In Guajajara it is limited to verbs with third person subjects (S or A). With first or second person subjects the independent verb form is still used. In 29, although the person marker which occurs with the transitive verb refers to a first person P (*ure-* '1EX'), it is the unexpressed third person A which requires the oblique-topicalized construction. In Tupinambá and Kayabi this construction occurs with both first and third person subjects. In 30 from Tupinambá, S is third person, in 31 S is first person, and in 32 A is third person.

(30) kwesé   **i-só-w**
     yesterday 3-go-OBTOP   'Yesterday he went.'
           Set2

(31) kwesé **jané-só-w**
     yesterday 1IN-go-OBTOP   'Yesterday we went.'
                Set2

(32) kwesé pajé   **syé-subán-i**
     yesterday shaman 1sg-suck-OBTOP   'Yesterday the shaman
                Set2   sucked (treated) me.'

2.3 CROSS-REFERENCING ON NOMINALIZATIONS. All the verbal constructions in section 2.2 use person markers from Sets 2 or 3 to refer to P in transitive verbs or S in intransitive verbs. We will now look at nominalizations, which are also cross-referenced by Set 2 markers. This is essentially the only set available to them as nominals. However, the referent of the markers in the various types of nominalizations is significant.

2.3.1 NOMINALIZATIONS OF ACTION, AGENT, AND CIRCUMSTANCE. Tupí-Guaraní languages have three closely related suffixes which are used to nominalize verbs: *-a, *-ár and *-áb. These affixes create nominalizations which refer to the action itself, the agent of the action, or its circumstances, respectively. The *-a suffix has two allomorphs: *-a following consonants and *-Ø following vowels. The *-ár and *-áb suffixes have three allomorphs each: *-ár and *-áb following consonants, *-cár and *-cáb following vowels, and *-tár and *-táb following diphthongs. The following examples from Tupinambá illustrate the three types of nominalizations.

Action

(33) s-epyák-a
     3-see-NOM   'his being seen'
     Set2

(34) oré   r-ekár-a
     1EX LK-search.for-NOM 'our being searched for'
     Set2

(35) né   só-Ø
     2sg   go-NOM   'your going'
     Set2

Agent

(36) i-moján-ár
     3-make-NOM   'its maker'
     Set2

Circumstance

(37) i-juká-sáb
    3-kill-NOM   'his death place, his death circumstance'
    Set2

(38) i-moján-áb
    3-make-NOM   'its making place'
    Set2

As mentioned above, the suffix used to create a nominalization which refers to the action itself (33-35) has two allomorphs. The allomorph *-a* is identical with the comparable allomorph of the suffix used to indicate serial verbs. Therefore 33 and 34 are identical with the serial verb forms. However those verb stems ending with a vowel, as in 35, have a *-Ø* (zero) suffix, distinct from the *-ábo* allomorph of the serial verb suffix. In all cases above, the possessor of the newly created nominal is P in transitive verbs and S in intransitive verbs.

2.3.2 NOMINALIZATIONS REFERRING TO THE PATIENT. Besides the types of nominalizations referred to in section 2.3.1, there are two affixes used to create nominalizations which refer to the P argument of a transitive verb. The first of these, formed by the suffix *-pýr*, refers to P without any reference to the A. It is preceded exclusively by the third person prefix from set 2, as in the following example from Tupinambá:

(39) i-juká-pýr-(a)
    3-kill-PAT-(NC)   'that which was killed'

The other nominalization is created by the prefix *emi-* which refers to P in relation to A. That is, this prefix is obligatorily preceded by a person marker from Set 2, indicating A, as in the following examples from Tupinambá:

(40) syé r-emi-'ú
    1sg LK-PAT-eat   'that which I eat; my food'
    Set2
    A   P

(41) s-emi-moján-(a)
    3-PAT-make-(NC)   'that which he makes; his handiwork'
    Set2
    A P

This type of construction is unlike any of the others discussed in this paper. In all other cases, whether verbal constructions or nominalizations, it is a suffix — not a prefix — which creates the particular construction. Furthermore, there are no other cases where Set 2 person markers reference A. These factors make the *emi*- construction appear more similar to noun incorporation, which detransitivizes the verb,[8] as can be seen in the following examples from Tupinambá:

(42) kunumí a-i-nupã
    boy   1sg-3-hit   'I hit the boy'
    P   A

(43) a-kunumí-nupã
    1sg-boy-hit   'I hit the boy'
    S(ag)

(44) syé r-emi-nupã
    1sg LK-PAT-hit   'the one whom I hit'

If the prefix *emi*- not only nominalizes the transitive stem but also detransitivizes it, the use of a person marker of Set 2 is straightforward. It refers not to A but to S.

2.4 OTHER MANIFESTATIONS OF ERGATIVITY. Up to this point we have discussed the use of person markers on various verb forms. In the constructions in 2.2 and 2.3 the person markers consistently refer to the S argument in intransitive verbs and the P argument in transitive verbs. There are two other constructions in Tupí-Guaraní languages in which the same association of S and P can be observed.

2.4.1 THE COMPLETIVE SUFFIX *-PAB*. The suffix *-pab* indicates that an action has been completed BY the S argument of an intransitive verb or that it has been performed ON all the possible P arguments of a transitive verb.[9] The following examples are reconstructed for Proto-Tupí-Guaraní:

(45) *o-có-pab   'he already went; they all went'
    3-go-COMPL

(46) *o-'ú-pab   'he ate it all'
    3-eat-COMPL

2.4.2 MONOSYLLABIC REDUPLICATION OF THE STEM. Reduplication of the last syllable of the verb stem indicates that the action is performed consecutively BY one S after another in intransitive verbs, or ON one P after another in transitive verbs.

In the following data from Tupinambá, 47 and 49 are simple forms of transitive and intransitive verbs, respectively. Examples 48 and 50 are the reduplicated forms.

(47) a-i-mokón
    1sg-3-swallow   'I swallowed it'

(48) a-i-mokó-kón   'I swallowed one after another'

(49) oro-pór   'we jumped'
     1EX-jump

(50) oro-pó-pór   'we jumped, one after another'

In contrast to this monosyllabic reduplication, there is a bisyllabic reduplication which does not associate S and P; the significance of this difference will be seen in section 3.3.6. Bisyllabic reduplication indicates that the action is performed frequently, as in 51 from Tupinambá.

(51) a-i-mokó-mokón   'I swallow(ed) them frequently'
     oro-pó-ro-pór   'we jump(ed) frequently'

2.5 SUMMARY. The interrelationship of A, S, and P characteristic of Tupí-Guaraní languages is summarized in Table 3. The squares indicate that the same form is used for all the referents indicated inside the square.

$S_{(ag)}$	$S_{(non-ag)}$	unmarked independent verbs
A	P	
A	$S_{(ag)}$	subordinate, serial, ob-top verbs
	$S_{(non-ag)}$	nominalizations
	P	monosyllabic reduplication
		completive aspect *(*-pab)*

Table 3. Organization of A, S, and P arguments in Tupí-Guaraní languages

3. CROSS-REFERENCING CHANGES IN SOME TUPI-GUARANI LANGUAGES

In section 2 I described the conservative Tupí-Guaraní interrelationships of A, S, and P arguments in various constructions. I will now show in detail what has happened in some languages which have undergone cross-referencing changes. These languages are Chiriguano, Kaiwa, and Mbya Guaraní from subgroup 1; and Wayampi and Urubu from subgroup 8. To generalize, the system used with unmarked independent verbs has replaced that which formerly occured in subordinate clauses. The extent of change varies with each of the five languages: Wayampi has changed the least, Urubu the most, with the other three languages somewhere in between.

3.1 PERSON MARKERS. In Table 1 (section 2.1) I showed four sets of person markers which have been reconstructed for Proto-Tupí-Guaraní. The descendents of these protoforms, as they occur in the five languages under discussion, appear in Table 4.

Set 1 person markers

	P-T-G	Chiriguano	Guaraní	Kaiwa	Wayampi	Urubu
1sg	*a-	a-	a-	a-	a-	a-
1IN	*ja-	ja-	ja-	ja-	ja-,si-	ja-
1EX	*oro-	ro-	oro-	oro-	oro-	
2sg	*ere-	re-	ere-	ere-	ere-	ere-
2pl	*pe-	pe-	pe-	pe-	pe-	pe-
3	*o-	o-	o-	o-	o-	(o-/u-)

Set 2 person markers

	P-T-G	Chiriguano	Guaraní	Kaiwa	Wayampi	Urubu*
1sg	*ce	xe	xe	xe	e	ihẽ
1IN	*jane	jane	jane	jane	jane	jane
1EX	*ore	ore	ore	ore	ore	
2sg	*ne	ne	ne	ne	ne	ne
2pl	*pe	pe	pe	pe	pe	pe
3	*i-,h-	i-,h-	i-,h-	i-,h-	i-,Ø-	i-,h-

* This set does not occur on Urubu verbs except in nonagentive intransitive verbs and in residual forms.

Set 3 person markers Nonexistent in all 5 languages

Set 4 person markers

	P-T-G	Chiriguano	Guaraní	Kaiwa	Wayampi	Urubu
1sg	*oro-	ro-	oro-	oro-	oro-	
2pl	*opo-	po-	oro-		poro-	
1sgA				apo-		
1plA				oropo-		

Table 4. Comparative person markers

The most striking thing that we see from Table 4 is that in all five languages, the set 3 prefixes, originally used on intransitive serial verbs, are no longer in use.

Chiriguano has deleted the initial vowel in bisyllabic prefixes (*ro-* and *re-* in Set 1 and *ro-* and *po-* in Set 4).

In all five languages, the forms in which proto *č-* and *c-* occurred reflect phonological weakening: *č* (ch) > *x* (sh) > *h* > ∅ (zero) in the first person singular form of Set 2. In the third person marker of the same set, *c* (ts) > *h* > ∅ (zero).

In Kaiwa two Set 4 prefixes *apo-* and *oropo-* replace the protoform *opo-*. This same form has been replaced by *poro-* in Wayampi and has neutralized with *oro-* in Mbya Guaraní (cf. note 6).

In Wayampi there are two first person inclusive prefixes, *ja-* which occurs with intransitive verbs and *si-* which occurs with transitive verbs. *Ja-* also occurs with both transitive and intransitive when its meaning is unmarked (generic), comparable to use of 'one' in the English sentence 'one does it this way.' In one dialect of Wayampi *ere-* has been replaced by *ne-* except when preceded by a prefix (*n-* or *t-*).

Urubu has lost the prefixes of Set 4. It has also lost the distinction between exclusive and inclusive in first person plural, leaving only the form which was originally inclusive. Furthermore, when the subject of a verb is third person, the subject (S or A) prefix only occurs with monosyllabic stems (Kakumasu 1986.392).

3.2 INDEPENDENT VERBS. Guaraní, Kaiwa, Chiriguano, and Wayampi have all retained the cross-referencing system characteristic of unmarked independent transitive verbs, as summarized in Table 2 (section 2.1). There is a split-S system for intransitive verbs and an agency hierarchy rule governing transitive verbs. Urubu has retained the split-S system but has eliminated the agency hierarchy rule. As a result, all cross-referencing on transitive verbs in Urubu is with the A, as in 52:

(52) a. a-sak   'I saw (you/him/her/them)'
     b. ja-sak   'we saw (you/him/her/them)'
     c. ere-sak   'you SG saw (me/us/him/her/them)'
     d. pe-sak   'you PL saw (me/us/him/her/them)'
     e. u-sak   'he/she/they saw (me/us/you/him/her/them)'
     f. a-petek   'I tapped (you/him/her/them)'
     BUT

(53)   ∅-petek   'he/she/they tapped (me/us/you/him/her/them)'

Whereas the first person prefix (52a-f) occurs with both monosyllabic and bisyllabic stems, the third person prefix occurs only with the monosyllabic one (52e but not 53).

3.3 REORGANIZATION OF THE VERBAL CROSS-REFERENCING SYSTEM.
3.3.1 TOPICALIZED OBLIQUE CONSTRUCTIONS. In Proto-Tupí-Guaraní the oblique-topicalized construction is signaled by a fronted adverbial or a post-positional phrase. The oblique-topicalized verb is suffixed by an oblique-topicalized affix and is prefixed by a person marker from Set 2, as illustrated in section 2.2.3.

In Mbya Guaraní, Kaiwa, Chiriguano, Wayampi, and Urubu, a fronted adverbial no longer requires a special construction (except in certain residual forms). The verb form currently used in this environment is identical with the independent verb, and is subject in each language to the same rules of cross-referencing as the independent verb. (When the P of a transitive verb is hierarchically superior to the A, the P is still expressed by set 2 patient markers, except in Urubu.)

Wayampi

(54) yapy-kyty ajã   o-o   amẽ
     upriver-to spirit 3-go consequently
                      Set1
     'Consequently the spirit went upriver.'

(55) ikeruã-wyi o-jenu
     afar-from   3-be.heard
                      Set1
     'He was heard from afar.'

Guaraní

(56) kuee   o-exa
     yesterday 3-see
                      Set1
     'Yesterday he saw it.'

(57) kuee   o-i-nupã
     yesterday 3-3-hit
                      Set1-Set2
     'Yesterday he hit it.'

(58) kuee   o-ke
     yesterday 3-sleep
                      Set1
     'Yesterday he slept.'

Kaiwa

(59) iro'y-ramo kyha-py   oke-ramo   **o-jara**   i-gwypy tata
     cold-when hammock-in slept-when 3-scraped 3-under fire
                              Set1
     'When it was cold, when he slept in his hammock, he scraped up fire beneath him.'

(60) o-membyry ndive   **o-ho** ho-'u kãgwi
     3-son   with   3-go 3-eat manioc beer
     Set3   Set1
     'With her (own) son she went to drink manioc beer.'

Chiriguano

(61) tenónde-roiko-kwe ore-ramy-réta   mbáety **ho-u** wáka
     before-our-time   our-grandfathers NEG   3-eat beef
                                   Set1
     'Before our time our grandfathers didn't eat beef.'

(62) karumboe **a-ju**   Paraguay-gui; hókope **o-mano** xe ru
     yesterday 1sg-came P.from   there   3-die   my father
          Set1   Set1
     'Yesterday I came from Paraguay. It was there that my father died.'

Urubu

(63) petaramo kaitã   ju'ipape pi'a **u-sak** o-ho tî
     today   Caetano turtle   egg 3-see 3-go again
                            Set1
     'Today Caetano went to look for turtle eggs.'

(64) pe-koty   **u-ár** o-ho tî
     that.side-at 3-fell 3-go again
             Set1
     'On that side it fell again.'

In spite of the general substitution of unmarked independent verbs for oblique-topicalized verbs in all five of these languages, residual (frozen) forms have been found in four languages (65-73). When they occur, these usually continue to function according to the original rules. However, a change of the fronting rule has occurred even with the frozen forms in 69 from Guaraní and 73 from Urubu. In 73 the adverbial does not occur initially to the clause, only to the verb itself. In 69 the adverbial does not occur initially at all; it follows the verb.

Wayampi

(65) *tu-i*, from **i-t-úb-i*, *(*júb)* 'to be lying down
eko-i, from **c-ekó-OBTOP*, *(*ikó)* 'to be in movement'

(66) pee-rupi   taiwĩgwe **ekoi**
path-along ancestor be.in.movement
'Our ancestor was going along the path.'

Guaraní

(67) *i-tu-i*, from **i-t-úb-i*, *(*júb)*, as above (65)
i-tury, from **i-t-úr-i*[10] *(*júr)* 'to come'

(68) xe-a   katy   **i-tury**
my-place toward 3-came i
'He came toward me.'

(69) **i-tui**   tupa py
3-be.lying bed on
'He is lying on the bed.'

Kaiwa

(70) *i-tu-i*, as above (65)
i-tury, as above (67)

(71) te'ogwe-rami **i-tui**   yvy-rupi   kunumi
corpse-like   3-be.lying ground-on boy
'The boy was lying on the ground like a corpse.'

Urubu

(72) *tu-i*, as above (65)
tur, as above in Guaraní *i-tury* (67)
i-ho-n, from **i-có-OBTOP*, *(*có)* 'to go'

(73) nasu   riki   ihe namo **i-ho-n**
Nasui EMPH me with 3-came
'Nasui went with me.'

Two factors may account for the resistance of these forms to change (i.e. substitution by the independent verb forms). All of these are commonly used verbs, which are learned at an earlier age than grammatical rules, making them more resistant to change. Second, three of the remnant forms have alternate roots, one for Set 2 person markers, the other for Set 1. This makes the oblique-topicalized forms less easily identifiable with the corresponding independent verb form. For instance, **t-ú(b)-i* 'to be lying down' corresponds to **o-úb*, **i-t-úr-i* 'to come' to **o-úr*, and **c-ekó-w* (or perhaps **c-ekó-n*) 'to be (moving around)' to **o-ikó*.

3.3.2 SUBORDINATE VERBS. In the original system (section 2.2.1) the subordinate verb is cross-referenced by Set 2 person markers, referring to the S and P arguments. This system has been replaced in Mbya Guaraní, Kaiwa, Chiriguano, Wayampi, and Urubu by the system used with independent verbs. In these languages (except for Urubu), transitive verbs may be cross-referenced by person markers from Sets 1, 2, or 4, depending on the relative position of A and P on the agency hierarchy. Urubu uses only Set 1 prefixes.

Wayampi

(74) tatarena rape **oro-inũ**   remẽ
    airplane path 1EX-make when   'when we made the airstrip'
          Set1

(75) **oro-esa**   remẽ
    1:2sg-meet when   'when I met you'
    Set4

(76) **a-mena**   paire
    1sg-marry(intr) after   'after I got married'
    Set1

Guaraní

(77) **a-porandu** ramo o-mbovai
    1sg-asked   when 3-replied   'When I asked, he replied.'
    Set1   Set1

(78) **o-exa** jave/ramo/vy
    3-saw when   'when he saw him/it'
    Set1

Kaiwa

(79) hoga   **o-me'ẽ-ramo**
    money 3-give-if/when   'if he gives (me) money'
          Set1

(80) **o-gwereko-ramo**
    3-have-if/when   'if he has it'
    Set1

(81) kwarahy **o-sẽ**   jave
    sun   3-come.out when   'when the sun comes out (rises)'
    Set1

Chiriguano

(82) heta   **a-ño-tỹˢ**-jave
     plenty 1sg-3-plant-when   'when I planted plenty'
             Set1

(83) o-**endu**-ramo o-iko-ve
     3-hear-if   3-be   'If he hears, he is alive.'
     Set1   Set1

(84) mbaety **o-ky**-jave
     NEG   3-rain-if   'if it doesn't rain'
             Set1

Urubu

(85) se   **a-jur**   we   rahã
     here 1sg-come again when   'when I come again'
          Set1

(86) **u-pa** aman **u-kyr** rahã   'when it stops raining'
     3-quit rain 3-rain when
     Set1   Set1

Examples 76, 77, 81, 84, 85, and 86 show that agentive S is prefixed by members of Set 1. The examples for transitive verbs (74, 75, 78, 79, 80, 82 and 83) illustrate those cases where A is hierarchically superior to P, since these are the conditions where Set 2 was replaced by Set 1 or Set 4. In 74, 79 and 82 a transitive verb is immediately preceded by the patient, expressed as a noun. According to the original system, no person marker would be necessary. In 75, 78, 80 and 83 the transitive verb occurs without the patient (as a noun) immediately preceding it. According to the original system, they would have required person markers from Set 2, referring to the patient.

Evidence in these languages of the original system for subordinate clauses is minimal. Though rare, the following constructions have been encountered:

Wayampi

(87) **i-'u**   paire
     3-eat after   'after eating it all' or
     Set2   'after (he/you/we,etc.) ate it'

(88) ije **Ø-esa** remẽ
     I   3-see when   'when I saw him'
         Set2

Kaiwa

(89) **nhande-ho** ramo   'when we all go'
     1IN-go   when
     Set2

For some reason the old system (with Set 2 person markers) was used instead of the new (with Set 1 markers) in each of these cases.

3.3.3 SERIAL VERBS. As explained in section 2.2.2, serial verbs occur together with an independent verb which has the same grammatical subject. Together they convey aspects of what is perceived as a single action. In searching for examples of serial verbs in Guaraní, Kaiwa, Chiriguano, Wayampi, and Urubu, I have looked for verbs which have the same relative position to the independent verb and the same function as the original serial verbs. That is, they occur in close association with the independent verb, with which they express a single action. They do not necessarily have the same prefixing rules or carry a serial verb suffix. But there is some indication that they have descended in some way from the original serial verbs. This explanation is particularly necessary in reference to the data from Mbya Guaraní.

In the original Tupí-Guaraní system, intransitive serial verbs are prefixed by a Set 3 (co-referential) person marker and suffixed by a serial verb marker. In Guaraní, Kaiwa, Chiriguano, Wayampi, and Urubu, Set 3 prefixes have been replaced by those of Set 1.

Wayampi

(90) a-jywy   **a-a**
     1sg-return 1sg-go   'I returned, going.'
     Set1   Set1

(91) o-o   **o-iporaka**
     3-go   3-hunt   'He went hunting.'
     Set1   Set1

Guaraní

(92) a-eka   **a-iko-vy**
     1sg-search.for 1sg-be-SER   'I went about looking
     Set1   Set1   for it.'

(93) kuaxia a-exa   **a-in-y**
     paper 1sg-see 1sg-be.located-SER
            Set1   Set1
     'I was reading, seated.'

Kaiwa

(94) a-jevy   **a-ha-vy**
    1sg-return 1sg-go-SER   'I returned, going.'
    Set1   Set1

(95) a-ha   **a-jahu-(vy)**
    1sg-go 1sg-bathe-(SER)   'I went bathing.'
    Set1   Set1

Chiriguano

(96) o-jaro-ma   **o-ho**
    3-approach-already 3-go   'He approached, going.'
    Set1   Set1

(97) a-ha   **a-guata**
    1sg-go 1sg-walk   'I went walking.'
    Set1   Set1

Urubu

(98) ihẽ ramuĩ   u-sak **o-ho**
    my grandfathers 3-see 3-go
                     Set1   Set1
    'My grandfathers went to see it.'

(99) xe   ihẽ ke   a-jupir   katu te   **a-xo**
    there I   FOC 1sg-climb well really 1sg-be.in.mvmt.
                 Set1   Set1
    'There I was really climbing well.'

Examples 90-99 have a main verb followed by an intransitive serial verb. In Wayampi, Chiriguano, and Urubu, there is no serial verb suffix at all; nevertheless, the second verb may justifiably be called a serial verb because of its behavior. Examples from Guaraní and Kaiwa have a suffix -*vy* which has descended from the suffix -*ábo*.[10] Another allomorph, -*ny* (93), was derived by a reassociation of the final consonant of the protostem with the allomorph *-*a* of the serial verb suffix. (Guaraní has eliminated final consonants.)

Although the class of potential serial verbs appears to have been an open class in Proto-Tupí-Guaraní, it has been reduced in Mbya Guaraní to a class of seven intransitive verbs, plus their derivatives (Dooley 1988).[11]

According to the original system, transitive serial verbs were preceded by either a noun or a person marker of Set 2 (referring to P). It is in this area that we see the greatest diversity among the five languages which have undergone change.

Wayampi

(100) a-a   pira **rekyi-ta**
       1sg-go fish pull-SER   'I went fishing.'
       Set1   (Set2)

(101) e-momo   **i-mono**
       imp-throw 3-send.away   'Throw it away.'
       Set2

(102) a-jo   **ne-resa**
       1sg-come 2s-see   'I came to see you SG.'
       Set1   Set2

Guaraní: New system

(103) o-jopy   **o-i-nupã**
       3-grasp 3-3-hit   'He grasped it to hit it
       Set1   Set1 Set2   (with an instrument).'

(104) o-o   tatu   **mbo'a vy**   'He went trapping
       3-go armadillo trap   SER   armadillos.'
       Set1   (Set2)

(105) o-o   **o-mbo'a vy**
       3-go 3-trap   SER   'He went to trap it.'
       Set1 Set1

Guaraní: Traditional system

(106) a-jopy   **h-era-vy**
       1sg-grasp 3-take-SER   'I got it and took it.'
       Set1   Set2

(107) a-mo-pu'ã   **i-mo'am-y**
       1sg-CAUS-stand 3-cause.to.stand.upright-SER
              Set2
       'I stood it up, causing it to stand upright.'

(108) a-mo-pu'ã   xe-ra'y **i-mo'am-y**
       1sg-CAUS-rise 1sg-son 3-cause.to.stand-SER
       Set1   Set2
       'I made my son stand up.'

Kaiwa

(109)   a-i-nupã   pira   **a-juka**
        1sg-3-hit fish   1sg-kill   'I hit the fish to kill it.'
        Set1-Set2   Set1

(110)   a-i-nupã   **a-juka hagwã/ -vy**
        1sg-3-hit 1sg-kill   -SER   'I hit it to kill it.'
        Set1-Set2 Set1

(111)   a-ju   **oro-hexa-vy**
        1sg-come   1:2sg-see-SER   'I came to see you SG.'
        Set1   Set4

From traditional system

(112)   a-ha   pira   **renohẽ-vy**
        1sg-go fish   bring.out-SER   'I went fishing.'
        Set1   (Set2)

Chiriguano

(113)   kua kuñatai o-u   **o-i-apo** kãgwyjy
        this girl   3-come 3-make manioc.beer
                            Set1   Set1
        'This girl came to make manioc beer.'

(114)   xe rembireko o-ho ñu-pe **o-eka**   vakareta
        my wife   3-go hill-to 3-search.for cows
                            Set1   Set1
        'My wife went to the hill to search for the cows.'

Urubu

(115)   ihẽ a-ho   ta   **a-sak**
        I   1sg-go FUT   1sg-see   'I will go to see him/it.'
            Set1   Set1

(116)   a'erehe   a-rur   **a-hjjar**   i-mai   pe
        for.that.reason 1sg-bring   1sg-leave(tr) 3-mother   to
                        Set1   Set1
        'For that reason I returned (him) to his mother.'

Wayampi (100-102) retains the original reference to P, either as a noun (100) or as a person marker (101-102). Examples 100 and 102 have stems of class II (section 1.2) and therefore have a linking prefix *r-* between the patient referent (noun or Set 2 person marker) and the stem. The stem in 101 belongs to class I, so it takes the *i*- allomorph for third person. The serial verb suffix *-ta* in 100 is the only allomorph of this suffix that has been retained in Wayampi; it follows diphthongs.

In 113-114 from Chiriguano and 115-116 from Urubu, the serial verb suffix has been deleted and the prefixing is identical with that in independent verbs. In 113 we see the occurence of the third person patient prefix *i*- between the agent prefix and the verb stem (section 2.1). Although Chiriguano data may not be sufficient to permit a generalization, 113-114 suggest that there is at least a tendency to put a noun referring to the patient after the serial verb, rather than before.

The situation in Guaraní is more complicated. There are two types of constructions, each of which retains some aspect of the original serial construction. The first type (106-107) is what Dooley 1988 considers to be true serial verbs in Guaraní. It involves a finite set of transitive verbs, which are derivations of the previously mentioned intransitive serial verbs. Like their protoforms, these verbs are cross-referenced with Set 2 person markers which refer to P. The new allomorphs of the serial verb suffix can be directly traced to the protoforms; there has been no regularization of any particular form. For these reasons they are indicated in this paper as instances of the old system. However, it is rare that a noun referring to the patient occurs between the independent verb and the serial verb in this language. Even when it does occur, as in 108, the person marker occurs as well.

In the second type of construction, the would-be serial verb is unprefixed when preceded by a noun referring to the P (104) as in the original construction. However, when not preceded by a noun, it is prefixed by a member of Set 1, referring to the A, as in independent verbs (105). I have referred to this construction as the new system because of certain other changes that have accompanied the cross-referencing change. Example 103 shows that the serial verb marker *vy* is not an absolute requirement. Dooley does not consider the verbs appearing in this type of construction to be serial verbs. He argues that the link between the two verbs is not as tight as in serial verb constructions. Furthermore, the *vy* morpheme carries independent stress and has lost the type of allomorphic variation which occurs in the construction type illustrated by 103-105.

Examples 109-111 from Kaiwa have similarities to both Chiriguano and to Guaraní. In 109 we see that a noun can precede the serial verb (or what descended from a serial verb), but the verb must still be prefixed. In 111 the serial verb is affixed by a portmanteau prefix of Set 4. Example 109 shows that, like Guaraní, the serial verb suffix is not always required. Example 112 contrasts with 109 in that the patient directly precedes the verb, with no agent prefix in between. The retention of the old system as expressed in *pira renohê-vy* 'fishing' could perhaps be due to a frequent reference to a very common activity. I do not have at my disposal any examples from Kaiwa which would be comparable to the first construction type in Guaraní.

Urubu, Guaraní, and Wayampi all have additional residual forms which are derivable from former serial verb forms. The cases in Guaraní (117-120) are different from the traditional set of serial verb forms illustrated above in that the third person prefix has been frozen to the stem, making the apparent cross-referencing irrelevant. In 118 the patient is really first person singular and in 120 it is really second person singular.

Guaraní

(117) *imondovy* from *i-mo-nó-ábo[10]   'sending it away'
                       3-cause.to.go-SER

(118) xe-mondyi-ve   **i-mondovy**
       1sg-scare-much   (3)-send
       Set2   (Set2)
       'He/it scared me so much that (he/it) made me go away.'

(119) **imoiny** from *i-mo-ín-a[10]   'causing to sit'
                        3-cause-sit-SER

(120) ava   ne-mo-ngaru **i-moiny**
       man   2s-cause-eat (3)-cause.to.sit   'The man made you
             Set2   (Set2)   sit down and eat.'

Wayampi

(121) **kupa** 'plural S or A' from *kúb-a   'being together'

(122) o-o   o-jau   **kupa**
       3-go 3-bathe plural   'They went bathing.'

Urubu

(123) *i-ndo* from *i-monó(-ábo)   'causing it to go'

(124) jangwate tiki mu-jan   **i-ndo**
       jaguar   AFF   3+CAUS-run 3-cause.to.go
                      Set1   Set2

       aja   ihẽ ke   '"It is the jaguar that chased
       thus I   FOC   it," thus I thought.'

Example 121 from Wayampi shows that the plural morpheme is derived from the former serial verb *kúb-a 'being together', without any prefix. The position in which this plural marker occurs is the same position as a serial verb (122). Examples 123-124 show the reduction of a former serial verb which still maintains its normal prefixing and position.

3.3.4 NOMINALIZATIONS. By way of review, all nominalizations in the proto-system were preceded by person markers from Set 2 (or by a noun referring to the patient in transitive verbs). Examples 125-144 illustrate nominalizations formed by suffixes which are descended from *-a*, *-ár*, and *-áb*. These nominalizations refer to the action itself, the agent of the action, and its circumstances, respectively. Examples 125-133 are nominalizations created from intransitive verb stems. Only Wayampi (125-126) retains the original prefixing (Set 2). In the other four languages (127-133) the original person markers have been replaced by Set 1 prefixes.

Intransitive verbs

Wayampi

(125)   e-jau-a
        1sg-bathe-NOM   'my (act of) bathing'
        Set2

(126)   e-reko-a-we
        1sg-be-NOM-PAST   'my past life'
        Set2

Guaraní

(127)   ere-o-a
        2sg-go-NOM   'your SG (act of) going'
        Set1

Kaiwa

(128)   ere-ho-ha
        2sg-go-NOM   'your SG (act of) going'
        Set1

(129)   o-iko-ma-ha-gwe
        3-be-already-NOM-PAST   'his birth'
        Set1

Chiriguano

(130)   a-ke-a
        1sg-sleep-NOM   'my sleeping place'
        Set1

(131)   kuaray o-ě-a-pe
        sun   3-go.out-NOM-to   'to the place where the
              Set1   sun comes out (east)'

Urubu

(132) a-ho-ha
       1sg-go-NOM   'my (act of) going'
       Set1

(133) ere-ho-ha
       2sg-go-NOM   'your SG (act of) going'
       Set1

Examples 134-142 are nominalizations created from transitive verbs. The examples from Wayampi (134-135) are nominalizations which refer to the agent and circumstance, respectively. In both of these cases the verbs are cross-referenced by Set 2 person markers referring to P, as in the original system. Nominalizations which refer to the agent in Mbya Guaraní, Kaiwa, and Chiriguano (136, 138, 141) also retain the Set 2 person markers, referring to P. However, in these three languages the nominalizations which refer to the action itself or its circumstances (137, 139, 140, 142) have undergone cross-referencing changes, and now use the prefixes which are used with independent verbs. Examples 137, 139, and 142 show that Set 1 prefixes (referring to A) are now used. Where it is grammatically required (139), the Set 2 prefix referring to the third person P follows the Set 1 prefix. The portmanteau prefixes (Set 4) also occur with nominalizations of this type, at least in Kaiwa.

Transitive verbs

Wayampi

(134) e-mo'e-are
       1sg-teach-NOM.PAST   'my former teacher'
       Set2

(135) i-juka-(a)-we
       3-kill-NOM-PAST   'the place where it was killed'
       Set2

Guaraní

(136) i-mbo'e-a
       3-teach-NOM   'his teacher'
       Set2

(137) o-mbo'e-a
       3-teach-NOM   'the action or place
       Set1   of his being taught'

Kaiwa

(138) i-mbo'e-ha
       3-teach-NOM   'his teacher'
       Set2

(139) o-j-apo-ha
       3-3-do-NOM   'the action of (something)
       Set1-Set2   being done'

(140) oro-mbogwera-ma-ha-gwe
       1:2sg-heal-already-NOM-PAST   'the action of my having
       Set4   healed you'

Chiriguano

(141) i-juka-a
       3-kill-NOM   'its (his) killer'
       Set2

(142) o-juka-a
       3-kill-NOM   'instrument which kills (knife)'
       Set1

Urubu

(143) a-kwa-ha
       1sg-know-NOM   'my knowing (of it)'
       Set1

(144) u-sak-iha
       3-see-NOM   'the one seeing him'
       Set1

Examples 143-144 from Urubu are nominalizations which refer to the action itself and the agent, respectively. In both cases, Set 1 prefixes have replaced Set 2 person markers in Urubu transitive verbs. The prefix *-ha* is still the basic form following vowels, but *-iha* has replaced *-a* following consonants. The former prefix *-*a* appears in the apparently frozen form *manioc sosok-a* 'manioc pounder' which also demonstrates the traditional option of an unprefixed transitive nominalization preceeded by its nominal object.

The suffix *-*pýr* which creates nominalizations referring to the patient is retained only in Guaraní (145) and Kaiwa (146-147). In Kaiwa the verb stem still requires a Set 2 prefix. But in Guaraní the Set 2 prefix has been replaced by that of Set 1, which in transitive verbs should refer to the agent. This is of

particular interest since the *-pýr construction was originally the one which
referred to the P independently of the A. In spite of the change in prefixing,
Dooley (182.157) states that this is still the case.

Guaraní

(145) ita   o-mboaty py-re
       rock 3-piled   PAT-PAST   'rocks which were piled up'
              Set1

Kaiwa

(146) i-juka-py
       3-kill-PAT   'something killed'
       Set2

(147) i-mombo-py-rã
       3-throw-PAT-FUT   'something to be thrown'
       Set2

The patient nominalization *emi- (148-149) occurs in all languages but
Urubu, and is prefixed by the original Set 2 person markers indicating the
subject. Urubu retains the nominalization only in one frozen form (154). The
former function of this nominalizer is handled in Urubu by another nominalizer
characteristic of the language family as a whole. This derives from *ba'e,
which nominalizes clauses as well. The loss of the *emi- prefix in Urubu is
consistent with the loss of other types of references to the P within a verbal
construction.[12]

Wayampi

(148) e-r-emi-tỹ
       1sg-LK-PAT-plant   'that which I planted; my plant'
       Set2

(149) Ø-emi-su'u
       3-PAT-bite   'the one that it bit'
       Set2

Guaraní

(150) xe-r-embi-'u
       1sg-LK-PAT-eat   'that which I eat; my food'
       Set2

(151) xe-r-emi-mbo'e
       1sg-LK-PAT-teach   'the one I teach; my student'
       Set2

Kaiwa

(152) xe-r-emi-tỹ-rã
       1sg-LK-PAT-plant-FUT   'that which I will plant'
       Set2

Chiriguano

(153) xe-r-embi-apo
       1sg-LK-PAT-make   'that which I make; my creation'
       Set2

Urubu (frozen form)

(154) h-imi-'u
       3-PAT-eat   'that which he eats; his food'
       Set2

3.3.5 THE COMPLETIVE SUFFIX *-PAB*. The completive suffix *-pab* is retained in Wayampi, Guaraní, and Kaiwa. For the most part it requires a reference to the S of intransitive verbs or the P of transitive verbs, as in the protosystem. Examples 155, 157, 158 and 162 have intransitive verbs; the suffix requires a reference to a completed action by all the possible subjects. Examples 156, 159, and 161 have transitive verbs; the suffix indicates that the action was completed on all possible patients. However, in Guaraní transitive verbs, the suffix sometimes appears to apply to the A rather than the P, as in 160.

Wayampi

(155) o-o-pa
       3-go-COMPL   'they all went; they already went'

(156) ere-'u-pa
       2s-eat(tr)-COMPL   'you ate it all'

(157) o-imi'u-pa
       3-eat(itr)-COMPL   'he/they finished eating'

Guaraní

(158) kunhagwe **o-u-pa**
       women   3-come-COMPL   'the women all came'

(159) oro-mombe'u-pa-ta
       1EX-tell-COMPL-fut   'we will tell everything'

(160) pe-mo-inge   opy, **pe-mbo-u-pa**   porã
       2pl-CAUS-enter   inside 2pl-CAUS-come-COMPL   well
       'Take him inside, all of you bring him, in a fitting manner.'

Kaiwa

(161) ho-'u-pa
     3-eat-COMPL   'they ate everything'

(162) o-ke-pa
     3-sleep-COMPL   'they all slept'

In Urubu (163-165) and Chiriguano (166) the suffix has been eliminated. In its place the intransitive verb *páb* 'to be finished, wiped out' in its third person form conveys the idea of completion (cf. note 9).

Urubu

(163) wyrahu   **upa**   u-'u
     king.hawk COMPL 3-eat   'The king hawk ate it all.'

(164) **upa**   nde ere-mujã tamũi
     COMPL you 2sg-make grandfather
     'Did you finish making it, old man?'

(165) **upa**   aman u-kyr rahã
     COMPL rain 3-rain when   'when it stops raining'

Chiriguano

(166) **ópa**   ó-ke
     COMPL 3-sleep   'they finished sleeping'

3.3.6 MONOSYLLABIC REDUPLICATION. Except for the occurrence of frozen forms, monosyllabic reduplication has disappeared from all five languages. Wayampi has the form *mokõ-kõ* 'swallow one after another' from *mokón* 'swallow'. However, this mechanism is no longer productive and has been replaced by a more common mechanism based on bisyllabic reduplication; this can be seen from the following comparative examples:

(167) o-nupã-nupã   'He clubbed it (a fish) repeatedly.'
     3-hit-RED

(168) o-nupã-nupã Ø-eraa   'He clubbed one (fish)
     3-hit-RED   3-taking   after another.'
     Set1   Set2

Urubu also has some frozen forms, including *mani' o sosoka* 'instrument for pounding manioc' from *sók* 'to pierce', though no nonreduplicated form of the verb appears in the language. Other examples (169-170) from Urubu also retain the monosyllabic reduplication in frozen forms. However, in the transitive verb (169) the reference is to repetitive action on a single patient, not on all possible patients. In the intransitive verb (170) the reference is once again to repetitive action by a single subject rather than all possible subjects. Thus the meaning of the frozen forms of monosyllabic reduplication has been changed to coincide with that of the still productive bisyllabic reduplication.

(169) tapi'ir ngã **u-sa-sak**   ta   tipe
       tapir   3PL 3-see-RED FUT unsuccessfully
       'They tried and tried to see the tapir, but didn't.'

(170) kwaraxi pe **i-ho-hon** me'ẽ u-hyk
       Icoaraci to 3-go-rep NOM 3-arrive
       'The one who repeatedly went to Icoaraci arrived.'

3.4 CROSS-REFERENCING INNOVATIONS IN GUAJAJARA. The five languages discussed in Sections 3.1-3.3 have shown a great deal of uniformity in the way they have undergone cross-referencing changes, though they have differed in the extent of change. The cross-referencing system used in unmarked independent verbs has been extended by replacing Set 2 or Set 3 person markers with those of Set 1. This means that transitive verbs have begun to be cross-referenced for A instead of P (at least where the agency hierarchy rule permits). It also means that the split-S system has been extended to constructions where it did not originally occur.

Guajajara (Tupí-Guaraní) is of interest because it has also undergone cross-referencing changes, but in a completely different way (Harrison 1986). The original cross-referencing system is essentially intact except for the Set 3 prefixes, which have been replaced by Set 1 prefixes on intransitive serial verbs. However, Guajajara has innovated clause-level nominative clitic pronouns; these occur at the end of the clause, as in 171-172.

(171) a-esak   kakwez   ka'i   **ihe**
       1sg-see distant.past.attested monkey I
       Set1
       'I saw the monkey.'

(172) he-kisi takihe-pupe **a'e**
       1sg-cut knife-with   he
       Set2
       'He cut me with a knife.'

In 171 the prefix on the verb refers to the A. The clitic pronoun at the end of the clause is *ihe* 'I', which refers to the A. In 172 the prefix on the verb refers to the P, but the clitic pronoun at the end of the clause, *a'e* 'he', still refers to the A.

Examples 173-175 show a transitive, an agentive intransitive, and a nonagentive verb, respectively. All three have a first person singular subject (A or S), and all three are cross-referenced at the end of the clause by the first person singular pronoun *ihe*.

(173)   a-esak ...   **ihe**   'I saw him'
        1sg-see   1sg
        Set1

(174)   a-ker ...   **ihe**   'I slept'
        1sg-sleep 1sg
        Set1

(175)   he-rurywete ...   **ihe**   'I was very happy'
        1sg-be happy   1sg
        Set2

(176)   he-resak ...   **a'e**   'he saw me'
        1sg-see   3
        Set2

Example 176 has a transitive verb whose prefix refers to the P, according to the demands of the agency hierarchy. However, it is cross-referenced at the end of the sentence by *a'e* 'he', which refers to the A. So even though the prefixing on the verb refers to the P, the sentence-level cross-referencing still refers to the agent. In summary, even though the verb prefixing is an active-stative or split-S system, the cross-referencing at the end of the sentence is strictly a nominative (A and S) system.

Harrison (1986.427,432-434) says that the current system applies as well to oblique-topicalized and subordinate clauses, even though the person markers occurring on the verbs in these clauses are still absolutive (as in Sections 2.2.1 and 2.2.3).

4. CONCLUSIONS ABOUT CROSS-REFERENCING CHANGES

Table 5 is a comparison of the cross-referencing systems used in Proto-Tupí-Guaraní and in Wayampi, Mbya Guaraní, Kaiwa, Chiriguano, and Urubu, showing which set of person markers is used in each syntactic condition. For each language there are four rows of information relating to nonagentive intransitive verbs (discussed briefly in the introduction), agentive intransitive verbs, transitive verbs in which the A is hierarchically superior to the P (A>P), and transitive verbs in which the P is hierarchically superior (P>A). (To facilitate comparison, only the nominalizations which are created by the *-a, *-ár, and *-áb suffixes are considered.)

Proto-Tupí-Guaraní

	Indep	Ob-Top	Subord	Serial	Nominal
Non-ag S	2	2	2	2	2
Ag S	1	2	2	3	2
A>P	1-2,4	2	2	2	2
P>A	2	2	2	2	2

Wayampi

	Indep	Ob-Top	Subord	Serial	Nominal
Non-ag S	2	2	2	2	2
Ag S	1	1	1	1	2
A>P	1,4	1,4	1,4	2	2
P>A	2	2	2	2	2

Mbya Guaraní

	Indep	Ob-Top	Subord	Serial	Nominal CIRC	Nominal AG
Non-ag S	2	2	2	2	2	
Ag S	1	1	1	1	1	
A>P	1-2,4	1-2,4	1-2,4	2,4*	1-2	2
P>A	2	2	2	2	2	2

*refers to restricted set only

Kaiwa and Chiriguano

	Indep	Ob-Top	Subord	Serial	Nominal CIRC	Nominal AG
Non-ag S	2	2	2	2	2	
Ag S	1	1	1	1	1	
A>P	1-2,4	1-2,4	1-2,4	1-2,4	1-2*	2
P>A	2	2	2	2	2	2

*4 also occurs in Kaiwa

Urubu

	Indep	Ob-Top	Subord	Serial	Nominal
Non-ag S	2	2	2	2	2
Ag S	1	1	1	1	1
A>P	1	1	1	1	1
P>A	1	1	1	1	1

Table 5. Comparative cross-referencing systems

In Proto-Tupí-Guaraní, independent verbs are characterized by a split-S system in intransitives and an agency hierarchy in transitives. Nonagentive intransitive verbs are affixed by Set 2 person markers, as are the transitive verbs with hierarchically superior P's. Agentive intransitive verbs are affixed by Set 1 prefixes, as are the transitive verbs with hierarchically superior A's. In transitive verbs, a Set 2 patient marker follows the Set 1 agent prefix, when the P was third person. The first person A plus second person P is expressed by the Set 4 prefixes.

In all other syntactic conditions, neither the split-S system nor the agency hierarchy is in effect. All verbs are cross-referenced by person markers of Set 2 (or 3), which refer to the S of an intransitive verb or the P of a transitive verb. This is an absolutive system.

In the Proto-Tupí-Guaraní section of Table 5, there are three boxes drawn to show where the split-S system, the agency hierarchy, and the absolutive system occur.

When we compare Proto-Tupí-Guaraní with its five descendents, we can make a number of observations. First of all, the changes in intransitive verbs are generally a step ahead of changes in transitive verbs. In Wayampi, the split-S system has been extended to intransitive serial verbs, by the substitution of Set 1 prefixes for Set 3 prefixes in agentive intransitive verbs. However, the transitive serial verbs retain the Set 2 person markers, referring to the P. Thus, the cross-referencing on transitive verbs is like that on nonagentive intransitive verbs, but not like that on agentive ones.

The cross-referencing on intransitive verbs is also out of step with that of transitive verbs in Chiriguano, Mbya Guaraní, and Kaiwa nominalizations. The agentive intransitive verbs take Set 1 prefixes, referring to the S. The transitive verbs are subdivided into two categories. Nominalizations referring to the action itself and its circumstance have also begun to use Set 1 (or Set 4) prefixes. However, nominalizations referring to the agent retain the Set 2 person markers (referring to P).

In Mbya Guaraní there has also been a subdivision of what were originally serial verbs. Only a restricted set of verbs retain the original cross-referencing. Other verbs occurring in the original syntactic position of serial verbs have been reinterpreted as something other than serial verbs and are now prefixed in the same way as independent verbs.

In Urubu, cross-referencing changes have extended to all constructions. The split-S system occurs even in nominalizations. In transitive verbs, all cross-referencing with the P has been replaced by referencing with the A, as expressed by Set 1 prefixes. This means that the S of nonagentive verbs use a prefixing system which is no longer associated with any other verb form.[13]

In summary, Wayampi has changed the least of the five languages, and Urubu the most, with Mbya Guaraní, Kaiwa, and Chiriguano in the middle.

Whereas Table 5 shows the degree of change in each of the five languages,

Table 6 proposes a relative order in which cross-referencing changes and other related changes have taken place. These features required some sort of absolutive interpretation in the original system, or they were characterized by some other strong association between the P and the transitive verb. Once an absolutive system begins to break down in one construction, it has ramifications in other constructions as well. A feature can be brought into line by a change in cross-referencing (substitution of person marker sets), by reinterpretation, or by elimination. Table 6 indicates, for each feature, what kind of change took place and in which languages.

Oblique-topicalized	substitution	Wa,Gu,Ka,Ch,Ur
Subordinate verbs	substitution	Wa,Gu,Ka,Ch,Ur
Monosyl. reduplication	elimination	Wa,Gu,Ka,Ch,Ur
IV Serial verbs	substitution	Wa,Gu,Ka,Ch,Ur
IV Nominalizations	substitution	Gu,Ka,Ch,Ur
TV Nominalizations		
(Action,circumstance)	substitution	Gu,Ka,Ch,Ur
TV Serial verbs	substitution	Ka,Ch,Ur
	partial reinterpretation	Gu
Completive suffix *-*pab*	elimination	Ch,Ur
	partial reinterpretation	Gu
TV Nominalizations		
(Agent)	substitution	Ur
Agency hierarchy	elimination	Ur
*-*emi*- (patient nom.)	elimination	Ur

Table 6. Proposed ordering and grouping of changes

Substitution of one set of person markers for another has been a major mechanism for bringing about change and reducing the extent of the absolutive system from that which occurred in Proto-Tupí-Guaraní. This move away from an absolutive system put pressure on the mechanism of monosyllabic reduplication and on the completive suffix *-*pab* since both require an absolutive interpretation. As a result, monosyllabic reduplication was eliminated as a productive feature in all five languages. The suffix *-*pab* has been eliminated from Urubu and Chiriguano, and in Guaraní there is evidence that the absolutive interpretation is weakening (160).

There is one nominalizer which could not easily be included in this ordering: the suffix which descended from *-pýr*, which created a nominalization referring to the P. This has been eliminated in three languages: Wayampi, Chiriguano, and Urubu. In the two languages which retain the suffix (Kaiwa and Mbya Guaraní), not even its cross-referencing is consistent. Kaiwa retains Set 2 while Guaraní has substituted Set 1.

Like Table 5, Table 6 shows that cross-referencing changes in agentive intransitive verbs have preceded changes in transitive verbs. There are two possible motivating factors for this. In transitive verbs, there are two possible referents, A and P, each with just one set of person markers. Set 1 refers to A and Set 2 to P. (Set 4 person markers are an exception, and refer simultaneously to A and P). Likewise, nonagentive S is referred to by just one set of markers, Set 2. On the other hand, agentive S can be referred to by three different sets of person markers, Sets 1, 2, and 3. It would be natural to simplify the cross-referencing of agentive S, by reducing the number of possible sets of person markers to one.

In one situation agentive S and nonagentive S are treated differently, which suggests that they are also perceived differently. Elsewhere they are treated alike. The change that occurred in Wayampi, Mbya Guaraní, Kaiwa, Chiriguano, and Urubu is that agentive and nonagentive S began to be treated differently in more environments. If they are perceived as different, this could provoke a move to treat them differently in all their cross-referencing environments.

Once this distinction is extended to some other verbal construction than the independent verbs, it would be natural to regularize the transitive verb conjugation to make it like that in independent clauses. In this way the split-S system is brought into association once again with the agency hierarchy. A is associated with agentive S, and P is associated with nonagentive S.

Urubu has gone one step further and eliminated all reference in the transitive verbs to the patient (by cross-referencing, by object incorporation, or by the patient nominalizer).

Cross-referencing changes in Guajajara are of a different nature. The original cross-referencing system is essentially intact, with active-stative in unmarked independent verbs and absolutive in other constructions. However, Guajajara has superimposed on this system a set of clause-level nominative clitic pronouns, which occur at the end of the clause.

NOTES

*No paper of this nature could be prepared without extensive preliminary descriptive field work by many linguists in many languages. The author wishes to thank all her colleagues working with various Tupí-Guaraní languages. Special thanks are due to Wolf Dietrich, Bob Dooley, Jim Kakumasu, and John Taylor for data or its clarification furnished in personal communication; and to Bob Dooley, Dan Everett, Terry Kaufman, Yonne Leite, Doris Payne, Tom Payne, Aryon Rodrigues, and Lucy Seki for criticisms which have been incorporated into the present version of this paper. The original version of this paper was presented at the Working Conference for Amazonian Languages held at the University of Oregon in August, 1987. This conference was funded by grants from NSF (BNS-8617854), NEH (RX-20870-87), and the University of Oregon Foundation.

[1] An attempt has been made to follow the conventions used for practical orthographies of Tupí-Guaraní languages in Brazil. Examples from Chiriguano, spoken in Bolivia, have been rewritten to coincide with the Brazilian Guaraní orthographies in order to avoid confusion. In all five languages the letter *y* represents the high central unrounded vowel [ɨ] and an apostrophe (') represents the glottal stop. The letter *j* is pronounced as [ž] in Tupinambá; [dž] in Mbya Guaraní and Kaiwa; and [y] in Wayampi and Urubu. The letter *b* in Tupinambá and Proto-Tupí-Guaraní represents the voiced bilabial fricative; *v* represents the same sound in Guarani and Kaiwa. The letter *x* represents the alveo-palatal fricative [š].

Hyphens indicate morpheme breaks. Where the morphology is not relevant to the discussion, I have not necessarily separated all morphemes. An asterisk (*) usually indicates a protoform. Occasionally an asterisk refers to an ungrammatical form; this is always made clear in the text of the paper.

The following abbreviations are used: 1sg first person singular, 1EX first person plural exclusive, 1IN first person plural inclusive, 2pl second person plural, 3 third person (singular or plural), 1:2sg first person A acting on second person singular P, A agent, AFF affirmation, CAUS causative, COND conditional, EMPH emphatic, FOC focus, FUT future or not yet realized state, IMP imperative, LK linking prefix (cf sec. 1.2), NC "nominal case" (occurring on stems functioning syntactically as nouns), NEG negation, NOM nominalizer (agent, circumstance, or action), OBTOP oblique-topicalized verb suffix, P patient, PAT patient nominalizer, RED reduplication, S(ag) agentive subject, S(non-ag) nonagentive subject, SER serial verb suffix.

[2] The phoneme indicated in Table 1 as *j corresponds to z in Guajajara and to some occurrences of s in Assurini. Linguists working in some languages separate the allophones of j in their practical orthography, writing nh or ñ and j. The phonemes *č and *c correspond in various languages to s, h, or Ø (zero).

³   The reconstructed forms for free pronouns and set 2 person markers for
Proto-Tupí-Guaraní are: 1sg *iče, *če; 1EX *ore, *ore; 1IN *jane, *jane
(Rodrigues, p.c.); and 2sg *ene, *ne; 2pl *pe..ẽ, *pe (Lemle, 1971).

⁴   Additional data from various languages has caused me to revise my reconstruction (Jensen 1984) of two prefixes from Set 3: *jere- '1IN' (jene-
Kamaiura, xere- Tapirape, jare- Kayabi, sere- Assurini); *peje- '2pl' (peje-
Kamaiura, pexe- Tapirape, peje- Kayabi, pese- Assurini). These occurrences of
x [č] in Tapirape and s in Assurini are derived from *j.

⁵   The *i- and *c- allomorphs of the third person prefix in Set 2 (Table 1)
occur with polysyllabic stems; monosyllabic stems have other allomorphs. The
third person patient prefix co-occurs with Set 1 agent prefixes in Tupinambá,
Guarayu, and the Guaraní subgroup. In the Guaraní subgroup the occurrence of
a third person prefix in class II transitive verbs is no longer apparent, since *c
has become Ø (zero) in these languages. Furthermore, in this subgroup the
prefix does not occur with the causative mo- prefix, whereas it does in
Tupinambá.

⁶   Whereas there is a high degree of consistency in the actual form of the
person markers in Sets 1, 2, and 3 from one language to another, the forms in
Set 4 show much less stability. Portmanteau prefixes occur in all languages but
Urubu and Kayabi. However, the actual form of these morphemes, particularly
the form corresponding to *opo-, deviates beyond the normally expected
phonological variation in several languages, including Kaiwa, Tapirape,
Guajajara, and Wayampi. The forms reconstructed for Proto-Tupí-Guaraní are
unaltered in Guarayu, Kamaiurá, Parintintin, and Tupinambá. In Assurini and
Guaraní, there has been a neutralization between *oro- and *opo-, with just
oro- occurring in these two languages. According to Dooley (p.c.), Mbya
Guaraní speakers recognize opo-, but they don't agree as to whether it should
be used, or only oro-, regardless of number.

⁷   The serial verb construction is referred to by Rodrigues 1953 for
Tupinambá as a gerund, by Nicholson 1975 for Assurini as a non-initiating
verb, and by Betts 1981 for Parintintin as 'construction #3'.

⁸   A transitive verb is detransitivized by noun incorporation as long as the
incorporated noun is not possessed. If it is a body part, it is obligatorily
possessed and the possessor becomes the patient of the transitive verb. In this
case the verb is not detransitivized.

⁹   The suffix *-pab is related to the agentive intransitive verb *páb 'to be
finished or wiped out'.

[10] The changes in the vowel of the oblique-topicalized and serial verb suffixes in Mbya Guaraní can be explained by a rule which neutralizes post-stressed vowels to a single high central vowel; this is written orthographically in Brazilian Indian languages as *y*.

(67) **túr-i* > *túry*

(92) **ikó-ábo* > *ikó>abo* > *ikó-bo* > *ikó-by*   (written in Guaraní as *ikovy*).

(93) **ín-a* > (by reanalysis) *í-na* > *i-ny*

[11] The intransitive verbs in this class (in Guaraní) are all verbs of being, position, or movement. The derivational prefixes are causative, comitative, or reciprocal.

[12] Urubu does not have noun incorporation or the nominalizer prefix **emi-* which occurs in the same position in relation to the verb stem. There are also no conjugated forms of transitive verbs in which the patient is cross-referenced, since the agency hierarchy has been eliminated.

[13] Set 2 person markers are used in Urubu to indicate the subject of nonagentive intransitive verbs, the possessor of nouns, and the object of postpositions.

REFERENCES

Bendor-Samuel, David. 1972. *Hierarchical structures in Guajajara*. Norman: Summer Institute of Linguistics and University of Oklahoma.

Betts, La Vera D. 1981. *Dicionário Parintintín-Português Português-Parintintín*. Brasilia: Summer Institute of Linguistics.

Comrie, Bernard. 1978. Ergativity. *Syntactic typology*. Ed. by Winfred P. Lehmann, 329-394. Austin: University of Texas Press.

Derbyshire, D. C. and G. K. Pullum (eds.). 1986. *Handbook of Amazonian languages, Vol. 1*. Berlin: Mouton de Gruyter.

Dietrich, Wolf. 1986. *El idioma chiriguano*. Madrid: Instituto de Cooperación Iberoamericana.

Dobson, Rose. 1977. Kayabi texts (T4). Brasilia: Archives of the Summer Institute of Linguistics.

Dobson, Rose. 1983. Nomes reflexivos Kayabi. Arquivo linguístico No. 139. Brasilia: Archives of the Summer Institute of Linguistics.

Dooley, Robert A. 1982. Vocabulário do Guaraní. Brasilia: Summer Institute of Linguistics.

Dooley, Robert A. 1988. Serial verbs in Mbyá. MS.

Harrison, Carl H. 1963. Pedagogical information and drills for the Asurini language. Brasilia: Archives of the Summer Institute of Linguistics. MS.

Harrison, Carl. 1975. *Gramática asuriní. (Série Linguística IV)*. Brasilia: Summer Institute of Linguistics.

Harrison, Carl. 1986. Verb prominence, verb initialness, ergativity and typological disharmony in Guajajara. *Handbook of Amazonian languages, Vol. 1*. Ed. by Derbyshire and Pullum, 407-439. Berlin: Mouton de Gruyter.

Jensen, Cheryl. 1984. *O desenvolvimento histórico da língua Wayampi*. Master's thesis. Campinas: Universidade Estadual de Campinas.

Kakumasu, James. 1986. Urubu-Kaapor. *Handbook of Amazonian languages, Vol. 1*. Ed. by Derbyshire and Pullum, 326-403. Berlin: Mouton de Gruyter.

Lemle, Miriam. 1971. Internal classification of the Tupí-Guaraní linguistic family. *Tupi studies I*. Ed. by David Bendor-Samuel, 107-129. Norman: Summer Institute of Linguistics.

Mallinson, Graham, and Barry J. Blake. 1981. *Language typology*. Amsterdam: North-Holland.

Nicholson, Velda. 1975. Initiating and non-initiating verbs in Assurini. Brasilia: Archives of the Summer Institute of Linguistics. MS.

Rodrigues, Aryon Dall'Igna. 1953. Morfologia do verbo Tupi. *Letras* 1:121-152. Curitiba.

Rodrigues, Aryon Dall'Igna. 1981. Estrutura do Tupinambá. MS.

Rodrigues, Aryon D. 1984/1985. Relações internas na família linguística tupi-guarani. *Revista de Antropologia* 27/28:33-53. São Paulo.

Schuchard, Barbara. 1979. *Ñande ñe, gramática Guaraní para castellano hablantes*. Santa Cruz de la Sierra: Ajuda para el Campisino del Oriente Boliviano/Centro Boliviano de Investigación y Acción Educativas.

Seki, Lucy. 1976. O Kamaiurá: língua de estrutura ativa. *Língua e Literatura* 5:217-227. São Paulo: Universidade de São Paulo.

Taylor, John and Audrey. 1966. Statement of Kaiwa grammar from clause to morpheme level. Archives of the Summer Institute of Linguistics (Brasilia), the Fundacão Nacional do Índio (Brasilia), and the Museu Nacional (Rio de Janeiro). MS.

II. Stress and Pitch-Accent Systems

Accent in Aguaruna*

David L. Payne

1. INTRODUCTION

This study describes the basic pattern of accent on substantives in Aguaruna, a Jivaroan language of the northern Peruvian Amazon region. Basic accent in Aguaruna involves the assignment of high pitch to one of the first three moras (=vowels) of the stem. When suffixes are adjoined there is a tendency to shift the accent rightward. This tendency is sensitive to the number of moras in the word and to suffix classes. Stress, which in Aguaruna does not completely co-incide with accent, is characterized by intensity or loudness. It is a surface feature of the syllable that is entirely predictable from the facts of accent assignment.

A cursory examination of Aguaruna accent may make it appear to be contrastive, and therefore marked entirely in the lexicon. This is, in fact, the analysis that Pike and Larson 1964 first proposed in their structural phonology of Aguaruna. However, they did not examine the details of accent distribution or perturbation. Consideration of more of the facts instead leads me to posit that accent is accounted for by counting moras from the beginning of the stem. Apparent exceptions are due to the occasional use of lexically marked irregularities and extrametrical segments (i.e. segments which are invisible when counting for accent assignment).

I first called attention to Aguaruna accent phenomena in Payne 1978 and 1981.336-7, though I did not flesh out the details in either of those works. Also, certain notions about 'stress shifting' in Aguaruna were first noted in Larson 1956.14. However Larson stated that her observations were tentative, undoubtedly because in that work and in her subsequent works on Aguaruna, vowel sequences were inconsistently marked as to whether the accent was on the first versus the second vowel. Furthermore, long vowels were not always consistently transcribed as distinct from short vowels. This significantly obscured the facts of accent placement. To my knowledge the details of accent have not elsewhere been conclusively treated for Aguaruna or other Jivaroan languages.

Following Pike and Larson 1964 and Payne 1974, the phonemes utilized in my transcription of Aguaruna are those shown in 1:

(1)

	bilabial	alveolar	(alveo)palatal	velar	glottal
stop	p	t		k	ʔ
affricate		¢	č		
fricative		s	š		h
nasal	m	n		ŋ	
glide	w		y	ǥ	
	front	central	back/rounded		
high	i	ɨ	u		
low		a			

There are three important allophonic rules which apply in the examples throughout this work. First, /a/ is raised to mid vowel position immediately preceding a high vowel, and assimilates to the fronting and rounding of the high vowel. Thus /ai/ is [ei], /aɨ/ is [əɨ], and /au/ is [ou]. Second, /m/ and /n/ are pre-nasalized stops in syllable initial non-nasal contexts. Thus /mušuk/ 'mushroom' is [ᵐbušuk]. Finally, /ŋ/ is realized as a nasalized laryngeal glide [ɦ] in syllable initial position. Thus /suŋkuŋ/ 'influenza' in the nominative case is [suŋkuŋ]. With an accusative suffix adjoined it is /suŋkuŋan/ [suŋkũɦãn]. Phonetic nasalization from the glide spreads to adjacent vowels.

Nasalized vowels contrast with oral vowel, and the nasalization spreads to adjacent non-consonantal segments. In the phonological representations I mark vowel nasalization on the rightmost vowel of a series with which the nasalization could be associated. Oddly enough, when /ŋ/ is in syllable final position, it morphophonemically denasalizes any preceding sequence of phonemically nasal vowels, as in 19b below. On the surface, other nasal consonants /m/ or /n/ do not significantly contribute to nasalize surrounding vowels, though one could posit an extremely abstract underlying level at which all phonemic vowel nasalization derives from nasal consonants. The details of nasality in Aguaruana are discussed in Payne 1974.

2. ACCENT ON SUBSTANTIVES WITH TWO OR THREE MORAS

In Aguaruna, nouns and adjectives consist primarily of two and three moras and are accented predominantly on the penultimate mora. There are a few pronouns which consist of a single mora. These are accented as well. I am not aware of any nouns or adjectives of this type. Straightforward examples of the apparent penultimate accent are in 2 below. (Accent, i.e. high pitch, is marked throughout with an acute accent.)

(2) a. núka   'leaf'
    b. kása   'thief'
    c. nápi   'snake'
    d. yúmi   'water'
    e. číŋki   'bird'

A regular elision process (Payne 1974, recapitulated in Corbera 1978) applies in words of three or more moras. This process somewhat obscures the facts of accent placement. The nominative column of 3 gives surface forms of substantives with three underlying moras. Each of these forms has undergone apocope.

(3)		NOMINATIVE	ACCUSATIVE	
	a.	čaŋkín	čaŋkinán	'basket'
	b.	namák	namakán	'river'
	c.	suŋkúŋ	suŋkuŋán	'influenza'
	d.	tutúp	tutupín	'back'
	e.	mučák	mučakín	'woman's dress'
	f.	ipák	ipakún	'achiote'
	g.	kučáp	kučapán	'wound, sore'
	h.	asíŋ	asiŋán	'firesticks'

The nature of the vowel before the final *-n* in the accusative column of 3 is non-predictable. This shows that this vowel is part of the underlying form and is elided in the nominative form. This analysis is preferred to one that inserts the vowel in the accusative form, or one that considers *-Vn* to be the accusative suffix. Further evidence that this elided vowel is part of the root is that in some dialects it is retained as a voiceless vowel. Underlying forms of the simple nominative case nouns in 3 are given below as having these final vowels:

(4) a. čaŋkina   'basket'
    b. namaka   'river'
    c. suŋkuŋa   'influenza'
    d. tutupi   'back'
    e. mučaki   'woman's dress'
    f. ipaku   'achiote'
    g. kučapa   'wound, sore'
    h. asiŋa   'firesticks'

The elision process also includes syncope, not merely apocope, as the above might suggest. Basically the elision rule looks at the third vowel from the beginning (or left) of the word, and elides that and every alternate vowel bounded

by consonants. At the end (or right) boundary of the word, Syncope stops short
of eliding a penultimate vowel. Instead the final vowel is elided, if that vowel
is immediately preceded by a consonant. The partial derivations in 5 illustrate
the application of syncope/apocope (accent is not marked):

(5) a. clay.pot   'pot'
        ičinaka   UNDERLYING FORM
                ø   SYNCOPE
        ičinak   SURFACE FORM

     b. clay.pot-ACC   'pot (accusative case)'
        ičinaka- na   UNDERLYING FORM
            ø   ø   SYNCOPE
        ičinkan   SURFACE FORM

     c. clay.pot-POS-2P-ACC   'your pot (accusative case)'
        ičinaka- ŋu -mi-na   UNDERLYING FORM
            ø   ø   ø   SYNCOPE
        ičinkaŋmin   SURFACE FORM

     d. clay.pot-POS-2P-ACC-ONLY   'only your pot (accusative case)'
        ičinaka- ŋu -mi-na -ki   UNDERLYING FORM
            ø   ø   ø   SYNCOPE
        ičinkaŋminak   SURFACE FORM

     e. basket   'basket'
        čaŋkina   UNDERLYING FORM
                ø   SYNCOPE
        čaŋkin   SURFACE FORM

     f. basket -ACC   'basket (accusative case)'
        čaŋkina-na   UNDERLYING FORM
                ø   SYNCOPE
        čaŋkinan   SURFACE FORM

     g. basket -POS-2P-ACC   'your basket (accusative case)'
        čaŋkina-ŋu -mi-na   UNDERLYING FORM
            ø   ø   SYNCOPE
        čaŋkinŋumin   SURFACE FORM

     h. basket -POS-2P-ACC-ONLY   'only your basket (accusative case)'
        čaŋkina-ŋu -mi-na -ki   UNDERLYING FORM
            ø   ø   ø   SYNCOPE
        čaŋkinŋumnak   SURFACE FORM

    The underlying form of the accusative case marker in 3 and 5 is -na. The
vowel of this suffix is elided in positions that would undergo Syncope. This includes all examples in the accusative column in 3 as well as 5b, 5c, 5f and 5g.

The full form of this suffix is seen in 5d and 5h. It is also demonstrated in the column marked ACC-ONLY in 6 below. The forms in this column mean 'only a leaf, thief, etc.' in the accusative case.

(6)

		NOM	ACC	ACC-ONLY	
	a.	núka	nukán	nukanák	'leaf'
	b.	kása	kasán	kasanák	'thief'
	c.	nápi	napín	napinák	'snake'
	d.	yúmi	yumín	yuminák	'water'
	e.	číŋki	čiŋkín	čiŋkinák	'bird'

Other alternations demonstrate that the underlying form of the suffix glossed 'only' is *-ki*, i.e. it has a vowel as well. For example, roots with a single vowel as in *nu-ki* 'this-ONLY', and *nu-na* 'this-ACC' do not undergo elision of the suffix vowel in second-mora position, as they do when the suffix vowel is the third mora or further toward the right in the word. In fact, it is necessary to consider that all noun stems and most suffixes have underlying final vowels, in order to generally account for their alternations, the accent placement and Syncope. Thus, the underlying form for the ACC-ONLY column of 6a is *nuka -na-ki* 'leaf-ACC-ONLY', and similarly for the other forms in that column.

In each of the above examples where there are CV or CVC syllables, a mora coincides with a syllable. The examples in 7 show the same accent patterns as in 2 and 3, except that syllables and moras do not coincide. Instead some syllables consist of two or three moras. In the examples in 7 pitch contours are shown; stress (intensity) is marked with a single quote before the stressed syllable.

(7)

		NOM	ACC		
	a.	['ču:] čúu	['ču:n] čuún	'monkey (choro)'
	b.	['wɨ:] wɨ́i	['wɨ:n] wɨ́ín	'salt'
	c.	['sou] sáu	['soun] saún	'foam'
	d.	['šu:t] šuút	[šu:'tan] šuután	'large cockroach (sp.)'
	e.	['kã:p] kãáp	[kã:'pin] kãapín	'gnat'
	f.	['səip] saíp	[səi'pin] saipín	'bark, skin'
	g.	[ka'wou] kawáu	[ka'woun] kawaún	'parrot'
	h.	[hiŋ'kei] hiŋkái	[hiŋ'kein] hiŋkaín	'fruit, seed'
	i.	['šo:u] šaáu	['šo:un] šaaún	'white'

Words with two moras, as in 7a-c in the nominative column, have high pitch on the first mora. They are considered to be accented on the first mora just as are the words in 2. Words with three underlying moras, as in the nominative column in 7g-h are accented (i.e. have high pitch) on the second underlying mora just as do forms in the nominative column of 3. The forms in the nominative column of 7d-f also have three underlying moras or vowels and undergo elision of the final vowel. These are also accented on the second underlying mora, like the forms in the nominative column of 3.

Note that the accent shifts one mora to the right when the accusative suffix is adjoined in 3 and 6. Similarly, the accent or high pitch on the forms in 7 is shifted one mora to the right when the accusative suffix is adjoined. These similarities confirm the interpretation of long vowels and vowel sequences as linked to two nuclear slots or moras, rather than one. In other words, they are interpreted as vowel sequences, not diphthongs.

Stress assignment in Aguaruna falls out predictably from the facts of accent placement. If the syllable is maximally defined as CVVVC, then it is possible to say that any syllable with an accented mora is stressed. It is, of course, necessary to stipulate that a single V is the only obligatory element of a word initial syllable, and that a medial syllable minimally consists of CV.

There are other reasons, aside from stress assignment, for considering this syllable structure to be the correct one for Aguaruna. The first reason has to do with constraints on vowel sequences within the syllable. Though there are no constraints on VV sequences within the syllable, sequences of VVV are highly constrained. Two types of sequences of VVV within a syllable are allowed. They are either identical vowels as in /tifik/ 'species of tree', or they have the first two vowels as /aa/ and the final vowel as high, as in 7i.

The syllable as a structural unit in Aguaruna is also justified by the fact that there are constraints on what consonants can occur in the coda. At an underlying level (i.e. before Syncope applies) the only types of codas allowed are those with nasal consonants. After Syncope has applied, syllable codas can contain any consonants except glides. For example, /namaka-numa/ 'river-locative' becomes [namaknum] 'at/to/in the river', where the second syllable has [k] in its coda. Justification for the syllable in Aguaruna also comes from the allophonic processes discussed in section 1 which have reference to onset and coda.

The majority of substantives with three moras exhibit the sort of underlying penultimate accent assignment shown in 2, 3 and 7. However, there are some nouns with three underlying moras which accent the initial mora. Examples are given in 8 below. The accusative forms show what the underlying final vowel of the stem is:

(8)   NOM   ACC

	NOM	ACC	
a.	púmpuk ['pumpūk]	pumpúkun [pūm'pukūn]	'owl'
b.	múšuk ['ᵐbušūk]	mušúkun [ᵐbu'šukūn]	'mushroom'
c.	káap ['ka:p]	kaápin ['ka:pīn]	'vine (tamshi)'
d.	háanc ['ha:nč]	haánčin ['ha:nčīn]	'cloth'
e.	kámau ['kaᵐboū]	kamáun [kaⁱᵐboūn]	'termite'

Observe that for these words as well, the accent is shifted one mora to the right when the accusative suffix is adjoined.

Words with three underlying moras and initial accent as in 8 are treated as exceptions with regard to accent assignment. There are roughly twice as many words of the type in 3 and 7d-i with three underlying moras and accent on the second mora, as there are of the type in 8 with three underlying moras with initial accent.

3. LONGER SUBSTANTIVES

Treating the examples in 8 as exceptions makes it appear that accent on the underlying penultimate mora is the norm in Aguaruna. Such a pattern does account for most nouns with two or three moras. This is true either when those nouns are suffixed or unsuffixed, as in all the columns of 2, 3, 6, and 7.

However, examination of longer substantives and of forms with a greater range of suffixes shows that penultimate accent is not the norm. The examples in 9 show a set of nouns with a variety of accent patterns. This set represents all of the accent patterns of Aguaruna substantives. The numbers in parentheses at the end of each line indicate the number of nouns of this canonical shape and accent pattern in Larson's Aguaruna vocabulary (1963); I consider this distribution to be fairly representative of the language. I have checked all of these forms in various paradigms with native speakers of Aguaruna. This was done to determine that the accent placements fit established patterns and that the shifting of accent from adjoining suffixes also fits the norms described in section 5.

In the schematized forms given first in 9, upper case 'V' represents the accented vowel or mora; lower case 'v' represents unaccented vowels or moras. The segments in parentheses in 9i and j are those elided by Syncope.

(9)		e.g.			
a.	Vv		núka	'leaf'	(224 examples)
b.	vVv		kawáu	'parrot'	(297 examples)
c.	Vvv		kášai	'paca'	(157 examples)
d.	vvVv		wampukái	'tadpole'	(82 examples)
e.	vVvv		maákai	'mud'	(123 examples)
f.	Vvvv		ámuntai	'buzzard'	(45 examples)
g.	vvVvv		apuúpuu	'dolphin'	(34 examples)
h.	vVvvv		wašíimau	'ocelot'	(24 examples)
i.	Vvvvv		áaŋkias(a)	'palm spear'	(14 examples)
j.	vVvvvv		agáikiam(pa)	'catfish'	(5 examples)

Most of the examples in 9 contain vowel sequences. These are utilized in the following section specifically so that the Syncope rule does not obscure the facts of accent placement. Whether or not a vowel occurs in a vowel sequence, the facts of accent placement remain the same. The only exception is when an accented vowel is deleted and there is a resulting shift of the accent to an adjacent mora. (Accent shifting which results from Syncope is dealt with in section 7.)

Several observations may be made for the data in 9. First, accent never falls on the final mora. Second, penultimate accent is the most common placement, at least superficially. To be specific, it occurs in 605 out of a total of the 1005 examples. This is due principally to the preponderence of nouns with two and three moras in the language. However, it is surely not coincidental that no nouns with five and six moras have penultimate accent and that it is not the most common accent pattern for words with four moras. In fact, a casual perusal of data for suffixed and non-suffixed words of more than four moras shows the accent normally falling on one of the first three moras.

4. THE BASIC PATTERN OF ACCENT ON AGUARUNA SUBSTANTIVES

Based on these facts, several hypotheses could be put forward:
(10)   A.   Accent is contrastive, i.e. marked for each lexical item.
       B.   Accent is penultimate; exceptions are marked either by the use of extrametricality and/or by lexically marked accent.
       C.   Accent is predictable based on rules assigning accent from the left of the word. Since accent is predominantly found on one of the first three moras, accent is assigned to one of the following:

            1.   The first mora of the word
            2.   The second mora of the word
            3.   The third mora of the word.

I reject Hypothesis A based on the severely restricted distribution of accent and the fact that for each canonical shape (particularly for those canonical shapes for which the most lexical items are attested), one accent pattern is clearly predominant. Therefore, it must be the case that accent is predictable. That is, metrical structure is built by rule, with exceptions being treated as such.

As for Hypothesis B, a majority of substantives exhibit penultimate accent when not suffixed. However, the facts of accent placement in longer words, as well as the facts of accent placement on suffixed forms, seem to indicate that metrical structure is built from left to right, i.e. from the beginning of the word. If penultimate accent were the unmarked case, then for all words of five or six moras 9g-j it would be necessary to presume a lexically marked accent on any one of the first three moras. To allow such would represent a theory that is too unconstrained. It would still fail to account for the fact that accent, even considering affixed forms, is very rarely found beyond the third mora of the word.

The remaining hypotheses predict accent assignment from the left (beginning) of the word, but which of the first three moras should be the one accented by regular rule? Consider the three alternatives:

At first glance the possibility of assigning word initial accent as the unmarked case (Hypothesis C1) appears plausible. This is the only pattern for two-mora nouns; it is a possible pattern for nouns of three to five moras (though admittedly not the predominant one for any of the canonical shapes). Under the terms of this hypothesis, irregular accent on the second mora would be accounted for by assuming the first mora on such words to be extrametrical. This certainly seems to be the wrong analysis for words of three moras, since it treats two thirds of these nouns as exceptions.

This hypothesis also encounters problems with the irregular accent on the third mora of some forms, as in 9d and 9g. Such forms could only be derived by lexically marking the accent on the third mora. However, under the terms of a theory such as in Halle and Vergnaud 1987, regular rules which build metrical structure from the left would accent the first mora anyway. Or if the first mora were marked as extrametrical, then the second mora would be accented. In either case it would take a bit of legerdemain, if not a significant alteration of the theory, to maintain the accent only on the third mora.

Except for words with two moras, initial accent assignment is not motivated. For words of three, four or five moras, those with initial accent are clearly in the minority and such accent appear to be exceptional. For these reasons Hypothesis C1 is to be rejected as well.

Hypothesis C3 might also be considered to have some plausibility since it describes the most common pattern for nouns with five moras and describes a common pattern for nouns of four moras as well (though not the most common). The theory advocated by Halle and Vergnaud 1987 provides a mechanism for deriving regular third-mora stress. First, all forms have their initial moras marked as extrametrical. Then, right-headed binary feet are constructed from left to right. This results in an accent on the third, fifth, seventh, etc., mora. Finally, all but the leftmost accent are suppressed. (The reader is referred to Halle and Vergnaud 1987.50-58 for the rationale for this machinery for deriving stress in languages that have no secondary stresses.)

Under this hypothesis, irregular accents on the first and second moras would have these moras lexically marked as accented. As might be expected, words with a lexically marked accent on the first mora would not undergo the rule assigning initial extrametricality.

Hypothesis C3 can adequately account for shorter words with some additional constraints. For words with three moras, a rule is needed to mark final moras as extrametrical so that they are not accented. Such a rule seems to be motivated since Aguaruna has no stems accented on the final mora. For words of three moras such as 9b, with both the inital and final moras marked extrametrical by rule, the only mora which could be accented would be the

second one. Words with only two moras, as in 9a, could be correctly derived
by assuming that final extrametricality applied before initial extrametricality.
Rules marking extrametrical segments are presumed not to apply if they would
result in an entire string being marked extrametrical (Halle and Vergnaud
1987.50). In the case of words with two moras, after final extrametricality has
applied, initial extrametricality cannot apply since the entire string would then
be marked extrametrical. In this way, initial accent on two-mora words is
achieved.

Hypothesis C3 accounts for the data adequately, as the above shows.
However, Hypothesis C2 better accounts for the data. To assign regular accent
to the second mora, the first mora may be marked as extrametrical by rule.
Then a single left-headed unbounded constituent is constructed to give the
accent on the second mora.

Irregular accent on the third mora may be achieved by marking that mora as
lexically accented. Another rule may be required to avoid an additional second-
mora accent from also surfacing in such words, next to the third-mora accent.

To derive the irregular initial accent under Hypothesis C1 would require a
lexically marked accent as well. Again, initial extrametricality could not apply
to such forms.

Under Hypothesis C2, accent on words of two or three moras falls out
correctly much the same as under Hypothesis C3 above. If final
extrametricality is assumed to apply before initial extrametricality, words with
two moras are accented on their initial mora. With both extrametricality rules
applying, the regular accent on words of three moras is on the medial mora.

Hypotheses C2 and C3 involve similar predictions for the shorter words.
Where they differ is with longer words. Regular second-mora accent is
preferable for at least two reasons. First, for words with four moras or more, it
correctly derives more forms in the sample (152 forms) than regular third-mora
accent does (116 forms). Second, it can assume a slightly simpler set of rules
in a framework such as Halle and Vergnaud 1987. Specifically, it does not
require a set of rules which constructs secondary accents and then suppresses
them, as the regular third-mora accent would. In general, what this seems to
correspond to is the notion that stress or accent closer to word boundaries (i.e.
initial, final, penultimate, or second-syllable) is more expected in language than
further into the word (i.e. antepenultimate or third-syllable or third-mora
accent). In section 7 I give further evidence in favor of Hypothesis C2.

In summary, Hypothesis C2, which predicts regular second-mora accent, is
the preferred one for accounting for accent placement in Aguaruna substantives. It predicts regular accent placement for roughly two-thirds of the sample
(673 of 1005 forms). Exceptions are constrained so as to have either their first
or third mora marked with an underlying accent.

5. ACCENT PERTURBATION RESULTING FROM ADJOINING SUFFIXES

The preceding section accounts for basic accent assignment in Aguaruna substantives. I now turn to the rightward shifting of accent that results from adjoining nominal suffixes. The analysis of nominal morphology draws heavily from Larson 1956.

Aguaruna nominal suffixes group into seven classes vis-a-vis accent shifting. Suffixes of one of these classes do not affect accent at all. In the second class, the suffix itself is always accented. A third causes accent on the preceding mora. Four other suffix classes result in some sort of rightward shifting of accent for short nouns. However, each of these four classes affects the rightward shifting differently. The differences arise from sensitivity to the number of moras in the noun stem, and in some cases sensitivity to the structure of the syllable containing the accented mora. I deal first with the classes of suffixes which shift accent to the right.

Nominal suffixes of one class result in a shift of accent one place to the right when adjoined to words with two and three moras, but do not shift the accent in longer words. Examples of this type of suffix given below are *-na* ACCUSATIVE (also previously illustrated in section 2), *-hai* COMITATIVE, and *-nuu* BELONGING TO X, each adjoined to the noun roots given in 9:

(11)

NOMINATIVE	ACCUSATIVE	COMITATIVE	BELONGING TO X	
a. núka	nukán	nukáhaí	nukánuu	'leaf'
b. kawáu	kawaún	kawaúhaí	kawaúnuu	'parrot'
c. káṣai	kaṣáin	kaṣáihaí	kaṣáinuu	'paca'
d. wampukái	wampukáin	wampukáihaí	wampukáinuu	'tadpole'
e. maákai	maákain	maákaihaí	maákainuu	'mud'
f. ámuntai	ámuntain	ámuntaihaí	ámuntainuu	'buzzard'
g. apuúpuu	apuúpuun	apuúpuuhaí	apuúpuunuu	'dolphin'
h. waṣíimau	waṣíimaun	waṣíimauhaí	waṣíimaunuu	'ocelot'
i. áaŋkias	áaŋkiasan	áaŋkiashaí	áaŋkiasnau	'palm spear'
j. agáikiam	agáikiampan	agáikiamhaí	agáikiamnau	'catfish'

The data in 11 constitute further evidence that penultimate accent is not the norm for words with four moras; none of the forms in the COMITATIVE or BELONGING TO X columns has penultimate accent.

Another class of suffixes behaves similarly to those illustrated in 11, except when adjoined to nouns of four underlying moras with a lexical third-mora accent. This is exemplified in 12 below by *-ŋu* POSSESSIVE and *-ṣakam* ALSO AN X. Other suffixes of this class are *-ma* DO/MAKE AN X (VERBALIZER), *-i* INTRUMENTAL, *-ki* ONLY AN X, *-api?* ISN'T IT AN X, and *-aṣi*

PERHAPS AN X (cf. 12k-o). With these suffixes a four-mora noun with a lexical third-mora accent, such as 12d *wampukái* 'tadpole', does indeed undergo an accent shift one place to the right. Note that this sharply contrasts with the lack of accent perturbation for the same form with the suffixes in 11d. Again, all other underlying four-mora and longer nouns undergo no accent perturbation when these suffixes are adjoined (12e-j). Two and three-mora nouns do undergo the normal shift (12a-c). The suffixes in 12 are again adjoined to the same noun roots as in 11:

(12)   NOMINATIVE   MY X (-ŋu)   ALSO AN X (-šakam)

	NOMINATIVE	MY X (-ŋu)	ALSO AN X (-šakam)	
a.	núka	nukáŋ	nukáškam	'leaf'
b.	kawáu	kawaúŋ	kawaúškam	'parrot'
c.	kášai	kašáiN	kašáiškam	'paca'
d.	wampukái	wampukaíŋ	wampukaíškam	'tadpole'
e.	maákai	maákaiŋ	maákaiškam	'mud'
f.	ámuntai	ámuntaiŋ	ámuntaiškam	'buzzard'
g.	apuúpuu	apuúpuuŋ	apuúpuuškam	'dolphin'
h.	wašíimau	wašíimauŋ	wašíimauškam	'ocelot'
i.	áaŋkɨas	áaŋkɨasaŋ	áaŋkɨasčakam	'palm spear'
j.	agáikiam	agáikiampaŋ	agáikiamšakam	'catfish'
k.	anɨntái		'heart'	
	anɨntaímat	'believe, think, consider'		

        (With -*ma* DO/MAKE AN X (VERBALIZER))

l.	wampukái	'tadpole'
	wampukaík	'only a tadpole'

        (With -*kɨ* ONLY AN X)

m.	šuŋkaím	'bird (arrendajo)'
	šuŋkaimái	'with the bird (arrendajo)'

        (With -*i* INTRUMENTAL)

n.	šuŋkaímáapiʔ	'Isn't it a bird (arrendajo) (object in sight)'

        (With -*apiʔ* ISN'T IT AN X)

o.	šuŋkaimáaš	'perhaps a bird (arrendajo)'

        (With -*aši* PERHAPS AN X)

Still another type of suffix is similar to the above except that it shifts the accent on regular three-mora nouns in an unusual way. It takes the accent on its own first mora, as illustrated in 13b. All other canonical shapes with this type of suffix behave identically to the forms in 12. This type of suffix is exemplified in 13 by -*numa* LOCATIVE. Another suffix of this class is -*maga* TO BECOME AN X AGAIN (VERBALIZER). However, this verbalizing suffix is always followed by other suffixes of the verbal morphology which somewhat obscures whether it actually is of the same accent perturbing class as -*numa*.

(13) NOMINATIVE   IN THE X (-numa)

a. núka	nukánum	'leaf'
b. kawáu	kawaunúm	'parrot'
c. kášai	kašáinum	'paca'
d. wampukái	wampukaínum	'tadpole'
e. maákai	maákainum	'mud'
f. ámuntai	ámuntainum	'buzzard'
g. apuúpuu	apuúpuunum	'dolphin'
h. wašíimau	wašíimaunum	'ocelot'
i. áaŋkɨas	áaŋkɨasnum	'palm spear'
j. agáikiam	agáikiamnum	'catfish'
k. kawaumágawai	'it became a parrot again' (cf. 13b)	

(With -*maga* TO BECOME AN X AGAIN (VERBALIZER))

Three other suffix types each behave distinctly vis-a-vis accent perturbations. One type, illustrated in 14 by -*ɨ* IS AN X (OBJECT NOT PRESENT, VERBALIZER), leaves the accent exactly as it is when the noun appears unsuffixed. Other suffixes of this class are -*čuu* NEGATIVE, -*¢u* MAYBE AN X, and -*a* IS AN X (OBJECT PRESENT, VERBALIZER). The second type always occurs word finally and is itself always accented. This is illustrated in 14 by -*á* THE X FIRST. This is the only suffix of this class of which I am aware. The third type also has just one member, the VOCATIVE. It copies the final vowel of the stem, adds a final glottal stop, and accents the penultimate vowel.

(14)

NOMINATIVE	IS an X (-ɨ)	X FIRST (-á)	VOCATIVE (-V?)	
a. núka	núkaɨ	nukaá	nukáa?	'leaf'
b. čaŋkín	čaŋkínaɨ	čaŋkinaá	čaŋkináa?	'basket'
c. áɲak	áɲakaɨ	aɲakaá	aɲakáa?	'seed'
d. šuŋkaɨm	šuŋkaɨmaɨ	šuŋkaɨmaá	šuŋkaɨmáa?	'bird (arren-dajo)'
e. apáič	apáičaɨ	apaičaá	apaičáa?	'leaf covering'
f. náyaan¢	náyaan¢aɨ	nayaan¢aá	nayaan¢áa?	'sea, lake'
g. kampaának	kampaánkaɨ	kampaankaá	kampaankáa?	'kind of palm'
h. taátaanč	taátaančii	taataančiá	taataančíi?	'water spider'
i. áaŋkɨas	áaŋkɨasaɨ	aaŋkɨasaá	aaŋkɨasáa?	'palm spear'
j. agáikiam	agáikiampaɨ	agaikiampaá	agaikiampáa?	'catfish'

   k. núkačuu   'not a leaf'
               (With -čuu NEGATIVE)
   l. núka¢   'maybe a leaf'
               (With -¢u MAYBE AN X)
   m. núkaa   'it's a leaf (object present)'
               (With -a IS AN X (OBJECT PRESENT, VERBALIZER))

When suffixes are adjoined to stems which have already been suffixed, the effect of the accent shifting of the subsequent suffix is identical to what it is when the suffix is adjoined to a root only. In 15 I repeat the same noun canonical shapes and accent patterns from the first two columns of 12. The third column shows the effect on accent from adjoining another suffix, this time of the type shown in 11. In each case the effect of adjoining -na ACC is the same as when -na as adjoined to a noun root with the same number of moras. For example, in 15a, -na is adjoined to nuká-ŋu- 'leaf-POSS-'; the accent shifts to the right, just as it does with the three-mora root in 11b. In 15b however, adjoining -na to kawaú-ŋu- 'parrot-POSS-' does not affect the stress, just as it does not when adjoined to the four-mora root in 11d.

(15)	NOMINATIVE	X-POS (-ŋu)	X-POS-ACC (-ŋu-na)	
a.	núka	nukáŋ	nukaŋún	'leaf'
b.	kawáu	kawaúŋ	kawaúŋun	'parrot'
c.	kášai	kašáiŋ	kašáiŋun	'paca'
d.	wampukái	wampukáiŋ	wampukáiŋun	'tadpole'
e.	maákai	maákaiŋ	maákaiŋun	'mud'
f.	ámuntai	ámuntaiŋ	ámuntaiŋun	'buzzard'
g.	apuúpuu	apuúpuuŋ	apuúpuuŋun	'dolphin'
h.	wašímau	wašímauŋ	wašímauŋun	'ocelot'
i.	áaŋkɨas	áaŋkɨasaŋ	áaŋkɨasŋun	'palm spear'
j.	agáikiam	agáikiampaŋ	agáikiamŋun	'catfish'

Adjoining several suffixes, and their effects on accent shifting, are further illustrated in 16. (These forms are originally from Larson 1956.)

(16) a. úči   'child'
     b. učín   (uči-na 'child-ACC') 'to the child'
     c. učináškam   (uči-na-šakam 'child-ACC-ALSO') 'to the child also'
     d. učíhainčuu   (uči-hái-čuu 'child-COMIT-NEG') 'not to the child'
     e. účičuuškam   (uči-čuu-šakam 'child-NEG-ALSO') 'not the child also'
     f. učíhaiŋkias   (uči-hái-kɨ-aši 'child-COMIT-ONLY-PERHAPS')
                    'perhaps only with (accompanying) the child'
     g. učiŋuík   (uči-ŋu-i-kɨ 'child-POS-INSTR-ONLY') 'only with (by
                    means of) my child'

In 16c the ACC suffix attracts the accent on the two-mora noun. Then the suffix glossed ALSO attracts the accent on the three-mora derived stem. Note here that with the suffix ALSO, Syncope begins its deletion at the fourth mora, i.e. at the first vowel of *-šakam*, rather than at the third vowel, as is usual. An alternative form *učínčakam* is also possible, showing a certain optionality to Syncope.

In 16d the comitative (COMIT) suffix again attracts the accent on a two-mora noun (in the same way that ACC does). NEG, the second suffix, does not further attract accent (nor would any suffix, since the stem now has four moras and the resultant accent is on the second mora). In 16e NEG is the first suffix and is of the class that does not perturb accent. This results in maintaining the initial accent. The addition of the accent perturbing suffix glossed ALSO does not further affect the accent, since there now are four moras and initial accent.

Example 16f illustrates ONLY and PERHAPS, suffixes which perturb accent in two and three-mora words. These suffixes also perturb accent in four-mora words with a lexical third-mora accent. Note that this class of suffix cannot further perturb the accent on the four-mora derived stem *uči-ha͡ɨ-*. This is because the form now has four moras with second-mora accent. Finally, 16g shows three single-mora suffixes, all of the class that perturb accent up to the fourth mora from the left.

6. ACCENT PERTURBATIONS IN WHICH SYLLABLE STRUCTURE IS RELEVANT

There are three distinct subregularities governing accent perturbation in Aguaruna which are sensitive to syllable structure, and not to number of moras alone. All three cases involve syllables with a complex nucleus.

The first type of evidence involves a suffix class not presented in section 5. As in many other Amazonian languages, nouns in Aguaruna naturally fall into one of two classes: inalienably possessed nouns (e.g. body parts, house, some kinship terms) versus 'regular' nouns. Regular nouns in Aguaruna utilize the possessive (POS) suffix *-ŋu* together with second person (2P) *-mi* or third persion (3P) *-ɨ* to indicate a possessed item. Inalienably possessed nouns may take a 2nd or 3rd person suffix directly without *-ŋu* to indicate possession. For both classes of nouns the POS suffix used without either 2P or 3P indicates first person possession. Examples 17a-d show regular nouns in a possessive construction; 17e-h exemplify inalienably possessed nouns.

(17) a. apái   'wild mango'
     b. apaíŋ   'my wild mango'   (apai-ŋu   X-POS)
     c. apaíŋum   'your wild mango'   (apai-ŋu-mi   X-POS-2P)
     d. apaíŋĭ   'his/her wild mango' (apai-ŋu-ɨ   X-POS-3P)

e. čiŋkún   'elbow'
f. čiŋkuníŋ   'my elbow'   (čiŋkuni-ŋu   X-POS)
g. čiŋkuním   'your elbow'   (čiŋkuni-mɨ   X-2P)
h. čiŋkuníɨ   'his/her elbow'   (čiŋkuni-ɨ́   X-3P)

From the above examples it would appear that 2P and 3P are of the same suffix class as ACC and others which on shorter words, perturb the basic accent onto the mora which precedes them, (though not onto a fourth mora). This is illustrated in 17c and 17d. However, unlike any of the other accent perturbing suffixes, the adjoining of 2P or 3P to two-mora nouns does not perturb the basic accent of the noun at all:

(18) a. máku   'thigh'
    b. makúŋ   'my thigh'   (maku-ŋu   X-POS)
    c. mákum   'your thigh'   (maku-mɨ   X-2P)
    d. mákuɨ́   'his/her thigh'   (maku-ɨ́   X-3P)

When 2P or 3P is adjoined to a three-mora noun whose second and third moras are in the same syllable, the accent is again unperturbed.

(19) a. máyáɨ́   'breath'
    b. mayáiŋ   'my breath'   (mayáɨ́-ŋu)
    c. máyáɨ́m   'your breath'   (mayáɨ́-mɨ)
    d. máyáɨ́   'his/her breath' (mayáɨ́-ɨ)
    e. págaɨ   'rib'
    f. pagáiŋ   'my rib'   (pagaɨ-ŋu)
    g. págaɨm   'your rib'   (pagaɨ-mɨ)
    h. págáɨ́   'his/her rib'   (pagaɨ-ɨ́)

This peculiarity only obtains with two-mora nouns (18) and with three-mora nouns with an initial lexical accent where the second and third moras are in the same syllable (19). The examples in 20 illustrate that when 2P or 3P is adjoined to other three or four-mora nouns, its behaviour is like that of the ACC class of suffixes in 11. The regular pattern holds for initially accented three-mora nouns whose second and third moras are in separate syllables (20a-d). It also holds for regular three-mora nouns (i.e. those with second-mora accent) whose second or third moras share a syllable with the preceding mora (20e-l). It holds as well for nouns with four or more moras (20m-p):

(20) a. úntuc   'umbilicus'   (untuči)
    b. untúčiŋ   'my umbilicus'   (untuči-ŋu)
    c. untúčim   'your umbilicus'   (untuči-mɨ)
    d. untúčiɨ   'his/her umbilicus'   (untuči-ɨ́)
    e. šiɨ́k   'mucus'   (šiiki)

f. šiikíŋ	'my mucus'	(šiiki-ŋu)
g. šiikím	'your mucus'	(šiiki-mɨ)
h. šiikíˀ	'his/her mucus'	(šiiki-í)
i. inái	'tongue'	
j. inaíŋ	'my tongue'	(inai-ŋu)
k. inaím	'your tongue'	(inai-mɨ)
l. inayíˀ	'his/her tongue'	(inai-í)
m. ɨpɨmuuk	'diaphragm'	(ɨpɨmuukɨ)
n. ɨpɨmuukɨŋ	'my diaphragm'	(ɨpɨmuukɨ-ŋu)
o. ɨpɨmuukɨm	'your diaphragm'	(ɨpɨmuukɨ-mɨ)
p. ɨpɨmuukɨˀ	'his/her diaphragm'	(ɨpɨmuukɨ-í)

There is another type of evidence from Aguaruna that syllable structure is relevant to accent assignment. This involves a rule that allows the accent to move one mora to the right on geminate vowels. This rule applies in four-mora nouns with normal second-mora accent when any of the accent perturbing suffixes such as ACC, POS, LOC, etc., are adjoined. These suffixes do not normally perturb the accent in similar words without geminate vowels. A comparison of such cases where the second and third moras consist of identical contiguous vowels (21a-c) with those where the vowels are disparate (21d-f), illustrates the process. Examples 21g-h show the same process with suffixes of other classes:

(21)   NOM   ACC

	a. pagáat	pagaátan	(pagaata-na)	'sugar cane'
	b. ¢aníim	¢aniímpan	(¢aniimpa-na)	'manioc stalk'
	c. wampúuš	wampuúšin	(wampuuši-na)	'cotton tree'
	d. ináuk	ináukan	(inauka-na)	'sweet potato'
	e. yukáip	yukáipin	(yukaipi-na)	'ceramic painting resin'
	f. kuŋkúim	kuŋkúiman	(kuŋkuima-na)	'turtle'
	g. pagaátaŋ	'my sugar cane'	(-ŋu -POS) (cf. 21a)	
	h. pagaátnum	'in/at the sugar cane'	(-numa -LOC)	

The forms in 21d-f behave regularly for four-mora nouns (cf. 11e, 12e and 13e). The phenomenon in 21a-c and 21g-h is limited to the second and third moras of four-mora nouns. Identical vowel sequences in longer words (22a), or in different positions in four-mora words (22b-d), do not undergo the shift:

(22)   NOM   ACC
    a. wašíimau   wašíimaun   (wašiimau-na)   'ocelot'
    b. sɨ̈taač   sɨ̈taačin   (sɨ̈taači-na)   'banana'
    c. múukɨa   múukɨan   (muukɨa-na)   'tarantula'
    d. taŋkakúu   taŋkakúun   (taŋkakuu-na)   'stalk of
                                                    plantains'

A form such as 22a shows that the rule in question is cyclic (i.e. will only apply in derived forms); the underived nominative form in 22a has the same number of moras, with the geminate vowels in the same position, as do the accusative (i.e. derived) forms in 21a-c which do undergo the rule.

In the sample corpus in 9 I register sixteen nouns which undergo the process defined for 21a-c. I also register two exceptions which do not undergo the accent shift. Such forms must be marked as lexical exceptions with regard to the process. The exceptions are *tūwíiŋ* 'ocelot species' (cf. accusative *tūwíiŋkun*), and *āwáan* 'young' (cf. accusative *āwáanin*).

The third case in which syllable structure is relevant is found where suffixes are adjoined to five-mora words with a lexical third-mora accent and where the third and fourth moras are nuclei of the same syllable. In this case, when any of the same accent-perturbing suffixes are adjoined, the accent shifts to the fifth syllable. Unlike the process described immediately above, the vowels do not have to be geminate in the five-mora words.

(23)   NOM   ACC
    a. waiwáaš   waiwáašin   (waiwaaši-na)   'squirrel'
    b. nahaɲáip   nahaɲaípan   (nahaɲaipa-na)   'yellow fruit species'
    c. uɲikíač   uɲikiáčan   (uɲikiača-na)   'bird species'
    d. wapuɲúuš   wapuɲuúšan   (wapuɲuuša-na)   'rabbit'

A comparison with other five-mora forms whose third and fourth moras are not in the same syllable in 11g, 12g, 13g, and in 24 below where no shifting occurs, shows how restrictive the process is.

(24)   NOM   ACC
    a. yantáanãa   yantáanãan   (yantaanãa-na)   'cayman'
    b. naikúu   naikúun   (naikuu-na)   'spoiled meat in broth'
    c. tiíik   tiíikan   (tiíika-na)   'tree species'

This results in the only case of fourth-mora accent for those suffix groups that include ACC and 2P.

7. ACCENT SHIFTS RESULTING FROM SYNCOPE

In section 4 I posited that the main accent rule in Aguaruna accents the second mora from the left of the word, and that there is no secondary stress or accentuation. The pervasive rule of Syncope could, in some sense, be said to function like secondary stress. As demonstrated in 4, the Syncope/Apocope rule elides the third and every alternate vowel bounded by consonants. It falls short of eliding a penultimate vowel and always elides a final vowel that is immediately preceded by a consonant.

Historically, Syncope may have developed from a vowel reduction process that eventually became an elision rule applying to non-initial unaccented vowels. If so, this confirms the analysis of basic accent assignment as applying to the second, rather than the third, mora. This assumes that at some stage of development the accent assignment rule accented even numbered moras from the left. Synchronically Syncope makes no reference to accent and can indiscriminately apply to delete an accented vowel.

From the accent patterns described in sections 4 and 5, an accent can result on the third mora. This is the result either from a lexically marked third-mora accent, or from perturbation by adjoining suffixes. It is this third mora that undergoes Syncope if it is the sole nucleus of the syllable, that is, if it is bounded by consonants. When an accented mora is elided, this will usually result in a shift of the accent leftward, as the following examples demonstrate:

(25) a. kuhánkun   <   kuhaŋúku-na   thorn-ACC

b. wiɲísman   <   wiɲisáma-na   frog-ACC

c. šaáɲmin   <   šaa-ɲú-mi-na   corn-POS-2P-ACC

d. ampúšɲum   <   ampušú-ɲu-mɨ   cricket-POS-2P

e. ampúšháí   <   ampušú-háí   cricket-COMIT

f. čaŋkínɲiɨn   <   čaŋkiná-ɲu-í-na   basket-POS-3P-ACC

g. kutáɲhaiŋkik   <   kutaŋká-háí-ki-ka   bench-COMIT-ONLY-FOC

h. aɲútčakam   <   aɲutá-šakam   old-ALSO

i. šuŋkaɨmnum   <   šuŋkaimá-numa   bird(arrendajo)-LOC

In cases where the accent falls on the fourth mora, and the vowel in this syllable undergoes Syncope, the accent is also normally shifted to the left, as in 25i.

There is a specific context, however, in which the accent on the elided vowel shifts rightward rather than leftward. The forms in 26 illustrate the shift on simple suffixed nouns:

(26) a. ampusɲúmin   <   ampušú-ɲu-mɨ-na   cricket-POS-2P-ACC

b. takumɲúmɨk   <   takumpɨ́-ɲu-mɨ-ka   macaw-POS-2P-FOC

c. pɨakɲúmnau   <   pɨaká-ɲu-mɨ-nuu   bed-POS-2P-BELONGING.TO.X

The forms in 27 illustrate the same process with compound nouns:

(27) a. uháŋkit   < uhaɲí-kiti   pubic.hair-CMPND 'palm species'

  b. uhaŋkítin   < uhaɲí-kiti-na   pubic.hair-CMPND-ACC

  c. šiwánkuč   < šiwanúku-ča   wild.plant-CMPND 'fruit species'

  d. šiwankúčan   < šiwanúku-ča-na   wild.plant-CMPND-ACC

  e. uŋúšnum   < uŋuší-numi   cmpnd-TREE 'tree species'

  f. uŋusnúmin   < unuší-numi-na   cmpnd-TREE-ACC

  g. uŋušnúmšakam< uŋuší-numi-šakam cmpnd-TREE-ALSO

The accent is generally shifted to the left when the accented vowel is deleted, as in 25. However, the accent will shift rightward from a deleted vowel if there are at least three underlying moras to the right, as in 26 and 27b, d, f, and g. If a rightward shift would have placed the accent on the first mora of a syllable with a complex nucleus, as in 25f and g, then the shift from the deleted vowel will be leftward instead.

8. CONCLUSION

To summarize, the basic pattern of accent assignment on Aguaruna substantives assigns high pitch to the second mora from the beginning of the word. Certain exceptions have lexically marked accents on the first or third moras. For words with two moras, a rule of final extrametricality results in the first mora being accented.

Nominal suffixes belong in one of seven classes according to how they affect accent. These are shown in 28:

(28) NOMINAL SUFFIX CLASSES REQUIRED BY ACCENT ASSIGNMENT

  a.   Suffixes which perturb accent on two and three-mora nouns, and on f o u r - mora nouns with lexical third-mora accent (cf. 12):

-ŋu	POS
-ma	VBLZR1 (DO/MAKE X)
-i	INSTR
-kɨ	ONLY
-api?	VBLZR2 (ISN'T IT X?)
-aši	PERHAPS
-šakam	ALSO

  b.   Suffixes which perturb accent on two and three-mora nouns, and on four-mora nouns with lexical third-mora accent, but which are accented on their own first mora with normal three-mora nouns (cf. 13):

-numa	LOC
-maga	VBLZR3 (BECOME X AGAIN)

  c.   Suffixes which perturb accent on three-mora nouns, except those with an initial lexical accent and whose second syllable contains two nuclei (cf. 17-20):

-mi	2P
-ɨ	3P

d. Suffixes which perturb accent on two and three mora nouns (cf. 11):

-na	ACC
-haí	COMIT
-nuu	BELONGING TO X

e. Suffixes which do no perturb accent (cf. 14)

-ɨ	VBLZR4 (IS AN X, OBJECT NOT PRESENT)
-čuu	NEG
-¢u	MAYBE
-a	VBLZR5 (IS AN X, OBJECT PRESENT)

f. Suffix which is always accented (cf. 14):

-á	FIRST

g. Suffix which is always pre-accented (cf. 14):

-V?	VOC

In general, the suffixes which do perturb accent (28a-d) do so only on relatively short nouns. A possible account of how the perturbation is effected considers that these suffixes are all 'pre-accenting.' That is, they accent the syllable immediately preceding them. In the case of short words, this often results in an accent clash, i.e. two nearby moras are both accented. To resolve the accent clash, the leftmost of these two accents is erased.

In longer words the accent in the noun root is usually further to the left, away from the pre-accentuation of the suffix. In most of these cases there is no accent clash to resolve. The leftmost accent in the word takes precedence and all others are suppressed (i.e. those generated by pre-accentuation of the suffixes). There must be some additional jockeying, of course, to account for the peculiarities of each of the four accent perturbing classes.

It would make for an orderly analysis if each of the nominal suffix classes in 28 constituted a morphological layer of affixation. If this were the case, then the rules accounting for accent shifting might be expected to each apply at a different cycle or stratum. However, it is not nearly so simple as this. Except for FIRST and VOC which are always adjoined last, the other suffixes adjoin in a rather mixed order. This adjoining order of suffixes is shown in 29. The flow chart in 29, adapted from Larson 1956, accounts for most of the nominal suffixes in the language.

(29) ADJOINING ORDER OF NOMINAL SUFFIXES
(Begin with POS, read left to right)

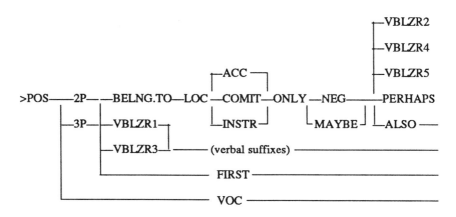

These facts appear to offer poignant support for the notion that concatenative morphology is planar rather than stratal (cf. Halle and Vergnaud 1987.77-84). Constraints on space in this anthology do not allow exploration of this topic here, however, so it will necessarily be relegated to a future study.

These data also appear to be relevant to other current issues in phonology. One is the nature of accent and pitch accent systems in general, and specifically, whether or not Aguaruna can be said to demonstrate a type of pitch accent. I propose that it does. Another concerns the interaction of mora counting with syllable structure as discussed in Hyman 1984. Several rules in Aguaruna are sensitive to both.

Another issue raised by these data concerns the shifting of accent from deleted vowels. Halle and Vergnaud (1987.28-34) claim that direction of such shifts is predicted by the consituency of metrical feet. In Aguaruna it also involves sensitivity to number of moras remaining in the word as well as to syllable structure. Finally, the data appear to be relevant in a more general way to to a formal theory of metrical structure such as in Halle and Vergnaud 1987. My initial approximation of rules accounting for the range of accent shifts (currently in manuscript form) stretches the formalisms significantly beyond what is attested in Halle and Vergnaud.

NOTES

* On an earlier draft of this paper I have benefitted from the helpful comments of Dan Everett, Larry Hyman, Doris Payne, Judy Payne and an anonymous reviewer. They are not responsible for any deficiency that remains. Because of limitations on length of articles in this anthology it was not possible to include a formal account of the accent phenomemon here. A preliminary formal account interacting with the theory espoused in Halle and Vergnaud 1987 is presently in manuscript form.

[1] Akin to penultimate accent assignment, another possibility for building metrical structure from the right is provided by the theory espoused by Halle and Vergnaud 1987. Left-headed feet (mora couplets) could be built from right to left. The leftmost of these heads could be designated as the primary accent and all secondary accents suppressed. This would result in accent on one of the first two moras from the left of the word. Marking some initial moras as extrametrical could then account for accents on the third mora, such as in 9d and 9g. It is possible to juggle some of the details of such an analysis to get the right moras accented in 9, e.g. marking certain initial or final moras as extrametrical, and having stray feet headed versus adjoined. However, none of the possible analyses of this nature that I can construct avoids seeming ad hoc.

[2] Another possibility for Hypothesis C2 is to construct right-headed binary constituents and suppress all but the leftmost accent. This would result in second-mora accent. Irregular third-mora accent could be derived by marking the initial mora as extrametrical. Irregular third-mora accent could be derived by marking the initial mora as extrametrical. Irregular first-mora accent would derive from lexically marking the initial mora. In Halle and Vergnaud's framework this may not be considered as more complex than the analysis proposed above. Until the theory has more time to undergo a constraining process, or until other aspects of the analysis in Aguaruna show otherwise, I consider this analysis to be bulkier.

[3] The alternation of the suffix BELONGING TO X in 11a-h versus 11i-j is a regular late process, fed by Syncope. Several suffixes show this type of alternation between CVV where the vowels are geminate high vowels, and CaV. For each of the suffixes exhibiting this alternation, the CaV form follows consonants and CVV form vowels.

[4] See section 7 for the reason for the resulting accent on the second mora.

[5] A comparison of 19d, 19h, and 20l with other 3P forms illustrates some other rules. The function of these rules is to avoid sequences of three vowels where possible. In 19d and 19h the rule deletes the middle vowel of a three vowel sequence when it is unaccented. In 20l the rule inserts a semivowel before the middle vowel when it is accented.

REFERENCES

Corbera Mori, Angel. 1978. Fonología aguaruna (jíbaro). (Centro de Investigación de Lingüística Aplicada, Documento 38). Lima: Universidad
Nacional Mayor de San Marcos.

Halle, Morris and Jean-Roger Vergnaud. 1987. *An essay on stress.*
Cambridge: The MIT Press.

Hyman, Larry. 1984. *A theory of phonological weight. (Publications in
Language Sciences, 19).* Dordrecht: Foris.

Larson, Mildred. 1956. Aguaruna noun suffixation: a tentative statement.
(Información de Campo 10c). Yarinacocha, Pucallpa, Peru: Instituto
Lingüístico de Verano.

Larson, Mildred. 1963. *Vocabulario Aguaruna de Amazonas. (Serie
Lingüística Peruana, 3).* Yarinacocha, Pucallpa, Peru: Instituto Lingüístico
de Verano.

Payne, David. 1974. Nasality in Aguaruna. M.A. Thesis, University of Texas
at Arlington. (Spanish translation published in 1976. *Nasalidad en
aguaruna. (Serie Lingüística Peruana, 15).* Yarinacocha, Pucallpa, Peru:
Instituto Lingüístico de Verano.

Payne, David. 1978. Aguaruna pitch accent. *(Información de Campo 373e).*
Yarinacocha, Pucallpa, Peru: Instituto Lingüístico de Verano.

Payne, David. 1981. Bosquejo fonológico del Proto-Shuar-Candoshi:
evidencia para una relación genética. *Revista del Museo Nacional* 45.323-
377. Lima, Peru.

Pike, Kenneth and Mildred Larson. 1964. Hyperphonemes and non-systematic
features of Aguaruna phonemes. *Studies in languages and linguistics in
honor of Charles G. Fries.* Ed. by A. H. Marckwardt, 55-67. Ann Arbor:
University of Michigan Press.

Asheninca Stress Patterns*

Judith Payne

1. INTRODUCTION

The purpose of this paper is to describe the pattern of stress assignment in Asheninca (Campa), a Pre-Andine Maipuran Arawakan language spoken in the high jungle of Peru. I utilize the formalisms proposed by Halle and Vergnaud 1987, but informally vary from the system somewhat by making reference to four different weights of syllables in Asheninca, some of which are determined by their onsets. Asheninca stress is a surface phenomenon applying post-cyclically.

Significant aspects of Asheninca stress assignment are: the need to make reference to syllable onsets in the stress rules; the formulation of a more complex set of non-cyclic stress rules than any cited by Halle and Vergnaud; stress rules involving optionalities and rapid speech adjustments; and a small set of exclamatory and imperative suffixes which carry an underlying line 2 asterisk.

The transcriptions of Asheninca words assume the phonemes[1] in 1.

(1)

	bilabial	alveolar	palatal	velar	glottal
stop	p	t		k	
affricate		¢			
fricative		s			h
nasal	m	n			
flap		r			
glide	w		y	ɡ̱	

	front	central	back
high	i		
mid	e		o
low		a	

Basic syllable structure is as given in 2, with the only obligatory element being a single vowel (o = onset, r = rhyme, n = nucleus, c = coda).

(2)

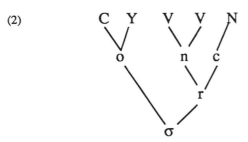

The branching nucleus can be either *ai, oi* or geminate. Non-initial syllables require an onset. The syllable final nasal is unspecified for point of articulation and only occurs word medially. All of the consonants except /ɡ/ occur word initially and before /y/. The sequence /yy/ is disallowed. The sequence Cy occurs preceding each of the four vowels.

2. SYLLABLE WEIGHT

Syllables in Asheninca can be ranged along a continuum based on their respective weights. I am using 'weight' to mean a syllable's propensity to take a stress pulse. The syllables fall naturally into four separate categories: Heavy, Normal, Light and Extra-light. In the following examples, syllables will be marked with a period between them.

a. Heavy syllables (H) are those which consist of a branching nucleus. They optionally can have any consonant for onset, and/or a syllable final nasal (N). For example:

(3) maa.ro.ni   'all'
     H
     pai.ra.ni   'long ago'
     H
     i.kyaa.piiN.ti   'he always goes in'
        H   H

b. Normal syllables (N) are any which have the single vowels *a, o,* or *e,* or the vowel *i* followed by a syllable final nasal. They may optionally have any onset, and following the *a, o* or *e* a syllable final nasal is also optional. For example:

(4) a.me.na.ke   'he/she saw'
     N N N N
     no.caN.ti   'I said'
     N N

```
pi.kiN.ki.¢a.ta.ko.ti.ri          'you told about him'
 N      NN N
koN.ti.ko.ta                      'split palm bark (pona)'
 N     N N
```

Within this category, there is also evidence of weight distinction; a syllable whose nucleus is the vowel *a* is heavier than the others (see section 7 and rule 47g) when it comes to resolving a clash with a Light syllable, but in other types of clash and in primary stress assignment it acts as a Normal syllable.

c. Light syllables (L) are those which have the single vowel *i* which is not followed in the same syllable by a nasal. They have a restriction that their onset cannot be the consonants *sy* or *¢* For example:

(5)
```
i.ri.ro.ri                        'he'
L L   L
ka.ni.ri.weN.ki                   'type of medicinal plant'
   L L      L
a.ti.ri                           'people/person'
 L L
```

d. Extra-light syllables (X) are *syi* and *¢*

(6)
```
¢i.ka                             'what, where'
X
syi.raN.pa.ri                     'man'
X
```

The reasons for this four-way division of syllables will become apparent as the rules are developed; briefly, Heavy syllables are stressed, Extra-light syllables are not stressed, and Light syllables surrender stress in a clash with a stronger syllable. The Asheninca syllable weight scale is given in 7.

(7)

H	> N	> L	> X
(C(Y))VV(N)	(C(Y))a(N)	(C$_i$)i	¢i
	(C(Y))e(N)		syi
	(C(Y))o(N)		
	(C(Y))iN	(where C$_i$ does not equal *¢* or *sy*)	

Four syllable weights might suggest that stress in Asheninca is simply phonetic prominence; however, these four syllable types interact with an alternating stress pattern by means of a set of phonological rules to produce secondary and primary stress. I am not suggesting that the symbols H, N, L and X are necessary formal devices needed to enrich the theory. Rather, they are intended as mnemonic devices for characterizing the natural class of features to

which the stress rules make reference. They thus characterize a set of syllable
projections, some of which make reference to onsets.

3. NORMAL STRESS PATTERN

Stress in Asheninca is characterized by a combination of loudness or
intensity, slight duration of the following consonant and sometimes higher
pitch. In a word which is composed of Normal syllables, the stress pattern
begins on the second syllable and stresses every second syllable which follows,
except the last syllable of the word. In this and following examples (sections
3-6) primary and secondary stress are not distinguished.

(8) σ ɗ σ ɗ σ ɗ σ σ

For example:

(9) pa.mé.na.kó.weN.tá.ke.ro   'take care of her'
     N N NN N NNN
     ha.má.naN.tá.ke.né.ro   'he bought it for her'
     N N N N NN N
     no.kó.wa.wé.ta.ka   'I wanted (it) in vain'
     N N N NN N
     no.tóN.ka.méN.to   'my gun'
     NN NN N
     ka.máN.ta.ke   'he/she said'
     N N NN
     há.ka   'here'
     N N

The final syllable is never stressed (except with three suffixes which have
underlying stress marked in the lexicon, see section 9), indicating that it must
be marked as extrametrical. It might also appear that a rule which deletes final
line 1 stress would account for the facts. But for reasons which will become
apparent later (see section 5) this is not a desirable solution.

As seen in 9, the stress pattern starts at the beginning of the word and moves
to the right, emphasizing every second syllable. This necessitates a rule which
builds binary constituents from left to right, marking the second member of
each as head. The combination of this alternation rule and the extrametricality
rule will occasionally cause a situation where two syllables near the end of the
word are both marked for stress, a clash. Therefore a rule of clash resolution is
also needed which deletes the stress on the second of the two syllables. These
three rules are given in 10. Following Halle and Vergnaud 1987 I am using the
formalism in which an asterisk on line 0 indicates a stressable element, an
asterisk on line 1 indicates a secondary stress, and an asterisk on line 2 (see

examples in section 7) indicates primary stress.

(10) a. EXTRAMETRICALITY: Mark the final syllable as extrametrical.

    b. ALTERNATION RULE: Line 0 elements are right-headed. On line 0 construct binary constituents from left to right.

    c. CLASH RESOLUTION: Delete a line 1 asterisk which dominates a syllable which is not Heavy and which immediately follows another line 1 asterisk.

Sample representations are given in 11.

(11) a. pa.mé.na.kó.weN.tá.ke.ro

```
  N  N N N  N  N N N
  *  *  * *  *   *  * *          Line 0  Extrametricality (10a)
  _____
  (*  *)(* *)  (*   *)(*)        Line 0  Alternation (10b)
  .  *  . *  .   * *              Line 1
  _____
  .  *  . *  .   * .              Line 1  Clash Resolution (10c)
```

  b. no.tóN.ka.méN.to

```
  N N  N  N  N
  * *  *  *                      Line 0  Extrametricality (10a)
  _____
  (* *)  (*  *)                  Line 0  Alternation (10b)
  *   .  *                        Line 1
```

Two-syllable words offer further justification that these rules are correct as stated. Two-syllable words are stressed on the first syllable, regardless of the weight of the syllables. Marking the final syllable as extrametrical leaves only one syllable to be stressed.

(12)
sá.ri		'green guacamayo'
N L		
máiN.to		'type of fish'
H N		
tí.so		'buzzard'
L N		
jí.ñaa		'water'
L H		
syí.ma		'fish'
X N		

Two-syllable words whose first syllable is Extra-light and whose second syllable begins with a voiceless consonant undergo vowel deletion in the first syllable, resulting in only one stressable syllable. The effect of vowel deletion on stress will be treated in section 6.

(13) ¢i.ka —> ¢ka   'what, where'
     X N
     syi.¢a —> sy¢a   'intestinal worm'
      X N

4. HEAVY SYLLABLES

Heavy syllables are always stressed except when they are word final, regardless of the pattern, and even when they are contiguous to one another. Following a strong syllable, the stress pattern begins again with the second syllable. In the following examples, stress on Heavy syllables is marked on the first of two vowels, although phonetically it is a single continuous long vowel.

(14) no.má.ko.ryáa.wái.ta.páa.ke   'I rested a while'
      N NN H HN H N
     pi.ñáa.páa.ke   'you saw on arrival'
      L H   H N
     i.kyáa.píiN.ti   'he always enters'
      L H   H   L
     póo.ka.ná.ke.ro   'you threw it out'
      H N N N N
     páa.ti.ká.ke.ri   'you stepped on him'
      H L N N L

A rule which assigns a line 1 asterisk to each Heavy syllable would work in conjunction with the Alternation rule given in 10b to produce the facts shown in 14. Since Heavy syllables affect the pattern of assigned stress, the rule must precede the Alternation Rule.

(15) a. EXTRAMETRICALITY: Mark the final syllable as extrametrical.
      b. HEAVY SYLLABLE STRESS: Assign a line 1 asterisk to each
         Heavy syllable.
      c. ALTERNATION RULE: Line 0 elements are right-headed. On
         line 0 construct binary constituents from left to right.
      d. CLASH RESOLUTION: Delete a line 1 asterisk which dominates a syllable
         which is not Heavy and which immediately follows another line 1 asterisk.

Sample representations are given in 16:

(16) a. no.má.ko.ryáa.wái.ta.páa.ke

    N N N H H N H N

*	*	*	*	*	*	*		Line 0 Extrametricality (15a)
.	.	.	*	*	.	*		Line 1 Heavy Syllable Stress (15b)

    (* *) (*   *) (*)(* *)   Line 0 Alternation (15c)

    . * . *   * . *   Line 1

  b. páa.ti.ká.ke.ri

    H L N N L

*	*	*	*	Line 0 Extrametricality (15a)
*	.	.	.	Line 1 Heavy Syllable Stress (15b)

    (*) (* *)(*)   Line 0 Alternation (15c)

    * . * *   Line 1

    * . * .   Line 1 Clash Resolution (15d)

When a Heavy syllable follows a Light syllable which the pattern has stressed, the Light syllable loses its stress:

(17) oN.ki.tái.ta.má.na.ke   'in the morning'

    N L HN N N N

    kaN.ti.mái.ta.¢ya   'however'

    N L H N N

When a Heavy syllable follows a Normal syllable which the pattern has stressed, the Normal syllable can optionally become unstressed:

(18) i.máN.¢i.yá.wái.ti   'he is sick'

    i.máN.¢i.ya.wái.ti

    L N X N H L

    a.tí.ri.pá.yée.ni   'people'

    a.tí.ri.pa.yée.ni

    N L L N H L

These two types of clash resolution are more weight governed than the normal Clash Resolution given in 15d in that these two show a weaker syllable being overshadowed by a stronger one. Two statements, given in 19, express the facts; these are ordered after the rules given in 15.

(19) a. LIGHT SYLLABLE CLASH RESOLUTION: Delete a line 1 asterisk which dominates a Light syllable if it immediately precedes a line 1 asterisk which dominates a Heavy syllable.

b. OPTIONAL NORMAL-HEAVY CLASH RESOLUTION: Optionally delete
a line 1 asterisk which dominates a Normal syllable if it immediately
precedes a line 1 asterisk which dominates a Heavy syllable.

Sample representations are given in 20.

(20) a. on.ki. tái.ta.má.na.ke
    N L H N N N N
    * * * * * *   Line 0 Extrametricality (15a)
    . . * . . .   Line 1 Heavy Syllable Stress (15b)

   (* *) (*)(* *)(*)   Line 0 Alternation (15c)
   . * * . * *   Line 1

   . * * . * .   Line 1 Clash Resolution (15d)

   . . * . * .   Line 1 Light Syllable Clash
                                       Resolution(19a)

   b. a.tí.ri.pá.yée.ni
    N LL N H L
    * * * * *   Line 0 Extrametricality (15a)
    . . .. *   Line 1 Heavy Syllable Stress (15b)

   (* *)(**)(*)   Line 0 Alternation (15c)
   . * . * *   Line 1
   or a.tí.ri.pa.yée.ni
   . * . * *   Line 1

   . * . . *   Line 1 Optional N-H Clash Resolution
                                       (19b)

5. LIGHT SYLLABLES

A Light syllable will accept the alternating stress pattern only in careful
speech when it is not in a clash situation with a stronger syllable. The tendency
during rapid speech is for a Light syllable to lose its stress, especially when
there are stronger syllables contiguous to it. In 21 are examples of Light
syllables which accept the alternating stress pattern:

(21) no.pí.to   'my canoe'
    N L N
    syoN.kí.ri   'type of partridge'
      N   L L

Examples of a Light syllable losing its stress in clash with a stronger syllable were given in 17 and 20. A similar situation occurs when a Light syllable clashes with a Normal syllable whose nucleus is the single vowel *a*. Again, the Light syllable loses its stress. Examples are given in 22:

(22) o.pi.ná.ta   'it costs'
    N L N N
    ka.ki.tá.ke   'he/she woke up'
    N L N N
    ka.ri.ná.ri   'colored'
    N L N L

In these examples, the Normal syllable with nucleus *a* is acting like the Heavy syllable in the Light Syllable Clash Resolution rule 19a. Therefore we can adjust that rule to allow both Heavy Syllables and the Normal syllables with nucleus *a* to draw the stress. A sample representation is given in 23:

(23) o.pi.ná.ta
    N L N N
    * * *   Line 0 Extrametricality (15a)
    ———————
    (* *)(*)   Line 0 Alternation (15c)
    . * *   Line 1
    ———————
    . . *   Line 1 Light Syllable Clash
                                    Resolution (19a)

If stress on a Light syllable clashes with stress on a following Normal syllable whose nucleus is a vowel other than *a* or with a following Light syllable, deletion of the stress on the first syllable is optional. The examples in 24 illustrate this.

(24) i.pí.¢o.ka   'he turned around'
    i.pi.¢ó.ka
    L L N N
    ka.wí.ni.ri   'cinnamon'
    ka.wi.ní.ri
    N L L L

o.kí.¢o.ki   'seed'
o.ki.¢ó.ki
N L N L
i.kí.te.ti   'he is clean'
i.ki.té.ti
L L N L

It is this situation which necessitates having the final syllable marked as extrametrical rather than deleting its line 1 asterisk.

The extrametricality sets up a clash on the antepenultimate and penultimate syllables which is resolved (sometimes optionally) by appealing to phonetic prominence. If the Light syllable retains its stress, then the regular rule of Clash Resolution (15d) deletes the stress on the following syllable.

These degrees of phonetic prominence in the Asheninca syllable in some ways reflect the sonority scale set up by Hogg and McCully 1987. The low vowel /a/ has the highest value, and always wins in a clash with a Light syllable. The mid and high vowels /e, o, i/ can only optionally take the stress in a clash with a Light syllable.

Because of the situations illustrated in 22 and 24, an adjustment of the Light Syllable Clash Resolution (19a) is needed. These two sets of examples showed that not only Heavy syllables will draw assigned stress from a preceding Light syllable, but that Normal syllables whose nucleus is *a*, optionally other Normal syllables, and even Light syllables can also draw stress from a preceding Light syllable.

(25) LIGHT SYLLABLE CLASH RESOLUTION: 1. Delete a line 1 asterisk which dominates a Light syllable if it immediately precedes a line 1 asterisk which dominates a Heavy syllable or a Normal syllable whose nucleus is the vowel *a*. 2. Optionally delete a line 1 asterisk which dominates a Light syllable if it immediately precedes a line 1 asterisk which dominates a Normal syllable (with nucleus *o, e, i*) or a Light syllable.

Sample representations are given in 26a of the option using the Light Syllable Clash Resolution, and in 26b using the Regular Clash Resolution (15d):

(26) a. o.ki.¢ó.ki
    N L N L
    * * *   Line 0   Extrametricality (15a)
    _____

    (* *)(*)   Line 0   Alternation (15c)
     . * *   Line 1
    _____

      . . *   Line 1   Light Syllable Clash
                                            Resolution (25)

```
b.o.kí.¢o.ki
N  LN  L
(*  *)(*)                    Line 0  Alternation (15c)
  .  *  *                    Line 1
─────────────────
    .  *  .                  Line 1  Regular Clash Resolution (15d)
```

6. EXTRA-LIGHT SYLLABLES

Extra-light syllables never accept the stress which the pattern would apply to them, except in the case given above (section 3) of a two-syllable word in which the second syllable begins with a voiced consonant. In longer words, any stress which would have fallen on an Extra-light syllable either falls on an adjacent syllable or is deleted in a fashion similar to the rule deleting stress in Light syllables.

```
(27) ó.¢i.ti                          'dog'
     N X L
     pí.¢i.¢i.ro                      'type of bird'
      L X X N
     pí.syi.tá.ke                     'he/she swept'
      L  X N N
     ká.¢i.tá.ke                      'he/she hurt'
     N XN N
     pí.syi.tá.¢i.ri                  'broom (that which sweeps)'
      L  X N XL
     í.syi.ta.né.ta.tya               'he has intestinal parasites'
     L  XN NN  N
     há.¢i.ka.wé.ta.ká.na             'he almost bit me'
     N XN NNN N
     áa.weN.tá.roN.¢i.tá.¢i.ri        'that which is medicine'
     H  N  NN   XN XL
     kó.¢i.ro                         'machete'
      N X N
     nó.¢i.ró.ne                      'my (type of) worm'
     N  XN N
     pí.¢i.rí.ne                      'your (type of) snake'
      L XL N
     kó.syi.ri                        'type of monkey'
      N  XL
```

nó.syi.ya.pí.¢a.táN.ta.ná.ka.ró.ri   'that I escaped from her'
N X N L N N   N N N N L
a.tí.ri.tá.¢i.ri   'it is a person'
N L L N X L

As can be seen in 27, Extra-light syllables differ from Light syllables in that a Light syllable will merely surrender its stress in a clash, but an Extra-light syllable will not even keep its stress in a non-clash situation. It transfers its stress to the preceding syllable. Light and Extra-light syllables differ physically only in the make-up of their onsets. Therefore, similar to the statements made by Everett and Everett 1984 about Pirahã, and by Davis 1985 with regard to two Australian languages, we claim that Asheninca stress must make reference to the entire syllable projection (2), and not just to the nucleus or rhyme[2]. A statement to this effect, given in 28 should precede the rules.

(28) Stressable elements are syllables.

I stated earlier that certain Extra-light syllables undergo vowel deletion (13); however not all Extra-light syllables do this. Deletion is a very late phonetic rule (following stress placement) that occurs only in Extra-light syllables preceding a voiceless consonant. Other Extra-light syllables retain the vowel but still reject stress. The last five examples in 27 have environments of this type. Because the vowel is not deleted, it would be impossible to merely let the rules of deletion account for the stress shifts on such words; therefore it is essential for the stress rules to have access to the syllable onset.

The only occasion when an Extra-light syllable retains its stress is in the case of a two-syllable word like *syima* 'fish'. The final syllable is extrametrical, so the stress falls on the Extra-light syllable *syi*. There is no preceding syllable to which the stress can transfer, nor is there a clash which would cause the stress on *syi* to be deleted. The following consonant is voiced, so the *i* is not deleted, and the syllable retains the stress. Compare this with the word *¢ika* 'what, where'. The final syllable *ka* is extrametrical, so stress falls on the first syllable *¢i*. The *i* is then deleted by the phonetic rules because the following consonant is *k*. This leaves a stressed syllable with no nucleus to carry the stress. The word is now phonetically a single syllable.

In order to allow for stress to fall on an Extra-light syllable in a word like *syima* 'fish', where the *i* is not deleted because of the voicing of the following consonant, the rule needs to be formulated so that the stress does not leave the word, but rather transfers to the preceding Light, Normal or Heavy syllable. If there is not a preceding syllable which is stressable, the stress will remain on the Extra-light syllable.

(29) STRESS TRANSFER: Transfer a line 1 asterisk which dominates an Extra-light
      syllable to the non-Extra-light syllable which precedes it.

This rule of Stress Transfer must precede the clash resolution rules, since it feeds them. Sample representations are given in 30:

(30) a. syí.ma

    X N

     *   Line 0 Extrametricality (15a)

    ———————

    (*)   Line 0 Alternation (15c)

     *   Line 1

b. ó.¢i.ti

    N X L

    * *   Line 0 Extrametricality (15a)

    ———————

    (* *)   Line 0 Alternation (15c)

    . *   Line 1

    ———————

    * .   Line 1 Stress Transfer (29)

c. pí.¢i.¢i.ro

    L X X N

    * * *   Line 0 Extrametricality (15a)

    ———————

    (* *)(*)   Line 0 Alternation (15c)

    . * *   Line 1

    ———————

    * . .   Line 1 Stress Transfer (29)

d. áa.weN.tá.roN.¢i.tá.¢i.ri

    H N   N N   XN X L

    * * * * * * * Line 0 Extrametricality (15a)

    * . . . . . . Line 1 Heavy Syllable Stress (15b)

    ———————

    (*) (* *)(* *)(* *) Line 0 Alternation (15c)

    * . * . * . * Line 1

    ———————

    * . * * . * . Line 1 Stress Transfer (29)

    ———————

    * . * . . * Line 1 Regular Clash Resolution (15d)

7. PRIMARY AND SECONDARY STRESS

Of the multiple stresses in an Asheninca word, only one is primary. The primary stress is given to the heaviest stressed syllable among the last four syllables in a word. If one of these syllables is not heavier, then the rightmost stressed syllable will receive primary stress. It is this situation which forces us to four syllable weights rather than five. If the fourth syllable from the end of the word is Normal and the penultimate is Light, the Normal syllable will receive primary stress. I stated earlier (section 2) that a Normal syllable with the nucleus *a* was heavier than a Normal syllable with the nucleus *e*, *o*, or *i*. However, in the matter of assigning primary stress, the weight difference between the two Normal syllables (with nucleus *a* and without nucleus *a*) is not considered. If the fourth syllable is Normal with the nucleus *a*, and the penultimate syllable is Normal with a different nucleus, the penultimate syllable will receive primary stress (cf. 31f). In the following examples, primary stress is marked with an acute accent (*á*) and secondary is marked with grave (*à*).

(31) a. sàa.sáa.ti   'type of partridge'
        H H L

     b. máa.ki.ri.ti   'type of bee'
        H LL L

     c. ñàa.wyàa.ta.wá.ka.ri.ri   'what he saw in a vision'
        H   H N N N L L

     d. nò.syi.ya.pì.¢a.tàN.ta.ná.ka.ri.ri   'I escaped from him'
        N X N L N N   N N N L L

     e. no.tòN.ka.méN.to   'my gun'
        N N   N   N

     f. iN.kìN.ki.syi.re.tà.ko.tà.wa.ké.ri   'he thought about it for a while'
        N N   L X N N N N N N L

     g. na.wì.sa.wè.ta.ná.ka   'I went in vain'
        N L N N N N N

     h. i.kàN.ta.syi.ta.rí.ra   'he said it without thinking'
        L N   N   X N L N

If we ignore for the moment 31b-d, where primary stress falls on the fourth syllable from the end of the word, we can formulate a Primary Stress rule as follows:

(32) PRIMARY STRESS: Line 1 constituents are right-headed. On line 1 construct an unbounded constituent.

This rule needs to follow the clash resolution rules since it depends on their output.

(33) a. on.ki.tài.ta.má.na.ke

```
N    L H N N  NN
*    * * * *   *          Line 0  Extrametricality (15a)
.    . *  . .  .          Line 1  Heavy Syllable Stress (15b)
_____

(*   *)(*)(* *) (*)        Line 0  Alternation (15c)
.    * * . *   *          Line 1
_____

.    * * . *   .          Line 1  Clash Resolution (15d)
_____

.    . * . *   .          Line 1  Light Syllable Clash Resolution (25)
_____

(.   . * . *  .)          Line 1  Primary Stress (32)
.    . . . *   .          Line 2
```

b. no.tòN.ka.méN.to

```
N N   N N   N
* *   * *                 Line 0  Extrametricality (15a)
_____

(* *) (* *)               Line 0  Alternation (15c)
. *   . *                 Line 1
_____

(. *  . *)                Line 1  Primary Stress (32)
. .   . *                 Line 2
```

Now, in order to account for 31b-d where the primary stress falls on the heaviest stressed syllable of the last four syllables of the word, a rule is needed which deletes the final asterisk on line 1 if the asterisk which precedes it dominates a stronger syllable.

(34) FINAL DELETION: Delete the final asterisk on line 1 if the line 1 asterisk which precedes it dominates a heavier syllable.

Example 35 (= 31b) illustrates this. This deletion rule must precede the Transfer rule in order to insure that primary stress is not assigned farther to the left than the fourth syllable from the end of the word. Take, for example, the word given in (31h=36), which has an Extra-light syllable as the fourth from the end of the word, and a Light syllable in penultimate position.

(35) máa.ki.ri.ti

```
    H  L  L  L
    *  * *                    Line 0  Extrametricality (15a)
    *  . .                    Line 1  Heavy Syllable Stress (15b)
    _____

    (*) (* *)                 Line 0  Alternation (15c)
     *   . *                  Line 1
    _____

     *   . .                  Line 1  Final Deletion (34)
    _____

    (*   . .)                 Line 1  Primary Stress (32)
     *   . .                  Line 2
```

(36) a. i.kàN.ta.syi.ta.rí.ra

```
    L  N  N  X N L N
    *  *  *  * * *            Line 0  Extrametricality (15a)
    _____

    (* *) (*  *)(* *)         Line 0  Alternation (15c)
     . *   .  * . *           Line 1
    _____

     . *  *  . . *            Line 1  Stress Transfer (29)
    _____

     . *  .  . . *            Line 1  Regular Clash Resolution (15d)
    _____

     . *  .  . . .            Line 1  Final Deletion (34)
    _____

    (. *  .  . . .)           Line 1  Primary Stress (32)
     . *  .  . . .            Line 2  INCORRECT RESULT
```

   b. i.kàN.ta.syi.ta.rí.ra

```
    L  N  N  X N L N
    *  *  *  * * *            Line 0  Extrametricality (15a)
    _____

    (* *) (*  *)(* *)         Line 0  Alternation (15c)
     . *   .  * . *           Line 1
    _____

     . *  *  . . *            Line 1  Stress Transfer (29)
    _____

     . *  .  . . *            Line 1  Regular Clash Resolution (15d)
    _____

    (. *  .  . . *)           Line 1  Primary Stress (32)
     . .  .  . . *            Line 2
```

Notice that if the Final Deletion rule (34) does not precede Stress Transfer (29) then the stress can be transferred from the fourth syllable to the one preceding it, and then even be deleted by the Regular Clash Resolution rule (15d). We are left, then, with a stress on the sixth syllable from the end of the word. If the following stressed syllable happens to be weaker, it can be deleted, allowing primary stress to fall six syllables from the end of the word, which is disallowed. The correct derivation (35b) illustrates the output when Final Deletion (34) is ordered preceding Stress Transfer (29). In this case the asterisk which precedes the final one dominates an Extra-light syllable, so Final Deletion (34) does not apply, and primary stress (32) applies to the penultimate syllable.

8. LIGHT SYLLABLES IN RAPID SPEECH

Stress patterns in Asheninca rapid speech move away from the alternating pattern described in section 3 toward a system of phonetic prominence. However, the basic alternating pattern still underlies. That is to say, rapid speech rules apply to the output of the careful speech rules; the rapid speech rules only affect certain sequences which contain Light syllables, after which the normal alternating pattern is still in evidence. In rapid speech a Light syllable which has not received primary stress loses its stress if it is contiguous to a stronger syllable, even if the contiguous syllable is unstressed. Note the examples in 37:

(37) Careful kiN.kì.¢a.réN.¢i   'story'
     Rapid kiN.ki.¢a.réN.¢i
            N L N N   X
     Careful ka.tì.ya.ná.ka   'he/she stopped'
     Rapid   ka.ti.ya.ná.ka
             N L N N N
     Careful no.pì.ya.ná.ka   'I returned'
     Rapid   no.pi.ya.ná.ka
             N L N N N

If the Rapid Speech stress deletion rule leaves more than three syllables in a row unstressed, then a rapid speech stress assignment rule will stress a normal syllable between the light ones (cf. the stressed syllables *tè* in 38a and *yà* in 38b). Following such a series of non-Heavy syllables, the stress will resume as it would have in slow speech. So, the phonetic prominence is only a rapid speech overlay on the basic alternating stress pattern.

(38) Careful i.kì.te.rì.ki.tá.ti   'he is pale/yellow'
     Rapid   i.ki.tè.ri.ki.tá.ti
             L L N L L N L

Careful i.pì.ya.pì.¢a.tà.na.ká.ro   'he returned because of her'
Rapid   i.pi.yà.pi.¢a.tà.na.ká.ro
        L L N L N N N N N

The rules governing Rapid Speech stress adjustment are stated in 39.

(39) a. RAPID SPEECH STRESS DELETION: In Rapid Speech delete a line 1
     asterisk which dominates a Light syllable if it is contiguous to a stronger
     syllable.

   b. RAPID SPEECH STRESS ASSIGNMENT: In Rapid Speech assign a line 1
     asterisk to a Normal syllable if the preceding and following syllables have no
     line 1 asterisk.

Rule 39a, Rapid Speech Deletion, may also apply to a Light syllable which
has received primary stress, but the deletion would be overruled by the line 2
asterisk which automatically fills the spaces on lower lines (see Halle and
Vergnaud 1987.51). Sample representations are given in 40 and 41.

(40) ka.tì.ya.ná.ka (careful speech)
     N L N N N
     * * * *   Line 0 Extrametricality (15a)
     _____
     (* *)(* *)   Line 0 Alternation (15c)
      . * . *   Line 1
     _____
     (. * . *)   Line 1 Primary Stress (32)
      . . . *   Line 2
     ka.ti.ya.ná.ka (rapid speech)
     N L N N N
     (. * . *)   Line 1 Primary Stress (32)
      . . . *   Line 2
     _____
     (. . . *)   Line 1 Rapid Speech Stress Deletion
                                               (39a)
      . . . *   Line 2

(41) i.kì.te.rì.ki.tá.ti (careful speech)
     L L N L L N L
     * * * * * *   Line 0 Extrametricality (15a)
     _____
     (* *)(**)(* *)   Line 0 Alternation (15c)
      . * . * . *   Line 1
     _____
     (. * . * . *)   Line 1 Primary Stress (32)
      . . . . . *   Line 2

i.ki.tè.ri.ki.tá.ti (rapid speech)

L L NL L N L

(. * . * . *)   Line 1 Primary Stress (32)

. . . . . *   Line 2

_____

(. . . . . *)   Line 1 Rapid Speech Stress Deletion
                                               (39a)

. . . . . *   Line 2

_____

(. . * . . *)   Line 1 Rapid Speech Stress Assignment
                                               (39b)

. . . . . *   Line 2

9. UNDERLYINGLY STRESSED SUFFIXES

Asheninca has a small set of underlyingly stressed exclamatory and imperative suffixes. These are illustrated in 42.

(42)

-vé 'exclamatory'

kitàiterivé	kitaiteri-vé	morning-exclamatory	'good morning!'
apàanivé	apaani-vé	one-exclamatory	'one!'

-Ntó 'distant'

haNtó	ha-Ntó	there-distant	'way over there'
iròNtó	iro-Ntó	that-distant	'that one far away'

-' (final stress) 'vocative/imperative'

¢yariné	¢yarine-'	grandfather-voc	'Grandfather(voc.)'
poyá	poya-'	eat-imperative	'Eat!'

The stress on these three suffixes has an intonational flavor in that raising the voice quite naturally goes along with exclaiming and commanding. However, the suffixes -vé 'exclamatory' and -Ntó 'distant' never occur without the stress, so I cannot justify separating these stresses onto an intonational level; I therefore consider them as part of the stress system.

These three suffixes each occur word finally. They always receive primary stress and require that the syllable preceding them (the penultimate) be unstressed if it is a Light syllable. It is usual in a situation of underlying stress to assign a line 1 asterisk to the lexical form. However, this approach in Asheninca would cause difficulties in the set of rules. Note, for example the incorrect derivations in 43.

(43) a. i.ròN.tó

    L N N

    * * *   Line 0

    . . *   Line 1 Underlying asterisk

    (* *) (*)   Line 0 Alternation (15c)

    . * *   Line 1

    . * .   Line 1 Regular Clash Resolution (15d)

    (. * .)   Line 1 Primary Stress (32)

    . * .   Line 2 INCORRECT RESULT

  b. a.pàa.ni.vé

    N H L N

    * * * *   Line 0

    . . . *   Line 1 Underlying asterisk

    * * * *   Line 0

    . * . *   Line 1 Heavy Syllable Stress (15b)

    (* *) (* *)   Line 0 Alternation (15c)

    . * . *   Line 1

    * . . .   Line 1 Final Deletion (34)

    (. * . .)   Line 1 Primary Stress (32)

    . * . .   Line 2 INCORRECT RESULT

In 43a the derivation goes wrong at the application of the Regular Clash Resolution (15d) which deletes the stress on the final syllable. An attempt to resolve this might insert a rule of penultimate stress deletion preceding Regular Clash Resolution. This rule would need to delete the asterisk which precedes a word final asterisk. However, in a word which has its final syllable marked as extrametrical, the 'word final' asterisk would be on the penultimate syllable, and an asterisk immediately preceding it would also be deleted by this rule. Note, for example the following representation of the word *oki¢oki* 'seed' which optionally has stress on the second syllable.

(44) o.kí.¢o.ki
   N L N L
   * * *   Line 0 Extrametricality (15a)
  _____

(* *)(*)   Line 0 Alternation (15c)
  . * *   Line 1
  _____

  . . *   Line 1 Penultimate deletion (not for
                                  mulated)
  _____

(. . *)   Line 1 Primary Stress (32)
  . . *   Line 2 INCORRECT RESULT

A rule of penultimate deletion would disallow the optional stress on the second syllable of forms such as the one in 44 unless it were ordered after the Regular Clash Resolution (15d). This ordering would, of course, ruin its application in 43a.

In 43b the problem arises when Final Deletion (34) is applied, deleting the final line 1 asterisk. An attempt to limit the Final Deletion rule so that it only applies to the penultimate syllable of a word is thwarted once again by Extrametricality. Marking a syllable as extrametrical makes it invisible to the rules, so that it becomes impossible to distinguish an actual word final line 1 asterisk from an asterisk on a penultimate syllable which precedes an extrametrical syllable.

Therefore, it appears that the best solution would be to mark these three suffixes with an underlying line 2 asterisk. This would allow all of the rules to apply without any complicated adjustments, but because of the line 2 asterisk, the final syllable would always receive the primary stress. Though unusual, this analysis is perhaps justified by the intonational-like character of these suffixes. The rule deleting the secondary stress on the penultimate asterisk is then formulated with reference to the line 2 asterisk.

(45) PENULTIMATE DELETION: Delete a line 1 asterisk which dominates a non-Heavy syllable if it immediately precedes a line 1 asterisk dominated by a line 2 asterisk.

This rule is illustrated in 46a, where the line 1 asterisk which dominates the syllable *ròN* is deleted because it immediately precedes a line 1 asterisk which is dominated by a line 2 asterisk. Example 46b suggests that it does not apply if the line 1 asterisks are not contiguous (though note that *pàa* is also a heavy syllable).

(46) a. i.ròN.tó

    L N N

    * * *   Line 0

    . . *   Line 1

    . . *   Line 2 Underlying asterisk

   (* *) (*)   Line 0 Alternation (15c)

   . * *   Line 1

   . . *   Line 2

   (. * *)   Line 1 Primary Stress (32)

   . . *   Line 2

  b. a.pàa.ni.vé

    N H L N

    * * * *   Line 0

    . . . *   Line 1

    . . . *   Line 2 Underlying asterisk

    * * * *   Line 0

    . * . *   Line 1 Heavy Syllable Stress (15b)

    . . . *   Line 2

   (* *) (* *)   Line 0 Alternation (15c)

   . * . *   Line 1

   . . . *   Line 2

   (. * . *)   Line 1 Primary Stress (32)

   . . . *   Line 2

10. SUMMARY

To conclude, Asheninca is a language whose stress system is an interaction between a regular alternating pattern and syllable weight sensitivity. The stress rules make reference to four weights of syllables, some of which are determined by their onsets.

The rules, although fairly complex, are non-cyclic and include optionalities and rapid speech rules. The complete set of rules is given in 47.

(47) a. Stressable elements are syllables.

   b. EXTRAMETRICALITY: Mark the final syllable as extrametrical.

   c. HEAVY SYLLABLE ASSIGNMENT: Assign a line 1 asterisk to each Heavy syllable.

   d. ALTERNATION RULE: Line 0 elements are right-headed. On line 0 construct binary constituents from left to right.

   e. FINAL DELETION: Delete the final asterisk on line 1 if the asterisk which precedes it dominates a syllable which is heavier.

   f. TRANSFER: Transfer a line 1 asterisk which dominates an Extra–light syllable to the non-Extra light syllable which precedes it.

   g. LIGHT SYLLABLE CLASH RESOLUTION: (1) Delete a line 1 asterisk which dominates a Light syllable if it immediately precedes a line 1 asterisk which dominates a Heavy Syllable, or a Normal syllable whose nucleus is the vowel *a*. (2) Optionally delete a line 1 asterisk which dominates a Light syllable if it immediately precedes a line 1 asterisk which dominates a Normal Syllable (with nucleus *o*, *e*, *i*) or a Light syllable.

   h. OPTIONAL NORMAL-HEAVY CLASH RESOLUTION: Optionally delete a line 1 asterisk which dominates a Normal syllable and which immediately precedes a line 1 asterisk which dominates a Heavy syllable.

   i. REGULAR CLASH RESOLUTION: Delete a line 1 asterisk which dominates a syllable which is not Heavy and which immediately follows a line 1 asterisk.

   j. PRIMARY STRESS RULE: Line 1 constituents are right-headed. On line 1 construct an unbounded constituent.

   k. PENULTIMATE DELETION: Delete a line 1 asterisk which dominates a Light syllable if it immediately precedes a line 1 asterisk dominated by a line 2 asterisk.

   l. RAPID SPEECH STRESS DELETION: In Rapid Speech delete a line 1 asterisk which dominates a Light syllable if it is contiguous to a stronger syllable.

   m. RAPID SPEECH STRESS ASSIGNMENT: In Rapid Speech assign a line 1 asterisk to a Normal syllable if the preceding and following syllables have no line 1 asterisk.

NOTES

* This paper has benefited a great deal from comments and suggestions by David Payne.

1 This paper deals with the Pichis dialect of Asheninca. A brief description of certain aspects of the phonology and morphology is given in D. Payne 1983. This differs from that analysis in that what we previously considered to be a palatalized set of consonants are here treated as a sequence of consonant plus /y/. This analysis, although it assumes a more complicated syllable structure (CYVVN rather than CVVN), trims the consonant inventory nearly in half. The /y/ occurs following every consonant but /g/ and /y/, and occurs preceding each of the four vowels. There are, however, some holes in the matrix. The contrast between /si/ and /syi/ is neutralized, as is the contrast between /¢i/ and /¢yi/. An argument could be made for either writing them both with /y/ or both without /y/, but phonetically the sequence /syi/ or /si/ is pronounced [ši] (although some dialect areas vary this freely with [si]), and the sequence /¢i/ or /¢yi/ is pronounced [tsi].

2 To date we have discovered no historical reason why the consonants /¢/ and /s/ affect syllable weight. However, phonetically /¢i/ and /syi/ are the only two syllables containing voiceless continuants and the vowel /i/; perhaps the voiceless continuant nature of the onset has in some way obscured the vowel. Of the set of /i/ syllables in the language, there are three which surface phonetically with the nucleus [i]. These are /¢i/ /syi/ and /ti/, phonetically [tsi], [si] and [tsi]. The first two delete their vowel in certain environments and the syllabicity is passed to the consonant. It should be noted here that Asheninca speakers who have learned to write Spanish consistantly write *i* in these syllables although phonetically it is absent. A reviewer has suggested that perhaps another way to handle the extra-light syllables without reference to onset would be to consider that Asheninca has a 3-vowel system /e, a, o/ and that /i/ is the default or epenthetic vowel. However, Asheninca already has a very productive morphophonemic epenthetic process by which /a/ is inserted to break up sequences of two consonants and /t/ is inserted to break up sequences of vowels. There is no other reason aside from stress to suggest an epenthetic vowel /i/.

REFERENCES

Davis, Stuart. 1985. Syllable weight in some Australian languages. *Proceedings of the Eleventh Annual Meeting of the Berkeley Linguistics Society* 11.398-407. Berkeley.

Everett, Daniel and Karen Everett. 1984. On the relevance of syllable onsets to stress placement. *Linguistic Inquiry* 15.705-711.

Halle, Morris and Jean-Roger Vergnaud. 1987. Stress and the cycle. *Linguistic Inquiry* 18.45-84.

Hogg, Richard and C.B. McCully. 1987. *Metrical phonology: a coursebook.* Cambridge: Cambridge University Press.

Payne, David L. 1983. Notas fonológicas y morfofonémicas sobre el ashéninca del Pichis. *Estudios lingüísticos de textos ashéninca (Serie Lingüística Peruana 21).* Ed. by David L. Payne and Marlene Ballena Dávila, 101-112. Yarinacocha, Pucallpa, Peru: Instituto Lingüístico de Verano.

Payne, David L., Judith K. Payne, and Jorge Sánchez Santos. 1982. *Morfología, fonología y fonética del ashéninca del Apurucayali. (Serie Lingüística Peruana 18).* Yarinacocha, Pucallpa, Peru: Instituto Lingüístico de Verano.

III. Morphological Studies

Morphological Characteristics of Lowland South American Languages

Doris L. Payne

1. INTRODUCTION

Lowland South American (SA) languages have been studied by Europeans for some 400 years. Del Rey (1971.285) affirms that documentation of indigenous languages began in earnest with the Jesuits whose earliest efforts were directed to Chibchan in Colombia and to Tupinambá spoken along the coast of Brazil. Attention to morphology was certainly part of these early studies. Anchietta 1595 puzzled over the meaning of Tupinambá verb prefixes (cf. Rodrigues, this volume) and Montoya 1693 documented numerous aspects of Guaraní. In describing Galibi (Carib) verb forms, Pelleprat 1655 noted that the first consonant of verbs was *s* for first person, *m* for second, and *n* for third. He further noted that, unlike familiar European languages, nouns and adjectives did not vary for number or case.[1]

During the past 400 years numerous morphological descriptions have accumulated. Often these have consisted in setting out verb paradigms or in listing affixes and describing their meanings. As a classic example of the former approach, von Kinder's 1936 grammar of Huitoto lists all the person and number conjugations in some 50 different tense, aspect and modality configurations just for the verb *iye* 'be'. Olza and Angel's 1986 grammar of Guajiro (Arawakan) is representative of the morpheme listing approach, presenting more than 140 verb suffixes along with a discussion of their meanings.

Several types of morphological studies, however, are generally lacking. There are almost no syntheses of morphological features typical of lowland SA, nor is there discussion of how these systems compare typologically with systems in other areas of the world. Such studies would be a step towards identifying whether lowland South (and possibly parts of Central) America forms a linguistic area in the technical sense (Sherzer 1973; Campbell, Kaufman and Smith-Stark 1986), and could be used in better evaluating proposed genetic groupings. Second, there are few discussions of how morphological systems in particular languages are organized. For example, neither the listing nor the simple paradigm approach makes verb-internal morphological

organization explicit. Third, there have been no studies on the acquisition of
morphology in highly polysynthetic languages, nor on the kind of cognitive
processing involved in morphology as opposed to that involved in syntax.[2]

In view of the types of morphological studies missing from the SA subfield,
the goals of this paper are extremely modest. Here I provide a general introduction based on selected languages representing the major, and some minor,
families of the region. Particular attention is paid to verb morphology.[3] The
features surveyed suggest that languages of lowland SA can be divided into two
broad TYPOLOGICAL groups, relative to morphology. These groups have a
roughly eastern versus a western geographical distribution, though some languages which belong to the western group are scattered in pockets throughout
the eastern region (e.g. some Arawakan languages). Languages of the western
group fall into a rough crescent defined by the eastern border of the Andes
mountains and belong to diverse families including Pano-Tacanan, Maipuran
Arawakan, Tucanoan, Saliban, Zaparoan, Yaguan, Huitotoan, and Cahuapanan.
This group is characterized by a high degree of polysynthesis, directionals in the
verb which may have tense/aspect/mode functions, and "western Amazonian"
noun classification systems (although the Pano-Tacanan families and some
Maipuran Arawakan languages lack noun classification systems). On a more
syntactic note, a number of genetically diverse languages in this group also have
verb-initial and postpositional constituent orders (some Maipuran Arawakan,
some Zaparoan, Taushiro, Yagua). This combination has rarely been attested
in other parts of the world and may be further evidence of a linguistic area.

Languages of the eastern group are comparatively more isolating, have
minimal or no directionals as part of verbal morphology, and generally lack
noun classification. These languages generally belong to the Jê-Bororo, Tupian, Cariban and Makú families. There are indications that at least Jê-Bororo,
Tupian, and Cariban are genetically related (see Kaufman, this volume, for
discussion). Thus, typological similarities in the eastern group conceivably
stem from genetic relatedness.

2. MORPHOLOGICAL TYPOLOGY

2.1 POLYSYNTHESIS. An isolating language tends toward having one morpheme per word, while a highly polysynthetic language has numerous morphemes per word. Indigenous SA languages are dominantly polysynthetic. In
most, modifications such as tense, aspect, mood, location, direction, type of
movement accompanying the action, causation and other valence-changing operations, and indication of person, number, and gender can, or must, be indicated by bound verbal affixes. In some languages, evidentiality, passive versus
active voice, negation, and registration of the semantic role or physical shape of
arguments must also be indicated by bound verbal affixes.

Arawakan languages are the most notorious for their high degree of synthesis. Some members of this family allow as many as eleven or twelve affixes on

a single verb (Wise 1986).[4] Depending on the particular language, position class approaches to Arawakan languages would require from 20 to more than 30 classes (Section 4.4). In a position class approach, Pirahã (Mura family) may have between 15 and 19 suffixal positions though not all these can co-occur in any given verb (Everett 1986). Tucanoan languages have suffixal categories for evidentiality (which simultaneously indicates person and number of subject), tense, aspect, direction, mood, negation, and valence changing formatives such as reciprocal, benefactive, and causative. Yagua (Yaguan) is somewhat lower on the scale of synthesis: excluding clitics and including the root, a verb rarely has more than four morphemes in natural text. However, more occur easily in elicited sentences. Cariban is slightly more toward the isolating end; generally there are two prefixal and three suffixal position classes. In Tupí-Guaranian the degree of synthesis is open for consideration, pending clarification of suffixal versus enclitic status for many verb phrase formatives. The Jê and Makú families are fairly isolating (Section 2.2).

Polysynthetic languages can further be characterized as to their degree of fusion, that is, the extent to which morphemes can be cut cleanly apart. Agglutinative (i.e. non-fusional) patterns clearly predominate throughout lowland SA, though there are isolated instances of fusion (e.g. Guahiro tense-gender suffixes, Olza and Jusayú 1986; Tucanoan evidential-gender-tense suffixes, Malone 1988; Yagua subject proclitics with verb roots, T. Payne 1983).

2.1.1 SUFFIXATION, PREFIXATION, INFIXATION. Languages tend to be morphologically asymmetrical. Morphology will be strung out predominantly to the left side of the root (right branching) or the right side (left branching). The latter is most common cross-linguistically, but left and right branching word forms are preferable to center embedding constructions (Greenberg 1966; Cutler, Hawkins and Gilligan 1985). Morphological asymmetry appears to be likely particularly when a language has a high degree of synthesis.[5]

Suffixation predominates over prefixation in the highly polysynthetic lowland SA languages. This is irrespective of whether object-verb is the basic order in main clauses (some Arawakan languages, Zaparoan, Panoan, Tucanoan, among others), or whether verb-object is the basic order (other Arawakan languages, Yagua, Cayuvava, possibly some Cariban langauges, among others).

Some languages are exclusively suffixing. Barnes and Malone 1987 suggest this is true in the Tucanoan language Tuyuca, although Gómez-Imbert 1982 shows that in Tatuyo, also Tucanoan, there is a small amount of prefixing. Verbal suffix categories in Arawakan include incorporated nouns or classifying roots, 'modals' of numerous types, applicatives which register the semantic role of the object argument, aspect, number, directionals, tense, and object agreement. In contrast, there are prefixes only for subject agreement, causation, and

other valence changing formatives (cf. Derbyshire 1986, Wise 1986). In
Mayoruna (Panoan), the only verb prefixes are incorporated body parts. Panoan
suffixal categories include the diminutive/emphatic, evidentiality, mood, aspect, type of movement or direction accompanying the action, causation, tense,
and agreement categories (Kneeland 1979, Loos 1969).

Tupí-Guaraní languages tend toward having a greater number of prefixes
than do most western Amazonian families. Tupinambá (Rodrigues 1953) had
prefixes for agreement, reflexive/reciprocal, permissive, and causative; nouns
were incorporated before the verb root. Nevertheless, according to Rodrigues'
analysis suffixal categories still outweighed prefixal categories. Suffixes included a second type of causative, mood (including indicative, subjunctive,
desiderative, intentional, and conditional), an adverbial 'very, much', and
aspect/manner categories (perfective, frustrative, iterative, continuative, action
about to take place, habitual, and action done for pleasure without a particular
reason). Negation may have been discontinuous, with one prefixal and one
suffixal formative. (Rodrigues does not discuss relative order and number of
'position classes' possible.) In Urubú-Kaapor (Kakumasu 1986), subject agreement, the reflexive, and causative are likewise prefixal categories. Kakumasu's
description of verbal suffixes is ambiguous. He first refers to the desiderative,
modals, negative, intensifiers, diminutive, tense and frustrative formatives as
'affixes', noting that some of these postposed elements can perturb stress
patterns in the verb. However, he chooses to treat them as clitics or particles and
writes them as separate words (1986.385). Although Tupí-Guaraní languages
do have more prefixing than many others of the region, Dietrich (this volume)
still describes them as 'rather isolating' and shows that derivational morphology is predominantly suffixal.

In Carib languages, the number of prefixal and suffixal categories in main
verbs is quite balanced. In Panare agreement and valence-decreasing morphemes are prefixes; aspect, tense, and some transitivity related formatives are
suffixes. Cariña (Mosonyi 1982) and Apalaí (Koehn and Koehn 1986) are
similar. Macuxi (Carson 1982) shows prefixal absolutive agreement and suffixal ergative agreement, along with prefixal detransitivizing and suffixal transitivizing morphemes.

Key (1967) describes Cayuvava (Bolivia, unclassified) as a VOS language
with six major prefix and five major suffix positions. Four of these are called
'modal':

(1)   6   5   4   3   2   1
    MODAL-TENSE/-LOCATIVE-SUBJECT-CLASS/-MODAL-   ROOT/
         ASPECT   AGRMT DEIXIS   REDUPLICATION

         1   2   3   4   5
    DERIVATION-MODAL:ASPECT-MODAL-OBJECT-LOCATIVE
                                        AGRMT

Affixes which occur in prefix positions five and six and suffix position two have further sub-ordering relationships. Some sixth position prefix modals can function as full verb roots themselves. This suggests that phonological collapsing of roots onto the verb as new prefixes may be a more recent historical process than the suffixation. If Key's analysis is correct, Cayuvava is an unusual language, allowing a roughly equal, and large, number of both prefixes and suffixes. It would be valuable to have data on the maximum and average number of prefixes vs. suffixes in particular verb tokens as well as to investigate whether any of these are actually clitics.

As in all areas of the world, infixation is uncommon in lowland SA. However, in the western Amazon region there is some apparent infixation of classifiers to numerals. In some Maipuran Arawakan languages, Yagua, Piaroa (Saliban), and perhaps some Tucanoan and Huitotoan languages, possible infixation is found for the numerals 'one', 'two' and/or 'three' (cf. Doris Payne 1987, Laurence Krute p.c.). For other numerals, and for other languages of these same families, classifiers are only suffixed to numerals. However, suffixal versus infixal analyses need to be carefully argued. In some cases the second part of the numeral root may have developed from a dual or plural morpheme. In Bora (Boran), the number 'one' simply suffixes a classifier (presumably because no singularizing morpheme is needed). But 'two' and 'three' take dual and plural morphemes, respectively, following the classifier (Thiesen 1975a, 1975b):

(2) a. tsa-jɨ   'one (button, coin, dish, etc.)'
        one-CL.disc

    b. mi-hé-cu   'two (trees)'
        two-CL.tree-dual

    c. pápichúú-wa-va   'three (boards, etc.)'
        three-CL.board-PLURAL

In Yagua, on the other hand, an infixal analysis is synchronically more motivated. For the numeral 'one', there is no recognizable singular morpheme corresponding to the material following the infixed classifier (ex. 3a). The final formatives for the numerals 'two' and 'three' most certainly have developed from a dual -*juy* and plural -*miy* (exs. 3b-c). However, the dual and plural morphemes which occur in the numerals have largely lost their independent meaning and are simply frozen as part of the numeral root. For example, as a plural, -*miy* is synchronically idiosyncratic. It occurs in *nijyąmiy* 'people' simply as part of the word (there is no free morpheme *nijyą*); it does not function as any type of agreement morpheme. The productive animate dual and plural suffixes are instead -*naada* and -*riy*, respectively.

(3) Yagua

    a. tá-juu-quïï   tuvári-vada   'one chicken egg'
       one-CL.egg-one chicken-egg

    b. ná-juu-júy   'two (eggs)'
       two-CL.egg-two

    c. múmu-júú-miy   'three (eggs)'
       three-CL.egg-three

2.1.2 NON-ADDITIVE MORPHOLOGICAL PROCESSES. Non-additive morphological processes are found throughout lowland SA, but none is particularly characteristic of the region. In Terena (Derbyshire 1986), vowel nasalization marks
1st person singular, replacive morphology marks 2nd person, and vowel har-
mony is the primary means for indicating potential mood. Subtractive morphology is perhaps found in Canela-Krahô (Jê; Popjes and Popjes 1986), though
it is not clear that any semantic commonality is attached to the subtraction.
Overlooking a number of details about verb classes, the basic rule is that a long
form of most verbs occurs in recent past and whenever the verb stem is non-final
in the verb phrase. Consider the verb *ton/to* 'to make' or 'do': *ca a-te ton* (2 2-
RECENT.PAST made) 'you made it', *a-mãton prãm* (2-TEMPORARY
make want) 'you want to make it'. A short form of the verb is found in all other
environments: *pê ca to* (DISTANT.PAST 2 make) 'you made it long ago', *quê
ha to* (3 FUTURE make) 'He will make it'. Thus, neither tense nor position is
sufficient by itself to account for the subtractive (or short) form.[6]

    Reduplication is not uncommon; nevertheless it is not as striking a charac-
teristic of this region as it is, say, of Oceanic languages. In all cases the reduplication is iconic, indicating plurality (e.g. Parecís, Derbyshire 1986; Tupí, Rodrigues 1953), imperfective action upon arrival (Asheninca; Payne, Payne and
Sánchez 1982), progressive aspect (Huitoto, von Kinder 1936; Parecís, Derbyshire 1986), iterativity or greater intensity (Guajajara, Bendor-Samuel 1972;
Palikur and Waurá, Derbyshire 1986; Tupian, Rodrigues 1953, Everett and Seki
1985). In Cayuvava, reduplication occurs in names for animals that are
associated with repeated sound or movement; different reduplication processes
convey the inception of action, inherently atelic actions, continuous action, or
an augmentative of the causative.

2.1.3 COMPOUNDING AND INCORPORATION. Compounding and incorporation
are common throughout the region. This is clearly the major historical source
of the rich verbal morphology found in numerous language families. In discussing Pirahã, Everett 1986 says that incorporation of one or two verb roots into
another verb is extremely productive, but that at times it can be difficult to
determine whether a particular element is an affix or an incorporated verb root.
In at least Arawakan, Harakmbet, Panoan, Cayuvava, and Tupí-Guaraní languages, noun roots may be compounded, or incorporated, with verb roots (cf.

Hart 1963, Weir, this volume; D. Rodrigues 1987). In some cases these function as incorporated classifiers (Derbyshire and Payne, this volume). Noun roots, or classifiers which derive historically from noun roots, may be compounded with noun roots (Doris Payne 1987).

2.2 ISOLATING LANGUAGES. Though languages of the region are dominantly polysynthetic, there are some at the isolating end of the spectrum.[7] These languages are relevant to a discussion of morphology since they illustrate the sources of what has ended up as morphology in other families. The two dominantly isolating families in the region are Jê and Makú. For instance, in Shokleng (Jê; Urban 1985), there is no verbal morphology showing agreement with person or gender of arguments of the verb. There are both free pronouns and non-bound nominative 'person markers' which can double with the free pronouns (e.g. in focus constructions); alternatively, they can occur as the only reference to a participant in certain situations. These 'person markers' can occur in both pre- and postverbal position.

In Canela-Krahô (also Jê), tense is marked by free particles. As is also true in Shokleng, several aspects and moods are expressed by free verb forms (some in subordinate clause constructions), and by postpositions. These possibilities are illustrated in the following examples from Canela-Krahô (Popjes and Popjes 1986):

(4) Canela-Krahô

    a. Ca ha   a-mã   ih-kĩn
       2 FUT 2-TEMPORARY 3-like
      'You will like him'.

    b. Pe   wa ajco   apu   to hane
       DIST.PAST 1 CUSTOMARY CONTINUOUS do thus
      'I always used to do that'.

    c. Wã pĩ   jakep to   mõ
       1   wood cut   SUBORDINATE go
      'I go along cutting wood'.

    d. I-ma   põhy kre   prãm
       1-TEMPORARY corn plant want`
      'I want to plant corn'.

In Shokleng, continuative aspect is indicated by free verbal particles which derive from the positional verbs *ñã* 'to stand', *nẽ* 'to sit', *nɔ* 'to lie', and *čɔ* 'to hang'. The verb *tẽ* 'to go' indicates imperfective or incompletive aspect.

Rather than increasing valence by adding an affix, Canela-Krahô can increase the valence of adjectival or intransitive clauses by employing the instrumental postposition. The transitivity of the resulting clause is shown by the past tense marker *te*, which occurs only in transitive and pseudo-transitive clauses:

(5) Canela-Krahô

> I-te   to   haka
>
> 1-PAST 3.INSTRUMENT 3.white
>
> 'I whitened it with (it)'.

In Hupda Makú, aspect, mood, location of action, and direction in which the action is done are conveyed by a second verb or free word. The separate word status of these morphemes is partly shown by the fact that they can vary in position (Moore and Franklin 1980). The following illustrate this with the habitual *big*.

(6) Hupda-Makú

> a. Kɔdɔh baktip tʌw   **big**   ñam-ah
>   ahead devil angry HABITUAL sing-Vh
>   'Up ahead the devil is always singing angrily'.
>
> b. waed nʌh   **big**.
>   eat   NEG HABITUAL
>   '(He) never eats'.
>
> c. **Big**   ʔay   tih-an   hid maeh waed-aeh
>   HABITUAL PROGRESSIVE 3SG-DIRECTION 3SO kill   eat-Vh
>   'They used to kill him to eat'.

3. NOMINAL MORPHOLOGY AND RELATED ISSUES

Nominal morphology is much less complex than verbal morphology in lowland SA languages. Adpositions are commonly encliticized to nouns (Arawakan, Panoan, Yagua, Zaparoan, among others). Depending on the language, classifiers are suffixed to numerals, demonstratives, nouns themselves, or incorporated into verbs (cf. Gómez-Imbert 1982; Hart 1963; Doris Payne 1986, 1987; Barnes, this volume; Derbyshire and Payne, this volume; Laurence Krute, p.c.). As these various works show, western Amazonian classifier systems differ from those of South East Asia by being affixal and by displaying both inflectional and derivational features. Thus, they are in some ways reminiscent of African noun class systems (cf. Doris Payne 1987).

Many languages of this region lack, or else have an extremely small set of morphologically simple adjectives. It hardly follows however, that there are no means of descriptively modifying nouns. Modification is often achieved by suffixing a classifier or other modifying affix to the noun. This is common in western Amazonian languages with classifier systems of the sort mentioned above. Other common nominal suffixes include diminuitives, number, and general quantification. Second, a syntactic noun can modify another noun. The modifying noun can be either morphologically simple or derived (Yagua, Arawakan, Cariban, Cahuapanan). Third, in Cariban languages a derived modifying word can be formed by adding various suffixes or prefixes to non-modifying stems. The resultant word belongs to a somewhat undifferentiated adjective/adverb class.

4. VERBAL MORPHOLOGY

In most lowland SA languages, verb morphology is rich and complex; morphology is where the action is. Sections 4.1 through 4.3 highlight some of the salient features of verbal morphology. Section 4.4 discusses data which do not lend themselves to a traditional position class approach and which, I argue, are not satisfactorily viewed either in terms of 'clause union' or of transformational merger of two clauses. The possibilities of a strict semantic approach to such morphology are also discussed. Finally, I sketch one type of verb-internal structure that (for at least some of these languages) is a descriptively and historically more adequate view.

4.1 VERB AGREEMENT AND OTHER PARTICIPANT REFERENCE. As mentioned previously, suffixation is the dominant morphological process in lowland SA. However, verb agreement is frequently prefixal. Prefixes agreeing with both subject and object are found in Cariban, Tupí-Guaraní, some Jê languages, Zaparoan, Andoke (Witte 1976), some Guaykuruan languages, and Makú. Prefixes indicate subject agreement, and suffixes or enclitics indicate object agreement, in Preandine Maipuran Arawakan, Cayuvava, Yagua, and the Guaykuruan language Toba. Agreement is exclusively suffixal in Guajiro (Arawakan), Tucanoan, Huitotoan, and Panoan. Various types of nominative-accusative and ergative-absolutive agreement systems are found (cf. Kneeland 1979; Urban 1985; Carson 1982; Derbyshire 1987; and the papers in this volume by Franchetto, Jensen, T. Payne, Rodrigues, and Seki).

4.2 PROMOTION TO OBJECT AND REFERENCING OF SEMANTIC ROLE. Bantu languages are often cited as some of the most productive in terms of being able to promote semantically oblique roles to direct object status with concomitant registering of this semantic role in the verb by an 'applicative' affix. However, Nomatsiguenga (Preandine Maipuran Arawakan) is at least, if not more, productive in this regard (Wise 1971). Direct object status is shown by a verb suffix which references the gender of the object. There are two gender classes: feminine (also including many inanimates) is marked by *-ro*; masculine (also including many animates) is marked by *-ri*. The most natural candidate for direct object is, of course, the patient. In general, there is no registration of this semantic role in the verb. In 7, *otsegoha* '(river) branch' is inanimate and the direct object suffix *-ro* occurs:

(7) Pablo i-komoke-ro   otsegoha
     Paul he-dam.stream-FEM branch
     'Paul dammed the river branch'.

However, there is specific registration of nine non-patient semantic roles.
Comparison of ex. 7 with exs. 11 and 15b shows the promotional function of the
suffixes which register these non-patient roles. Exs. 11 and 15b clearly demonstrate that the verb no longer agrees with the patient, but with the promoted noun
phrase. This noun phrase, rather than the patient, must now occur in immediately post-verbal position (EP=epenthetic formative; FRUST = frustrative;
INDIC = indicative).

(8) LOCATIVE-1
     Pablo i-hoka-TE-ta-be-ka-ri   Ariberito i-gotsirote
     Paul he-throw-TOWARD-EP-FRUST-RFLEX-MASC Albert   his-knife
     'Paul threw his knife toward Albert'.

(9) LOCATIVE-2
     Pablo i-kenga-MO-ta-h-i-ri   Ariberto
     Paul he-narrate-IN.PRESENCE.OF-EP-again-TENSE-MASC Albert
     'Paul narrated it in Albert's presence'.

(10) INSTRUMENT
     ora pi-nets-AN-t-i-ma-ri   hitatsia negativo
     that you-look.at-INST-EP-TENSE-FUT.RFLEX-MASC name   negative
     'Look at it (the sun during an eclipse) with that which is called a negative'.

(11) ASSOCIATIVE
     Juan i-komota-KA-k-e-ri   Pablo otsegoha
     John he-dam.stream-ASS-INDIC-TENSE-MASC Paul river.branch
     'John dammed the river branch with Paul'.

(12) PURPOSE
     a. Pablo i-ata-SI-k-e-ri   Ariberito
        Paul he-go-PURP-INDIC-TENSE-MASC Albert
        'Paul went with Albert in mind (e.g. to see him)'.

     b. Ni-ganta-SI-t-ĕ-ri   hompiki
        I-send-PURP-EP-TENSE-MASC pills
        'I sent him for pills'.

(13) REASON
     a. Pablo i-kisa-BIRI-k-e-ri   Juan
        Paul he-be.angry-REASON-INDIC-TENSE-MASC John
        'Paul was angry on account of John'.

b. Pablo i-atage-BIRI-k-e-ri   Juan
   Paul   he-go-REASON-INDIC-TENSE-MASC John
   'John was the reason for Paul's going'.

(14) BENEFACTIVE
   Pablo i-pë-NE-ri   Ariberito tiapa   singi
   Paul   he-give-BEN-him Albert   chicken corn
   'Paul gave the chickens corn for Albert'.

Relative to exs. 15a-b, Wise states that *-ko* INCLUDED 'specifies only that the action has some reference [to the participant]. Sometimes the function appears to be co-agent, sometimes direction, or sometimes beneficiary':

(15) INCLUDED (with reference to)
   a. Pablo i-samë-KO-k-e-ro   i-gisere
      Paul   he-sleep-INC-INDIC-TENSE-FEM his-comb
      'Paul went to sleep with reference to the comb'
      (he was making it and dropped it).

   b. Pablo i-komoto-KO-k-e-ri   pabati otsegoha
      Paul   he-dam.stream-INC-INDIC-TENSE-MASC father river.branch
      'Paul dammed the river branch with reference to father'.

(16) WITH REFERENCE TO (WRT):
   Pablo i-pëna-BEN-ta-h-i-ri   yaniri   kireki
   Paul   he-pay-WRT-EP-again-TENSE-MASC howler.monkey money
   'Paul paid money for the howler monkey'.

4.3 MOVEMENT, LOCATION, AND DIRECTION.   Common in the western Amazonian region (cf. Section 1) are morphemes which indicate the type of movement accompanying the action of the verb, the location of the action (especially 'upriver' and 'downriver'), or the directional orientation of the action or agent carrying out the action. Some or all of these categories are found in Panoan, Yaguan, Arawakan, Makú (though probably in serial verb constructions), Cayuvava, Tucanoan, probably Andoke, Pirahã, Guaykuruan, and others.

The location, direction, orientation, and especially movement formatives commonly (if not always) derive from verbs.[8] The stages in development from full verb roots which occur in serial-like constructions, to compounding, to bound affixes, could be illustrated from a single language. For instance, Yagua *siiy* 'run' is an independent verb root. As such, it can function as the only verb root in a clause. However, it also occurs in compound constructions such as *siiy-maasiy* (run-go.out) 'rush out'. Further, a related form *-siy* occurs as a derivational suffix indicating that an action was done upon departure, as in *sa-suuta-siy* (3SG-wash-upon.departure) 'he washed upon (or just prior to) leaving'. Movement affixes of the set to which *-siy* belongs add a perfective sense to the verbal action, and thus do not easily co-occur with affixes that impart an imperfective sense. In what follows, I discuss data from several languages to illustrate stages in the development of affixes from verbs.

Hupda-Makú is an isolating language with minimal verb morphology. Nevertheless, it illustrates the verbal origins of what end up as affixes. Moore 1980 states that:

'... Hupda puts special emphasis on the direction of an action, the position it is done in and the relationship to other parts of the environment. The morphemes used are verbs in their own right and can take all the usual verb endings... When any of the positional, directional or relational verbs combine with other verbs, they often suggest nothing more than that the main verb was done in that position, direction or relation.'

Moore lists the following 'positional', 'directional', and 'relational' verbs:

POSITIONAL: *ket* 'to stand; person has legs, body and head all in alignment; could be used for person lying on bed'; *pem* 'to sit, body is bent in such a way to make sitting possible'.

DIRECTIONAL (includes more than those listed here): *ham* 'to go'; *naen* 'to come'; *cak* 'to go straight up'; *tuu* ' to go straight down (this cannot occur as the only verb of a sentence); *hiy* 'to go down an incline'; *bay* 'to return'; *cɔp* 'to ascend'; *dob* 'to descend'.

RELATIONAL: *wob* 'to be laying on some other object'; *yaet* 'to be laying on the ground (not on another object)'; *kä* 'to be suspended from something that allows free movement (as in a hammock)'; *dak* 'to be up against something'; *kʌd* 'to pass someone or something else'.

With the one exception noted, these roots can occur as the only predicate in a sentence. When combined with other verbs, the positional, directional or relational verbs occur either before or after the accompanying verb. Moore notes that it is not uncommon to find three or four of these verbs in a string.

(17) a. tih   **ket**   ñam-ah   tíh-an-ah
        3SG stand sing-Vh 3SG-DIR-Vh
        'He stood singing to her'.

    b. nɔɔ yo'   tih   'ɔt **wʌd**   naen-aeh
        say circumstance.same.agent 3SG cry arrive come-Vh
        'So saying,she arrived here crying'.

    c. tih-an   yu-p   hɔhɔh wʌd bi'id **hiy**   bay
        3SG-DIR that-ADJ frog   old blow incline.down return
        'That old frog blew down on him again'.

    d. 'ɔt **kä'**   koʔ-oy: 'ip   wʌd
        cry suspend ʔ-Vy   father old
        'Old father lay (in his hammock) and cried'.

Pirahã illustrates the next stage of development in which verb roots are compounded into single verb words. In Pirahã, verb roots can be phonologically incorporated immediately following the main verb root to indicate the type of movement accompanying the action of the main verb root. Everett 1986 notes that it is common to find up to three roots in the same stem.

In numerous languages, what were independent movement or positional verb roots at one stage are now found only as affixes (e.g. Yagua as discussed above and in Doris Payne 1985; various Panoan languages, Loos 1969, Kneeland 1979). Toba (Guaykuruan) verbs have affixes which indicate orientation in space as seen from the speaker's viewpoint and direction of the action. Toba verb prefixes primarily indicate subject agreement. However, choice of prefix also depends on whether the subject is performing an 'inward' action (often with reflexive meaning), or an 'outward' action. For example, pouring out perfume or syrup is done with care, often with direction toward the body. In contrast, liquid may be thrown out of a pail or other container, with direction away from the body (Klein 1973.94). Secondly, there is a set of position suffixes which indicate: *-a'a* 'unchanging position of the subject participant during the action', *-pe* 'subject participant moves about in a circle during the action', and *-o* 'subject participant moves to knees from sitting or standing position during an action'. Thirdly, direction suffixes indicate either the direction in which the subject participant moves during the action, or a movement in a direction towards the subject participant. These suffixes are: *-wek* 'action done in an outwards direction', *-wo* 'action done in an inward direction', *-ñi* 'action from up to down', *-sigem* 'action from down to up', *-lek* 'action done on top of or over a space', *-'oga* 'vision directed across a space', and *-get* 'toward speaker'.

The difficulty of separating categories of tense, aspect, and mood from each other has been noted throughout the literature. DeLancey (1982) has shown that tense and aspect notions commonly develop from movement verbs; in lowland SA bound suffixes whose primary semantic component is one of movement, direction, orientation, or even stationary location often also have tense-aspect-mood functions. Mattei-Muller (p. c.) discusses Yanomamɨ directional formatives which also have tense and evidentiality functions. I cite here a few additional examples.

As noted above, the Toba suffix *o'*- indicates that the subject moves to a kneeling position during the action. This suffix also implies futurity. It frequently co-occurs with a future time adverb, though the adverb is apparently not required in order to convey the future meaning (Klein 1973):

(19) si-yogotak-o'   qome
   1SG-wash-kneel later
   'I'm going (to bend my knees) and wash later on' /
   'I've decided to wash up later'.

In Yagua there are BOUNDED and UNBOUNDED movement suffixes. The bounded movement suffixes bound the inception, the termination, or both inception and termination of a movement trajectory over which the main action of the verb is carried out (the exact semantics of -nuvįį and -nuvee are discussed in T. Payne 1984, 1985):

(20) -nuvįį   'action done upon arrival at the current scene'
               (bounds termination of movement trajectory)

     -nuvee   'action done upon arrival at a new scene'
               (bounds termination of movement trajectory)

     -rįį   'action done enroute, interrupting a journey'
               (bounds the termination of one movement trajectory and
               its subsequent resumption)

     -siy   'action done upon departure'
               (bounds inception of movement trajectory)

In addition to their primary meaning, these suffixes have perfective overtones. Thus, most are incompatable with UNBOUNDED movement suffixes which have inherent imperfective aspect.[9] The two UNBOUNDED movement suffixes are -tītyiiy 'action done while going along directly to some location' and -nayąą 'action done while going along aimlessly' or 'all over the place'.

It is entirely possible that movement meaning features could become bleached or broadened over time, resulting in forms whose primary meanings are aspectual. In fact, Judith Payne (1982) argues that the basic meanings of Asheninca directionals are now aspectual. With motion verbs the suffix -apa means that the action was done towards a specific point. With non-motion verbs it indicates that the action was done upon arrival at a specific point. But with verbs of time or quantity it indicates finality in that the endpoint of a sequence has been reached. Its basic meaning can thus be synthesized as 'finality'. Similarly, J. Payne argues that the basic meaning of the directional -aw is 'receptive' and that of the directional -an is 'non-final'.

Affixes indicating type of movement, location, or directional orientation are apparently not characteristic of Cariban, Tupí-Guaraní, and Jê families. Sometimes, however, auxiliary verbs (Tupí-Guaraní, Jê), imperative forms (Cariban), and tense affixes may convey positional or movement meanings. For example, the Panare suffix -ñe has both tense and movement/directional meanings. With transitive verbs it indicates non-past and/or narrative present tense. But with intransitive verbs it indicates that the action will be done in some other location.

4.4 INTERNAL VERB STRUCTURE. 4.4.1 THE PROBLEM. We now turn to a descriptive 'problem' in the organization of some of the more complicated verbal affix systems, such as those found in Panoan, Arawakan, and Yagua.

The basic issue is that verbs in these languages are not amenable to traditional position class analyses. At first glance, certain affixes seem to 'move around', though not just any order can occur. Further, certain suffixes can occur more than once in a given verbal string, but the occurrences need not be contiguous. Since the occurrences are non-contiguous, it cannot be argued that they constitute a simple case of reduplication.

For some languages a position class approach would require positing a horrendous number of classes. Wise 1963 claims it would have to be 33 for Amuesha (Arawakan).[10] However, she also argues that if a sequence of 33 orders were given, it would obscure common semantic components among groups of suffixes. A position class approach also says nothing about the empirically noted limitation on the number of affixes that may occur in any particular verb, nor about co-occurrence possibilities among suffixes. For Asheninca (also Arawakan), David Payne 1981 mentions 21 positions just for what he terms 'modal' suffixes. Perhaps the most significant problem he notes with a position class approach is that 'It ... appears that no reality is represented by stringing together twenty-one optional suffixal slots as the output to a structure rule'.[11] Under a strict position class approach there would be approximately 13 positions for Yagua, and somewhere around the same number for Capanahua (Panoan; based on the description in Loos 1969).[12]

We will first illustrate the apparent movability of certain suffixes, using data from Capanahua and Yagua. For Capanahua, Loos (1969.25) lists some 29 'aspectual' and 'adverbial' suffixes. The 'adverbial' suffixes are heavily concerned with movement, direction, orientation, and to some extent aspect. The 'aspectual' suffixes are somewhat concerned with modality.[13] Loos posits four subtypes of 'adverbial' and four subtypes of 'aspectual' suffixes. Presumably these subtypes correlate with general order. Loos suggests that the 'adverbial' and 'aspectual' suffix series are differentiated by a causative suffix. This causative suffix follows the 'adverbials' but precedes the 'aspectuals'. However, other data from Eugene Loos (p.c.) show that at least some affixes from both sets can occur on both sides of the causative suffix:

(21) a. bich-xon-hue

    get-BENEFACTIVE-IMPERATIVE

    'Get it for me!'

  b. bich-ma-xon-hue

    get-CAUSE-BENEFACTIVE-IMPERATIVE

    'Make him take it for me'.

  c. bich-xon-ma-rihbi-hue

    get-BENEFACTIVE-CAUSE-again-IMPERATIVE

    'Again make him get it for me'.

(22) a. mapet-ma-hi
      ascend-CAUSE-PRESENT
      'He causes it to ascend (e.g. he brings it up the bank)'.

    b. mapet-ma-yama-hue
      ascend-CAUSE-NEG-IMPERATIVE
      'Do not bring it up the bank!'

    c. mapet-yama-ma-hue
      ascend-NEG-CAUSE-IMPERATIVE
      'Make him stay down below (i.e. cause him not to come up)'.

(23) a. pi-catsihqu-i
      eat-DESIDERATIVE-PRESENT
      'He wants to eat it / he's hungry'.

    b. pi-catsih-ma-hue
      eat-DESIDERATIVE-CAUSE-IMPERATIVE
      'Make him hungry (i.e. make him want to eat it)'.

    c. pi-ma-catsihqu-i
      eat-CAUSE-DESIDERATIVE-PRESENT
      'He wants to feed it'.

In all the Capanahua examples involving 'moveable' suffixes that have been so far available, the causative is involved.[14] The same may also be true for Arawakan: David Payne 1981 notes that in Asheninca the RESOLVED MODAL usually follows ARRIVAL, but the order of these two can be reversed if the CAUSATIVE is also used.

In Yagua there are three different suffixes that behave like the Capanahuan causative. These are -*tániy* CAUSATIVE, -*rỵỵy* POTENTIAL (which includes 'ability to', 'thought concerning', and 'desiderative' meanings), and -*nayạạ* 'going all over aimlessly'. For ease of reference I will refer to these as POSTBASES. Certain suffixes can appear to either the right or the left of these postbases.[15] The causative and potential derive historically from verbs which took the now-main verb root as a complement. For example, Yagua -*rỵỵy* POTENTIAL is related etymologically to the verb root *nirỵỵy* 'love, desire'. (Note that semantically -*nayáá* forms a set with -*títyiiy* 'going directly'; however, -*títyiiy* does not appear to have the same morphological properties as -*nayáá*.)

(24) a. rá-jasiríỵvay-tániy-jancha-ráy
      INAN-sneeze-CAUSE-CONTINUATIVE-1SG

    b. rá-jasiríỵvay-jancha-tániy-ráy
      INAN-sneeze-CONTINUATIVE-CAUSE-1SG

    Both: 'This is making me sneeze for a considerable time'.

(25) a. sa-quiivʉ́ʉ́y-su-rʉ́ʉ́y-muuy-janu
    3SG-deceive-TRANS-POTENTIAL-COMPLETIVE-DISTANT.PAST
    'He stopped wanting to deceive (someone) long ago'.

  b. sa-suuta-muuy-rʉ́ʉ́y-ra
    3SG-wash-COMPLETIVE-POTENTIAL-INAN
    'He wants to stop washing it'.

(26) a. sa-suuta-nuvi̧i̧-naya̧a̧
    3SG-wash-on.arrival.here-going.aimlessly
    'He washes here, over here, over here, whenever he arrives here'.

  b. sa-suuta-naya̧a̧-nuvi̧i̧
    3SG-wash-going.aimlessly-on.arrival.here
    'She (used to) come to every place to wash'.

Yagua postbases differ from auxiliary verbs in that the latter precede the semantically main verb and take subject pro-clitics (the clitic does not then occur on the semantically main verb). One also might question whether the postbases are not clitics, rather than verb suffixes. If clitics should not be able to change the syntactic category of their host (cf. Muysken 1981), then at least the causative would clearly not qualify as a clitic since it derives transitive verbs from intransitive, and ditransitive verbs from transitive (this can be shown by participant reference morphology; cf. Doris Payne 1985).

As noted, a second 'problem' is that the same suffix can occur more than once in a given verbal string; these repetitions may or may not be contiguous. In 27a there is little or no evidence that the verb root plus the postbase closest to it are lexicalized, regardless of the fact that the most idiomatic English translation is 'bring' rather than 'make ascend' (judgments about Capanahua data come from Eugene Loos, p.c.).

(27) Capanahua (Eugene Loos, p.c.)

  a. mapet-**ma**-**ma**-hue
    ascend-CAUSE-CAUSE-IMPERATIVE
    'Make him bring it up (the bank)'.   OR:
    'Allow him to bring it up (the bank)'.
    (Literally: 'Make him make it ascend (the bank)')

  b. pi-**yama**-ma-catsihqu-**yama**-hi
    eat-NEG-CAUSE-DESIDERATIVE-NEGATIVE-PRESENT
    'He[i] doesn't want to make him[j] not eat it'.

  c. pi-**yama**-**ma**-catsihqu-**ma**-**yama**-hi
    eat-NEG-CAUSE-DESIDERATIVE-CAUSE-NEGATIVE-PRESENT
    'He[i] doesn't want him[j] to make him[k] not eat it'.

(28) Yagua

sa-jimyiy-**rų́ų́y**-tániy-muuy-**rų́ų́y**-níí

3SG-eat-POTENTIAL-CAUSE-COMPLETIVE-POTENTIAL-3SG

'He [i] thinks that he [i] should finish making him [j] eat everything'.

Wise 1963 notes that in Amuesha (Arawakan), certain members of an affix class can also occur repeatedly.

4.4.2 PREVIOUS APPROACHES. In purely formal terms, some might argue that the behavior of these postbases could be modeled via a relational clause union analysis (Aissen and Perlmutter 1983), or via a transformation which collapses two clauses into one (Marantz 1985).[16] Loos 1969 describes the Capanahua causative suffix in a transformational framework. On the surface the causative simply appears to be a suffix co-occurring with other possible suffixes on a single verb root. However, this is conceptualized as resulting from a transformation which derives a single word from two distinct underlying sentences; the causative is the main verb in one of the underlying sentences. In Loos' analysis, order issues are handled via the arrangement of suffixes in the causative and the caused clauses prior to the transformation which collapses them into a single verb word. Loos 1973 and 1976 take a generative semantics approach to Capahanua verbal morphology. Although transformational approaches to word formation have come into question since Chomsky (1970), Marantz (1985) continues to advocate such solutions, particularly with reference to causative morphology.

Such solutions are, in actual fact, better viewed as HISTORICAL scenarios of verb formation — not, as they imply, synchronic ones (which actually obscure the synchronic reality). The current reality that we should like to model is, first, that postbases are historically RELATED to full verb roots. However, the postbases are NOT synchronically verb roots. Unlike lexical and even auxiliary verbs, Yagua postbases cannot occur unless there is some other verb root simultaneously in the verb word, and they cannot take subject clitics. Further distributional evidence differentiates postbases from verb roots which are compounded with other verb roots. In compound verb forms, the two roots occur necessarily contiguous to one another. Postbases, on the other hand, necessarily follow any highly idiosyncratic derivational suffixes, locational suffixes, and iterativity suffixes (Doris Payne 1985). Clause union and transformational analyses overlook these distinctives of postbases. Fourth, as we shall see below, postbases are yet distinct from other (productive) derivational suffixes in that a postbase can potentially take its own suffixes, distinct from those of the main verb root. To summarize, we should like to emphasize that these are bound suffixes, and yet that not all suffixes have lost their full verbal properties to the same extent. That is, we should like an analysis which fairly reflects the GRADUAL nature of the development of bound derivational morphology from lexically free verb roots.[17]

Wise's 1963 approach to the descriptive problem in Amuesha (Arawakan) is to posit six levels of structure or 'affix complexes', rather than strict position classes. Each successive affix complex has within its scope all previous complexes. Thus, the affix complexes are hierarchically, as well as linearly ordered relative to one another. Each complex has a common semantic component. For some (but not all) complexes the internal members may have further varying orders relative to one another. This general approach is most certainly on the right track.[18] It is possible that solutions which are different in detail will be needed for the Arawakan case, from that needed for Yagua and Panoan.

David Payne 1981 and Wise 1986 present a 'semantic class' approach to the morphology of Peruvian Arawakan languages. This does not explicitly spell out order possibilities, but rather gives a general order in which semantically grouped suffixes tend to occur. Doris Payne 1985 independently takes a similar approach for Yagua verbs. The semantic class approach is ultimately inadequate. Although some insights may be captured relative to co-occurrence restrictions and general order, it remains inexplicit; it falls short of saying what is a good verb and what is not.

4.4.3 TOWARDS A SOLUTION. The above approaches either fail to explicitly predict what counts as a possible verb, or else treat as a synchronic process what should be acknowledged as a historical process.[19] Most crucially perhaps, none of them serves as a production model of how a speaker puts a verb together. Here I will try to mark the broad outlines of what I believe is a more satisfactory approach to these questions.

For these languages, verb structure is most insightfully viewed in terms of successively embedded layers of morpho-semantic structure. More than one suffix may occur in a given layer. What demarcates different layers, however, is not simply semantics. Rather, certain suffixes, which for ease of reference I have termed POSTBASES, have the privilege of 'marking off' a new layer of structure. Historically speaking, these have retained more independent verbal properties in that they have a high degree of lexical content and they can take their own suffixes, distinct from suffixes specific to the main verb root or stem. This is schematically represented in 29 (**STM** = stem, **SUFX** = suffix(es); **PB** = postbase):

(29) [[[STEM]-STM.SUFX]- [PB -PB.SUFX]- CLAUSAL.SCOPE.SUFX]

The levels of embedding suggested here are not necessarily equivalent to layers or levels in the sense of Lexical Phonology (Mohanan 1982). In Lexical Phonology, levels are determined by the interaction of phonological and morphological rules and by morpheme order possibilities. What I am suggesting here, rather, are layers of a morpho-semantic nature.[20] If 29 is correct, it reflects the fact that a complex of affixes - as a unit - can be put onto an extended stem. The relationship between the stem complex and the postbase complex is not really one of coordination, as the postbase complex is an operator on the stem complex:

(29')   VERB

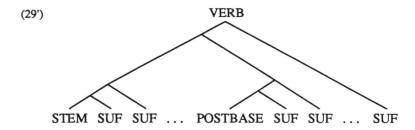

STEM SUF SUF ... POSTBASE SUF SUF ... SUF

At the outermost layer of structure are suffixes which have scope over the entire clause. These may include mood, aspect, tense, and agreement categories. One might question whether these are not clitics to the rest of the verbal complex. One argument against this for Yagua comes from the fact that at least some of the outermost Yagua aspectual morphemes can alternatively occur as stem and/or postbase affixes (cf. 24a). A clitic analysis would be possible only if the postbase itself were a cliticized verb; otherwise we would have the possibility of an aspectual clitic, say, occurring inside of a morphologically complex word. In Section 4.4.1 I argued that such an analysis would not be possible for at least the causative postbases. (Yagua does have other aspectual-modal second position clitics which can attach to the verb as well as to other categories; D. Payne 1985.)

Certain suffix categories are strictly stem suffixes. In Yagua these include locational and iterativity morphemes. Other suffix categories may serve either as stem suffixes or as postbase suffixes. In Yagua these include certain types of movement and other aspectual morphemes. Thus, there need not be a categorical difference between stem suffixes versus postbase suffixes. Instead, whether something functions as a stem versus postbase suffix in any particular verb depends on whether it has scope over the stem (and occurs before any postbases), versus has scope over the postbase (and occurs after any postbases).

The following pairs of Yagua sentences briefly illustrate this 'syntax of morphology'. In 30a the completive has semantic scope only over the POTENTIAL postbase -rúúy and not also over the main verb root. The sentence does not imply that the subject actually stopped deceiving anyone - only that he stopped wanting to deceive. In 30b the completive has semantic scope just over the main verb root. Cases like 31a, b are similar, though one might argue that 31b is sufficiently ambiguous such that 'stop making Y do X' is tantamount to Y ceasing to do X.

(30) a. sa-quiivúúy-su-rúúy-muuy-janu
       3SG-deceive-TRANS-POTENTIAL-COMPLETIVE-PAST3
       'He stopped wanting to deceive (someone) long ago'.

     b. sa-suuta-muuy-rúúy-ra
       3SG-wash-COMPLETIVE-POTENTIAL-INAN
       'He wants to stop washing it'.

(31) a. sa-júnay-muuy-tániy-níí   Mario
       3SG-cry-COMPLETIVE-CAUSE-3SG
       'He makes Mario stop crying'.

    b. sa-júnay-tániy-muuy-níí   Mario
       3SG-cry-CAUSE-COMPLETIVE-3SG
       'He stops making Mario cry'.

The structure in 29 accounts for why certain suffixes appear to 'move': formatives such as the Yagua completive in 30-31 can function as suffixes to the main verb root (i.e. between the main verb root and the postbase), or as suffixes to the postbase (i.e. following the postbase). This also partially accounts for why certain suffixes can occur twice in a given verb: they can occur once as a suffix to the main verb root, and again as a suffix to the postbase (27b). Alternatively, a postbase itself can occur more than once (27a, c). Thus, depending on the language, the general approach given in 29 needs to be amended to allow at least a limited amount of postbase recursion.

Could morphological order in these languages be accounted for strictly in semantic terms? That is, could one read the order of morphemes directly off of the semantic structure? A pure semantic solution would simplify the description without need for additional 'morpho-semantic' structure. If this were possible in suffixing languages, each morpheme to the right should have semantic scope over the entire complex to the left. That is, we would expect only leftward binary branching in terms of semantic structure.

Semantic scope over the entire verbal string to the left is often the case (e.g. Wise 1986:583 on Amuesha). In the following Capanahua example, each instance of the negative -*yama* has scope over the entire complex to its left:

(32) a. miin bene   queen-yama-yama-hue
       your husband love-NEG-NEG-IMPERATIVE
       'Do not not love your husband (i.e. don't reject him)'.

However, there are a few potential problems with predicting order simply on the basis of semantics. A minor difficulty noted by Wise 1986 is that 'there are examples where orders are reversed with no apparent difference in meaning or scope relations' (cf. ex. 24). However, I do not see this as a serious problem. Lack of clear meaning differences despite differences in order is particularly likely when the non-postbase suffix involved is an imperfective aspectual. As in 24, it is very likely that an imperfective causative action would also be interpreted as conveying an imperfective caused action, and vice versa. A serious problem would be a case where a leftward suffix clearly had scope over a rightward suffix; but no such cases have yet surfaced.

A more substantive problem for the pure semantic view are those cases where a suffix has scope just over its postbase, and not over everything to the left. This is the case in 30a, b.

A further problem, which rules out a strong form of a pure semantic solution, is that only certain formatives can occur as suffixes to both stems and postbases. Other formatives can occur only as affixes to the root or stem. This is the case with Yagua locationals, despite the fact that they are totally productive and are not idiosyncratic in meaning. Nevertheless, they cannot occur rightward of the postbase.

Further, in Yagua there are derivational valence changing suffixes which are only root suffixes. In terms of semantics and what they do to the argument structure of the verb, these are very like the productive causative postbase *-tániy*. However, they differ markedly in their morphological properties, both in terms of lexicalization with certain verb roots (i.e. lack of productivity), and in their position. Semantics alone cannot account for the difference. Rather, diachronic history and the concomitant higher degree of lexicalization found with historically older suffixes accounts for the restriction.

For at least these reasons, then, verb structure cannot be accounted for by an oversimple mapping from semantics to the morphological form. Rather, there is morphological structure, which to a large degree correlates with semantic meaning. Each successive suffix necessarily has semantic scope over everything to the left only when there are no postbases.

A further question raised by these data is: To what extent is the cognitive processing involved in the production of such verbs the same as, or different from the cognitive processing involved in the syntactic production of both simple and complex sentences? For example, is morphology in these languages more akin to syntax in an Indo-European language? It is commonly assumed that the possibilities in word formation are highly restricted and often 'frozen'. Syntax, on the other hand, is creative and allows for recursion. There are rules, but there are few 'frozen forms'.[21] For example, it has been claimed that the notion of 'possible but non-existent word' is relevant for morphology, while 'possible but non-existent sentence' has no relevance for syntax (Scalise 1984, Halle 1973). But in Arawakan languages, where speakers can produce long and novel verb forms quite freely, is there such a thing as a 'possible but non-existent' verb?

5. SUMMARY

Here we have briefly reviewed some of the more salient features of lowland SA morphology. These include: (a) a high degree of polysynthesis in the western Amazon and less towards the east; (b) the prevalence of verb affixes indicating location, direction, position or orientation, and type of movement associated with the action; (c) the temporal, aspectual, and modal functions of these suffixes; and (d) the nearly syntax-like nature of certain verbal suffixes in some western Amazonian languages.

NOTES

1   For a general history of early European views on Latin American indigenous languages see Pottier 1983. The ideas presented in this paper have benefited from comments by participants in the Working Conference on Amazonian Languages, particularly Terrence Kaufman, Wolf Dietrich, Daniel Everett, and Tom Payne. I am grateful to Peter Austin and Robert Carlson for additional commentary, and especially to Eugene Loos and Harold Shaver for sharing data.

2   But see Cutler, Hawkins and Gilligan 1985 for review of the literature and some hypotheses on morphological processing.

3   Due to space limitations, only selected claims are illustrated with examples; the reader is referred to the cited works for further exemplification.

4   See also note 10.

5   Why morphological asymmetry should be the norm is likely related to the overall preference for suffixation (cf. Cutler, Hawkins and Gilligan 1985). The reasons for such an asymmetry should be sought in at least two directions. First, the length of time during which a language is dominantly OV vs. VO could certainly have a bearing on the number of suffixes vs. prefixes. However, if time were the only factor, we would expect a greater number of polysynthetic languages with a balanced number of prefixes and suffixes. This suggests the existence of cognitive processing factors which impede the development of heavy prefixation when a language already has heavy suffixation, and vice versa. For example, if words are NOT learned and stored as single wholes (cf. Bybee 1985.111-114), but the speaker must instead synthetically process (at least some of) the morphology, the relative difficulty of computing center-embedded constructions will mitigate against piling on both prefixes and suffixes.

6   Examples in Popjes and Popjes 1986 show that long forms usually end in *-n* or *-r*, suggesting an old morphological element.

7   Abreu 1941 claims that Cashinahua (Panoan) is largely monosyllabic and can thus be compared with Chinese. Evidentaly he means that morphemes in the language are largely monosyllabic. Panoan languages have quite complex morphology (cf. Section 4.4).

8   Some may derive from postpositions, which in turn may have derived from verbs (cf. Doris Payne 1985 for discussion of Yagua).

9   The suffix -rįį 'action done enroute' is not so limited. In combination with an unbounded movement suffix the resultant action must be interpreted as iterative performance of a perfective action.

[10]   For Machiguenga (also Preandine Maipuran Arawakan), Betty Snell (p.c.) cites examples of verbs with nearly 20 affixes in spontaneous unelicited speech.

[11]   Regardless of whether or not any analysis is "real", stringing out 21 suffix slots is still not conceptually adequate.

[12]   Everett 1986 suggests that Pirahã has somewhere between 15 and 19 position classes. Cayuvava must be similar.

[13]   The term MODAL has been used in Arawakan for what appears to be a similar eccelctic range of items; (cf. David Payne 1981).

[14]   Though Eugene Loos has suggested in personal communication that there might be others.

[15]   It can be shown that the postbases evoke the apparent moveability: if there is no postbase, the remaining suffixes occur in a fixed order. The term POSTBASE is borrowed from Eskimo-Aleut linguistics, though I use it in a narrower sense here to refer just to morphemes which (a) have heavy lexical content (not just a grammatical function), and (b) delimit a new layer of morpho-semantic structure (cf. Section 4.4.2).

[16]   I don't know of any independent evidence for bi-clausal properties in such Yagua clauses, other than translation equivalence into English and the variable placement possibility itself. Like Marantz, Baker 1985 also rejects a strong form of the lexicalist hypothesis, arguing that if morphology and syntax are completely disassociated then there is no explanation for the fact that order of morphemes in a single word reflects the semantics of performing syntactic operations in one order, rather than another. It is worth pointing out that in many cases order of morphemes reflects the HISTORICAL sequence in which morphemes collapsed onto the verb. Baker is primarily concerned with noun incorporation; it remains to be seen to what extent his approach can be extended to the postbase issue.

[17]   It is, in fact, a synchronic oversimplification to posit a sharp three-way distinction between free verb roots, postbases and more traditional derivational suffixes. The finer distinctions cannot be taken up here.

[18]   Wise's discussion is presented in terms of a 'Voegelin decade' grammar. Although explicit in one sense of the word, it is difficult to visualize the exact structure that Wise conceives of. Further, it is possible that some of the 'affixes' Wise described in 1963 as 'stem closure' morphemes are epenthetic elements which complicated the description of the morphology (cf. Wise, this volume).

[19]   Though with further clarification Wise 1963 may be more adequate than the rest.

[20]   One feature of this proposal potentially different from claims made by LP is that it allows for specific formatives to occur in two different layers of structure.

[21]   This is not to deny that lexicalized phrases, sentence frames and sentences exist.

REFERENCES

Abreu, J. Capistrano de. 1941. *rãtxa hu-ni-ku-ĩ A lingua dos caxinauás* (2nd edition). Sociedade Capistrano de Abreu, Livraria Briguiet (Brazil).

Aissen, Judith, and David Perlmutter. 1983. Clause reduction in Spanish. *Studies in Relational Grammar 1*. Ed. by D. Perlmutter, 360-403. Chicago: University of Chicago Press.

Anchietta, Joseph de. 1595. *Arte de grammatica da lingua mais usada na costa do Brasil*. Coimbra: Antonio de Mariz.

Baker, Mark. 1985. The Mirror Principle and morphosyntactic explanation. *Linguistic Inquiry* 16.373-416.

Barnes, Janet and Terrell Malone. 1987. El tuyuca. MS.

Bendor-Samuel, David. 1972. *Hierarchical structures in Guajajara. (SIL Publications in Linguistics and Related Fields 37.)* Norman, OK: SIL and University of Oklahoma.

Bybee, Joan. 1985. *Morphology*. Amsterdam: J. Benjamins.

Campbell, Lyle, Terrence Kaufman, and Thomas C. Smith-Stark. 1986. Meso-America as a linguistic area. *Language* 62.530-70.

Carson, Neusa. 1982. Phonology and morpho-syntax of Macuxi Carib. University of Kansas doctoral dissertation.

Comrie, Bernard. 1981. *Language universals and linguistic typology*. Chicago: University of Chicago Press.

Chomsky, Noam. 1970. Remarks on nominalization. *Readings in English Transformational Grammar*. Ed. by R. Jacobs and P. Rosenbaum, 184-221. Waltham, Mass.: Ginn and Co.

Cutler, Anne, John Hawkins, and Gary Gilligan. 1985. The suffixing preference, a processing explanation. *Linguistics* 23.723-58.

DeLancey, Scott. 1982. Aspect, transitivity and viewpoint. *Tense/Aspect*. Ed. by Paul Hopper, 167-83. Amsterdam: J. Benjamins.

Derbyshire, Desmond. 1986. Comparative survey of morphology and syntax in Brazilian Arawakan. In Derbyshire and Pullum (eds.), 469-566.

Derbyshire, Desmond. 1987. Areal characteristics of Amazonian languages. *International Journal of American Linguistics* 53.311-26.

Derbyshire, Desmond, and Geoffrey Pullum (eds.). 1986. *Handbook of Amazonian languages*, 1. Berlin: Mouton de Gruyter.

Everett, Daniel. 1986. Pirahã. In Derbyshire and Pullum (eds.), 200-325.

Everett, Daniel and Lucy Seki. 1985. Reduplication and CV skeleta in Kamaiurá. *Linguistic Inquiry* 16.326-330.

Gómez-Imbert, Elsa. 1982. De la forme et du sens dans la classification nominale en Tatuyo. Paris: Universite Sorbonne doctoral dissertation.

Greenberg, Joseph. 1966. Some universals of grammar with particular reference to the order of meaningful elements. *Universals of language*. Ed. by J. Greenberg, 73-113. Cambridge, MA: MIT Press.

Halle, Morris. 1973. Prolegamana to a theory of word formation. *Linguistic Inquiry* 4.3-16.

Hart, Raymond. 1963. Semantic components of shape in Amarakaeri grammar. *Anthropological Linguistics* 5.1-7.

Kakumasu, James. 1986. Urubu-Kaapor. In Derbyshire and Pullum (eds.), 326-403.

Key, Harold. 1967. *Morphology of Cayuvava. (Janua Linguarum.)* The Hague: Mouton.

von Kinder, Leopoldo. 1936. *Gramática y vocabulario de la lengua huitota*. (Boletin de Estudios Históricos, suplemento No. 4.) Pasto, Colombia: Imprenta del Departamento de Nariño.

Klein, Harriet E. M. 1973. *A grammar of Argentine Toba: verbal and nominal morphology*. Columbia University doctoral dissertation.

Kneeland, Harriet. 1979. *Lecciones para el aprendizaje del idioma mayoruna*. (Documento de Trabajo 14.) Pucallpa, Perú: Instituto Lingüístico de Verano.

Koehn, Edward and Sally Koehn. 1986. Apalai. In Derbyshire and Pullum (eds.), 33-127.

Loos, Eugene. 1969. *The phonology of Capanahua and its grammatical basis. (SIL Publications in Linguistics 20.)* Norman, OK: SIL and the University of Oklahoma.

Loos, Eugene. 1973. *Estudios Panos I*. Dallas: Summer Institute of Linguistics.

Loos, Eugene. 1976. *Estudios Panos V: Verbos Performativos*. Dallas: Summer Institute of Linguistics.

Malone, Terrell. 1988. The origin and development of Tuyuca evidentials. *International Journal of American Linguistics*. 54.119-40.

Marantz, Alec. 1985. Lexical decomposition versus affixes as syntactic constituents. *Causatives and agentivity*, 154-71. Chicago: Chicago Linguistic Society.

Matthews, P. H. 1974. *Morphology*. Cambridge: Cambridige University Press.

Mohanan, K. P. 1982. *Lexical phonology*. Cambridge, Mass: MIT doctoral dissertation.

Moore, Barbara J. 1980. Positional, directional and relational verbs in Hupda Makú. MS.

Moore, Barbara J. and Gail Louise Franklin. 1980. Verbal and nominal inflection in Hupda Makú. MS.

de Montoya, Antonio Ruiz. 1639. *Tesoro de la lengua guaraní*. Madrid.

Mosonyi, Jorge C. 1982. Morfología verbal del idioma cariña. MA Thesis. Caracas: Universidad Central de Venezuela.

Myusken, P. 1981. Quechua word structure. *Binding and filtering*. Ed. by F. Heney, 279-327. Cambridge, Mass: MIT Press.

Olza A., Jesús, and Miguel Angel Jusayú. 1986. *Gramática de la lengua guajira (morfosintaxis)*. San Cristóbal, Venezuela: Universidad Católica del Táchira.

Payne, David L. 1981. *The phonology and morphology of Axininca Campa (SIL Publications in Linguistics 66.)* Arlington: University of Texas at Arlington and SIL.

Payne, David L., Judith K. Payne, and Jorge Sánchez S. 1982. *Morfología, fonología y fonética del asheninca del apurucayali (Campa - Arawak pre-andino)*. Pucallpa, Perú: Instituto Lingüístico de Verano.

Payne, Doris L. 1985. *Aspects of the grammar of Yagua: a typological perspective*. UCLA doctoral dissertation.

Payne, Doris L. 1986. Noun classification in Yagua. *Noun classes and categorization in typological perspective*. Ed. by Colette Craig, 113-131. Amsterdam: J. Benjamins.

Payne, Doris L. 1987. Noun classification in the western Amazon. *Language Sciences* 9.21-44.

Payne, Doris L. and Thomas E. Payne. 1989. A grammatical sketch of Yagua. *Handbook of Amazonian languages, 2.* Ed. by Desmond Derbyshire and Geoffrey Pullum. Berlin: Mouton de Gruyter.

Payne, Judith K. 1982. Directionals as time referentials in Ashéninca. *Anthropological Linguistics* 24.325-37.

Payne, Thomas E. 1983. Subject inflection of Yagua verbs. MS.

Payne, Thomas E. 1984. Locational relations in Yagua narrative. *Work Papers of the Summer Institute of Linguistics, University of North Dakota.* 28.157-192.

Payne, Thomas E. 1985. *Participant coding in Yagua discourse.* UCLA doctoral dissertation.

Pelleprat, P. Pedro, S. J. 1655. *Introducción a la lengua de los galibis, salvajes de tierra firme de America Meridional.* Paris. (Reprinted in *Aportes Jesuíticos a la filología colonial venezolana, Tomo II.* 1971. Ed. by José del Rey, 9-23. Caracas: Universidad Católica Andrés Bello.)

Popjes, Jack and Jo Popjes. 1986. Canela-Krahô. In Derbyshire and Pullum (eds.), 128-99.

Pottier, Bernard. 1983. Perspectiva histórica: Introducción. *América latina en sus lenguas indígenas.* Ed. by B. Pottier, 17-39. Caracas: Monte Avila Editores.

del Rey F., José, S. J. 1971. Introduction. *Aportes Jesuíticos a la filología colonial venezolana, Tomo I.* Caracas: Universidad Católica Andrés Bello.

Rodrigues, Aryon. 1953. Morfologia do verbo Tupi. *Revista Letras* 1.121-52. Curitiba, Brazil.

Rodrigues, Danielle. 1987. Incorporation in Ancient Guaraní. Paper presented at the Working Conference on Amazonian Languages, Eugene, Oregon.

Scalise, Sergio. 1984. *Generative morphology.* Dordrecht: Foris Publications.

Sherzer, Joel. 1973. Areal linguistics in North America. *Current trends in linguistics.* Ed. by Thomas Sebeok, 10.749-95. The Hague: Mouton.

Thiesen, Wesley. 1975a. El sistema numérico del bora (huitoto). *Datos Etnolingüísticos* 1. Pucallpa, Perú: Instituto Lingüístico de Verano.

Thiesen, Wesley. 1975b. Un informe breve de la morfología bora. *Datos Egnolingüísticos* 18. Pucallpa, Perú: Instituto Lingüístco de Verano.

Urban, Greg. 1985. Ergativity and accusativity in Shokleng (Gê). *International Journal of American Linguistics* 51.164-87.

Wise, Mary Ruth. 1963. Six levels of structure in Amuesha (Arawak) verbs. *International Journal of American Linguistics* 29.132-52.

Wise, Mary Ruth. 1971. *Identification of participants in discourse: a study of aspects of form and meaning in Nomatsiguenga. (SIL Publications in Linguistics 28.)* Norman, OK: SIL and the University of Oklahoma.

Wise, Mary Ruth. 1986. Grammatical characteristics of Preandine Arawakan languages of Peru. In Derbyshire and Pullum (eds.), 567-642.

Witte, Paul. 1976. Andoke clause, phrase, and word. MS.

Noun Classification Systems of Amazonian Languages

Desmond C. Derbyshire and Doris L. Payne

1. INTRODUCTION

In this survey we discuss noun classification systems of Amazonian[1] languages in terms of two of the four types of classifier languages proposed by Allan 1977: **numeral classifier** languages and **concordial classifier** languages. We also discuss a third type not discussed by Allan: **verb-incorporated classifiers** (Mithun 1986). The chief characteristic of most of the Amazonian classification systems discussed here is that they cannot be labelled discretely as any one type, but are a mixture of two or all three types. Two other characteristics are:

(1) Classifiers of all three types frequently serve a discourse anaphoric function. That is, they refer to entities which are not explicitly expressed in the noun phrase or sentence in which the classifier occurs, but in some other part of the discourse. (Sometimes these entities are not linguistically expressed at all, but are recoverable from the nonlinguistic context of the speaker-hearer situation.) It may well be that this is a near universal function of classifiers. Although it was not highlighted in earlier sources, more recent work has drawn attention to it (e.g. Downing 1986; Payne 1987). An interesting exception to the anaphoric function of classifiers is found in written Malay (Hopper 1986), where the use of classifiers appears to be restricted to cooccurrence with a noun when that noun introduces a new entity that is to be an important topic of the discourse. In the subsequent discourse, however, the classifier is not used to refer back to that noun. Jacaltec classifiers are also used in a special way to signal thematic saliency of a newly introduced entity (Ramsay 1985), but in Jacaltec classifiers are also more generally used anaphorically in the subsequent discourse (see sect. 4 for fuller discussion). Craig 1986a refers to the anaphoric role of classifiers as a restricted one. But the anaphoric function is especially prominent in Amazonian languages, which are characterized by the scarcity of fully-identifying nominal expressions in natural discourse. (See, for example, Krute-Georges 1983 and Moore 1984.204.)

(2) The semantic basis for classification varies in detail from language to language, but in general the primary categories reflected in the various systems follow Allan's groupings: material (animate vs. inanimate), shape (long, flat, round, etc.), consistency (flexible, rigid), size (big, medium, small), location, arrangement (configuration, position) and quanta (single, dual, plural, etc.). There is one additional category which occurs in Amazonian languages: function (vehicles, instruments, houses) (cf. Payne 1986).

This paper is organized as follows: section 2 reviews the established criteria for identifying classifier systems and shows how these fail to account for the systems found in the Amazon area; section 3 gives an overview of the classifier systems of Amazonian languages, groups the languages that follow similar patterns, and sets out all the necessary data; section 4 concludes by summarizing the distinctive areal characteristics, summarizing the patterns found in the major language families of the region, and suggesting directions for future research.

While we refer to a variety of languages and families, the paper is not in any sense comprehensive in its scope, either in the number of languages surveyed or in the detail with which individual languages are presented. We discuss about twenty languages (the Arawan, Campa, Huitotoan and Tucanoan families are counted as single units) in the Amazon area that have some system for classifying nouns. These represent 13 language stocks or families.[2] There are four other major families that do not have a developed classifier system: Cariban, Gean, Panoan and Tupí-Guaranian. Some languages in these families appear to have an incipient system: verb-incorporated body parts in Cariban and Panoan and the use of generic possessed nouns in Cariban.

2. CRITERIA FOR IDENTIFYING CLASSIFIER SYSTEMS

Allan 1977 defines classifiers of all types as meeting two criteria: (a) they occur as morphemes in surface structures under specifiable conditions; and (b) they have meaning, in the sense that a classifier denotes some salient perceived or imputed characteristic of the entity to which an associated noun refers. He specifically excludes European gender inflections on the grounds that they are semantically empty. We shall, however, include gender systems as a sub-type of concordial system in this discussion of Amazonian languages, since gender markers do carry some meaning and also are not totally independent of the other systems in at least some languages. In fact, gender systems are common in the area, although a number of languages also have nongender concordial systems (in some cases in addition to a gender system).

The three classifier systems on which we focus have their own specific sets of criteria. We now summarize these as they have been generally accepted in the literature (e.g. Allan 1977, Craig 1986a, Dixon 1986, Mithun 1986).

Numeral classifiers are lexico-syntactic forms, as distinct from closed grammatical systems. They are often obligatory in expressions of quantity (though not limited to such expressions) and they are normally separate words. They result in a relatively large number of distinct classes. They are associated primarily with typologically isolating languages (e.g. Austronesian, Burmese, Chinese, Japanese, Tai and other south-east Asian languages). It is a modified type of such numeral classifier system that occurs in Amazonian languages (see below).

Concordial classifiers constitute a closed grammatical and paradigmatical system. Morphologically the classifiers are affixes or clitics which occur on constituents of the noun phrase and/or verb phrase. They express class agreement with some head noun, but do not always occur on the noun itself. There are usually only a few classes (up to 20) and this kind of system is associated with agglutinative or inflectional languages (e.g. Australian, Bantu and Niger-Congo languages). In this discussion we will distinguish two sub-types of concordial system: gender (including the animate/inanimate distinction) and nongender.

Verb-incorporated classifiers are lexical items incorporated into the verb stem which signal some classifying characteristic of the entity referred to in an associated noun phrase. This is usually the (nonactive) intransitive subject or the object of the clause (though it is not necessarily overtly expressed as a separate clause constituent). Verb-incorporated classifiers are functionally similar to **predicate classifiers**, another of Allan's four types and found in Athapascan languages. The latter, however, are complete stems, being a composite of verbal event plus classifying characteristic of an associated entity. Verb-incorporated classifiers do not occur in noun phrases and do not express concord in the generally accepted sense. They do, however, function to classify the nouns with which they are associated, and the semantic range of the characteristics in focus is similar to that found in numeral and (nongender) concordial systems. They are found in languages as genetically and geographically distinct as Ngandi and Gunwinggu (Australian), Caddo (Caddoan, Oklahoma), Cayuga (Northern Iroquoian, Ontario) and Munduruku (Tupí, Brazil) (Mithun 1986).

In section 1 we noted that Amazonian classifiers do not fit discretely the three categories as defined above. We now specify some of the ways in which the Amazonian systems diverge from the traditionally established systems.

(1) Some have general characteristics of numeral systems but either do not occur with numerals at all (Arabela) or do so only when the numeral is the predicate in a predicate-adjective type of construction (Sanuma).

(2) Some have general characteristics of numeral systems but they take the form of affixes, not separate words. (Except for Sanuma and Gavião, this is generally the case.)

(3) Languages which have some of the characteristics of numeral systems are not typologically isolating. This is obviously the major reason for (2) above.

(4) There is often a single set of classifier forms with the functions of two, or even all three, systems (excluding gender systems). These constitute a single, integrated system, rather than two or three separate systems. This is the case in Amarakaeri, Nomatsiguenga, Chayahuita, Huitotoan, Piaroa, Tucanoan, Munduruku, Waorani, Yagua and Arabela. Palikur is an exception in that it has distinct forms for the numeral system and the verb-incorporated system.

(5) Gender systems are usually distinct from all other systems, but in at least one family the gender system is complementary to, and integrated with, the nongender concordial and numeral systems (Tucanoan).

(6) Some languages have both types of concordial system, gender and nongender, functioning independently of each other (Arawan, Nomatsiguenga, Tucanoan, Yagua).

(7) In some languages, what are primarily verb-incorporated systems have developed numeral and/or concordial functions (Munduruku, Amarakaeri, Chayahuita, Waorani).

(8) In some languages and families, the same set of classifiers may have both derivational and inflectional functions (Yagua, Huitotoan, Tucanoan, Cahuapanan). Mufwene 1980 makes a similar claim for Bantu classifiers.

3. OVERVIEW OF CLASSIFIER SYSTEMS IN AMAZONIAN LANGUAGES

In this section we present a summary, with illustrative data, of the types of classifier systems found in Amazonian languages. Some languages have systems with the characteristics of only one basic type: numeral (3.1), concordial (3.2), or verb-incorporated (3.3). Others have systems with the characteristics of two types: numeral and concordial (3.4), numeral and verb-incorporated (3.5), or concordial and verb-incorporated (3.6). Yet others have systems with characteristics of all three types (3.7). Finally, there is a group of languages and families that appear not to have any clearly defined classifier system, although there is some evidence that the beginnings of a system may be emerging in a few of these languages (3.8).[3]

3.1 NUMERAL CLASSIFIER SYSTEM ONLY: SANUMA (AND OTHER YANOMAMI LANGUAGES), GAVIAO (TUPI).[4] Sanuma (Yanomaman family) has a modified numeral classifier system. Classifiers only occur with numerals or quantifiers in predicate adjective constructions in which the numeral is the predicate and the classifier is part of the subject noun phrase. As with the canonical type of numeral classifier system, the classifiers occur as separate lexical items in the noun phrase (and they are inflected only for singular, dual and plural number). There is no concord with other constituents of the noun phrase or the verb. Nor is there any verb-incorporation of classifiers. While not strictly an isolating language, Sanuma appears to be less polysynthetic than many Amazonian languages.

Each noun has a classifier pronoun which indicates the class to which the noun belongs. There are four types of classifier pronouns, designated by Borgman (to appear) as: specific, general, characteristic, and body part. The first three types have singular, dual and plural forms. With some nouns the dual is rarely used and with another set of nouns the plural form is infrequent.

The specific classifier pronouns are: *a* 'singular', *kökö/kö* 'dual', and *pö* 'plural'. These are used with nouns that are specific in nature, such as common objects, animals, heavenly bodies and proper names.

The general classifier pronouns are: *te* 'singular', *tökö* 'dual', and *töpö* 'plural'. These are used with nouns that are general in nature, including uncommon objects, nominalizations, mass nouns, a collective group of spirits or people, or one belonging to such a group, e.g., 'female', 'non-Indian', 'Brazilian'.

According to Borgman, **specific** and **general** do not necessarily correlate with **definite** and **indefinite** categories of reference as found in many languages, although English glosses sometimes suggest that they do. Some examples of the use of these two types of classifiers are shown in 1-3. Kinship terms usually take the specific classifier in the singular and the general classifier in the plural.

(1) sai   a
    house SPCFC.CL.3SG   'It is a/the house.'

(2) a. ulu te
      child GEN.CL.3SG   'a child'

    b. ipa ulu a
      my child SPCFC.CL.3SG   'my child'

(3) a. opo   te
      armadillo GEN.CL.3SG
      'the/an armadillo' (a covered basket which looks like an armadillo)

    b. opo   a
      armadillo SPCFC.CL.3SG
      'the/an armadillo' (animal)

Characteristic classifier pronouns indicate some general property of the object (4a, 4b). Borgman says there are about sixteen different classifiers in this category.

(4) a. nasi   koko   su- a- mö a- su- lö- ma
      cassava CHAR.CL(root) take-DUR-PURP leave-FOC-DIR-CMP
      '(They) left to get bitter cassava.'

b. söpala sa   asö-   kö te- li   ke
   metal 1SG CHAR.CL(thin) DL receive-FOC I
   'I received the scissors.'

The object noun is regularly separated from its classifier (i.e. forming a discontinuous noun phrase) by the subject of the clause when that subject is a short form personal pronoun, as in 4b and 5. A possible explanation is that the subject pronoun is a second place clitic.

(5) hama sama   töpö   se kite
     visitor 1PL.EXCL GEN.CL.3PL hit FUT
     'We will hit the visitors.'

It is common in Sanuma for classifiers to substitute for the nouns to which they refer, as well as to cooccur with them in the noun phrase. They thus frequently serve a significant anaphoric discourse function.

There are two Tupian languages (outside of the Tupí-Guaraní family) for which we have data on classifiers: Gavião (Moore 1984) and Munduruku (Gonçalves 1987). Munduruku has a single set of classifier forms which have numeral, nongender concordial and verb-incorporated functions; this is discussed in section 3.7.

Gavião has only a numeral classifier system. The semantic range of the Gavião numeral classifiers includes 'small round object (6a)', 'long thin object', 'fruit-like object', 'hollow/convex object', 'liquid', 'root', 'powder' (6c) and 'leaf' (6d). In a few cases the classifier has a corresponding noun stem which is more semantically and syntactically constrained, e.g. the regular noun is inalienably possessed, as in 6b, where the possessor must be something that lays an egg; the classifier on the other hand can be alienably possessed, but only by using what Moore calls a dummy noun, meaning 'thing, possession' (6a).

(6) a. ę-bát   káp
       2-thing/possession CL.small.round.object 'your egg'

    b. ę-gáp   'your egg'

    c. sép kę̀ac kǫ̀òp
       hair burnt CL.powder   'powder of the burnt hair'

    d. e-gó   sep
       2-mouth CL.leaf   'your book'

3.2 CONCORDIAL CLASSIFIER SYSTEMS ONLY. There are two language subtypes which have only concordial classifier systems. The first has just a gender system (some Maipuran Arawakan language such as Apurinã and Piro). The second has both gender and nongender systems (some members of the Arawan

family such as Deni, Jamamadi, Madija Culina, and Paumari). Although both
Maipuran and Arawan have been generally called 'Arawakan', they show quite
different characteristics with regard to noun classification. In fact, Aryon
Rodrigues (p.c., and see Rodrigues 1982) maintains that there is no solid
evidence for even a remote genetic relationship between these two groupings,
such as has been generally accepted in the recent literature. Even within the
Maipuran family, there is considerable diversity, as is evident from the fact that
languages of this branch are found in four of the eight groupings in section 3.

3.2.1 GENDER CONCORDIAL SYSTEMS: APURINA, PIRO (MAIPURAN ARAWAKAN).
Apurinã and Piro (Maipuran) have only gender concordial systems. In
Apurina, there is no overt marking of gender on nouns, but their inherent gender
is signalled by the form of the subject prefixes (7a,b) and object suffixes (7b,d)
in the verb and also of the demonstratives (7b,c) in the noun phrase. Nominalizing suffixes are also marked for gender (7e,f). The Apurinã data are taken
from Aberdour 1985 (7a-c), Pickering 1973 (7d,f) and Pickering 1977 (7e).
(Minor orthographical changes have been made in the Pickering data, in order
to conform with the current orthography that is used by Aberdour.)

(7) a. xamina   o-   iopotokaka
        firewood 3.S.FEM-light
        'She lit the firewood.'

     b. i-   makatxaka-ro   ãto   sito
        3.S.MASC-remove-3.O.FEM   another.FEM woman
        'They removed another woman.'

     c. xãta ãti   ĩtopati
        fast another.MASC jungle(MASC)
        'He fasts in another jungle.'

     d. nota apa- ri   anana
        I   fetch-3.O.MASC pineapple(MASC)
        'I fetch pineapple.'

     e. kiki ma- ereka-ti   apopeka
        man NEG-good-NOMLZR.MASC arrive.PERF
        'The bad man has arrived.'

     f. anio   Pedro jorota-karo   okapeẽ-ka
        mosquito(FEM) Peter bite- NOMLZR.FEM kill-   PASS
        'The mosquito which bit Peter was killed.'

3.2.2 GENDER AND NONGENDER CONCORDIAL SYSTEMS: DENI, JAMAMADI,
MADIJA CULINA, PAUMARI (ARAWAN). The languages of the Arawan family

(Deni, Jamamadi, Madija Culina and Paumari) have only concordial systems, and all four have both gender and nongender systems. The two systems are independent of each other, but interact to produce complex intra-clausal agreement patterns. Signalling of gender is much more complex than any other language in the Amazon area. It is not marked on the nouns themselves, but their inherent gender is marked on other constituents of the noun phrase, as in Madija (8) and Paumari (13), including demonstratives and adjectives. It is also marked on various clausal and verbal categories, including interrogative markers in Deni and Madija (9), subordinators in Deni and Paumari, imperative markers in Jamamadi and Madija (11), aspect markers in Deni and Madija (10), evidential markers in Jamamadi and discourse-related theme/perspective markers in Jamamadi and Paumari (13). In the case of the verbal categories, the agreement is governed by the absolutive constituent in the clear-cut cases. This is illustrated by the Madija imperative suffixes in 11; in 11a, the feminine form agrees with the intransitive subject; in 11b, the masculine form agrees with the direct object, which is not otherwise overtly expressed in the clause. In less clear cases of superficially transitive clauses in which agreement is with the subject, Adams and Marlett 1987 argue fairly convincingly that these are antipassive constructions, so that agreement is still with the absolutive constituent

Madija Culina data:

(8) a. amonehe onii
         woman   other.FEM   'another/the other woman'

     b. makhidehe owaa
         man   other.MASC 'another/the other man'

(9) a. to-kha ko
         3- go   Q.MASC   'Did he go?'

     b. to-kha ki
         3- go   Q.FEM   'Did she go?'

(10) a. (powa) dzoho i-na-   ni- hari
         he/him carry 3-AUX-back-IMPF.MASC
         'She/he carried him back.'

     b. (poni)   dzoho i-na- ni-haro
         she/her   IMPF.FEM
         'She/he carried her back.'

(11) a. ohi ti-ki-ne-   hera-   hi
       cry 2- PL-AUX-NEG.FEM-IMP.FEM
       'Don't you all cry!'

   b. daphi   ti-na-   ho
       swallow 2- AUX-IMP.MASC
       'Swallow it.'

(12) a. o-kha   odza ti-ka-naato- hi
       1-GEN house 2- CL-   make- IMP.FEM
       'Make my house!'

   b. odza   bika-ni   0-ka-itta
       house good-INCMPL 3-CL-sit
       'I have a good house.' (lit. 'My good house sits.')

Paumari data:

(13) o-   ka-nofi- hi   oni   vanami   ka-karaho
     1SG-CL-want-THEME.FEM DEM.FEM paddle.FEM CL-big
     'I want the big paddle.'

The nongender concordial system found in these Arawan languages is restricted to a small class of nouns. (It appears to be less consistently implemented in Deni, Madija and Jamamadi than in Paumari.) The concord is expressed by the same form in each language: the prefix *ka-*, which occurs on verbs and (at least in Paumari) on noun modifiers. The Madija examples 12a-b show the absolutive case noun phrase as governing the *ka-* prefix in the verb. The verbal concord in Paumari is also with the absolutive constituent. The Paumari example 13 shows the two systems (gender and nongender) in operation in the same sentence: the inherent feminine gender of *vanami* 'paddle' is overtly marked in the form of the demonstrative *oni* and in the verbal theme suffix *-hi*; the same word *vanami* belongs to the *ka-* noun class and this is marked by the *ka-* prefix occurring on both the verb *nofi* 'want' and on the adjective *karaho* 'big'. In Deni, Madija and Paumari, items associated with water, especially rivers, fall into this *ka-* class; but for other items in the class it is difficult to see any uniform semantic basis. Thus, in Deni the class includes items meaning 'house', 'knife' and 'bow' (G. Koop 1976) and in Paumari it includes 'rainbow', 'dove', 'species of lizard', 'alligator', 'watermelon', 'corn', 'thigh', 'intestines', 'salt' and 'spoon' (Chapman and Derbyshire, to appear). In Paumari, there are pairs of homophonous nouns with associated meanings (central mass vs. appendages), where only one of the pair (central mass) belongs to the *ka-* class (cf. the discussion in Zubin and Köpcke

1986.146-49 on the role of gender in German for differentiating between superordinate and basic level categories):

	ka- class	non-ka-
sa'ai	'hand'	'finger'
'damai	'foot'	'toe'
moroboi	'inner ear'	'outer ear'
siho	'fire'	'firewood'

In this restricted concordial system, the *ka-* prefix can be the only overt reference in the clause to the entity, so that a useful anaphoric function is also served by this noun class marker. The same is true of the gender markers in these languages.

3.3 VERB-INCORPORATED CLASSIFIER SYSTEM ONLY: TERENA (MAIPURAN ARAWAKAN), PIRAHA. Terena (Maipuran) has only verb-incorporated classifiers and these can refer to subjects of nonactive intransitive verbs and to oblique constituents (14a,b). The Terena sources consulted say little about the classifiers and it is possible that they can be used to refer to other clause constituents. (Ekdahl & Butler 1979.184-86 contains a number of classifiers in a miscellaneous listing of verbal elements.) Terena is the only Brazilian Arawakan language that does not have a gender system of any kind.

(14) a. movó-cava
      dry- CL.branch
      'It (branch) is dry.'

   b. neve- nó'e-   co-ti   nĭca
      select-CL.liquid-PL-DUR food
      'They are picking food (from the water).'

Information about Pirahã (Mura family) comes from Keren Everett (p.c.). The language appears to have only a verb-incorporated classifier system, with the classifiers taking the form of verb-initial proclitics (15). Their semantic domains include plants and plant food, animals and animal products, liquids, and items newly introduced into the culture. The noun to which the classifier refers is the subject of an intransitive verb or the direct object of a transitive verb.

(15) a. ti xá-   ohoái-baaí, xágaísi
      I CL.plant.food-eat- a.lot farinha
      'I eat a lot of farinha.'

b. xís-   igi-   hai
CL.meat-carry-RELATIVE.CERT
'He will carry the meat.'

c. xís-   ahabopita
CL.meat-run.out
'The meat runs out.'

3.4 NUMERAL + CONCORDIAL CLASSIFIER SYSTEMS: YAGUA (PEBA-YAGUAN), TUCANOAN FAMILY, ZAPAROAN FAMILY, HUITOTOAN FAMILY AND PIAROA (SALIBAN). Yagua (Peba-Yaguan) has both a numeral and a concordial system. Payne 1986, 1987 and Powlison and Powlison 1958 have provided a fairly complete description of Yagua noun classification and only some of the main characteristics are given here.

There is a gender-type of concordial system which is expressed by means of subject and object cross-reference clitics. These agree in animacy with their referents, distinguishing animate and inanimate and, for animate, person and number (16a,b). The masculine/feminine distinction normally associated with gender is lacking.

(16) a. sa-   jimyiy-níí   quiivą
3SG.S.ANIM-eat-   3SG.O.ANIM fish
'He is eating the fish.'

b. sa-   jimyiy-rà
3SG.S.ANIM-eat-   O.INAN
'He ate it (a thing).'

There is another set of 40 or more classifiers that is an amalgam of a numeral system and a concordial system. All items which do not have a more specific classifier take the neutral classifier *-ra*. These classifiers take the form of infixes or suffixes (Yagua is a highly polysynthetic language) which are phonologically related to noun roots and semantically reflect distinctions of shape, function or internal arrangement of the referent. Syntactically, they may occur both in predicate nominal constructions (17a) by virtue of having served to derive a noun, and also in noun phrases, where they are attached to numerals (17b), demonstratives (17c) and sometimes descriptive modifiers (17d). Normally, they express concord with the head noun (of the subject NP in the case of predicate nominals), but they can also occur within a sentence independently of the noun to which they refer, serving a discourse anaphoric function. In addition to showing characteristics of both numeral and concordial classifier systems, they tend to obscure distinctions between inflectional and derivational processes, since they are inflected for animacy and number (17c), but also sometimes function as nominalizers. This is also true in Chayahuita (Cahuapanan) and the Huitotoan, Zaparoan and Tucanoan families.

254   DESMOND C. DERBYSHIRE AND DORIS L. PAYNE

(17) a. súduu-bii-   numaa naváá- bii
     ripe- CL.sprout-now   banana-CL.sprout
     'The stalk of bananas is now ripe.'

   b. ray-tááryûy dá-ra-jųy   quínuu jazúcaru
     1SG-buy   two-CL.NEUT-DL kilo   sugar
     'I bought two kilos of sugar.'

   c. naada- júúryįį   ru- nu-jųy   dapúúy-ñuuy
     3DL- arise.early that-CL.SG.ANIM-DL hunt-CL.DL.ANIM
     'Those two hunters arose early.'

   d. jįtyąą-jąą   vánuqui-jąą
     breast-CL.liquid hot-CL.liquid
     'hot milk'

   e. vuyajuuy-nu ninuuy
     ten-CL.pole tree
     'ten trees'

Tucanoan languages have characteristics of two classifier systems: numeral and concordial. The primary distinction is animate vs. inanimate. For animate nouns there is only a gender concordial system. For inanimate nouns there is an integrated numeral and nongender concordial system. Gómez-Imbert's 1982 discussion of Tatuyo suggests that it also has verb-incorporation of nominal roots to some verbs (though not all). It is not clear what range of nouns can be incorporated and thus to what extent it is approaching a (verb-incorporated) classificatory system.

In Tuyuca (Barnes and Malone 1987), there are more than 80 inanimate classifiers that are suffixed to numerals, inanimate demonstratives and nouns, including nominalized verb roots and genitives (18a-g). The semantic categories to which classifiers refer include shape and arrangement, topological, botanical and anatomical features, and a few other domains. Within this system, the concordial function is relatively weak, since nouns rarely occur in normal discourse and, when they do (as newly introduced participants), they usually occur without classifiers. There are, however, some cooccurrences of nouns and numerals or demonstratives which show concordance in the noun phrase and there is also concordance between a subject noun and/or its classifier and the evidential suffix in the verb (Janet Barnes, p.c.). Animate nouns are classified by gender and number, following patterns similar to those described below for Tucano. A fuller description of Tuyuca classifiers by Janet Barnes is included in this volume.

(18) a. hoa-   ri-   boka
     sweep-NOMLZR-CL.cluster   'broom'

   b. kɨ-   ya-   pɨ́
      3SG.MASCPOSS-CL.2D.long   'his (machete)'

   c. sika-da
      one- CL.1D.flexible   'one string'

   d. sõã-   re-   pa
      be.red-NOMLZR.PL-CL.PL.3D   'the red (balls)'

   e. hoo-   pū-   ñ
      banana-CL.leaf-PL   'banana leaves'

   f. yoa-   ri-   yãbɨ́
      be.long-NOMLZR-CL.night   'long night'

   g. ti- gɨ-   wãsõ-gɨ- pɨ́ -re   yãã- pea- yɨ́ra   kɨä
      that-CL.tree waso-CL.tree-LOC-RE fall- rest- EV.3.PL they
      'They (the birds) lit in the waso tree.'

In Tucano (West 1980), there are two principal classes of nouns, animate and inanimate. Animate nouns have inherent gender, masculine or feminine, which is marked on numerals (19c,d) and other modifiers in the noun phrase and also on certain verbal categories. The animate nouns are further divided into two main groupings on the basis of the plural forms they take: a general class of humans, animals and celestial bodies; and the class of kinship terms. The general class is further subdivided into: individual, for which the singular is the morphologically unmarked form; and group, for which the plural is the unmarked form.

There are three main groupings of inanimate nouns based on the plural suffixal forms they take (either *-ri* or *-pa* or, in the case of mass or abstract nouns, the absence of a plural form). The *-pa* class has additional classificatory suffixes which occur with both the singular and plural forms of the noun and there is concord within the noun phrase (19a,e,f); there are five such suffixes which classify nouns on the basis of shape (round, long and straight, extended) and function (pots, vehicles and instruments). Ex. 19b is a special case of the head noun *baka* 'village' being repeated as a free form classifier. There are just a few nouns which function as classifiers in this way.

(19) a. yukɨ́-gɨ pahi-kʰɨ
      tree-CL big- CL   'a big tree'
      (CL = 'long and straight')

b. bāká pahi-rí   bākā
   village big- NOMLZR CL.village   'a big village'

c. diʔ-kí   íbí   cf: piá-rā íbí-á
   one-MASC man 'a man' two-PL man-PL 'two men'

d. diʔ-kó   dúbíó
   one-FEM woman   'a woman'

e. itiá- gí yukí-gí
   three-CL tree-CL   'three trees'

f. bipáriti-se-   pa-gí yukí-pa-gí
   four- PL.NOMLZR-PL-CL tree-PL-CL 'four trees'

Classificatory, number and gender suffixes in Tucano constitute a concordial system, occurring with nouns (including nominalized verb forms), as well as with adjectives, demonstratives, numerals and possessives, either with or without the nouns to which they refer. Verbs have suffixes which agree with the subject of the clause in person, number and animacy and, where they refer to animate entities, in gender also. Both the nominal concordial system and verb agreement system clearly serve an anaphoric discourse function, since in many clauses they constitute the only overt reference to the entity.

Siona and Orejon are other Tucanoan languages that are reported to have numeral and concordial classifier systems (Payne 1987, citing Wheeler (Siona) and Velie (Orejon)), though the system in Siona appears to be less developed (or more moribund?) than that in other Tucanoan languages (David Weber, p.c.).

Arabela (Zaparoan) has primarily a concordial system, but the fact that it has some 30 classifier suffixal forms suggests it should also be considered a numeral system rather than merely a closed grammatical system. The classifiers do not, in fact, occur with numerals, nor with demonstratives or head nouns. They occur on modifying nominals in noun phrases (20a) and on predicate nominals, showing agreement with the subject noun (20c). They also function to derive nouns from verbs (20b; Payne 1987, citing data from Edgar Pastor and Furne Rich).

(20) a. posu- nee   mueruu
        short-CL.metal.INST machete
        'short machete'

     b. taka- tu
        go.up-CL
        'ladder'

   c. nio riuriuquiu seca- jajau
      this egg   small-CL.small.round
      'This egg is small.'

Our Huitotoan data are restricted to three dialects: Ocaina (21, Leach 1963); Bora (22, Thiesen 1975a, 1975b); and 'Huitota' dialect (23, von Kinder). All three have a single set of classifier forms which appear to have both numeral and nongender concordial functions. The concordial system is expressed by suffixal forms that occur on modifying nominals. In some cases it seems that the classifiers are also functioning as nominalizers (21a-c; 23a,b). Ocaina classifiers are infixed to numerals (21d). Bora classifiers are infixed to the numerals 'two' and 'three' and suffixed to nouns (22a), demonstratives (22c) and the numeral 'one' (22b).

(21) a. juhto-ca   tsovaca
       new- CL.cloth dress   'new dress'

    b. ohfo-tya-voco
       head-for-CL.disc   'head pill'

    c. juman-tyá-tsica
       write-for-CL   'typewriter'

    d. jañaan-ca-   h
       two- CL.cloth-two   'two dresses'

(22) a. múciici   'caimito (type of fruit)'
       múciici-pa   'caimito fruit'
       múciici-kwa   'caimito seed'
       múciici-'e   'caimito tree'

    b. tsa-ji
       one-CL.flat.round   'one (e.g., button, coin, dish)'

    c. í'- pa
       this-CL.oblong   'this (a fruit)'

(23) a. moko-na
       green-CL.trunk   'green tree'

    b. naima eicho-ma
       caiman big-CL.ANIM.MASC 'big caiman'

    c. da- keyna
       one-CL.time   'one time'

    d. mena-keyna
       two- CL.time   'two times'

    e. da- ko-   amany
       three-CL.house-three   'three houses'

    f. da- keyna- amany
      three-CL.time-three   'three times'

    Like the Huitotoan languages, Piaroa (Saliban) also seems to have a single set of classifiers which combines numeral and (nongender) concordial functions. There are well over 100 different forms. Classifiers are suffixed to nouns (only plural suffixes can follow them) and all modifiers in the noun phrase (24b). As in Yagua and the Huitotoan languages (cf. 23c-f), they are infixed or suffixed to numerals (24a). Further, as is true throughout the western Amazon region, classifiers correspond etymologically to the last one or two syllables of noun roots. This is also illustrated in 24a. In Piaroa, two different classifiers can occur in a single noun (and its modifiers), but only a small subset of the classifiers can function in the second position. This information comes from Krute-Georges (1983), who refers to the anaphoric function of classifiers, noting that 'full lexical nouns are fairly rare in conversational Piaroa and even rarer in narrative ... in place of nouns stand only modifier plus classifier.'

(24) a. kurodæ hidætetæ   'one machete'
       todære   'two machetes'
       himutewæ'dæ   'five machetes'

    b. kʰoromæ tuʰmæ saræmæ himæ
      other.CL red.CL plate.CL that.CL
      'that other red plate'

3.5 NUMERAL + VERB-INCORPORATED CLASSIFIER SYSTEMS: CHAYAHUITA (CAHUAPANAN) AND WAORANI (UNAFFILIATED). Chayahuita (Cahuapanan) has a single set of classifiers which has both numeral and verb-incorporated functions. There are at least twenty classifiers, many of them derived from body part nouns and the same forms occur both suffixed to numerals (25a,b) and incorporated into verb stems (25c,d) (data from Helen Hart, p.c.). They do not occur with demonstratives. Classifiers are also used to derive nouns from verbs. Like Munduruku (sect. 3.7), Chayahuita classifiers appear to constitute primarily a verb-incorporated system that has developed characteristics of a numeral system (Payne 1987, citing from Helen Hart, p.c.).

(25) a. cara- raya
       three-CL.disc   'three (e.g., plates)'

b. cara- rin
   three-CL.long.flexible   'three (e.g., pieces of string, vine)'

c. a'pë-raya-   t-   ër-   in
   burn-CL.disc-TRANS-INDIC-3S 'He burned (his) face.'

d. i'sho-rin-   in
   peel- CL.long.flex.-3S   'He peeled vines.'

Waorani (unaffiliated), like Chayahuita, has numeral and verb-incorporated classifier systems. Peeke 1973 lists 35 classifiers, all shortened forms of nouns and referring mainly to body parts, but also to plants, natural phenomena (river, sky, territory), house, and a few other items. The classifiers are infixed to numerals (26a) and interrogative words (26c), suffixed to demonstratives (26d) and adjectives (26e), and incorporated into verb stems (26f), in which case they sometimes function as nominalizing affixes (26b). Like Munduruku (sect. 3.7), the Waorani system appears to be primarily a verb-incorporating one which has developed characteristics of numeral systems.

(26) a. ado-ba-   ke
        one-CL.palm.leaf-one   'only one palm leaf'

b. ŏkĭ-   bĕ
   3.make-CL.vine   'string which he will make'

c. kĭ- bĕ-   dŏ
   what-CL.vine-Q   'what vine/string?'

d. ĩbæ̃-bŏka
   this-CL.ear   'this ear'

e. giyæ̃-ka
   small-CL.stone   'small stone'

f. ko-   wa
   pierce-CL.foot   'to pierce foot'

3.6 CONCORDIAL + VERB-INCORPORATED CLASSIFIER SYSTEMS: PARECIS (MAIPURAN ARAWAKAN), AMARAKAERI (HARAKMBET). Rowan and Burgess 1979 give descriptive statements that lead us to conclude that Parecis (a Brazilian Arawakan language) has both gender concordial and verb-incorporated systems, but there are no clear examples of either type of system. Such examples as are available relate only to the gender system, which is restricted to certain nominalizing suffixes (27a,b). These nominalized forms function as modifiers, like relative clauses, and we assume that the head noun, which governs the gender agreement, can be overtly expressed in the sentence. The sources do not, however, provide examples of these nominalized words in phrases or clauses. Verb-incorporated classifiers are reported to refer to concepts such as 'round object', '(certain) species of animals', 'birds' and 'long-stemmed plants'. Their occurrence must be infrequent since, again, there is not a single example given by Rowan and Burgess, even though their description includes three texts totalling 128 sentences.

(27) a. tona-re
        walk-NOMLZR.MASC   'one (male) walking'

     b. tona-lo
        walk-NOMLZR.FEM   'one (female) walking'

Amarakaeri (Harakmbet) is primarily a verb-incorporated classifier system, but the single set of classifiers also functions as a nongender concordial system. In 28b, the same form -po 'CL.round' is found in the verb and in the direct object noun. Verb-incorporated classifiers refer to intransitive subjects, direct objects, or semantic obliques. Classifiers also occur with adjective roots (28d; cf. -pi 'CL.stick' with the same form in 28c, where it occurs in both the verb and the direct object noun). Data are lacking to show whether there is concordance within the noun phrase. The classifier appears clearly to have a derivational function in 28c, where it is attached to another formative wa- to form a noun. It is not clear whether it has a similar function when attached to adjectives. It is reported that classifiers do not nominalize verb roots, but they can be affixed to verb roots that have already been nominalized (Hart 1963; Payne 1987). There are about 50 classifier forms. The reasons why we consider this primarily a verb-incorporated system that has developed concordial characteristics are similar to those stated for Munduruku (see sect. 3.7).

(28) a. o'-ku-   tiri
        he-CL.head-aches
        'He has a headache.'

     b. pera'-po   o'-po-   yakai'e
        rubber-CL.round he-CL.round-kick.try
        'He tries to kick the ball.'

     c. wa-pi   ih-pi-   ka'i
        WA-CL.stick I- CL.stick-make
        'I make an arrow.'

     d. wa-pi-   men-na
        WA-CL.stick-red-ADJ
        'red (e.g. stick, pencil)'

3.7 NUMERAL + CONCORDIAL + VERB-INCORPORATED CLASSIFIER SYSTEMS: MUNDURUKU (TUPI), SOME MAIPURAN ARAWAKAN LANGUAGES (INCLUDING AMUESHA, CAMPA LANGUAGES AND PALIKUR). Munduruku (Tupian) classifiers are suffixed to head nouns (29a-c), numerals (29b) and demonstratives (29c), thus showing concordance in the noun phrase. They may also be incorporated in the verb (29a). The referent of verb-incorporated classifiers is the subject of an intransitive verb or the direct object of a transitive verb. In general, incorporation takes place only when the verb has a past tense form and there is a cooccurring prefix signalling absolutive case (there are also cooccurring subject and object person-marking prefixes).

(29) a. bekitkit ako-   ba   o'-su- ba-dobuxik
        child   banana-CL.arm/long.object 3- REF-CL-find
        'The child found the banana.'

   b. xepxep-'a   wexik- 'a
      two-   CL.round.object potato-CL   'two potatoes'

   c. ija- ba ako-   ba
      this-CL banana-CL   'this banana'

Most of the Munduruku classifiers pertain to body parts (Gonçalves 1987 lists 98 such forms), but there are also others which refer to plants (13 forms), natural elements such as liquid and cloud/smoke (6 forms) and certain culturally significant items (9 forms). Body part and plant classifiers have become more generalized to refer to physical aspects such as shape or items associated with plants; e.g. 'a front part of head, round object' (cf. 29b); *kape-di* 'coffee (drink)' and *kape-da* 'coffee (seed)'; *ako-ba* 'banana (fruit, long object)', *ako-dot* 'banana (stalk)', *ako-'ip* 'banana (plant)' and *ako-dip* 'banana (plantation)'.

Munduruku classifiers occur with numerals and have some of the characteristics of numeral systems. We consider them, however, to constitute primarily a verb-incorporated system which has developed to the stage of also classifying constituents of the noun phrase. The evidence for this lies mainly in the large number of body part classifiers. At some intermediate stage the meaning of these predicate classifiers has shifted from specific body part to some general quality, of the kind that is typical in numeral systems. See Mithun 1986 for fuller discussion on verb-incorporated systems, including specific reference to Munduruku. These arguments in favor of the primacy of a verb-incorporated system for Munduruku, seem to apply also to the systems found in Amarakaeri, Chayahuita and Waorani.

The Peruvian Maipuran Arawakan languages Amuesha and most members of the Campa sub-group (specifically Ashaninca, Caquinte, Machiguenga and Nomatsiguenga) and the Brazilian Arawakan languages Palikur and Waurá have characteristics of all three types of classifier system. The evidence is

inconclusive for determining whether the systems in these languages are
primarily numeral or verb-incorporated.

The Nomatsiguenga data (fairly typical for the Campa languages) show that
the same set of formatives occurs in all three systems: numeral (30a),
nongender concordial (30b) and verb-incorporated (30c). There is also a
gender concordial system with a different set of morphological markers
indicating masculine and feminine gender (e.g. *-ro* 'FEM' in 30a,c and *i-*
'MASC' in 30c; data from Harold Shaver and Mary Ruth Wise, p.c.).

(30) a. pa- tso-   ro
        one-CL.spoken-FEM
        'a word'

     b. soga-tsa   kosho-tsa-   ri
        rope-CL.linear.flexible hard- CL.linear.flex.-ADJ
        'strong rope'

     c. oka i-   ri- sitiga-tsa-   ngi-ro- ka
        this MASC-put-tie- CL.linear.flex.-ASP-FEM-this
        'He will tie him with this (rope).'

The Palikur examples illustrate numeral (31a), gender concordial (31b,c),
nongender concordial (31f) and verb-incorporated (31d) systems. The gender
system in Palikur is quite complex (31b,c), showing agreement (a) within the
noun phrase — the nouns that govern the agreement are not overtly marked but
have inherent gender that governs the overt marking on demonstratives,
numerals and adjectives (demonstratives and numerals do not normally occur
in the same phrase), and (b) between the subject noun phrase and the aspect
suffix in the verb. Palikur verb-incorporated classifiers usually refer to the
shape of an object (31d), plants, or human attributes or body parts, and refer to
either the non-volitional subject of an intransitive verb or to the direct object.
The classifier forms that occur in verbs also occur with prepositions (31e) and
with adjectives (31f). Numeral classifiers appear to be formally distinct from
the verb-incorporated classifiers and for certain classifying characteristics each
numeral has its own unique form (Harold and Diana Green, p.c.). These facts
suggest quite independent origins for numeral and verb-incorporated classifiers
in Palikur.

(31) a. pugunkun-maku   umuh
        six-   CL.pointed.object canoe   'six canoes'
        cf. pugunkun-mabu
                     CL.flat.object
                     -maki
                     CL.large.cluster
                     -a
                     CL.animate.being (also some shapes of objects)

b. ig ner   awayg sukuh-ape-   ne
   he that.MASC man   wash- CL.concave-CONT.MASC
   barew- yo   tumawri
   pretty -DUR.FEM gourd.FEM
   'That man is washing a pretty gourd bowl.'

c. eg no   tino   sukuh-pta-   no
   she that.FEM woman wash- CL.IRREG- CONT.FEM
   barew-ye   epti
   pretty-DUR.MASC chair.MASC
   'She that woman is washing a pretty chair.'

d. su-   sukuh-bet-   as-   ape-   p-   ka
   REPET-wash- CL.particle.shape-CAUS-SIMULT.GROUP-CMP-PASS
   '(The clothes) were all caused to be repeatedly washed all over.'

e. a-bet   murok
   in-CL.particle.shape rain
   'in the rain'

f. eg sukuh-mine   ennetet, in barew-min
   she wash- CL.cylindrical pencil   be clean CL.cylindrical
   'She washed the pencil; it is clean.'

The Waurá verb-incorporated classifier system (data not presented here) is similar to that of Palikur. The gender system is much less complex, like Parecis, being found only in nominalizing suffixes and a few other nouns (Richards 1976).

The gender system in the Peruvian Maipuran languages is also less complex than in Palikur. It appears to be completely lacking in Amuesha (as in Terena, see above); in Piro and the Campa languages it is similar to what is found in Apuriná, being restricted to personal pronouns (including person-marking affixes in the verb), demonstratives and adjectives.

3.8 NO CLASSIFIER SYSTEMS: CARIB, GE, PANO AND TUPÍ-GUARANÍ FAMILIES. The Carib family, along with the Ge, Pano and Tupí-Guaraní families, is listed as not having any kind of classifier system. There is, in fact, evidence of an incipient system of classification in some languages in these families, including Carib. Hixkaryana (Carib; Derbyshire 1985) has verb-incorporation of body parts, which Mithun (1986.383) argues to be a preliminary stage in the development of a classificatory system. In Hixkaryana also, generic possessed noun forms are used in a way similar to that described below for Panare.

The Panare (Carib) data in 32 show the use of generic possessed forms (='classifiers') juxtaposed to obligatorily nonpossessible items of that generic

class: *a-yɨkɨ... kërënëpën* 'your pet ... the dog' (32a). The same construction is
found in the first option shown in 32c: *yu-kon ka'ka* 'my weapon, a bow', but
in this case the word for the specific item 'bow', can also be possessed, as
indicated by the other two possibilities in 32c. In 32b, the word for 'canoe' can
be possessed, but when it is, the nonpossessed form of the word, *kanowa*,
obligatorily follows the possessed form (in the case of 'bow' it may optionally
follow the possessed form, as seen in the last example of 32c). The referential
items for which these constructions are used form a resricted sub-set of
semantic groupings, relating to food, animals, weapons, vehicles ('canoe') (and
possibly a few others, according to Marie-Claude Mattéi-Muller, p.c., who is
the source of our data for Panare; cf. also Muller 1974). This restriction of
semantic domains, together with the limitation to a single grammatical
construction (possession), the variability in the forms that occur (note the three
alternative ways of expressing the same thing in 32c), and the widespread use
of phrasal juxtaposition in Cariban languages all point to this being not yet a
developed classifier system in the language.

(32) a. a-yɨkɨ t-an- ya'   yu (kërënëpën)
      2-pet 1-take-PAST 1   dog
      'I took your pet, the dog.'

    b. yu-kanowae kanowa
      1- canoe   canoe   'my canoe'

    c. yu-kon   ka'ka / yu ka'kae / yu ka'kae ka'ka
      1-weapon bow   / 1 bow   / 1 bow bow
      'my weapon, a bow'/ 'my bow' / 'my bow, a bow'

Panoan languages are also listed as not having classifier systems. As
exemplified by Capanahua (Payne 1987, citing Loos 1963), however, there is
incorporation of body parts in the verb, which could be a preliminary stage in
the development of a classification system (Mithun 1986).

4. CONCLUSION

In Table 1 we summarize the types of classification systems and the
language families in which each type is found to occur. Numeral, concordial
and verb-incorporated classifier systems are all represented. Individual
languages often have at least two of the systems (Munduruku and some
Maipuran Arawakan languages have all three of them); the systems can interact
with each other, sometimes to the point of constituting an integrated single
system. Concordial systems are of two types: gender and nongender. Both
types cooccur in the Arawan, some Maipuran (Campa and Palikur) and
Tucanoan languages, and in Yagua (in which gender is restricted to the ani-
mate-inanimate distinction). Only the nongender type occurs in Amarakaeri,

Amuesha, Huitotoan languages, Piaroa, Munduruku and Arabela (Zaparoan).
Only the gender type occurs in Apurinã, Piro and Parecis.

NUMERAL	CONCORDIAL	VERB INCORPORATION
Yanomaman	Arawan	Pirahã
Tupí	Maipuran Arawakan	Maipuran Arawakan

NUMERAL + CONCORDIAL	NUMERAL + VERB INCORPORATION	CONCORDIAL + VERB INCORPORATION
Peba-Yaguan	Waorani	Harakmbet
Tucanoan	Cahuapanan	Maipuran Arawakan
Zaparoan		
Huitotoan		
Saliban		

**NUMERAL +
CONCORDIAL +
VERB INCORPORATION**

Tupí

Maipuran Arawakan

Table 1. Summary of Amazonian noun classification systems

None of the classifier systems reported here have all the typical
characteristics of canonical numeral systems. In particular, the occurrence of
the classifiers with numerals is somewhat marginal in some languages.
Nevertheless, we have used the term 'modified numeral classifier' system for
such languages because they do have other features of what has come to be
known as a characteristic numeral classifier system. From this perspective,
Sanuma comes closest to a traditional numeral system, even though it is a case
where classifiers do not occur with numerals. There are free forms for
classifiers and there are no features of a concordial system (except for number).
The Sanuma system shows marked similarities to the Jacaltec noun classifier
system described by Craig 1986b, both as to their lexico-syntactic status (free
forms) and their anaphoric function. We note, however, that the set of classifiers in Sanuma is not large (between twenty and thirty) and it does not appear
to be an open-ended set. Further, the Sanuma system differs from the Jacaltec
system in that Sanuma classifiers do not enter into syntactic processes related
to coreferentiality and deletion (i.e. they do not systematically occur in

syntactic structures where they encode information other than their primary classificatory function).   In general, numeral classifiers have not been 'syntacticized' in this way in Amazonian languages. (At least, the sources we have used do not report any such function, but some of these sources give rather meagre information on the classification system and it is possible that not all the facts have been investigated.)

Most languages are highly polysynthetic and in these, classifiers of all three types take the form of affixes (Sanuma and Gavião are exceptions).

There are a number of these languages in which the classifiers have a nominalizing function: these include Amarakaeri, Chayahuita, Huitotoan languages, Waorani, Yagua and Arabela. As Payne 1987 points out, the use of classifiers in some of these languages blurs the distinction between derivational and inflectional processes and, more generally, between the two categories that Dixon 1986 wants to keep separate: grammatical **noun class** (i.e. gender and concordial systems) and lexico-syntactic **noun classification** (i.e. numeral classifier systems).

There are reasonable grounds for a preliminary hypothesis about the origin and development of some of these Amazonian classifier systems.   In Munduruku, which has a single set of classifier forms with all three functions, the verb-incorporated function is dominant and it is largely composed of body-part classifiers. This is *prima-facie* evidence that classifiers originated in that language as verb-incorporated elements and later developed numeral and concordial functions (cf. Mithun 1986). Concordial characteristics appear to have developed from a verb-incorporated system in Amarakaeri, Chayahuita and Waorani. In the Maipuran languages (e.g. Nomatsiguenga), which also have characteristics of all three classifier systems, the evidence in most cases is less conclusive as to which was original or which should be regarded as the primary function in the languages of today. In Palikur, however, the distinct forms in the numeral and verb-incorporated systems suggest that the two developed independently, as two separate systems. More comparative studies within families and higher level groupings are needed, however, in order to trace the development of classifier systems in the area with any degree of confidence.

Finally, we refer again to the discourse-pragmatic factors that influence the use of classifiers. It is clear that classifiers have an important role in the referential system, serving an anaphoric or related function. Most Amazonian languages leave out head nouns and noun phrases unless they are needed to disambiguate or for some other marked pragmatic purpose. Various devices are used to substitute for the noun, including pronouns and person- and/or number-marking affixes. Classifiers also often occur as the only overt marker of a referent. Both gender and nongender concordial affixes often reflect a considerable amount of referential redundancy.

In their discussion of Jacaltec classifiers, Craig 1986b and Ramsay 1985 have drawn attention to another pragmatic function which they call **thematic saliency.** Thematic saliency has to do with the signalling of important discourse topics when they are newly introduced. In Jacaltec, this is accomplished by the use of a marked indefinite construction that contains a classifier, as against use of the unmarked indefinite construction that does not have a classifier. In the case of the written Malay texts discussed by Hopper 1986, highlighting the introduction of a new topic of importance into the discourse is the only function classifiers seem to have. Thematic saliency could well be the explanation in Sanuma for determining the use of what Borgman calls the **specific** and **general** classifiers (illustrated in 1-3). It may be relevant for other languages in the area. More text studies are needed in individual languages.

The significance of verb-incorporated classifiers as a discourse back-grounding device needs to be explored. For these and other types of classifiers, our sources sometimes refer in general terms to a 'discourse function'. There is little evidence, however, that an in-depth study of this function of classifiers has been undertaken for a single language in the Amazon area. This could be another rewarding objective of future research.

NOTES

[1]   The term 'Amazonian' is used in this paper to denote a natural ecological subregion of lowland South America, drained by the Amazon and Orinoco rivers and their tributaries, and including the Guianas, northern Brazil, and eastern portions of Colombia, Ecuador, Peru and Bolivia. For a fuller description of the 'Amazonian area', see Derbyshire and Pullum 1986. We sincerely thank all those who shared with us the data that are found in this paper, and Keith Allan and Marianne Mithun for comments on a previous version. This research was partially supported by NSF Grant No. BNS-8617854, NEH Grant No. RX-20870-87, and the University of Oregon Foundation.

[2]   We make no claims here about larger genetic connections between these families. The reader is referred to Kaufman (this volume) for detailed discussion of the various hypotheses and a conservative assessment of what is actually known about larger affiliations.

[3]   It may be of interest to compare these Amazonian classification systems with some of those reported in neighboring language groups: Quechuan languages do not have classifier systems (David Weber, p.c.); Chibchan languages have numeral classifier systems (cf. Bertoglia Richards 1983); and Toba has what Klein 1979 describes as 'classifiers', but which are forms that primarily signal visual, spatial and temporal perceptions of the speaker in a given speech situation, rather than intrinsic semantic characteristics pertaining to the referent of a noun.

[4]   The transcriptions of vernacular data in this paper are as found in the sources; in only a few cases have we changed glosses, punctuation or diacritics. The following abbreviations are used in the glosses: ADJ adjective marker, ANIM animate, ASP aspectual, AUX auxiliary verb, CAUS causative, CERT certainty, CHAR characteristic, CL classifier, CMP completive, DEM demonstrative, DIR direction, DL dual, DUR durative, EV evidential, EXCL exclusive, FEM feminine, FOC focus, FUT future, GEN general (Sanuma only) or genitive, IMP imperative, IMPF imperfect, INAN inanimate, INCMPL incompletive, INDIC indicative, INST instrument, IP immediate past, LOC locative, MASC masculine, NEG negative, NEUT neutral, NOMLZR nominalizer, NONDUR nondurative, O object, PASS passive, PERF perfect, PL plural, POSS possessive, PURP purpose, Q question marker, REF reference (to absolutive constituent), REPET repetitive, S subject, SG singular, SIMULT simultaneous, SPCFC specific, TRANS transitivizer, 1 first person, 2 second person, 3 third person, 1D one-dimensional, 2D two-dimensional, 3D three-dimensional.

REFERENCES

Aberdour, Catherine. 1985. Referential devices in Apuriná discourse. *Porto Velho Workpapers*. Ed. by David L. Fortune, 43-91. Brasília: Summer Institute of Linguistics.

Adams, Patsy and Stephen Marlett. 1987. Gender agreement in Madija. *Native American languages and grammatical typology. Papers from a Conference at the University of Chicago*. Ed. by Paul D. Kroeber and Robert E. Moore, 1-18. Bloomington: Indiana University Linguistics Club.

Allan, Keith. 1977. Classifiers. *Language* 53.284-310.

Barnes, Janet and Terrell Malone. 1987. El Tuyuca. MS.

Bertoglia Richards, Mafalda. 1983. Los clasificadores numerales en los dialectos cabécares de Ujarrás y Chirripó. *Estudios de Lingüística Chibcha* 2.3-13. San José: Universidad de Costa Rica.

Borgman, Donald. To appear. Sanuma. In Desmond C. Derbyshire and Geoffrey K. Pullum (eds.).

Chapman, Shirley and Desmond C. Derbyshire. To appear. Paumari. In Desmond C. Derbyshire and Geoffrey K. Pullum (eds.).

Craig, Colette. 1986a. Introduction. In Colette Craig (ed.).

Craig, Colette. 1986b. Jacaltec noun classifiers. *Lingua* 70.241-284.

Craig, Colette, ed. 1986. *Noun classes and categorization*. Amsterdam: John Benjamins.

Derbyshire, Desmond C. 1985. *Hixkaryana and linguistic typology*. Dallas: Summer Institute of Linguistics and University of Texas at Arlington.

Derbyshire, Desmond C. and Geoffrey K. Pullum (eds.). 1986. *Handbook of Amazonian languages*, 1. Berlin: Mouton de Gruyter.

Derbyshire, Desmond C. and Geoffrey K. Pullum (eds.). To appear. *Handbook of Amazonian languages*, 2. Berlin: Mouton de Gruyter.

Dixon, Robert M.W. 1986. Noun classes and noun classification in typological perspective. In Colette Craig (ed.), 105-112.

Downing, Pamela. 1986. The anaphoric use of classifiers in Japanese. In Colette Craig (ed.), 345-375.

Ekdahl, Muriel and Nancy Butler. 1979. *Aprenda Terêna*, Vol. 1. Brasília: Summer Institute of Linguistics.

Gómez-Imbert, Elsa. 1982. *De la forme et du sens dans la classification nominale en tatuyo*. Universite Sorbonne doctoral dissertation.

Gonçalves, Cristina Helena R.C. 1987. *Concordância em Mundurukú*. Campinas: Editora da UNICAMP.

Hart, Raymond E. 1963. Semantic components of shape in Amarakaeri grammar. *Anthropological Linguistics* 5.9.1-7.

Hopper, Paul J. 1986. Some discourse functions of classifiers in Malay. In Colette Craig (ed.), 309-325.

Kinder, Leopoldo von. 1936. *Gramatica y vocabulario de la lengua huitota. (Boletin de Estudios Historicos, Suplemento No. 4.)* Pasto: Departamento de Nariño, Republica de Colombia.

Klein, Harriet E. Manelis. 1979. Noun classifiers in Toba. *Ethnolinguistics: Boas, Sapir and Whorf revisited*. Ed. by M. Mathiot, 85-95. The Hague: Mouton.

Koop, Gordon. 1976. *Deni person affixes*. Arquivo Lingüístico No. 031. Brasília: Summer Institute of Linguistics.

Krute-Georges, Laurence. 1983. Metaphor, morphology, and the organization of classifier systems. MS.

Leach, Ilo. 1963. Outline of Ocaina syntax. *Informaçion de Campo*, No. 134. Peru: Instituto Lingüístico de Verano.

Loos, Eugene. 1963. Capanahua narration structure. *Studies in literature and language* 4.699-742. Austin: The University of Texas.

Mithun, Marianne. 1986. The convergence of noun classification systems. In Colette Craig (ed.), 379-397.

Moore, Dennis. 1984. *Syntax of the language of the Gavião Indians of Rondônia, Brasil.* The City University of New York doctoral dissertation.

Mufwene, Salikoko S. 1980. Bantu class prefixes: inflectional or derivational? *Chicago Linguistic Society* 16.246-58.

Muller, Marie-Claude. 1974. El sistema de posesion en la lengua panare. *Antropológica* 38.3-14.

Payne, Doris. 1986. Noun classification in Yagua. In Colette Craig (ed.), 113-131.

Payne, Doris. 1987. Noun classification in the Western Amazon. *Language Sciences* 9.21-44 *(special issue): Comparative linguistics of South American Indian languages,* edited by Mary Ritchie Key.

Peeke, Catherine. 1973. *Preliminary grammar of Auca. (Summer Institute of Linguistics Publications in Linguistics 39.)* Norman, Oklahoma: Summer Institute of Linguistics and the University of Oklahoma.

Pickering, Wilbur N. 1973. Command in Apurina. MS.

Pickering, Wilbur N. 1977. Relativicacão em Apurinã. *Serie Lingüística* 7. Brasília: Summer Institute of Linguistics.

Powlison, Esther and Paul Powlison. 1958. El sistema numérico del yagua (pebano). *Tradición: Revista Peruana de Cultura* 8.21.69-74. Cuzco, Peru.

Ramsay, Violeta. 1985. Classifiers and referentiality in Jacaltec. *Proceedings of the First Annual Pacific Linguistics Conference,* 289-312. Eugene: University of Oregon.

Richards, Joan. 1976. Waura verb structure. MS. (Portuguese version: 1988. A estrutura verbal Waurá. *Serie Lingüística* 9.2. Brasília: Summer Institute of Linguistics.)

Rodrigues, Aryon D. 1982. A família Aruák. *Porantim.* Brasília: Conselho Indigenista Missionário.

Rowan, Orland and Eunice Burgess. 1979. Parecis grammar. MS. (Portuguese version: *Gramática Parecís.* Arquivo Lingüística 146. Brasília: Summer Institute of Linguistics.)

Thiesen, Wesley. 1975a. El sistema numérico del bora (huitoto). *Datos Etnolingüísticos*, 1. Peru: Instituto Lingüístico de Verano.

Thiesen, Wesley. 1975b. Un informe breve de la morfología bora. *Datos Etnolingüísticos*, 18. Peru: Instituto Lingüístico de Verano.

West, Birdie. 1980. *Gramática popular del Tucano*. Bogota: Instituto Lingüístico de Verano, Ministerio de Gobierno, Republica de Colombia.

Zubin, David and Klaus M. Köpcke. 1986. Gender and folk taxonomy: the indexical relation between grammatical and lexical categorization. In C. Craig (ed.), 139-180.

Classifiers in Tuyuca

Janet Barnes

1. INTRODUCTION

The Tuyuca[1] language of Colombia has a rich classifier (CL) system pertaining to the world of the inanimate, but has only three animate classifiers. In this paper the Tuyuca classifiers are first listed according to their semantic categories. Following that, the regular and irregular plural forms are presented, and the distinction between classifiers and nouns is explored (Section 2). Both inanimate and animate classifiers occur suffixed to numerals, demonstrative adjectives, genitives, nouns and nominalized verbs (Sections 3 and 4). Classifiers also play an anaphoric role in discourse (Section 5).

According to Allan (1977.285), classifiers '(a) occur as morphemes in surface structure under specifiable conditions; (b) they have meaning, in the sense that a classifier denotes some salient perceived or imputed characteristic of the entity to which an associated noun refers (or may refer).' However, in Tuyuca the 'associated noun' of Allan's definition is not necessarily expressed explicitly in the sentence or discourse in which the classifier occurs; nevertheless, the referent is understood from context or by gesture. Noun phrases which include both the referent and a descriptive word containing the classifier are rare in natural speech, as are phrases made up of two descriptive words each containing the same classifier.

According to Allan's four types of classifier languages (Allan 1977.286), Tuyuca is primarily a 'numerical classifier language', so called because classifiers in such languages occur in expressions of quantity, as well as in anaphoric or deictic expressions. In Tuyuca, classifiers also occur in other adjective-like expressions. Tuyuca also has some characteristics of a concordial system, as all the references to the same item, whether nouns, stems with classifiers suffixed to them, or suffixes on certain verbal categories, agree in at least one of the following: animacy, person, number and/or gender.

Classifiers in Tuyuca always occur as suffixes. When a classifier is suffixed to a root or stem, the result is a single phonological word. (The phonological word in Tuyuca is defined as an utterance containing two or more syllables and having one and only one syllable with high pitch.) The classifiers presented in this paper never occur as phonological words; they are always suffixes.

By contrast, morphemes that are referred to in this paper as nouns do occur as phonological words. A subset of the nouns in Tuyuca, in addition to functioning as phonological words, can also be suffixed to the same roots or stems to which classifiers are suffixed, forming a single phonological word with that root or stem. In this paper such nouns are referred to as 'nouns which may function as classifiers'. For example, *-ri* is the classifier for 'pot-shaped item', and *wesé* is the noun for 'field'. The word *wesé* 'field' is a noun which may function as a classifier, and may be suffixed to roots such as *biki* 'old', and *ati* 'this', in the same way as a classifier:

biki-ri	biki-wese[2]
'old pot'	'old field'
ati-ri	ati-wesé
'this pot'	'this field'

In general, each physical object in the Tuyuca world is associated with one and only one classifier. Even so, there are instances when a noun is used in place of its corresponding classifier. For example, one might choose to use the word 'head' in the classifier slot of a given construction rather than using the corresponding classifier that denotes a saliently three dimensional object.

Generally, items which are new to the culture are quite readily assigned a classifier, although at times a loan word is used as both noun and classifier (ex: *bésa* 'table' from Spanish *mesa*). Only occasionally will a Tuyuca speaker search around, unsure as to the classifier he should assign to a new item in the culture.

Inanimate classifiers occur in singular form when referring to one, two or three items, and in plural form when referring to four or more items. The grammatical categories to which inanimate classifiers may be suffixed are listed below. Note that all of the categories are non-verbal constructions.

1. nouns
2. demonstratives
3. numerals
4. genitives
5. nominalized verbs

The three animate classifiers denote 'masculine singular', 'feminine singular' and 'plural'. Animate entities pluralize when referring to two or more animate objects, rather than at four like the inanimate classifiers. Animate classifiers are found suffixed to the same grammatical categories as the inanimate classifiers, one difference being that the verbs are not suffixed first by a nominalizer. Rather the animate classifiers themselves function as nominalizers of the verbs.

2. INANIMATE CLASSIFIER CATEGORIES

The inanimate classifiers are divided into ten semantic categories: shape, collection, arrangement, anatomical, botanical, geographical, container, manufactured item, consistency and time. The term 'collection' is here used to refer to a group of items as a whole, whether or not the items are bound together in some way. The term 'arrangement' is used to mean that the item(s) so classified was not originally in its present configuration, but rather has, by deliberate action or otherwise, come to be in that configuration. The classifier groups are presented in Tables 1 through 9.[3]

Singular	Plural	Gloss:	examples
		Saliently 1D:[4]	
-da	*-dári*	FLEXIBLE:	string, thread,a hair
-wakã[5]	*-wakári*	RIGID:	splinter, dart, nail
		Saliently 2D:	
-ro/-rõ	*ø*[6]	FLEXIBLE:	cloth, cassava bread
-pĩ	*-pírĩ*	RIGID, FREE:	split firewood, piece of board, machete
-pãbã́	*-pãbárĩ*	CONNECTED:	door, hand, foot
		Saliently 3D:	
-póro	*-póri*	CYLINDRICAL:	banana, ear of corn
-pe	*-péri*	NON-SPHERICAL:	seed, pebble
-píõrõ	*-píõrĩ*		egg or heart shaped
-ga/-gã	*-pa*	GENERALLY SPHERICAL:	ball, head, calf of leg, toe, finger, outboard motor
-ki	*-kíri*	ALL SURFACES FLAT:	coin, button, aspirin, brick

Table 1. Shape classifiers

Singular	Plural	Gloss: examples
-ba	*-bári*	pair: earrings, shoes, woven leg bands
-bādá	*-bādárī*	bits: flying ash, crumbs
-bākā'	*-bāké*	object(s) that belong to a person or to another object
-bĕ	*-bérī*	fire
-boká	*-bokári*	small bundle of long viny things
-bu	*-búri*	animate group: tribe, herd
-butú	*-butúri*	hanging cluster: lemons, grapes
-dotó	*-dotóri*	large bundle: firewood, cane
-dúriro	*-dúriri*	disorderly pile: rocks, vines
-kĕ	*-kérī*	package of small thing wrapped up and tied: fishhooks, matches
-pokáro	*-poká(ri)*	pieces: wood chips, coarse manicoc flour
-putí	*-putíri*	small box of little things: fishhooks, matches
-sa	*-sári*	package of edible ants wrapped up in leaves

Table 2. Collection classifiers

Singular	Plural	Gloss: examples
-betó	*-betóri*	coil: vine (by extension: ring, tire)
-boró	*-borí*	object damaged through use or misuse: basket, clothes, canoe
-biriá	*-biriári*	spherical from previous configuration: cloud
-kāyīró	*-kāyīrí*	badly dented object
-kuyúro	*-kuyúri*	head after the hair has been shaved off, or nearly so
-kírŏ	*-kírī*	long layers or rows: clouds, waves
-sasíro	*-sasíri*	bristled: messed up hair, crest of bird
-sitía	*-sitíri*	crumpled mass: cloth, bark
-sísírŏ	*-sísírí*	wrinkled, gathered, pleated
-tĕrŏ	*-tĕrī*	cross (i.e., two items tied together to form a cross)
-tūdū	*-tūdūrī*	rolled up: scroll
-wogoró	*-wogorí*	bark, or other substance, that is not clinging as tightly as it should
-yawíro	*-yawíri*	twisted, deformed
-yirírō	*-yiríri*	object not properly closed: house, box with lid
-yibiá	*-yibiári*	spherical, shaped by hand: clay

Table 3. Arrangement classifiers

Singular	Plural	Gloss: examples
-bõ	*-bṍrĩ*	arm (including the hand)
-dasí	*-dasíri*	wounded or infected feet causing a limp
-di	*-díri*	flesh (or meat)
-dubú	*-dubúri*	appendage: arm, leg
-kíro	*-kírori*	crest
-sáro	*-sári*	horn (by extension: horn-shaped)
-sawéro	*-sawéri*	ear of animal (by extension: ear shaped)
-siriá	*-siriári*	lump: swelling, hive
-siriá	*-siriári*	joint
-yuriró	*-yurirí*	permanent limp

Table 4. Anatomical classifiers

Singular	Plural	Gloss: examples
-dipí	*-dipíri*	branch (by extension: comb)
-gi/-gĩ	*-yukí*	tree or stick (by extension: hammock, fishnet, pencil)
-ke	*-kéri*	palm leaf
-kobéa	*-kobepá*	joint or knot (by extension: a tied knot, elbow, knee)
-kóro	*-kóri*	flower
-popéro	*-popéri*	center part: heart of tree, corncob
-pũ	*-pṹrĩ*	leaf (by extension: paper)
-satí	*-satíri*	bush or any other multi-trunk plant
-sãdá	*-sãdárĩ*	unopened leaf
-tõ	*-tṍrĩ*	stalk of bananas
-wõ	*-wṍrĩ*	palm tree

Table 5. Botanical classifiers

Singular	Plural	Gloss: examples
-bǎ	-bári	path, river
-bedó	-bedóri	a nearly circular bend in a river
-bóa	-bóari	flat area that floods when the river rises
-dīyá	-dīyárī	side of river (by extension: of person, cassette tape)
-du	-dúri	an area where 'umar'i' palms have been planted
-dudí	-dudíri	bend in a river (by extension: arc-like path taken in follow-the-leader type dance)
-gi/-gī	-īñyukí	hill
-ko	-kóri	a wide place in a river
-kotó	-kotóri	previous house site or village site
-kutíro	-kutíri	bed of river (by extension: bottom of canoe)
-páro	(not used)	patio (traditionally the area around the long-house that is cleared of grass)
-pōrérō	-pōrérī	projection
-tabé	-tabéri	temporary place; area where large trees do not grow
-táro	-tári	body of water: puddle, lake
-tatá	-tatári	an area where only one kind of palm grows
-tutí	-tutíri	geologically stratified area (by extension: book)
-tidí	-tidíri	steep incline (by extension: wall)
-wo	-wóri	section of a garden, area of jungle replete with leaf cutter ant holes

Table 6. Geographical classifiers

Singular	Plural	Gloss: examples
-pi	-piséri	deep basket
-po	-póri	pocket, bag
-rí	-párí	pot
-sidá	-sidári	recipient that is more or less flat
-tibá	-tibári	box
-wa	-páwa	shallow container with wide mouth: gourd, cup, basket
-wí	-páwí	item with hollow interior: blowgun, canoe, balsam tree (by extension: pipe, shotgun, car, airplane)

Table 7. Container classifiers

Singular	Plural	Gloss: examples
-ka	*-kári*	row of like things joined together: fish trap, fence
-píró	*-pírí*	bench carved from a log
-ro/-ró	/⁶	device or machine: knot, stove
-sodóro	*-sodóri*	painted or woven design
-wi	*-wiséri*	building

Table 8. Manufactured item classifiers

Singular	Plural	Gloss
		Consistency
-kebéro	*-kebéri*	consistency of mud
		Time
-to	*-tóri*	time of an event, season
-túro	*-túri*	regular time of doing something

Table 9. Miscellaneous classifiers

2.1 PLURALS OF INANIMATE CLASSIFIERS. The plurals of the classifiers are formed in various ways. The majority are formed by the addition of the suffix *-ri/-rí* 'inanimate plural'. With the exception of *-kíro* 'crest', those that terminate in *-ro/-ró* in the singular, replace *-ro/-ró* with *-ri/-rí* in the plural.

Three classifiers have suppletive forms in the plural:

-ga	*-pa*	'3D, generally spherical'
-gí	*-yukí*	'tree'
-gí	*-ídyukí*	'hill'

One of the classifiers has only a singular form: *-ro/-ró* 'device'. When the plural of this classifier would normally be required, the plural of the specific item referred to is used instead.

sika-ró
one -CL.device
'one device (such as a sewing machine)'

peé sutí   hee-ré
lots clothes sew-PL.NOM
'lots of sewing machines'

The remaining irregular forms are presented in Table 10.

Singular	Plural	Gloss
-kobéa	-kobepá	'joint'
-bãká	-bãké	'object(s)'
-wi	-wiséri	'building'
-pi	-piséri	'deep basket'
-ri	-pári	'pot'
-wɨ	-páwɨ	'hollow interior'
-wa	-páwa	'shallow container'

Table 10. Irregular plurals

The form -kobéa may have been -kobé-ga at one time, indicating that -kobé may have been a classifier suffixed by the three-dimensional general classifier -ga/-pa in both the singular and the plural. Comparative studies as well as dialect differences among Tuyuca villages indicate that /g/ is being elided in some environments.

Whether or not the -pa in the plural of the last three forms listed above is diachronically related to the plural three-dimensional (general) classifier -pa is open to speculation. If so, this might indicate that these items have historically been viewed as saliently three-dimensional.

2.2 DISTINCTION BETWEEN NOUNS AND CLASSIFIERS. As was discussed in section 1, there is a subset of nouns that function as classifiers. Some of the nouns are presented in Table 11.

bireko	day
kaseró	skin, bark
kopé	hole
sopé	doorway
wesé	field
yãbí	night
yepá	earth

Table 11. Nouns/classifiers

These nouns, though they may occur as phonological words, may also occur suffixed to demonstratives, numerals, etc., in the same way that classifiers are suffixed. None of the classifiers in Tables 1 through 9 denotes the salient characteristics of these nouns which may function as classifiers. For example, no classifier denotes the salient characteristics of a doorway. Therefore, the word *sopé* 'doorway' occurs suffixed to demonstratives, numerals, etc., to indicate 'one doorway', 'this doorway', etc.

sik á-sope   ati -sopé
one -doorway   this-doorway

This is not generally the case with other nouns, such as 'banana'. To say 'one banana', generally the three-dimensional shape classifier *-póro* is used:

siká-poro
one -CL.cylindrical

However, it is not incorrect to suffix the specific noun, although in such a situation both the root and the suffixed noun are stressed, indicating that the 'suffix' is neither a classifier nor a noun which may function as a classifier.

siká-hoó   -poro
one -banana-CL.cylindrical
'one banana'

atí -hoó   -poro
this-banana -CL.cylindrical
'this banana'

Some classifiers are morphologically similar to the nouns which share all or some of the same meaning components. Some of these noun/classifier pairs are presented in Table 12. The differences between the members of these pairs in phonological structure and semantics, as well as analogy from root/suffix pairs elsewhere in the language indicate that the classifiers in Table 12 are indeed suffixes rather than noun roots. This is discussed in further detail in the following paragraphs.

Noun root		Classifier suffix	
bãã́	path	*-bã*	path, river
diı́	meat, flesh	*-di*	meat, flesh
hoó	banana	*-ho*	banana
koóro	flower	*-kóro*	flower
piı́	deep basket	*-pi*	deep basket
pṹũ	leaf	*-pũ*	leaf
toó	anaphoric time or place	*-to*	time of an event
waá	gourd	*-wa*	shallow container with a wide mouth
wiı́	building	*-wi*	building
poká	coarse manioc flour	*-poká*	pieces: wood chips, coarse manioc flour
wãbố	arm, including hand	*-bõ*	arm, including hand

Table 12. Nouns and corresponding classifiers

The pairs in Table 12, with the exception of *poká/-poká*, are phonologically distinct. For example, the first two phonemic syllables of the noun *koóro* 'flower' constitute a long, rising phonetic vowel ['kŏ·rò]. The first syllable in the classifier *-kóro* 'CL.flower' is short, and is only stressed[9] when the rules governing stress assign it to that morpheme.[10]

> siká-koro   pia-kóro
> 'one flower'   'two flowers'

The same is true for pairs such as *piı́* ['pĭ·] 'basket' and *-pi* 'CL.basket':

> siká-pi   pia-pí
> 'one basket'   'two baskets'

Some of the nouns in Table 12 differ semantically from their corresponding classifiers in that the classifier may be more general in meaning than the noun. For example, the noun *bãã́* 'path' refers only to paths on land (and roads and highways by extension), whereas *-bã* 'CL.path, river' may refer to a land path or a river. The noun *wáa* refers only to a gourd, whereas the classifier *-wa* refers to any shallow container which, like a gourd split in half lengthwise, has a wide mouth.

The fact that some classifiers correspond to nouns of a similar phonological shape is analogous to root/suffix pairs in verbs. For example, many verb roots, among them *sáá* 'to enter' and *yaá* 'to eat', appear in shortened form as suffixes to other verb roots:

    basá -sã   -yira
    dance-enter-3PL.PAST.EV
    'they entered the house dancing'

    ãbá   -ya -ki
    search-eat -3M.SG.PRESENT.EV
    'he looks for (food) and eats'

3. DISTRIBUTION OF INANIMATE CLASSIFIERS

As mentioned in section 1, inanimate classifiers may be suffixed to 1) nouns, 2) demonstratives, 3) numerals, 4) genitives, and 5) nominalized verbs. In this section each of these categories is discussed.[11]

3.1 INANIMATE CLASSIFIERS SUFFIXED TO NOUNS. Nouns do not require classifiers; however classifiers may be suffixed to nouns in order to specify part of a whole:

    hoó   -tõ
    banana-CL.stalk
    'banana stalk'

    hoó   -pũ
    banana-CL.leaf
    'banana leaf'

    hoó   -poro
    banana -CL.cylindrical
    'banana'

Classifiers may also be suffixed to nouns to show the configuration of the object referred to by the noun:

    yãké -da
    beads-CL.1D.flexible
    'necklace'

    yãké -beto
    beads-CL.coil
    'arm band of beads'

Classifiers may be suffixed to the dummy noun *opá* when the features of the classifier are the only features being referred to:

opá   -bã
dummy.noun-CL.path
'unspecified stream'

3.2 INANIMATE CLASSIFIERS SUFFIXED TO DEMONSTRATIVES. Classifiers may
be suffixed to demonstrative roots and to the root *ape-* 'other/another'. The
singular demonstrative roots and *ape-* 'other/another' require a classifier (or a
noun functioning as a classifier); the plural demonstrative roots do not. The
demonstratives are presented in Table 13.

		Singular	Plural
Exophoric	'this'	*ati-*	*ate*
	'that'	*i-*	*iye*
Anaphoric	'that'	*ti-*	*tee*

Table 13. Demonstrative adjectives

In conversation, constructions with exophoric demonstratives refer to items
that are visible, or that would be visible if one looked outside or if nothing were
in the way:

ati -wí
this-CL.building
'this house'

i   -wó
that-CL.palm
'that palm'

ate   -dudí   -ri
those-CL.bend-PL
'those bends (in the river)'

Constructions using anaphoric demonstratives or *ape-* 'other/another' refer to
something which has been referred to, however obliquely, in the course of the
discourse:

ape -dĩyá
other-CL.side
'other side'

ti -wí
that-CL.building
'that house (that I just mentioned)'

3.3 INANIMATE CLASSIFIERS SUFFIXED TO NUMERALS. Numerals are obligatorily suffixed by a classifier or a noun functioning as a classifier.

Although numerals beyond four (4) can be elicited, in actual conversation they are rarely used. Rather, the term 'a lot' is used.

sika-dá
one -CL.1D.flexible
'one string (or rope,...)'

pɨa -dá
two-CL.1D.flexible
'two strings (or ropes,...)'

itiá -da
three -CL.1D.flexible
'three strings (or ropes,...)'

bapári[12] -da   -ri
four   -CL.1D.flexible-PL
'four strings (or ropes,...)'

peé-da   -ri
lots -CL.1D.flexible -PL
'lots of strings (or ropes,...)'

In general, the referent of the classifier in a numeral construction is clear from the context; however there are situations where the referent must be mentioned in a noun phrase with the numeral construction, as in the following listing of items that were purchased:

sapátu sika-bá,[13]   sirúra   pɨa-ró,
shoes one -CL.pair trousers two-CL.2D.flexible
    pũũgɨ   pɨa-gɨ
hammock two-CL.tree, hammock,...
'one pair of shoes, two pair of trousers, two hammocks'

3.4 INANIMATE CLASSIFIERS SUFFIXED TO GENITIVES. Genitives are formed by suffixing first the genitive marker -ya/-ye 'sg./pl. genitive' to the noun, noun phrase or pronoun which refers to the possessor, and then suffixing a classifier which refers to the thing possessed. The only exception to this is in the first person singular, in this case the pronoun is omitted and the genitive appears as a stem: *yáa/yée* 'first person singular genitive'.[14]

bāríya-ya   -da
María -SG.GEN -CL.1D.flexible
'Mary's string'

kɨ́[15]   paki -ya   -wɨ
3M.SG father -SG.GEN -CL.hollow.interior
'his father's canoe (car, blowgun,...)'

bɨ́ -ye   -pābā   -ri
2SG -PL.GEN -CL.2D.rigid -PL
'your doors'

yáa   -boka
1SG.GEN -CL.bundle
'my bundle (broom,...)'

3.5 INANIMATE CLASSIFIERS SUFFIXED TO NOMINALIZED VERBS. When a classifier is suffixed to a verb that has been nominalized with -ri/-re 'singular/ plural nominalizer', the resulting word functions as a relative clause.[16]

pai -rí   -sawero   wáa-yiro
be.big -SG.NOM -CL.ear.shaped go -INAN.PAST.EV
'An ear-shaped area that was big was left
(in the cassava bread after a piece had been torn out).'

yɨ̃ká   dííkɨti   -ri   -ga   dɨ̃́-yiro
calf.of.leg flesh.having-SG.NOM -CL.3D.general be -INAM.PAST.EV
'The leg was the one that had had the fleshy calf. (i.e., not the shriveled leg).'

ãyã́ bako -á   -ri   -gɨ   dií
snake bitten-recently-SG.NOM -CL.stick flesh
   yãá-hõã   -yiro
   fall -completely-INAM.PAST.EV
'The flesh had come completely off the leg that had been bitten by the snake.'
(The calf-less leg had the appearance of a stick.)

ti -bã   -ré ãdõ -pé kɨ́   atí -a   -ri   -bã   -pɨ
that-CL.path-RE here -TC 3M.SG come-recently -SG.NOM -CL.path-LOC
   hoá   -wa-yigɨ
   start.down.path-go -3M.SG.PAST.EV
'He started down that path over here that he had recently come on.'

3.6 CLASSIFIERS SUFFIXED TO CLASSIFIERS. While classifiers may be suffixed to classifiers, semantic considerations do not allow the suffixing of very many classifiers to other classifiers.

ati -gɨ̃   -dɨpɨ
this -CL.tree -CL.branch
'the branch of this tree'

4. ANIMATE CLASSIFIERS

The three categories of animate classifiers: masculine singluar, feminine singular, and plural, also signal tense (see Table 14). The present animate classifiers are found suffixed to all five of the grammatical categories listed in section 1; the past and future animate classifiers are found suffixed only to verbs. The animate classifiers, when suffixed to categories other than nouns, function as nominalizers. When animate classifiers are suffixed to any category except for verbs, irregularities occur. These will be described in the following sections.

	Masculine	Feminine	
	Singular	Singular	Plural
Present	-gi/-gɨ	-go/-gŏ	-ra/-rã̃
Past	-rígɨ	-rígo	-ríra
Future	-ɨ́dɨ	-ŏdo	-ádara

Table 14. Animate classifiers

4.1 ANIMATE CLASSIFIERS SUFFIXED TO NOUNS. Singular animate classifiers are suffixed to the name of an animal only when it is desirable to make explicit the animal's sex. The following forms were elicited:

aké   'monkey'
aké-go   'female monkey'

wekɨ   'tapir (bull)'
wekɨ-go   'female tapir, (cow)'

The plural morpheme used with animals is, with rare exceptions, -*a* 'animate plural', rather than the animate plural classifier -*ra*.

aké-a   'monkeys'
wekɨ-á   'tapirs'

Singulars and plurals of terms referring to human beings are highly irregular; these remain to be studied in depth.

4.2 ANIMATE CLASSIFIERS SUFFIXED TO DEMONSTRATIVES. One would expect that the exophoric demonstratives in Table 13 could be combined with the animate suffixes; for the feminine forms, that is in fact what occurs:

ati-gó	'this female'
i-gó	'that female'

However, the following expected masculine singular forms are ungrammatical:

*ati-gí	'this male'
*i-gí	'that male'

Instead, the masculine singular forms are:

ãdí	'this male'
ídĩ	'that male'

The plural forms follow from these latter forms by the addition of the suffix -*a* 'animate plural':

ãdíã	'these people (or animals)'
ídĩã	'those people (or animals)'

The anaphoric demonstrative of Table 13 is not used with animate classifiers. For anaphoric reference to animate entities the personal pronouns are used instead.

4.3 ANIMATE CLASSIFIERS SUFFIXED TO NUMERALS. As mentioned in section 3.3, the root for the number 'one' is *sika-*. However, the masculine and feminine singular forms are irregular:

sīkí	'one male'
sīkó	'one female'

The animate forms for 'two' and 'three' are irregular in that the animate plural classifier is nasalized:

pia-rã́	'two people (or animals)'
itiá-rã	'three people (or animals)'

The numeral four does not take a classifier when referring to four animate beings: *bapári*.

As discussed in section 3.3 the root for 'lots (inanimate)' is *peé*. When referring to more than four animate beings, the word *paí* 'lots (animate)' is normally used. However, if the person is recounting his many children or the number of relatives that he has, he indicates the specific number on his fingers or his fingers and toes. (Those who have learned some Spanish freely use the Spanish numbers.)

4.4 ANIMATE CLASSIFIERS SUFFIXED TO GENITIVES. The genitive construction for animate classifiers is identical to the construction for inanimate classifiers (see section 3.4) except that the singular genitive is used for both singluar and plural.

bãríya-ya   -gɨ
Mary -SG.GEN-CL.M.SG
'Mary's male creature (dog, bird, ...)'

bɨ́ -ya   -go
your-SG.GEN-CL.F.SG
'your female creature (dog, hen, ...)'

bɨ́ -ya   -ra
your-SG.GEN-CL.ANIM.PL
'your creatures'

yáa   -gɨ
1.SG.GEN-CL.M.SG
'my male creature'

4.5 ANIMATE CLASSIFIERS SUFFIXED TO VERBS. As with inanimate classifiers, when animate classifiers are suffixed to verbs, they result in words that function as relative clauses. The verb stem may be inflected for aspect or mood before one of the animate classifiers from Table 14 is added.

basoká yaa-gɨ   dɨ́ɨ-yigɨ
people eat -CL.M.SG be -3M.SG.PAST.EV
'He was one who eats people.'

koó bãdɨ́ dɨ́ɨ-bɨ -a   -rigɨ
her husband be -FRUS-RECENT.PAST-CL.M.SG.PAST
  utɨ́-ko   -pɨtɨa -yigɨ
  cry-movement-return-3M.SG.PAST.EV
'The one who recently had frustratedly been her husband returned crying.'

yɨɨ húpda-ye   bué -ɨdɨ   -bɛ̃dã wáa-wɨ
1.SG hupda-language study-CL.M.SG.FUTURE-with go -1,2PAST.EV
'I went with the man who is going to study the Hupda language.'

5. USE OF CLASSIFIERS

I have observed that in general the referent of the entity referred to by a classifier is not mentioned in each sentence that contains the classifier unless the statement might be unclear without it. Thus, noun phrases as such are not common in Tuyuca. One example which illustrates this occurs in a short discourse of only 14 sentences. The topic of the discourse is a small shell that had holes drilled in it and was used as a musical instrument. At the time of the recording of the discourse, the snail shell had already been passed around, the speaker was holding it, he was going to be playing a tune on it, and as he spoke into the recorder his first reference to the shell was *ati-gá* 'this 3D object'. He continued to describe its use in dances, and compared its sound with *ti-gá* 'that 3D object', referring to the type of shell that used to be used. In the 14 sentences there are nine occurrences of the classifier *-ga* '3D object'. The only time that the name of the snail shell was used was when he told me what to say when I played the recording for my friends:

> bií -ro   bií -wɨ   ati -gá
> like -ADV like-INAM.PAST.EV   this -CL.3D.general
>   sɨ̃ -gã   hɨ̃ -wa
>   snail -CL.3D.general say-IMP
> 'Say, "This snail was like that."'

In this example the anaphoric function of classifiers is quite evident. The anaphoric function of classifiers in Amazonian languages in general is emphasized in the introduction of the paper by Derbyshire and Payne (this volume).

When no anaphoric referent is possible, such as in the 600 illustrative sentences that were written by a Tuyuca for a Tuyuca-Spanish school dictionary, noun phrases freely occur. For example:

> suti -ró   bãbã -ró   -rẽ
> clothes-CL.2D.flexible new -CL.2D.flexible   -re
>   ãyú -rõ   tɨsa ´-ga
>   good-ADV   like -1.PRESENT.EV
> 'I like the new article of clothing.'

Though detailed studies on the function of classifiers in Tuyuca discourse have yet to be undertaken, it may be that the use of classifiers contributes to the low frequency of full noun phrases, and expanded noun phrases in particular (cf. Payne 1987.39 for some similar ideas).

6. CONCLUSION

Tuyuca is a numerical classifier language with a weak concordial system. The more than 90 classifiers, supplemented by many nouns that function as classifiers, are suffixed to numerals, demonstrative adjectives, nouns, nominalized nouns and genitives. Except for the suffixation to genitives, these are all features which Payne 1987 describes as characteristic of a number of other languages in the Western Amazon area. Semantically there are ten categories of classifiers in Tuyuca. These include some categories discussed by

Allan (1977.297) such as shape and arrangement. Botanical and geographical categories, which are perhaps not highly characteristic of numeral classifier systems in many other areas of the world, are also well attested in Tucanoan languages.

NOTES

[1]   The Tuyuca language is spoken by some 800-1000 people in Colombia and Brazil who live in small villages along the Papurí and Tiquié Rivers and their tributaries. Tuyuca is a Tucanoan language of the Eastern Tucanoan branch. It is basically SOV, but allows alternate orders of sentence constituents. The Tuyuca classifier system is, in general, typical of the eastern and central Tucanoan languages. For a synopsis of Tuyuca phonology and grammar see Barnes and Malone, to appear.

[2]   For a brief discussion of the phonology of Tuyuca, see Barnes and Malone, to appear.

[3]   The labels for the ten semantic categories of classifiers are adapted from Allan 1977.297ff.

[4]   In this paper the following abbreviations are used: ADV adverbializer, ANIM animate, CL classifier, D dimension, EV evidential, F feminine, FRUS frustrative, GEN genitive, IMP imperative, INAN inanimate, LOC locative, M masculine, NEG negative, NOM nominalizer, PL plural, RE specificity marker, SG singular, TC thematic contrast. Examples are given in phonemic notation. Voiced consonants have nasal allophones in nasal morphemes. The stressed syllable of each phonological word is marked in the examples.

[5]   Stress on the multi-syllable classifiers indicates the syllable which is stressed if the morpheme to which the classifier is suffixed is a stress rejecting morpheme.

[6]   See section 2.1 for a discussion of forms marked with Ø.

[7]   The singular form is restricted to occurring suffixed to nouns or nominalized forms. When suffixed to other forms, its referent is to the homophonous form *bãkã* 'town', which is a noun that may function as a classifier.

[8]   Nasalization is a feature of the morpheme, and nasal spreading occurs across morpheme boundaries. The morphemes *-ri* and *-ro* are unspecified with respect to nasalization and nasalization will spread to them.

[9]   Stress in Tuyuca co-occurs with high pitch. A more precise study of the correlates of stress remains to be done.

[10]   For rules of stress see Barnes and Malone, to appear.

[11]   Source materials for the observations in this paper are mainly two long legends for which I have a concordance, supplemented by shorter texts, plus some elicited information.

[12]   Attempts to divide *bapári* 'four' into two morphemes *bapá* and *-ri* have thus far not been conclusive. (The noun *bapá* means 'dish', the verb *bapákiti* means 'to accompany', and *bapákeo* means 'to count'.)

[13]   The reverse order, i.e., *sikabá sapátu,* has also been observed.

[14]   Other closely related Tucanoan languages (Northern Barasano, for example) retain the first person singular pronoun that Tuyuca omits.

[15]   Genitives are not employed when relationship rather than possession is in focus, as with kinship terms.

[16]   For a brief discussion of relative clauses in Tuyuca, see Barnes and Malone, to appear.

REFERENCES

Allan, Keith. 1977. Classifiers. *Language* 53.285-311.

Barnes, Janet and Terrell Malone. El tuyuca. Bogotá: Instituto Caro y Cuervo. (To appear.)

Payne, Doris L. 1987. Noun classification in the Western Amazon. *Language Sciences 9.1 (special issue): Comparative linguistics of South American Indian languages.* Edited by Mary Ritchie Key.

Tamayo L., César. 1988. *Mi primer diccionario: español-tuyuca, tuyuca-español (primera edición).* Janet Barnes, editor. Bogotá: Instituto Lingüístico de Verano.

Chiriguano and Guarayo Word Formation

Wolf Dietrich

1. INTRODUCTION

1.1 GRAMMATICAL DESCRIPTION of South American Indian languages seldom has paid special attention to word formation[1] as a specific field of study. Word formation suffixes and prefixes generally are treated in separate chapters, without being discussed from the perspective of any particular theory of word formation. Descriptions thus often lack a clear distinction between grammatical determinations of one and the same word (sometimes known as 'inflection' - especially in American linguistics) and word formation processes leading to new words (sometimes known as 'derivation'). In this paper I will describe word formation in two closely related Tupí-Guaraní languages from the perspective of Coseriu's 1981 theory. In part, this description suggests that a single morpheme can be either a lexical item, a grammatical suffix, or a word formation suffix - all depending on its use in a particular context. This study may further serve as a sample of word formation in any canonical Tupí-Guaraní language (e.g. Mbyá, Kaiwá, or Tembé). Tupí-Guaraní languages are rather isolating in terms of traditional language typology; the word formation morphemes that do exist are mostly highly agglutinative suffixes.

1.2 I CHOSE CHIRIGUANO AND GUARAYO as samples for this description because I know Chiriguano from my own field work in Argentina and could take advantage of Bárbara Schuchard's work on Bolivian Chiriguano (Tapyi or Izoceño dialect; Schuchard 1979). The only extensive description of Guarayo is that of Father Alfredo Hoeller, which dates from more than half a century ago. As his grammar and dictionary of Guarayo are not accessible to linguists who do not read German, these works have not been widely assimilated in Tupí-Guaraní studies.[2] Examples of recently spoken Guarayo have been taken from texts published by Newton 1978.

2. EUGENIO COSERIU'S THEORY OF WORD FORMATION

Traditional theories of morphology classified word formation morphemes according to formal categories such as suffixes, prefixes, or types of composition; however, they did not really describe the semantics of word formation. In this paper, I refer to Eugenio Coseriu's theory of word formation (Coseriu 1981) which does address semantics; it is a purely functional theory in the sense that it is not based on formal categories like derivation and composition, but on three types of intrinsic word formation structures.

2.1 MODIFICATION in Coseriu's scheme is an intrinsic word formation type which does not include an actual syntactic determination. This means that it does not change the syntactic category (word class) of the basic word, but only modifies its meaning quantitatively. For instance, modification may express a constant diminutive, augmentative, approximative (*yellowish, oldish*), collective (*mileage, flowerage*), or repetitive function (*to re-write, to re-open*). Other modifications are not excluded; rather, the specific functions depend on the language studied.

2.2 DEVELOPMENT means that the principal purpose of a word formation process is to effect a change from the word class of the basic word. That is, the basic word is 'developed' from one word class to another. In Coseriu's terms this includes an actual syntactic determination like PREDICATIVITY, as in *ill* + 'predicative' —> *illness* 'the fact of being ill', *to arrive* + 'predicative' —> *arrival* 'the fact of arriving'; or 'ATTRIBUTIVITY', as in *nation* + 'attributive' —> *national* 'relating to a nation'. Under this view, it is not sufficient to say that *illness* is a nominalization of an adjective; instead it must be recognized that it includes the nominalization of an underlying sentence (with subject deletion): '(Someone) is ill' —> '(his) being ill' —> 'the fact of being ill' = *illness*. All kinds of word formation that maintain the lexical meaning of the basic word in another word class are developments. In many cases, in addition to the change in part of speech or word class, there may be a change in specific semantic shade; reference may be made to object, time, instrument, manner, or secondary meanings like passive or resultative. It is important to note that development does not cover reference to an agent or instrument like *teacher*; the noun *teacher* does not mean 'to teach' + 'syntactic determination (predicative)', but instead 'somebody who teaches'; it is composed of both a lexematic and a prolexematic element (see 2.3.1).

2.3 COMPOSITION means both the formal and the semantically determined composition of two lexical morphemes. Coseriu distinguishes two types of composition.

2.3.1 GENERIC COMPOSITION is the combination of a specific basic lexeme and a generic lexeme; the result generally refers to an agent (nomina agentis), an instrument (nomina instrumenti), or any kind of material thing (tree, receptacle, and so on) that is related to the basic lexeme. GENERIC COMPOSITION is different from modification in that composition does not mean a specified kind of the basic word, but instead a composition of 'the one who' or 'the thing

which does something or is related to something'. It differs from development
in so far as it need not include a change of word class; if it does, it includes more
than this because there always is a relation to someone or something outside the
basic notion. This 'someone' or 'something' is expressed by the generic
morpheme. Thus, *teacher* is a composition of the lexical element *(to) teach* and
the generic element *-er,* which means 'personal or instrumental agent';
gardener is 'the one who has to do with/works in the garden'; *container* is a
composition of '(to) contain' and 'that which (contains), instrument, thing
which (contains)'.

2.3.2 SPECIFIC COMPOSITION is the composition of two specific lexemes,
regardless of the kind of determination that exists between them: *Dealer* and
trader are generic compositions, whereas *tradesman* expresses a similar notion
by specific composition; *storekeeper* is a specific composition as far as *store +
keeper* is concerned, though *keeper* itself is a generic composition.

2.4 IN COSERIU'S theory all kinds of word formation in all languages can be
associated with one of these four functional types. Nevertheless, it is clear that
the specific kinds of modification, development, and composition may differ
from language to language. We will further see that a single morpheme in
Chiriguano and Guarayo may seem to leap over the functional boundary between development and generic composition (see 5.1 below). This
phenomenon must be explained by other functional criteria. In Coseriu's
theory, at least, it would appear to be a peculiar phenomenon because his theory
does not use more general terms like 'nominalizer'. For Coseriu a nominalizing
function is a 'development' whenever it involves nothing more than changing
word class (e.g. *to fish* —> (the act of) *fishing*); it is a generic composition
whenever there is a second argument designating, in a very generic manner, an
agent or thing related to the first argument (*to fish* —> (to) *fish* + 'generic agent'
—> *fisher*). Functionally, these are very different kinds of nominalizations.

With Coseriu I conceive of word formation as the grammar of vocabulary.
This means that the linguistic faculty places at the speaker's disposal systematic
grammatical processes (derivation and composition) for making new words
from basic words. It is sometimes difficult to establish the boundary line
between grammar (inflection) and word formation (derivation and composition). For instance, linguists do not always agree on whether the formation of
adverbs is a case of inflection or of word formation. Payne (1985.248, 253,
citing various other linguists) states a common view that inflectional formatives
'correlate with something elsewhere in the syntactic structure' while
derivational formatives 'do not correlate with something elsewhere in the
syntactic structure'. Nevertheless, in Chiriguano and Guarayo word formation,
we have to ask ourselves whether forms created by means of one and the same
morpheme are new lexical items in all cases, or whether in some cases that same
morpheme might not simply create paradigmatic forms of a basic lexical item

(see 3.2-3.4 and 4.2.2). The difficulty mainly arises from the different categories of word structure and from the syntactic structure of Tupí-Guaraní languages which do not always allow us to clearly see where derivation ends and where inflection begins.

In what follows I use the terms 'grammar' and 'grammatical' with reference to all morphemes that express inflectional categories within a word (such as 'tense' or 'mood') and to derivational functions that form new words (such as 'diminutive' or 'generic composition'). Grammatical morphemes may be bound (synthetic inflection) or free (analytic inflection). 'Syntax' differs from grammar in that syntax refers to the functions which constitute a phrase (such as 'predicate', 'subject', and 'object'). Both 'syntax' and 'grammar' are opposed to lexical meaning. However, lexical 'meaning' can be an ambiguous term. Depending on context, it can refer to different extralinguistic objects and notions; Coseriu calls this semantic relation 'designation'. On a higher level of linguistic analysis, 'meaning' can refer to the semantic structure of a language; this semantic relation is called 'signification'. For example, although a chair may be designated as a chair, a seating accomodation, or a piece of furniture, the significations ('meaning' in this restricted sense) of *chair, piece of furniture*, and *seating accomodation* are not identical; rather they describe different aspects of the same extralinguistic object.

Finally, I use the term 'lexicalization' to refer to a diachronic phenomenon which consists in a loss of transparent semantic motivation. The meaning of a lexicalized compound or derivation may be no longer predictable from the lexemes and morphemes once used in the word formation process.

3. MODIFICATION[3]

3.1 DIMINUTIVES. As in European languages, diminutive function means the real or figurative diminution of a given linguistic concept. If real diminution is not possible in a particular context, the diminutive will lead to a figurative diminution; this means that the concept will have an affective or even intensified meaning. A small or reduced sample of a thing, person, or notion may be more pleasant than a normal or big one. Alternatively, a notion may be reduced to its critical point, so that the resulting meaning is concentration or focussing.

3.1.1 NOMINAL DIMINUTIVES. Chiriguano has a diminutive formation identical with the lexical root *táy* 'son' (an absolute form, not marked for person), *che-ráy* 'my son', originally 'seed, offspring, little thing' (see Montoya, Tesoro, 351). The original meaning is still found in Mbyá (see Dooley 1982.46: *okě ra'y'i* 'window', lit. 'little son of the door'). In Paraguayan Guaraní we have syntactic constructions with *-ra'y* 'ATTRIBUTIVE-son' which may be interpreted as diminutive forms (though the suffix *-'i* is more frequent). Chiriguano *-ráy* is not clearly a diminutive suffix, but is close to an element of syntax (attributive construction). For example, in *mburíka-ráy*, there is no morphological distinction between 'donkey's offspring' and 'little donkey'. It is always the context which clarifies whether the hearer has to understand 'offspring, son', or 'small piece of', that is 'diminutive'. Of course, in the case of *íta-ráy* 'stone-DIM' there would never be any ambiguity. Other examples are *gwyra-ráy* 'little bird', *kuñatāi-ráy* 'little girl', *mīchia-ráy* 'little child', *íporáy* 'his little hand' *haywi-ráy* 'it is drizzling, there is a drizzle'.

The diminutive suffix functions as an intensifier when used with qualities. Diminution of qualities means reduction to the point where the focus is on the quality: *póchy-ráy* 'pretty bad, wicked, evil', *chútu-ráy* 'quite short', *mīchi-ráy* 'quite small'.

3.1.2 GUARAYO does not have the lexical innovation *-ráy* of Paraguayan Guaraní and Chiriguano (*che-ráy* 'my son, my seed'). Instead it uses the widespread Tupí-Guaraní suffix *-i* (see Tupinambá *pirá-í* 'little fish', *añur-í* 'little neck', *kumandá-í* 'little bean'; Mbyá *ava'í* 'little boy', *peteí* just one'; Wayãpi *tamanuwa-i* 'small ant-bear'). In Old Tupí (Tupinambá) the suffix was *-í* or *-i*, but we cannot tell whether there was a morphologic rule of distribution or a semantic difference between the forms (see Lemos Barbosa 1956.63). In Old Guaraní we find *-í* as a diminutive suffix (Montoya, *Arte*, 73: *poriahubí* 'pobrecito') and *-i* as a suffix which means 'identification' (Montoya, *Tesoro*, s.v. 5 Y: *che-roba-pe-í* '1 p-face-in-IDENTIF', 'right in my face'). But there are two other suffixes *-í*, quoted by Montoya as '3 Y, Al fin del verbo dize perseverancia: *a-jerure-í* "pídolo con perseverancia"' and '4 Y, Al fin del verbo hazer sin duda la cosa: *a-ha-í-ne* "sin duda yré"' ('1 p-go-FOCUS-FUT', 'I certainly will go'). From this I conclude that Montoya's *-i$_3$* is different from his *-í$_4$* and *-í$_5$*; however, the last two suffixes must be identified as being the same, because the functions 'identification' and 'absoluteness' can easily be explained as contextual variants of the diminutive function. This is likely the diminutive suffix of Tupinambá, which was not used with nouns but with verbs.

In Guarayo, we find some evidence for the hypothesis that there were two suffixes in Old Tupí. Diminutive *-i* is short and unstressed (*ybyrá-i* 'tree-DIM, small tree', *oporavýky atá-i* 'he worked pretty/very hard'), whereas long and stressed *-í* means 'insistence' like Montoya's *-i$_3$* (Hoeller 1932b.87: *amombeú-í* 'I tell it once more with insistence'). So, there certainly are two different suffixes in Guarayo even though both push stress to the syllable preceding the suffix. Sometimes *-i* has a clearly diminutive function as in *pirá-i* 'small fish', *ybyrá-i* 'little tree'. But depending on the context, *avá-i* could be translated by 'little man' or it could refer to a young man. Similarly, *kunāi* 'woman-DIM' can designate a girl or a small woman. As both contextual meanings do not depend on any formal distinction, we must argue that there is only one morpheme 'diminutive'. The reference to a young man by means of 'man-DIM' can easily be explained on the basis of the diminutive function inasmuch as the basic meaning 'diminution' can also refer to the imperfect or unaccomplished state of an object.

3.2 POSSIBLE PREDICATIVE DIMINUTIVES. There are no diminutives on predicative expressions in either Chiriguano or in Guarayo. I will discuss expressions that come into question in order to show the problems which arise here.

3.2.1 THE QUESTION about the nature of the suffix -*i* (discussed in 3.1.2) also arises when -*i* is used with predicative expressions. On the basis of semantics, it seems that it is not the same suffix -*i* as we find with nouns. The examples given by Hoeller (1932a.137) show that -*i* on verbs is long and means 'insistence' or 'perseverance'. This is not a word formation suffix; it does not form new words, but makes a grammatical determination within the paradigm of a lexical item, akin to determinations like number, tense, or mood. For example, *a-ikó-i* '1.p-be/live-PERSEVERANCE', 'I still am, remain' is not a new word compared to *á-iko* 'I am/live'. Morphological evidence for this claim comes from forms like *aikó-i* which cannot themselves be determined by modal verbs like *aikátu* 'I am able, can'. It is possible to say:

```
ko    che aikátu íko
here  I   1p.can live
'here I can live'
```

and also

```
ko    che aikatú-i        íko
here  I   1p.can-INSIST   live
'here I am quite able to live'.
```

But it would be agrammatical to say **ko che aikátu aikó-i* in order to express 'here I can remain'; there is no lexical item *aikó-i* 'I remain' in Guarayo. Hoeller's dictionary (1932b) gives the false impression that there are lots of independent lexical items, such as *áiko é (ichúi)* lit. 'I am apart from him' (also translatable as 'I differ from him') or *áiko tẽi* 'I am unemployed, jobless'. However, the latter is nothing more than *áiko* 'I am/live' + -*tẽi* 'FRUSTRATIVE'. The suffix -*téi, -tẽi* is very common in Guarayo and Chiriguano (see Dietrich 1986.148-9), and is itself composed of -*(é)te* 'absolute superlative' and -*i* 'PERSEVERANCE'(?), 'INSISTENCE'(?), or 'DIMINUTIVE'(?). This expresses a high degree of intensity of a quality or an action such that it yields a negative result 'FRUSTRATION'. Therefore, the actual meaning of *áiko-tẽi* can be paraphrased by 'all my existence is for nothing; I am/live very much (and this includes a big struggle for life), but just like this, without any result'. It is evident that this is a paradigmatic variation on a single lexical item, rather than a derivational process.

Other Guarayo examples are:

opa-katú-i   ogweráco
3p-finish.well-INSIST 3p.take.away
'he took it all away, he took away just all of it'

ajeruré-i   Tũpa-upe
1p.beg/pray-INSIST   God-DIRECTION
'I constantly pray to God'.

The conclusion of all this is that *-i* with predicative expressions is not a word formation suffix, but a grammatical suffix that must be described in syntax. The suffix can be found with this grammatical function also in Chiriguano; for example:

má-i   áiko   kwá-pe
PERFECTIVE-PERSEVERANCE 1p.be/live this-LOCATIVE'
'I have been being here and I still am here'.

3.2.2 'EXTENUATIVE' is a paradigmatic grammatical determination, used mostly with imperatives. It has a smoothing effect on the order or request, which we may translate by adding 'please!' in the case of requests, or by 'a litte bit', 'for a moment', or the like. The very semantic description argues that this cannot be a case of word formation because use of the affix on a verb form depends on context. In Chiriguano we find the clitic *-mi* (< Proto-Tupí-Guaraní *mirim* 'small') used in this way:

embóu-mi awáti! 'give (me) a little bit/please corn!'

embóu-mi y táu! 'give (me), please, water that I may drink!'

ché agwáta-mi áiko yãka ijéwy-rupi 'I was walking a bit by the riverside'.

In Chané this suffix is frequently used as an intensifier on all kinds of word classes (see Dietrich 1986.178). Because it is not restricted to a single word class and not even to lexical items, but also occurs with suffixes of textual comment, it cannot be a word formation suffix:

kõi-mi   õi
near-EXTENUAT 3p.be
'it is quite near'

che-ramĩ-ño-mi
1p.PRON-like-EXCLUS-EXTENUAT
'exactly the same as me'.

In Guarayo the equivalent *mini* (*mĩnĩ* in Newton 1978) still exists as a full lexical word: *mĩni mĩni* 'the kids', *i-miní-ce* 'inasmuch as he is small/as it is little'. But it also functions as a suffix *-mĩni* which is not restricted to certain syntactic contexts like imperatives; it therefore could be an element of word formation. Examples of the suffixal use of *-mini* in Guarayo are:

> *arakáe* 'formerly, long ago, for a long time (before the life time of the speaker, late)' —> *arakáe-mini* 'for a short time, for a moment, soon, a bit late'

egwápy-mini chéu-rane 'sit down for a while close to me!'

ério-mini áve! 'come here for a moment!'

ijapúa-mini 'he, she, it is a small ball, dumpling'

tere' u-mĩnĩ! 'you may eat it, please!'

teresãrõ-mĩnĩ! 'that you guard it, please!'

In modern texts (Newton 1978) we also find the allomorph *-mi*. The phonological reduction is explained by a general phonological rule in both languages by which /n/ and /r/ are neutralized in contact with nasal vowels and tend to be dropped (see Dietrich 1986.70). The following data are from Guarayo:

eraso-mĩ 'take it, please!'

a'u-mĩ-tẽi
1p.eat-EXTENUAT-FRUST
'I eat some of it, and I do this with frustrating intensity'

t-aru-mĩ   ja'u-no!
HORTATIVE-1p.bring-EXTENUAT   1p.pl.incl.eat-again
'that I may bring a bit we may eat again!'

amombe'u-pota-mĩ
1p.tell-want-EXTENUAT
'I would like to tell'

ajembo'e-mĩ   che-poravyky-ãwã
1p.learn-EXTENUAT   my-work-PURPOSE
'I learn(ed) a little how to work'

pe-japysáka-mĩ-ra!
2.pl.p.think.on-EXTENUAT-FUT
'please think on it!'

t-a-mombe'u-mĩ   pẽu!
HORTATIVE-1p-advise-EXTENUAT 2pl.p-OBJ.PRON
'let me advise you!/I would like to advise you'.

3.3 AUGMENTATIVES. Augmentative function is the opposite of diminutive function. It means that a notion is enlarged or amplified, which may involve negative connotations in some contexts; big samples of a species used to be experienced as unpleasant, clumsy, and so on.

3.3.1 *WÁSU* (AVA DIALECT OF CHIRIGUANO), *GWÁHU* (IZOCEÑO-TAPYI DIALECT) have a lexical origin[4] but can no longer be used as a predicate. Thus, formations by means of -*wásu* and -*gwáhu* in Chiriguano now belong to the domain of word formation. The lexical item 'big' now is only *túicha* (= Parag. Guar. *tuvixá*). One could argue that -*wásu*, *gwáhu* form compounds and thus are not a kind of modification. But semantic study shows that this would not be correct; *mburíka-gwáhu*, for instance, does not mean *'donkey bigness' but refers to a kind of donkey, 'big/giant (and therefore threatening) donkey'. Other Chiriguano examples are:

    Yãka-Wásu 'Big-River, Tartagal (place-name)'

    nẽ-wásu 'stench-AUGM', 'an awful stench'.

An augmentative form itself can be a predicate: *1-ne-wásu* 'there is an awful stench'. Hoeller 1932b gives similar data for Guarayo:

    takúra 'hen' —> *takúra-gwácu* 'peahen'

    áwa-gwácu 'big man' or 'great man'.

Examples of Guarayo -*wasu*, -*wusu* taken from Newton 1978 include the following (-*wusu* is based on the allomorph -*usu* of Old Tupí; see note 4):

    ojáty-wasũ-ño 'he exactly shed/threw it greatly'

    yúpa-wúsu 'a large lake'.

3.3.2 AS A LEXICAL MORPHEME Guarayo *ái* means 'bad, ill' (*che-júru ái* 'my mouth is ill', that is 'sore, ulcerous'). In a sort of improper (that is, figurative) usage it is added, perhaps one could say suffixed, to other words; it then functions as a degree term, parallel to the catachrestic *pretty* or *awfully* in colloquial English (*pretty bad, an awfully pretty girl*): *púku* 'long', *puku-ái* 'terribly long', *ipuku-ái* 'he/she/it is awfully long'. This is a common absolute superlative in Guarayo. But thirdly, -*ái* may be regarded as a word formation suffix whenever a lexical item + -*ái* can grammatically be determined as a whole. For example, Guarayo *mbae-káru* 'the one who eats, eater' —> *mbae-káru-ái* 'great eater', may be determined by -*éta* 'many' as in *mbae-karu-ái-éta* 'great eaters'. Another example is *mbae-poro-u-ái* 'NOM-HUMAN.OBJ-eat-AUGM', 'cannibal/monster-AUGM', 'a terrible monster'.

In summary, we see that the nature of a unit like *ái* depends on its use: it is lexical when it is used as an attributive or predicative adjective, it is a grammatical suffix when it functions as an absolute superlative, and it is a word formation suffix whenever the result is a new word; the latter is only possible with nouns.

3.3.3 IN TUPÍ-GUARANÍ LANGUAGES reduplication of lexemes is a common technique for intensifying lexical meaning. This is particularly frequent with verbs, but can be found with predicative nouns as well. This is never a word formation technique because the reduplication does not form new lexical units; rather, it conveys aspectual meaning. For instance, with Guarayo *oñ-apỹchi-pỹchi* 'he tied and tied, he tied extraordinarily' or *i-apajére-jére* 'he rolled over and over,' we cannot say that these are new, derivative verbs as against the simple *oñ-apỹchi* or *i-apajére*. Reduplication is limited to the last two syllables so that the reduplicated part is not always a complete root: Chiriguano *ei-nūpa-nūpa* 'beat him hard!', *ára hyápu-ápu* (sky-3 p thunder-REDUPL) 'it is thundering heavily'. The same kind of reduplication is found on numerals (Chiriguano *mopēti-pēti* 'one by one', *pa-jandépo-ndépo* 'ten by ten' (see Schuchard 1979.59). These last constructions are not new words, nor do they have an intensifying meaning. Unlike reduplication in many other language families, reduplication in Tupí-Guaraní never has an augmentative function in the sense defined earlier. Augmentation is a function which appears on new constant lexical nouns, whereas reduplication in Tupí-Guaraní is a phenomenon that is found on word classes other than nouns. Further, a verbal construction like Chiriguano *ai-nūpa-nūpa* 'I beat him and beat him, I beat him hard', cannot be determined by another verb (cf. **aipóta ainūpa-nūpa* 'I want to beat him hard'); only the determining verb can be reduplicated: *aipóta-póta ainūpa* 'I want very much to beat him'. In contrast to this, an augmentative noun can be determined either by a demonstrative (*kwa mburíka-gwáhu* 'this huge donkey') or a plural morpheme (*kwa mburíka-gwáhu-réta* 'these huge donkeys').

3.4 LEXICAL NEGATION. Many of the actually existing Tupí-Guaraní languages have inherited from Old Tupí and Guaraní a distinction between predicative negation and lexical negation; this is comparable to the same distinction in European languages (*she does NOT come* versus *UNlawful, NONcooperation*). Predicative negation is a matter of syntax. Lexical negation belongs to modification as a subcategory of word formation, inasmuch as modification covers all shapes, states, or manifestations of a given notion including its negation. Under this view, *unlawful* is an extreme kind of *lawful, noncooperation* is an extreme form of *cooperation*.

3.4.1 THE SUFFIX USED for lexical negation in Chiriguano is not the common one of most of the other Tupí-Guaraní languages. Chiriguano has ~*a* (with nasalization of and stress on the syllable preceding the suffix) in the Ava and

Chané dialects and an oral allomorph *´-a* (with stress on the preceding syllable) in the Tapyi-Izoceño dialect. The suffix itself is oral in all the dialects but it nasalizes the preceding syllable in Ava and Chané.[5] Chiriguano data are: *káwi* 'good' —> *kawĩ-a* 'bad', *typy* 'deep' —> *typ'y-a* 'undeep, shallow', *púku* 'long' —> *pukú-a* 'not long, short'.

The suffix *´-a/~a* forms negative modifications of notions that designate qualities. Functionally it is not a word formation suffix when it negates verbal or nominal predicates. For example, *hoũ-a* 'they did not eat' is not a new word but rather a syntactically determined form of the paradigm of *háu* 'I eat/ate'. The same is true for *hehá-a* '3.p-eye-NEG', 'he is eyeless'. In contrast, *yãka typ'y-a* 'shallow river' can be the result of a word formation process. This is decidedly the case if we have *yãka typ'y-a-pe* 'in(to) the shallow river' because there is no predication. But if the whole predication is *yãka typ'y-a* (without 3p marking in this case), we must understand it as 'the river is shallow'; then it is an actual paradigmatic form, not a lexical unit. Chiriguano, unlike European languages, does not mark this syntactic difference morphologically.

Another common suffix for lexical negation in Chiriguano is *-mbae*. As can ʋɛ seen throughout this paper, the lexeme *mbáe* 'thing' is widely used as a word formation affix (prefix, infix, and suffix). But *mbáe* is used in Chiriguano also as a negative indefinite pronoun 'nothing' (*mbáety mbáe aécha* 'NOT anything 1.p-see, I did not see anything'). There is a clear distributional difference between *´-a/~a* and *-mbáe*. The suffix *-mbáe* appears with verbs and those nouns that designate things which can be possessed. It always has a personal prefix. Thus, formations with *-mbáe* cannot be modifications: they contain two arguments, a grammatical person and a negative lexical morpheme which reveals that they are generic compositions (see below 5.1). For instance, *héha-mbáe* is not a negation of 'eye' but means 'the one who has no eyes' (or, 'the one who has nothing eye(s)'). Formations with *-mbáe* do not function as actual predicates. For example, a form like *ij'ywa-mbáe* '3p.arm-NOTHING, armless' is not a predicate by itself but must be determined by the identification suffix *-ko* to become a predicate:

ij'ywa-mbáe-ko   háe
3p.arm-NEG-IDENTIF 3p.PRON
'he is armless, does not have arms'.

Ij'ywa-mbáe is a nominal form which emphasizes lack or absence of a possessable thing. In contrast, *´-a/~a* negates the lexical meaning of the word it determines. The resulting word form is an attributive noun (*jywá-a* 'armless'), showing that *´-a/~a* belongs to the domain of word formation.

3.4.2 GUARAYO has the traditional suffix *-eỹ* of most Tupí-Guaraní languages for lexical negation. We find *-eym* in Old Tupí, *-eỹm* in Old Guaraní, and cognate forms in Mbyá, Kaiwá, Wayãpi, Kamayurá, Parintintin, Tapirapé,

Guajajara, Urubú (see Jensen 1984.107), but not in Chiriguano. Guarayo examples are:

táta-eȳ 'fireless'

táta-eȳ-me 'fire-NEG-LOC' 'where there is no fire'

mbáe porã 'thing good/beautiful, something good/beautiful' —>
mbáe porã-eȳ 'something bad/ugly'.

Formations with the suffix *-eȳ* in Guarayo have the same meaning and similar syntactic behavior as do formations with *'-a/~a* in Chiriguano. They allow the attributive suffix *-vae*, together with a personal prefix, as in *c-ecap'yco-eȳ-vae,* 3p-(eye)sight-NEG-ATTR, 'he who has no sight, who is blind'. Since there are two arguments (3p and (eye)sight-NEG), this is not an example of modification, but of generic composition (see below 5.1).

3.5 MODIFICATION OF VERBS BY INCORPORATION OF AN OBJECT. Incorporation of an object noun into the verb is a typological characteristic of many Amerindian languages, and of Tupí-Guaraní languages in particular. In Tupí-Guaraní languages incorporation means the insertion of an object between the personal prefix and the verbal root. When the object is expressed outside of the verb, it denotes an actual object. When the verb is modified by an incorporated object, it refers to the generic object of an habitual action. Incorporation is a kind of modification; only the verb is modified and there is only one argument (not two as in compounds). The derived verbs are syntactically intransitive in the sense that they do not admit a further direct object.

3.5.1 CHIRIGUANO EXAMPLES of incorporation include:

ai-asói '1p-cover', 'I cover(ed) it' —> *añ-aka-asói* '1p (nasal allomorph)-head-cover' —> *añakasói* 'I head-covered', 'I cover(ed) my head, I use(d) a head-covering'

ai-kwãwa 'I hug(ged) him/her' —> *añ-añu-kwãwa* 'I neck-hugged(him/her)', 'I hug(ged) his/her neck'.

Chiriguano, more than other languages of the same family, has systematized the differentiation of generic and actual objects. Since each transitive verb form implies an object, which is not marked morphologically whenever it is actual, speakers used to distinguish personal and non-personal generic objects. Personal generic objects include domestic animals, non-personal generic objects include all other kinds of animals.

Generic non-personal objects are expressed by *-mbáe-* 'thing' (with the allomorph *-mae-* in nasal contexts):

a-mbow'ywy 'to sew (a definite object)' —> *a-mbae-mbow'ywy* 'to sew (what generally has to be sewn)' *a-júka* 'to kill (a definite object)' —> *a-mbae-júka* 'to kill any kind of animals, to hunt'

a-putúka 'to wash (a definite piece of clothes) —> *a-mbae-putúka* 'to wash (any kind of clothes)'

a-moãky 'to wet, moisten' —> *a-mae-moãky* 'to irrigate.'

Generic personal objects are expressed by *poro-*, which is composed of the clitics *-po-* '2 pl p object' and *-ro-* '2 sg p object':

ai-póta 'to desire' —> *a-poro-póta* 'to be in love with someone'

a-epēña 'to approach to s.o. definite' —> *a-por(o)-epēña* 'to approach (to people)'

ai-nūpa 'to beat s.o./s.th. definite' —> *a-poro-nūpa* 'to beat (people, dogs, animals)'

a-mbóe 'to teach (one or more definite persons)' —> *a-poro-mbóe* 'to teach (people), to be a teacher'

a-júka 'to kill (a definite object)' —> *a-poro-júka* 'to be a murderer'

háe gwy-rówia 'he/she believes it' —> *háe o-poro-gwy-rówia* 'he/she believes'; *háe-ko o-poro-gwy-rówia-wae* 'he/she is believing, faithful'.

3.5.2 GUARAYO does differ fundamentally from Chiriguano with respect to object incorporation. For both languages it is not always possible to make clear the difference between syntax and incorporation via an English translation. As described above, the difference is that between an actual object on the one hand, versus generic, non-referential objects, or habitual or commonly referred to actions that are considered as unitary on the other hand. Generally, the verbs resulting from incorporation are intransitive because the object is already incorporated; they do not admit any further object. However, sometimes the object-incorporated action refers to another, personal object; then the incorporated verb must be interpreted as transitive (among the following Guarayo data, see exs. 6 and 7):

(1) *ai-pycy Tūpa* 'I receive God' —> *a-tūpa-pycy* 'I God-receive, communicate'

(2) *ai-kwáa c-éko* 'I know his nature' —> *a-céko-kwáa* 'I his-nature-know'

(3) *a-mõta ñ-ãka* 'I hit his head' —> *a-ñãka-mõta* 'I head-hit him, I used to hit his head'

(4) *a-aycu Tūpa* 'I love God' —> *a-tūpa-r-aycu* '1p-God-RELATION-love, I God-love, I am a God-lover'

(5) *a-rója Tūpa ñěe* 'I believe in God's word' —> *a-tūpa-ñěe-re-rója* '1p-
God-speech-RELATION-believe', 'I God's-word-believe'

(6) *a-mõpe i-jywa* 'I break his arm' *a-jywa-mõpe Pedro* 'I arm-break Pedro'

(7) *tõ ajóo Pédro-cui* 'sand-flea 1p-cut out Pedro-from', 'I cut out a sand-
flea from Pedro' —> *ai-tõ-õ Pédro* 'I sand-flea-cut Pedro'

(8) *a-cépia ywa* 'I see the heaven' —> *a-ywa-épia* 'I look toward heaven, I
heaven-look'

(9) *o-gwápy che-pya* 'my heart is sitting, rests, I am calm' —> *ché pya-
gwápy* 'my heart-sitting, calmness; I am calm'.

The last example does not involve object incorporation, but incorporation of
a generic locative which makes the original action a stative-like construction.

I argue that all these derived verbs are new lexical items; they have a unitary
meaning and syntactically behave in the same way as simple verbs. So, *acépia*
is a transitive verb and can take the causative suffix *-uka*: *a-c-epiá-uka*
(1p.SUBJ-3p.OBJ-see-CAUSATIVE) 'I make him/her see it', but *a-ywa-épia*
cannot take *-uka* without being first made transitive by the morpheme *mbo-*: *a-
mbo-ywa-epiá-uka* 'I make him look toward heaven'. In any case, *a-ywa-épia*
is treated as a whole, as a lexical unit, not as a syntactic construction.

Unlike Chiriguano, in Guarayo we found only a few examples of
incorporated non-personal generic objects expressed by *mbae-*; *poro-* seems to
occur quite frequently:

á-u 'I eat/ate it' —> *a-mbaé-u* 'I eat/ate (without referring to a determinate
object)'

ja-mõi 'let's cook it' —> *ja-mbae-mõi* 'let's cook (something)'

a-poro-aycu 'I am loving (someone)'

a-poro-júka 'I am hunting (animals)'

a-poro-jokwái 'I am commanding (people)'

o-ápy 'he is burning it' —> *(táta) o-poro-ápy* 'the fire is burning and may
burn people'.

Even if there is a specific object, *poro-* may be used and is combined with the
specific object + *-rece* 'DIRECTION':

a-poro-júka '1p-GENERIC.PERSONAL.OBJ-kill' —> *a-poro-júka wáka -
rece* '1p-GENERIC.PERSONAL.OBJ-kill cow-toward', 'I used to
slaughter (on behalf of) cows'.

As this last example shows, in Guarayo *poro-* refers to a generic object
which may be specified by a circumstancial complement; this is not possible in
Chiriguano. Besides this, *poro-* does not seem to be strictly bound to personal
objects in Guarayo. As shown by *(táta) o-poro-ápy* 'the fire is burning (intr.)',

the literal meaning 'the fire is burning people' actually conveys stative-like meanings of *o-ápy* 'to burn (tr.)'.

3.6 GENERIC MODIFICATION OF NOUNS. In Chiriguano, as well as in Guarayo, there is a type of word formation which appears to be functionally an equivalent to the generic incorporation of *mbáe-* (see 3.5.1). Unpossessed nouns taken in a general sense are opposed to possessed nouns designating the same things as particular, specific items. When taken in a general or generic sense, they are marked by the prefix *mbáe-*. The following examples are from Chiriguano:

(ij)agw´yje 'perfection, ripeness (of something)' —> *mbagw´yje* 'product, result, ripe fruit (in general)'

(i)póty 'blossom, flower (of a determinate plant) —> *mbaepóty* 'a blossom, blossoms, a flower, flowers (in general)

(i)mbáe 'his belongings, possession' —> *mbaembáe* 'possession, wealth (in general)'

che-ăka-rásy 'there is an ache of my head', 'I have a headache', *che-mbae-rásy* 'there is a generic ache with me, I am ill'

m'ymba '(a special or determinate) domestic animal' —> *mbaem'ymba* '(any) domestic animal'

(i)píre 'skin, pelt (of a determinate animal or man)' —>*mbaepíre* 'skin, pelt (in general, as a material or stuff)'.

In the case of an actual, referential object one can say *kwa-píre* 'this skin', *háe-ko ipíre* 'this is his/her/its skin', but one cannot say **kwa mbaepíre** 'this skin (in general)' nor **imbaepíre** 'his skin (in general)'. The demonstrative or personal reference is inconsistent with the generic character of the modification made by means of *mbáe-*.

The following examples are from Guarayo:

(i)k´yra 'a fat, grease, the fat or grease of something' —> *mbaek´yra* 'fat, grease (in general)'

(i)pótyr 'a determinate blossom or flower' —> *mbaepótyr* 'blossom(s), flower(s) (in general)'

(i)kángwer 'the bone(s) of someone or something' —>*mbaekángwer* 'bone (as a material)'

(i)pírer 'his/her/its skin, pelt' —> *mbaepírer* 'skin, pelt (as a material)'

m´ymba '(a determinate) domestic animal' —> *mbaem´ymba* '(any domestic animal)', and therefore e.g. *mbaem´ymba ´ygwa* 'watering-place (of the domestic animals)' [see 4.4.2]

c-óo 'his, its meat', *t-óo* 'a (determinate) meat' —> *mbae-róo* 'meat (in general)'.

4. DEVELOPMENT

4.1 DEVERBAL NOUNS which express the result of a process, the object of a process, or the process as a whole, are formed by means of the prefix *tem(b)i-* (the initial consonant may alternate: *t-* for absolute, *r-* for attributive use or determination by 1p or 2p, *h-* for 3p determination). Thus, *(t)em(b)i-* is a nominalizer of verbal stems. In many studies this prefix is described as a present passive participle because the formation means 'that which is done'. But the general definition of participles does not include the restriction to the designation of things, concrete or abstract, that we find with this prefix. Other than passive participles formed by *-pyr* (as occurs in Guarayo, for instance), it appears that participles do not exist in Tupí-Guaraní languages. Formations with *-tem(b)i* undoubtedly are nouns.

The following examples are from Chiriguano:

> *há-u* 'I eat it' —> *tembí-u* 'food, meal', *che-rembí-u* 'my food, meal', *hembí-u* 'his food, meal'

> *a-mónde* 'to put on, clothe, dress' —> *temi-mónde* etc. 'clothing, clothes'

> *ai-ápo* 'I make it' —> *tembi-ápo* etc. 'creation, creature'

> *ai-póta* 'I desire' —> *temi-mbóta* etc. 'desire, the object of a desire'

> *a-écha* 'I see it' —> *tembi-écha* etc. 'spectacle, panorama, view'.

The following are from Guarayo:

> *a-mbóe* 'I teach him/her' —> *che-remi-mbóe* 'the personal object of my teaching, my pupil' (see *che-poro-mbóe-ca* 'the material object of my teaching, my lessons', see also 4.2.1.)

> *a-aycu* 'I love him/her/it' —> *che-rembiaycu* 'the object of my loving, my favorite'

> *ai-pótar* 'I desire it' —> *che-remimbótar* 'the object of my desiring, my desire'

> *ai-ápo* 'I make, create it' —> *jande-rembi-ápo* 'our workmanship'.

4.2 DEVERBAL NOUNS WITH PREDICATIVE FUNCTION

4.2.1 DEVERBAL NOUNS with predicative function in its canonical form (on the model of *to make* —> *the making*, i.e. 'the fact of making') exist only in Guarayo. The Old Tupí suffix *-saba* (Montoya's *-hab(a)* 'nomen actionis' or 'place, instrument or way of making something') was preserved distinct from Old Tupí *-sara* (Montoya's *-har* 'nomen agentis'; see below 5.1.2). In Guarayo, Old Tupí *-saba* appears as *-ca* (this must reconstructed as a Proto-Tupí-Guaraní *-caβ,* see Jensen 1984.109):

a-cépia 'I see him/her/it' —> *cépia-ca* '(the) seeing him/her/ it'

añ-ǒ-ty 'I sow it' —> *tỹ-ca* '(the) sowing'

a-ñangaréko 'I attend him/her/it' —> *che ñangaréko-ca* 'my being attended', *iñangaréko-ca* 'his welfare, being attended'

a-mbóe 'I teach' —> *che-poro-mbóe-ca* 'the material object of my teaching, my instructions, lessons' (see above 4.1.2 *che-remimbóe*)

a-káru 'I eat, have a meal' —> *káru-ca* 'eating, meal, the things eaten; place where people eat, dining-room'

á-kie 'to sleep' —> *kíe-ca* 'sleeping-place'.

The last examples show that Guarayo *-ca* generally means 'nomen actionis', but also can nominalize verbs referring to the place of the action.

Newton 1978 has some examples of nominalizing *-sa* without any further reference:

aporavyky 'I work' —> *mboravyky-sa* 'the work'

amombry-sa-ve 'in that far-away one, in that far away place'

ătắ-sa-ve 'hard-NOM-LOC' 'on the hard one'.

4.2.2 IN CHIRIGUANO, Proto-Tupí-Guaraní *-caβ* and *-car* merged into two homonymous suffixes *-a*, as final consonants were dropped. We find examples of nominalizations with *-a* which make reference to place:

á-ke 'to sleep' —> *che-á-ke-a* 'my sleeping-place'

ắ-i 'to be (located)' —> *che-ắ-iñ-a* '1p.PRON-1p-be.located(allomorph)-NOM', 'my home'.

The suffix *-a* in this function is added to personal verb forms and can be used with the local suffixes *-pe* and *-gwi* to form complex local expressions:

ja-w'ya   kátu-a-pe
1.pl.p.incl-rejoice very.much-NOM-LOC
'where we are/were happy'

ó-ho   mbáety kía   ó-iko-a-pe
3p-go (is) not   anybody 3p-live-NOM-LOC
'he went to where nobody was living'

mbáety pe-puére pé-o   ché a-há-ta-a-pe
not   2.pl.p-can 2.pl.p-go I   1.p.sg-go-FUT-NOM-LOC
'you cannot go where I will go to'

kwaráy ŏ-e-a-pe
sun 3p-go.out-NOM-LOC
'where the sun rises, east'

kwaráy ói-ke-a-pe
sun 3p-go.in-NOM-LOC
'where the sun sets, west'

gwé-ru y ŏ-i-a-gwi
3p-bring water 3p-be-NOM-SEP
'he brings/brought water from where it is'

However, one must question whether these are true nominalizations; the derivations are made on personal, actual verbal forms and, therefore, are not the result of word formation, but of conversion.[6] When these forms appear without verbal personal markers, they become constant nominalizations:

ké-a 'sleeping-place, bed', *che-ké-a-pe* 'in my sleeping-place, bed'

ché áke ãi ĭru i-ké-a-pe 'I am sleeping in another one's bed'

4.3.1 NOUNS WITH PREDICATIVE FUNCTION, but without any other reference, are formed in Chiriguano by means of *mbáe-* (see above 3.5, 3.6). This prefix again illustrates the even synchronic transition from lexicon to morphology because its use as a prefix always reflects part of its lexical meaning. The morpheme can appear either with actional or stative word stems, so that one might argue that there are two homonymous morphemes. With actional word stems *mbae-* forms a nominal generalization of the action ('the fact of doing x') or a generic composition setting off the agent (see below 5.1.1). With stative word stems *mbae-* forms a nominal generalization of a quality which has a predicative function (*i-k´yra* 'it is fat'—>*mbaek´yra* 'fatness, the fact of being fat'). However, this is modification by generic incorporation if the basic word is syntactically used as a non-predicative noun (*k´yra* 'a (determinate) fat, grease' —> *mbaek´yra* 'fat, grease (in a generic sense)'. Other examples are:

a-mŏña 'to pursue' —> *mbaemŏña* 'persecution'

i-káwi 'it is good' —> *mbaekáwi* 'the being good, beauty'

ai-ápo 'to make, do' —> *mbaápo* 'that what is done, work'

che-rásy 'I am sick', *hásy* 'he/she is sick' —> *mbaerásy* 'sickness', *che-mbaerásy* 'my sickness'.

4.3.2 IN GUARAYO we find the same kind of formation and function. The same issues of identifying such word formations as developments or as generic modifications arise. The answer depends on the syntactic context:

c-éta 'it is much' —> *mbaeéta* 'the fact of being much,multitude, wealth, fortune'

porã 'beautiful, good' —> *mbaeporã* 'something good, beauty' —> *mbaeporã-eỹ* 'something bad'.

4.4 FORMATION OF ATTRIBUTIVE FORMS (ADJECTIVES) INDICATING ORIGIN OR RELATIONSHIP. The nominalizers *-(i)gwa* and *-pegwa* have the same origin, which explains why they have the same functions.   In Old Tupí the nominalizing suffix of adverbials had several allomorphs. One of these, when bound to a preceding /y/ or even /i/, surfaced as *-gwara* (instead of *-swara*, *-ndwara*; see Lemos Barbosa 1956.288-89).   The characteristic vowel then fused together with the suffix itself, such that we now have *-(i)gwa* in Chiriguano and *-ygwar* in Guarayo. In both languages, the respective suffix is a nominalizer of circumstantial complements (adverbials) of time and localization. On the other hand, *-pegwa* seems to be nothing more than *-(i)gwa* (see Montoya, Tesoro, *guâra* 'utilidad, pertenecer a cosas, y personas y tiempos ...') preceded by the locative suffix *-pe*. Thus, *-pegwa* has the local determination in itself and is translated by 'belonging to'. It is reduced to *-gwa* if the expression it operates on already contains the local suffix *-pe* (see the first example below). The nominalized forms can be used as nouns or as adjectives, as in the following Chiriguano examples:

kwápe 'here' —> *kwapé-gwa* '(which is) from here, herebeing', *mb´ya kwapé-gwa* 'the man from here'

ñana-rupi 'in, through, by the savanna' —> *ñana-rupí-gwa*'(which is) from in the savanna, wild, savage'

ñana 'wild land, savanna' —> *ñaná-igwa* '(which is) from the wilderness'(designation of the Ayoréode tribe in the Bolivian Izozog)[7]

káa 'woodland' —> *káa-pégwa* 'belonging to the woodland', *mbae-póty káa-pég*wa 'a flower of the woodland'; 'growing in the woodland'

mopẽti kuñatãi Bolívia-pégwa 'a Bolivian girl', *mb´ya Agwaráy-pegwa* 'a man from Aguaray, an Aguarayan'

ché aikwã-a péa tẽta-pégwa 'I don't know those who belong to that house'.

The function of the suffix *-´ygwar* (*´ygwa* in Newton 1978) in Guarayo is quite similar to that in Chiriguano:

ywa-´ygwar 'heaven + belonging to/coming from', 'heaven-dwelling'

Ascensión-´ygwar 'coming from, living in Ascensión'

kaa-´ygwar 'woodlander, living in the woods'

jana-´ygwar 'thicket-dwelling, inhabitant of the thicket'.

4.5 FORMATION OF VERBS BY MEANS OF *MBO-, MO-*. The prefix *mbo-, mo-* is one of the most productive word formation morphemes in all traditional Tupí-Guaraní languages. When operating on transitive verb stems, it is a grammatical marker of the causative voice; on non-transitive stems (intransitive verb stems, nouns, or 'adjectives') it is a causativizer that derives new word forms.[8] Both in Chiriguano and in Guarayo the prefix derives transitive verbs from 'adjectives', i. e. from nouns which designate a quality. These verbs are 'causative' in their lexical meaning, in the sense that the quality they express is 'made' by the action they imply; they are not causative in the grammatical and syntactic sense of the term. This prefix is always preceded by the verbal person marker. The following are from Chiriguano:

apúa 'round' —> *ambopúa* 'I make it round, to turn it'

púku 'long' —> *ambopúku* 'I lengthen it'

chútu 'short' —> *ambochútu* 'I shorten it'

pyáu 'new' —> *ambopyáu* 'I make it new, renew it'.

The following are from Guarayo:

yu 'yellow' —> *ambóyu* 'I make it yellow'

awáete 'ugly' —> *amboawáete* 'I make it ugly'

púku 'long' —> *amopúku* 'I lengthen it'

pyácu 'new' —> *amopyácu* 'I make it new, renew it'.

ãtã'hard' —> *amoãtã* 'I make it hard, stretch, bend it'.

The prefix *mbo-, mo-* can also form transitive verbs from noun stems. The resulting verbs contain the same 'causative' meanings as described in the preceding paragraph, such as 'to make, give, put the thing to someone or something'. Chiriguano data are:

che-résa (Ava), *se-réha* (Tapyi) 'my eye' —> *amboésa* (Ava), *amboéha* (Tapyi) 'I give eyes, eyesight to s.o.'

hépy 'it has a price, costs' —> *amboépy* 'I give the cost to s.o., pay'

'ypy 'ground, foundation, origin' —> *ambóypy* 'I give origin,found, begin s.th.'.

Guarayo data are:

pái 'priest' —> *amopái* 'I make s.o. a priest'

mbáe 'things' —> *amombáe* 'I make s.o. have things, give things to s.o.', literally 'to "thing" somebody'

céta, -réta 'multiplicity, many' —> *amboéta* 'I multiply, increase'

cépy(r) 'price, cost' —> *amboépy* 'I pay, buy it'.

The same prefix can also form transitive verbs from other kinds of morphemes, including grammatical morphemes and borrowed words:

Spanish *cambiar* —> Chir. *ambokámbio* 'I change'

Spanish *ganar* —> Chir. *amongăna* 'I gain, earn, win'

Guarayo *kóije* 'late(r)' —> *amokóije* 'I postpone, delay'

Guarayo *-raŋgwer* 'which was destinated (to be x), idle, fruitless' —> *amorangwer* 'I ruin, foil, frustrate'

Spanish *respectar* —> Guar. *amborepéta* 'I respect it'

Spanish *afinar* —> Guar. *amoafína* 'I plane it'

Spanish *cepillo* 'plane' —> Guar. *ambosepíju* 'I plane it'.

5. COMPOSITION

5.1 GENERIC COMPOSITION. We will first consider nouns formed by means of *mbae-*. The morpheme *mbae-* was described earlier with reference to non-personal incorporation (see 3.5.1) and with reference to generic modification (see 3.6). However, *mbae-* can also derive nouns from verbal bases or from nominal bases with process meaning. Therefore, it is difficult to interpret *mbae-* as having a single function. The fundamental lexical meaning of *mbae* is 'thing'; this is a generic non-personal meaning, which surfaces when *mbae-* functions as a grammatical morpheme. Thus, it may be difficult to understand how it can also function as a personal nominalizer. Nevertheless, some formations appear where it has a clear meaning of personal generic composition, as in 'nomina agentis', 'the one who ...'.

In Guarayo we find formations like

a-káru 'to eat, have a meal' —> *mbae-káru* 'eater' —>*mbae-karu-ái* 'great eater'

á-u 'to eat it' —> *mbae-poró-u* 'eater' —> *mbae-poro-u-ái* 'the one who eats (generally) much' (see above 3.6).

The following examples are from Chiriguano:

ái-kwa 'to know him/her/it' —> *mbaé-kwa* 'the one who knows, wise man'

ai-nũpa 'to beat, hit' —> *mbae-nũpa* 'that which hits, whip, stick', *há-u* 'to eat/drink it' —> *mbae-poró-u* 'NOM-PERSONAL.GENERIC OBJ-eat', the one who eats everybody, cannibal'.

At the same time *mbae-nũpa* can mean '(the fact of) whipping, thrashing': This is a kind of development (changing of the word class from 'to whip' to '(the fact of) whipping, see 4.3). It is not a generic composition, which would include the designation of an acting person or thing ('the one who whips, that which whips'). The same issue arises for *mbae-mõña* 'persecution'; depending on the context *mbae-poro-mõña* can mean the 'persecution of people' (which is a generic modification of the development *mbae-mõña*) or 'the one who pursues people, pursuer' (which is a generic personal modification of the generic composition *mbae-mõña* 'pursuer').

Such examples show that we cannot isolate just a single function for *mbae-*. The morpheme *mbae-* has an object function when it is a generic modification morpheme (generic object incorporation, see 3.5); but it can have a subject function whenever it is a nominalizer. As a nominalizer it can have either a development function (*mbae-mõña* 'to pursue as a thing/substance/substantive' —> 'persecution'; 'the thing/matter is *moña* "pursue"') or a generic composition function (*mbae-mõña* 'something/someone pursues', 'the thing/person that pursues').

We will now consider a second type of generic composition. In Chiriguano, generic composition with reference to persons (nomina agentis) is made by means of *-a* (< Proto-Tupí-Guaraní *-car*, see Jensen 1984.108-109):

ai-ápo 'to make' —> *(ij)ápo-a* 'the maker (of s.th.)'

a-ráha 'to take (away)' —> *waka-réta rerahá(-a)* 'the one who takes away the cows, the cows' taker'

á-ru 'to bring' —> *waka-réta rerú-a* 'the bringer of the cows'

a-ñangaréko 'to attend' —> *waka-réta iñangaréko-a* 'guardian of the cows, cowboy, herdsman'

póchy 'evil' —> *póchy-a* 'the evil, the evil man'

a-júka 'to kill' —> *(i)juká(-a)* 'the killer (of s.o.)', *(o)juká (-a)* 'that which kills, knife'

(a)káru 'to eat, have a meal' —> *(ja)karú-a* 'that we eat from/ with, our plate, fork'.

Personal nomina agentis get nominal personal markers (*che-, nde-, i-juká-a* 'my, your, his killer' etc.), whereas non-personal ones are marked by verbal personal prefixes (*o-juká-a* 'that which kills him, the knife (which kills him)').

In Guarayo the formation is made by means of *-car*, which corresponds to the unreduced form of the Proto-language:

a-aycu 'to love (s.o.)' —> *che-r-aycú-car* '1p PRON-REL-love-NOM','my lover, friend'. *Tũpa o-c-aycu c-aycú-car* 'God 3pSUBJ-3pOBJ-love 3pREL-love-NOM', 'God loves him who loves him'

a-mbóe 'to teach (s.o.)' —> *che-mboé-car* 'my teacher', *che-mboé-car-ér* 'my ex-teacher, former teacher', *che-mboé-ca-rã* 'my future teacher', *che-mboé-ca-rangwér* 'the one who had to be my teacher'.

In more recent Guarayo (Newton 1978) the suffix is *-sa;* this is homonymous with the simply nominalizing *-sa*, which has a development function (see above 4.2.1.):

ajó' o yvy 'to dig the soil' —> *yvy'ó-sa* 'hole-digger'

amoafína 'to plane it' (see 4.5.3.) —> *i-moafína-sa* 'its plane'.

In Old Tupí (Lemos Barbosa 1956.260) the allomorph of *-sara* after nasal consonants was *-ndara*. The reflex of this suffix in Guarayo is *-ndar, -na*:

´ypy 'beginning, origin' —> *ypyndar* 'the first one, ancestor'

amõi 'to cook it' —> *mba' emõina* 'that which cooks, cooking-pot'

vyry-rupi-na-rã 'that which is to be its top braces'.

5.2 SPECIFIC COMPOSITION

5.2.1 IN PARAGUAYAN GUARANI and Guarayo syntax, the juxtaposition of nouns is understood as an attributive syntagma with a determined element preceded by its determinant (Guaraní *óga jára* 'house lord', 'the lord/master of the house'). Specific composition has the same structure, being expressed by simple juxtaposition: Guarayo *gw´yra pépo* 'bird feather' may be translated by 'a bird's feather' (free syntax) or by 'bird-feather' (composition). In Chiriguano, on the other hand, attributive juxtaposition of nouns without 3p personal marking in the determined element is unusual (instead of *gw´yra pépo* speakers prefer *gw´yra i-pépo* 'bird's feather'); this seems to be restricted to fixed expressions, and belongs to the domain of word formation.

There are two more types of juxtaposition in Chiriguano, which, however, cannot be understood as types of word formation (composition). Firstly, there are lexemes which never have any kind of 3p marker, as, for example *´y(y)* 'water'; thus *yãka 'yy* 'river water' must be interpreted only as an attributive construction ('the water of the river'). Secondly, as in Paraguayan Guaraní, in Chiriguano we find juxtapositions of nouns where the usual order 'determinant' + 'determined' is inverted. In these constructions the second element follows the determined noun like an adjective determinant:

mb'ya parawéte-wa óu owãe
man poor-ATTRIB 3p.come 3p.arrive
'a poor man arrived'

úru kũña 'chicken-wife', 'hen'

kúa háe-ko ñãe tujuápo
DEM.PRON 3p.PRON-IDENTIFICATION bowl clay
'this is a bowl made from clay (characterized by clay)'

kúa   háe-ko   ó   tujuápo
DEM.PRON 3p.PRON-IDENT house clay/mud
'this is a house built up with mud'.

5.2.2 SPECIFIC COMPOSITION is not formed by juxtaposition of nouns alone but
is also characterized by a different stress which marks the close union of the
compound: there is only one stress on the penult. This is especially striking
when the second element consists of a monosyllable, which thus loses its stress.
In Chiriguano we find:

Tũpa 'God' + sy 'mother' —> Tupãsy 'God('s) Mother, Blessed Virgin'

Tũpa 'God' + ó(o) 'house' —> tupáo 'church'

táta 'fire' + ṫi 'white' —> tatãti 'smoke'

ãka 'head' + áo 'clothing' —> akandáo 'hat'

kwarásy 'sun' + ãa 'shadow' —> kwarasỹa 'shade'

tỹma 'leg' + ãka 'head' —> tymãka 'shinbone'

tỹma 'leg' + sã 'string' —> tymãsa 'cord, rope'

'ywy 'earth, soil' + ṫi 'white' —> ywỹti 'fog, snow'

ywykúi 'dust' + ṫi —> ywykwĩti 'sand'

po 'hand' + ãka 'head' —> poãka 'finger'

se-pytía 'my spirit/humor/mood' + ãka 'head' —> se-pytiãka 'my chest'
   (Tapyi-Izoceño dialect)

che-résa 'my eye(s)' + píre 'skin' —> che-resapíre 'my eye lid(s)'

yásy 'moon' + táta 'fire' —> yasytáta, yatáta 'star'

'yy 'water' + ãka 'head' —> yãka 'river'.

The same type of composition is found in Guarayo:

ñãna 'thicket' + por 'contents, filling' —> ñanámbor 'thicket +filling,
   contents of the thicket', which usually designates the 'savages'[9].

táta 'fire' + chĩ 'white' —> tatãchi 'smoke'

yácy 'moon' + táta 'fire' —> yacytáta 'star'

ápi'a 'globe, testicle' + a'ỹi 'seed, nut' —> api'ã'ỹi 'testicles' (with stress
   on ã, the nasal diphthong ỹi being unstressed).

The examples show that specific composition in Chiriguano and Guarayo
tends to lexicalize. Some of the compounds are not the result of a productive
process of composition, but are inherited from Old Guaraní or even from a

proto-language. For example, 'star' is already *yasytatá* in Montoya's dictionary and is *zahytatá* in Tembé (see Dietrich 1986.346). (The lexicalization of 'moon' and 'fire' —> 'star' may be explained by mythology.) Other compounds designate different notions in different languages; for example, *poãka* is 'finger' in Chiriguano, 'wrist' in Paraguayan Guaraní (*poakã*) and Tembé (*poakãng*), 'fist' and 'back of the hand' in Guarayo (*poãkã*, see Dietrich 1986.322). I argue from this that there is an inherited pattern of compounding *po* and *akã/ãka*, but each language has its own tradition of what kind of extralinguistic object the linguistic meaning of the literal expression 'head of the hand' may refer to. In such cases the meaning of the compound is only partially motivated.

6. CONCLUSION

Chiriguano and Guarayo word formation has well established structures representing all kinds of traditional word formation types; these include derivation (chiefly by suffixation in our case, but also by prefixation) and composition. In terms of Coseriu's functional theory of word formation, both languages have developed morphemes in each type: MODIFICATION is exemplified by diminutive, augmentative, and negative functions, and especially by processes of object incorporation. One of the most interesting features is generic modification of nouns, which allows one to distinguish between particular instances of an object (e.g. the blossoms of a tree) and the same object in a generic sense (e.g. blossom in general). DEVELOPMENT is far from being as rich as in Indo-European languages. This may be partly a consequence of a smaller number of word classes (for instance, there is no special class of adjectives or adverbs), but also due to the lack of differentiation between subtypes of nominalization. Nevertheless, there are some word class changing morphemes in Chiriguano and Guarayo; word classes like nouns and verbs are well established and are even reinforced by means of word formation processes. GENERIC COMPOSITION is a traditional category in Tupí-Guaraní languages. In Chiriguano and Guarayo there is one productive suffix (-*a* and -*car*/-*sa*, respectively); however, formations made from verbal bases by means of the prefix *mbae-* may belong to the domain of either development or generic composition, according to the context. This means that *mbae-* has a general nominalizing function when operating on verbal stems and nominal bases which designate processes, but its function goes beyond such distinctions as development or generic composition. SPECIFIC COMPOSITION can be distinguished from free syntactic juxtaposition insasmuch as there is only one stress on the compound instead of two, as in syntactic juxtaposition. It is not clear, however, to what extent specific composition is a productive word formation technique in contemporary Chiriguano and Guarayo.

NOTES

¹   See A.D. Rodrigues 1951, 1952, and 1953.

²   Chiriguano is spoken by about 15,000 people in the Northeastern part of
the Argentine province of Salta and by 40,000 to 50,000 people in the Bolivian
Oriente, between the Rio Grande Guapay, South of Santa Cruz de la Sierra, and
the Pilcomayo River. Guarayo is spoken by 7,000 to 8,000 people northeast of
Santa Cruz, between the San Pablo (San Miguel) and Blanco Rivers.

³   Chiriguano data were taken from Schuchard 1979 and Dietrich 1986, and
Guarayo data from Hoeller 1932a,b and Newton 1978. Newton's transcription
is different from Hoeller's; Newton uses <s> instead of <c> and writes <'> ,
which is absent in Hoeller. I normalize the different transcriptions for <ɨ> and
use <y> instead, as in Guaraní; for the semivowel /j/, I use <j> instead of <y>.
Stress is marked by ´ on oral vowels and by ~ on nasal vowels. Unstressed
nasal vowels are not marked because, within a word, all vowels preceding a
stressed nasal vowel are nasalized. <1p> = '1st person sing.', <1 pl p> = '1st
person plural'.

⁴   *Guasú* is translated by 'grande' in Montoya's dictionary. In some of
Montoya's examples the word is used predicatively, but in most cases it is an
augmentative suffix. In old Tupí it is only an augmentative suffix;
morphological evidence for its affixal status comes from the allomorph *-usu*
which is used after consonants (see Lemos Barbosa 1956.62).

⁵   The cognate suffix expresses predicative negation in Siriono, Guayaki, and
Guajajara; in Chiriguano it refers to lexical as well as to predicative negation,
according to the context. In some other languages (Wayãpi, Parintintin, Juma)
it is part of more complex negative forms. Its origin may be related to
Montoya's *ãã* 'pequeño, ruin' and *ãng 4* 'sombra, abrigo, ausencia de' (Ruiz de
Montoya, *Tesoro*, 1639). Chiriguano does not have the traditional predicative
negation *nd(a) ...i* of most Tupí-Guaraní languages, but has *mbáety* (< *-mbáe*
'NEG' and Old Guaraní *hetyp* 'not to agree, not to intend', see Montoya,
Tesoro, s.v.), which expresses negation in the verb and its object. The suffix
´-a/~a negates only the action or state expressed by the predicate, not the object
(for example, *mbáety hóu júky* 'they did not eat salt' means that there was no
salt to eat, but *júky hoũ-a* means 'they did not eat the salt', maybe because they
spared it and put it by).

⁶   This term was first used by Sweet 1892-96.38 and means what others call
syntactic transposition or functional change, as in cases *like the poor, the
British, at his best* (see Marchand 1969.360). Conversion has to be
distinguished from zero derivation.

[7]   Most of the examples in this section come from B. Schuchard 1979.60-61.

[8]   See W. Dietrich 1986.103-104 and P.A. Hoeller 1932a.130-131, although Hoeller actually does not make the functional distinction between grammar and word formation. Grammar establishes relations within the paradigm of the word stem, whereas word formation places new word stems at the speaker's disposal. The causative or factitive voice ('to make s.o. do s.th.') is a grammatical category, since Chir. *a-mo-měe chú-pe* 'I make him give it to him' belongs to the paradigm of *a-měe* 'I give'; the same is true for reflexive, reciprocal and comitative voice. On the other hand, new words are characterized by the possibility of being operated on by grammatical categories, such as the reflexive. For example, a syntagm like Chir. *ó-iko kátu* '3p-be well', 'he is well' in the sense of 'he is rich' can be the base of the word formation *a-mbo-iko-kátu* 'I make him rich'; this must be considered a new word, since it can be operated on by reflexive (*o-ñe-mbo-iko-kátu* 'he makes himself rich') or by reciprocal voice (*o-ño-mbo-iko-kátu* 'they make themselves rich' or *o-ño-mbo-iko-katú-ta* 'they will make themselves rich').

[9]   In nasal contexts /p/ has the allophone [mb], /t/ > [nd], /k/ > [n]. This phonological rule works only with inflectional morphemes and word formation morphemes.   It does not apply when syntactically separate words are juxtaposed. Therefore, it distinguishes these two domains.

REFERENCES

Barbosa, P. A. Lemos. 1956. *Curso de Tupí antigo*. Rio de Janeiro: Livraria São José.

Coseriu, Eugenio. 1981. *Las estructuras lexemáticas, principios de semántica estructural* (2nd edition). Ed. by E. Coseriu, 162-184. Madrid: Gredos.

Dietrich, Wolf. 1985. Las categorías verbales (partes de la oración) en tupí-guaraní. *Anales del Instituto de Lingüística* 12.5-24. Mendoza (Argentina).

Dietrich, Wolf. 1986. *El idioma chiriguano. Gramática, textos, vocabulario*. Madrid: Instituto de Cooperación Iberoamericana.

Dooley, Robert A. 1982. *Vocabulário do Guaraní (Mbyá)*. Brasília: Summer Institute of Linguistics.

Grenand, Françoise. 1980. *La langue wayãpi (Guyane française). Phonologie et grammaire*. Paris: Société d'Etudes Linguistiques et Anthropologiques de France.

Hoeller, P. fray Alfredo. 1932a. *Grammatik der Guarayo-Sprache*. Guarayos, Bolivia: Verlag der Missionsprokura der PP. Franziskaner, Hall (Tyrol).

320WOLF DIETRICH

Hoeller, P. Fray Alfredo. 1932b. *Guarayo-Deutsches Wörterbuch.* Guarayos, Bolivia: Verlag der Missionsprokura der PP. Franziskaner, Hall (Tyrol).

Jensen, Cheryl Joyce S. 1984. O desenvolvimento histórico da língua Wayampi. Campinas: UNICAMP Master's Thesis.

Marchand, Hans. 1969. *The categories and types of present-day English word-formation. A synchronic-diachronic approach.* (Second edition.) Munich.

Montoya, see Ruiz de Montoya

Newton, Dennis. 1978. *Guarayu discourse. Work Papers of the Summer Institute of Linguistics.* Ed. by Ursula Wiesemann et al., 252-268. Riberalta (Bolivia).

Payne, Doris L. 1985. Inflection and derivation: is there a difference? *Proceedings of the First Annual Meeting of the Pacific Linguistics Conference,* 247-260. Eugene: University of Oregon.

Rodrigues, Aryon Dall'Igna. 1951. A composição em Tupí. *Logos* 6.63-70. Curitiba.

Rodrigues, Aryon Dall'Igna. 1952. Análise morfológica de um texto Tupí. *Logos* 7.56-77. Curitiba.

Rodrigues, Aryon Dall'Igna. 1953. Morfologia do verbo Tupí. *Letras* 1.121-52. Curitiba.

Rodrigues, Aryon Dall'Igna. 1985. Relações internas na família lingüística Tupí-Guaraní. *Revista de Antropologia* 27/28.33-53. São Paulo.

Ruiz de Montoya, P. Antonio. 1876. *Vocabulario y tesoro de lengua guaraní, ó más bien tupí. En dos partes: I. Vocabulario español - guaraní (ó tupí), II. Tesoro guaraní (ó tupí) - español.* New Edition by Francisco Adolfo de Varnhagen, Visconde de Porto Seguro. Viena: Faesy & Frick - Paris: Maisonneuve. (First edition, 1639. Madrid: Iuan Sánchez.)

Schermair, P. Fr. Anselmo. 1958. *Vocabulario sirionó-castellano.* Innsbruck: Innsbrucker Beiträge zur Kulturwissenschaft, no. 5.

Schermair, P. Fr. Anselmo. 1962. *Vocabulario castellano-sirionó.* Innsbruck: Innsbrucker Beiträge zur Kulturwissenschaft, no. 11.

Schuchard, Bárbara. 1979. *Ñane ñẽ, gramática guaraní para castellano hablantes.* Santa Cruz de la Sierra: Ayuda para el Campesino del Oriente Boliviano.

Sweet, Henry. 1892-98. *A new English grammar.* 2 vols. Oxford.

Incorporation In Nadëb*

E.M. Helen Weir

1. INTRODUCTION

The phenomenon of noun incorporation (NI) was noted as long ago as the early seventeenth century. Father Antonio Ruiz de Montoya, in his grammar of Ancient Guaraní, observed 'El primer modo de composición es de los verbos activos, que se componen con acusativo incorporado entre la nota y el verbo' (1876.53, a new publication without alteration of the grammar and vocabulary originally published in 1640); that is, he noted that a direct object ('acusativo') may be incorporated between the person prefix ('nota') and the verb root of a transitive ('activo') verb. NI has been reported in a wide variety of languages from different genetic families and geographical areas (for references see Woodbury 1975, Mardirussian 1975, Mithun 1984, Miner 1986). Until comparatively recently, however, there has been little attempt at a systematic study of the phenomenon in general.

The term 'incorporation' has been variously defined by different linguists. Sadock and others who have worked with Eskimo languages use the term to refer to a derivational process whereby an 'incorporated' noun and a verb-forming suffix combine to form a predicate. These verb-forming suffixes are not independent verbs in their own right (Sadock 1980.306).

The most generally accepted use of the term, however, follows Sapir's early work (1911) on NI. Based on this, Mithun defines the phenomenon as the compounding of a noun stem with a verb stem 'to yield a more specific, derived verb stem' (1986.32). Within this definition, there are differences of detail. For example, some definitions have limited the relationship between the incorporated noun (IN) and the V to that of direct object (e.g. Kroeber 1909.569, Campbell et al. 1986.550) or 'logical object' (Mardirussian 1975.387). Some specify that NI applies to 'a full NP argument of a predicate' (e.g. Mardirussian 1975.383), whereas Frantz speaks of 'the head noun of a nominal' appearing 'as a constituent of the verb of a clause'. He specifies that it is the head N (or its root), rather than a full NP, which is incorporated because 'in some languages the "remainder" of the noun phrase may be intact' (1979.54; cf. also Allen et al. 1984.292).

A few writers have used the term 'incorporation' to apply to elements of the clause other than nominals. Baker gives a very broad definition of incorporation as 'the process by which one semantically independent word comes to be found "inside" another word' (1985b.10; see also Comrie 1973.243). Baker discusses preposition and verb incorporation as well as noun incorporation.

Sapir 1911 distinguishes NI from (i) affixing of 'elements of pronominal signification', (ii) lexical affixes, and (iii) N stems used as V stems (Sadock's 'incorporation'). Miner 1986 also distinguishes it from what he terms 'noun stripping', whereby Ns in Zuni are stripped of certain normally obligatory suffixes and enter into some sort of unit with the V, though they are not regarded as part of the V.[1]

Mithun distinguishes between two formal variations of incorporation, viz. 'compounding by juxtaposition' in which the incorporated element, although syntactically bound to the V, remains a phonologically separate word retaining its own stress, and 'morphological compounding' in which the formal bond between the two constituents is much tighter and all regular word-internal phonological rules apply (1984.849, 854). Mithun's compounding by juxtaposition corresponds roughly to Miner's 'loose incorporation' (1986.244, 252).

In this paper, I describe the phenomenon of incorporation and its purpose in Nadëb and examine the implications for some recent theoretical issues . Nadëb incorporation fits partially with Frantz' definition of NI in that the head of a phrase, rather than a full phrase, is incorporated. Incorporated elements in Nadëb do not normally lose their status as phonologically separate words, although they do form syntactic units with their hosts (Mithun's 'compounding by juxtaposition'; Miner's 'loose compounding'). The resulting construction can show considerable complexity. For these reasons, I prefer to speak of the resulting construction as a 'verb complex' (VC), rather than a verb word; incorporated elements are generally written as separate words from the V stem.[2] For purposes of this paper, I define incorporation in Nadëb as the process whereby the head of a NP or of a PP combines with the V to form a new VC.[3]

Two unusual facets of Nadëb incorporation discussed in this paper deserve special mention:

i)   NI can take place only with possessed Ns. There must always be a possessor left after incorporation to assume the grammatical relation vacated by the IN.

ii) Incorporation is not restricted to Ns; postposition incorporation (PI) also occurs as a transparent and productive phenomenon.

I discuss Nadëb NI and PI in sections 2 and 3, respectively. Justification for the interpretation of these constructions as incorporation is considered in section 4. In section 5, I examine combinations of incorporation patterns and later in the paper suggest that pragmatic considerations govern the allowable combinations. The development of lexicalized compound Vs is mentioned in section 6. Section 7 discusses the purpose of incorporation in Nadëb and section 8 discusses whether it is a morphological or syntactic phenomenon. Section 9 turns to the implications of the Nadëb data for three recent theoretical works on incorporation: Mardirussian's universals of NI, Mithun's evolution of NI and Baker's theory of incorporation. I show that Nadëb incorporation agrees partially with each of these three theories, but not completely with any.

2. NOUN INCORPORATION IN NADËB

2.1 DESCRIPTION OF NI. The head N of the absolutive NP of a clause may be incorporated into the VC, provided the said NP is a genitive construction, i.e. provided it has the structure NP ->P + N.[4] Generally the phonological form of the IN is identical or almost identical to that of its unincorporated counterpart.[5] The IN, while forming a syntactic unit with the V stem, remains a phonologically separate word retaining its own stress. The possessor NP in the original absolutive NP ascends to become the new absolutive NP. There is no change in the valence of the VC; an intransitive V remains intransitive and a transitive V remains transitive. There is, however, always a change in the grammatical relations within the clause, since the possessor NP in the original absolutive NP ascends to the status of absolutive NP. This is generally known as 'possessor raising' or, in Relational Grammar terms, 'possessor ascension'.

Example 1 illustrates this process with the intransitive V *da-tés* 'hurt'. The head N *tug* 'tooth' of the subject NP of 1a is incorporated into the VC in 1b; its modifier (possessor) *ǐ* '1SG' becomes the new subject of the VC *tug da-tés* 'tooth-hurt' in 1b. The form of the pronoun changes from that of possessor in 1a to that of subject/object in 1b. This change in pronoun form is discussed further in section 4.3.

(1) a. tug   ǐ   da-tés
        tooth 1SG+POSS   THEME-hurt
        'My tooth hurts'.

     b. ǐih   tug   da-tés
        1SG   tooth THEME-hurt
        'I have toothache'. (Lit. 'I tooth-hurt'.)

Example 2 illustrates the same process of incorporation of the head N of the absolutive NP with the transitive V *hi-jxüt* 'wash'. The head N *mooh* 'hand' of the object NP of 2a is incorporated into the VC in 2b, while its modifier (possessor) *a* '2SG' becomes the new object of the VC *mooh hi-jxüt* 'hand-wash' in 2b.

(2) a. a   mooh ɫïh   hi-jxïit
        2SG+POSS hand 1SG THEME+ASP-wash
        'I wash your hands'.

     b. õm ɫïh mooh hi-jxïit
        2SG 1SG hand THEME+ASP-wash
        'I wash your hands'. (Lit. 'I hand-wash you'.)

2.2 CONSTRAINTS ON NI. Five restrictions apply to the incorporation of Ns into
a VC. First, a distinctive and unusual facet of Nadëb NI is that it can take place
only with possessed Ns. Nadëb Ns may be classified in terms of their
possessability: a) obligatorily possessed Ns require a possessor (but may be
stranded from their possessors under incorporation; cf. section 4.1);[6] b)
unpossessable Ns cannot occur with a possessor; c) possessable Ns may occur
with or without a possessor. Example 3 illustrates the incorporation of the
obligatorily possessed N tɨ́ 'food'; 3b shows that tɨ́ must have a possessor.

(3) a. Subih tɨ́   ɫïh i-tïi
        Subih food 1SG ASP-fish
        'I am fishing Subih's food'.

     b. * tɨ́ ɫïh i-tïi

     c. Subih ɫïh tɨ́ i-tïi
        'I am fishing Subih's food'. Or, 'I am fishing food for Subih'.
        (Lit. 'I am food-fishing Subih'.)

Unpossessable Ns cannot incorporate, as exemplified in 4 with the N *lakonan*
'tucunaré (sp. of fish)'; 4b shows that *lakonan* cannot be possessed. In 4c,
lakonan would be interpreted as subject, giving the semanticaly unacceptable
reading 'the tucunaré is fishing me' (contrast with 3 above).[7]

(4) a. lakonan ɫïh i-tïi
        tucunaré 1SG ASP-fish
        'I am fishing tucunaré'.

     b. * Subih lakonan ɫïh i-tïi

     c. * ɫïh lakonan i-tïi

A possessable N may incorporate into a V only when it leaves behind a
possessor, as exemplified in 5 with the possessable N *tób* 'house'; 5a,b show
that *tób* may be used with or without a possessor.

(5) a. Subih tób ɫïh ta-ma
        Subih house 1SG THEME-make
        'I am making Subih's house'.

b. tób łih ta-ma

'I am making a house'.

c. Subih łih tób ta-ma

'I am making Subih's house'. Or 'I am making a house for Subin'.

(Lit. 'I am house-making Subih'.)

The form 5d, which is also grammatical, might appear to be an instance of incorporation of an unpossessed N. It is not, however, derived from 5b by incorporation of the unpossessed *tób*, giving a reading 'I am making a house' ('I am house-making'). Rather it is derived from 5e by incorporation of the possessed *tób* followed by obligatory deletion of the third person pronominal object. All the tests for transitivity show that 5d is a transitive clause.

(5) d. łih tób ta-ma

'I am making his house'. (Lit. 'I am house-making him'.)

e. ta   tób   łih   ta-ma

3SG house 1SG THEME-make

'I am making his house'.

These examples demonstrate that NI can take place only with possessed Ns.

Second, pronouns, proper names, unpossessable Ns, and complex nominalizations, such as relative clauses, cannot be incorporated into the VC; this is in accordance with the rule which allows NI only from the head of a NP whose structure is of the form NP —> NP + N.

Third, heads of transitive subjects are never incorporated. Only heads of intransitive subjects and of direct objects are incorporable. This prohibition of incorporation from transitive subjects is reported to be universally true (cf. Baker 1985b.105-6).

Fourth, the process of incorporation of the head N of the absolutive NP is not permitted to produce a structure which would violate the general rule which states that the subject and direct object of a clause cannnot be coreferential. Instead, a reflexive construction is used, as in 6.

(6) a. tú   łi   łih   i-tüi

food 1SG+POSS 1SG ASP-fish

'I fish my food'.

b. * łih łih tú i-tüi

c. łih   tú   ki-tüi

1SG food REFL/REC+ASP-fish

'I fish my food'. (Lit. 'I food-fish myself'.)

Fifth, it is not common to find animate Ns incorporated into most VCs. An exception to this is with the simple V *a-ning* 'exist', which is often used with an IN to indicate possession, as in:

(7) a. Subih txaah niŋ
         Subih son   exist
         'Subih has a son'. (Lit. 'Subih son-exists'.)

It is also possible to have animate INs in relative clause structures, such as:

(8) txaah hiŋ   doo
     son   go.downriver the.one
     'the one whose son went downriver'

(9) masxãah i-tïip   doo
     pet   ASP-lay.egg the.one
     'the one whose pet (e.g. chicken) is laying an egg'

The fact that animate Ns are, in general, not commonly incorporated into VCs may be explained in terms of the purpose of incorporation (see section 7).

3. POSTPOSITION INCORPORATION IN NADËB

3.1 DESCRIPTION OF PI. The head (postposition) of a PP may be incorporated into the VC, while its dependent NP is advanced to direct object of the new VC. The direct object, if any, of the original V is demoted to become the dependent of the P *hã* 'dative' or *me* 'by means of'. The new VC is always transitive. Thus, in the case of an original intransitive V, there is a change in valence of the VC. As with the incorporation of Ns, there is always a change in the grammatical relations within the clause.

The process of PI is illustrated for the intransitive V *a-hiŋ* 'go downriver' in 10. The head of the PP in 10a, i.e. the P *sii* 'with', is incorporated into the VC in 10b to form the new transitive VC *sii hiŋ* 'with-go-downriver'. At the same time, the dependent NP in the PP in 10a *kad* 'uncle' becomes the direct object of the new VC.

(10) a. Subih a-hiŋ   kad   sii
         Subih FORM-go.downriver uncle with
         'Subih went downriver with uncle'.

     b. kad Subih sii hiŋ
         'Subih went downriver with uncle'. (Lit. 'Subih with-went-downriver uncle'.)

The process of PI with an already transitive V is illustrated with the V *a-wuh* 'eat' in 11. The head of the PP in 11a, i.e. the P *sii* 'with', is incorporated into the VC in 11b to form the new transitive VC *sii wuh* 'with-eat'. At the same time, the dependent NP in the PP in 11a *kaat* 'aunt' becomes the direct object of the new VC; the original direct object *kalaak dab* 'hen meat' is demoted to become the dependent of the P *hã* 'dative'.

(11) a. kalaak dab   Subih a-wuh   kaat sii
       hen   meat Subih FORM-eat aunt with
       'Subih is eating chicken with aunt'.

   b. kaat Subih sii   wuh kalaak dab hã
      aunt Subih with eat hen   meat DAT
      'Subih is eating chicken with aunt'.
      (Lit. 'Subih is with-eating aunt with respect to hen meat'.)

3.2 RELATIONSHIP BETWEEN PI AND SOME V PREFIXES. The simple Ps *go* 'inside', *me* 'by means of', and *bú* 'ablative' as such are not found incorporated into a VC. Instead they are replaced by the V prefixes *ga-*, *ma-*, and *ba-*, respectively.[8] Such prefixes are here called relational prefixes, because they alter the grammatical relations within the clause. Some linguists have used the term 'applicative' for this type of prefix (see, for example, Baker 1985b.342). The prefixation of the IP *go* 'inside' is illustrated in 12.

(12) a. éé   a-hing   hxóóh go
       father FORM-go.downriver canoe in
       'Father goes downriver in a canoe'.

   b. * hxóóh éé go hing

   c. hxóóh éé   ga-hing
      canoe father in-go.downriver
      'Father goes downriver in a canoe'. (Lit. 'Father in-goes-downriver a canoe'.)

In addition to the obligatory prefixation of these three IPs, the P *hã* 'dative' is preferentially prefixed as *ha-*; *yó* 'on top of' is optionally prefixed as *ya-* with some Vs.[9] This prefixation process is described more fully in Weir 1986, where it is argued that all relational, and some other, V prefixes have been derived diachronically from IPs.

3.3 CONSTRAINTS ON PI. Four restrictions apply to the incorporation of Ps into a VC. First, as stated in section 3.2, certain simple Ps are not found incorporated into VCs. Instead the equivalent relational V prefix is used.

Second, Ps cannot be incorporated into a VC from a comparative construction. This is illustrated with the P *bahinh* 'in front of' in 13.

(13) a. Subih a-eh   kad bahinh
       Subih FORM-be.big uncle in.front.of
       'Subih is bigger than uncle'.

   b. * kad Subih bahinh eh

This non-incorporation of Ps from a comparative construction is in accordance with the NP accessibility hierarchy of Keenan and Comrie, which states that the NP least accessible to relativization is the object of comparison (1977.66). Incorporation in Nadëb is closely linked with relativization (cf. section 7.2).

Third, I have no clear examples of compound Ps, such as *ithã* 'under', *noogo* 'in the time of', incorporated into a VC.[10]

Fourth, there are also restraints on multiple incorporations into the same VC involving PI. These are dealt with in sections 5.2 and 5.3.

4. SYNTACTIC UNITY OF THE VC

Some justification is needed for interpreting these NV and PV constructions as incorporation, rather than simply an alternative word order. This is especially necessary since, in most cases, the incorporated elements remain phonologically separate words, retaining their own stress; they do not present any phonological or morphological changes which would not occur in contexts larger than a word. Six arguments are given here for the syntactic unity of the VC. Further arguments apply to those VCs which have become lexicalized as compound Vs; these are considered in section 6.1.

4.1 STRANDING OF OBLIGATORILY POSSESSED Ns FROM THEIR POSSESSORS. Obligatorily possessed Ns cannot normally occur without an immediately preceding possessor. However, in the construction under question an obligatorily possessed N may be stranded from its possessor by incorporation into the VC, as in 2b above, where the obligatorily possessed N *mooh* 'hand' is incorporated into the VC.

When the possessor of the IN is a third person pronoun, this is obligatorily deleted, in accordance with the rule which deletes a third person pronominal absolutive NP in main clauses. In this case, the possessor of the IN is not even overtly expressed in the same clause (14b), although the reference would normally be clear from the linguistic or extra-linguistic context.

(14) a. ta   mooh łih   hi-jxïit
        3SG   hand 1SG THEME+ASP-wash
        'I wash his hands'.

    b. łih mooh hi-jxïit
        'I wash his hands'. (Lit. 'I hand-wash him'.),*'I wash my hands'.

4.2 STRANDING OF Ps FROM THEIR DEPENDENT NPs. In a similar way, Ps must normally be immediately preceded by their dependents; however, they can be stranded from their dependents under incorporation, as in 10b and 11b above.

4.3 CHANGE IN GRAMMATICAL RELATIONS WITHIN THE CLAUSE, AND SOME-TIMES IN THE VALENCE OF THE V. Under incorporation there is always a change in grammatical relations within the clause (cf. sections 2.1 and 3.1).[11] This may be seen by alterations in word order and, in some circumstances, by different use of Ps. It is perhaps most clearly demonstrated, however, by the forms of certain pronouns used under incorporation and in the non-incorporated paraphrase, as illustrated below.

First and second person singular and third person plural pronouns have two distinct forms each: one used for subject or object of a clause, and a different one for possessor in a genitive construction or dependent of a P. These forms are:

pronoun	subject/object	possessor/dependent of P
1st sing.	ḭh	ḭ
2nd sing.	õm	a
3rd pl.	la-	sa

When a N possessed by, or a P whose dependent is, one of these personal pronouns is incorporated into the VC, the form of the pronoun changes from possessor to subject/object; this indicates a change in grammatical relations within the clause. This is illustrated in example 2 above, where the second person singular pronoun has been advanced from possessor of the N *mooh* 'hand' in 2a to object in 2b. The N *mooh* 'hand' has lost its status as an argument of the clause and becomes part of the VC syntactic unit.

There is also a change in valence of the VC when a P is incorporated into an intransitive V (cf. section 3.1). This also indicates the syntactic unity of the VC.

4.4 INTERACTION BETWEEN INCORPORATED ELEMENTS AND SUBORDINATION PREFIXES. Nadëb V prefixes are classified into six types, as follows:

i) The formative prefix *a-* is generally attached to a main V root in the absence of other prefixes or incorporated elements. Any proclitic pronoun attached to the V will combine with the formative prefix when nothing else intervenes.

ii) The multi-function 'aspect' prefix *i-* occurs obligatorily with some V roots in all contexts and only in certain contexts with other V roots. As with the formative prefix, the 'aspect' prefix will be combined with any proclitic pronoun when nothing else intervenes.

iii) Derivational prefixes introduce a further dimension of meaning, such as *ka-* 'reflexive/reciprocal'. With several of the derviational prefixes there is a change in valence of the V.

iv) Thematic prefixes occur obligatorily with certain V roots, but not at all with others. It is often difficult or impossible to isolate the meaning of a thematic prefix from its V root.

v) Relational prefixes alter the grammatical relations within the clause, such as *ga-* 'inside'.

vi) Subordination prefixes occur only in certain embedded clauses. In the case of relative clauses they indicate the grammatical relation of the relativized constituent, e.g. *ha-* 'relativized subject'.

In general, subordination prefixes are not realized in the presence of any derivational, thematic, or relational prefix. This is illustrated for the subordination prefix *ha-* 'relativized subject' in 15 and 16. Example 15b shows the presence of *ha-* in the absence of any derivational, thematic, or relational prefix. In 16, the derivational causative prefix *da-* is present, blocking the realization of *ha-* in 16b.

(15) a. kad   a-sooh
         uncle FORM-be.on.something.above.the.ground
         'Uncle is sitting'. (Lit. 'Uncle is on something above the ground'.)

     b. ha-sooh   doo
         RS-be.on.something.above.the.ground   the.one
         'the one who is sitting'

(16) a. kad   da-sooh
         uncle CAUS-be.on.something.above.the.ground
         'Uncle puts (it) on something above the ground'.

     b. da-sooh doo
         'the one who put (it) on something above the ground'

     c. * da-ha-sooh doo

Any incorporated element in a VC also blocks the realization of any subordination prefix. This is illustrated in 17, with the incorporated N *nahǽǘh* 'illness' and the same subordination prefix *ha-*.

(17) a. ǂih   nahǽǘh ning
         1SG   illness exist
         'I am ill'. (Lit. 'I illness-exist'.)

     b. nahǽǘh ning doo
         illness exist the.one
         'the one who is ill'

     c. * nahǽǘh ha-ning doo

Thus, incorporated elements behave in the same way as derivational, thematic, and relational prefixes with respect to subordination prefixes. This supports the claim that the VC behaves as a syntactic unit.

4.5 PROCLITIC PLACEMENT. Mithun cites the placement of affixes and clitics which normally attach to the V as evidence for incorporation in some Oceanic languages (1984.850). In Nadëb, only V prefixes and proclitic pronouns are relevant in this respect, since the IN precedes the V. There is a difference between the behaviour of V prefixes and proclitics in an incorporation construction.

Proclitic pronouns are attached to the first constituent of the VC, viz. the IN, rather than to the V stem. Example 18 illustrates the attachment of the proclitic pronoun *ta-* '3SG' to the first element of the VC. This cliticization to the VC as a whole is evidence for the syntactic unity of the VC.

(18) a. ta-tá   i-tïï

    3SG-food ASP-fish

    'He is fishing his (i.e. someone else's) food'.

   b. * tá ti-tïï

On the other hand, the behaviour of V prefixes in Nadëb in no way indicates the syntactic unity of the NV complex. Prefixes which are permitted to occur with incorporation are still attached to the V stem rather than to the first constituent of the VC. This is illustrated with the V prefix *na-* 'negative' in 19.

(19) a. tá   ni-tïï   doo

    food NEG+ASP-fish the.one

    'the one who is not fishing (someone else's) food'

   b. * na-tá i-tïï doo

Nothing other than the permitted verb prefixes (and, in the case of multiple incorporations, other incorporated elements) can come between an incorporated element and the V root.

4.6 PREFIXATION OF CERTAIN IPs. The prefixation of certain IPs (cf. section 3.2) shows that, in these cases, a tighter formal bond has developed between the incorporated element and the V stem, thus emphasizing the syntactic unity of the VC. This prefixation has parallels in the NN compounds where a tight bond has developed as in *batxúúh* 'type of caterpiller' from *bxaah* 'tree' and *txúúh* 'something which clings'. The prefixed IPs, however, are part of a productive system in that they can occur with many different Vs; the resulting VC is not to be regarded as a frozen form. The tight NN compounds, on the other hand, are frozen forms.

5. MULTIPLE INCORPORATIONS INTO THE SAME VC

5.1 NI-NI INTERACTIONS. The head N of the absolutive NP may be incorporated into the VC provided the said NP has the structure NP —> NP + N (cf. section 2.1). This process of NI may be continued in the same clause as long as the conditions for incorporation are met, i.e. as long as the NP in question has the structure NP —> NP + N. The process of recursive NI into the same VC is illustrated with the transitive V *ga-jṳ* 'close' in 20. Each newly incorporated N appears in the left-most position of the VC.

(20) a. a   hoonh   tób   nooh kad ga-jṳṳ   dák

    2SG+POSS grandmother house mouth uncle THEME-close be.suspended

    'Uncle closed the door of your grandmother's house'.

b. a hoonh tób kad nooh ga-juu dúk
'Uncle closed the door of your grandmother's house'.
(Lit. 'Uncle mouth-closed your grandmother's house'.)

c. a hoonh kad tób nooh ga-juu dúk
'Uncle closed the door of your grandmother's house'.
(Lit. 'Uncle house-mouth-closed your grandmother'.)

d. õm   kad   hoonh   tób   nooh   ga-juu   dúk
2SG uncle grandmother house mouth THEME-close be.suspended
'Uncle closed the door of your grandmother's house'.
(Lit. 'Uncle grandmother-house-mouth-closed you'.)

In practice, not all of the forms cited in this example are commonly used, the most common being 20b. This is presumably because the participant most affected by the action of closing the door is normally to be regarded as the house, rather than the door itself or the people involved (see section 7.1). However, all forms cited are acceptable to a native speaker; it would be possible to describe circumstances under which the focus of the result of the action could be shifted to another participant. Any of the cited forms could be used in a relative clause, for example:

(21) kad   hoonh tób   nooh   ga-juu   dúk   doo
uncle grandmother house mouthTHEME-close be.suspended the.one
'the one whose grandmother's house door uncle closed'

There appears to be no theoretical limit to the number of Ns which may be incorporated into one VC, the practical limit being when the NP in question no longer has the structure NP —> NP + N, as is the case in 20d above. The INs resulting from multiple NI are in the same relationship to each other as they were before incorporation. It is not common, however, to find VCs with more than one IN. This corresponds to the fact that the majority of genitive constructions in Nadëb have only one level of possession. More than two levels, although not ungrammatical, is rare.

5.2 PI-PI INTERACTIONS. There is no PI-PI interaction in Nadëb. Once a P has been incorporated into a VC, this cannot be followed by the incorporation of another P into the same VC. For example, from the form 22a, either the P *mahang* 'among' (22b) or the P *sii* 'with' (22c) may be incorporated into the VC, but not both (22d,e).[12]

(22) a. tih a-wút   nadub mahang éé   sii
1SG FORM-be.in.movement Nadëb among father with
'I live among the Nadëb with father'.

b. nadᵾb łᵼh mahang wᵾt éé sii
'I live among the Nadëb with father'.
(Lit. 'I among-live the Nadëb with father'.)

c. éé łᵼh sii wᵾt nadᵾb mahang
'I live among the Nadëb with father'.
(Lit. 'I with-live father among the Nadëb'.)

d. * éé łᵼh sii mahang wᵾt nadᵾbhã

e. * nadᵾb łᵼh mahang sii wᵾtéé hã

The same restriction applies in the case of relational prefixes, which are derived from the incorporation of Ps into the VC (cf. section 3.2). An IP and a relational prefix cannot occur in the same VC, as illustrated in 23.

(23) a. łᵼh   a-hing   hxóóh go kad   sii
1SG FORM-go.downriver canoe in uncle with
'I go downriver in a canoe with uncle'.

b. hxóóh łᵼh   ga-hing   kad   sii
canoe 1SG in-go.downriver uncle with
'I go downriver in a canoe with uncle'.
(Lit. 'I in-go-downriver a canoe with uncle'.)

c. kad łᵼh sii hing hxóóh go
'I go downriver in a canoe with uncle'.
(Lit. 'I with-go-downriver uncle in a canoe'.)

d. * kad łᵼh sii ga-hing hxóóh hã

e. * hxóóh łᵼh sii ga-hing kad hã

The Advancee Tenure Law of early Relational Grammar theory, which states that 'an advancee cannot be placed in chômage by an advancement' (Perlmutter and Postal 1984.82), would have accounted for this PI-PI prohibition. This law, however, was later abandoned in favour of the less restrictive 1-Advancement Exclusiveness Law. In section 9.3.3, I offer a pragmatic explanation for the restrictions on incorporation interactions in Nadëb.

5.3 NI-PI INTERACTIONS. In examining the possibilities of interaction between NI and PI, there are two cases to be considered: (i) when PI is followed by NI of the head of the new ('applied') absolutive NP, and (ii) when NI of the head of the original absolutive NP is followed by PI.

5.3.1 PI FOLLOWED BY NI. PI may be followed by the incorporation of the head of the new ('applied') absolutive NP, provided the said NP has the structure NP —> NP + N (cf. ex. 24). The P *yó* 'on top of' in 24a is incorporated into the VC

in 24b, while its dependent NP *a tïng* 'your seat' is advanced to the status of absolutive NP of the new transitive VC *yó sooh* 'on-sit'. In 24c, the head *tïng*
'seat' of the new absolutive NP is incorporated into the VC, producing a new
VC with the structure N + P + V.

(24) a. kalapéé a-sooh   a   tïng   yó
         child   FORM-be.sitting 2SG+POSS support on.top.of
         'The child is sitting on your seat'.

   b. a tïng kalapéé yó sooh
         'The child is sitting on your seat'. (Lit. 'The child is on-sitting your seat'.)

   c. õm kalapéé tïng   yó   sooh
      2SG child   support on.top.of be.sitting
         'The child is sitting on your seat'. (Lit. 'The child is seat-on-sitting you'.)

   After incorporation the IP and IN have the same relationship to each other as
they had before incorporation.

5.3.2 NI FOLLOWED BY PI. On the other hand, the incorporation of a N into a VC
cannot be followed by the incorporation of a P into the same VC:

(25) a. Subih tá   tïh i-tïi   kad   sii
         Subih food 1SG ASP-fish uncle with
         'I fish Subih's food with (i.e. in the company of) uncle'.

   b. Subih tïh tá i-tïi kad sii
         'I fish Subih's food with (i.e. in the company of) uncle'.
         (Lit. 'I food-fish Subih with uncle'.)

   c. * kad tïh sii tá i-tïi Subih hã

6. LEXICALIZATION OF VCs WITH AN IN AS COMPOUND Vs

6.1 EVIDENCES OF LEXICALIZATION. Several VCs with an IN appear to have
been lexicalized as compound Vs since they present one or more of the
characteristics discussed in 6.1.1-6.1.6.

6.1.1 IDIOMATIC MEANING. The meaning of the VC may not be immediately
obvious from the meaning of its constituents. An example of a VC which has
taken on an idiomatic meaning is *mooh wát* 'work, do, make (with the hands)'.
The meaning of this compound form is not immediately obvious from the
meanings of its two components, *mooh* 'hand, arm' and *wát* 'be in movement',
although there is evidently some connection.

6.1.2 NO EQUIVALENT NON-INCORPORATED PARAPHRASE OF VC. There may be
no equivalent non-incorporated form of the VC, even though both the IN and
simple V are found independently in other contexts. The VC *mooh wát* 'work,
do, make (with the hands)' displays this characteristic also. The form 26a

would appear to have been derived from a non-incorporated form such as 26b; however, the non-incorporated form is unacceptable to all speakers.

(26) a. kad mooh wát
     uncle hand be.in.movement
     'Uncle is working'.

    b. * kad mooh a-wát
      uncle hand FORM-be.in.movement

6.1.3 IN OCCURS ONLY IN INCORPORATION CONSTRUCTIONS. The IN may be used only in incorporation constructions, as in the case of *txïïd*. As far as I know, this morpheme occurs only in the VC *txïïd mi-hlin* 'be sorry for, be concerned for' and its corresponding reflexive *txïïd ka-mi-hlin* 'be sorry for oneself, be concerned for oneself'. Native speakers cannot give any meaning for the morpheme *txïïd* in isolation, but their intuition is that it must refer to some part of the body or to some personal faculty or property.[13,14]

With a very few Ns, one (perhaps older) form is used when incorporated and another form when non-incorporated, as in the case of *tï*. Although this morpheme does not normally occur in isolation, native speakers say it refers to the eyes or the face. The non-incorporated forms most commonly used for eye and face are the obligatorily possessed Ns *matïm* and *mamej*, respectively. Example 27 illustrates the use of the alternative forms *matïm* and *tï* in paraphrases, without and with incorporation, respectively.

(27) a. a   matïm i-wúíh
     2SG+POSS eye ASP-be.big+MULT
     'Your eyes are big'.

    b. õm tï i-wúíh
     2SG eye ASP-be.big+MULT
     'You have big eyes'. (Lit. 'You are eye-big'.)

6.1.4 IN WITH WIDER RANGE OF MEANINGS WHEN INCORPORATED. The IN may have a much wider range of meaning when incorporated into various VCs than it has when used independently. This is the case with the N *nuuh* 'head'; it often refers to spherical objects when incorporated but may also have other, more obscure, reference. Examples of VCs containing this IN are: *nuuh düng* 'arrive' (cf. *a-düng* 'fall'), *nuuh ga-la-leem* 'be circular, be square', *nuuh ga-suu* 'put ridge on thatch roof' (cf. *ga-suu* 'put the lid on'), *nuuh ha-hót* 'have a bald head' (cf. *ha-hót* 'be bare'), *nuuh i-üí* 'start motor' (cf. *i-üu* 'shake, beat'), *nuuh ka-wung* 'have a headache', *nuuh sa-bok* 'gather together'.

6.1.5 VIOLATION OF INCORPORATION INTERACTION RESTRICTIONS. Sometimes an element may be incorporated into the VC and result in a VC whose incorporated elements are not in a genitive relationship. For example, the VC *mooh wɨ́t* 'work, do, make (with the hands)' allows the incorporation of Ps, as illustrated in 28. This conflict with the general NI-PI prohibition, described in section 5.3.2, indicates that *mooh wɨ́t* is no longer analysed into a N + V incorporation structure; rather it is treated as a single frozen item in the lexicon.

(28) a. kad   mooh wɨ́t   éé   sii
        uncle hand be.in.movement father with
        'Uncle is working with father'.

   b. éé kad sii mooh wɨ́t
      'Uncle is working with father'. (Lit. 'Uncle is with-working father'.)

6.1.6 UNEXPECTED CHANGE IN VALENCE OF VC. There may be an unexpected change in the valence of the VC. This occurs with the VC *mooh wɨ́t* 'work, do, make (with the hands)'. Since the V *a-wɨ́t* 'be in movement' is intransitive, it would be expected that the VC *mooh wɨt* would also be intransitive if it were a case of true productive incorporation. It is, however, ambivalent; that is, at times it behaves as an intransitive V and at times as a transitive V. For example, in 29 the third person subject pronoun *ta-* '3SG' is deleted. This is a characteristic of intransitive clauses. By way of contrast, in 30 *mooh wɨ́t* occurs with a direct object *ta waa* 'his food' and the third person singular subject pronoun *ta-*, as in the normal transitive clause structure.

(29) mooh wɨ́t
     hand be.in.movement
     '(He) is working'.

(30) ta   waa ta-mooh   wɨ́t
     3SG food 3SG-hand be.in.movement
     'He is making his food'.

6.2 LEXICALIZED VCs AND PRODUCTIVE INCORPORATION. It is worthy of note that in their primary sense, all Ns which occur in lexicalized VCs seem to be parts of wholes. These include body parts, such as *hóóh* 'liver', *hxɨɨb* 'chest' (also 'thought, desire, reason, intention, etc.'), *id* 'underneath', *jɨɨm* 'foot'. Alternatively, they may be faculties or properties closely associated with a person or animal, such as *babuu* 'smell', *kɨɨh* 'speech, words', *maɨj* 'shadow, spirit'. Compounds of some of these with the nominalizer *nxaa* 'that which functions in the capacity of' also occur, as *hɨbnxaa, kɨnxaa.*

The dividing line between true productive incoporation and lexicalized VCs is not always very clear. Some structures such as *mooh wɨ́t* 'work, do, make (with the hands)' are clearly lexicalized VCs. Other structures are clear cases of productive incorporation. However, some combinations could be interpreted either as lexicalized forms or as incorporation. This is the case with *nuuh ka-wɨng* 'have a headache', from *nuuh* 'head' and *ka-wɨng* 'ache'. *Ka-wɨng,* however, occurs only in a very limited number of incorporation structures and never in non-incorporated paraphrases. These incorporation structures could be analyzed as frozen lexical forms; alternatively, it could be specified that incorporation is obligatory with the V stem *ka-wang*. In contrast with this is the VC *tug da-tés* 'have toothache', which does have a non-incorporated paraphrase (cf. ex. 1). This somewhat fuzzy line between productive incorporation and lexicalization is to be expected if lexicalization is a continuing process in the language.

7. PURPOSES OF INCORPORATION

Mithun (1984.848) states that 'A comparison of the process [of incorporation] across languages reveals that...speakers always incorporate for a purpose; however, the purpose is not always the same'. The purposes and consequences of incorporation noted by various linguists and in various languages include the following, some of which are very closely related to each other:

i)　Creation of new words, especially the naming of events, qualities, or actions which have come to be regarded as recognizable, unitary concepts (e.g. Huauhtla Nahuatl 'lexical incorporation', Merlan 1976.183-4; Chukchee, Comrie 1973.243). These lexical items may develop idiomatic meanings which are not equal to the sum of the meanings of the constituents.

ii)　The expression of permanent or general activity, as opposed to specific activities (e.g. Mainland Comox, Hagège 1978.60; Chiriguano, Dietrich 1986.179-80).

iii)　A device for reducing the referentiality of the N (e.g. Ute, Givón 1984.72-3; Swedish, Hagège 1980.244).

iv)　'Object removal or object demotion', i.e. a detransitivizing device (e.g. Coptic, Givón 1984.416).

v)　A device for changing the grammatical relations within a clause (e.g. Blackfoot, Frantz 1979.30; Southern Tiwa, Allen et al. 1984.306).

vi)　A discourse reference strategy (e.g. Huauhtla Nahuatl, Merlan 1976.184).

vii)　A device for differentiation of an automatic or unpremeditated action from a deliberate one (e.g. Huauhtla Nahuatl, Merlan 1976.188; Dutch, Weggelaar 1986.303).

viii)　A method of classifying Ns, in which a relatively general IN stem (classifier) is accompanied by a more specific external NP which identifies the argument (e.g. Mohawk, quoted by Mithun 1984.869-71; traces in Dutch, Weggelaar 1986.303).

ix)   A stylistic device (e.g. Swedish, Hagège 1980.245).

The purpose of true productive incorporation in Nadëb is to change grammatical relations within the clause; a N or a P is incorporated in order for another participant of the clause to advance or ascend to the status of the absolutive NP. There are two reasons for changing another participant to the status of absolutive NP: (i) to reflect its greater affectedness, and (ii) to permit its relativization.[15]

7.1 GREATER AFFECTEDNESS. The first main reason for changing grammatical relations within the clause is to reflect the degree of affectedness of the advanced participant. Under incorporation, the effect of the state or action on the advanced or ascended participant is perceived as greater than its effect on the demoted participant. This is particularly the case when the incorporated element is head of an absolutive NP of the form whole-part, such as possessor-body part. For example, in 1a above the speaker is focusing more on the fact that his tooth is hurting, while in 1b he is emphasizing more the effect the toothache has on him as a whole. In 31a the speaker regards the effect of the action of closing the door to be more important to the door itself, while in 31b the effect on the house as a whole is seen as more important. In each case, the 'b' form is the more commonly used.

(31) a. tób   nooh kad ga-juu   dúk
         house mouth uncle THEME-close be.suspended
         'Uncle closed the door of the house'.

     b. tób kad nooh ga-juu dúk
         'Uncle closed the door of the house'. (Lit. 'Uncle mouth-closed the house'.)

Benefactives in Nadëb are generally expressed by using an incorporation structure. For example, in 5c (above) the effect on the person benefitted by the house-making is regarded as more significant than the effect on the house itself.

This purpose of incorporation, viz. to reflect greater affectedness of one participant by demotion (incorporation) of another, explains why animate Ns, in general, are not often incorporated in Nadëb. The tendency against (in some cases, total lack of) incorporation of animate Ns has been observed in many other languages (e.g. Anderson 1985.54). Other languages which use incorporation to reflect greater affectedness of the advanced or ascended participant include Blackfoot (Frantz 1971.72-6), Huauhtla Nahuatl (Merlan 1976.188), Koryak, Chukchi and Mohawk (quoted by Mithun 1984.862,868).

7.2 RELATIVIZATION. The second main reason for the advancement or ascension of another participant to the status of head of the absolutive NP has to do with the formation of relative clauses. In Nadëb there are only three clause constituents which can be relativized: subject, direct object, and adverbial. Only the first two cases are relevant to the discussion here.[16] In these cases, the relative clause usually contains as head either *doo* 'the one' indicating specific reference (ex. 32), or *péh* 'a one' indicating non-specific or hypothetical reference, such as 'type of, member of the class of' (ex. 33). The head of the relative clause may, under some circumstances, be deleted.

Relativization of the subject of a clause is indicated (potentially) by the V prefix *ha-* (exs. 32b, 33b). In the presence of most other V prefixes or incorporated elements, the relativized subject prefix *ha-* is not realized. Relativization of the object of the clause is indicated by the absence of this V prefix (ex. 32c).

(32) a. manaiin Subih a-wa
     cará   Subih FORM-eat
     'Subih is eating cará (sp. of edible tuber)'.

    b. manaiin ha-wa doo
      cará   RS-eat the.one
      'the one who is eating cará'

    c. Subih a-wa doo
      'that which Subih is eating'

(33) a. ta   ag   i-guuh
     3SG fruit ASP-be.sweet
     'The fruit is sweet'.

    b. hi-guuh   péh
      RS+ASP-be.sweet a.one
      'one which is sweet, a sweet one'

In order to relativize any nominal clause element other than subject or direct object, that element must first advance or ascend to one of these two positions; it then becomes eligible for relativization. For example, in order to relativize the dependent *kad* 'uncle' of the P *sii* 'with' in 10a above, *kad* must first be advanced to the status of direct object by incorporation into the VC of the P *sii* (10b). It can then be relativized as in 10c, given here:

(10) c. Subih sii hing   doo
     Subih with go.downriver the.one
     'the one with whom Subih went downriver'
     (Lit. 'the one Subih with-went-downriver')

Comparison of 1a-b above with 1c, given here, illustrates the ascension and relativization of the possessor of the subject.

(1) c. tag   da-tés   doo
        tooth THEME-hurt the.one
        'the one who has toothache' (Lit. 'the one who tooth-hurts')

In the case of the Ps *go* 'in', *me* 'by means of', *bú* 'ablative', and
(optionally) *yó* 'on top of', the dependent of the P is advanced to the status of
direct object by use of the corresponding relational V prefix, as illustrated by
comparison of 12a,c above with 12d (given here).[7]

(12) d. éé   ga-hing   doo
        father inside-go.downriver the.one
        'the one in which father goes downriver'
        (Lit. 'the one which father in-goes-downriver')

In view of the limitations on which clause constituents can be relativized, it
is not surprising that there is a very productive device for advancing other
participants to the status of subject or direct object. Compare, for example,
Keenan's statement that many Bantu languages which restrict the relativizable
positions to subject and direct object 'have very productive means for
presenting oblique NPs as surface direct objects' (1985.158-9).

7.3 COMPOUND Vs IN THE LEXICON. Arising out of the process of productive
incorporation, some VCs have become lexicalized as compound Vs denoting
common concepts (cf. section 6). In this way the lexicon is expanded. These,
however, are frozen forms which have arisen out of, but are not instances of,
true productive incorporation.

8. NATURE OF THE PROCESS OF INCORPORATION IN NADËB

There has been considerable discussion in recent years as to whether
incorporation should be regarded as a morphological or syntactic phenomenon.
Some recent treatments assume that incorporation is a result of a syntactic rule
(e.g. Rigsby 1975, Woodbury 1975). Comrie describes incorporation in
Chukchee as an optional transformation (1973.243). On the other hand, Anderson states that a syntactic rule of incorporation 'would be a rule of quite an
unusual type, since it would apply to incorporate only intransitive subjects or
transitive objects (just those elements which are marked as "absolutive" in an
ergative language...), but not transitive subjects, which are not known to be
incorporated in any language.' He goes on to argue that general and
idiosyncratic constraints on incorporation, together with the uses of incorporation in some languages, are best explained in terms of a word formation rule
rather than a syntactic movement rule (1985.54).

It does not always seem clear, in practice, just where the line should be
drawn between morphological and syntactic processes. Mithun describes NI as
'perhaps the most nearly syntactic of all morphological processes', yet insists
that it is a 'morphological device that derives lexical items, not sentences'

(1984.847). Baker argues strongly that incorporation is 'the result of standard movement rules applying to words rather than to entire phrases'; he shows, contrary to Anderson, how syntactic principles can explain the limitations on just what can be incorporated (1985b). He points out that incorporation, although basically a syntactic process, also has a morphological aspect in that it 'creates a complex category of the X-o level' (1985b.42). Baker unites the morphological and syntactic aspects of grammatical relation changing (which he explains in terms of incorporation) in his 'Mirror Principle' (1985a). Sadock 1986 argues for the syntactic nature of incorporation in some languages and states that 'noun incorporation is a phenomenon that straddles the boundary between syntax and morphology' (1985.432). He proposes that syntax and morphology are autonomous components of grammar, the interaction between them being regulated by universal principles of 'autolexical syntax' within the framework of Generalized Phrase Structure Grammar; this system has no place for movement rules.

I have argued that in Nadëb, incorporation is a very productive device for changing the grammatical relations within a clause, which reflects the greater affectedness of the advanced participant (section 7.1). I have also shown it to be closely related to the formation of relative clauses (section 7.2). The process of incorporation in Nadëb must precede relativization, since the former feeds the latter. It must also precede reflexivization, since this rule will act upon the output of the incorporation process if relevant (cf. section 2.2). On the other hand, there is clearly a morphological aspect involved in the formation of the complex verb and prefixation of certain IPs.[17] Thus, in accordance with Baker, I regard productive incorporation in Nadëb as basically a syntactic process which interacts with morphology. Those VCs which have become lexicalized as compound Vs are items in the lexicon rather than examples of true incorporation.

9. IMPLICATIONS OF THE NADËB DATA FOR SOME GENERAL WORKS ON INCORPORATION

I now turn to a consideration of the Nadëb data in the light of three recent works on the phenomenon of incorporation cross-linguistically. The first two deal only with NI; the third is more general. Mardirussian's 1975 work is an attempt to formulate universals for NI. Mithun's 1984 work classifies the different types of NI which occur cross-linguistically and proposes a universal path for the historical development of NI. Baker's 1985b and 1988 works are a formal treatment of incorporation in general within the government-binding framework of Chomsky 1981.

9.1 MARDIRUSSIAN'S UNIVERSALS. Mardirussian 1975 proposes a number of universals for NI. Although he speaks of 'object incorporation', he intends by this a 'logical object' which is 'the noun which undergoes the action of the verb' rather than the syntactic direct object of the clause (1975.387). His proposed universals concern phonological, morphological, and syntactic characteristics, semantic properties, and characteristics of the N that undergoes incorporation. The phonological and morphological characteristics apply only to certain languages and, for the most part, are not relevant to Nadëb. The second morphological characteristic, viz. that the IN 'may be moved between bound morphemes' (1975.384) does apply to Nadëb; INs are placed between the proclitic pronoun (if any) and the V stem (cf. section 4.5).

Mardirussian gives a hierarchy of accessibility for INs: a language incorporating indirect objects will also incorporate non-agental subjects and direct objects; a language incorporating non-agental subjects will also incorporate direct objects (1975.387). As we have seen, Nadëb allows incorporation of only head Ns of direct objects and intransitive subjects. Mardirussian implies that agental subjects are not incorporable. However, in Nadëb at least some agental intransitive subjects are incorporable under certain circumstances (cf. section 2.2 exs. 8 and 9).

The two aspects of Mardirussian's work most relevant to the Nadëb data are the syntactic and semantic proposals; I consider these in more detail in the following two subsections.

9.1.1 SYNTACTIC CHARACTERISTICS.

PLACEMENT OF THE IN RELATIVE TO THE V STEM

Mardirussian's first syntactic universal of incorporation is that the IN 'attaches to the right of the verb stem in verb-initial languages' and otherwise 'to the left of the verb stem' (1975.384). This is true of Nadëb; it is a V-final language and the IN always precedes the V stem.

TRANSITIVITY OF THE COMPOUND

Mardirussian's second syntactic universal of incorporation states that 'after incorporation of the noun the V becomes intransitive (if it was not already so)' (1975.384). This issue has also been addressed by several other linguists and it is said to be true for many languages. It does not, however, hold true for Nadëb. Productive NI never changes the valence of the VC. Even most of the lexicalized VCs which have arisen out of incorporation show the same pattern of case manipulation, without change of valence, which is characteristic of productive NI in Nadëb. Mithun 1984 cites several other languages (including Tupinambá, Yucatec Mayan, Blackfoot, Huauhtla Nahuatl, Mohawk, Southern Tiwa) in which incorporation does not always affect the transitivity of the V.

MARKING OF THE IN FOR PLURALITY

Mardirussian specifies that the IN 'cannot pluralize, take adjectives, determiners, etc.' (1975.386). The category of 'adjective' does not exist in Nadëb; the only 'determiners' are demonstrative pronouns, which do not modify the N but stand in apposition to it as a separate NP. Thus the only relevant factor here is pluralizing. Most Ns in Nadëb are not marked for number, the exceptions being a few animate Ns such as *txaah/taah* 'son/s', *ɨim/ɨy* 'wife/wives', *masxãah/masãah* 'domestic animal/s', etc. Ns which are marked for number when non-incorporated are also so marked when incorporated into a VC, as illustrated by comparison of 7a above with 7b, below. The V root *ning* is singular in both cases, agreeing in number with the subject of the clause *Subih* rather than with the IN. This incorporation of plural Ns appears to be contrary to Mardirussian's claim, but it should be pointed out that Nadëb has no productive inflectional morphological marking of plurals.

(7) b. Subih taah ning
      Subih sons exist
      'Subih has sons (children)'. (Lit. 'Subih sons-exists'.)

9.1.2 SEMANTIC PROPERTY - REFERENTIALITY OF THE IN.   The only basic semantic property Mardirussian lists as a universal of NI is the non-referentiality of the IN; he uses this to explain some of the syntactic characteristics of NI (1975.386).

The question of referentiality in relation to NI has given rise to some recent controversy. Sadock (1986.22-6) challenges Mithun's (1984) treatment of the subject. Mithun herself later admits that 'the referentiality of IN's is a subtle issue. Obviously it is not the case that they are never related to a referent...IN's are not marked for referentiality, and this is why external determiners appear so often with such constructions: they are used to supply overt referential specification' (1986.34). It is not clear to me from this whether she is claiming that INs are necessarily non-referential. Sullivan makes the claim that all INs are necessarily non-referential in Yucatec Maya, although he states that 'the texts and contexts within which incorporation occurs may limit the range of possible (implicit) referents for INs to the point of virtual referentiality' (1984.142). That being the case, it seems to me that there is little ground for claiming non-referentiality for all INs. Frantz makes a weaker statement, viz. that 'incorporation of a noun is often accompanied by a difference in referential status of the launching pad nominal in the discourse as compared to the counterpart without incorporation' (1979.54).

In Nadëb, it appears that the IN is regarded as less highly affected, rather than as non-referential. Except for a few idiomatic compounds (see below), the IN must belong to the person or thing referred to by the absolutive NP. For example, in 34 the incorporated *mooh* 'hand, arm' must be that of the subject of the clause (Subih), while in 35 the incorporated *mooh* must be that of the object (child).

(34) Subih mooh wa-yes
     Subih arm   THEME-be.scarred
     'Subih has a scarred arm'. (Lit. 'Subih is arm-scarred'.)

(35) kalapéé Subih mooh i-yóóh

    child   Subih arm   ASP-pierce

    'Subih pierced the child's arm (i.e. gave an injection)'.

    (Lit. 'Subih arm-pierced the child'.)

Only in a few cases of lexicalized VCs which have taken on an idiomatic meaning not equal to the sum of the meanings of its components can the IN have any other reference (or perhaps no reference at all). For example, in the ambivalent VC *mooh wúit* 'work, do, make (with the hands)', whether used intransitively or transitively, if the IN has any connection at all with the independent N *mooh* 'hand, arm',then the IN must be understood as the hand of the agent (subject); this V is used only when the activity involves the hands of the agent.

The relevant syntactic characteristics which Mardirussian explains in terms of the non-referentiality of the IN can, in Nadëb, be explained by other factors. For example, the constraint against the incorporation of proper names and personal pronouns in Nadëb is a consequence of the fact that these are non-possessable nominals, and therefore cannot function as head of a NP of the structure which allows incorporation, viz. NP —> NP + N.

9.1.3 SUMMARY. Thus, Nadëb NI agrees with some of Mardirussian's universals, particularly with regard to the placement of the IN. It also agrees partially with his accessibility hierarchy for INs, but contradicts the implication that agental subjects are not incorporable. The Nadëb data also contradict the statements that the V formed by incorporation becomes intransitive and that the IN becomes non-referential.

9.2 MITHUN'S CLASSIFICATION AND EVOLUTION OF NI. As a result of Mithun's 1984 study of NI across a wide range of geographically and genetically diverse languages, she finds that NI is used for four different but related purposes: lexical compounding (Type I), the manipulation of case (Type II), the manipulation of discourse structure (Type III), and classificatory NI (Type IV). She claims that 'these four types of NI fall into an implicational hierarchy, which in turn suggests a path along which NI develops historically' (1984.848). In the following subsections, I examine the phenomenon of incorporation in Nadëb in the light of Mithun's hypothesis.

9.2.1 TYPE I NI - LEXICAL COMPOUNDING. Mithun states that 'if a language exhibits any NI at all, it will contain basic lexical compounds'. A verbal compound is formed to designate an activity or quality which 'is viewed as a recognizable, unitary concept, rather than the chance co-occurrence of some action or state and some entity'. In such compounding 'the VN bond is both semantic and syntactic'. The IN is always non-referential, losing 'its individual salience both semantically and syntactically', and serving to qualify the V by limiting its scope. The effect of Type I NI extends no further than the VN complex itself. It simply lowers the valence of a transitive V, deriving an intransitive predicate from a transitive one (1984.848-56).

It might appear, at first glance, that the Nadëb lexicalized verbal compounds fit into Mithun's Type I NI. However, a closer examination reveals two basic differences between the Nadëb compounds and what Mithun describes, viz. in referentiality of the IN and transitivity of the compound.

First, Mithun specifies that the nominal constituent of a Type I NI compound is always non-referential. In productive NI in Nadëb, an IN is to be regarded as less highly affected rather than non-referential (cf. section 9.1.2). Although this is not true of all lexicalized compounds, it does seem to be true for several, for example, *hxuub nim* (cf. *hxub* 'chest, thoughts, desire, spirit, etc.', *a-nim* 'be good, pretty') 'be in a good mood'. The more highly idiomatic the lexicalized VC, the more likely the N is to be non-referential.

Second, Mithun specifies that the compound formed by Type I NI is always intransitive. This, however, is not true of Nadëb lexical compounds; there is no change in valence of the VC, except in a few cases where a very idiomatic expression has developed (cf. sections 2.1 and 6.1.6).

Mithun quotes as typical examples of Type I NI such compounds as 'to water-drink', 'to fish-spear', 'to door-close', 'to hand-wash', etc. The first two of these are impossible in Nadëb, since 'water' and 'fish' are unpossessable Ns in Nadëb; as such, they cannot appear either in productive incorporation structures or in lexicalized compounds (36; cf. also the first restriction in section 2.2).

(36) a. naung ʉ̈h   i-uuk
       water 1SG ASP-drink
       'I drink water'.

   b. * ʉ̈h naung i-uuk

Such compounds as 'to door-close' and 'to hand-wash' do occur in Nadëb, but the construction is subtly different from that described by Mithun as Type I NI. Rather than being necessarily intransitive as in Mithun's description, these VCs in Nadëb are always transitive; the direct object of the VC is the possessor of the IN. Thus, in Nadëb, 'to hand-wash' will always mean washing someone else's hands, unless a reflexive construction is used (2b, 14b above, and 37a given here). These constructions in Nadëb are instances of productive incorporation (of Mithun's Type II), rather than lexical compounds.

(37) a. ʉ̈h   mooh ki-jxʉ̈t
       1SG hand REFL/REC+ASP-wash
       'I wash my hands'. (Lit. 'I hand-wash myself'.)

The form 37a is derived from 37b below by incorporation of the head N of the absolutive NP. Since this would result in a clause in which the subject and object would be coreferential, the reflexive construction in 37a must be used.

(37) b. mooh ⱡi   ⱡih   hi-jxüt
       hand 1SG+POSS 1SG THEME+ASP-wash
       'I wash my hands'.

9.2.2 TYPE II NI - THE MANIPULATION OF CASE. The second type of NI identified by Mithun affects the structure of the entire clause. The essential difference between the two types of incorporation is that Type I 'simply lowers the valence of the V when it derives intransitive predicates from transitive ones; but Type II NI advances an oblique argument into the case position vacated by the IN. When a transitive V incorporates its direct object, then an instrument, location, or possessor may assume the vacated object role. When an intransitive V incorporates its subject, another argument may be advanced to subject status' (1984.856).

We have seen that the basic purpose of productive incorporation in Nadëb is to change the grammatical relations within the clause. In all cases of productive NI in Nadëb, the possessor of the incorporated element ascends to the vacated grammatical relation, whether the simple V is transitive or intransitive. This is in accordance with Mithun's definition of Type II incorporation.

9.2.3 TYPE III NI - THE MANIPULATION OF DISCOURSE STRUCTURE. The purpose of Mithun's Type III NI is 'to background known or incidental information within portions of discourse' (1984.859). This type of NI reduces the IN's 'salience...within a particlar portion of the discourse' (1984.862). As far as I know, this type of NI as described by Mithun does not occur in Nadëb.

9.2.4 TYPE IV NI - CLASSIFICATORY NI. Mithun's Type IV NI is the use of an incorporated 'relatively general N stem...to narrow the scope of the V...accompanied by a more specific external NP which identifies the argument implied by the IN'. This often results in a classificatory system, whereby 'nominals are classified according to the particular general N stem that is incorporated to qualify V's directed at them' (1984.863).

There is no general classificatory system of this type in Nadëb, although traces of such a system can be found. For example, the V *a-eh* 'be big' may be found with the following incorporations: *kxʉʉ eh*, referring to the length of certain objects, such as fish hooks (cf. *kxʉʉ* 'bone'); *nuuh eh*, referring to spherical objects, such as fruit (cf. *nuuh* 'head'); *ti eh*, referring to a hole or wound, etc. (cf. *ti* 'eye, face', although, as we have seen, this morpheme does not exist independently); *tʉʉg eh*, referring to the girth of a tree (cf. *tʉʉg* 'tree, wood, fire'); etc. To illustrate in more depth, consider *nuuh* whose primary meaning is 'head'. When incorporated, it may indicate spherical objects or may have more obscure uses (cf. section 6.1.4). Examples are: *nuuh eh* 'be big (spherical object)' (cf. *a-eh* 'be big'); *nuuh nüw is* 'be pretty (small spherical object, e.g. fruit)' (cf. *a-nɨm* 'be pretty', *is* 'diminutive'); *nuuh i-sóm* 'pound (spherical object, e.g. fruit)' (cf. *i-sóm* 'pound'); *nuuh i-tɨɨ* 'weigh' (cf. *i-tɨɨ* 'measure'). Mithun states that 'classificatory systems often originate as N's with narrower scope. When incorporated as qualifiers, they assume a much wider scope' (1984.865). This can be seen not only in the examples with *nuuh*, but also with *kxʉʉ*, and *ti*. Neverthless, this use of NIs as a classificatory system is restricted to certain Ns and certain Vs.

9.2.5 NADËB NI AND MITHUN'S THEORY OF NI EVOLUTION. From her comparison of NI processes across a wide range of languages, Mithun proposes that once NI appears in any language,

> it develops along a specific path. The beginning is a type of lexical compounding, in which a N stem and a V stem are combined to form an intransitive V denoting a nameworthy, unitary activity (Stage I). The IN loses its individual salience and syntactic role, becoming simply a component of the V. Next, the system may be extended to permit a significant oblique argument to assume the syntactic role vacated by an IN (Stage II). At this stage, NI affects case relationships within the clause - backgrounding one argument by NI while moving another into a more prominent case role.

Type III NI may then develop in polysynthetic languages; finally a classificatory system (Type IV) may arise (1984.874).

However, I suggest that Nadëb NI has not developed in the way Mithun postulates. The basic type of incorporation is that which changes grammatical relations within the clause (Mithun's Type II), with lexical compounds (not identical to Mithun's Type I) having arisen out of Type II incorporation structures which have become lexicalized as compound Vs. Type III NI does not occur in Nadëb but there are traces of Type IV. Thus, incorporation in Nadëb does not conform to the path Mithun traces for the universal development of NI. Weggelaar 1986 notes that the same is true for Dutch, although in this case, the process of incorporation is not nearly as productive as it is in Nadëb. Dutch does, however, present some similarities to the Nadëb situation; Types I, II, and traces of IV NI are found; only possessable Ns may incorporate.

9.3 BAKER'S THEORY OF INCORPORATION. Baker (1985b, 1988) proposes a theory of incorporation as a 'grammatical function changing' mechanism.[18] By it he explains the various grammatical relation changing devices in language, viz. NI (including possessor raising), antipassives, morphological causatives, applicatives, dative shift alternations, double object constructions and passives, as 'side-effects of the general process of movement ("Move Alpha") when it applies so as to take a word level category from its original phrase and adjoin it to a governing word level category' (1985b.2). In other words, he eliminates all other grammatical relation changing rules from the grammar, explaining these processes in terms of a general theory of incorporation, rather than explicit transformational or lexical rules. Baker's theory is based on the Government-Binding theory. The range of permissible grammatical relation changing processes is limited by the Empty Category Principle (see sections 9.3.1 and 9.3.2).

This appears to be a very neat theory, resulting in simplification of grammar. Nadëb incorporation is completely consonant with Baker's tenet that incorporation is a mechanism for changing grammatical relations. At the same time the Nadëb data raise certain problems which require further consideration of some of Baker's claims.

9.3.1 NADËB NI AND BAKER'S THEORY. Baker gives the following 'prototypical Noun Incorporation structures', stating that 'Noun Incorporation involves syntactically moving the structurally lower lexical item (the noun) in order to combine with the higher lexical item' (i.e. the verb) (1985b.103-4)[19]; further 'the Projection Principle requires that a trace be left in this movement' (1985b.116).

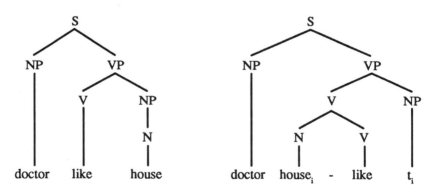

Baker notes that the process of NI 'has a limited distribution' (1985b.104), which he explains in terms of the Empty Category Principle. Excluded by the theory are the incorporation of: i) transitive subjects;[20] ii) a N root out of a prepositional phrase contained within the VP; iii) a N root out of a NP adjunct that appears in the VP; iv) subjects of unergative transitive Vs. In each of these cases the trace would not be properly governed by its antecedent, thus violating the ECP. In the first three cases, Nadëb NI presents no problem for the theory, since NI can only take place from the head of the absolutive NP (cf. section 2.1). The fourth case, however, requires further discussion.

Baker notes that in some incorporating languages, certain intransitive subjects may be incorporated, while others may not. This he explains in terms of the Unaccusative Hypothesis. Subjects of unaccusative Vs, which are claimed to be 'internal arguments' (i.e. D-structure objects), may incorporate; subjects of unergative Vs, which are 'external arguments' (i.e. subjects at all levels of representation), may not; the latter would violate the ECP in exactly the same way as would the incorporation of transitive subjects. Baker notes that 'there is a strong correlation to the effect that unergative verbs take an agentive (or experiencer) argument, while unaccusative verbs take a patient/theme argument'. He concludes that 'the argument of agentive intransitive verbs should never be incorporated' (1985b.113-4); this is indeed true for the incorporating languages he examined. We have seen, however, that Nadëb agentive subjects may, under certain circumstances, be incorporated, as in examples 8 and 9 above (cf. section 2.2).

Nevertheless, Rosen 1984, demonstrates that, although there is a strong tendency cross-linguistically for certain semantic roles to be associated with unaccusative Vs and others with unergative Vs, intransitive Vs cannot be designated as unaccusative or unergative on purely semantic grounds. In some languages certain syntactic tests provide the basis for making such a split. Since syntactic tests for unaccusativity in Nadëb have not yet been established, it is not clear at present whether the Vs in examples 8 and 9 are unaccusative or unergative. Thus, these examples may or may not present a problem for Baker's theory. However, if there is a distinction between unaccusative and unergative Vs in Nadëb, I would think it reasonable for both types to allow subject incorporation, on the grounds that this would appear necessary for the formation of certain relative clauses. This is an area which awaits further research.

It should be noted here that Baker's theory assumes that the language has a syntactic VP node where 'patient arguments are canonically internal to the VP and agent arguments are external' (1985b.673). Other deep structures have been postulated for some languages. In deep (or true) ergative languages the argument internal to the VP would be the agent, while the patient would normally be an external argument. In non-configurational (or flat) languages there would be no structural difference between the two arguments. Baker points out that, if such languages do exist, they should behave very differently with respect to incorporation, then do the languages he examined. In a deep ergative language, 'Ns associated with agent roles will freely incorporate, whereas Ns associated with patient roles will be unincorporable. In 'non-configurational' languages, on the other hand, either or both types of N should incorporate. Similar variation would be seen in...PI structures as well' (1985b.673). Baker, however, is doubtful as to the existence of languages with these deep structures on the grounds that he has not found empirical evidence from the behaviour of incorporation in languages claimed to have them. This raises the interesting question as to what the deep structure of Nadëb is. Discussion of this aspect is outside the scope of this paper; there are several factors to be considered other than the behaviour of incorporation.

9.3.2 NADĚB PI AND BAKER'S THEORY.   Baker argues that applicative
constructions are derived from preposition incorporation, although he gives no
concrete examples of adposition incorporation as a transparent phenomenon in
any language.   According to his hypothesis, prepositions and applicative
prefixes are alternative forms of one morpheme in the lexicon. Choosing the
preposition form results in a prepositional phrase construction, while choosing
the prefix form results in an applicative construction. Some languages have
only one or the other type of lexical item; other languages have both.

In this paper, I have shown that incorporation in Naděb is not restricted to
Ns, but that adpositions (in this case, postpositions) may also be incorporated.
I have further shown that some simple Ps are not found in incorporation
constructions, but are replaced by relational prefixes (Baker's 'applicative'
prefixes). Based on synchronic variation of certain Ps and their corresponding
prefixes, I have described elsewhere the diachronic process by which some V
prefixes (including all the relational prefixes) have developed from the
incorporation of Ps (Weir 1986). Thus, Naděb PI provides supporting evidence
for Baker's claim that applicatives originate as adposition incorporation.

According to Baker's theory, the ECP predicts that PI should not be
possible: i) from subject position (but this is a rather vacuous prediction, since
PPs are not likely to be found in subject position anyway; 1985b.351); ii) out of
an embedded PP (1985b.351); iii) out of an adjunct (1985b.353). The first two
cases do not occur in Naděb PI and present no problem for the theory. The third
requires further discussion.

In his consideration of which types of PP can allow incorporation, Baker
admits that 'it is not easy to tell which PPs are adjuncts, and which are
actually arguments of the verb' (1985b.353). However, he presents evidence
that dative/goal, benefactive/malefactive, instrumental and some locative
('inner' locative) PPs are arguments, while other locative ('outer' locative),
temporal, manner and reason PPs are adjuncts. According to his theory, the
former should allow PI, while the latter should not; he does mention in a
footnote some possible exceptions to this in the data available to him. We have
seen that in Naděb Ps cannot be incorporated out of a comparative construction
(cf. section 3.3). There are, however, instances of incorporation from some
reason phrases; for example, in 38b the reason P pxãa is incorporated. There is
also a restricted use of an applicative construction with temporal and manner
phrases.

(38) a. a-óót   ta   ib   pxãa
       FORM-cry 3SG father reason
       'He is crying for his father'.

     b. ta   ib   ta-pxãa   óót
        3SG father 3SG-reason cry
        'He is crying for his father'. (Lit. 'He is for-crying his father'.)

Baker claims that dative applicative constructions are 'perhaps the most common and syntactically regular class across languages'. This he accounts for on the basis that it is 'universally acknowledged' that the goal PP in dative constructions is a component of the verb (1985b.348-9). It is comparatively rare to find a Nadëb verb with incorporated dative P *hã* or its equivalent prefixed version *ha-*. More commonly the morpheme *ma* is incorporated (cf. 39a,b).[21]

(39) a. ̃Ih i-lih   ̃uun   hã
     1SG ASP-write mother DAT
     'I am writing to mother'.

   b. ̃uun   ̃Ih   ma i-lih
     mother 1SG GL ASP-write
     'I am writing to mother'. (Lit. 'I am goal-writing mother'.)

With certain Nadëb verbs, the goal may be expressed as the possessor in the direct object NP, rather than the dependent of a P. This goal may ascend by NI (possessor raising):

(40) a. Subih waa hoonh   a-nxoo   dúk
     Subih food grandmother FORM-give be.suspended
     'Grandmother gave food to Subih'. (Lit. 'Grandmother gave Subih's food'.)

   b. Subih hoonh waa nxoo dúk
     'Grandmother gave Subih food'. (Lit. 'Grandmother food-gave Subih'.)

Baker discusses at length the differences in the behaviour of benefactive and instrumental applicatives, accounting for these differences in terms of 'a universal difference in how thematic roles are assigned' (1986.90). There is also a fundamental difference in these two constructions in Nadëb, but not the same as that investigated by Baker. While instrument phrases appear as PPs in Nadëb, benefactives (like some datives, mentioned above) are generally expressed in NPs; the benefactee appears as 'possessor' in the direct object NP. Thus, the raising of the benefactee to direct object is an instance of possessor raising, as in example 3 above.

Baker's theory explains two syntactic characteristics which he claims for applicative constructions:

   i) 'applicative constructions always make the designated semantically oblique nominal into the direct object, rather than the subject or the indirect object, or some other kind of oblique phrase' (1985b.374);

   ii) 'applicative constructions should not be possible when the verb that hosts the P incorporation is not a Case assigner' (1985b.379), i.e. verbs which are basically intransitive cannot undergo PI. He accounts for apparent exceptions to this prediction by saying that such 'must be derived in the lexicon', and are 'generally idiosyncratic in semantic interpretation' (1985b.387).

The first of these syntactic characteristics is true of Nadëb PI. As we have seen, the dependent NP of an IP is advanced to direct object (cf. section 3.1). However, Nadëb PI does present a problem for the second characteristic; intransitive verbs, as well as transitive ones, can freely undergo PI, resulting always in a new transitive VC.[22] This is a very productive process and does not show evidence of idiosyncratic semantic interpretation. The problem here would not appear to be in the basic statement that the derived V in an applicative construction must assign accusative Case to the stranded NP (1985b.378); rather the problem concerns the manner in which the derived V is assumed to acquire this capability, viz. that it inherits this from the original V root. The argument behind this is that since the derived V does not exist in the lexicon as such, it inherits the property of being able to assign Case from its components. It is claimed that since a P will assign oblique Case, and since the derived V cannot inherit the property of being able to assign such a Case, the derived V will only 'be able to assign Case by inheriting that ability from the verb root it is based on' (1985b.379). Thus, according to Baker's argument, only transitive Vs can undergo PI.

In later works Baker accounts for the occurrence of certain applicatives with intransitive Vs in some languages in terms of the manner in which those languages assign Case. He observes that 'prepositional elements may be structural Case assigners rather than oblique Case assigners in some languages'. This property of assigning structural Case 'could potentially be inherited by the applied verb' (1988.469). He shows that in Popoluca 'verbs can assign structural Case to a governed NP even if they do not take a direct NP argument' (1986.83), i.e. some basic intransitive Vs can assign Case to a NP argument. To allow for PI with intransitive Vs in Nadëb, it would seem that a derived V which is based on an intransitive V root must in some way acquire the ability to assign accusative Case in the process of incorporation of the P.[23] In the case of a transitive base V root, the original direct object can no longer receive accusative Case from the derived V. It is always demoted to oblique, as shown by the presence of the dative or instrumental P following it in the clause with PI (cf. section 3.1).

9.3.3 NADËB INCORPORATION INTERACTIONS AND BAKER'S THEORY. Baker specifies two conditions by which he accounts for the behaviour of incorporation interactions:

i) 'in general only one noun may be incorporated into a single verbal stem' (1985b.473);

ii) 'incorporation of the head of the complement of a category which has previously been incorporated' is not permitted (1985b.474).

Both conditions rule out the incorporation of a raised possessor, i.e. 'the possessor of an incorporated noun cannot itself incorporate' (1985b.478).

However, in Nadëb this may indeed occur, provided the conditions for NI are met. Possessor raising with concomitant NI is recursive; there is apparently no theoretical limit to the number of Ns which may be incorporated into a single V (although in natural discourse multiple incorporation is not common; cf. section 5.1). In a footnote, Baker mentions that the possessor of a possessor may, under certain circumstances, be raised in Kinyarwanda, but he claims that the construction involved is different from the one he is discussing (1985b.526).

Baker's two conditions on the behaviour of incorporation interactions allow the incorporation of the basic object (NI), followed by PI. He specifies that 'some type of Noun Incorporation is generally obligatory under these circumstances, because of the Case filter' (1985b.480). However, he rules out interactions between applicatives and possessor raising (= NI in Nadëb) for those languages whose Vs can only assign one accusative Case, on the grounds that both the raised possessor and the applied object would need to receive accusative Case from the V (1988.387). Although Nadëb appears to be a language which assigns only one accusative Case, the problem of Case assignment would not prohibit the combination of NI followed by PI; PI would require the raised possessor to be demoted to become the dependent of the P *hā* 'dative' or *me* 'instrument' (cf. section 3.1). Thus NI followed by PI would not be ruled out on syntactic grounds. However, this combination does not occur in Nadëb (cf. section 5.3.2).

On the other hand, NI of the applied object after PI is ruled out by Baker's second condition. He states 'all of the kinds of NI are predicted to be uniformly ungrammatical when they are fed by PI in this way, even though PI seems on the surface to create the sort of direct object NP which would be incorporable' (1985b.486). However, this combination does occur in Nadëb (cf. section 5.3.1).

For most languages, Baker's theory rules out double PI constructions on the grounds that this would require the incorporation (overt or covert) of two Ns into the V to escape the Case filter, which, in turn, is forbidden by his first condition. However, he shows that languages such as Kinyarwanda, whose Vs have the property of being able to assign two accusative Cases, do, in fact, permit double PI constructions. As in the case of NI + PI, the problem of Case assignment would not rule out PI + PI in Nadëb, since the applied object after the first PI would be demoted to become a dependent of a P by the second PI. Thus double PI would not be ruled out on syntactic grounds. However, this combination does not occur in Nadëb (cf. section 5.2).

Thus, of the four logically possible incorporation interactions, viz. NI + NI, NI + PI, PI + NI, and PI + PI, Baker's conditions make the wrong prediction for Nadëb in two cases (NI + NI and PI + NI). In the other two cases, the grounds on which the interactions are ruled out by the theory are inapplicable in Nadëb.

E. M. HELEN WEIR

It is not the purpose of this paper to discuss in detail all the theoretical implications of these facts, or to consider how Nadëb incorporation relates to the phenomenon of incorporation cross-linguistically. However, some simple observations relevant to the Nadëb data are noted here for further investigation.

Baker's first condition on the behaviour of incorporation interactions, viz. that only one N may incorporate into a single V, is based on the generalized Case filter and on the claim that 'a single item cannot morphologically identify two NPs in the same way' (1985b.164). Thus, a single V will normally be allowed to assign a theta role to only one NP, ensuring that theta role assignments are recoverable. In this respect, most of Baker's discussion relates to the incorporation of two Ns from two different NPs, such as patient and means. This situation, however, does not arise in Nadëb, where recursive NI can take place only from the same original absolutive NP. Under these conditions, if a VC with an IN were, as a unit, able to assign a theta role to another N, then there would be no problem from recursive NI; each successive IN would receive its theta role from the (composite) verb into which it was incorporated. Thus, in the structure $N_2 + N_1 + V$, N_1 would receive its theta role assignment from V, while N_2 would receive its theta role from the composite form $N_1 + V$. Thus, Baker's first condition would be unnecessary for Nadëb. Baker's second condition, viz. that an item and the head of its complement cannot both be incorporated, rules out double NI and also PI followed by NI of the head of the applied object; both of these occur in Nadëb. Thus this condition, as formulated, does not hold true empirically for Nadëb.

We have seen that Nadëb permits NI + NI and PI + NI, but not NI + PI and PI + PI. We have also seen that, in the case of multiple incorporations, all incorporated items will have come originally from the same NP or PP. If the purpose of incorporation in Nadëb (cf. section 7) has been correctly perceived, there is a very simple pragmatic explanation for the occurrence of the permitted (and only the permitted) incorporation interactions. I claimed that the purpose of incorporation in Nadëb is to change grammatical relations within the clause in order to reflect greater affectedness of the advanced participant or permit relativization of the advanced participant. Thus, if in any clause a N or P is incorporated precisely in order to reflect greater affectedness of, or relativize, another participant, there would be no pragmatic justification for incorporating a P from a **different** PP. Thus NI + PI and PI + PI are ruled out because, in both cases, the two elements would come from two separate phrases. However, the incorporation of a N or P could be followed by that of the head N of the possessor or dependent NP from the **same** original phrase in order to reflect greater affectedness of, or relativize, the latter's possessor. In this case, the first incorporation would merely be a necessary intermediate step towards advancing the required participant.

In section 6.1.5 we saw that lexicalized compound Vs can sometimes occur with incorporated elements which appear to violate the incorporation interaction restrictions. For example, in 28b above, the VC has the structure P + N + V, suggesting that NI has been followed by PI. This apparent violation of the incorporation interaction restrictions can be accounted for pragmatically. The compound *mooh wǘt* is a frozen form, no longer analysed into a N + V combination; the apparently 'incorporated noun' *mooh* 'hand' has not been incorporated in order to reflect greater affectedness of another participant. Hence, pragmatics will not rule out the possibility of another element being incorporated for this purpose.

9.3.4 SUMMARY. In summary, Nadëb provides much evidence in support of Baker's theory, but also raises some questions for further consideration. The main issues are:

i)   the incorporation of intransitive subjects, the question of unaccusativity and the nature of Nadëb deep structure;

ii) the occurrence of PI with intransitive Vs and the manner in which the derived verb acquires its capability to assign Case;

iii) Baker's conditions on incorporation interactions, which, for Nadëb, are either inapplicable or make the wrong predictions; such interactions in Nadëb are governed by pragmatic considerations.

10. CONCLUSION

The study of the phenomenon of incorporation in Nadëb is far from complete. However, the present work has revealed some unusual features from this little known language. Three areas are worthy of special note: the fact that NI can take place only with possessed Ns in Nadëb, the occurrence of PI as a transparent and productive phenomenon, and the restrictions on the permitted combinations of incorporation. I have mentioned some areas of theoretical interest which merit further study. Little is known at present about other languages related to Nadëb. As data becomes available from these languages and as research into Nadëb continues, it should become possible to determine whether or not some of the characteristics discussed in this paper are also found in related languages.

NOTES

*   Nadëb is an indigenous language spoken in the state of Amazonas in northwest Brazil. Although little comparative work has been done with other languages, Nadëb has been classified as belonging to the Makú-Puinave family (see, for example, Rivet and Tastevin 1920, Mason 1950.257-8, Tovar 1961.156-7, Loukotka 1968.190-3). The data on which the present analysis is based were collected by the author from speakers of the Upper Uneiuxi dialect during various field trips between September 1975 and December 1976, and

between October 1980 and December 1982, under the auspices of the Summer Institute of Linguistics and the Universidade Estadual de Campinas. I wish to thank the Fundação Nacional do Indio and the Conselho Nacional de Desenvolvimento Cientifico e Tecnológico for authorization to live and work in the indigenous area. This paper was partially supported by NSF Grant No. BNS-8617854, NEH Grant No. RX-20870-87, and the University of Oregon Foundation. It was originally presented in preliminary form at the Working Conference on Amazonian Languages held at the University of Oregon (1987). I wish to thank other partcipants of the conference for their comments and discussion; also Mark Baker, Loraine Bridgeman and Doris Payne for their helpful suggestions on how to improve this paper. The abbreviations used are: ABL ablative; ADV adverbial; ASP multi-function 'aspect' prefix; CAUS causative; CMPL completive; DAT dative; ECP Empty Category Principle; FORM formative prefix; GL goal; IN incorporated noun; IP incorporated postposition; MULT multiple; N noun; NEG negative; NI noun incorporation; NP noun phrase; OSV object subject verb; P postposition; PART partitive; PI postposition incorporation; POSS possessive; PP postpositional phrase; RA relativized adverb; REFL/REC reflexive/reciprocal prefix; RS relativized subject; THEME thematic prefix; TR transitivizer prefix; UNIT unitary; V verb; VC verb complex; VP verb phrase; 1SG first person singular pronoun; 2SG second person singular pronoun; 3SG third person singular pronoun. The terms 'ablative' and dative are glosses for the Ps and V prefixes *bʉ́/ba-* and *hā/ ha-*, respectively; their range of meaning is, however, considerably wider than these terms might imply.

[1]   In practice, it seems possible to distinguish between stripping and incorporation in Zuni only when a V prefix is present. In the case of stripping, the prefix is attached to the V; in the case of incorporation, it is attached to the NV construction as a whole (Miner 1986.251-3).

[2]   The term 'verb-complex' was used in this sense by Kroeber 1909 and Sapir 1911.

[3]   I regard the postposition as head of the PP and the accompanying NP as its dependent. The basic structure of the genitive construction in Nadëb is NP -> NP + N (possessor-possessed); that of the PP is PP -> NP + P. As in many languages, the term 'possessor' in Nadëb has wider scope than strict ownership. It extends to the relationship between any modifying NP and its head N in a NP ->NP + N 'genitive' construction, including kinship, part-whole, social role, etc., as well as ownership. There is an obligatory rule which moves a first person singular pronominal possessor or dependent of a P to the position immediately following the head of the phrase (possessed N or P); cf. *a txaah* (2SG+POSS son) 'your son', *txaah ʉ̃* (son 1SG+POSS) 'my son'; *a hā* (2SG+POSS DAT) 'to you', *hā ʉ̃* (DAT 1SG+POSS) 'to me'.

⁴   By 'absolutive' I mean the subject of an intransitive V or the direct object of a transitive V. There is no morphological case marking on subjects or objects in Nadëb.

⁵   In a few instances there is a phonological change in the form of the IN, as in *bu bi-niim* 'smell nice' (cf. *babuu* 'smell', *i-niim* 'be pretty, good (pl.)'). A few INs are nominalized forms of other Vs which are seldom found as nominalizations other than in VCs. An example of this is the VC *dijṻh bi-niim* 'be bitter but good' (cf. the nominalized form *dijṻh* of the V *di-jṻng* 'be bitter', and the V *i-niim* 'be pretty, good (pl.)').

⁶   Obligatory possession is not the same as inalienable possession. With some obligatorily possessed Ns the referent of the possessor may change, but there must always be a possessor. Examples of obligatorily possessed Ns which may change ownership are *masxãah* 'pet', *naam* 'louse', *tṵ* 'food', *yóóm* 'plant'.

⁷   Further evidence that unpossessable Ns cannot incorporate comes from relative clauses. It is stated in section 7.2 that a relativized subject is (potentially) marked by the V prefix *ha-*. This prefix is not realized in the presence of certain other V prefixes or incorporated elements. In the grammatical form (i), the presence of *ha-* indicates that the object *lakonan* is not incorporated. The form (ii) without *ha-* is ungrammatical, showing that incorporation is not permitted. In (ii) *lakonan* would be interpreted as subject, giving the semantically unacceptable reading 'the one the tucunaré is fishing'.

(i)   lakonan hi-tii   doo
       tucunaré RS+ASP-fish the.one
       'the one who is fishing tucunaré'

(ii)   * lakonan i-tii doo

⁸   The change in vowel quality when prefixation occurs is in accordance with the general form of all V prefixes *Ca-*. This is a partially neutralized vowel in pretonic syllables. Any prefix which immediately precedes the multi-function 'aspect' prefix will combine with it yielding the form *Ci-*.

⁹   See also the discussion of dative applicatives in section 9.3.2.

¹⁰   A possible exception is the appearance of the compound *hɨbnxaa* in VCs which have been lexicalized as compound Vs, such as *hɨbnxaa ni-wɨɨ* 'think about', *hɨbnxaa tón* 'be sad'. These, however, are not cases of productive incorporation. It is also not clear whether *hɨbnxaa* should be regarded as a compound N or a compound P in all these cases.

¹¹   Incorporation is often described as a special case of compounding (see, for example, Sapir 1911.257, Anderson 1985.43). However, in Nadëb the change in grammatical relationships which always takes place under incorporation

distinguishes it from compounding. Compare Sullivan's claim that, in Yucatec Maya, incorporation and compounding are two syntactically distinct processes with different semantic consequences (1984.139). Baker 1985b also makes a distinction between incorporation and compounding.

[12]   It is not very common to find a clause with more than one PP, unless these are coreferential.   One speaker considered the following forms better alternatives to 22a, though he seemed to accept 22b and 22c without question.

(i)   ƚih   a-wút   nadub mahang, éé   dahééh
       1SG FORM-be.in.movement+UNIT Nadëb among, father also
       'I live among the Nadëb, and so does father'.

(ii)   ƚih   a-bok   nadub mahang, éé   dahééh
       1SG FORM-be.in.movement+MULT Nadëb among, father also
       'I live among the Nadëb, and so does father'.

[13]   There are a few other morphemes which occur only incorporated into VCs; the clauses in which they appear have no non-incorporated paraphrases. These include the partitives *hãd* and *baah* (exs. i and ii) and the resultative morpheme *wén* 'therefore' (ex. iii).

(i)   ta   txaah hãd   eeh   dúk
       3SG son   PART be.big CMPL
       'His son is quite big already'.

(ii)   kad   baah ƚh   wút
       uncle PART sleep CMPL
       'Uncle slept a bit'.

(iii) ta   ib   Subih hi-gxãas,   ta   wén   hing
       3SG father Subih THEME+ASP-see, 3SG therefore go.downriver
       'Subih went downriver to see his father'.

These morphemes, however, are not to be regarded as having disappeared from the lexicon except in compounds, since they enter into incorporation constructions very productively. They also behave in a different manner from normal INs or IPs in that they are not subject to the usual restrictions on multiple incorporations (see section 5).

[14]   A special case of morphemes which occur in VCs but not in non-incorporated forms arises in onomatopoeic compound Vs such as *mi ha-mi* 'roar'. Here the complete compound is the onomatopoeic representation of the roaring; *mi* is not to be interpreted as having any significance apart from the compound, even though there is a homophonous N *mi* 'type of fruit'. This onomatopoeic verbal compound parallels onomatopoeic compound names of birds, animals, etc.

15   In this paper I use the term 'participant' in a very broad sense to mean any nominal (animate or inanimate) in the clause.

16   The relativization of an adverbial constituent is not relevant to the present discussion since a clause constituent can never be raised to the status of adverbial. The following example illustrates the relativization of an adverbial constituent. This type of relativization is indicated (potentially) by the presence of one of the relativized adverbial V prefixes *ba-* and *ha-*. The latter is used only to indicate a contrastive locative or temporal phrase. Relativized adverbial clauses are always headless and generally appear as dependents of Ps.

(i)   kad   a-hing   jém   hě
      uncle FORM-go.downriver yesterday ADV
      'Uncle went downriver yesterday'.

(ii) kad   ba-hing   bʉ́
      uncle RA-go.downriver ABL
      'when uncle went downriver'

17   There is some evidence that prefixing of INs may also have taken place under certain circumstances.

18   Baker's 'grammatical function changing' corresponds to my 'grammatical relations changing'.

19   Compare Sadock's constraint on incorporation, viz. 'it is the deepest governed phrase from which an incorporated element must be drawn' (1985.414).

20   Myhill 1988 argues that a construction in Indonesian which has traditionally been referred to as 'passive' is, in fact, 'agent incorporation'; that is, he argues for the existence of incorporation of transitive subjects. However, it seems that this construction could be interpreted as passivization followed by agent incorporation. If this is the case, the constituent incorporated would be an oblique nominal (similar to instrument incorporation cited by several authors), rather than a surface transitive subject.

21   It is not completely clear whether *ma* should be regarded as an IP or an IN. By comparison with ex. 40, it would seem reasonable to interpret it as a N. There is a (probably related) N *ma* 'belongings'. Incorporated *ma* has other uses, as in *ma i-na* (*ma* ASP-come) 'make a noise', *ma i-niim* (*ma* ASP-be.pretty) 'sound pleasant', *ma ba-doh hʉ̄m* (*ma* THEME-be.nonexistent go) 'die', *ma ka-yaa* (*ma* THEME-arrive) 'know how to', etc. Some of these are idiomatic.

22   Yagua is another language which allows a productive PI construction with Vs which are basically intransitive (Doris Payne; personal communication).

[23] A similar situation arises with transitivizing prefixes, which turn a few basic intransitive Vs into transitive ones, as in:

(i) Subih i-łim　　　　　awad hã
     Subih ASP-be.afraid.of jaguar DAT
     'Subih is afraid of the jaguar.'

(ii) awad Subih yi-łim
     jaguar Subih TR+ASP-be.afraid.of
     'Subih fears the jaguar.'

Transitivizing prefixes may have arisen diachronically from incorporated Ps, but their origin is not as clear as that of relational prefixes.

REFERENCES

Allen, Barbara J., Donna B. Gardiner and Donald G. Frantz. 1984. Noun incorporation in Southern Tiwa. *International Journal of American Linguistics* 50.292-311.

Anderson, Stephen R. 1985. Typological distinctions in word formation. In Shopen, ed., vol. 3, 3-56.

Baker, Mark C. 1985a. The mirror principle and morphosyntactic explanation. *Linguistic Inquiry* 16.373-415.

Baker, Mark C. 1985b. Incorporation. A theory of grammatical function changing. MIT doctoral dissertation.

Baker, Mark C. 1986. Incorporation and the syntax of applicative constructions. MS.

Baker, Mark C. 1988. *Incorporation. A theory of grammatical function changing.* Chicago: University of Chicago Press.

Campell, Lyle, Terrence Kaufman and Thomas C. Smith-Stark. 1986. Meso-America as a linguistic area. *Language* 62.530-570.

Chomsky, Noam. 1981. *Lectures on government and binding.* Dordrecht: Foris.

Comrie, Bernard. 1973. The ergative: variations on a theme. *Lingua* 32.239-253.

Dietrich, Wolf. 1986. *El idioma chiriguano: gramática, textos, vocabulario.* Madrid.

Frantz, Donald G. 1971. *Toward a generative grammar of Blackfoot. (Summer Institute of Linguistics Publications in Linguistics 34.)* Norman, OK: Summer Institute of Linguistics and Univ. of Oklahoma.

Frantz, Donald G. 1979. *Grammatical relations in universal grammar. Summer Institute of Linguistics Work papers 23, supplement.* SIL. University of North Dakota. (Also published by Indiana University Linguistics Club. Bloomington. 1981.)

Frantz, Donald G. 1985. Syntactic constraints on noun incorporation in Southern Tiwa. *Proceedings of the eleventh annual meeting of the Berkeley Linguistics Society,* 107-116. Berkeley.

Givón, T. 1984. *Syntax: a functional-typological introduction.* Amsterdam: John Benjamins.

Hagège, Claude. 1978. Lexical suffixes and incorporation in Mainland Comox. *Forum Linguisticum* 3.57-71.

Hagège, Claude. 1980. On noun incorporation in universal grammar (further comments on a previous article). *Forum Linguisticum* 4.241-245.

Keenan, Edward L. 1985. Relative clauses. In Shopen, ed., vol. 2, 141-170.

Keenan, Edward L. and Bernard Comrie. 1977. Noun phrase accessibility and universal grammar. *Linguistic Inquiry* 8.63-101.

Kroeber, Alfred L. 1909. Noun incorporation in American languages. *XVI Internationaler Amerikanisten-Kongress.* Ed. by Frantz Heger, 569-576. Vienna & Leipzig: Hartleben.

Loukotka, Čestmir. 1968. (J. Wilbert, ed.). *Classification of South American Indian languages.* Los Angeles: University of California/Centro Latinamericano de Venezuela.

Mardirussian, Galust. 1975. Noun incorporation in universal grammar. *Papers from the eleventh regional meeting of the Chicago Linguistics Society,* 383-389. Chicago.

Mason, J. Alden. 1950. The languages of South American Indians. *Handbook of South American Indians, Vol. 6.* Ed. by J.H. Steward, 157-317. Washington DC: Smithsonian Institution. US Bureau of American Ethnology.

Merlan, Francesca. 1976. Noun incorporation and discource reference in modern Nahuatl. *International Journal of American Linguistics* 42.177-191.

362 E. M. HELEN WEIR

Miner, Kenneth L. 1986. Noun stripping and loose incorporation in Zuni. *International Journal of American Linguistics* 52.242-254.

Mithun, Marianne. 1984. The evolution of noun incorporation. *Language* 60.847-894.

Mithun, Marianne. 1986. On the nature on noun incorporation. *Language* 62.32-37.

Myhill, John. 1988. Nominal agent incorporation in Indonesian. *Journal of Linguistics* 24.111-136.

Perlmutter, David M. and Paul M. Postal. 1984. The 1-Advancement Exclusiveness Law. In Perlmutter and Rosen, eds., 81-125.

Perlmutter, David M. and Carol G. Rosen (eds.). 1984. *Studies in Relational Grammar* 2. Chicago: University of Chicago Press.

Rigsby, Bruce. 1975. Nass-Gitksan: an analytic ergative syntax. *International Journal of American Linguistics* 41.346-354.

Rivet, P. and C. Tastevin. 1920. Affinités du Makú et du Puináve. *Journal de la Société des Américanistes de Paris* 12.69-82.

Rosen, Carol G. 1984. The Interface between Semantic Roles and Initial Grammatical Relations. In Perlmutter and Rosen, eds., 38-77.

Ruiz de Montoya, Antonio. 1876. *Arte de la Lengua Guaraní.* Leipzig: B.G. Teubner. (Originally published in 1640.)

Sadock, Jerrold M. 1980. Noun incorporation in Greenlandic: a case of syntactic word formation. *Language* 56.300-319.

Sadock, Jerrold M. 1985. Autolexical Syntax: a proposal for the treatment of noun incorporation and similar phenomena. *Natural Language and Linguistic Theory* 3.379-439.

Sadock, Jerrold M. 1986. Some notes on noun incorporation. *Language* 62.19-31.

Sapir, Edward. 1911. The problem of noun incorporation in American languages. *American Anthropologist* 13.250-82.

Shopen, Timothy (ed.). 1985. *Language typology and synctatic description* Vols. 2, 3. London: Cambridge University Press.

Sullivan, Paul R. 1984. Noun incorporation in Yucatec Maya. *Anthropological Linguistics* 26.138-160.

Tovar, Antonio. 1961. *Catálogo de las lenguas de América del Sur.* Buenos Aires: Editoral Sudamericana.

Weggelaar, C. 1986. Noun incorporation in Dutch. *International Journal of American Linguistics* 52.301-304.

Weir, E. M. Helen. 1984. A negação e outros tópicos da gramática Nadëb. Universidade Estadual de Campinas. Master's thesis.

Weir, E. M. Helen. 1986. Footprints of yesterday's syntax: diachronic development of certain verb prefixes in an OSV language (Nadëb). *Lingua* 68.291-316.

Woodbury, Hanni. 1975. Onondaga noun incorporation: some notes on the interdependence of syntax and semantics. *International Journal of American Linguistics* 41.10-20.

IV. Transitivity and
   Grammatical Relations

Kamaiurá (Tupí-Guaraní) as an Active-Stative Language*

Lucy Seki

INTRODUCTION

An active system (also known as active-stative, agent-patient and split-system) is frequently treated in the linguistic literature as a variant of an ergative system (Comrie 1978; Dixon 1979). The soviet linguist G. A. Klimov has a different opinion; he claims that the active type is a typologically separate system defined by a set of related structural features on different levels of the language. According to Klimov (1972, 1977), the semantic determinant of active languages consists in an opposition between the active and inactive roles, which manifests itself on different levels in the linguistic structure. The structure of active languages is oriented to the expression of relations between the active and inactive roles, and not to the relations between subject and object. The last are expressed in active type languages only indirectly.

Among others, the characteristic features of active languages include a lack of adjectives, a division of nouns into active and inactive, and a division of verbs into active and stative. Apart from that, there are different sets of person markers for expressing the active and the inactive participants and two main types of sentence constructions: active and inactive, according to the relations of activity or inactivity expressed. In active languages the subject of active verbs is marked differently from the subject of statives; the subject of statives is marked in the same way as the object of active verbs (Klimov 1972, 1977, 1979).

Our purpose in this paper is to describe person marking in Kamaiurá, a Tupí-Guaraní language spoken by 150 Indians located in Upper Xingu River, Central Brazil[1] and show that Kamaiurá is, in Klimov's terms, an active type language.[2] In Section 1 we will give some grammatical information necessary as background for the subsequent discussion. We will particularly consider the distinction between two verb classes - active and stative - and show that this distinction correlates with a semantic one involving control versus lack of control. In Section 2 we introduce the devices that code grammatical roles in simple constructions. Finally, in Section 3 we focus on the person marking system in Kamaiurá independent clauses and splits in the system. It will be shown that, contrary to Dixon's (1979.91) expectations, the splits in the Kamaiurá system are partially conditioned by the semantic content of NPs and manifested by cross-referencing on the verb (cf. Section 2.8).

1. PRELIMINARY REMARKS

Kamaiurá nouns are distinguished from other word classes by specific syntactic and morphological properties. Nouns may occur as subject or direct object of a clause, as a possessor in a genitive construction and as an object of a postposition. When used in any of these functions nouns are marked with the suffix -*a*, which I label 'nominal function marker' (NF).[3] Other function markers are the locative suffix -*(i)p* ∞ -*(i)m* and the predicative -*(r)am:*

(1) wyrapy-a ka'i-a   tete   o-'u[4]
     eagle-NF monkey-NF only 3-eat
     'The eagle eats only monkey.'

(2) lusi-a   pyr-im   oro-ho-n   a'ewa oro-ja-m-e   ko'
     Lucy-NF house-LOC 1EX-go-INT PART 1EX-say-GER-EP PART
     'We'll go to Lucy's house, we said.'

(3) moi-ram   o-je-'apahwapahwat o-ho-m-e   ko'y kwãj
     snake-PRED 3-REFL-coil   3-go-GER-EP PART PART
     'They were coiling themselves like a snake.'

Nouns are further characterized by morphemes such as -*(h)et* 'nominal past', -*(r)ám* 'nominal future', -*i* 'diminutive', etc.

While Kamaiurá lacks an independent class of adjectives, it distinguishes a class of transitive verbs and two classes of intransitive verbs. I refer to these classes as (active) transitives, active intransitives and descriptive verbs. In indicative and hortative moods transitive verbs occur with subjective prefixes (Set I forms) and with dependent pronouns (Set II forms), which are reduced forms of the independent pronouns (Set III). Active intransitives take only Set I forms; descriptives take only Set II forms. Set II forms are also used to express the possessor in genitive constructions and the object of postpositions. The sets of subjective prefixes, dependent pronouns and independent pronouns are given in Table 1:

	Set I	Set II	Set III
1 singular	a-	je	ije
1 inclusive	ja-	jene	jene
1 exclusive	oro-	ore	ore
2 singular	ere-	ne	ene
2 plural	pe-	pe	pehe
3	o-	-	-

Table 1. Set I, Set II and Set III pronominal forms

There is no third person dependent or independent pronoun. This absence is supplied in Set II by the relational prefix *i-∞ t-∞ h-*[5] and in Set III by the demonstratives *a'e* 'this, that' and *a'ewan* 'these, those', which syntactically are like nouns. The prefix *i-∞ t-∞ h-* will be treated in detail in Section 2, together with other relational prefixes.

Descriptives behave as verbs and not as nouns since 1) they cannot occur with function markers and cannot fill the role of a noun in a clause unless they are nominalized, and 2) they share many characteristics in common with active verbs.

The observed similarities between descriptives and active verbs may be summarized as follows:

First, both types of words occur directly as predicates:

(4) a. kunu'um-a o-jan
     boy-NF   3-run
     'The boy is running.'

   b. ywyrapar-a i-katu
      bow-NF   3.REL-good
      'The bow is good.'

Second, both types of words may occur in clauses with the sentential negative marker *na ... ite* and with the sentential interrogative particle *po*. These markers do not appear in nominal clauses.

(5) a. kunu'um-a n-o-jan-ite
     boy-NF   NEG-3-run-NEG
     'The boy is not running.'

   b. ywyrapar-a n-i-katu-ite
      bow-NF   NEG-3REL-good-NEG
      'The bow is not good.'

(6) a. po posto katy ere-o
       Q posto DIR 2SG-go
       'Are you going to the Posto?'

     b. po ne   r-opeyj
       Q 2SG REL-be sleepy
       'Are you sleepy?'

Third, both may cooccur with tense/aspect markers. These usually occur as second position particles and are characteristic of verbal clauses:

(7) a. a-ha   rak-e   ko'yt
       1SG-go T/A-EP PART
       'I went.'

     b. je   katu rak-e   ko'yt
       1SG good T/A-EP PART
       'I was good.'

Fourth, both active intransitives and descriptives may be nominalized with the relative morphemes *ma'e* 'atributive' and *uma'e* 'negative atributive':

(8) a. o-'ata ma'e
       3-walk NOM
       'one who walks'

     b. i-katu   ma'e
       3REL-good NOM
       'one who is good'

On the other hand, descriptives and active verbs exibit differences:
First, descriptives and active intransitives use two different sets of person markers in the indicative mood (see details in Section 2).
Second, descriptives do not occur in the circumstantial form. This form, which is used when the verb is preceded by an adverbial in the clause, is restricted in Kamaiurá to active verbs with a third person participant:

(9)   ikue   rak i-maraka-w
       yesterday T/A 3CIRC-sing-CIRC
       'He sang yesterday.'

Third, unlike active verbs, in the imperative mood the descriptive occurs in a third person form and the imperative is indicated in the auxiliary verb *-ko* :

(10) a. e-jan
       2SG.IMPER-run
       'Run!'

b. i-katu   e-ko
3REL-good 2SG.IMPER-be
'Be good!'

Fourth, descriptives may occur in adverbial function. In this case they are always marked with the prefix *i-:*

(11)   i-katu   i-maraka-w   (cf. ikatu ere-maraka)
       3REL-well 3.CIRC-sing-CIRC   2SG-sing
       'He sings well.'   'You sing well.'

These formal differences between the two classes of intransitive verbs correlate with a semantic distinction similar to Klimov's active vs. non-active situations (Klimov 1977). The exact definition of the semantic distinction relevant for Kamaiurá is still under investigation, but some conclusions may be advanced.

The descriptive class consists largely of verbs which predicate qualities and relations, including concepts that would be expressed by adjectives in other languages. Some examples are:

-uwijap	'to be big'	-ayk	'to be short'
-oryp	'to be glad '	-'amot	'to be longing for'
-'arõ	'to be good tasting'	-'akym	'to be wet'
-ciŋ	'to be white'	-powyj	'to be heavy'
-jym	'to be smooth'	-kyra	'to be fat'
-akup	'to be hot'	-pyau	'to be new'
-myratã	'to be old'	-kaneõ	'to be tired'

Other members of descriptive class in Kamaiurá are:

-earaj	'forget'	-eakwap	'remember'
-'aŋekyj	'sigh'	-'aŋeraha	'mourn'
-kororõ	'snore'	-ryryj	'tremble'
-ay	'feel pain'	-aem	'shout'

The active intransitive class contains typically volitional verbs like *-je'eŋ* 'talk', *-jan* 'run', *-maraka* 'sing', *-'ata* 'walk', etc., but also such verbs as *-manõ* 'die', *-in* 'be sitting', *-kuj* 'fall down', *-kyje* 'be afraid of', *-ko* 'be in a place.'

Although the two classes cannot be characterized in an absolute way by their lexical content, an opposition between control vs. lack of control seems to be generally true.

On the other hand, a contrast between participant in control vs. participant not in control is manifested in the use of different sets of person markers: Set I forms express that the participant is in control, while Set II forms and the relational prefixes express that the participant is not in control. Clear examples of this contrast are found for third person in constructions involving active verb stems and the relative nominalizing morpheme *uma'e* 'negative atributive':

(12) a. i-je'eŋ   uma'e
        3REL-talk NOM
        'one who does not talk'

    b. o-je'eŋ   uma'e
        3 Set I-talk NOM
        'one who does not talk'

The first example refers to a person who cannot talk, that is, a dumb person; the second example refers to a person who can talk but does not like to.

2. PARTICIPANT CODING DEVICES IN KAMAIURÁ

In this section we introduce the participant coding devices of Kamaiurá used in simple constructions. Among the verbal constructions, only those with the verb in the indicative will be considered. The coding devices include full NPs, free pronouns, dependent pronouns, affixes and zero.

Following Dixon 1979, we use the terms A, Sa, O and So to refer to the semantico-syntactic roles associated with the participants. A and O stand for the participants in a two argument clause usually refered to as subject and object, respectively. Sa stands for the core argument of a single argument clause with an active verb, and So stands for the core argument of a single argument clause with a descriptive verb. Besides these four roles, we also present the devices used to code possessors and oblique objects.

2.1 A AND SA CODING. A and Sa participants are primarily refered to by the Set I prefixes given in Table 1. The prefix may be the only reference to A and Sa, or A and Sa may be additionally referred to via noun-phrases or independent pronouns.

2.1.1 SET I PREFIXES. Set I prefixes are characteristic of active verb stems and are used only in the indicative and hortative moods. The examples below illustrate the use of Set I prefixes:

(13)   a -manõ korin a'ewa jyjryp (Sa)
        1SG-die FUT PART friend
        'I will die, (my) friend.'

(14)   ita   o-momot (A)
        stone 3-throw
        'He throws stones.'

(15)   o-kutuk (A)
       3-pierce
       'He pierces it.'

2.1.2 NOUN-PHRASE PLUS SET I PREFIX. A noun-phrase usually occurs preceding the verb and is marked with the suffix -*a* 'nominal function marker':

(16)   kara'iw-a   rak o-yk   tenone (Sa)
       non.indian-NF T/A 3-come   before
       'The non-indian came first.'

(17)   kunu'um-a ka'i-a   r-uwaj-a   w-ekyj (A)
       boy-NF   monkey-NF REL-tail-NF 3-pull
       'The boy is pulling the monkey's tail.'

   Where all NPs are third person, as in 17, the grammatical relations are coded
by SOV word order or by semantics.

2.1.3 PRONOUN PLUS SET I PREFIXES. Independent pronouns are used mostly in
nominal clauses. They can occur as clause constituents to code A or Sa
participants, usually in situations expressing contrast, as illustrated in 18, or to
highlight the participant, as in 19:

(18)   ije a-je'eŋ   ene ere-karãj
       I   1SG-speak you 2SG-write
       'I speak and you write.'

(19)   ije te   awa   n-a-'amotare'ym-ite   kowa
       I   FOC people NEG-1SG-argue-NEG   PART
       'As for me, I do not argue with people.'

2.2 O AND So CODING. In Kamaiurá, O and So participants are treated in much
the same way. However, in simple clauses with the verb in the indicative, the
set of devices used to code So is wider than that used to code O.

2.2.1 DEPENDENT PRONOUNS (SET II FORMS) PLUS RELATIONAL PREFIX *R-∞ Ø*.
The forms of dependent pronouns used to code O and So are those given in
Table 1. When a dependent pronoun is used, the verb stem has a prefix attached
to it. This is a relational prefix with two allomorphs: *r-* and *Ø*. These two
allomorphs provide a division of the verb stems (as well as the noun and
postposition stems) in two major morphological classes: the *r-* class and the *Ø*
class:

(20) a. akwama'e-a je   r-ecak (O, r-class)
        man-NF   1SG REL-see
        'The man saw me.'

   b. wararuwijaw-a je   Ø-u'u (O, Ø-class)
       dog-NF   1SG REL-bite
       'The dog bit me.'

(21) a. je   r-oryp (So, r-class)
       1SG REL-glad
       'I am glad.'

   b. je   Ø-katu (So, Ø-class)
       1SG REL-good
       'I am good.'

2.2.2 INDEPENDENT PRONOUN PLUS DEPENDENT PRONOUN. An independent pronoun may be used in addition to a dependent pronoun to code first and second person So and O participants. This occurs only in cases of contrast, as in the following examples:

(22)   ije ruẽj je   r-ecak (O)
       I   NEG 1SG REL-see
       'It is not me that he sees.'

(23)   ene ne   Ø-hwaratã (So)
       you 2SG REL-strong
       'You are strong.'

2.2.3 RELATIONAL PREFIX *I-∞ T-∞ H-*. Another device for coding So and O participants is the relational prefix *i-*. As mentioned earlier, there is no third person dependent pronoun. Although the prefix *i-* supplies this absence, it is not analysed as a person marker of Set II, but as a relational prefix; unlike the dependent pronouns, it is a prefix and has the same distribution as other relational prefixes, being mutually exclusive with them. The dependent pronouns behave as nouns in that they co-occur with a stem prefixed with the relational prefix *r- ∞ Ø-*.

Unlike other Tupí-Guaraní languages, in Kamaiurá the prefix *i-* does not code O participants in independent clauses with the verb in the indicative mood. Instead, it is frequently used to code O participants in constructions with a non-indicative verb form (Seki, to appear).

The prefix *i-* has three main allomorphs: *i-*, *t-* and *h-*. All stems which occur with the allomorph *i-* belong to the *Ø* class and the stems which occur with allomorphs *t-* and *h-* belong to the *r-* class. The following examples illustrate the use of prefix *i-∞ t-∞h-* in So function:

(24) a. i-katu
       3.REL-good
       'He is good.'

b. h-oryp
   3.REL-glad
   'He is glad.'

c. t-uwijap
   3.REL-big
   'He is big.'

2.2.4 NOUN PHRASE PLUS RELATIONAL PREFIX *I-∞ T-∞ H-*. The relational prefix *i-* may be accompanied by a full coreferent NP to code an So participant:

(25) a. akwama'e-a i-katu
        man-NF   3.REL-good
        'The man is good.'

b. kujã   h-oryp
   woman 3.REL-good
   'The woman is good.'

c. jay-a   t-uwijap
   moon-NF 3.REL-big
   'The moon is full.'

2.3 A AND O CODING. There are some devices used to code A, but not Sa, and O, but not So participants. These are: 1) noun phrase, 2) portmanteau prefixes and 3) zero. These devices occur only with respect to certain combinations of person in A and O, related to an hierarchy of personal reference (see section in 2.8). This hierarchy governs the agreement with A, with O or with both. When the verb agrees with A, O is coded by only NP or Ø; when the verb agrees with O, A is coded by only NP or Ø. The portmanteau prefixes are used when the verb agrees with both A and O.

2.3.1 NOUN PHRASE. The following examples illustrate the use of a noun phrase in A and O function, occurring in absence of a coreferential marker on the verb:

(26)   a'e ramuẽ mojũ-a   jene   r-ekyj   typy katy (A)
        that when sucuri-NF 1.INCL REL-pull deep DIR
        'Then the sucuri (kind of snake) pull us to the deep.'

(27)   yrypary-a ane a-'awyky-n   a'ewa (O)
        basket-NF first 1SG-make-INT PART
        I will make baskets first.'

2.3.2 PORTMANTEAU PREFIXES. Two portmanteau prefixes, *oro-* and *opo-*, are used to code a first person A participant acting on a second person O participant. The prefix *oro-* refers to a first person singular A participant acting on a second person singular O participant. The prefix *opo-* refers to a first person singular or plural A participant acting on a second person plural O participant. Note that the prefix *oro-* has the same shape as the first exclusive Set I subjective prefix.

(28) oro-ecak   (cf. oro-ecak)
      PM.1/2SG-see   1EX-see
      'I see you (sg.).' 'We (ex.) see him.'

(29) opo-ecak
      PM.1/2PL-see
      'I see you (pl.)'; 'we(excl.) see you (pl.).'

In Kamaiurá the portmanteau prefixes occur only with two argument verbs in the indicative or hortative moods and are added directly to the verb stem. Distributionally they are mutually exclusive with Set I and Set II forms and with the relational prefixes.[6]

Comparison with data from Guajajara, a language closely related to Kamaiurá, suggests that the portmanteau prefixes resulted from the fusion of Set I prefixes with an object marker. In Guajajara the corresponding forms for Set I and Set II markers and for the portmanteau prefixes of Kamaiurá are (Bendor Samuel 1966):

	Set I	Set II	Portmanteau prefixes	
1 sg.	a-	he	a) 1/2 sg.	uru-
1 ex.	uru-	ure	lex./2 sg.	uru-
1 in.	ei	zane	b) 1/2 pl.	apu-
2 sg.	ere-	ne	c) lex./2 pl.	urupu-
2 pl.	pe-	pe		

The forms of the portmanteau prefixes *apu-* and *urupu-* reflect a stage in which it is still possible to distinguish the prefixes *a-* and *uru-*, as these forms are also found in the Set I paradigm.

2.3.3 ZERO. Zero is here considered as the absence of any morphological marker. Examples 30 and 31 illustrate zero coding of A and O participants:

(30) kunu'um-a o-me'eŋ i-upe (O)
      boy-NF   3-give 3REL-to
      'The boy gave (it) to him.'

(31) ne   r-ecak (A)
      2SG REL-see
      '(He) sees you (sg.).'

In 31 the relational prefix on the verb indicates that the grammatical relation of the pre-verbal constituent is O. Given the hierarchy of persons operating in Kamaiurá (see 2.8), the A participant in 31 can only be interpreted as a third person which is identified by context. Where both participants are third person, as in 30, some ambiguity may arise, which must also be solved by context.

2.4 A, SA AND SO CODING. There is one device used to code the categories A, Sa and So: the morpheme *awa* 'person, people.' Unlike all other devices, *awa* occurs postverbally and indicates an indeterminate third person participant:

(32)   o-api   awa (A)
       3-shot 3.INDET
       'People shot him.'

(33)   o-jomuhur   awa   je ko'yt (Sa)
       3-go (more than one) 3.INDET HS PART
       'People went.'

(34)   n-i-katu-ite   awa (So)
       NEG-3.REL-good-NEG 3.INDET
       'They are not good.'

2.5 POSSESSOR CODING. In relation to their possessed items, possessors are coded by 3 devices. In all of them the relational prefixes are involved.

2.5.1 DEPENDENT PRONOUN PLUS RELATIONAL PREFIX *R-∞ Ø*. The dependent pronouns introduced in Table 1 are used to code first and second person possessors and occur in exactly the same way as when used in O or So function. Like the verbs, the head (possessed) noun is preceded by the relational prefix *r-∞ Ø-*. Two major classes of noun stems are distinguished by their ability to occur with each of these two allomorphs: the *r-* class and the *Ø* class. The *r-* class contains only inalienably possessed nouns while the *Ø* class includes both inalienable and alienable possessed nouns. The following examples illustrate the use of dependent pronoun plus the relational prefix *r-∞ Ø* with noun stems from each class:

(35) a. ne   r-up (r-class; inalienable)
         2.SG REL-father
         'your father'

     b. ore   Ø-akaŋ (Ø class; inalienable)
         1.EX REL-head
         'our (excl.) head'

     c. je   Ø   kye'i (Ø class; alienable)
         1.SG REL   knife
         'my knife'

2.5.2 NOUN PHRASE PLUS RELATIONAL PREFIX *R-∞ Ø*. When the possessor is coded by a noun phrase, the head noun must be preceded by the relational prefix *r-∞ Ø*. The noun phrase occurs with the function marker *a-*.

(36) a. kunu'um-a r-ea (r-class; inalienable)
         boy-NF   REL-eye
         'the boy's eye'

     b. jawar-a   Ø-pit (Ø class; inalienable)
        jaguar-NF REL-skin
        'the jaguar's skin'

     c. kara'iw-a   Ø-yat (Ø class; alienable)
        non.indian-NF REL-canoe
        'the non-indian's canoe'

2.5.3 DEMONSTRATIVE *A'E* PLUS RELATIONAL PREFIX *R-∞ Ø*. Possesssors may be coded by the demonstrative *a'e*, which occurs in a genitive construction with a noun preceded by the relational prefix *r-∞ Ø*. The demonstrative is coreferential with a left-dislocated NP:

(37)   kuikuro a'e-a   r-etam-a   amoete ucu
        K.   DEM-NF REL-village-NF far   INTENS
        'The Kuikuro, their village is very far.'

2.5.4 THIRD PERSON RELATIONAL PREFIXES. Third person possessors may be coded by one of two relational prefixes attached to the head noun: *i-∞ t-∞ h-* or *o-∞ w-*. The prefix *i-∞ t-∞ h-* is the same relational prefix used in So function. It codes a possessor which is not coreferential with any A or Sa participant either in the same clause or outside the clause. The three allomorphs of the prefix divide the nouns into three morphological subclasses: 1) *i-* subclass, 2) *h-* subclass and 3) *t-* subclass. The last two subclasses contain only inalienable possessed nouns of the *r-* class. The *i-* subclass includes both inalienable and alienable possessed nouns of the *Ø* class:

(38) a. i-nami-a   o-kutuk (Ø class; inalienable)
         3.REL-ear-NF 3-pierce
         'He$_i$ pierced his$_j$ ear.'

     b. i-yar-a   o-moŋatu (Ø class; alienable)
        3.REL-canoe-NF 3-repair
        'He$_i$ repaired his$_j$ canoe.'

(39)   h-etymakaŋ-a w-e'ỹj (r-class; inalienable)
        3.REL-leg-NF 3-scratch
        'He$_i$ scratches his$_j$ leg.'

(40)   t-a'yr-a nite   i-'ata-w   (r-class;   inalienable)

3.REL-son-NF   with   3.CIRC-walk-CIRC

'He$_i$ walks with his$_j$ son.'

The prefix *o-* (*w-* preceding unstressed vowels) codes a third person possessor which is coreferent with the A or the Sa participant of the same clause or outside the clause. This prefix may occur with any possessed noun.

(41) a. o-nami-a   o-kutuk (Ø class; i-subclass; inalienable)
3.REL-ear-NF 3-pierce
'He$_i$ pierced his$_i$ ear.'

b. o-yar-a   o-monatu (Ø class; i-subclass; alienable)
3.REL-canoe-NF 3-repair
'He$_i$ repaired his$_i$ canoe.'

(42)   w-etymakaŋ-a w-e'yj (r-class; h-subclass; inalienable)
3.REL-leg-NF 3-scratch
'He$_i$ scratches his$_i$ leg.'

(43)   w-a'yr-a   nite i-'ata-w (r-class; t-subclass; inalenable)
3.REL-son-NF with 3.CIRC-walk-CIRC
'He$_i$ walks with his$_i$ son.'

2.6 OBLIQUE CODING. Oblique nominals have as their heads a postposition which indicates the semantic role of the noun. Obliques are coded basically with the same set of devices used to code possessors. All of them involve a relational prefix.

2.6.1 DEPENDENT PRONOUNS PLUS RELATIONAL PREFIX *R-∞* *Ø*. Like nouns and verbs, postpositions fall in two classes according to the allomorph of the relational prefix they can take: 1) *r-* class and 2) Ø class. The *r-* class contains the postposition *-ehe* which has a range of meanings. The remaining postpositions belong to the Ø class.

(44)   je   r-eakajym-ite   ne   r-ehe
1.SG REL-forget-NEG 2.SG REL-ABL
'I will not forget you.'

(45)   po mo'yr-a   ere-me'eŋ potat je   Ø-upe
Q necklace-NF 2.SG-give want 1.SG REL-DAT
'Do you want to sell me a necklace?'

2.6.2 RELATIONAL PREFIX *I-∞ T-∞ H-*. Postpositions fall into subclasses according to the allomorph of the relational prefix they can take. However no postposition occurs with the *t-* allomorph, and only *-ehe* was found with the *h-* allomorph. The remaining postpositions belong to the *i-* subclass:

(46) a. ka'aher-a e-karãj   i-upe
        letter-NF 2.SG.IMPER-write 3.REL-DAT
        'Write a letter to him.'

     b. wararuwijaw-a o-jarõ h-ehe
        dog-NF   3-bark 3.REL-ABL
        'The dogs barked on it.'

2.6.3 NOUN PHRASE PLUS RELATIONAL PREFIX *R-∞ Ø*. Obliques may be coded by a noun-phrase with the nominal function suffix followed by a postposition with the relational prefix *r-∞ Ø* attached to it:

(47) a. kunu'um-a o-jae'o i-potaw-a   r-ehe
        boy-NF   3-cry 3.REL-food-NF REL-ABL
        'The boy is crying because of his food.'

     b. kamaiurá-a Ø-pupe   e-je'eŋ   je   Ø-upe
        K.-NF   REL-INSTR 2.SG.IMPER-speak 1.SG REL-DAT
        'Speak to me in Kamaiurá.'

2.6.4 DEMONSTRATIVE *A'E* PLUS RELATIONAL PREFIX *R- ∞ Ø*. Like possessors, obliques may be coded by the demonstrative *a'e* which is coreferential with a left dislocated NP. The postposition is preceded by the relational prefix *r-∞ Ø*:

(48) moiacĩ   a'e-a   Ø-wi   a-kyje a'ia'ip
      kind of snake Dem-NF REL-ABL 1.SG-be afraid INTENS
      'Chumbeguaçu (kind of snake), I am very afraid of it.'

2.6.5 RELATIONAL PREFIX *O- ∞ W-*. The relational *o- ∞ w-* prefix codes a third person oblique which is coreferent with an A or Sa participant of either the same clause, or outside it. Unlike the possessed noun, the postposition must occur with the reflexive prefix *je-:*

(49) o-mepy o-je-upe
      3-buy 3REL-REFL-DAT
      'He bought for himself.'

The relational prefixes, including the morphologically conditioned allo-morphs, are shown in Table 2:

Poss., Obl.	So, (O), Poss., Obl.	So, Poss., Obl.
o-	r-	t- h-
	∅	i-
intra/inter sentence	intra phrase	intra/inter sentence

Table 2. Relational prefixes and their allomorphs

The relational prefix *r-∞ ∅* is added to a stem whenever the So, O, Possessor or Oblique is expressed by a dependent pronoun (1st or 2nd person) or by a full NP (3rd person). In this case Kamaiurá groups together NPs and dependent pronouns, treating both in the same way. The relational prefix *i-∞ t-∞ h-* is used only to express a third person So, Possessor or Oblique.

In the preceding discussion we have introduced the devices used in Kamaiurá to code participants in simple constructions. The coding possibilities for A, Sa, O, So, Possessors and Obliques are summarized in Table 3:

	Sa	A	O	So	Poss.	Obl.
Verb coding	+	+				
PRO + verb coding	+	+				
NP + Verb Coding	+	+				
PROnoun	-	+				
NP + Rel. i-			-	+		
PRO + Dep.PRO + Rel. r-			+	+		
Dep. PRO + Rel. r-			+	+	+	+
Rel. i-			-	+	+	+
NP + Rel. r-					+	+
NP + a'e + Rel. r-					+	+
Rel. o-∞w-					+	+
NP	-	+	+	-		
Portmanteau	-	+	+	-		
Zero	-	+	+	-		
Morpheme awa	+	+	-	+		

Table 3. Coding possibilities for A, Sa, O, So, Possessor and Oblique

We have grouped together A with Sa and O with So based on the correspondence between the sets of coding devices used to code them. However this
correspondence is not exact. The relational prefix *i*- alone or accompanied by a
preceding coreferential NP is used to code So, but not O. On the other hand, zero,
portmanteau prefixes and also independent pronouns and NPs occurring without
a coreferential marker on the verb may code A, but not Sa. Except for the
pronouns in cases where contrast is not involved, these same devices are used to
code O, but not So. Thus we have another grouping: that of A with O participants.
This occurs only with respect to certain combinations of A and O in terms of the
persons involved and is related to an hierarchy of personal reference and to splits
in the personal system of Kamaiurá. Both these aspects will be treated in section
2.7.

Another observation concerns the correspondence between the categories O/
So and Possessor/oblique, as opposed to A/Sa categories. In what has been
presented so far, O/So and Possessor/Oblique have in common only the Dep.
PRO + Rel. *r*-, and, except for O, also the Rel. *i*- devices. The other two devices,
however, NP + Rel. *r*- and NP + *a'e* + Rel. *i*- are commonly used to code O and
So participants in certain non-indicative constructions. These are not represented in Table 3.

2.7 RESTRICTIONS ON COOCCURRENCE OF PERSON MARKERS. It has been shown
that A participants are coded by Set I forms (verbal prefixes), O participants are
coded by Set II forms (dependent pronouns) necessarily accompanied by the relational prefix *r*- attached to the verb stem, and that both A and O participants can
be coded by two portmanteau prefixes.

With regard to coding of A and O participants in two argument verbs
Kamaiurá is similar to other Tupí-Guaraní languages (Monserrat 1976; Leite
1987). There is a general restriction such that only one participant, either A or
O, may be marked on the verb in the indicative form. That is, Set I forms (A) and
Set II forms (O) may not cooccur in any one verb:

(50) a. ne   r-ecak
        2sg. REL-see
        'He saw you.'

   b. * o-ne-r-ecak

   c. * ne o-ecak

The choice between coding of A versus O in Kamaiurá is made according to
the following schema:

(51)   Participant   Coded on the verb by
         A   0   Set I   Set II   Portmanteau
1.   1, 2   3   A
2.   3   1, 2   O
3.   3   3   A
4.   2   1   O
5.   1 excl.   2 sg.   A
6.   1 sg.   2 sg.   A/O
7.   1   2 pl.   A/O

The alternations between A and O marking are determined in most cases by the hierarchy in 52 below (Silverstein 1976), whereby a) first person is higher than second person, which is higher than third person, and b) A is higher than O.

(52) a. 1st > 2nd > 3rd
     b. A > O.

Thus, given two participants A and O, the higher one on the hierarchy is coded on the verb by the corresponding marker from Set I or Set II. If the two participants have the same value for person, the A participant will be marked.

The hierarchy accounts for the alternations indicated in rows 1 through 5, as illustrated in the following examples:

(53) a. a-ecak 'I see him'
     b. ja-ecak 'we (incl.) see him'
     c. oro-ecak 'we (excl.) see him'
     d. ere-ecak 'you (sg.) see him'
     e. pe-ecak 'you (pl.) see him'

(54) a. je r-ecak 'he sees me'
     b. jene r-ecak 'he sees us (incl.)'
     c. ore r-ecak 'he sees us (excl.)'
     d. ne r-ecak 'he sees you (sg.)'
     e. pe n-ecak 'he sees you (pl.)'

(55)   o-ecak 'he sees him/it'

(56) a. je r-ecak 'you (sg./pl.) see me'
     b. ore r-ecak 'you (sg./pl.) see us (excl.)'

(57)   oro-ecak 'we (excl.) see you (sg.)'

With regard to rows 6 and 7 in 51, we might expect the forms in 58 and 59 where the A participant is marked, since A is higher than O on the hierarchy in 52:

(58) a-ecak   a. * 'I see you (sg.)'
      1.SG.SET I-see b. * 'I see you (pl.)'

(59) oro-ecak   a.   'we (excl.) see you (sg.)'
      1.EX.SET I-see   b. * 'we (excl.) see you (pl.)'

However, except for 59a, the examples above are ungrammatical with the indicated meaning. The correspondent grammatical forms are those in 60 and 61 which use the portmanteau prefixes *oro-* and *opo-* (notice that the prefix *oro-* has the same shape as the Set I first exclusive prefix):

(60) oro-ecak 'I see you (sg.)'
      PM.1SG/2SG-see

(61) opo-ecak 'I see you (pl.)'
      PM.1/2PL-see 'we (excl.) see you (pl.)'

In fact, portmanteau prefixes are limited to cases when second person equals or is greater than first person in number; that is, those cases where 1st and 2nd persons are both singular, both plural or when 1st person is singular and 2nd person is plural. In such instances the hierarchy does not apply.

Thus a restriction must be added to the hierarchy in 52: first person outranks second person if first person is greater in number.

There is a basic opposition in Kamaiurá involving 1st and 2nd person versus 3rd person, or, in terms of Benveniste 1976, involving [+person] vs. [-person] categories: whenever O is [-person] (i.e. 3rd), A is marked and whenever O is [+person] (i.e. 1st or 2nd), O is marked. Next, there is an opposition within the [-person] category: whenever A and O are [-person], A is marked. Then we have oppositions within the [+person] categories, or, between [+tu] and [+ego]: whenever O is [+ego], O is marked; when O is [+tu], both A and O are marked, unless [+ego] is greater in number. Thus, in these cases the feature 'plural' is relevant.

3. CASE-MARKING

In this section we will address the case marking system in Kamaiurá independent clauses and the splits existing in the system.

In preceding sections we have seen that in Kamaiurá the inflection (the function marker) of core nominals does not help to distinguish participants. Rather, case marking in this language is realized by cross referencing person markers (prefixes and dependent pronouns) on the verb. We have also seen that the Kamaiurá system of personal reference includes independent pronouns,

dependent pronouns, subjective prefixes, relational prefixes and two portmanteau prefixes. The set of subjective prefixes (Set I) have different forms for first
person singular, first inclusive, first exclusive, second singular, second plural
and third person. The sets of independent and dependent pronouns lack a third
person form; this is supplied by noun phrases and third person relational prefixes,
respectively.

We can classify Kamaiurá pronominal forms as in 62, using the features [+/
-person], [+/- ego], [+/- tu] and [+/- plural] (Benveniste 1976), related to the
Hierarchy (52) and to the oppositions indicated in 2.8 above:

(62)

	ß1 incl.	1 excl.	1 sg.	2 pl.	2 sg.	3
Person	+	+	+	+	+	-
Ego	+	+	+	-	-	-
Tu	+	-	-	+	+	-
Pl.	+	+	-	+	-	-

In what follows, the pronominal forms are grouped in tables according to the
participant they mark and the basic opposition involved, that is, the relationship
among the participants governed by the hierarchy 52, which in turn depends on
the features of the participants. Thus, each table includes all the forms used for
participants with one argument verbs (Sa, So) as well as the forms used with two
argument verbs (A, O). In the last case the forms vary, depending on the
particular opposition involved.

Let's consider first the basic opposition [+/- person]. The table in 63 displays
all the forms that convey [+person] categories, either [+ego] or [+tu] alone (in
case of Sa and So function) or considered in opposition to [-person]; that is, the
forms for first and second persons used with two argument verbs, when the other
participant involved is third person.

(63) [+person] vs. [-person]

		A	Sa	So	O
A	1 sg.	a-	a-	je	je
B	1 incl.	ja-	ja-	jene	jene
C	1 excl.	oro-	oro-	ore	ore
D	2 sg.	ere-	ere-	ne	ne
E	2 pl.	pe-	pe-	pe	pe

Rows A through D identify A with Sa and O with So. This pattern defines an
active-stative system (also known as an agent/patient system).

Row E, involving second person plural, shows a neutral system since it has
a single form which encodes A, Sa, So and O.

The forms related to the opposition within the [-person] category are summarized in 64. Here we observe that there is a single form for A and Sa, and different forms for So and O. Third person thus shows a tripartite subsystem.

(64) [-person] vs. [-person]

	A	Sa	So	O
3	o-	o-	i-	Ø

Let us now turn to the oppositions within the [+person] categories. The forms that convey the [+ego] categories are shown in 65a and the forms that convey [+tu] categories are given in 65b:

(65) a. [+person] vs. [+person], [+Ego]

	A	Sa	So	O
A. 1 sg. vs. 2 pl.	opo-	a-	je	je
B. 1 sg. vs. 2 sg.	oro-	a-	je	je
C. 1 excl. vs. 2 pl.	opo-	oro-	ore	ore
D. 1 excl. vs. 2 sg.	oro-	oro-	ore	ore

The pattern in rows A through C identifies So with O and distinguishes A from Sa, forming a tripartite subsystem. In row D the first exclusive person displays an active/stative system, since it identifies A with Sa and So with O. Notice that this is the only case in which second person is smaller than first person in number.

(65) b. [+person] vs. [+person], [+Tu]

	A	Sa	So	O
A. 2 sg.	Ø	ere-	ne	oro-
B. 2 pl.	Ø	pe-	pe	opo-

Row A shows that the second person singular distinguishes all four functions, defining a quadripartite subsystem. Row B shows that the second person plural has a tripartite subsystem, since the pattern distinguishes A from Sa, and So from O, but makes no distinction between Sa and So.

It should be noted that the portmanteau prefixes *oro-* and *opo-* were analysed into separate forms and were included in 65a as A forms and in 65b as O forms. This is in disagreement with Dixon (1979.14) who states that portmanteau prefixes 'cannot be analysed into separate A and O forms and cannot be related to S affixes.' However, even if we analyse the Kamaiurá portmanteau prefixes only as O forms, the system for first person in 65a rows A through C will remain tripartite since in this case we would have a zero A form, distinct from the Sa form.

To summarize, the Kamaiurá case system includes different subsystems. First we have an active/stative pattern basically involving the opposition [+/- person]; this pattern also applies to first exclusive in relation to second singular, involving the feature [+/- plural].

Second, there are three tripartite subsystems. One is within the domain of [-person] and results from a distinct marking for So and O. The two others are within the domain of [+person]: one is related to first person and results from a distinct marking for A and Sa; the other is related to second person plural and results from a single marking for Sa and So and distinct marking for A and Sa.

Third, there is neutral subsystem for second person plural; this system makes no distinctions.

Fourth, there is one of maximal distinctions—the quadripartite subsystem for the second person singular.

It is worth noting that in all the subsystems, S is never treated as a coherent category. The subsystems of Kamaiurá are summarized in Table 4:

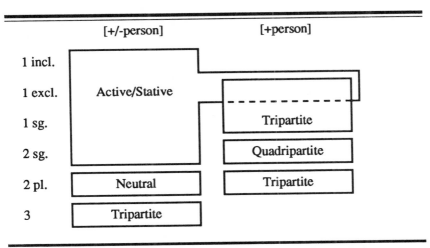

Table 4. Subsystems in Kamaiurá case marking

4. KAMAIURÁ AS AN ACTIVE/STATIVE LANGUAGE

The facts examined in this paper support Klimov's claim that Kamaiurá is basically an active/stative language, at least relative to independent clauses. According to Klimov 1977, the structure of languages of this type is oriented to express the relations between active and inactive participants, rather then the relations between subjects and objects.

In fact, we have seen that this language distinguishes two classes of one argument verbs—the active and the descriptive—by their lexical content; this distiction is related to an opposition between control and lack of control by participants or, in Klimov's terms, between activity and inactivity. We have also seen that there are different sets of person markers which express either the

participant in control or the active participant (Set I prefixes), and the participant not in control or the inactive participant (Set II and the relational prefixes).

It is clear from the preceding discussion that Set I forms (subjective prefixes)
can be associated only with one argument and two argument active verbs and
are related to A and Sa categories; Set II forms (dependent pronouns) and the
relational prefixes can be associated with two argument active verbs, with
descriptive verbs, and with possessed noun and postposition stems and are
related to So, O, Possessor and Oblique categories. NPs may express any of the
six categories, but when the NP expresses So, O, Possessor or Oblique, the
associated stem must have a relational prefix attached to it.

If we assume together with Klimov (1973, 1977) that Kamaiurá is a language
of active structure, then it can be stated that a) Set I forms mark an active
participant (A, Sa) while Set II forms mark a non-active participant (So, O, Pss.,
Obl.), and b) a correlation is observed between the type of stems and the
activity/inactivity of the participant (Seki 1987). This is summarized in Table
5:

Stem	Participant	
	active	inactive
one argument active verb	+	
two argument active verb	+	+
descriptive verb		+
possessed noun		+
postposition		+

Table 5. Activity of participant correlated with type of stem

When the relational prefixes are added to roots/stems, they specify that the
stem is related to an inactive participant. Syntactically this participant may be
a subject, an object or a modifier in a genitive or in a postpositional phrase. The
prefix *r-* indicates that the inactive participant is expressed in the same phrase,
immediately preceding the stem. Synchronically this prefix appears to have
only grammatical content. It encodes no semantic information about the participant itself, except that it is a first or second person inactive participant if
expressed by a dependent pronoun, or a third person inactive perticipant if
expressed by a NP.

The remaining relational prefixes code third person inactive participants. The
prefix *i-* marks a stem as related to an inactive participant in So, Possessor or

Oblique function. This participant must be mentioned previously in the sentence or is otherwise known by the context. When the participant is a possessor or an oblique, it must be distinct from the A or Sa participant in the same or in a previous sentence. In Kamaiurá, unlike Tupinambá and other closely related languages, the relational prefix *i-* is not used in O function in independent clauses (it does not cooccur with Set I prefixes); however, it is commonly used in dependent constructions, cooccurring with Set II forms. The prefix *o-* indicates that a stem is related to an inactive participant in Possessor or Oblique function, and the prefix has the same referent as the A or Sa participant of the same sentence or of a preceding one.

Case marking in Kamaiurá is manifested by person markers (Set I prefixes, Set II dependent pronouns and relational prefixes) on the verb. The case system in this language is basically an active-stative one, with splits of different kinds conditioned by the semantic nature of the verb (in case of one argument verbs) and by the semantic content of NP's (in the case of two argument active verbs). If the analysis presented here is correct, then contrary to Dixon's expectations, a split conditioned by the semantic content of the NP and manifested by cross-referencing on the verb is not so rare, since similar splits are also found in other Tupí-Guaraní languages Moreover, Kamaiurá appears to be a counterexample to Dixon's findings (p.91): 'I know no examples of languages that combine a split conditioned by semantic content of verb with a split conditioned by semantic content of NP's, where both splits are realized in terms of morphological marking of the same kind.'

NOTES

*   This paper was prepared during the Working Conference on Amazonian Languages and was partially supported by NSF Grant Nº BNS-8617854, NEH Grant Nº RX-20870-87, and the University of Oregon Foundation. The paper has greatly benefited from comments and suggestions by Doris Payne, Tom Payne, Dan Everett and Terry Kaufman.

[1]   All the data on which this paper is based were colected by the author from Kamaiurá native speakers during intermitent contact (1968, 1980-1983), totalling aproximately five months.

[2]   In his works Klimov classifies Kamaiurá and other Tupí-Guaraní languages as active type languages. Relative to Kamaiurá, in 1969-1972 Klimov had access to only a small amount of data collected by Seki at that time (quoted in Klimov's works as Ferreira, Lucy Soares).

[3]   The suffix *-a* is usually dropped when it follows a stem ending in a stressed *a* or when it precedes a stem beginning in a vowel.

⁴   The abbreviations used are: ABL ablative, CIRC circumstantial, DAT dative, DEM demonstrative, DIR directional, EP epenthetic, EX exclusive, FUT future, GER gerund, HS hearsay, IMPER imperative, INCL inclusive, INDET indeterminate, INSTR instrument, INT intentive, INTENS intensifier, LOC locative, NEG negative, NF nominal function, NOM nominalizer, PART particle, PL plural, PM portmanteau, PRED predicative, REFL reflexive, REL relational, SG singular, T/A tense/aspect.

⁵   The term 'relational' for refering to these prefixes is common in Tupian Studies.

⁶   In Seki 1982 an attempt was made to treat the two portmanteau prefixes as relational.

REFERENCES

Bendor-Samuel, David. 1966. *Hierarchical structures in Guajajara.* Doctoral Dissertation. London: School of Oriental and African Studies.

Benveniste, E. 1976. Estrutura das relacões de pessoa no verbo. *Problemas de Lingüística Geral,* 247-259. São Paulo: Companhia Editora Nacional e Editora de Universidade de São Paulo.

Comrie, Bernard. 1978. Ergativity. *Syntactic typology.* Ed. by W. P. Lehmann, 329-94. Austin: University of Texas Press.

Dixon, R. M. W. 1979. Ergativity. *Language* 55.59-138.

Klimov, G. A. 1972. K kharacteristike jazykov aktivnogo stroja. *Voprosy Jazykoznanija* 4.3-13.

Klimov, G. A. 1977. *Tipologuija jazykov aktivnogo stroja.* Moscow: Nauka.

Klimov, G. A. 1979. On the position of the ergative type in typological classification. *Ergativity – towards a theory of grammatical relations.* Ed. by F. Plank, 327-332. London: Academic Press.

Leite, I. 1978. Para uma tipologia ativa do Tapirapé. Paper presented at II Encontro Nacional da Associação Nacional de Pós-Graduação e Pesquisa em Letras e Lingüística. Rio de Janeiro.

Merlan, Franchesca. 1985. Split intransitivity: functional oppositions in intransitive inflection. *Grammar inside and outside the clause.* Ed. by J. Nichols and A. C. Woodbury, 324-362. Cambridge: Cambridge University Press.

Monserrat, R. M. F. 1976. Prefixos pessoais em Aweti. *Publicações do Museu Nacional,* Série Lingüística III. Rio de Janeiro: Museu Nacional.

Seki, Lucy. 1982. Marcadores de pessoa do verbo Kamaiurá. *Cadernos de Estudos Lingüísticos* 3.22-40. Campinas: Unicamp/Funcamp.

Seki, L. 1987. Para uma caracterização tipológica do Kamayurá. *Cadernos de Estudos Lingüísticos* 12.15-24. Campinas: Unicamp/Funcamp.

Seki, L. *The Kamaiurá language.* (To appear).

Silverstein, Michael. 1976. Hierarchy of features and ergativity. *Grammatical categories in Australian languages.* Ed. by R. M. W. Dixon, 112-171. Canberra: Australian Institute of Aboriginal Studies.

You and I = Neither You nor I: The Personal System of Tupinamba

Aryon D. Rodrigues

In Tupinambá, a Tupí-Guaraní language spoken in the 16th and 17th centuries along the Brazilian coast, the personal pronouns, the person markers on the verb, and the referential prefixes manifest a situation that, as far as I know, has not been reported for any other language. It would be worthwhile to check other lowland South American languages, particularly - but not only - the Tupí ones, for discovering analogous cases.

The missionaries who attempted 400 years ago[1] to describe Tupinambá were puzzled by the fact that what they interpreted as the verbal form for the first person plural inclusive, marked by *ya-* (exs. 1-2), was used also for the third person (ex. 3):[2]

(1) ya-só
     1.IN-go
     'We (incl.) went'

(2) pirá ya-y-pisík
     fish 1.IN-REL-catch
     'We (incl.) caught fish'

(3) móya kuyã ya-y-suʔú
     snake woman 1.IN?-REL-bite
     'A snake bit the woman'

On the other hand, the verbal form interpreted by the missionaries as third person, marked by *o-* (exs. 4-5), was also employed in constructions whose meaning included the speaker (ex. 6):

(4) o-só
     3-go
     'He went'

(5) kunumĩ pirá o-y-pisĩk
     boy   fish 3-REL-catch
     'The boy caught fish'

(6) asé   pirá o-y-pisĩk
     we.all fish 3?-REL-catch
     'We all caught fish'

An examination of the data available in the two grammars and in the texts written by the missionaries leads us to the conclusion, presented summarily in a previous paper (Rodrigues 1978), that the system of personal reference of Tupinambá is characterized by a set of features that includes the contrast between the speaker and the hearer as one parameter, and the focality of the third person as another parameter.

Before proceeding to a closer examination of the facts of Tupinambá, we would like to sketch the general pragmatic and discourse setting for the linguistic distinction of person.

The pragmatic setting for the discourse consists of events that may involve one or more elements including or not, the speaker, the hearer or addressee, and a third class of elements - persons like the speaker and the hearer or other living beings or things. This third class of elements is traditionally termed the 3rd person, in the same way as the speaker is named the 1st person and the hearer, the 2nd person.

For the pragmatic setting he is going to refer to, the speaker takes as a subject of his discourse either the only element acting or being acted upon, or one or more of several elements acting or being acted upon. This is what we call focus: the speaker brings into focus one or more elements of the pragmatic setting (see also Fillmore 1977). By so doing he promotes such elements into persons of his discourse.

The process of focusing a person in discourse therefore implies the selection of that person from a given pragmatic setting; the setting may actually include one or more other elements, which are thereby left out of focus. The discourse does not represent every detail of the pragmatic setting, but sifts this setting according to the intention of the speaker.

Seven basic combinations of the personal elements focused upon in discourse may be distinguished. If we symbolize the speaker by the number 1, the hearer by the number 2, and the third person by the number 3, we can mark these combinations as follows:

1	Only the speaker is in focus.
13	Only the speaker and 3rd person are in focus.
2	Only the hearer is in focus.
23	Only the hearer and 3rd person are in focus.
12	Only the speaker and the hearer are in focus.
123	The speaker, the hearer, and 3rd person are in focus.
3	Only 3rd person is in focus.

It should be kept in mind that any element not included in a combination may be part of the pragmatic setting, but is left out of focus in the discourse. Two third persons may also be distinguished in this way. That is, since third person is a concept that may apply to one or more than one entity, only one entity (or possibly one group of entities) may be brought into focus; one or more others are left out of focus.

The contrast between speaker and hearer, basic to any discourse, may be highlighted or neutralized by means of focusing. The contrast is highlighted when either the speaker or the hearer is brought into focus, to the exclusion of the other; this is the case in combinations 1, 13, 2, and 23 above. The contrast is neutralized when both the speaker and the hearer are conjointly focused, as in combinations 12 and 123, or when both are left out of focus, as in combination 3.

Each of the seven basic combinations of personal elements in discourse presented above are, as we have seen, a reduction imposed on the pragmatic setting. Once the speaker has made the reduction, it must then be expressed by means of the grammatical devices of his language. These devices are language-specific and impose a second sifting, now on the elements selected by the speaker: they either give the selected elements explicit manifestation in the sentences or leave them simply implicit in the syntactic context.

As far as the discourse persons are concerned, languages show a moderately large variety of sets of coding devices, such as the personal pronouns and personal markers. Besides personal pronouns, Tupinambá also has personal markers prefixed on the verb and relational markers prefixed on both verbs and nouns. The relational markers will be touched upon in this paper only in so far as one of them may participate in shifting the focus from 3rd person agent to 3rd person patient, or vice-versa, in transitive verbs (see Seki, this volume, for discussion of relational markers in another Tupí-Guaraní language).

There are six personal pronouns in Tupinambá; these cover the following combinations of personal elements:

isé	1	oré	13
ené	2	pe?ẽ	23
yané	12	asé	123

(AG 10v-11, 12; F 6-7)

This set constitutes a well defined morphological paradigm, characterized among other things by being the only words in the language to have a morphological dative:

iséβe	'to me'	oréβe	'to me and him'
enéβe	'to you'	pe?ẽme	'to you and him'
yanéβe	'to you and me'	aséβe	'to you, me and him'

(AG 10v-11, 12; F 6-7)

This set does not include pronouns for either a focal 3rd person or a non-focal one. A 3rd person is expressed either by a nominal phrase or by a demonstrative; alternatively it can be simply referred to by a relational prefix. (Other sets of personal pronouns show the same distinctions or are subsets of the set above.)

In independent clauses, both intransitive and transitive verbs have person markers for the subject. These person markers agree with the personal pronouns given above and distinguish, therefore, the same combinations of personal elements:

a-	1	oro-	13
ere-	2	pe-	23
ya-	12	o-	123

(cf. AG 20v; F 10)

Here enters the question that vexed the old missionary grammarians: *ya-* and *o-* are used also for agreement with NP subjects, as in exs. 3 and 5. On an intransitive verb *ya-* is consistently understood as 12, as in ex. 1; but on a transitive verb it may be understood as either 12 or 3, as in exs. 2 and 3, respectively. As to *o-*, on intransitive verbs it is consistently interpreted as 3, as in ex. 4; but on transitive verbs it may be interpreted as either 3 or 123, as in exs. 5 and 6, respectively.

Luis Figueira (1621), one of the two missionary grammarians of Tupinambá, appears to be satisfied in saying that the use of *ya-* on transitive verbs for the 3rd person is an idiomatic one, without any further explanation.[3] He presents the following examples for the two ways of expressing a third person subject in transitive main clauses:

(7) Pedro móya o-Ø-yuká
     Peter snake 3-REL-kill
     'Peter killed a snake'. (F 99)

(8) Pedro móya ya-Ø-yuká
     Peter snake 3-REL-kill
     'Peter killed a snake'. (F 99)

(9) o-erasó temõ sapiʔá iβák-ipe tupána syé r-úβa   mã
     3-carry OPT soon sky-LOC God   1   REL-father oh
     'Oh would soon God take my father to heaven!' (F99)

(10) ya-rasó temõ sapiʔá iβák-ipe tupána syé r-úβa   mã
     3-carry OPT soon sky-LOC God   1   REL-father oh
     'Oh would soon God take my father to heaven!' (F99)

Figueira remarks that 10 is better than 9. This remark makes sense if we consider that a sentence with the meaning of 9 and 10 is most likely to occur in a discourse whose focus is 'my father' rather than in one focusing on 'God'.

Joseph de Anchieta (1595), the other missionary grammarian, tries to show the nature of the difference between *ya-* and *o-* when both are used for the 3rd person on transitive verbs. Initially, Anchieta states that *ya-* is used when the subject is of lesser esteem than the object; he gives the following examples:[4]

(11) syé r-úβa   t-oβayára   ya-Ø-ʔú
     1   REL-father REL-adversary 3-REL-eat
     'The enemies ate my father'. (AG 36v)

(12) móya Pedro ya-y-suʔú
     snake Peter 3-REL-bite
     'The snake bit Peter'. (AG 36v)

(13) Pedro t-aʔíra   ya-y-nupã
     Peter REL-son 3-REL-beat
     'His (i.e. Pedro's) son beat Pedro'. (AG 36v)

However, in the next paragraph Anchieta goes on to remark that *ya-* may also be used when the subject is of greater esteem than the object, in accord with the subject matter, and gives two contrastive examples:[5]

(14) moruβisáβa moná ya-y-namí-ʔók-ukár
     judge   thief 3-REL-ear-take.off-CAUS
     'The judge ordered the thief's ear to be taken off'. (AG 36v)

(15) moruβisáβa moná o-y-namí-ʔók-ukár
     judge   thief 3-REL-ear-take.off-CAUS
     'The judge ordered the thief's ear to be taken off'. (AG 36v)

Our interpretation of Anchieta's statements and examples is that the factor governing the choice of *ya-* or *o-* on transitive verbs is focus: if the subject, i.e. the agent, is in focus, it is marked on the verb by *o-*; if conversely the object, i.e., the patient, is in focus, the subject is marked by *ya-*. Thus, *o-* means '3rd person subject in focus' and *ya-* means '3rd person subject out of focus'. This interpretation is compatible with exs. 11-13: in 11 the discourse would most likely be focusing on the father, in 12 on 'Peter', and in 9 on 'Peter' again. As to exs. 14-15, it is equally likely that the speaker is commenting on the severeness of the judge, bringing this judge into focus (15), or on the unhappiness of the thief, putting the thief into focus and leaving the judge out of focus (14).

This interpretation is also compatible with the use of *o-* and *ya-* as markers of 3rd person agents in texts such as the poetic compositions by Father Anchieta:[6]

(16) maratawã-me   t-ekw-ára   o-Ø-eroβyá   syé Ø-yeʔéŋa
     Maratawã-LOC REL-be-AG 3-REL-believe 1   REL-speech
     'Those living in Maratawã believe my words'. (AT 123)

(17) piná-eytɪk-ára...   o-y-moyaʔók o-emiára
     fishhook-throw-AG 3-REL-divide REL-catch
     'The fishers divide their catch'. (AT 130)

(18) i-sɪ̂   y-asoʔí-katw-áβo   o-yo-pyá   roʔ̃ suí i-poreawsú-miñ̃
     REL-mother REL-cover-good-GER 3-REL-defend cold from REL-poor-little
     'His mother defended from the cold the poor little one by covering him well'.
     (AL 150)

In ex. 19, 'sinners' is the focus of the discourse, whereas 'our fire', the subject of the clause, is incidental. In 20 'his mother' is the focus and subject of the first three clauses; she is the object of the fourth clause, whose subject, *pitáŋĩ*, is out of focus. Examples 21-22 are said of Jesus, who is the focus of the discourse from which they are taken.

(19) opá emonã t-ekw-ára   yané r-atá   ya-yá rõ
     all thus   REL-be-AG 12   REL-fire 3-take then
     'Then our fire takes all that live this way'
     (said by a devil about the sinners). (AT 219)

(20) i-sɨ́   n i-memɨr-asɨ́-y   na s-uwɨ́-y   n i-maraʔár-i
REL-mother not REL-son-pain-NEG not REL-blood-NEG not REL-sick-NEG

n ya-y-mo-marã-potár-i   pitáŋ-ĩ   morawsuβára
not 3-REL-CAUS-harm-wish-NEG child-DIM merciful

'His mother did not feel any childbirth pain, did not bleed, was not sick; the
merciful baby did not wish to cause her any harm'. (AL 150)

(21) ya-y-pó-pwár-atã   i-moaŋaipápa,   s-uwɨ́   momukápa;
3-REL-hand-tie-hard REL-maltreating REL-blood pouring

ya-y-nupã-nupã
3-REL-beat-beat

'They tied up his hands tightly, maltreating him, pouring his blood; they beat
him repeatedly'. (AL 212)

(22) ya-y-pó-asá-sá   i-pɨ́   r-eséβé
3-REL-hand-transfix-transfix REL-foot REL-together

'They transfixed (one after the other) his hands and his feet'. (AL 213)

A brief comment on the *ya-/o-* distinction for the 3rd person is found in the
Tupinambá dictionary of the Jesuits;[7] in the entry for *'Eclypsar-se a lua'*
(eclipsing of the moon), four ways of saying it are given:

(23) yasɨ́   maʔé   ya-Ø-ʔú
moon animal 3-REL-eat

(24) maʔé   yasɨ́   ya-Ø-ʔú
animal moon 3-REL-eat

(25) yasɨ́   maʔé   o-Ø-ʔú
moon animal 3-REL-eat

(26) maʔé   yasɨ́   o-Ø-ʔú
animal moon 3-REL-eat

The comment offered is as follows:

These are among the most obscure ways of speaking in this language, for they mean
that the moon is eaten by something, but they are so ambiguous that they mean also
that it is the moon which eats something... As for the eclipse of the moon they say
that it is eaten by a beast of the sky. Some, like the Tupinambá, say it is a jaguar.
The Tupí say it is a snake.

Two main questions are at issue here: (a) the possibility of both SOV and
OSV word order, which entails for every construction the interpretation of
either nominal phrase as the subject; and (b) the use of *ya-* and *o-* independently
from word order as a subject marker for 3rd person. As the Tupinambá

meaning of 'eclipse of the moon' (as well as the Tupí one) rules out any
interpretation of 'moon' as the agent of the verb -?ú 'to eat', we must admit that
all four constructions mean basically 'the animal ate the moon'. The difference
between 23 and 24, as well as between 25 and 26, may be due to topicalization
or another stylistic device. The difference between the sentences with *ya-* (23
and 24) and those with *o-* (25 and 26) must correlate with the examples
previously discussed; the subject marked by *ya-* is not focal whereas the subject
marked by *o-* is focal. My assumption is that 23 and 24, the two sentences
presented first by our source, should occur in a discourse in which the moon is
the focus. This would most probably be the case when a moon eclipse is taking
place. Accordingly, the subject/agent is out of focus and would be marked by
ya-. Sentences 25 and 26 would occur, for instance, when one would tell about
the existence of that animal present in the sky that can sometimes eat the moon.
In instances like this, the animal, besides being the subject/agent of the
sentence, would also be the focus of the discourse and would therefore be
marked by *o-*.

The distinction between *ya-* and *o-* argued for in this paper is also compatible
with other information added by Anchieta in his grammar, namely that *ya-* is
also used for marking "impersonality" without an expressed subject,[8] as in 27:

(27) ya-Ø-yuká
    3-REL-kill
    'Somebody kills' (Portuguese: 'Matam') (AG 36v)

An indetermined subject as in 27 is of course non-focal. Analogous
examples occur in the Catechism (Araujo 1952; examples identified by C and
page number):

(28) emonã t-ekw-ár-wéra   ya-y-pe?á
    thus   REL-be-AG-EX 3-REL-separate
    'Who has been thus (married against his/her will) will be separated'. (C 128)

(29) o-mená teyẽ   s-ér-ók-ipɨra   s-ér-ók-ipɨr-e?ɨma   r-esé
    3-marry in.vain REL-name-take-PAT REL-name-take-PAT-NEG REL-to
    i-mená   riré ya-y-pe?á   yẽ
    REL-marry after 3-REL-separate simply
    'A baptized one marries in vain an unbaptized one: after their marriage they will
    simply be separated'. (C 130v)

The prefix *o-*, which was assumed by the old grammarians to be basically a
3rd person marker, means clearly 123 when it occurs in agreement with the
pronoun *asé*. An example like 30 illustrates how Anchieta understood *asé:*

(30) asé yuká
123 kill
Anchieta's translation: 'Somebody kills one, i.e. me, us, etc.' (Portuguese
original: 'A homem matão, i. a mĩ, a nos, &c.') (AG 12)

The following is an example from Figueira in which both values of *o-* are
present, as 3 and as 123:

(31) tupã o-manõ, memē-tipó   asé o-manõ-mo
God 3-die   so.much-more 123 123-die-GER
'(If even) God died, so much more we shall die'. (F 163)

Exs. 32-37 are additional instances of *o-* '123' taken from the Catechism:

(32) o-yerokĩ pe   asé Jesus ?é-reme?
123-bow INT 123 Jesus say-when
'Do we bow when we say (the name of) Jesus?' (C 23)

(33) o-yerokĩ
123-bow
'We bow'. (as an answer to ex. 32) (C 23)

(34) aβá pe   amē   asé o-s-enõy   o-ykóteβē-mo
who INT always 123 123-REL-call 123-be afflicted-GER
'Who do we always invoke when we are afflicted?' (C 23)

(35) Jesus o-s-enõy.
Jesus 123-REL-call
'We invoke Jesus'. (as an answer to ex. 34) (C 23)

(36) o-s-epĩy   βé pe   asé tiβĩ   ?ĩ-karaíβa pupé?
123-REL-sprinkle too INT 123 grave water-saint with
'Do we also sprinkle the graves with blessed water?' (C 24v)

(37) o-s-epĩy   βé
123-REL-sprinkle too
'We sprinkle them too'. (C 24v)

A relational prefix *s-, i-, y-, yo-* or *Ø*[9] in transitive verbs refers to a 3rd
person object, irrespective of whether the object is in focus or out of focus. Its
focal value in transitive constructions is automatically the inverse of whatever
focal value the respective subject person marker has. If we employ [+f] and [-f] as
a device for marking the sentence constituents that are in focus or out of focus,
we can label exs. 14-15 as follows:

(14a) moruβisáβa moná ya-y-namí-ʔók-ukár
       judge⁻ᶠ   thiefᵗᶠ 3⁻ᶠ-REL⁺ᶠ-ear-take.off-CAUS

(15a) moruβisáβa moná o-y-namí-ʔók-ukár
       judge⁺ᶠ   thiefᶠ 3⁺ᶠ-REL⁻ᶠ-ear-take.off-CAUS

BOTH: 'The judge ordered the thief's ear to be taken off'. (AG 36v)

In conclusion, in Tupinambá the verbal person marker *o-* means that 3rd person is in focus and that there is no contrast between the speaker and the hearer; that is to say, it means {(you, I, and he)⁺ᶠ } as well as {he⁺ᶠ}. Analogously, *ya-* means that 3rd person is out of focus and that there is no contrast between the speaker and the hearer; it means {(you and I)⁺ᶠ and he⁻ᶠ}. In both cases, then, a single form indicates both 'you and I (and he)' and 'neither you nor I (but he)'. This system of personal marking can be clearly presented in a matrix constructed with the parameters of (a) contrast between speaker and hearer and (b) focality of the 3rd person. This is shown in Figures 1 and 2.

		Contrast 1/2		
		+		-
		1	2	
3ᶠ	-	isé	ené	yané
	+	oré	peʔẽ	asé

Figure 1. Matrix of personal pronouns

		Contrast 1/2		
		+		-
		1	2	
3ᶠ	-	a-	ere-	ya-
	+	oro-	pe-	o-

Figure 2. Matrix of personal prefixes

The neutralization of the contrast between speaker (1) and hearer (2), as it obtains with the personal prefixes on transitive verbs, may also be visualized by means of a tree-diagram. In Figure 3 the confluence of branches indicates one single output for two different semantic situations.

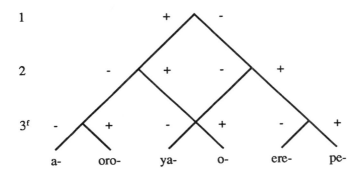

Figure 3. Tree-diagram of personal prefixes

NOTES

[1]   The first grammar of Tupinambá was written by Father Joseph de Anchieta, S. J., and was published in Coimbra in 1595 under the title *Arte de grammatica da lingua mais usada na Costa do Brasil.*   Several facsimile reproductions of this book are now available, the most recent of them made by the Federal University of Bahia in 1980 and reprinted in 1981. A second grammar was composed by Father Luis Figueira and published in Lisbon in 1621 under the title *Arte da lingua brasilica* and in 1687 as *Arte de grammatica da lingua brasilica.* A facsimile reproduction of Figueira's grammar was published in Leipzig in 1878, under the title *Grammatica da lingua do Brasil.* Examples cited from Anchieta's grammar will be identified by AG followed by the corresponding page number; those taken from Figueira's grammar by F followed by the page number of the (facsimile of the) 1687 edition.

[2]   "Ainda que o comum das linguas seja concordar o nome singular com o verbo singular; & o de multidão com o verbo no plural, com tudo nesta lingua todas as vezes que se ajuntão dous nomes terceiras pessoas, hum dos quaes aja de ser nominativo, & outro accusativo, o que he nominativo do singular pode ter o verbo na primeira pessoa inclusiva, do plural." (Although the usual in the

languages is the agreement of the singular noun with the verb in the singular
and of the noun of multitude with the verb in the plural, in this language
however every time when two nouns of the third person meet, one of them
being nominative and the other accusative, the one that is nominative of the
singular may have the verb in the first person inclusive of the plural.) (Figueira
1697.98-99).

Abbreviations are as follows: AG agent, CAUS causative, DIM
diminutive, EX former, GER gerund, IN inclusive, INT interrogative, LOC
locative, NEG negative, OPT optative, PAT patient, REL relational.

[3]   "Parecera barbaria, concordar terceira pessoa no singular, com a primeira
do plurar. Mas não he de estranhar, pois tambem na lingua Grega elegantissima
temos exemplo semelhante, porque comummente os nomes neutros no plurar,
pedem o verbo no singular: ut Zóa tréki, Animalia currit; são modos de fallar
de varias linguas." (It would seem a barbarism to make the third person singular agree with the first plural, but we should not find it so strange, since we have
a similar example in the very elegant Greek language, for [in this] neuter nouns
in the plural usually ask for a verb in the singular, e.g. Zóa tréki, 'the animals
runs'; these are ways of speaking of different languages.) (Figueira 1687.99).

[4]   "Quando as cousas de menor valia, são nominativos usase da primeira
plural, ya." (When things of lesser value are subjects the first plural ya- is used.)
(Anchieta 1595.36v).

[5]   "Ainda que tambem se pode usar deste, quando o nominativo he de maior
estima, secundum subiectam materiam." (However this [i.e., ya-] may also be
used when the nominative is of greater esteem, according to the subject matter.)
(Anchieta 1595.36v).

[6]   Examples from Anchieta's poetic works in Tupinambá are taken from
Anchieta 1977 (identified by AT and page number) and 1984 (identified by AL
and page number).

[7]   The Tupinambá dictionary was preserved in a few manuscript copies of
the 17th century. There were two editions of it, both under the title *Vocabulário
na língua brasílica;* the first (1938) was edited by Plinio Ayrosa and reproduces
a manuscript of 1621; the other (1942-1943) was edited by Carlos Drumond
and combines the same manuscript with another undated one. The quotation
given here is from this latter edition (Anonymous 1942-1943), in which it
occurs on page 108 of the first volume: "*Eclypsar-se a lua.* Jacîbaeyaû, vel,
Baejacigyâû, ou Jacigbae, 1, Baejacîoû. Estes são dos mais escuros termos de
fallar que ha nesta lingoa, porq. querem dizer que a lua he comida dalgũa cousa,
e são tam ambiguos q. iuntamente querem dizer que ella he a que come algũa
cousa... O eclypse da Lua dizẽ elles q. a come algũa fera do Ceo. Outros como
os Tupinambâs dizem q. he hum tigre. Os Tupîs dizem que he hũa serpente."

⁸ "Tambem se usa desta primeira plural por terceira impersonaliter, ut yajucâ, matão, sem ter nominativo expresso." (This first plural is also used impersonally for the third, without an expressed nominative.) (Anchieta 1595.36v).

⁹ The forms *s-*, *i-*, *y-*, *yo-* and *Ø* are allomorphs of one and the same prefix: *s-* occurs with stems of class II; *i-* occurs with stems of class I (these are lexically defined morphological classes); *y-* is a variant of *i-* occurring after vowels; *yo-* replaces *i-* between the prefixed person marker and a monosyllabic stem; and *Ø* replaces *i-* between the prefixed person markers and a very restricted set of verbal stems.

REFERENCES

Anchieta, Joseph de. 1595. *Arte de grammatica da lingua mais usada na costa do Brasil.* Coimbra: Antonio de Mariz.

Anchieta, Joseph de. 1977. *Teatro de Anchieta.* Complete works, 3rd volume. Originals accompanied by translation in verses, introduction and notes by P. Armando Cardoso, S. J. São Paulo: Edicões Loyola.

Anchieta, Joseph de. 1984. *Lírica portuguesa e tupi.* Complete works, 5th volume, I. Originals in Portuguese and in Tupi, accompanied by translation in verses, introduction and annotations to the text by P. Armando Cardoso, S. J. São Paulo: Edicões Loyola.

Anonymous. 1952-1953. *Vocabulário na língua brasílica.* 2nd edition reviewed and compared with the MS fg., 3144 of the Biblioteca Nacional de Lisboa by Carlos Drumond. 1st volume (A-H), Bulletin 137; 2nd volume (I-Z), Bulletin 164, Universidade de São Paulo, Faculdade de Filosofia, Ciências e Letras. São Paulo: Universidade de São Paulo.

Araújo, Antônio de. 1952. *Catecismo na língua brasílica.* Facsimile reproduction of the 1st edition (1618) with introduction by Pe. A. Lemos Barbosa. Rio de Janeiro: Pontifícia Universidade Católica do Rio de Janeiro.

Figueira, Luiz. 1878. *Grammatica da lingua do Brasil.* Republished by Julio Platzmann. Facsimile of the 1687 edition. Leipzig: B. G. Teubner.

Fillmore, Charles. 1977. The case for case reopened. *Grammatical Relations (Syntax and Semantics 8).* Ed. by Peter Cole and Jerrold Sadock, 59-81. New York: Academic Press.

Rodrigues, Aryon D. 1978. O sistema pessoal do Tupinambá. *Ensaios Linguísticos* 1.167-73. Brazil, Belo Horizonte.

Ergativity and Nominativity in Kuikúro and Other Carib Languages

Bruna Franchetto

1. INTRODUCTION[1]

Kuikúro is one of the dialects of the Upper Xingu Carib (north of Mato Grosso, Central Brazil). It is spoken by nearly two hundred individuals living on the left bank of the middle Culuene river, headwaters of the Xingu river.

The aims of this paper are 1) to describe the system of split ergativity in Kuikúro at the semantic, syntactic and morphological levels, and 2) to compare the Kuikúro system to systems of coding grammatical relations in several other Carib languages of Central Brazil. Kuikúro is unique among these languages in that in declarative clauses it exhibits ergativity in three distinct morphosyntactic systems: nominal case marking, pronominal clitics and basic constituent order. The other languages investigated exhibit, with some variation, a semantically determined person hierarchy dominated by nominativity. Nevertheless, Kuikúro also exhibits a similar person hierarchy in a class of non-declarative verb forms which I have termed 'interactive moods'. This synchronic comparative study suggests a hypothesis concerning the diachronic relationship between nominativity and ergativity in Carib languages, namely that the ergative system is older than the nominative system and that the 'interactive moods' represent an embryonic nominative pattern that is fully developed in other Carib languages. Future detailed comparative analysis of these and other languages of the same family will be necessary to confirm or reject this hypothesis.

2. ERGATIVITY IN KUIKÚRO[2]

In discussing ergativity and nominativity in Kuikúro, I will follow Comrie 1978a in using the terms A, S and P to refer to transitive subject (the most agent-like participant), intransitive subject and transitive object respectively. Any system that treats S and P as members of a morphosyntactic category as opposed to A is said to be an 'ergative' system. Any system that treats S and A as a morphosyntactic category as opposed to P is said to be a 'nominative' system.

Kuikúro clearly manifests ergativity in nominal case marking, anaphoric clitics and word order. In 2 the suffix -*héke* marks the ergative case on noun phrases and pronouns. In exs. 1b-d and 2c-f the anaphoric proclitics *i*- (third person) and *u*- (first person) refer to absolute arguments (the conjunction of S and P as defined above). Observe in 1c and 2e that the verbal suffix *ko*- 'plural' refers exclusively to absolutive arguments.

Furthermore, these examples show that in terms of neutral word order Kuikúro treats S and P alike (preverbal position) and A differently (post-verbal position). Although there is some freedom of order of the A argument, as seen in 2b where the noun phrase marked by -*héke* is left-dislocated, the intranstive subject and transitive object rigidly occur in pre-verbal position. These facts are a clear manifestation of 'syntactic' ergativity.

Intransitive Clause:

(1) a. karaihá   kacun-tárâ
        non.indian work-CONT
        'The non-indian is working.'

     b. cué   i-kacun-tárâ
        hard 3-work-CONT
        'He is working hard.'

     c. cué   i-kacun-tarâ-ko
        hard 3-work-CONT-PL
        'They are working hard.'

     d. cué   u-kacun-tárâ
        hard 1-work-CONT
        'I am working hard.'

Transitive Clause:

(2) a. kuk-aki-sâ   ta-lâígo léha karaihá-héke
        1INC-word-REL hear-FUT ASP   non-indian-ERG
        'The non-indian will hear our words.'

     b. karaihá-héke   kuk-aki-sâ   ta-lâígo   léha
        non-indian-ERG   1INC-word-REL hear-FUT   ASP
        'The non-indian will hear our words.'

     c. i-ta-lâígo léha karaihá-héke
        3(P)
        'The non-indian will hear it.'

     d. i-ta-lâígo léha i-héke
                       3-ERG
        'He will hear it.'

e. i-ñomó-ko-héke   titá   i-ta-lâ-ko
   3-husband-PL-ERG there 3(P)-hear-PUNCT-PL
   'Their husbands there heard them.'

f. u-ta-lâígo léha i-héke, karaihá-héke
   1-   3-ERG non-indian-ERG
   'He will hear me, the non-indian.'

Although absolutive arguments are not marked morphologically, there is suprasegmental absolutive case marking. This is coded by a stress shift from the penultimate to the ultimate syllable of the preverbal noun phrase (*kukakísâ —>kukakisâ* , transitive object in 2a and 2b; *karáiha —> karaihá* intransitive subject in 1a), combined with a general rising intonation. These suprasegmental features code the link between absolutive nominals and the verb.

Table 1 illustrates the pronominal clitics and free pronouns of Kuikúro. The etymological relationship between the pronouns and clitics is evident from this Table.

The morphological and syntactic ergative system illustrated in 1 and 2 and

	Free Pronouns	Pronominal Clitics	
		S/P	A
1 person	úre	u-	u-héke
2	ére	e-	e-héke
1INC	kukúre	ku-	kupéke
1EXC	tisúre	ti-	ti-héke
3	íre	i- (or Ø)	i-héke
	(ekíse, âgéle, etc.)		

Table 1. Pronominal devices in Kuikúro declarative clauses

in Table 1 is the dominant pattern, functioning in all declarative finite clauses, either independent or subordinate, which code actual events.

Semantically, the most general function of *-héke* is to mark a causing or initiating source of an action carried through to a terminating patient. In addition to transitive agents, *-héke* also marks a kind of locative that indicates a measured distance between two points, as in the following example:

(3) eté   iháki ipá-héke
   village far   lagoon-LOC
   'The village is far from the lagoon.'

As a device for marking transitive agents, the locational character of *-héke* is metaphorically applied to the cognitive movement from initiating agent to a distinct patient. In other words, full transitivity in Kuikúro involves filling up the 'space' between the two arguments of a transitive clause.

Furthermore, transitive subjects marked by *-héke* need not necessarily function as agents in the strict sense of Fillmore 1968. That is, they need not act with volition or control and they need not be animate. They must, however, refer to the causing source of the action:

(4) a. tarí-héke   u-e-tárâ
        hunger-ERG 1-hurt-CONT
        'The **hunger** is hurting me / I am hungry.'

     b. tehú-héke   u-e-pârâ
        stone-ERG   1-hurt-PERF
        'The **stone** hurt me.'

     c. tugá-héke   léca ate-lâ-ko   léha
        water-ERG   ASP encircle-PUNCT-PL ASP
        'The **water** encircled them.'

     d. u-igkuri-cárâ táka koníre   e-i-ñarâ-héke léha, o-kotú-héke léha
        1-deceive-CONT yesterday 2-be-PUNCT-ERG 2-mad-ERG
        'Your yesterday's feeling is deceiving me, the fact that you went mad.'

Thus we see that **causer** or **source** is the central semantic property of nominals marked with *-héke*.

It is interesting to note that in Kuikúro one of the most common transitivizing/causativizing devices is simply to add a *-héke* argument to an intransitive clause. For example:

(5) a. hâré   té-lâ
        arrow go-PUNCT
        'The arrow goes.'

     b. hâré   té-lâ   i-héke
        arrow go-PUNCT 3-ERG
        'He made the arrow go/He shot the arrow.'

On the other hand, the absence of an ergative nominal with a normally transitive verb indicates that the A argument is non-specific. I consider this construction type to be a 'middle passive' construction. It is used mainly in procedural or didactic texts:

(6) lepéne kwirí   hihí-jâ
     after   manioc peel-PUNCT
     'Afterwards, people peel the manioc roots/manioc roots are peeled.'

3. DETRANSITIVIZATION

As in all Carib languages, the transitive/intransitive dichotomy is central in Kuikúro. There are many constructions that involve formal detransitivization of inherently transitive roots. The verbal prefix *t-* (VC = valence change) derives an intransitive verb from a transitive verb; it has a valence changing (VC) function that often codes reflexivity.

In 7b and 7c the transitive verb *ikaín* 'to raise' is detransitivized to mean 'to get up'. The same prefix indicates reflexivity of possessor when attached to nouns, as in example 7a:

(7) a. t-umu-rú   ikaín-jâ   isí-héke
        REFL-son-POSS raise-PUNCT mother-ERG
        'The mother $_i$ raised her $_i$ son.'

     b. i-mu-rú   t-ikaín-jâ   léha
        3-son-POSS VC-raise-PUNCT
        'Her son got up.'

     c. i-t-ikaín-jâ   léha
        3-VC-raise-PUNCT
        'He got up.'

Example 8a illustrates a transitive construction with two distinct arguments, while 8b illustrates the same verb with the detransitivizing prefix *r-*, an allomorph of *t-*. The clause in 8b has two possible interpretations; one is reflexive, i.e. the doer and the undergoer of the action must be the same person, while the other is that the action is not carried over to a specific patient. Marantz 1984 considers this phenomenon to be convincing evidence of a 'truly ergative' language.

(8) a. áiha u-ikucé-lâ   léha e-héke
        ASP 1-paint-PUNCT   2-ERG
        'You finished painting me.'

     b. áiha u-r-ikucé-lâ   léha
        ASP 1-VC-paint-PUNCT
        'I finished painting myself' / 'I finished painting (something).'

The same detransitivizing/reflexivizing process is at work in a classic example of an antipassive construction (Comrie 1978a, Kalmar 1979, inter alia). In 9a the plain ergative construction implies that the action is directed towards some specific piece of paper. In 9b the attention of the hearer is intended to be focussed on the doer of the action and the action itself. The identity of the piece of paper is inconsequential to the intention of the speech act. Nevertheless, the same clause can have a reflexive meaning, as in 9c:

(9) a. papé ahehi-carâ u-héke
   paper write-CONT 1-ERG
   'I'm writing on the paper.'

b. u-t-ahehi-cárâ (papé-ki)
   1-VC-write-CONT (paper-INST)
   'I'm writing (on a paper).'

c. u-t-ahehi-cárâ
   'I'm writing (on something)' / 'I'm writing on myself.'

4. DE-ERGATIVIZATION

There is a process in Kuikúro which has some but not all properties of detransitivization. I will term this process 'de-ergativization'. Like the detransitivization process, de-ergativization applies to inherently transitive verbs and results in the verb agreeing with the **actor** or **agent** of the event described by the verb. De-ergativization is formally marked by the verbal prefix *ñ-* or *g-*; the prefixed verb occurs immediately after the unmarked subject. The prefix can be considered a general object marker or an object agreement marker. Unlike the detransitive constructions, the **patient** associated with a de-ergativized verb does not appear in an oblique case and retains all other syntactic properties of transitive patients. However, unlike the ergative constructions, the agent of the de-ergative construction does not take *-héke*. Hence, I conclude that the de-ergative construction represents an alternative transitive clause type that reflects a **nominative** rather than **ergative** system for encoding grammatical relations. Examples of de-ergative constructions according to their various functions are given in the following two subsections.

4.1 PRAGMATICALLY MARKED CONSTRUCTIONS. As illustrated in examples 10-12, de-ergativization is obligatory in cleft constructions, relative clauses and content questions in which the direct object is questioned. Each of these constructions is based on nominalized verb forms. In 10 and 12 the verb 'eat' is transfomed into a predicate nominal by the copular form *-i*. In 11 the verbal suffix *-pârâ* is a perfective nominalizer. In other words, this sentence could be translated literally as 'you will bring your taken water'. In relative constructions, the nominalized verb is frequently dislocated to the rightmost position in the sentence (11a). The regular ergative versions of these sentences are ungrammatical (10b, 11c and 12b):

(10) a. sahúnta-ha iré-i e-g-ege-tarâ-i
    tucunaré-EMPH DEIC-COP 2-DERG-eat-CONT-COP
    'It's tucunaré that you are eating.'

b. *sahuntá-ha iré-i ege-tarâ-i e-héke

(11) a. tugá igi-nâm-ígo   e-heké-ni   a-g-ame-pârâ-ko
       water bring-PUNC-FUT 2-ERG-PL 2-DERG-take-PERF-PL
       'You will bring the water that you will take.'

OR b. tugá a-g-ame-pârâ-ko igi-nâm-ígo e-heké-ni

   c. *tugá ame-pârâ-ko e-héke-ni igi-nâm-ígo e-heké-ni

(12) a. tâ   e-g-ege-tarâ-i
        QW 2-DERG-eat-CONT-COP
        'What are you eating?'

   b. *tâ ege-tarâ-i   e-héke

4.2 THE INTERACTIVE MOODS.   As is common in dominantly ergative languages, Kuikúro exhibits split-ergativity.   In Kuikúro, the factors conditioning the split are a person hierarchy and the presence of certain performative speech act markers which I will call **interactive moods**.

The intentional mood is illustrated in 13a-f:

(13) a. ku-ñ-api-rái   âgéle
        1INC-DERG-hit-INT he
        'We shall hit him.'
        *âgéle api-rái kupéke
                        1INC.ERG

   b. ku-ñ-api-ramíni   âgéle
      1INC-DERG-hit-INT.PL he
      'We all shall hit him.'
      *âgéle api-ramíni kupéke

   c. ñ-api-rái   âgéle
      DERG-hit-INT he
      'I shall hit him.'
      *âgéle api-rái u-héke
                      1-ERG

   d. akiñá ti-ñ-iha-tái   e-íña
      story 1EXC-DERG-show-INT 2-PURP
      'We (excl) shall tell the story to you.'
   OR akiñá iha-tái ti-héke   e-íña
                      1EXC-ERG

   e. akiñá iha-tái e-héke   u-íña
                      2-ERG   1-PURP
      'You shall tell the story to me.'
   OR akiñá   e-g-iha-tái   u-iña
                  2-DERG

f. akiñá iha-tái   i-héke   u-íña
   3-ERG
'He shall tell the story to me.'
*akiñá (i)-ñ-iha-tái u-íña

In 13a-c the prefix *ñ-* indicates 'de-ergativization'. Constructions headed by a verb with this prefix manifest a nominative rather than ergative system in that the A argument may not occur in the ergative case, and the verbal proclitic, normally reserved for S or P arguments, refers to the A argument. Word order in de-ergativized clauses manifests neither ergativity nor nominativity in that the position of the P argument is genuinely free.

As illustrated in 13a-c de-ergativization is obligatory for transitive intentional mood verbs in which the subject is first person singular or inclusive. However, if the transitive subject is first person exclusive or second person, there is alternation between an ergative and a nominative pattern (13d and 13e). Finally, when the transitive subject is third person, de-ergativization may not occur (13f).

In the hortative mood, in which the transitive subject is necessarily first person plural inclusive, the nominative construction must occur. Compare 14b with the corresponding intransitive sentence in 14a and the regular ergative construction in non-hortative mood 14c:

(14) a. INTRANSITIVE   ku-tiñamapá-ni   hóho
                        1INC-eat-HORT EMPH
                        'Let's go eat.'

     b. TRANSITIVE   ku-g-ege-tâgi   hóho   kága
                        1INC-DERG-eat-HORT.PL EMPH fish

                        or kága hóho ku-g-ege-tâgi
                        'Let's go eat fish.'

     c. NON-HORTATIVE   kagá egé-lâ   kupehé-ni
                        fish eat-PUNCT 1INC.ERG-PL
                        'We all eat fish.'

The same de-ergativizing process occurs in the imperative mood, but only with a small class of highly transitive verbs such as 'eat':

(15) a. INTRANSITIVE: e-tiñampá-ke hóho
                        2-eat-IMP
                        'Eat!'

     b. TRANSITIVE: e-g-egé-ke   kága
                        2-DERG-eat-IMP fish
                        'Eat fish!'

A possible explanation of the presence of nominativity in interactive moods is both semantic and pragmatic. The interactive moods all constitute a kind of irrealis in that they describe events that, at the time of speaking, are yet to be realized. Universally, if there is a realis/irrealis distinction that correlates with a concomitant distinction between ergative and non-ergative morphosyntax, the realis clauses will be ergative and the irrealis clauses will be non-ergative. This fact is a consequence of the resultative character of ergative constructions: ergative clauses typically describe a situation from the perpective of the result or **endpoint**, normally the **patient**, of whatever action, if any, the situation involves (DeLancey 1985). Speakers are much more likely to view yet-to-be-realized events from the perspective of their (potential) inception, since the result of such a situation is likely to be even more irrealis than its inception. This is another way of saying that high transitivity is associated with highly realis clauses, whereas low transitivity is associated with highly irrealis clauses (Hopper and Thompson 1980). In Kuikúro, ergative constructions are the most common vehicles for expression of the main, transitive events in narrative discourse. De-ergative constructions are typically less transitive in terms of their discourse functions. Hence it is understandable that split ergativity in Kuikúro should be such that declarative clauses are ergative while interactive mood clauses allow a nominative pattern.

The above semantic line of reasoning motivates split ergativity between declarative and interactive mood clauses. An explanation for split ergativity within the domain of the interactive moods is more complex. Table 2 summarizes the pattern of ergativity/nominativity with the interactive moods in Kuikúro. The person/number categories are specified according to the feature system proposed by Silverstein (1976.117):

+ego	+ego	+ego	-ego	-ego
-tu	+tu	-tu	+tu	-tu
-pl	(+pl)	+pl	±pl	±pl

1SG, 1INC	1EXC, 2	3
Nominative	Ergative/Nominative	Ergative

Table 2. Split ergativity in Kuikúro interactive moods

This schema is generally consistent with Silverstein's (1976.122) observations concerning the relation between hierarchies of lexical features and split ergativity. However, the relative positions of the first person singular and first person exclusive categories are problematic from the point of view of Silverstein's observations. Since the pattern found in Kuikúro is previously unattested, and since this pattern pertains crucially to wider issues within the Carib family, some discussion of the nature of this apparent counterexample to observed universal tendencies is in order.

Silverstein's observation (which has been validated for a large number of languages) is that if a language exhibits lexically conditioned split ergativity, the least marked categories will exhibit the ergative system while more marked categories will exhibit a non-ergative system. Although the split may occur at any point on the hierarchy, wherever the split occurs, the least marked category will appear on the ergative side of the split. If Silverstein's observation is to be taken as a prediction of possible grammatical patterns (and it is not clear whether Silverstein intended it to be taken as such or not), the claim can be stated schematically as follows: in any language L, where L exhibits split ergativity conditioned by the lexical person/number of some verbal arguments, given two lexical person/number categories, c_1 and c_2 in L, such that c_1 is more marked (according to Silverstein's hierarchy) than c_2, and the lexical person/ number split in L occurs between c_1 and c_2, then c_1 will condition a non-ergative system, while c_2 will condition an ergative system.

Kuikúro clearly violates this prediction. As the diagram in Table 2 shows, first person singular conditions a nominative pattern, while first person exclusive plural allows an ergative pattern as well. Since, according to Silverstein's hierarchy, first person exclusive plural is more marked than first person singular, we would expect the positions of these categories with respect to the split to be reversed. This particular pattern is, as far as I am aware, attested only in Kuikúro. In the following section I will suggest that this pattern is due to the fact that the first person exclusive category is, in the Carib family in general, **pragmatically** less marked than the first person singular or inclusive categories. That is, first person exclusive has more in common with third person than with the other first person categories.

Note further that the prefixes which can manifest either a nominative or an ergative pattern (1EXC and 2) express the interaction between participants of the speech act (first and second person). These allow for competing perspectives on transitivity such that whenever there is a stronger conception of 'actorness', it may comparatively weaken the salience, if not the very perceived existence, of an affected patient; a delicate face-to-face relationship can always have an uncertain outcome. Hence, syntactically there are both nominative and ergative possibilities. Table 3 summarizes the entire system of split ergativity in Kuikúro.

Speech act type:	Person:	Formal Pattern:
Interactive Mood	1 (SG, INC)	Nominative (DERG)
	1 (EXC)	Either nom. (DERG)
	2	or erg
	3	Ergative
Descriptive Mood	(all)	Ergative

Table 3. Kuikúro system of split ergativity

5. AN INTER-LINGUISTIC COMPARISON

I will turn now to a comparison of Kuikúro with four other Carib languages of central Brazil. Of the four Carib languages for which recent and detailed descriptions are available, none exhibits exactly the same split-ergative system as Kuikúro. These languages are: Galibí (Hoff 1968, Boutle 1963, Renault-Lescure 1984); Hixkaryâna (Derbyshire 1979); Waiwai (Howard 1986); and Apalaí (Koehn 1962, 1974).

These languages do not exhibit case marking of free noun phrases in basic declarative clauses. Word order and the pronominal proclitics are the means by which grammatical roles are distinguished. However, all of these languages exhibit some constructions in which the A argument is marked by a special suffix. These constructions constitute ergative constructions. For example, in Hixkaryâna the A is marked with the dative post-position *-wya* in dependent nominalized clauses and causativized verbs. In Apalaí the A is marked by the form *-a* in dependent clauses, causativized verbs and in the completive aspect.

Furthermore, the verbal cross-referencing systems of these languages all display what I will call a 'split nominative' system in that part of the paradigm manifests a nominative/accusative system while part manifests a tripartite system. The interesting observation from the point of view of this paper is that in the verbal cross-referencing systems of declarative mood clauses in all of these languages, the third person and first person exclusive categories are isomorphic (they are distinguished only by means of free nominal elements, either pronouns or fully-specified noun phrases). For these categories S, A and P arguments are not distinguished at all, hence neither an ergative nor a nominative system is realized.

The following tables and examples illustrate the verbal cross-referencing paradigms for declarative mood clauses in these four Carib languages. (The tables present only the most basic forms.)

A \ O	1INC	1SG	2	1EXC	3	S
1INC					kɨsi-	kɨ-
1SG		kɨ-		s-		y-,0
2		kɨ-			m-	a-
1EXC		a-			n-	n-
3	kɨ-	y-,0	a-	n-	n-	n-

Table 4. Galibí pronominal proclitics

Galibí examples:

(16) a. moxko kari'na ene:yan
         he   Indian   saw
         'He saw the Indian.'

     b. moxko kari'na kɨn-ene:yan
                            3A/3P
         'The Indian saw him.'

     c. kai'tsusi k-ene'nuyɨ
         jaguar   3S-drink
         'The jaguar is drinking.'

     d. pero y-'kaⁱ
         dog 1P-bit
         'The dog bit me.'

     e. o:ma m-epo:lɨi
         path 2A-found
         'You found the path.'

A \ O	1INC	1SG	2	1EXC	3	S
1INC					tɨ-	tɨ-
SG		kɨ-		i-		k-, w-
2		mɨ-		mɨ-	mɨ-	mɨ-, ow-
1EXC		o-			n-	n-
3	kɨ-	r-	o-	n-	n-	n-

Table 5. Hixkaryâna pronominal proclitics

Hixkaryâna examples:

(17) a. Biryekomo y-otaha-no wosi
        child   3-hit-i.p.   woman
        'The woman hit the child.'

    b. ni-amryeki-no romuru
       3S-hunt-i.p.   my.son
       'My son went hunting.'

    c. ni-otaha-no
       3P-hit-i.p
       'She hit him.'

    d. r-ahe-no
       1P-seduce-i.p.
       'He seduced me.'

    e. amna ni-otaha-no
       1EXC 3P-hit
       'we hit him.'

    f. amna ni-niki-no
       1EXC 1EXC.S-sleep.i.p.
       'We slept.'

    g. ti-onye-no
       1INC-see-i.p.
       'We saw him.'

A \ O	1INC	1SG	2	1EXC	3	S
1INC					s-	s-
1SG			?		Ø	Ø
2		w-		m-	m-	m-
1EXC			o-		n-	n-
3	ki-		o-	n-	n-	n-

Table 6. Apalaí pronominal proclitics

Apalaí examples:

(18) a. y-rato pepekah-no papa
        1-knife buy-i.p.   father
        'The father bought my knife.'

    b. papa n-oturu-no aimo maro
       3S-talk-i.p. child with
       'The father talked with the child.'

    c. o-pi'po?-no
       2P-hit-i.p.
       'I hit you.'

    d. mi-pi'po?-no
       2A-
       'You hit me.'

    e. kaikusi ki-eseka-no
       jaguar 1INC.P-bite-i.p
       'The jaguar bit us all.'

    f. yna eseka-no kaikusi
       1EXC
       'The jaguar bit us (exc.).'

    g. ynan-epuka-no
       1EXC-fall-i.p.
       'We fell.'

A \ O	1INC	1SG	2	1EXC	3		S
-------	------	-----	---	------	---		---
1INC					t-		t-
1SG		k-		w-			k-, w-
2		m-		m-	m-		m-
1EXC			a-		n-		n-
3	ki-	oy-	a-	n-	n-		n-

Table 7. Waiwai pronominal proclitics

Waiwai examples:

(19) a. ša'pari oy-eska
    dog   1P-bit
    'The dog bit me.'

  b. 'wewe w-aknipu
    wood 1A-burn
    'I burned the wood.'

  c. k-etapesi
    1A2P-hit
    'I hit you.'

  d. ša'pari amna ñ-eska
    dog   1EXC 1EXC.P-bit
    'The dog bit us.'

  e. 'wewe amna n-akñipu
    wood 1EXC 3-burn
    'We burned the wood.'

For all of these languages there exists a person hierarchy whereby certain person categories override others in the verb marking system, regardless of the grammatical role (S, A or P) exhibited by the elements representing those categories. This pattern is reminiscent of the Algonquian verb system where transitive verbs agree with whichever argument is higher on a hierarchy (generally 2 > 1 > 3) regardless of which argument is in the A role and which is the P role. The unmarked case is where the argument higher on the hierarchy is taken to be the A, while the other argument is taken to be the P. If this typical situation is reversed such that a lower ranked argument acts upon a higher ranked argument, a special marker (some variation of -k, depending on the language) appears on the verb. This is known among Algonquianists as the 'inverse' marker.

In Carib languages no special verbal morphology is used when the person hierarchy and the agentivity hierarchy do not coincide. Instead, the Carib system can be generally described as follows: when speech act participants, i.e. 1st and 2nd persons, are in the A role the prefixes that appear on transitive verbs vary with the person of the A in the same way that prefixes on intransitive verbs vary with the person of the S. I will define this set of prefixes as 'prefix set 1'. This pattern defines a 'nominative' category in terms of cross-referencing on the verb, and is represented in Figure 1.

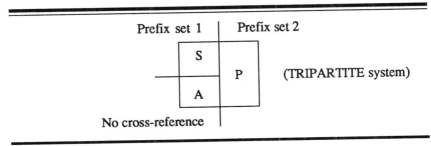

Fig.1. Pattern of person marking: A = speech act participant
(less first person exclusive)

It is important to note that for all the Carib languages which I have investigated, the first person exclusive category is treated exactly like the non speech act participant categories. That is, there is no distinction, in terms of verbal cross-referencing morphology, between the third person and first person exclusive categories. This fact will be important in understanding the apparent anomaly in the Kuikúro system.

When speech act participants (less the first person exclusive category) are in the P role, special transitive prefixes (prefix set 2) vary according to the person of the P. This is represented in Figure 2.

Fig.2. Pattern of person marking: P = speech act participant
(less first person exclusive)

In both of these situations, the P role is distinguished from S and A: however, Figure 1 exhibits a nominative-accusative system while Figure 2 exhibits a 'tripartite' system (Comrie 1978a).

When only third persons or 1st person exclusive are involved, a single prefix *n-* occurs. Hence in this situation neither an ergative nor a nominative system is employed, as indicated in Figure 3.

```
┌─────────────┐
│  S          │
│          P  │
│  A          │
└─────────────┘
```

**Fig.3. Pattern of person marking: A, S and P = third person or
first person exclusive**

Given that a transitive relation between first exclusive and third persons can
be neutrally marked (by a form that is cognate to the Kuikúro object marker *g-*
in the de-ergativized constructions), a closer look at the behavior of the *n-*
prefix may now reveal an ergative logic. Compare the Hixkaryâna examples
17a-c: *n-* occurs only when there is no independent noun phrase in the patient
role. When an independent P does occur, the verbal prefix is *y-*, the unique
manifestation of agreement in such a case (compare 17a and c). In sum, A is
never marked and *n-* may refer to P in certain cases if the verb is transitive, or
to S if the verb is intransitive (17c vs. b). Hence we can see in the domain of
1 exclusive and 3 persons, at the bottom right of Tables 3-7, a non-nominative
system with some ergative traces.

The languages vary in how they treat situations where speech act
participants appear in both the A and the P role. For Hixkaryâna and Waiwai
the verb agrees with the participant in the A role, regardless of the relative
persons of the A and P. In general (though the situation is complicated by
allomorphic and phonological variation due partially to systematic differences
between the stem shapes of transitive versus intransitive verbs), the cross-
reference prefixes employed are the same as those used of S participants of
intransitive verbs. Hence, when speech act participants interact a nominative-
accusative system prevails (cf. Figure 4).

```
        Prefix set 1  │
              ┌───────┼─────┐
              │  S    │     │
              │       │  P  │
              │  A    │     │
              └───────┼─────┘
```

**Fig.4. Hixkaryâna and Waiwai person marking: A, S and P =
speech act participants (less first person exclusive)**

In Galibí whenever first and second persons interact, the prefix employed for first person inclusive intransitive subject, *ki-*, is used. In this case the question of a nominative, ergative or tripartite system is moot. Apparently the language is simply sensitive to the fact that a first and second person are involved in a situation. Whether that situation is intransitive with first and second person acting cooperatively in an S role, or whether the situation is transitive and one speech act participant is acting upon the other, is not directly reflected in the verbal cross referencing system.

The data for speech act participants in interaction for Apalaí transitive verbs is incomplete insofar as no clear examples of first person acting on second person occur in Koehn and Koehn 1986. In any case, the prefix *w-*, indicating second person acting on first person, appears to be distinct from any prefix in the intransitive set.

Table 8 illustrates the general pattern of nominative and non-nominative patterns in the four languages discussed in this section. The pattern represented in Table 8 has two characteristics in common with the patterns of verbal cross-referencing in Kuikúro (summarized in Table 1). First, the observations of Silverstein 1976 are generally upheld, i.e. the nominative system is used for the more marked marked categories according to Silverstein's hierarchy, while the non-nominative system is used for the least marked categories. Second, first person exclusive surprisingly appears on the non-nominative side of the split.

+ego	+ego	-ego	+ego	-ego
-tu	+tu	+tu	-tu	-tu
-pl	(+pl)	±pl	+pl	±pl

1SG, 1INC, 2	1EXC, 3
Nominative	Non-nominative

Table 8. 'Split nominativity' in four Carib languages

From these facts I conclude that the feature +other (i.e. the presence of a third person referent) is of greater significance in the placement of the first person exclusive category on the hierarchy than is the presence of a +ego feature. In other words, third person and first person exclusive have the feature +other in common, i.e. they both include reference to a non speech act participant. This commonality seems to override the fact that first person exclusive also includes reference to a speech act participant.

The addition of the feature **+other** to Silverstein's hierarchy need not result
in a more complex system than previously proposed. This is because with the
addition of the feature **other**, the feature ±**plural** may be eliminated. This is
consistent with the fact that ±**plural** itself never distinguishes categories for a
given person in the system of verbal proclitics in any of these languages. That
is, there is no second person plural or third person plural category. The first
person 'plural' categories can be inferred from the presence of a +**tu** or +**other**
feature in addition to the +**ego** feature. The proposed ±**other** feature, on the
other hand, itself accomplishes what might be seen as the most significant
distinction in the entire system — the distinction that defines the split between
nominativity and non-nominativity. The revised system according to the hierarchy as manifested in these Carib languages is schematized in Table 9.

+ego	+ego	-ego	+ego	-ego
-tu	+tu	+tu	-tu	-tu
-other	-other	-other	+other	+other

1SG, 1INC, 2	1EXC, 3
Nominative	Non-nominative

Table 9. The person hierarchy of Carib languages, declarative moods

6. CONCLUSION

In this paper it has been shown that Kuikúro is unique among the Carib
languages of central Brazil insofar as it presents a strictly ergative system of
encoding grammatical relations in basic, declarative clauses. This ergativity is
manifested in the following ways:

1. **Verbal cross-reference**: verbs consistently cross-reference the ABSOLU-
   TIVE argument, regardless of the relative person/agentivity, etc., of the
   participants.

2. **Nominal case marking**: the ERGATIVE nominal occurs with a special
   post-positional marker -*héke*.

3. **Basic constituent order**: transitive subjects follow the verb, whereas
   intransitive subjects and transitive objects precede the verb.

Despite this basic ergativity in declarative clauses a nominative-accusative system appears in certain verb forms formally marked as **de-ergative**. De-ergative constructions occur primarily in a set of irrealis categories which I have termed the 'interactive moods', though they also appear in such environments as clefts, relative clauses and content questions. De-ergativization in the interactive moods is required only when the subject is first person singular or inclusive. It is 'optional' when the subject is first person exclusive or second person, and it is precluded when the subject is third person.

A comparison with several other Carib languages of Central Brazil shows that the general pattern of nominativity that prevails in Kuikúro interactive moods is found as the basic pattern in other languages in declarative moods. This fact leads to a revision of Silverstein's hierarchy of person features that makes special use of the feature ±**other**.

The special status of the first person exclusive category in conditioning a non-nominative system of coding grammatical relations both in Kuikúro interactive moods and in the declarative paradigms of verbal proclitics in other Carib languages leads to a hypothesis concerning the diachronic development of ergativity and nominativity in these languages. This hypothesis is that nominativity in Kuikúro is a relatively recent phenomenon, and that the present system of interactive moods represents the beginning of the nominative pattern fully developed in the other non-ergative Carib languages. In those languages the older ergative pattern is still found in dependent clauses and its traces can be found in the non-nominative cross-referencing system of first person exclusive and third persons in Hixkaryâna. This hypothesis will have to await detailed comparative and historical analysis of many Carib languages in order to be confirmed or rejected. One can only hope that such work will be forth-coming in the very near future.

NOTES

[1] My special thanks to those colleagues whose collaboration has been fundamental to the realization of this work. First I must recognize the intelligent and patient collaboration of Thomas Payne, who is responsible not only for an accurate revision of the English translation, but above all for analytical suggestions, many of which I have incorporated into the final version.

I also thank Yonne Leite and Marcia Damaso Vieira for discussions and for a comparative vision that provided the basis for developing the ideas contained in my doctoral thesis (Franchetto 1986).

²   The Kuikúro consonantal phonemes are: p, t, k, kʷ, s, ts, dʸ, h, ɟ (ɾ), m, n, ñ, ŋ, ɸ, w. The vocalic phonemes are: a, o, u, i, e, ə.

The graphic symbols for these phonemes are the above, with the following exceptions: kʷ —> kw, ts —> c, dʸ —> j, ɟ/(ɾ) —> r, ŋ —> g, ɸ—> p, ə—> â.

The labels used to translate the Kuikúro morphemes in the examples are: ASP aspectual particle; CONT continuative aspect; COP copula; DEIC deictic; DERG de-ergativizer; EMPH emphatic; ERG ergative; FUT future; HORT hortative mood; IMP imperative mood; INST instrumental; INT intentional mood; PL plural; POSS possessive suffix; PERF perfective nominalizer; PUNCT punctual aspect; PURP purpose; QW question particle; REFL reflexive; REL relative; VC valence change.

³   Silverstein defines markedness in person/number systems in terms of Jakobson 1936.

REFERENCES

Boutle, P. and W. 1963. Formulário dos vocabulários padrões. Galibí. Arquivo do Setor de Lingüística do Museu Nacional, UFRJ, Rio de Janeiro. MS.

Comrie, Bernard. 1978a. Ergativity. *Syntactic typology.* Ed. by W. Lehmann, 329-94. Austin: University of Texas.

Comrie, Bernard. 1978b. *Aspect.* (Second printing). Cambridge: Cambridge University Press.

Comrie, Bernard. 1981. *Language universals and linguistic typology.* Chicago: University of Chicago Press.

DeLancey, Scott. 1985. *Agentivity and syntax. Causatives and agentivity.* Ed. by William Eilfort, Paul Kroeber, and Karen Peterson, 1-12. Chicago: Chicago Linguistic Society.

Derbyshire, Desmond C. 1979. Hixkaryâna. *Lingua descriptive series I.* Amsterdam: North Holland.

Dixon, R.M.W. 1979. Ergativity. *Language* 55.59-138.

Fillmore, Charles J. 1968. The case for case. *Universals in linguistic theory.* Ed. by E. Bach and R. Harms, 1-88. New York: Holt, Rinehart and Winston.

Franchetto, B. 1986. Falar Kuikúro. *Estudo etnolingüístico de um grupo karíbe do Alto Xingu.* Doctoral dissertation, Departamento de Antropologia, Museu Nacional, UFRJ, Rio de Janeiro.

Jakobson, Roman. 1936. Beitrag zur allgemeinen Kasuslehre: gesamtbe-deutung der Russischen Kasus. *Travaux de Cercle Linguistique de Prague* 6.240-88.

Hoff, Berend J. 1968. *The Carib language.* The Hague: Martinus Nijhof.

Hopper, Paul J., and Sandra A. Thompson. 1980. Transitivity in grammar and discourse. *Language* 56.251-99

Howard, K. F. 1986. Formulário do vocabulários padrões. Arquivo do Setor de Lingüística do Museu Nacional, UFRJ. Rio de Janeiro. MS.

Kalmar, Ivan. 1979. The antipassive and grammatical relations in Eskimo. *Ergativity.* Ed. by F. Planck, 117-43. London: Academic Press.

Koehn, E. 1962. Formulário do vocabulários padrões. Apalaí. Arquivo do Setor de Lingüística do Museu Nacional, UFRJ. Rio de Janeiro. MS.

Koehn, E. 1974. Processes and roles in Apalaí clause structures. Brasília, SIL. MS.

Koehn, Edward and Sally Koehn. 1986. Apalai. *Handbook of Amazonian languages*, 1. Ed. by Desmond Derbyshire and Geoffrey Pullum, 33-127. Berlin: Mouton de Gruyter.

Marantz, Alec. 1984. *On the nature of grammatical relations.* Cambridge, MASS: MIT Press.

Renault-Lescure, O. 1984. *Évolution lexicale du Galibí, langue Caribe de Guyane Française.* Paris: Ed. Orstrom.

Silverstein, Michael. 1976. Hierarchy of features and ergativity. *Grammatical categories in Australian languages.* Ed. by R.M.W. Dixon, R. M. W. 112-171. Canberra: Australian Institute of Aboriginal Studies.

Transitivity and Ergativity
in Panare

Thomas E. Payne

1. Introduction[1]

In Panare (Carib, Venezuela) there is a pair of verb suffixes, *–sa'* and *–se'ña*, that synchronically function to 1) form a nominalization that refers to the PATIENT of the verb root, 2) indicate perfect aspect, and 3) form a passive clause. For example:[2]

NOMINALIZATION:

(1) tosen-pĕkĕ pu'ma-sa' t- u'- se   e'ñapa i'yakae-úya
     big-part kill-NOM1 IRR-give-HAB people family-DAT
     'Part of the large killed (thing) the people give to the relatives.'
       (nominalization on PATIENT of 'kill')

(2) tĕna upa-sa' karoma-ñe   paka
     water dry-NOM1 drink.water-NONPAST.TRANS cow
     'The cows drink dry (i.e. stagnant) water.'

PERFECT ASPECT:

(3) wu-ch-irema-sa'   yu
     1-DETRANS-feed-ANT.PERF   1SG
     'I have eaten.'

(4) a-wĕ'-sa'   kam
     2-arrive-ANT.PERF   Y/N.2
     'Have you arrived?'

(5) wĕ-s-awatĕ-sa'   yu
     1-DETRANS-hang.hammock-ANT.PERF 1SG
     'I have hung in a hammock.'

When the verb suffixed with *–sa'* or *–se'ña* is formally transitive, the AGENT, if present, is expressed in the dative case.[3] I will argue that these constructions can be insightfully regarded as passive clauses. For example:

PASSIVE:

(6) y-amaika-sa'   mĕn   y-úya
     3-keep-PASS   INAN.INVIS   1SG-DAT
     'I keep it/it is kept by me.'

(7) y-an-sa'   y-úya   mankowa
     3-get-PASS   1SG-DAT   poison
     'I got the poison/the poison was gotten by me.'

(8) y-an-se'ña   ó-ya
     3-get-POST.PASS   2-DAT
     'It is (destined to be) gotten by you.'

(9) nkai'wa nkai' y-o'ma-sa'   kĕ'
     precisely thus 3-change-PASS   DEF.ANIM
     'Exactly like that they were changed.'

An ergative system is one in which the most agent-like argument of a multi-argument clause receives special morphosyntactic treatment, as distinct from intransitive subjects and transitive objects (Comrie 1978, Dixon 1979, inter alia). Since in exs. 6-8 the most agent-like argument occurs in the DATIVE case, the question arises whether these might be more appropriately analyzed as ergative constructions, with the DATIVE case marker doubling as an ergative marker. I will show that, though these constructions do exhibit some properties of ergative constructions, both morphosyntactic and discourse functional evidence makes it clear that they are best analyzed as passives.

The definition of a passive clause to be employed in this paper is based on a prototype (Comrie 1981, Givón 1984.164). A prototypical passive clause is characterized both morphosyntactically and in terms of its discourse function. Morphosyntactically a passive is a semantically transitive (two core argument) clause for which the following three properties hold: 1) the AGENT (or most Agent-like argument) is either omitted or demoted to an oblique role,[4] 2) the other core argument (termed P for expository purposes) possesses all properties of subjects relevant for the language as a whole, and 3) the verb possesses any and all language-specific formal properties of intransitive verbs. In terms of discourse function a prototypical passive is used in contexts where the A (most AGENT-like argument) is relatively low in topicality with respect to the P. It is crucial to note that this is not a criterial definition. Rather it defines a prototype against which passive-like constructions can be compared. A particular construction may exhibit many or few of the morphosyntactic properties. Similarly, a particular passive-like construction may sometimes occur in contexts where a passive would be unexpected, given the above characterization. However, this would not negate the fact that constructions that possess the morphosyntactic properties of passives also generally exhibit the discourse functional properties mentioned above. Givón (1981, 1982, 1984.164 and forthcoming) provides a relatively comprehensive typology of various passive-like phenomena according to a definition similar to the one given here.

Morphosyntactic evidence that sentences such as 6 through 9 are passives rather than ergatives includes, 1) the AGENT in these clauses is seldom expressed, 2) the PATIENT exhibits some subject properties (e.g. it controls coreference in infinitival complements), and 3) there are no discernable subject properties possessed by the dative-marked AGENT. Furthermore, these constructions have more in common functionally with passive clauses than with ergatives. For example, they are relatively infrequent in discourse, and tend to occur in contexts where the PATIENT is high in topicality with respect to the AGENT. Arguments that these constructions are becoming more like ergatives are 1) the verb remains formally transitive, and 2) these clauses can function to code main events in narrative discourse.

This particular constellation of functions encoded with a single form illustrates a synchronic connection from the universally least transitive clause type — nominal predicates — to the most transitive clause type — multi-argument clauses coding main events in discourse. The existence of this connection in Panare provides crucial insight into two problems within the Carib family: 1) It documents a source for true ergative constructions, and 2) potentially explains why, in some Carib languages, passives have not been attested — either they do exist, masquerading as ergatives, or they have recently begun to function as ergatives and the languages have yet to replace them with new passive constructions.

In summary, in this paper I will argue that a) the suffixes *-sa'* and *-se'ña* have three related but distinct functions, b) that dative-AGENT constructions are more appropriately analyzed as passives than ergatives, and c) that Panare offers a relatively clear example of formal isomorphism spanning the entire functional cline from the least transitive to the most transitive clause type in discourse.

2. TRANSITIVITY

Panare verbs are especially sensitive to transitivity in the traditional sense; intransitive (single argument) verbs are formally distinct from transitive (multi-argument) verbs in several respects. The most obvious of these are distinct tense/aspect/mode suffixes and person marking prefixes, e.g. a NONPAST suffix has the form *-ñe* for transitive verbs and *-n* for intransitive verbs;[5] an IMPERFECTIVE suffix has the basic form *-mpë'* for transitive verbs and

-*nĕpĕ'* for intransitive verbs. The following examples illustrate the different tense/aspect suffixes characteristic of each type:

TRANSITIVE:

(10) y-ani'-ñe   yu
     3O-fill-NONPAST.TRANS   1SG
     'I'm gonna fill it.'

     *y-ani'-n yu

INTRANSITIVE:

(11) wu-tĕ-n   yu
     1-go-NONPAST.INTRANS   1SG
     'I'm gonna go.'

     *wu-tĕ-ñe yu

TRANSITIVE:

(12) wĕ -mpĕ'   chu[6]
     kill-IMPERF.TRANS   1SG
     'I'm killing it.'

     *wĕ-nĕpĕ' chu

INTRANSITIVE:

(13) tĕ-nĕpĕ'   chu
     go-IMPERF.INTRANS   1SG
     'I'm going.'

     *tĕ-mpĕ' chu

Another formal test for grammatical transitivity is that agreement prefixes in affirmative, declarative, non-imperfective clauses are drawn from distinct sets depending on whether the verb is grammatically transitive or intransitive. Table 1 illustrates the prefix sets for non-past agreement forms. Although the markers for third person are similar between the transitive and intransitive prefix sets, it is clear that the sets as a whole are distinct from one another. That is, they reflect neither a clear nominative/accusative nor an ergative/absolutive system. This generalization holds for all agreement paradigms in the language. I have presented only the non-past paradigm as this is the one which is relevant for verbs suffixed with -*sa'* and -*se'ña*.

ABBREVIATIONS:

   y^- = Prefix y- plus stress on first syllable of root.

   yĕC^- = Prefix yĕ- plus stress on first syllable of root.

	Transitive object	Intransitive subject
1	y^-/yĕC^-/yĕC^	w-/u-/wĕ-
2	ay-/a-/a-	o-[7]
3	y-/yĕ-/yĕ-	y-/Ø-/i-

**Table 1. Person marking for Panare
regular verbs, non-past tense/non-imperfective aspect
no pre-verbal object noun phrase[8]**

A second important typological feature of Panare (and Carib generally) verb structure is that many intransitive verbs are derived from transitives. For example, the verb root *amaika*[9] 'to keep/put/store' is transitive in its underived form:

(14) y-amaika-ñe   yu
    3O-keep-NONPAST.TRANS   1SG.PRO
    'I will keep it/store it.'

This root commonly occurs with the derivational prefix *s-* to form an intransitive verb:

(15) wĕ-s-amaika-n   yu
    1S-DETRANS-keep-NONPAST.INTRANS   1SG.PRO
    'I will sit down/stay.'

This formal detransitivization of inherently transitive stems is a very common feature of Panare. In fact, it seems that MOST intransitive verbs in the lexicon are derived from transitives, though there are exceptions, notably verbs of motion and position.

The following table lists some typical transitive verbs and their detransitivized counterparts grouped according to the detransitivizing prefix employed. To my knowledge, each transitive verb only occurs with a particular detransitivizing prefix.

PREF.	TRANSITIVE		DETRANSITIVE	
ch–/s–	incha	'beware of, fear'	chinchama	'think'
	ipa	'feed'	chipa	'overeat'
	irema	'feed'	chirema	'eat'
	irepa	'touch (tr)'	chirepa	'touch (itr)'
	amaika	'keep/put'	samaika	'sit'
	an	'take'	san	'ascend'
	apĕ	'begin' (nominal O)	sapĕ	'begin' (clause complement)
	awa	'hit'	sawa	'hit oneself'
	ĕwachíka	'make sneeze'	sĕwachíka	'sneeze'
	awantĕ	'endure X'	sawantĕ	'be sick/die'
	e'ka'	'bring'	se'ka'	'come'
	i'nampa	'adorn X'	si'nampa	'adorn self'
	inampa	'fight X'	sinampa	'fight (recip)'
	mĕnka	'finish X'	sĕmĕnka	'arrive/finish'
	o'koma	'raise'	so'koma	'rise'
	o'nama	'move X'	so'nama	'move self'
	o'renka	'dampen'	so'renka	'dampen self'
	uka'	'kill'	suka'	'die'
	ukinka	'paint X'	sukinka	'paint self'
	uru	'gripe at'	suru	'worry'
	etc.			
t–	ĕka	'fatten'	tĕka	'be fat'
	ani'	'fill X'	taani'	'fill' (as a river rising)
	aru'ma	'cause to swing'	taru'ma	'swing'
	ĕsa	'straighten'	tĕsa	'be straight'
	ayapa	'to make shout'	tayapa	'to shout/make noise'
	in	'to charge'	tin	'to cost'
	inaan	'to hide X'	tinaan	'hide self'
	iñan	'raise'	tiñan	'rise'
	u'	'give (tr.)'	tu'	'give (itr)'
	—	—	tĕnĕ	'get sick'
	—	—	taka	'leave'
w–	marapa	'to chase'	wĕmarapa	'to escape / become lost'
	muku	'to close X'	wumuku	'close' (itr)
	utu'	'to break X'	wutu'	'break' (itr)

Table 2. Typical transitive verbs & their detransitivized counterparts

Though there do seem to be some general semantic principles that underlie these detransitivizing prefixes (e.g. reflexive for *ch-/s-*, anticausative for *t-*), there are numerous exceptions. None of the prefixes is fully productive.

3. THE FUNCTIONS OF -SA'

In the preceding section I have shown that a) Panare verb structure is particularly sensitive to grammatical transitivity, and b) that many intransitive verbs are derived from transitives. These properties constitute 'tests' for grammatical transitivity, and therefore will be useful in determining whether particular constructions are passives or ergatives. In this section, I will discuss the three major functions of verbs suffixed with the formative -*sa'*. The functional distinctions discussed here often overlap and are difficult to isolate. In fact the three functions proposed are little more than convenient reference points along a continuum extending from 'things' (formally correlated with concrete nouns) through 'states' (sometimes correlated with predicate nominals and sometimes with stative verbs) to 'events' (formally correlated with active transitive verbs) (Hopper and Thompson 1980, 1984). At any given point along the continuum, functional similarity may be high enough to motivate analogical shift of the use of a particular formal structure between one function and the next, whereas the extremes represent functions which are absolutely distinct. It is precisely these points of functional similarity that both motivate diachronic shift between unrelated functions and make it difficult to discern precise boundaries between functions at any given juncture.

Before discussing the various functions of -*sa'*, a few definitions are in order. I will use the term 'event chain' to mean a series of events that occupy temporal space on the 'time line' of a narrative text (Hopper 1979, Hopper and Thompson 1980). An 'event chain clause' is a clause which expresses one of the events in an event chain. This distinction is independent of the distinction between 'eventive' vs. 'stative' clause. An 'eventive' clause is one which expresses an event AS AN EVENT (ex. 7), whereas a stative clause expresses a state that may incidentally have been brought about by some event (e.g. 19 below). That is, a stative clause may contain an event as part of its presuppositional background, but does not itself express the event as its main assertion (see section 4 for further discussion). The value of introducing the event chain vs. non-event chain distinction is that it is more empirically verifiable than the eventive vs. stative distinction. When a verb marked with -*sa'* or -*se'ña* occurs as a link in an event chain, it is likely to be coding an eventive clause. Similarly, when one of these verb forms occurs outside of an event chain, it is more likely to be coding a semantically stative clause.

3.1 THE NOMINALIZER -SA'. In this section I will demonstrate that the verbal suffix -*sa'* derives a noun (or adjective) that refers to an entity in a state brought about by the action of the verb. This characteristic holds whether the verb is formally transitive or intransitive. In this function -*sa'* can be considered a past participle suffix:

Participle of an INTRANSITIVE verb:

(16) Tĭna upa-sa'   karoma-ñe   paka
     water stagnate-NOM1   drink-NONPAST.TRANS   cow
     'The cows drink stagnant water.'

(17) Y-o'koma-ñe   nkĕ kĕn   tikon i'yakae y-upu'ma-sa'[10]
     3-raise-NONPAST.TRANS also INVIS.ANIM child family 3-fall-NOM1
     'The child's companions also lift the fallen one.'

Participle of a TRANSITIVE verb:

(18) Tosen-pĕkĕ   pu'ma-sa'   t- u'- se   e'ñapa i'yakae-úya
     big-DIM   kill-NOM1   IRR-give-HAB   people family-DAT
     'Part of the large killed (thing) the people give to the relatives.'

(19) monam yĕ-menkĕ-sa'   pícha
     exist   3-write-NOM1   little
     'There is little written.'

(20) T-ĕnaní-se   kĕn   kaemo   kĕn
     IRR-withhold-HAB INVIS.ANIM celebration:meat INVIS.ANIM
     yu-warupŭtĕ-sa' uya
     3-initiate-NOM1 DAT
     'They withhold the celebration meat from the initiated one.'

In each of these examples a verb suffixed with -sa' functions in a syntactic role of a noun or nominal modifier. In 16, 17 and 18 the role of the nominalized verb is direct object. In 19 the nominalized verb functions as the subject of an existential clause, and in 20 it functions as an oblique (dative) adjunct.

The suffix -se'ña(pe) can also derive a resultative noun from a verb. However, the noun that results from -se'ña(pe) nominalization refers to an entity that is 'destined' to be in a state as a result of the yet to be accomplished event described by the verb.[11] For the time being I will refer to -se'ña(pe) as the 'posterior' counterpart to -sa'. For example:

(21) yĕ-karoma-se'ña   e'ke'   ch-in-pĕ'
     3-drink-NOM2   NEG.EXIST 3-drink-for
     'There wasn't anything to drink.' (i.e. 'There was no thing-to-be-drunk
         there to drink.')

     cf. e'ke'   yĕ-karoma-sa'
     NEG.EXIST 3-drink.water-NOM1
         'There was nothing drunk.' (i.e. 'No drinking took place' though there may
         or may not have been something there to drink)

Nominalized verbs, like all nominals, can function as nominal predicates. In Panare, nominal predicates require a copula only in the past tense. Ex. 22 illustrates a simple nominal predicate formed from an inherently nominal stem, while exs. 23 through 25 illustrate nominal predicates formed with -*sa*' nominalizations:

(22) Maesturo we'cha   kën
     teacher   COP.PAST INVIS.ANIM
     'He was a teacher.'

(23) yu-w-utú-sa'   we'cha   kën
     3-DETRANS-break-NOM1 COP.PAST INVIS.ANIM
     'It was (in the state of having been) broken.'

(24) uto   y-anmɨ-sa'   we'cha   mën   uto
     manioc 3-plant-NOM1 COP.PAST INVIS.INAN manioc
     'The manioc was (already) planted.'

(25) y-akama-sa'   we'cha   mën   pake
     3-teach-NOM1 COP.PAST INVIS.INAN before
     'It was taught a long time ago.' (i.e. I already knew it).

Exs. 22 through 25 are from texts in which it is clear that what is referred to is a STATE rather than an EVENT. For example, 25 is from a text in which the speaker recounts the story of how animals were formed from people. The sentence in 25 is a meta-comment on the source of the information contained in the discourse — not an event in the story itself. The pragmatic force of this sentence is approximately, 'I already knew this a long time ago', i.e. 'I didn't have to go to school to learn it.' The clause does not, in this context, describe a specific event of teaching. Nevertheless, some event of teaching is a part of the background that this clause assumes.

Speakers can choose to view events from many different 'perspectives' (Fillmore 1977). For example, rather than simply asserting a 'state', as in 25, a Panare speaker may choose to present the same scene from the perspective of the event that resulted in the state. This may involve using a different clause type, or using the same clause type with an intonational pattern that foregrounds the event. Alternatively, Panare hearers might interpret the event, rather than the state, as foregrounded and begin to use a clause like 25 to describe specific events. The fact that the verb meaning 'teach' occurs in this clause renders such a reinterpretation more likely than in a clause such as 22 where no verb is present, but for which it could be argued that events of teaching are also part of the presuppositional background.

In fact, in my corpus there are 17 instances of clauses with a -*sa*' nominalization plus *we'cha* 'COP.PAST' that occur as links in 'event chains' (as

defined above) and which therefore can be interpreted as coding events. For
example, 26 initiates a text about the formation of a community known as
Camana:

(26) yu-wĕ-muku'ma'-sa'   we'cha   e'ñapa pake atawĕn
     3- DETRANS-begin-NOM1 COP.PAST person before all
       Kamána pana
       Camana towards
     'All the people started out for Camana a long time ago.'

Conceivably one could interpret this sentence as referring to a state, i.e. 'the
people were embarked towards Camana', or something of the sort. However,
I contend that this would be to assume that a clause is either stative or non-
stative and that the copula always signals a stative clause. The fact of the matter
is that this clause occurs at the beginning of an event chain involving the
establishment of the community. It has formal properties of stative clauses,
perhaps because of its discourse-initial position, or the **distant past** temporal
setting (as is also the case in ex. 27 below).

Ex. 27 is completely ambiguous out of context as to whether it refers primarily to a state of being full, or to an event of filling.

(27) y-ot-aani'-sa'   we'cha   mĕn   ano' atawĕn
     3-DETRANS-fill-NOM1 COP.PAST INVIS.INAN earth all
       pake   tina-ke
       before water-with
     'The earth filled completely with water.'

Like the sentence illustrated in 26, 27 occurs within an event chain. Therefore, given our operational hypothesis that a clause that constitutes a link in an
event chain represents an 'eventive' clause, we can surmise that 26 and 27 are
'more eventive' than clauses such as 25.

An important feature of this construction type is that when the participial
verb (i.e. the one suffixed with -sa') is both transitive AND eventive, the copula
does not occur (see Table 3). Thus there exists formal asymmetry between
intransitive and transitive verbs suffixed with -sa'. Intransitives enter easily
into the nominal predicate pattern in that they can always occur with the copula,
regardless of whether they refer to events or states. Transitive verbs marked
with -sa', on the other hand, only occur with the copula when they refer to
states. In these instances -sa' can always be interpreted as a nominalizer, and
the whole construction understood as a predicate nominal. When the copula
does not occur it is often ambiguous whether -sa' is a nominalizer or a perfect
aspect marker. It is this ambiguity, I contend, that leads to the possibility of
reinterpretation, and hence of diachronic shift from one function to the other.

There are 58 instances in my corpus of constructions which are formally identical to predicate nominals without *we' cha* that occur in event chains. Such clauses occur in past as well as non-past contexts, so the use of *we' cha* cannot be accounted for on the basis of tense, as it can with true predicate nominals. I contend that such constructions convey 'perfect' aspect or passive voice (as described in the following sections). That is, although they may describe a state, they do so in terms of the event that resulted in the state (Comrie 1978). As such these constructions are open to reinterpretation as 'eventive' clauses whereas 'pure' nominal predicates (i.e. those based on inherently nominal stems) are not.

Table 3 summarizes the occurrence of the copula with participial verbs according to the distinction between 'event chain' and 'non-event chain' clauses:

	Event chain	Non-event chain	Total
With copula:	17	54	71
Without copula:	58	0	58
Total 'participial' verbs:			129
Total verbs in corpus (approx):			3,500

Table 3. Summary of participial verbs

From the data in Table 3, I conclude that the copula in participial clauses strongly correlates with 'stative' semantics while the lack of a copula correlates with 'eventive' semantics (χ^2 with Yates' correction 77.58, p = < 10^{-6}).

3.2 THE ANTERIOR PERFECT -SA'. In this section I will argue that -*sa*' in addition to functioning as a nominalizer, also functions as a perfect aspect marker when it occurs on main, independent verbs.

For purposes of this paper perfect aspect is defined as a grammaticalized means of expressing a STATE (i.e. a non-dynamic situation) in terms of some other situation that has a **causal** relationship to the state being described. For example, the sentence 'I've seen that movie before' describes a state in terms of (i.e. by reference to) the event that brought the state about; the event of 'seeing the movie' brought about a state described as 'having seen' the movie. Note that the clause 'I've seen that movie before' does **not** primarily express the event of seeing the movie. Instead the state resulting from that event is being asserted. The event is simply a natural means of identifying the state.

As noted by Givón (1984.278ff), individual languages may 'load onto' the perfect category a number of additional functions. Anderson (1982) also discusses the various functions that tend to cluster around aspect categories commonly known as perfects. Here I take the 'state in terms of another situation' function to be basic to the notion of perfect aspect. This definition departs somewhat from previous characterizations of perfect aspect in that there is no necessary requirement that the 'other situation' be temporally prior to the state. This departure is based on the fact that, according to my analysis, Panare exhibits two 'perfect' categories. The category represented by -*sa'* expresses a more-or-less prototypical 'anterior perfect' in which the causing situation precedes (or is anterior to) the state. The category represented by -*se'ña*, on the other hand, expresses a state that is the 'result' of a yet-to-be-accomplished event. A near translation equivalent in English would be the pattern 'to be VERBed', as in 'this water is to be thrown away'. I will refer to -*se'ña* as a marker of 'posterior perfect' aspect.

As illustrated in examples 16 through 20, verbs suffixed with -*sa'* may function as nominal clause constituents. However, such verbs can also function as the main verb of a sentence (see exs. 3 through 8). As such they encode either anterior perfect aspect, or passive voice. These two functions are so similar that often particular examples are ambiguous, at least to a non-native speaker working with transcribed texts supplemented by elicitation. Nevertheless, I will attempt to show that the unclear cases provide exactly the locus needed to motivate the diachronic shift from one function to the other.

In a discussion of hunting monkeys with a blowgun, two dative-AGENT constructions occur in contexts where they are most naturally construed as coding mainline events. The interactant initiates the exchange by asking the speaker (a 20 year old man) what he puts on the darts to kill the monkeys. The response is as follows:

(28) a. Mankowa T-amonka-ñe   mankowa pe'ñi'-cha
     poison   IRR-hurt-INF   poison   quickly-in
     yu-s-awantë-n   arakon
     3-DETRANS-kill-NONPAST.INTRANS   monkey
     'Poison. The painful poison by which the monkeys die quickly.'

    b. **Y-an-sa'**   **y-úya**   **mankowa** Kandelária-po pake
     3-get-PASS   1SG-DAT   poison   Candelaria-at   before
     cinquenta-pe   t-in-se
     fifty-for   IRR-cost-HAB
     'I got the poison in Candelaria that costs fifty (Bolívares).'

    c. Y-an-ñe   nkë   yu tonkwanan asa'-tye
     3-get-NONPAST.TRANS   again 1SG other   two-CL ?
     'I'm going to get another two.'

    d. A-ri-ñëpë'   E'ke'   amen
     A-finish-IMPERF.INTRANS   NEG.EXIST now
     'It's running out. There isn't any more now.'

e. **Y-iri-ma-sa'**   **y-úya**
3-finish-CAUS-PASS   1SG-DAT
'I finished it.'

Whether the emphasized clauses in this excerpt are functioning as anterior perfects or as passives is not crucial. In fact, as mentioned above, functional similarity is a necessary prerequisite to diachronic shift from one function to another. The important fact is that the verbs marked with -*sa'* are clearly functioning as main verbs. They are so far removed from their nominal function that a translation that reflects nominalization sounds extraordinarily affected, i.e. 'the poison is a gotten thing by me' and 'it is a finished thing by me.' These translations are odd not just because they are odd turns of phrase in English, but because they seem to imply a stative relationship (in this case class membership) between subject and predicate, whereas the Panare clauses in this excerpt refer to actual events.

This analysis is independently validated by the presence of a locative adjunct 'in Candelaria' in ex. 28b. If the poison is 'gotten' , it is in the state of 'having been gotten' at all times and places after the event of getting. It only makes sense to express the location of 'getting' if it is the event itself that is being referred to, rather than the state that results from that event. That is, the speaker 'got' the poison in Candelaria, but it did not cease to 'be gotten by him' when he entered the jungle to shoot monkeys. For a more straightforward example, an unquestionably stative clause such as 'the poison was green in Candelaria' would not make sense unless the poison was some other color elsewhere. From this I conclude that ex. 28b must be an EVENTIVE clause.

To summarize, it is clear that there exists formal asymmetry between intransitive and transitive verbs suffixed with -*sa'* in that the former enter easily into the nominal predicate pattern whereas the latter do not. This formal asymmetry correlates with a functional distinction between 'stative' and 'eventive' semantics: intransitive participles, true to their nominal prototype, tend to express only states; transitive participles, in approaching the main verb prototype, tend to express events (as well as the states that result from those events).

3.4 THE PASSIVE -*SA'*. In this section I argue that the dative-AGENT construction type is properly considered a 'non-promotional' passive clause (Givón 1981). By this I mean that the AGENT fails to exhibit any formal subject properties, while the PATIENT retains formal characteristics of transitive objects. This construction tends to occur in discourse contexts where the PATIENT is high in topicality with respect to the AGENT. Since another possible analysis of these constructions is that they represent ergative clauses, I will specifically address this alternative hypothesis.

3.4.1 MORPHOSYNTACTIC EVIDENCE FOR THE PASSIVE ANALYSIS. Morphosyntactic evidence that a construction type is a passive rather than an ergative would consist of 1) showing that the most AGENT-like nominal has morphosyntactic properties of oblique adjuncts rather than of subject arguments, and 2) that the semantic PATIENT does have subject properties. I will show in this section that at least the first of these criteria hold for Panare dative-AGENT constructions.

First, dative-AGENTs in Panare have all and only the distributional privileges of oblique adjuncts: 1) They are 'optional' in the sense that the sentence is complete and independent even if no mention of the AGENT is made (see ex. 9). Subjects of independent verbs not marked by -sa' or -se'ña, on the other hand, must be overtly expressed either by a full noun phrase, a postverbal enclitic pronoun or a verbal prefix. 2) The AGENT of the dative-AGENT constructions need not be contiguous to the verb; it may occur either pre- or post-verbally, though most commonly as the last element in the clause. Full NP or pronoun subjects, on the other hand, most neutrally occur immediately after the verb, and only in very unusual circumstances may be separated from the verb.

No other commonly applied morphosyntactic 'tests' for subject status are applicable to Panare dative-AGENT constructions. This is primarily because these constructions are so limited in their distribution. For example, dative-AGENT constructions (as defined above) do not occur in object complements, reflexive clauses or imperative mode. Hence such tests as 'omissibility' in complement clauses, control of reflexive or addressee of imperative clauses (Keenan 1976) simply do not apply to Panare dative-AGENT constructions.

Second, evidence that the Panare passive is non-promotional is that the passive PATIENT is registered on the verb with the same set of prefixes as transitive objects:

(29) ay-a'tĕ-sa'   amĕn   mĕk-úya
     2SG-chase-PASS 2SG.PRO 3.VISIB-DAT
     'You are chased by him/it.'

In this example the second person singular PATIENT is coded on the verb by the prefix ay-. This is the prefix used for transitive objects. The prefix o- is used for second person singular intransitive subjects.

In summary, the AGENT in Panare dative-AGENT constructions has no formal subject properties. The PATIENT, on the other hand, has formal properties of regular transitive PATIENTs, e.g. control of verb agreement.

3.4.2 DISCOURSE FUNCTIONAL EVIDENCE FOR THE PASSIVE ANALYSIS. To this point we have seen morphosyntactic evidence that argues for classifying the Panare dative-AGENT constructions as non-promotional passives. In this section we will look at the discourse function of these constructions in a corpus of ethnohistorical and personal experience narratives. Though the discourse data are as yet sparce, due to the relative paucity of dative-AGENT constructions in texts, indications are that a major function of these constructions is to encode semantically transitive situations in which the PATIENT is high in anaphoric topicality in relation to the AGENT.

In languages for which the identification of an ergative construction is unproblematic, the ergative is the most transitive clause type in discourse. It is the most common multi-argument construction type, and typically codes the main events of a narrative (Hopper 1979, Cooreman, Fox and Givón 1984, DuBois 1987, inter alia). Ergative subjects are highly topical, both in terms of 'Referential Distance' (anaphoric topicality, Givón 1983a,b,c) and 'Persistence' (cataphoric importance). Absolute PATIENTs are typically less topical, according to every metric, than ergative subjects.

Passive clauses, on the other hand, typically function to downplay the topicality of an AGENT. 'Promotional' passives also upgrade the topicality of the PATIENT. Usually this is accomplished by AGENT omission and/or PATIENT promotion to subject status, but occasionally expression of the AGENT is allowed in an oblique role.

A pilot study of 358 clauses of ethnohistorical and personal experience narratives and five Panare 'Pear Stories' (Chafe 1980) yields the topicality figures given in Table 4 for the various arguments in verbs marked with *-sa'* and *-se'ña*.

	Semantically intransitive	Semantically transitive	
	Intrans. Subj.	dative-AGENT	PATIENT
Referential distance:	6.25	10.5	1.79
Persistence:	3	5.33	5.36
N =	4	10	14

Table 4. Mean topicality of arguments: *-sa'* and *-se'ña* verbs

A high index of Referential Distance (RD) indicates low anaphoric topicality, whereas a high index of Persistence indicates high cataphoric topicality. The figures in Table 4 suggest that dative-AGENTS are low in anaphoric topicality, with respect both to expectations for transitive AGENTS (Givón 1983a) and to the figures for PATIENTS in dative-AGENT clauses. The high RD index for dative-AGENTS is due largely to the fact that four of the ten examples (40%) in this small corpus constitute first mentions. According to procedures outlined in Givón (1983a) and elaborated by Payne (1985), each of these receives the maximum RD of 20. By contrast, only 9 of the 160 transitive subjects of non-participial verbs (5.6%) in the same corpus code new mentions. Hence we can hypothesize that one of the functions of the dative-AGENT construction is to introduce participants into the text in the semantic role of AGENT.

Each of the four examples of dative-AGENTs that introduce participants into the discourse are situations where a topic chain is broken by the introduction of the new AGENT. One illustrative example is included here:

(30) a. Ñen pɨ   peña
        see NEG before
        'I didn't see it before.'

    b. T-ini-ya'   chu mĕn   pericura
       1O3A-see-PAST   1SG INAN.INVIS   movie
       'I saw this movie.'

    c. T-ini-ya'   chu tato   e'chipen yĕ-kɨtɨ-'
       1A3O-see-PAST   1SG white.person   fruit   3-cut-INF
       'I saw a white person picking fruit.'

    d. Nĕ-kɨtɨ-ya'   mĕn   e'chipen asa' tye   tu'ke
       3A3O-cut-PAST   INAN.INVIS   fruit   two   basket   full
       'He picked two baskets full of fruit.'

    e. Y-ankɨ-se'pe   ña'   ana-pana
       3-take-RELFUT1   there   earth-towards
       'Then he takes them to the ground.'

    f. Kawĕ chi', chi'che tyo'-po   chi'che
       high very very   plant-in   very
       'He was high in the tree.'

    g. Y-an-se'ñape   mĕn   tɨkon-uya
       3-grab-POST.PASS   INAN.INVIS   child-DAT
       'It is (destined to be) taken by a child.'

    h. N-an-ya'   tikon mĕn
       3A3O-grab-PAST   child INAN.INVIS
       'The child took it.'

In clauses c. through f. of this excerpt the man picking fruit is the main topic. In g. the boy is introduced as the AGENT in a dative-AGENT construction. The child then becomes a major topic for the rest of the text.

The excerpt in 30 illustrates two dative-AGENT constructions in situations where the PATIENT is highly topical. In these cases the AGENT is first person, hence is of course 'given' information. The situational context makes it clear, however, that 'poison' is the most highly topical entity 'on stage' at this point in the discourse — the entire excerpt is a response to the question 'what do you put on the darts?'

Although this study is far from conclusive, indications are that the dative-AGENT constructions occur in those atypical discourse contexts where a PATIENT is highly topical with respect to an AGENT. As such, these constructions have more in common functionally with passive clauses than with ergatives.

4. DISCUSSION

In the following discussion I assume a view of lexical semantics akin to Fillmore's (1977) 'scene semantics'. Under this view particular lexical items induce 'scenes' composed of various elements, including participants, props, events, states, etc. In the case of a pure nominal predicate such as 'it is a dish', the scene induced by the predicate 'be a dish' involves no more than the state of belonging to the class denoted by the incorporated term 'dish'. A predicate based on a nominalized verb, on the other hand, in addition to conveying a state of identity or class membership, also potentially conveys some aspects of the scene induced by the nominalized verb. So, for example, the scene induced by a nominal predicate such as 'he is an IBM employee' includes not only a state of class membership (x is an element of class Y), but also potentially a scene involving the participant being employed by IBM. Similarly, a nominal predicate of the form 'it is a broken dish' not only predicates a state of brokenness of the dish, but also includes, in a peripheral way, reference to the event which brought about that state.

This last type of nominal predicate is functionally closer to a passive than one that does not involve a nominalized (for English one might say 'adjectivized') verb. The choice between a nominal predicate based on a nominalized verb and a passive expressing the same scene is based on a slight difference in point of view. For example, the difference between 'he is an IBM employee' and 'he is employed by IBM' is that in the first, the state of class membership ('he belongs to the class of entities denoted by the term 'IBM employee") is in perspective, whereas in the second, the same state is described in terms of an 'event' of his employment. Parallel observations can be made concerning such pairs as 'it is a broken dish' (nominal predicate, state = class membership) and 'the dish is broken' (passive, state = result of an event).

It is widely observed that perfect and passive constructions universally tend to refer to events as well as to states. In French, for example, a perfect has been reinterpreted as an eventive past. The *passé composé* construction, formed with the auxiliary *avoir* and a past participle, is the contemporary reflex of the Latin perfect. In other Romance languages, e.g. Spanish, this construction type still functions as a stative perfect, alongside other non-composite eventive constructions (e.g. the Spanish 'preterite'). In modern conversational French the *passé composé* replaces the *passé simple* as the unmarked mode of expressing simple past events. This reinterpretation is eminently understandable in terms of the semantic characteristics of perfect aspect. The perfect is a stative clause that is so close to the eventive end of the continuum that speakers commonly reinterpret it as expressing a pure event.

English provides a ready example of ambiguity between stative and eventive uses of passive constructions. An English sentence like 'the vase was broken' can refer to a state, as in 'When I came into the room I noticed that the vase was broken', or to an event, as in 'The vase was broken by the workers when they moved the table'. There is some sense in which we (and our English teachers) want to say that the 'stative' use of this construction is not a passive, but simply a 'predicate adjective' based on an adjectival (in this case past participle) verb form. Even given this analysis, the obvious functional and formal similarities between predicate adjectives based on past participles and passive constructions cannot be ignored.

The functional distinction between predicate nominal and perfect/passive is that in a predicate nominal a pure state is in perspective — any events that may have given rise to that state are incidental to the speaker's communicative purposes. In perfect aspect or passive voice, on the other hand, the state is described IN TERMS OF (i.e. by reference to) the situation that brought it about.

The distinction between perfect aspect and passive voice universally is that passive functions not only along the continuum of 'state' versus 'event', but also in the related domain of AGENT and PATIENT topicality; a passive is a clause type that downplays the topicality of an AGENT with respect to some PATIENT. The concomitant enhanced topicality ascribed to the PATIENT in a passive clause renders such a clause more 'stative'. This is, of course, because it is typically the PATIENT which displays the resultant state of a transitive event. It is often the case that passive voice and perfect aspect are isomorphic, or that one only occurs in the presence of the other (Comrie 1978).

We return now to the discussion of the Panare data. Since with intransitive verbs there is no AGENT (distinct from the PATIENT) to be de-topicalized, -sa' must be a marker of perfect aspect. Grammatically transitive verbs with -sa' can be either perfect aspect or passive voice, in the same sense that English 'be + past participle' constructions can be either passives or predicate adjectives.

When one wishes to express a STATE in terms of some semantically transitive event with the AGENT of that event in perspective, grammatical detransitivization must take place. See ex. 3 and the following:

(31) wĕ-sĕ-mĕnka-sa'   yu
     1-DETRANS-finish-ANT.PERF 1SG
     'I have finished.'

All that constructions such as 31 lack in order to be properly termed 'antipassives' (Comrie 1978.361ff) is the possibility of expressing the PATIENT in an oblique case. Research to date indicates that this does not happen in Panare. These construction types are used in situations where the identity of the PATIENT is so unimportant that it can be omitted entirely. For the purposes of this paper we can consider this grammatically intransitive construction type to be in the same category as constructions based on nominalizations of inherently intransitive verbs (see ex. 4).

The often-advanced hypothesis that passive constructions give rise to ergatives (e.g. Chung 1976, Anderson 1977), presents the following conceptual problem for a functional approach to syntactic change. The passive is prototypically an intransitive clause type, often with formal similarities to the most intransitive clause type in any language, namely nominal predicates. Ergatives, on the other hand, are highly transitive, under any definition of the term 'transitive'. If we assume that diachronic change involves formal restructuring due to functional similarities between closely related formal structures, it is not sufficient to reconstruct only the formal structures. We must also propose functional paths along which restructuring proceeds. In the case of the passive to ergative reanalysis, the functional path at first blush appears impossibly difficult. The Panare data, however, provide a key to the path by exhibiting a single form whose functions, and consequent formal behavior, vary between stative, perfect/passive and transitive.[12]

The Panare INTRANSITIVE perfect constructions exhibit all formal characteristics of plain nominal predicates, e.g. they require the copula in the past tense. Functionally, they can code events in discourse (see exs. 26 and 27, as well as Table 3), though they normally assert a state of identity or class-membership. The transitive perfect constructions (a.k.a. passives), on the other hand, lack at least one formal quality of nominal predicates — they fail to occur with the copula.

The most highly transitive clauses in any language are those in which a conscious AGENT acts upon a PATIENT to produce a change of state in the PATIENT (Hopper and Thompson 1980). Both perfect/passive and ergative clauses express scenes involving a transitive event. The perspective in ergative constructions is on the 'event' element of the scene rather than the resultant state. The perspective in perfect and passive constructions, on the other hand, tends to be on the 'resultant state' element of the scene. In fact ergatives can code events in which the PATIENT undergoes no discernible change in state, as in 'I saw the mountain'. I have no examples of such expressions with -*sa'* or -*se' ña* verbs in Panare.

So we see that a functional continuum exists between pure state (nominal predicate, state as class membership) to pure event (verbal predicate, event in perspective). Nominal predicates based on nominalized verbs and perfect/passive constructions form key links between the two extremes of this continuum. The schema presented in Table 5 outlines this proposed functional continuum and its formal correlates. In Table 5, boxes extending across construction types represent the functional links, whereas multiple boxes appearing under a single construction type indicates 'ambiguity', i.e. one construction functioning, or potentially functioning, in two distinct ways.

	Plain Predicate nominal	Predicate nominal formed with nominalized verb	Perfect aspect	Passive	Ergative
Perspective:					
STATE:	STATE	STATE resulting from event	STATE in terms of event.		
EVENT:			EVENT resulting in a state		EVENT may or may not result in a state.

Table 5. Functional chain from nominal predicate to transitive clause and its instantiation in Panare

5. CONCLUSION

In this paper I have presented basic data on the system of grammatical transitivity in Panare verbs, and a class of 'dative-AGENT' constructions based on verbs suffixed with -sa' or -se'ña. I have shown that -sa' functions in three logically related ways: 1) as a PATIENT nominalizer, 2) as a perfect aspect marker, and 3) as a marker of passive voice.

Since AGENTs have no case marker in ordinary transitive constructions, and since the Panare dative post-position is cognate with the ergative suffix in some other Carib languages, the question arises as to whether these constructions are properly categorized as 'ergative' clauses. An alternative analysis is that these constructions constitute passives. Various arguments show that these Panare constructions share more characteristics, both morphosyntactically and functionally, with prototypical passives than with ergatives. Hence, I conclude that Panare dative-AGENT constructions are more insightfully termed 'passives,' and that they probably represent a conservative reflex of Proto-Carib.

NOTES

Research for this paper was conducted under the auspices of the school of
Anthropology and the Philological Institute "Andrés Bello" of the Central
University of Venezuela, and the Catholic University of Táchira Venezuela,
with funding from U.S. National Science Foundation grants BNS-8609304 and
BNS-8617854, National Endowment for the Humanities grant RV-20870-87,
and the Oregon Foundation. Many thanks to our colleagues Andrés Romero
Figueroa, Omar Gonzales Ñañez, Paola Bentivoglio, María Teresa Rojas and
many others for help and encouragement with the research in Venezula; to
Monseñor Medardo Luzardo, Father José Pulido, Father José del Rey Fajardo,,
Paul and Ginny Witte, and Raúl Prieto, for logistical support in Caicara del
Orinoco, and to Scott DeLancey, Des Derbyshire, T. Givón, Marie-Claude
Mattéi-Muller, Doris Payne and Sandy Thompson for helpful comments on
earlier versions of this paper. Finally, I'd like to thank the Panare people for the
privilege of learning their beautiful and intricate language. In particular, I thank
Pragedes Salas of Caicara (originally of Caño Amarillo West, see Henley
1985), Miguel Castillo of Santa Fé (also originally of Caño Amarillo West),
Manuel Castro of Camana, Tosé of Maniapure, his son Těna (José Gregorio),
and the families of all of these men.

   The dialect represented by the examples in this paper is that of Pragedes
Salas and Miguel Castillo. The dialects spoken around the Colorado Valley on
the West (near Maniapure) and Camana on the East (near Caicara) both diverge
slightly from the Central dialect in pronunciation and lexicon. The few
grammatical differences that were noted mostly involved simplifications in the
outlying areas. For example, in the 'Central' dialect (Salas and Castillo), a verb
prefix *k-* marks first person inclusive intransitive verbs in non-past tenses. In
both the other dialects the first person inclusive merges with the singular.
Although not all examples in this paper have been checked with speakers from
both Eastern and Western dialects, I am fairly certain that claims made here will
hold for these outlying areas as well.

2   Examples with *-sa'* will dominate the following presentation, though the
syntactic generalizations hold for both *-sa'* and *-se'ña*. The distinction between
the two kinds of nominalization is parallel to the distinction between the tense
markers *-ya'* 'immediate past' on the one hand and *-se'pe* 'relative future' on
the other. The first suffix anchors fully independent verbs according to their
temporal relation to the time of speaking, while *-se'pe* indicates futurity with
respect to an event described by the immediately previous clause. That is, a
-se'pe clause describes an event that NECESSARILY follows the event
described in the previous clause, even though in a given instance the event
described by the *-se'pe* verb may or may not have occurred at the time the
sentence is uttered. Similarly, the noun that results from *-se'ña* nominalization
refers to an entity that is 'destined' to be in a state as a result of a potential event
described by the verb.

Examples cited in this paper appear in a modified form of the official Venezuelan Ministry of Education, Department of Indigenous Affairs orthography for Carib languages. Most symbols represent more or less standard phonetic values, with the following exceptions:

ě — [ə] (schwa)
n — [ŋ] / _#, _C[-dental]
    [n]/__
’ — ʔ (Glottal stop)

3   Although in elicitation situations speakers consistently maintain that the AGENT, when expressed in this construction type, must occur in the dative case, 5 of 12 examples in the corpus leave the AGENT without a case marker. The function of the use versus non-use of the dative postposition in discourse is a topic for future investigation.

4   By using the term omit here I exclude the phenomenon often called ‘zero-pronominalization’. A zero pronoun does consitute a mention of a participant, whereas omission does not. Zero pronominalization is typically used in situations where the referent is so obvious, i.e. so highly activated in the hearer’s consciousness, that it need not receive any overt coding. On the other hand, a reference to a participant is omitted in exactly the opposite kind of situation, namely when the participant is extremely unimportant to the speaker’s communicative task. So, for example, reference to the object argument in a clause like ‘I already ate’ has been omitted. This is because the identity of the food eaten is not important to the speaker’s task at this point. However, in a conjoined construction like ‘he came in and sat down’ the ‘zero’ preceding the verb ‘sat’ has a very clear and important referent. In fact the zero can only be used in this kind of situation in English precisely because its referent is so specific (Givón 1983).

5   In addition to these NONPAST suffixes, there are other suffixes -ñe and -n that occur on either transitive or intransitive verbs. However, these are clearly distinct from the NONPAST -ñe and -n. For example, when the form -ñe occurs on an intransitive verb the interpretation necessarily involves displacement in space. Furthermore, the verb does not register the person of the subject:

(a)   a-ch-irema-ñe   yu   ‘I’m going to go over there to eat.’
      A-DETRANS-feed-DISPLAC 1SG

Similarly, when the suffix -n occurs on a transitive verb, it indicates a dependent clause type that we refer to as ‘INFINITIVE’. A major use of this -n suffix is in complement clauses:

(b) Y-akama-ñe   t-incha   kĕn   we'-tyope
     3-teach-NOPAS.TRANS   IRR-know ANIM.INVIS be-PURP

   o'   chawa-*n*
   beer prepare-INF

   'They teach her so that she will know how to prepare manioc beer.'

It is clearly the case, however, that the normal way of expressing events in NONPAST tense is -*ñe* for transitive verbs and -*n* for intransitive verbs.

⁶ *Chu* is the allomorphic variant of the enclitic pronoun *yu* that occurs following stems that end in a glottal stop.

⁷ Intransitive verbs with vowel-initial stems drop the initial vowel and replace it with the prefix *o-* when subject is second person. Verbs with consonant-initial stems simply add *o-* to the stem.

⁸ For most of the prefixes illustrated in this table, three forms are given. These forms are allomorphs based on the phonological form of the verb stem. The first allomorph in each group occurs with vowel-initial stems, the second with stop-consonant initial stems and the third with continuent-consonant initial stems. The prefix vowel here represented as *ĕ* varies in quality depending on the form of the following syllable.

   In imperfective intransitive verbs (i.e. verbs with the suffix -*nĕpĕ'*), as well as in all negatives, interrogatives and irrealis clauses, the verb agreement prefixes are neutralized. In all these contexts a prefix *a-* replaces a stem initial vowel. For consonant-initial stems no prefix occurs.

⁹ In fact, this root itself is probably complex, deriving from the root *ama* 'to throw out/knock down/damage' plus the negative -*ika*. That the root *amaika* is synchronically not considered a negative is evidenced by the fact that it is followed by the normal tense/aspect/mode suffixes, and occurs with the normal person marking prefixes. True negatives trigger the prefix *a-/0-* that neutralizes person marking and does not allow the normal tense/aspect/mode suffixes.

¹⁰ There is some evidence that the syllable *up-* in the verbs *upa* 'stagnate' and *upu'ma* 'fall' is another detransitivizing prefix. However, to date that evidence is inconclusive. Even if these verbs are not formally detransitivized, they share the semantic property that their subjects undergo a change in state or location. In my entire text corpus (about 3,500 clauses) there are no examples of intransitive verbs with -*sa'* that do not have this property. Further research will be necessary to determine whether this is a fully grammaticalized requirement, or simply a statistical fluke of my sample.

¹¹ Many thanks to Marie-Claude Mattéi-Muller (p.c.) for this insight.

¹² Note that I am not necessarily suggesting that in Panare the diachronic path is from nominal predicate to transitive verb. In fact, for reasons that go beyond the scope of this paper, I suspect that the directionality of change is as follows:

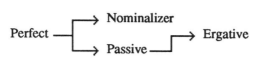

One argument for not accepting a path from ergative to passive is that such a development is universally unattested, whereas the opposite, from passive to ergative, is quite common. The main argument that the 'perfect' function is chronologically prior is that the source for *-sa'* (and *-se'ña'*) is fairly clearly a verb that has become an auxiliary, and subsequently an aspectual suffix. Currently there exists a set of modal/evidential auxiliaries *ma'*, *wa'*, and *na'* and a past tense marker *-ya'*. Since *m-*, *w-*, *n-*, *y-* and *s-* are all common verbal prefixes, it is highly likely that all of these forms derive from a verb *a'*.

In any case, the main point of this paper is not to argue for or against any particular chronological path of change — much more research is needed on the Carib family as a whole in order to accomplish this worthwhile task. Here I simply wish to point out that in Panare a set of interlocking functions coded by a single form motivates an otherwise complex and unintuitive diachronic connection between functionally distinct construction types.

REFERENCES

Anderson, Stephen R. 1977. On mechanisms by which languages become ergative. *Mechanisms of word order change*. Ed. by C. Li, 317-63. Texas: University of Texas Press.

Chafe, Wallace L. 1980. *The pear stories*. New York: Academic Press.

Chung, Sandra. 1977. On the gradual nature of syntactic change. *Mechanisms of word order change*. Ed. by C. Li, 3-55. Texas: University of Texas Press.

Comrie, Bernard. 1978. Ergativity. *Syntactic typology: studies in the phenomenology of language*. Ed. by Winfred P. Lehmann, 329-394. Austin: University of Texas Press.

Cooreman, Anne, Barbara A. Fox and T. Givón. 1984. The discourse definition of ergativity. *Studies in Language* 8.1-34.

Derbyshire, Desmond C. 1985. *Hixkariana and linguistic typology*. Dallas: Summer Institute of Linguistics.

Dixon, R. M. W. 1979. Ergativity. *Language* 55.59-138.

Fillmore, Charles J. 1977. Topics in lexical semantics. *Current issues in linguistic theory*. Ed. by Roger Cole, 76-138. Bloomington: Indiana University Press.

Givón, T. 1981. Typology and functional domains. *Studies in Language* 5.163-93.

Givón, T. 1983a. Topic continuity in discourse: an introduction. *Topic continuity in discourse: a quantitative cross-language sudy.* Ed. by T. Givón, (Typological Studies in Language 3), 1-41. Amsterdam: John Benjamins.

Givón, T. 1983b. Topic continuity in discourse: The functional domain of switch reference. *Switch reference and universal grammar.* Ed. by J. Haiman and P. Munro (Typological Studies in Language 2), 51-82. Amsterdam: J. Benjamins.

Givón, T. 1983c. Topic continuity and word-order pragmatics in Ute. *Topic continuity in discourse: a quantitative cross-language study.* Ed. by T. Givón (Typological studies in language 3), 141-214. Amsterdam: J. Benjamins.

Henley, Paul. 1985. *The Panare: tradition and change on the amazonian frontier.* New Haven and London: Yale University Press.

Hopper, Paul J. 1979. Some discourse origins of ergativity. *Hawaii Working Papers in Linguistics* 11.137-53.

Hopper, Paul J. and Sandra A. Thompson. 1980. Transitivity in grammar and discourse. *Language* 56.251-99.

Hopper, Paul J. and Sandra A. Thompson. 1984. The discourse basis for lexical categories in universal grammar. *Language* 60.703-52.

Keenan, Edward L. 1976. Towards a universal definition of "subject". *Subject and topic.* Ed. by C. Li, 303-33. New York: Academic Press.

Keenan, Edward. 1985. Passive in the world's languages. *Language typology and syntactic description 2: complex constructions.* Ed. by T. Shopen. Cambridge: Cambridge University Press.

Mattéi-Muller, Marie Claude. 1974. El sistema de posesión en la lengua panare. *Antropológica* 38.3-14.

Payne, Thomas E. 1985. *Participant Coding in Yagua discourse.* UCLA doctoral dissertation.

V. Morphosyntax in Its Wider Context

The Positioning of Non-pronominal Clitics and Particles in Lowland South American Languages*

Robert A. Dooley

1. INTRODUCTION

In descriptions of languages of lowland South America, items loosely identified as 'particles' (sometimes as clitics) often figure prominently. As a reflection of this fact, the outline for descriptions in the *Handbook of Amazonian Languages* (Derbyshire & Pullum 1986.31f) lists 'Particles' as one of the six major headings, whereas the *Lingua Descriptive Questionnaire*, designed for more general use, has no heading at all for particles and only a minor one for clitics. This raises the question as to whether 'particles' (clitics or otherwise) might be especially characteristic of languages of this area, having distinctive syntax or an especially heavy functional load.

Languages of the area are not uniform in the frequency or number of particles they present. Languages of the Arawakan family seem to have very few of these elements (Derbyshire 1986a, Wise 1986), whereas certain languages in the Tupí and Carib families have many (Bendor-Samuel 1972; Bontkes & Dooley 1985; Brandon & Seki 1984; Dooley 1977, 1982; Jensen 1982; Derbyshire 1985; Hoff 1986 and in this volume; Koehn & Koehn 1986).

This paper deals specifically with the syntax of particles and non-pronominal clitics in a sample of lowland South American languages (this sample will be described shortly). Considering these elements as one-place operators, we ask what determines or influences the way they are positioned with respect to their operand (the expression that corresponds to their semantic scope). In many cases, semantic and discourse-pragmatic considerations provide partial or complete motivation for what would otherwise simply be a formal grammatical rule of positioning. A useful starting point is the distinction between narrow-scope items, and wide- or sentential-scope items (the terminology is due to Hoff 1986). Some items have split scope: wide in some instances and narrow in others.

The positioning of one clitic subtype (found, for example, in Mbyá Guaraní, Tupí family) does not appear to be controlled by grammatical rule at all, but rather by considerations of discourse-pragmatics. Clitics of this type have the

following properties:
- a. they are phonologically enclitic;
- b. they have sentential semantic scope;
- c. their positioning, along with their phonological and semantic prop-
      erties, gives them the function of 'spacers' which signal divisions in
      the information structuring of the utterance;
- d. the component parts in c. seem to be frequently identifiable with
      particular pragmatic functions.

Still other elements are positioned under split control: their positioning is
sometimes controlled by grammar and sometimes by discourse-pragmatics. It
is, in principle, impossible to prove the nonexistence of a grammatical rule
which produces a given output, except in highly formal theoretical frameworks.
In this paper, therefore, I will simply present evidence to show that the
positioning of the elements in question is not accounted for by grammatical
rules that have been found to determine the position of similar elements in other
languages.

This paper, then, has two aims: (i) to identify parameters that influence the
positioning of non-pronominal, non-affixal, single-place 'particle'-like elements in a genetically and geographically diverse sampling of lowland South
American languages; and (ii) to discuss in some detail those elements whose
positioning is apparently controlled by discourse-pragmatics rather than, or in
addition to, grammar. After an initial discussion of the linguistic status of
particles in the sample, I consider the positioning of narrow-scope items
(section 2), wide-scope items positioned under grammatical control (section 3),
and wide-scope items positioned under discourse-pragmatic control (section 4).
Data is taken from fifteen languages in seven families:

Arawakan:	Amuesha
Carib:	Apalaí, Carib, Hixkaryana
Ge:	Apinajé, Canela-Krahô
Maku:	Nadeb
Mura:	Pirahã
Peba-Yaguan:	Yagua
Tupí	Guajajara, Kamaiurá, Mbyá Guaraní, Suruí,
	Urubu- Kaapor, Wayampi

PARTICLES, WORDS, AND CLITICS. It is common to find the term 'particle' in
descriptions of lowland South American languages, used in the sense of a
syntactic category or a level in the hierarchy of grammatical units. Cross-
linguistically, it is doubtful that such a category or level can be justified, even
though Zwicky 1985 identifies the following properties for the (mostly
English) 'particles' he considers: they are 'odd on distributional grounds',
differing in this respect from prepositions and adverbs; semantically, they are

'function', rather than 'content' items; phonologically, they 'tend to be 'dependent'; 'some... cannot occur in complete isolation' (p. 290f). This clustering of properties, Zwicky claims, is not sufficient to establish particles as a grammatically significant category, nor is he aware of any 'generalization about the grammar of any language which requires reference to such a level'. He concludes that 'everything to which the "particle" label has been attached falls somewhere else on the hierarchy of units', and that 'most of the things that have been labeled particles are in fact independent words'.

When we examine items that are called 'particles' in languages of lowland South America, we find that many of them are phonologically enclitic, and others, notably modifiers, appear to function as full words. But certain of these elements are difficult to assign to another level. Derbyshire's description of particles in Hixkaryana may be taken as a case in point, even though he treats them as a word class (1985.21):

> Particles...follow words of any class other than the ideophone, and never occur as free forms or in isolation. They are noninflected, nonderived words...Particles are like clitics in that they are phonologically bound to their head word...they are mobile compared with bound affixes, and...at their boundaries they are not subject to the same morphological processes that apply at morpheme boundaries within words.

Derbyshire is careful to distinguish Hixkaryana particles from affixes, but, considering their distributional and phonological characteristics, there seems to be as much reason for grouping them with clitics as for analyzing them as words.

There is a major point of difference between the 'particles' discussed by Zwicky and the type discussed by Derbyshire: while both are distributionally idiosyncratic, this is true in two entirely different senses. Whereas English verbal elements like *off* in *send off* and *up* in *give up* are limited in occurrence to idiomatic combinations with a very few stems, Hixkaryana particles seem to have practically unconstrained co-occurrence patterns. It is this 'mobility', a property cited for 'particles' in other area languages as well, which distinguishes the Hixkaryana type of particles. Since it is a syntactic property, it raises the possibility that particles of a particular kind may function as a grammatical category in a given language or group of languages. While the focus of this paper is not on the categorial status of particles, it is an important question for certain languages of the area.

The category of clitic in linguistic description also requires careful interpretation. Fortunately, recent studies have shed light on these elements, not only formal generative studies of pronominal elements (various papers in Borer 1986; Everett 1987), but also studies of more general types of clitics in other frameworks (Kaisse 1982; Klavans 1982, 1985; Zwicky & Pullum 1983; Zwicky 1985). In this paper I assume Klavans' characterization of cliticization as, essentially, 'affixation at the phrasal level' (Klavans 1985.117). In particular, I do not use the term 'clitic' in the superordinate sense which includes word-level affixes; diagnostic tests between these two categories are provided in Klavans 1982 and Zwicky & Pullum 1983. Although Klavans distinguishes between a clitic's syntactic ('structural') host and its phonological host, and although this distinction is useful for at least one language in the area (Yagua, cf. Payne and Payne, to appear), it does not turn out to be crucial in general for the present study. In recent treatments, a clitic's phonological attachment does not necessarily imply that it is unstressed; it may be bound to its host in other ways (Klavans 1982, chapter 5; Zwicky 1985, section 2.2).

2. NARROW-SCOPE ITEMS

For non-pronominal elements which are single-place operators, we can inquire into their semantic scope. A narrow-scope operator is one whose semantic scope (in logical terminology, its operand) is less than the sentence; in this paper, narrow-scope operands are phrasal. For all elements under discussion, both wide- and narrow-scope, the expression 'control of positioning' has to do with positioning with respect to the operand. For narrow-scope operators, we are interested in their positioning with respect to the phrase to which they attach; for wide-scope operators, we are interested in their positioning within the sentence (sometimes understood to refer to the clause).

With this understanding, in the language descriptions at hand it appears that the positioning of all narrow-scope operators can be described by grammatical rule. In fact, all such narrow-scope items occur juxtaposed to their operand. The following types of narrow-scope operators can be identified: lexical modifiers, labels of grammatical status, and labels of discourse-pragmatic status.

2.1 LEXICAL MODIFIERS. Adjectival and adverbial modifiers which can occur with a variety of construction types are common in many of the languages of the area. The three examples below from Mbyá Guaraní (Tupí family) contain the narrow-scope modifier *rive* 'merely':

(1) yy   r-upi   rive   ma   jaxy   o-o   o-iko-vy yya   py
     water EP-along merely BDY moon 3-go   3-be-SER water.NR in
     '(And so when the flood came,) the moon simply went off in a boat on the surface of the water.'(3.23)[1]

(2) apy rive   'rã   ko   nhande-r-o-fã   a-j-apo
     here merely FUT opinion 1+2-EP-house-FUT 1SG-3-make
     'It's right here that I'll build our house.'(27.129)

(3) ajukue vai-kue   rive   tu   a-r-eko
     cloth   bad-COLL   merely   discontent   1SG-COM-life
     'I only have old clothes.'

In 1 and 2, *rive* modifies an adverbial expression; in 3, it modifies a noun phrase. In each case this item is positioned following the phrase it modifies.

For Hixkaryana (Carib), Appendix I of Derbyshire 1985.245-6 lists 'five forms which clearly belong to the set of modifying particles': *heno* 'dead' or 'set of', *komo* 'collective', *tho* 'devalued', *txho* 'diminutive', and *ymo* 'augmentative'. These items likewise follow the word or phrase they modify (21): *toto ymo* (person-AUG) 'the big man'. Apalaí (Carib) has a similar set of 'modifying particles' (Koehn & Koehn 1986.88f, 111).

2.2 LABELS OF GRAMMATICAL CATEGORY OR STATUS. Case markers on noun phrases are also narrow-scope items, but differ from the above in the sense that their semantic content does not convey lexical, but rather grammatical, information. In Yagua (Peba-Yaguan family, Peru), object clitics immediately precede their operand or syntactic host, which is a free NP object, but 'they always cliticize leftward, regardless of the syntactic category of the [phonological] host' (Payne & Payne, to appear). In 4a the phonological host of the object marker *níí* is the free subject; in 4b it is an adjunct of location:

(4) a. sa-jimyiy Alchico-níí   quiivą
       3SG.S-eat Alchico-3SG.O fish
       'Alchico is eating the fish.'

    b. sa-jimyiy sinu-mu-níí   quiivą
       3SG.S-eat land-LOC-3SG.O fish
       'He is eating the fish on land.'

There are a few other details regarding the positioning of the Yagua object marker: when there is no free object, the marker occurs clause-final; when the free object is sentence-initial, the marker does not occur at all. But as with other narrow-scope operators, its positioning is clearly under grammatical control and is based on juxtaposition of operator to operand.

2.3 LABELS OF DISCOURSE-PRAGMATIC STATUS. In this section we consider narrow-scope operators which convey discourse-pragmatic rather than either lexical or grammatical information. Like other narrow-scope items, they occur juxtaposed to their operand.

An initial illustration is provided by the English definite article *the:*

(5) a. The cats saw dogs in houses.

    b. Cats saw the dogs in houses.

    c. Cats saw dogs in the houses.

This element behaves syntactically like the other types of narrow-scope items under consideration in that it occurs juxtaposed to its operand. The only difference is that its semantic content (definiteness, discussed in more detail in 4.1) is in the area of discourse-pragmatics.

In the same way, most 'discourse particles', as they are referred to in the sources, can be analyzed as narrow-scope labels of discourse-pragmatic status. In Pirahã, *(x)agia* 'principal participant' is a 'discourse particle' of this narrow-scope type:

(6) hi koab-áo-b-á-há taío   xis   agía
    3 die   CERT.RES animal PRINCIPAL.PARTICIPANT

    hi kahá-p-í-hiab-a-há-   taío
    3 leave   CERT.RES

    'He died therefore (the panther which we are discussing), therefore he didn't get away.' (Everett 1986.305f)

Four Hixkaryana 'discourse particles' discussed by Derbyshire 1985 (Appendix J) appear to label constituents as to pragmatic role or status. These are: *rma* 'same referent' or 'continuity', *ryhe* 'emphatic prominence' or 'mild contrast', *xa* and *haxa* 'contrast':

(7) towahke rma   totokom hok   nehxakoni karaywa
    friendly CONT people occ.with he.was   non.Indian
    'Yet the non-Indian was still friendly towards the people.'

(8) xenyheni   ryhe   mokyamo
    one.not.to.be.seen EMPH those
    'Those are (creatures) we should never look at.'

(9) ohetxenhir   xe   xa   wehxaha
    your.wife.PAST desirous.of CONTR I.am
    'I want the one who has been your wife (not this other woman).' (251)

(10) Waraka haxa   nehurkano asama yawo
     Waraka CONTR he.fell   trail on
     'It was Waraka (not someone else) who fell on the trail.'

Each of these elements follows its operand. This is true for *ryhe* 'emphatic prominence', for example, whether its operand is initial in the sentence as in 8 and 11, or final as in 12:

(11) yawaka ryhe   wimyako,   Waraka wya
     axe   EMPH I.gave.it   Waraka to
     'It was the axe I gave to Waraka.' (149)

(12) yaskomo foryeni̵ rma   uro ryhe
     shaman chief.of SAME I   EMPH
     'I am still the chief shaman.'

In Urubu-Kaapor (Tupí-Guaraní), the enclitic *ke* is glossed 'focus' (Kakumasu 1986.401):

(13) xe   ihẽ ke   a-jupir   katu te   a-xo
     there I   FOC 1SG-climb well truly 1SG-move
     'There I was really climbing well.'

(14) a-'u   ym ihẽ ke   ma'e ke
     1SG-eat NEG I   FOC thing OM
     'I didn't eat a thing.'

(*Ke* is also glossed 'object marker' when it occurs with a direct object.)[2]

In Amuesha (Arawak) of Peru, 'the local theme or topic of a sentence is marked by fronting and the affixation of the clitic *-pa?* 'theme/topic marker' to the last word of the constituent which is topicalized ... If there is no change of theme or of agent *-pa?* can be omitted' (Wise 1986.629f):

(15) po?-se-na-pa?   aw-o?
     3SG-brother-SEQ-THEME AUX-REPORT
     ø-e-mas-a.n   po-was-e.r
     3SG-CAUS-dry.up-OBJ   3SG-dam.area-GEN
     'Her brother went ahead and caused the dam area to dry up.' (626f)

Many lowland South American languages appear to have no elements which label phrases as to discourse-pragmatic status. Mbyá Guaraní is one language which does not, and of the seventeen Arawakan languages surveyed by Derbyshire 1986a and Wise 1986, only one, Amuesha as illustrated above, is reported to have this type of marker.

2.4 ITEMS ASSOCIATED WITH PRAGMATIC CATEGORIES; SPIKERS. The mere fact that a certain element collocates with a phrase that has a particular discourse-pragmatic status, say Focus, does not mean that its semantic content need be 'focus'. English once more provides an example:

(16) a. John gave his daughter a new bicycle.
     b. Even John gave his daughter a new bicycle.

Example 16 is from Jackendoff (1972), who states that 'the interpretation of words such as *even, only,* and *just* is intimately tied up with focus and presupposition' when they occur before a simple NP (1972.247f). These items are modifiers whose meanings strongly suggest an interpretation of Focus. In the Prague School tradition, such items have been called 'rhematizers': 'For instance, Czech *i*, English *even*, German *sogar*, Russian *daže* would come under this heading. They render the element they accompany rhematic' (Firbas 1974.20), that is, the most informative element in the sentence.

Focus often has phonological signals. In many languages, including English (Chomsky1971.200f) and Mbyá (Dooley 1982), a Focus component, when present, is given the intonation center. In languages where this is the case certain morphemes can have the effect of drawing the intonation center either to themselves or to their operand. For the purpose of discussion, I label these elements **spikers**. Some spikers are described as having 'focus', 'emphasis', etc., as their semantic content; others are simply associated with Focus through collocation.

In Apinajé (Ge) the form *mãr*, described by Callow as a 'free emphasizing particle', appears to be a spiker. It is free in the sense that 'it is not confined to functioning as a constituent of a particular type of phrase or piece but may be attached to any ... It functions as a retrogressively emphatic particle, so that the last major word in the preceding phrase or piece occurs as the peak' of a descending intonation contour (1962.215f).

(17) tã   mãr   ka añ   ixpumu
     now EMPH you still   me.see
     'Nevertheless, you will continue to see me.'

(18) nà, pa   mẽ pa ja   mãr   mẽ'pãnh-ã
     no 1.PL PL ?   this.one EMPH instead.of.them
     o   mõ
     away.with   go
     'Okay, we indeed will take him away instead of them.'

(19) nà, pu   mẽ ma kẽnkrã 'prêkti wỳr   mãr
     no INCL PL away rock   high   to   EMPH
     o   mõ
     away.with   go
     'No, let us take him away to the mountain.'

In 17, *mãr* follows a paragraph marker *tã* 'now', in 18 a pronoun *ja* 'this one', and in 19 a locational phrase *kẽnkrã 'prêkti wỳr* 'to the mountain'.

In Mbyá Guaraní (exs. 1-3), *rive* is a spiker with the gloss 'merely'. It has lexical stress and draws the intonation center to itself, so that its operand is identified as the most informative part of the sentence (actually Focus, 4.1.2).

There is a large area of overlap between the class of spikers and a semantic class which Roland Hall 1963 calls excluders: excluders are modifiers that '(1) are attributive as opposed to predicative, (2) serve to rule out something without themselves adding anything, and (3) ambiguously rule out different things according to the context' (67). *Only* and *just* in English, as well as Mbyá *rive* 'merely', are excluders which are also spikers.

The Apalaí 'discourse particle' *roro* 'alone, only just' also appears to be an excluder, and may be a spiker if it has stress with discourse-pragmatic significance:

(20) ywy roro   koih   a-ṽko
    I   alone paddle do-CONT
    'I (was) the only one paddling.' (Koehn & Koehn 1986.117)

2.5 SPLIT-SCOPE ITEMS. Certain operator types are narrow-scope items in some languages and wide-scope items in others. This can be illustrated by yes-no interrogative particles in languages of the Tupí family. In Asuriní, Kayabí, Sataré-Mawé, and Mundurukú, these particles have been analyzed as having narrow scope, whereas in others, such as Kamaiurá (ex. 21), they have wide scope (Brandon & Seki 1984):

(21) po petyma ere-'u-potat
    Q tobacco 2SG-drink-want
    'Do you want to smoke?'

There also exist elements which, in a single language, function at times as wide-scope items and at other times as narrow-scope items. Such elements can be spoken of as having split scope. One such item is the negative morpheme *e'ỹ* in Mbyá Guaraní. In 22, *e'ỹ* occurs as a narrow-scope item:

(22) João   anho e'ỹ   o-guata
    John   only NEG 3-travel
    'It wasn't just John that traveled.'

In 22, the scope of *e'ỹ* is *João anho* 'only John'. In 23, however, *e'ỹ* has wide scope:

(23) João gu-a'y   o-eja-xe   e'ỹ   vy ogue-raa ng-upive
    John REFL-son 3-leave-want NEG SS 3-take   REFL-with
    'Since John didn't want to leave his son, he took him with him.'

In 23, *e'ỹ* negates the entire subordinate clause, which would otherwise be translated 'Since John wanted to leave his son'. It is primarily in subordinate clauses that *e'ỹ* functions as a wide-scope negator, but in subordinate clauses as well as main clauses it can have narrow scope:

(24) João   anho e'ỹ   o-guata vy o-vy'a.
    John   only NEG 3-travel SS 3-be.happy
    'Since it wasn't just John that was travelling, he was happy.'

In Hixkaryana (Carib family), there are five evidential clitics (called 'verification particles' in Derbyshire 1985) whose positioning in the sentence reflects split scope: *ti* 'hearsay', *na* 'uncertainty', *mpini* 'certainty/prediction/ warning', *we* 'opinion/recollection/counteraffirmation', *mpe* 'positive doubt, scepticism'. 'The basic order of constituents is OVS, with adjuncts normally following the subject. There is an optional rule which moves the subject or an adjunct to the clause-initial position for purposes of emphasis' (Derbyshire 1985.74f). When an evidential occurs 'it is often placed in the verb phrase, which may or may not be the initial phrase of the sentence; however, when a subject or adjunct phrase is fronted for emphasis, the verification particle is usually placed in that initial phrase' (129). In 25a *ti* 'hearsay' occurs in the verb phrase; in 25b it occurs with a fronted adjunct:

(25) a. mana   yonahyatxkon hati, ohoryen   heno komo
        manna they.ate.it   HSY your-ancestor dead COLL
        'Your ancestors ate manna.'

    b. Focus   —Presuppposition — —— Tail——
        ito   ti   nehxakon ha   kamara yohi
        there HSY   he.was   INTENSFR jaguar chief.of
        'The jaguar chief was there.' (147)

Ex. 25 illustrates that 'the *ha* part of the sequence,' glossed as 'intensifier', 'is never moved to the left' (79).

In 26 the subject is, in Derbyshire's terms, 'fronted for emphasis' and followed by *ti*. The context is provided in Derbyshire 1986b:

(26) Context: The preceding sentence indicated that the sloth was not in the village where he might have been expected to be. That sentence, in which the sloth is referred to by a pronoun, together with the following one, reintroduce the sloth into the discourse:
        Focus-   —Presupposition —
        xofrye mah   ti   ehxera n-ehxakoni
        sloth   CTEXP HSY be.NEG 3S-be+DP
        'The sloth was not there.'

In discussing this example, Derbyshire states that 'the clause-initial, preverbal subject noun phrase [*xofrye* 'sloth'] is a grammatical device that correlates with the semantic factors to indicate that there is some sort of thematic break at this point' (1986b.250).

The five Hixkaryana evidential clitics listed above are split-scope items: when they occur postverbally, their scope 'relates to the whole clause'; 'when they occur in a dislocated phrase, the scope relates to that phrase'. A sixth one, *mi* 'deduction', is a wide-scope clitic which only occurs postverbally (Derbyshire 1985.79).

2.6 SEMANTIC MOTIVATION.   Steele (1975.225) states the principle that 'surface position reflects semantic scope', meaning that one-place operators often, or characteristically, occur juxtaposed to their operands, as opposed to occurring within them or being separated from them by intervening material. For narrow-scope items, as we have seen, that principle holds up well. Hence we can say that a grammatical rule which positions these narrow-scope items is fully motivated with respect to semantic scope. The principle does not operate as pervasively for wide-scope items, as is shown in section 3.

3. WIDE-SCOPE ITEMS POSITIONED UNDER GRAMMATICAL CONTROL

Whereas the positioning of narrow-scope items is fully motivated by the principle of juxtaposition of operator and operand, the positioning of wide-scope items is, in many cases, not fully motivated by any principle. However, we can sometimes recognize a significant partial motivation for it. This is discussed in Section 4.3, following a survey of discourse-pragmatic factors.

The languages in the sample present various possibilities for the grammatical positioning of wide-scope items. These are illustrated in the following sections.

3.1 FIRST POSITION. Steele says that 'modals ... tend as a class to positions at either end of a sentence', and that other elements which behave like modals in this regard are tense markers, negatives, and quotation margins (1975.224, 227). The Kamaiurá yes-no interrogative marker provides an illustration (ex. 21). This kind of positioning is analogous to that of narrow-scope items, in the sense that operator is juxtaposed to operand. Hence, this positioning is fully motivated by semantic scope.

3.2 SECOND POSITION. Steele includes second position items among those occurring 'toward the beginning of the sentence', hence having their positioning also motivated by semantic scope (1975.234). Inasmuch as they divide up their operand, however, other analyses are preferable. Motivation for second positioning is treated in 4.3 after the discussion of certain discourse-pragmatic phenomena. The present section furnishes examples of second position items.

Carib of Suriname is reported to have seventeen evidential (more broadly, modal) particles which 'are only found after the first constituent of the utterance' (Hoff 1986.50). One of these is *hkuru* 'certainly':

(27) yuʔpa hkuru   man
     good certainly it.is.INTROSP.strong
     'I assure you that it is right' (57).

'The "first constituents" have been found to be either a single word, or a word group held together by syntactic cohesion of such strength, that the group is impenetrable to evidential particles' (64). An impenetrable word group can, for example, consist of a finite verb and patient:

(28) a:mu wori:wori kahtan   hkuru   mohko
     a   fan   he.will.make.INTROSP certainly he
     'He will make a fan' (67).

This illustrates the fact that second position must be carefully defined for the language in question.

Weir (1984.108 and p.c.) reports several second-position elements in Nadëb (Maku), including the wide-scope tense marker *paah* 'past', the verfication marker *mih* 'second-hand information', and *séh* 'reaction'. This last element occurs in the following example, which also has a correlative element *éh* (only found question-final):

(29) õm séh   naiñ   éh
     2SG reaction NEG.sleeper reaction
     'Aren't you sleeping?'

Nadëb second position elements, normally unstressed, follow such first position constituents as verb, postpositional phrase, adverbial, transitive object, intransitive subject, sentence-initial connective, and conditional (subordinate) clause. Two factors seem to indicate that the positioning of these elements is highly grammaticalized: they appear to be quite limited as to freedom of movement (although *paah* and *mih* can also occur following the verb), and their placement does not appear to correlate highly with pragmatic functions. In Nadëb topicalization, for example, the Topic is not normally followed by particles, but by a phonological juncture (indicated in 30 by a comma):

(30) ta-kolãay, ta-t-ʉ́   ta-mi-soo   ta-kolãay me
     3SG-claw   3SG-food 3SG-means-get 3SG-claw   means
     'As to his claws, he gets his food with his claws.'

Wayampi (Tupí-Guaraní) has several wide-scope modal particles, such as *ipo* 'doubt', *sie~je* 'hearsay', *no* 'logical step', *ko* 'deliberative', *kua* 'resolve, duty' (Jensen 1982). These all occur in second position:

(31) aparai ipo   oo   upi
     Apalaí doubt 3.go 3.by.means.of
     'It appears that an Apalaí Indian went because of him.'

Wayampi also has a second position interrogative particle *po* which appears to be a split-scope item. When one particular constituent is being questioned, it occurs sentence-initial and is followed by *po*:

(32) saa   po   ere-pota
    knife INTERR 2SG-want
    'Is it a KNIFE you want?/Do you want a knife?'

(33) ere-pota   po   saa
    2SG-want INTERR knife
    'Is it that you WANT a knife?'

(34) ene po   saa   ere-pota
    2SG INTERR knife 2SG-want
    'Is it YOU that wants a knife?'

However, fronting occurs with other types of elements as well. Wayampi word order is determined primarily by discourse-pragmatic considerations: items which the speaker is treating as particularly informative (in certain specifiable senses) precede the verb, while others follow it (Payne 1987). In particular, a noun will occur preverbally if it is referential-indefinite (Jensen 1980, Payne 1987); the second free translation of 32, 'Do you want a knife?' is apparently meant to reflect this situation. Hence, the two readings of 32 correspond to two possibilities for the scope of *po*: narrow for the first reading and wide for the second. What is constant is that, in each case, (i) the scope of *po* is what is being questioned, whether it is a single constituent or the proposition as a whole; and (ii) *po* occurs in second position under grammatical control. There is a difference, though, in functional motivation: when *po* is a narrow-scope item, its second positioning is motivated by semantic scope, whereas the same positioning has no such motivation when *po* has wide scope.

3.3 OTHER POSITIONS. So common is it crosslinguistically to find wide-scope clitics in second position, that Ellen Kaisse has hypothesized that 'All languages with S' clitics [wide-scope, sentential-scope clitics, RAD] place those clitics in second position, after the first stressed constituent (or word) of the clause, regardless of the category of that constituent (or word)' (Kaisse 1982.4, cited in Zwicky 1985). Not all wide-scope clitics, however, occur in second position, not even all those whose positioning in the sentence is under grammatical control. We have already noted sentence-initial elements in 3.1. Wide-scope clitics can also be positioned in the verb phrase. Steele cites three languages in which particles/clitics (she doesn't distinguish between the two) occur in the verb phrase: the Mon-Khmer language Chrau and the two Eastern Oceanic languages Rarotongan and Nguna (1975.204).

Examples of clitics in the verb phrase can be found in lowland South America as well. In Mbyá Guaraní, the future marker *va'erã* occurs in the verb phrase between the main verb and a 'gerundive' serial-type verb:

(35) ko'ẽ   rã   ja-vy'a   va'e-rã   ja-kua-py
     dawn DS   1+2-be.happy REL-FUT 1+2-be.PL-SER
     'Tomorrow we will celebrate together.'

But when the speaker is expressing strong interpersonal feeling — lack of patience, for example — the contracted monosyllabic form 'rã can be used instead.

(36) ne-kane'õ   vy   nd-ere-o-ve-i   'rã
     2SG-tired   SS   NEG-2SG-go-more-NEG   FUT
     'When you get tired, you won't go on any farther.' (Said in a disparaging way; 4.12)

(37) ha'e   rami   teĩ   xee a-a   tema   'rã
     3.ANA like   but   1SG 1SG-go CONT FUT
     'Even so, I'll keep right on going.' (Said in reply to an utterance like 36; 4.236)

Both va'erã and 'rã are unstressed enclitics.

Another possibility for positioning of wide-scope clitics is found in Suruí (Tupí). There is a class of tense/aspect (T/A) markers (including the form jé ~ dé) which only occurs enclitic to the free subject (Bontkes & Dooley 1985). This is true regardless of where the free subject occurs in the sentence:

(38) Zebel-dé   étígá   gúdgúda
     Zebel-T/A then   take.pictures
     'Zebel took pictures of them.'

(39) áyab-éy   iwe-pámí   tóy-jé
     then-PL   that-afraid   1PL.EXCL-T/A
     'So we were afraid of them.'

In 38, the free subject Zebel is sentence-initial, and in 39 tóy 'we' is sentence-final, but the tense/aspect enclitic occurs on both.

Similar to Suruí, in Canela-Krahô (Ge) 'recent past is expressed in transitive clauses by the postposition te 'PAST', which follows a free form subject or has the subject person prefix attached to it' (Popjes & Popjes 1986.180). (Here, 'postposition' refers to a class of enclitics whose semantic content includes, in addition to tense, certain meanings commonly associated with adpositions.)

(40) hũmre   te   cakwĩn
     man   PAST 3.beat
     'The man beat it' (129).

(41) i-te   rop cakwĩn
     1-PAST dog beat
     'I beat the dog' (180).

Guajajara (Tupí-Guaraní) has several different kinds of elements called 'particles' which are grammatically positioned within the sentence (Bendor-Samuel 1972 and Harrison, p.c.) The basic word order in the clause nucleus is VSOAux; adjuncts of time normally occur before the nucleus, and adjuncts of place after it. There are three positions where particles are likely to occur: in second position, whether the clause-initial constituent is an adjunct or part of the nucleus; postnuclear, following the auxiliary; and clause-final, after the postnuclear adjunct. Particles in second position commonly indicate tense, or tense and evidentiality, such as *rakwez* and *roko* 'recent past', *kakwez* 'distant past attested', and *zekaipo* 'distant past unattested'; there are others as well, such as *zepe* 'unfortunately, without result'. In 42, *rakwez* occurs following the first position adverbial *karumehe* 'yesterday':

(42) karumehe rakwez   ama'ereko aha ko   pe ihe ri'i
     yesterday REC.PAST I.work   I.go field to 1SG REC.PAST
     'Yesterday I went to the field to work.'

The particle which can occur in the postnuclear position is the tense marker *kwez* 'immediate past':

(43) uhem   wà   kwez   kury
     3.arrived3.coming IMMED.PAST CHANGE
     'He just arrived.' (Harrison, p.c.)

Guajajara clause-final particles show more variety and structure. 'Their relative order is rigidly fixed ... in terms of nine positions ... No more than four final particles have, however, been found in a sentence ... In conversational speech, the vast majority of sentences conclude with one or more final particles' (Bendor-Samuel 1972.152). These elements, in their nine respective positions, are described as follows: (1) personal pronouns; (2) *wà* 'plural'; (3) *nehe* 'future time'; (4) *miamo* 'in vain'; (5) certain tense/aspect markers, apparently including *ri'i* 'recent past' (ex. 42); (6) *kury* 'now, then action or state at point of change'; (7) *no*, a form with 'no semantic reference, but ... very generally related to change of topic'; (8) vocative and other elements with 'a certain weak, exclamative sense'; and (9) 'plural' modifying an element in position eight (153ff).[3] Some of these elements appear to be narrow-scope phrasal modifiers; some are likely full words. But it is clear that all of the Guajajara wide-scope particles are positioned in the sentence under the control of the grammar.

The following, then, are positions in the sentence where wide-scope clitics and particles have been found to be grammatically positioned: initial position, second position, in the verb phrase, following an auxiliary element, sentence final, and attached to the free subject. Those non-second position items identified as clitics would appear to give difficulty for Kaisse's claim referred to at the beginning of the present section.

4. WIDE-SCOPE ITEMS POSITIONED UNDER DISCOURSE-PRAGMATIC CONTROL

In addition to wide-scope particles which are positioned in the sentence by grammatical rule, there are wide-scope items for which no grammatical rule of positioning is apparent, but whose positioning is fully motivated by discourse-pragmatic factors. The positioning of these elements brings about a discourse-pragmatic effect, more or less independently of their semantic content (although, as will be seen, the fact of their sentential scope may contribute to this effect).

As far as can be determined from the data and sources available, all of the wide-scope items positioned under discourse-pragmatic control are enclitics. In 4.1, we initially survey some discourse-pragmatic notions which the positioning of these elements might reflect. In 4.2, we see how this can work out in practice. And in 4.3, we consider how these same discourse-pragmatic effects can serve as partial motivation for grammatically-positioned items.

4.1 DISCOURSE-PRAGMATIC NOTIONS. Three types of discourse-pragmatic notions will be sketched out here: cognitive statuses which particular concepts might be assumed to have in the mental representation of the hearer; pragmatic functions (and the configurations in which they occur) which involve syntagmatic relationships; and the division of utterances as a means of information structuring.[4]

4.1.1 COGNITIVE STATUSES. Chafe 1976 describes several cognitive statuses that noun phrases may have vis-à-vis their context, such as givenness, contrastiveness, and definiteness. In a given sentence, the status of a particular element may or may not be reflected linguistically; and linguistic signalling of a status may be scalar or more or less discretized. The four cognitive statuses Chafe describes will be briefly introduced here.

Following Chafe 1976, **given** information is 'that knowledge which the speaker assumes to be in the consciousness of the addressee at the time of the utterance', whereas '**new** information is what the speaker assumes he is introducing into the addressee's consciousness by what he says' (1976.30). Obviously, this distinction does not claim to include everything that the addressee might have cognitive access to; certain kinds of information may be neither in consciousness nor in the process of being introduced into consciousness. But the given/new distinction is nevertheless useful. Both Prince 1981 and Chafe 1987 have elaborated on it further, especially in combination with other categories that relate to definiteness.[5]

In an act of **definite** reference, 'the speaker assumes that the addressee will be able to identify the referent' (Chafe 1976.55); in **indefinite** reference, that is not the case. In discourse-pragmatic studies, generic reference is often grouped with definite reference (Li and Thompson 1976.461; Givón 1978.298 and 1984, ch. 11).

Givenness and definiteness can be formulated within a schema model of cognitive representation, in which nominal-type 'concepts' are represented by interconnected slots, or nodes, to which different pieces of information attach. A slot 'can accept any of the range of values that are compatible with its associated schemata. The comprehension of a specific situation or story involves the process of instantiation whereby elements in the situation are bound to appropriate slots in the relevant schema' (Adams & Collins 1979.4). A nominal concept which is given is one whose slot or node in the schema is activated or 'lit up' (Chafe 1987.25) by having been recently instantiated or referred to, and is thereby in consciousness or short-term memory. A concept which is new is only being activated by means of the utterance. In definite reference, the addressee is expected to be able to find a particluar slot that already exists in his schema, although perhaps it is empty up to that point. New but definite references involve already-existing slots which have, at the beginning of the utterance, either never been filled or are filled but not activated. An indefinite (but specific) reference is an instruction to create a new slot.

Contrastiveness can also be characterized in a schema model. One type, which Chafe 1976 calls 'double-focus contrast', involves attaching unlike propositions, one by one, to distinct slots/nodes: *The living room* (node 1) *was beige, but the hall* (node 2) *was light blue.* A second type, Chafe's 'single-focus contrast', specifies a value for a position in a propositional structure whose other elements already exist and are, in fact, given: *It was more of a cream color* (in contrast to beige) *in the living room.* There is often one (sometimes more) alternative value for the position which is present in the schema in some form, perhaps already stored in the position in question.

The cognitive status of **informativeness** can be seen as a composite of several other parameters. It correlates with new as opposed to given, indefinite as opposed to definite, contrastive as opposed to noncontrastive; and in general it involves information that is less predictable, less accessible, more urgent. Informativeness often gives rise to rather subtle scalar nuances in language, such as in Givón's (1983) scale of referring devices which code less informativeness in their descending order:

(44) MOST INFORMATIVE
    full noun phrase
    stressed/independent pronoun
    unstressed/clitic pronoun/affix
    zero anaphora
    LEAST INFORMATIVE

There is a strong correlation between informativeness and coding weight: the more informative a certain bit of information is, the more attention is likely be demanded by signals used to encode it. In a more concise statement: informational prominence is reflected in linguistic prominence (cf. Givón 1984.416). In schema terms, informativeness relates to what part of the schema is under attention as undergoing change (substitution, addition, etc.) at a given moment.

4.1.2 PRAGMATIC FUNCTIONS AND CONFIGURATIONS. Sometimes sentences occur which have been 'packaged' into a **pragmatic configuration**, an information structure for an utterance that is based on discourse-pragmatic categories. The constituents can be identified within a small set of **pragmatic functions or relations**, of which Topic and Focus are the most commonly cited. What most clearly distinguishes pragmatic functions from cognitive statuses (section 4.1.1) is that functions enter into syntagmatic relation with one another within the utterance, and can only be characterized in relation to the configuration in which they occur. Thus, only certain well-formed configurations occur; we find Topic-Comment and Focus-Presupposition, but not Focus-Comment or Presupposition-Topic. As in the case of particles (1.1), 'ontological parsimony' dictates that the concept of pragmatic functions should not be introduced unless it would capture significant linguistic generalizations; otherwise, it would be better to describe an utterance's information structuring directly in terms of the cognitive statuses which various parts might have. In this paper I will not attempt to justify pragmatic functions in general, and even for particular examples any explanation will be brief (for a first attempt at this for Mbyá Guaraní, see Dooley 1982). However, the examples may at least serve to illustrate how utterances might be parsed into pragmatic functions, and the contexts should give some indication as to the motivation for such structuring.

Although the claim here is that pragmatic functions and configurations are fully motivated discourse-pragmatically, languages differ along such lines as the following:

(45) frequency of sentences with pragmatic configurations

   inventory of those configurations

   types of contexts in which each configuration is used

   the choice of one configuration as neutral, with others as special-purpose kinds

   linguistic signals used to identify pragmatic functions

Certain universals, though, do seem to hold. I take it as a working hypothesis that all languages use configurations of pragmatic functions in some contexts. In fact, it may be that the Focus-Presupposition configuration, such as is found in English cleft sentences like 46, is found in every language:

(46) -Focus- ——————————Presupposition—————

   It's me you're supposed to be going out with tonight.

In this section I will briefly sketch out a notional description of six pragmatic functions: Core, Topic, Presupposition, Setting, Connective, and Tail. These characterizations borrow heavily from the analyses of others; Dik 1978 deserves the most general citation.

I use **Core** as a cover term for two traditional terms which manifest a particular function in different configurations: **Comment** when in syntagmatic relation with Topic, and **Focus** in relation with Presupposition. That is, I claim that the pragmatic function referred to by the traditional terms Comment and Focus is the same in a fundamental sense. Core is defined in terms of the cognitive status of informativeness (4.1.1): when a sentence is structured in a pragmatic configuration, Core is the constituent that is the most informative. The Core furnishes the communicative 'point' of the sentence; it is the part of the sentence that is calculated to effect the most change in the cognitive representation (schema) of the hearer. Two facts follow from this characterization. First, Core constituents cannot be omitted (undergo deletion) from a configuration, whereas other functions, such as Topic (Huang 1984) and Presupposition (Chomsky 1971) sometimes do. Second, in many languages the intonation center falls within the Core (see Daneš 1967.225f; Chomsky 1971.200ff for English). There exist other languages, however, such as tonal Aghem (Watters 1979.138) and non-tonal Hixkaryana (Derbyshire 1979.164), in which Core is not signalled in any systematic way by the intonation center.

The function **Topic** occurs in a configuration with **Comment** (which is simply Core in syntagmatic relation with Topic). In this kind of configuration, sentence Topic can be characterized within the schema model as a reference to the slot or node to which the speaker sees the Comment as principally attaching (cf. Linde 1979.345ff; Reinhart 1982.2f; Chafe 1987.36ff). This characterization also has two empirical consequences. First, Topics are (prototypically) nominal, since they address a node. Second, Topics are definite (or generic) (Steele 1975.239; Li and Thompson 1976.461), since the addressee is assumed to be able to find the node referred to. Topics are not, however, restricted to given information; so-called 'marked topics' are often new (Duranti and Ochs 1979.396ff; Pontes 1982.141ff), either 'semi-active' in Chafe's (1987) terms or 'inferrable' in Prince's (1981).

Presupposition, when this term designates a constituent in a pragmatic configuration, is a propositional framework in which one item of information is not deemed to be correct as represented in the hearer's schema; the item of information may be incorrect or missing altogether (present only as a variable, Chomsky 1971.200ff). The correct item for this position is furnished as the **Focus** constituent, as in example 46 above. Information contained in a Presupposition seems to require given status. As a result, the informativeness of the Focus is set off in sharp relief as a gestalt phenomenon, in view of the high degree of contrast between figure (Focus) and ground (Presupposition). Focus, then, can be characterized as Core in syntagmatic association with Presupposition. The difference between Presupposition and Topic is the distinction between a propositional framework somewhere in a schema and a nominal reference to a node or slot. Many languages use the configurations Topic-Comment (in some order) and Focus-Presupposition for distinct discourse-pragmatic purposes.

A Core constituent of some type, along with its primary concomitant, Topic or Presupposition (if such is present), makes up the **nucleus** of a pragmatic configuration. At least three nonnuclear or adjunct functions have been usefully distinguished: Setting, Connective, and Tail. These pragmatic functions are exemplified in detail for Mbyá Guaraní in Dooley 1982.

A **Setting**, when it is a pragmatic function, gives a spatial, temporal, or perhaps logical frame of reference within which the pragmatic nucleus is contextualized. It points the hearer to a particular section of his mental representation where the accompanying information is to be stored. This characterization points up its functional affinity with Topic (Reinhart 1982.4). If such a section is not already in the current schema, the Setting may create it, or even create a new schema altogether.

A **Connective** can be thought of as a special type of abbreviated Setting, linking the utterance to its preceding context, or rather to some section of the schema that was referred to in the preceding context.

A **Tail** is a right-dislocated expression giving an afterthought, clarification, correction, amplification, or some other kind of 'material added after a premature closure' of the utterance (Chafe 1987.40).

It is often relevant to analyze some instance of a certain pragmatic function along the additional parameter of a cognitive status. Thus, for example, we can speak of Topics which differ along the parameter of informativeness. In general, the more informative a Topic is, the more distinctly it will be set off as a separate constituent; this is one implication of Givón's (1983) scale given in 44. In particular, new or contrastive Topics are often fronted, given a secondary peak of intonation, and set off from the rest of the sentence by a phonological break. In principle, however, a highly informative Topic is still distinguishable from Core, especially if Core has distinctive signals of its own, such as the intonation center in Mbyá and English.[6]

It seems to hold that pragmatic functions (with the exception of one which is final in the pragmatic nucleus or in the sentence), taken in the order in which they occur in a sentence, have the rest of the sentence as their semantic scope. That is, the semantic scope of pragmatic functions is typically right-branching. This can be indicated by nested parentheses:

(47) —Conn— (———Setting——— (Top Comment))
       Afterwards, when I finished eating, I   simply left.

Sometimes when a Comment or Presupposition occurs finally in the pragmatic nucleus, it is structured as an embedded nucleus:

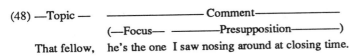

(48) —Topic —   ————————— Comment—————————
                  (—Focus— —————Presupposition—————)
        That fellow,   he's the one I saw nosing around at closing time.

In one-line form, this can be written Topic (Focus-Presupposition). In Mbyá Guaraní, nesting of this type is frequent (Dooley 1982). Neither Topic nor Focus seem to be amenable to this kind of restructuring.

For present purposes — the demonstration of discourse-pragmatic motivation for clitic positioning — it would be possible to dispense with the notion of pragmatic functions and configurations. I would merely try to show how such clitic positioning indicates motivated but unlabelled divisions of information structuring. However, pragmatic functions and configurations are a frequent feature in Mbyá Guaraní data, the principal source of illustrations in the next section; labelling utterances with these notions makes the motivation clearer.

4.2 'IN THE CRACKS' BETWEEN UNITS; SPACERS. There are different ways of indicating the division of an utterance for purposes of information structuring. First, an argument can be realized as a phrase (NP, PP) even though the grammar does not require it; one motivation for this might be so that the phrase can constitute a component in information structuring. Second, a certain phrase could be maneuvered into a position that makes a particular division feasible; movement rules such as topicalization are of this type. Third, a non-final constituent can be given some type of phonological closure; thus, topicalized elements in languages like Mbyá and English typically have a secondary peak of intonation or a distinctive intonation contour. Fourth, syntactic adjustments can give to each division of the utterance what might be called 'syntactic self-containment'; for example, a cleft sentence in English may be thought of as a single underlying clause which 'has been divided into two separate sections, each with its own verb' (Crystal 1985.50). Fifth, the components of the utterance can be physically separated from each other.

The most obvious physical separation between expressions is pause; 'it is almost trite to say that nearness in time operates to determine units in messages — the longer the pause between two speech events, the less likely they are to belong to the same unit' (Osgood & Sebeok 1954.52). But pause is not the only means of separation: 'The linguistic distance between expressions is reflected not only in the number of milliseconds that elapse between them, but also in the nature and number of the morphemes that lie between them' (Haiman 1985.105). I give the name **spacers** to phonologically attenuated elements which occur between components in the information structuring of an utterance and have the function (possibly one among others) of indicating the division of the utterance into such components. By 'phonologically attenuated' I mean typically short items of one or two syllables that carry no special suprasegmental phenomena, such as stress which might indicate a high degree of informativeness. Metaphorically, we could say that spacers are 'pause-like' elements. The function of their positioning is to indicate discontinuity in the information structure.

Parenthetical expressions, although not short expressions in general, are otherwise phonologically attenuated and many times seem to function as spacers:

(49)   however,
             to my great surprise,
    John,   in short,   wasn't at his desk.
             wouldn't you know?
             and this always happens,

Parenthetical expressions, by definition, bring about semantic discontinuity; this kind of discontinuity also contributes to the division of the utterance into separate components.

As spacers par excellence, however, we consider wide-scope clitics whose positioning is free from grammatical control. They are typically phonologically attenuated (short and unstressed). Like parenthetical elements, they involve semantic discontinuity simply by virtue of being wide-scope items in sentence-medial position. We will consider such elements in Mbyá Guaraní.

Mbyá employs a large variety of enclitic elements as spacers: clitics of mood such as *ke* 'imperative'; of evidentiality, such as *je* 'hearsay' and *ko* 'opinion'; of speaker attitude, such as *nda* 'amusement', *ta'vy* or *tu* 'disapproval', *katu* 'lack of patience', and *ty* 'surprise'; of tense, such as *'rã*; and of aspect, such as *tema* 'continuously', *ra'e* 'just verified', and *ta* 'about to'. Another such element, *ma*, seems merely to function as the semantically neutral choice for a spacer (Dooley 1977). These elements are illustrated more fully in Dooley 1982 than it is possible to do here. In Mbyá, components of information structuring, as indicated by spacers and other phenomena, can generally be labelled by pragmatic functions in a contextually-motivated configuration.

In order to demonstrate that such elements are positioned under discourse-pragmatic instead of grammatical control, I will present evidence that (i) the positioning of such an element is not the result of any apparent rule of grammar, and (ii) the resulting information structuring is motivated by discourse-pragmatic factors. In particular, I will indicate how these information structures can be interpreted as motivated pragmatic configurations. In Mbyá, the basic word order is SVO and the basic or neutral pragmatic configuration is Topic-Comment. There exist other, special-purpose configurations which are used only under certain specifiable discourse conditions; these include Focus-Presupposition and a type of Topic-Comment configuration with the Topic given more salient coding (Dooley 1982, 1987).

We will begin by considering the hearsay enclitic *je*, showing a variety of pragmatic configurations that can be indicated by its positioning. In 50, it separates Topic from Comment:

(50) Context: A hawk (unrecognized as such) was buying chickens from local farmers. He told the farmers that he would come to get them one by one, and that he didn't want them enclosed. He left, and afterwards when other farmers asked what had transpired, the farmers who had talked with the hawk said:

—Topic—— ——— Comment ———
uru   je   nha-mboty   eme
chicken HSY 1+2-enclose NEG.IMPER
'In regard to the chickens, as he said, let's not enclose them.' (17.61)

Ex. 50 shows a fronted direct object *uru* 'chicken' as Topic, in the context a new or resumptive topic of conversation. The particle *je* occurs 'in the cracks' between Topic and Comment.

In 51 *je*, in combination with the aspect enclitic *tema* 'continuously', occurs between Focus and Presupposition:

(51) Context: A group of Mbyá were on a long journey.
—— Focus ————   — Presupposition —
ka'aguy anho tema je   o-axa o-je'oi-vy
woods   only CONT HSY 3-pass 3-go.PL-SER
'They were only going through woods' [in contrast to open roads and fields].
(30.10)

In 51 the intonation center is on *anho* 'only', which is acting here as a spiker (2.1.2). In Mbyá, when a nonfinal constituent in the nucleus of a pragmatic configuration has the intonation center, Focus-Presupposition is always indicated.

In 52, *je* follows a sentence-initial connective:

(52) Context: The local 'chief of police' had sent his men out to lie in wait at every crossroads for a certain wanted man.
Connective-   Topic ——Comment ——
ha'e   rire je   Ø   o-arõ o-kua-py
3.ANA after HSY Ø   3-wait 3-be.PL-SER
'After that, they all waited for him.' (22.54)

In 52 the subject 'they', represented by zero anaphora, is treated as an unmarked (not especially informative) Topic (see Huang 1984 for zero Topics). In English there is often a pause following a sentence-initial connective, setting it off from the rest of the utterance. Mbyá effects a similar discontinuity by means of spacer clitics like *je*.

In the examples thus far it would be possible to analyze *je* either as a second position clitic or as an element which is positioned before the main verb, that is, as being positioned by grammatical rule. It turns out, however, that Mbyá has no items whose positioning can be described in either of those ways; the following examples show that something further is happening with *je*. In 53 it occurs after a Setting expression which is itself in second position:

(53) Context: A woman and her brother, in danger, were having to flee to another location.

Connective -	— Setting —				Topic	Comment-
ha'e	rire	o-vaẽ	rã	je	Ø	o-porandu
3.ANA	after	3-arrive	DS	HSY	Ø	3-ask

'Afterwards when they had arrived, they [the people of that place] asked: ['Why have you come?']' (7.29)

In 54 *je* occurs both after an initial connective 'after that' and between Focus and Presupposition:

(54) Context: The preceding paragraph spoke of a group of Mbyá travelling for one day. The following sentence begins a new paragraph:

Connective—			——— Focus ———					
ha'e	rire	je	peteĩ	jaxy	ha'e	javi	re	je
3.ANA	after	HSY	one	moon	3.ANA	all	for	HSY

— Presupposition —	
o-guata	o-je'oi-vy
3-travel	3-go.PL-SS

'After that, it was for a whole month that they travelled.' (12.32)

In 54 the intonation center is on the word *javi* 'all', indicating that the constituent *peteĩ jaxy ha'e javi re* 'for a whole month' is the Core (here, Focus). Ex. 55 has four occurrences of *je*:

(55) Context: Text-initial sentence: 'Once a certain man went to the woods and saw a lot of wild game animals.'

Second sentence:

—Conn—			——— Setting ———				
ha'e	vy	je	o-juka	ta	o-iko-vy	jave	je
3.ANA	SS	HSY	3-kill	about.to	3-be-SER	when	HSY

——— Setting ———						— Setting —	
peteĩ	ava	o-vaẽ	ha'e	py	vy	je	ij-ayvu	vy	je
one	man	3-arrive	3.ANA	in	SS	HSY	3-speech	SS	HSY

Topic —— Comment ——		
Ø	aipo-e'i	ix-u-pe
ANA	thus-3.say	3-OBL-to

'And so, just as he was about to kill them, a certain man arrived there, and he [the second man] spoke up and said to him: ['Don't kill them.']'   (11.2-3)

Note that the second occurrence of *je* in 55 is not juxtaposed to any verb. There does not appear to be any theoretical limit to the number of occurrences of *je* in Mbyá sentences; all occurrences do set off plausible pragmatic functions.

Other wide-scope enclitics in Mbyá behave similarly. Exs. 56a and 56b are alternative ways of forming equative clauses, either with or without the copula:

(56) a. Topic   - Comment —
        xee   ma   Tupã r-a'y
        1SG   BDY Tupã EP-son
        'I am the son of Tupã.'

    b. Topic   (— Focus ——— - Pres—)
        xee ma   Tupã r-a'y   a-iko
        1SGBDY   Tupã EP-son   1SG-be
        'I am the son of Tupã.' (5.12)

The pattern in 56a is more common for equatives, but sentences like 56b are not rare.   In the latter, the copula *aiko* functions pragmatically as a Presupposition constituent, indicating that the complement *Tupã ra'y* 'son of Tupã' has a somewhat higher degree of informativeness than in 56a. In both equative sentences, the neutral spacer *ma* occurs between Topic (subject) and Comment (complement); this is typical in equatives. Note that in 56 *ma* does not occur juxtaposed to a verb.

Ex. 57 presents a 'double-focus contrast' (4.1.1) in which *ma* (and here, the hearsay enclitic *je*) separates Topic and Comment:

(57) Context: Our father and his rival, Xariã, decided to go on a journey to the end of the world.
    Connective   Topic   ——— Comment ———
    ha'e   gui Xariã ma je o-o t-akykue
    3.ANA   from Xariã BDY HSY 3-go NPOSSD-behind
    Conn-   —Topic—   ——— Comment ———
    ha'e   nhande-r-u   ma je o-o t-enonde
    3.ANA   1+2-EP-father BDY HSY 3-go NPOSSD-ahead
    'And so Xariã went behind, while our father went in front.' (4.224)

In 'double-focus contrast', the occurrence of *ma* or some other wide-scope enclitic is all but required. In the sentences of 57, unlike 56, the enclitics do not occur in second position. That is, clitics like *je* and *ma* in Mbyá are not positioned by any of the grammatical rules which we surveyed in Section 3. In the absence of a plausible grammatical rule and in the presence of pervasive motivation from discourse-pragmatics, it seems fair to conclude that these elements are positioned according to discourse-pragmatic considerations.

In 3.3, we saw that the Mbyá future marker *va'erã* (or its contracted form *'rã*) occurs in the verb phrase after the main verb, a sentence position which is determined by grammatical rule. Consider, however, the sentences of 58 (ex. 3 is repeated as 58b):

(58) Context: A young lady was to throw a flower to indicate her choice of a husband. Her sisters were to do the same. At different points in the text, she told both her mother and her sisters which young man was her choice:

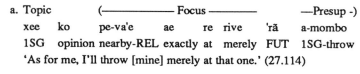

    a. Topic   (——————— Focus ———————   —Presup -)
       xee   ko   pe-va'e   ae   re rive   'rã   a-mombo
       1SG   opinion nearby-REL exactly at merely FUT 1SG-throw
       'As for me, I'll throw [mine] merely at that one.' (27.114)

    b. ——————— Focus ———————   (Top (Topic— Comment))
       pe-va'e   re rive   'rã ko   xee yvoty   a-mombo
       nearby-REL at merely FUT opinion 1SG flower   1SG-throw
       'It's merely at that one that I will throw my flower.' (27.84)

In neither 58a nor 58b does the future marker *'rã* occur in its grammatically determined postverbal position. Rather, it is positioned as a spacer to help indicate constituent boundaries in the pragmatic configurations that are labelled. The enclitic *ko*, which indicates that the speaker recognizes that what is being said reflects a personal viewpoint, is also used as a spacer. The difference between *'rã* on one hand and *ko, je,* and *ma* on the other, is that the last three are always spacers, while the positioning of *'rã* is under **split control** (split between grammar and discourse-pragmatics). When an element is under split control, there is a grammatically determined position in which it occurs when it is not particularly needed as a spacer; but when pressed into service by discourse-pragmatics, it functions as a spacer. When the Mbyá future marker is used in this way, the contracted form *'rã* generally occurs. Hence, when used as a spacer, the future marker is not capable of encoding the nuance of strong vs. weaker feeling; paradigmatic opposition of the contracted form with the longer form can convey this when in postverbal position. In 60, another sentence from the same text but spoken by young lady's sisters, the future marker *'rã* is not employed for discourse-pragmatic ends; hence it occurs in its postverbal position:

(59) —— Focus —   (Top — Comment——)
     pe-va'e   re ko   xee a-mombo 'rã
     nearby-REL at opinion 1SG 1SG-throw FUT
     'It's at that one that I will throw mine.' (27.104)

Sentences 58a, 58b, and 59 have essentially the same semantic content. In 58a, however, the top-level pragmatic configuration (Topic-Comment) indicates a 'double-focus' contrast whose nodes of origin are the speaker and her sister. In 58b, the top-level configuration shows 'single-focus' contrast, pointing out the young man at which the speaker was going to throw her flower. The configuration which is on the top level of structuring in one is shown on an embedded level in the other. In this way, both kinds of contrast get coded in both sentences. Example 59 is similar in its pragmatic configuration to 58b, although more simple.

4.3 PARTIAL MOTIVATION. Following Nunberg 1981, **partial motivation** involves (i) a phenomenon under grammatical control and (ii) a functional justification which holds only part of the time. The functional domain, which could be semantic or discourse-pragmatic, is said to provide partial motivation for the phenomenon. When phenomena are partially motivated from discourse-pragmatics, 'we can calulate SOME rationale for them, ... but the rationale is not sufficient to explain the circumstances or frequency of their actual use' (1981.203). Any attempt to describe such a phenomenon as being in the area of discourse-pragmatics would be 'a bad pragmatic explanation' (loc. cit.) — it would leak. Grammatical control must be recognized as such, even when partial motivation is present. But, once grammatical control is recognized, we may want to recognize partial motivation as well, depending on the goals we are pursuing. Partial motivation adds nothing to a description which seeks to provide the minimum formal description; but it may have much to say about how the formal system likely arose, or what ends it serves. In this sense, partial motivation can play an important role in a functional or non-minimal language description, which seeks to achieve a broader understanding of how language works.

In this paper I have indicated that the positioning of certain particles and clitics in the sentence is describable as a grammatical rule (section 3), but this does not rule out the possibility that such positioning can, in many instances, serve discourse-pragmatic ends. This possibility will be illustrated in the case of second position items.

In regard to wide-scope clitics, Newmeyer states: 'There is no obvious reason why the exigencies of communication or the structure of the human perceptual apparatus would demand second position as opposed to third, fourth, or last; or, for that matter, why there should be sentential clitics at all. Those taking a reductionist approach to grammar have the obligation to demonstrate that, in some sense, the occurrence of sentential clitics in second position 'reflects' the function of such clitics' (1983.103). Actually, two reductionist approaches are to be avoided: one which cites the presence of any motivation as proof of full motivation, and another which cites any lapses in motivation as proof that there is none at all. An alternate approach would be to ask if there is any significant partial motivation in the grammatical phenomenon of second positioning. I believe that in many cases, such can be seen via the notion of spacers (4.2).

Consider the Wayampi interrogative marker *po*, which is positioned under grammatical control in second position (exs. 32-34, section 3.2). When questioned items occur in first position, such as in ex. 33 and 34, *po* has the effect of a spacer in setting off that (Focus) constituent from the rest of the question (Presupposition). Only when there is no demonstrable fronting will a Focus-Presupposition configuration not be demonstrable. Thus, the grammatical second positioning of *po* is partially motivated by discourse-pragmatics. If, as proposed in 3.2, *po* has narrow-scope semantics when following a fronted item, then its second positioning can be said to be partially motivated by narrow-scope semantics as well. It could as well be said that when following a fronted item, the second positioning of *po* is fully motivated, by semantics and discourse-pragmatics simultaneously — a felicitous arrangement.

Guajajara also has second position clitics, as we have seen in 3.2. In 42, repeated below, the recent past marker *rakwez* occurs after the initial temporal adjunct *karume*he 'yesterday'; this may be analyzed as having the pragmatic function Setting in contexts that come typically to mind.

(42) karumehe rakwez   ama'ereko aha ko pe ihe ri'i
     yesterday REC.PAST I.work   I.go field to 1SG REC.PAST
     'Yesterday I went to the field to work.'

Another second position element, *roko* 'recent past', occurs in 60; it appears that the initial expression *a'e* is a left-dislocated subject:

(60) a'e roko   ce a'i i-in a'e ri'i   no
     3   REC.PAST there very 3-sit 3   PAST TOP.CHANGE
     'He was sitting just there' (Bendor-Samuel 1972.186).

If *a'e* in 60 is in fact left-dislocated for discourse-pragmatic reasons, then *roko* is functioning as a spacer by setting off *a'e* from the remainder of the utterance. In other Guajajara examples, however, it seems doubtful that this effect is discourse-pragmatically motivated:

(61) u-hem   zekaipo wà   wà
     2-arrive DP   3.coming PL
     'They arrived' (Harrison, p.c.)

In 61 the second positioning of *zekaipo* has no obvious pragmatic motivation or effect; that is to say, the discourse-pragmatic motivation of Guajajara second position clitics is only partial; but it does seem to be that.

Discourse-pragmatic motivation of second positioning should not be surprising, since sentence-initial position is often a highly significant one for discourse-pragmatic purposes. The fronting of informative Topics and Focus expressions is highly universal cross-linguistically (cf. Givón 1983). As Steele puts it, 'the tendency of modals, specifically, to sentential second position is a function of the importance of first position' (1975.238).

Hixkaryana evidential clitics, when they occur in second position following a fronted item, differ from the second position items considered earlier in this section in that at times they occur in another position (postverbally). Nevertheless, when in second position they show partial motivation as spacers. In 25b and 26 (Section 2.5), *ti* 'hearsay' occurs with fronted elements. The second positioning of such elements in Hixkaryana is motivated by both narrow-scope semantics and discourse-pragmatics, the latter because of their function as spacers.

Figure 1 below summarizes the findings and analyses of this paper in regard to positioning of particles and clitics in the languages sampled.

5. CONCLUDING DISCUSSION

In describing the sentential positioning of non-pronominal, operator particles and clitics in lowland South American languages, reference must be made to grammatical, semantic, and discourse-pragmatic factors. I assume that, for the purposes of minimal or basic description, a phenomenon should be described in purely grammatical terms if that is possible. This reflects a metatheoretical principle (a kind of Occam's Razor for description) which roughly says: Given alternative descriptions of a phenomenon, use the level of description that brings in the smallest range of other facts. In other words, a minimal description should involve the minimal range of facts necessary to describe the phenomenon at hand. Following Fillmore (1981.144), grammar can be seen as dealing with facts of linguistic form, semantics as dealing with relations between linguistic form and meaning, and pragmatics as dealing with relations involving linguistic form, meaning, and contextual factors. Hence the order of preference for minimal description is grammar, semantics, discourse-pragmatics.

There is a further metatheoretical principle, however, which says that rule motivation is of interest. This is a functionalist credo, an expression of the basic human desire to see why things work as they do. Since this often brings in a range of facts from broader human experience, it is in tension with the principle of minimal description. In this paper, I have included more than minimal facts.

I have shown that in the sample of languages under consideration, the positioning of narrow-scope particles and clitics can be described by a grammatical rule involving juxtaposition to the operand; we consider this kind of rule as being motivated by semantics. This holds not only for 'modifying particles', but for narrow-scope 'discourse particles' as well.

The positioning of most wide-scope items can also be described by grammatical rule. These include items in sentential first, second, or final

SCOPE OF OPERATOR	Control of positioning with respect to operand	Motivation (partial or complete) for positioning from other domains
NARROW	grammar	1 semantics (juxtaposition to operand)
		2 discourse-pragmatics (as spacer)
WIDE		3 none identified
		4 semantics (juxtaposition to operand)
		5 discourse-pragmatics (as spacer)
	discourse-pragmatics	6 none identified

SELECTED EXAMPLES:
  Items positioned under the control of a single domain:
    line 1:   Mbyá *rive* 'merely' (2.1)
    line 2:   —
    line 3:   Mbyá *va'erã* 'future', Suruí *jé* 'tense/aspect' (3.3)
    line 4:   Kamaiura *po* 'interrogative' (2.5, 3.1)
    line 5:   Guajajara *rakwez* and *roko* 'recent past' (3.3, 4.3)
    line 6:   Mbyá *je* 'hearsay', *ma* 'boundary', *ko* 'opinion' (4.2)

  Items with split scope:
    lines 1 + 3:   Mbyá *e'ỹ* 'negation' (2.5)
    lines (1 + 2) + 3: Hixkaryana *ti* 'hearsay' (2.5, 4.3)
    lines (1 + 2) + 3: Wayampi *po* 'interrogative' (3.1, 4.3)

  Item with split control:
    lines 3 + 6:   Mbyá *'rã* 'future' (3.2, 4.2.1)

Figure 1. Control and motivation of positioning

position, whether in the verb phrase, attached to an auxiliary, or attached to a free subject. Not all rules for this type of positioning show obvious motivation, at least not from the domain of semantics; however, second positioning often seems to be partially motivated from discourse-pragmatics and the notion of a 'spacer'. Principally because of its phonological and semantic properties, a spacer effects a discontinuity which segments the sentence into processing units. In many cases, these units can be identified with specific pragmatic functions.

In at least one language of the area, Mbyá Guaraní, there are wide-scope clitics whose positioning apparently cannot be described by grammatical rule; instead they are positioned according to discourse-pragmatic considerations, functioning as spacers between components in a contextually motivated information structuring of the utterance.

Some elements have split scope (sometimes narrow and sometimes wide), and others have split control of positioning (sometimes grammatical and sometimes discourse-pragmatic).

The incidence of clitics and particles varies widely, somewhat according to language family. Arawakan languages generally report few of these elements, whereas languages of the Tupí and Carib families tend to have many. And within a language family, even among closely-related languages, there are differences in the kinds of positioning rules that are operative. In Suriname Carib, for example, there are seventeen evidentials and modals which are second position items (Hoff 1986); corresponding items in Hixkaryana, another Carib language, are positioned according to different grammatical rules. Among Tupí-Guaraní languages, Mbyá Guaraní has many wide-scope clitics whose positioning is under discourse-pragmatic control; in closely related Guajajara and Wayampi, corresponding items are positioned under grammatical control.

The existence of discourse-pragmatic positioning should not be completely anomalous when considered in analogy with languages that are sometimes described as having free or flexible word order. Such a language 'will generally turn out, upon closer inspection, to be one in which pragmatic factors determine the position of major constituents' (Thompson 1978.23). In a similar vein, elements which lend themsleves to an initial description as free or mobile particles could turn out to have their positioning controlled or motivated, at least in part, by discourse-pragmatic considerations.

NOTES

*   This research was partially supported by NSF Grant No. BNS-8617854, NEH Grant No. RX-20870-87, and the University of Oregon Foundation. The author gratefully acknowledges helpful suggestions and clarification of language data he received from Des Derbyshire, Dan Everett, Talmy Givón, Pat Ham, Carl Harrison, Cheryl Jensen, Yonne Leite, Doris Payne, Lucy Seki, and Helen Weir. All remaining errors are his own.

[1]   Many of the examples in Mbyá are accompanied by text and line number. Any of these texts may be obtained from: Summer Institute of Linguistics, SAI/No, Lote D, Bloco 3, 70770 Brasília, DF, Brazil.

The following abbreviations are used in glosses throughout this paper.

Since they are taken from different authors, some terms have two abbreviations. ANA anaphora, ATTN attention, AUX auxiliary, auxiliary verb, BDY boundary marker, CAUS causative, CERT certainty, COLL collective, COM comitative, CONT continuative, CONTR contrast, CTEXP contraexpectative, DIMIN diminutive, DP distant past, DS different subject, EP epenthesis, EMPH emphasis, EXCL exclusive, FOC focus, FUT future, GEN genitive, HSY hearsay, IMMED.PAST immediate past, IMP imperative, INCL inclusive, INTENSFR intensifier, INTROSP introspective, INTERR interrogative, LOC locative, NEG negative, NPOSSD nonpossessed, NR nominalizer, O object, OBJ object, OBL oblique, OM object marker, PL plural, Q question marker, REC.PAST recent past, REFL reflexive, REL relativizer, RES result, S subject, SEQ sequence, sequential, SER indicator of serial verb, SG singular, SS same subject, T/A tense/aspect, TOP topic, 1 first person, 1+2 first person plural inclusive, 2 second person, 3 third person.

[2]   Derbyshire (p.c.) suggests that both Urubu-Kaapor *ke* and Amuesha *pa?* could possibly be better analyzed as items associated with a certain discourse-pragmatic status (section 2.4) instead of actual labels of such a status.

[3]   Although certain features of this description, such as the exact number of positions for clause-final particles, may vary with different Guajajara dialects, the general outline is true for all of them (Harrison, p.c.).

[4]   These three types of discourse-pragmatic notions correspond closely with what Payne 1987 has identified as 'three types of discourse-pragmatic statuses or operations' which are signalled by word order variation: 'the CURRENT COGNITIVE STATUS of some information in the mind of the hearer'; 'the speaker's attempt to CHANGE the hearer's mind with regard to the RELATION that one item of information has to some other, usually presupposed, piece of information'; and 'CHUNKING OF DISCOURSE into hierarchical units'.

[5]   Chafe 1987 is 'an update and, I would like to think, an improvement of that earlier attempt' (1987.21). In the recent paper, Chafe doesn't mention definiteness except in a footnote, but one of his cognitive statuses, 'semi-activated', correlates closely with it. His three-way division of the former binary parameter of givenness is reminiscent of Prince 1981. Chafe further discusses functional correlations between cognitive statuses/operations and processing units, such as intonation unit, clause, and paragraph. In the present paper, for purposes of exposition, I have opted to retain a framework which deals in more familiar terms and in which givenness and definiteness are initially presented as separate parameters. On the other hand, my use of schemata in explicating cognitive statuses and pragmatic functions owes much to Chafe, as well as to others.

⁶   As a methodological decision, I do not analyze any constituent in a pragmatic configuration as having more than one pragmatic function. In this I follow Dik 1978 and van Dijk 1977. The latter, in discussing *No, Peter has stolen the book,* says that 'For such sentences the grammatical subject or the first noun phrase does not carry the topic function ... [the utterance is] not about Peter but about someone who has stolen the book, intuitively speaking, whereas it is asserted that ... Peter is [an] individual satisfying the particular ... relation' (p. 115). In the terminology of the present paper, I would analyze this sentence as Focus-Presupposition, without a Topic constituent of any kind. The identification of the Core (of some variety) is always prior to the identification of its concomitants. In this sense, Core can pre-empt Topic. Of course, there can be languages which do not formally distinguish between Core and a highly informative Topic; one is Hixkaryana (Derbyshire 1985). But there are others that do (English and Guaraní, Dooley 1982); the theoretical framework must be set up to allow for this distinction.

REFERENCES

Adams, Marilyn Jager and Allan Collins. 1979. A schema-theoretic view of reading. *New directions in discourse processing.* Ed. by Roy O. Freedle, 1-22. Norwood, NJ: Ablex.

Bendor-Samuel, David. 1972(1966). *Hierarchical structures in Guajajara.* (University of London doctoral thesis.) Norman, Oklahoma: Summer Institute of Linguistics and University of Oklahoma.

Bontkes, Willem and Robert A. Dooley. 1985. Verification particles in Suruí. *Porto Velho workpapers.* Ed. by David Lee Fortune, 166-88. Brasília: Summer Institute of Linguistics.

Borer, Hagit (ed.). 1986. *Syntax and semantics, 19. The syntax of pronominal clitics.* New York: Academic Press.

Brandon, Frank Roberts and Lucy Ferreira Seki. 1984. Moving interrogatives without an initial +WH node in Tupí. *Syntax and semantics, 16. The syntax of native American languages.* Ed. by E. D. Cook and D. B. Gerdts, 77-103. New York: Academic Press.

Callow, John. 1962. *The Apinayé language: phonology and grammar.* University of London doctoral thesis.

Chafe, Wallace L. 1976. Givenness, contrastiveness, definiteness, subjects, topics, and point of view. *Subject and topic.* Ed. by Charles N. Li, 25-56. New York: Academic Press.

Chafe, Wallace L. 1987. Cognitive constraints on information flow. *Coherence and grounding in discourse.* Ed. by Russell Tomlin, 21-51.

Amsterdam: John Benjamins.

Chomsky, Noam. 1971. Deep structure, surface structure, and semantic interpretation. *Semantics.* Ed. by Danny D. Steinberg and Leon A. Jakobovits, 183-216. Cambridge: Cambridge University Press.

Cole, Peter (ed.). 1981. *Radical pragmatics.* New York: Academic Press.

Crystal, David. 1985. *A Dictionary of linguistics and phonetics.* 2nd edition. Oxford: Basil Blackwell and London: André Deutsch.

Daneš, František. 1967. Order of elements and sentence intonation. *To honor Ramon Jakobson: Essays on the occasion of his seventieth birthday,* 499-512. The Hague: Mouton. [Reprinted in *Intonation,* ed. by Dwight Bolinger, 216-32, (Harmondsworth: Penguin, 1972), from which my citations are taken.]

Derbyshire, Desmond C. 1977. Discourse redundancy in Hixkaryana. *International Journal of American Linguistics* 43.176-88.

Derbyshire, Desmond C. 1979. *Hixkaryana syntax.* University of London doctoral thesis.

Derbyshire, Desmond C. 1985. *Hixkaryana and linguistic typology.* Arlington: Summer Institute of Linguistics and U. of Texas at Arlington.

Derbyshire, Desmond C. 1986a. Comparative survey of morphology and syntax in Brazilian Arawakan. In Derbyshire and Pullum (eds.), 469-566.

Derbyshire, Desmond C. 1986b. Topic continuity and OVS order in Hixkaryana. *Native South American discourse.* Ed. by Joel Sherzer and Greg Urban, 237-306. Berlin: Mouton de Gruyter.

Derbyshire, Desmond C. 1987. Morphosyntactic areal characteristics of Amazonian languages. *International Journal of American Linguistics* 53.311-26.

Derbyshire, Desmond C. and Geoffrey K. Pullum (eds.). 1986. *Handbook of Amazonian languages, 1.* Berlin: Mouton de Gruyter.

Dik, Simon C. 1978. *Functional grammar.* Amsterdam: North-Holland.

Dooley, Robert A. 1977. A constituent boundary marker in Guaraní. *Arquivos de Anatomia e Antropologia, Instituto de Antropologia Professor Souza Marques* 2.147-55.

Dooley, Robert A. 1982. Options in the pragmatic structuring of Guaraní sentences. *Language* 58.307-31.

Dooley, Robert A. 1987. Basic configurations of pragmatic structuring. *1987 Work Papers of the Summer Institute of Linguistics, University of North*

Dakota session 31.1-27. Grand Forks, ND: Summer Institute of Linguistics.

Duranti, Alessandro and Elinor Ochs. 1979. Left-dislocation in Italian conversation. *Syntax and semantics, 12. Discourse and syntax.* Ed. by Talmy Givón, 377-416. New York: Academic Press.

Everett, Daniel L. 1986. Pirahã. In Derbyshire and Pullum (eds.), 200-325.

Everett, Daniel L. 1987. Pirahã clitic doubling. *Natural Language and Linguistic Theory* 5.245-276.

Fillmore, Charles J. 1981 (1974). Pragmatics and the description of discourse. In Cole, 143-66. [Originally published in *Berkeley Studies in Syntax and Semantics, Vol I*, ed. by Charles Fillmore, George Lakoff, and Robin Lakoff. U. of California, Berkeley.]

Firbas, Jan. 1974. Some aspects of the Czechoslovak approach to problems of functional sentence perspective. *Papers in functional sentence perspective (Janua Linguarum Series Minor 147)*. Ed. by František Daneš, 11-37. Prague: Academia and The Hague: Mouton.

Givón, Talmy. 1978. Definiteness and referentiality. *Universals of human language, vol. 4: syntax.* Ed. by Joseph H. Greenberg, 291-330. Stanford: Stanford University Press.

Givón, Talmy. 1981. Typology and functional domains. *Studies in Language* 5.163-93.

Givón, Talmy. 1983. Topic continuity in discourse: an introduction. *Topic continuity in discourse: a quantitative cross-language study.* Ed. by Talmy Givón, 1-41. Amsterdam: John Benjamins.

Givón, Talmy. 1984. *Syntax: a functional-typological introduction.* Amsterdam: John Benjamins.

Haiman, John. 1985. *Natural syntax: iconicity and erosion.* Cambridge: Cambridge University Press.

Hall, Roland. 1963. Excluders. *Philosophy and ordinary language.* Ed. by Charles E. Caton, 67-73. Urbana: Univ. of Illinois.

Halliday, Michael E. K. 1967. Notes on transitivity and theme in English, part 2. *Journal of Linguistics* 3.199-244.

Harrison, Carl H. 1986. Verb prominence, verb initialness, ergativity and typological disharmony in Guajajara. In Derbyshire and Pullum (eds.), 407-39.

Hoff, B. J. 1986. Evidentiality in Carib: particles, affixes and a variant of Wackernagel's law. *Lingua* 69.49-103.

Huang, C.-T. James. 1984. On the distribution and reference of empty pronouns. *Linguistic Inquiry* 15.531-74.

Jackendoff, Ray S. 1972. *Semantic interpretation in generative grammar.* Cambridge, MA: MIT Press.

Jensen, Cheryl. 1980. Word order in Oiampí. University of Oregon. MS.

Jensen, Cheryl. 1982. Partículas em Wayapí. Universidade Estadual de Campinas. MS.

Kaisse, Ellen M. 1982. Sentential clitics and Wackernagel's law. *West Coast Conference on Formal Linguistics* 1.1-14.

Kakumasu, James. 1986. Urubu-Kaapor. In Derbyshire and Pullum (eds.), 326-403.

Klavans, Judith L. 1982. *Some problems in a theory of clitics.* Bloomington: Indiana Univ. Linguistics Club.

Klavans, Judith L. 1985. The independence of syntax and phonology in cliticization. *Language* 61:95-120.

Koehn, Edward and Sally Koehn. 1986. Apalaí. In Derbyshire and Pullum (eds.), 33-127.

Li, Charles N. and Sandra A. Thompson. 1976. Subject and topic: a new typology of language. *Subject and topic.* Ed. by Charles N. Li, 457-89. New York: Academic Press.

Linde, Charlotte. 1979. Focus of attention and the choice of pronouns in discourse. *Syntax and semantics, 12. Discourse and syntax.* Ed. by Talmy Givón, 337-54. New York: Academic Press.

Newmeyer, Frederick J. 1983. *Grammatical theory: its limits and its possibilities.* Chicago: University of Chicago Press.

Nunberg, Geoffrey. 1981. Validating pragmatic explanations. In Cole (ed.), 199-222.

Osgood, Charles E. and Thomas A. Sebeok. 1954. *Psycholinguistics: a survey of theory and research problems. (International Journal of American Linguistics, Memoir 10).* Baltimore: Waverly Press.

Payne, Doris L. 1987. Meaning and pragmatics of order in selected South American Indian languages. Paper presented at Conference no. 105, Wenner-Gren Foundation for Anthropological Research, The Role of Theory in Language Description, Ocho Rios, Jamaica.

Payne, Doris L. and Thomas Payne. to appear. A grammatical sketch of Yagua. *Handbook of Amazonian languages, 2.* Ed. by Desmond C. Derbyshire and Geoffrey K. Pullum. Berlin: Mouton de Gruyter.

Pontes, Eunice. 1982. Anacoluthon and "double subject" sentences. Paper presented at the XII International Congress of Linguists, Tokyo, 1982. *Ensaios de Lingüística* 7.138-52.

Popjes, Jack and Jo Popjes. 1986. Canela-Krahô. In Derbyshire and Pullum (eds.), 128-99.

Prince, Ellen F. 1981. Toward a taxonomy of given-new information. In Cole (ed.), 223-55.

Reinhart, Tanya. 1982. *Pragmatics and linguistics: an analysis of sentence topics.* Bloomington: Indiana Univ. Linguistics Club.

Steele, Susan. 1975. On some factors that affect and effect word order. *Word order and word order change.* Ed. by Charles N. Li, 197-267. Austin: University of Texas Press.

Thompson, Sandra A. 1978. Modern English from a typological point of view: some implications of the function of wort [sic] order. *Linguistische Berichte* 54.19-35.

van Dijk, Teun A. 1977. *Text and context.* London: Longman.

Watters, John R. 1979. Focus in Aghem: a study of its formal correlates and typology. *Aghem grammatical structure. (SCOPIL 7).* Ed. by Larry M. Hyman, 137-97. Los Angeles: UCLA.

Weir, E. M. Helen. 1984. *A negação e outros tópicos da gramática Nadëb.* Master's thesis. Universidade Estadual de Campinas.

Wise, Mary Ruth. 1986. Grammatical characteristics of PreAndine Arawakan languages of Peru. In Derbyshire and Pullum (eds.), 567-642.

Zwicky, Arnold M. 1985. Clitics and particles. *Language* 61.283-305.

Zwicky, Arnold M. and Geoffrey K. Pullum. 1983. Cliticization vs. inflection: English *n't. Language* 59.502-13.

The Non-modal Particles of the Carib Language of Surinam and Their Influence on Constituent Order*

Berend Jacob Hoff

1. INTRODUCTION

The twenty-four non-modal particles of Carib[1] constitute one of the ten word classes which together accommodate all the words of this language. Six of these classes have their own characteristic morphological paradigms, as described in Hoff 1968: verbs, nouns, postpositions, adjectives/adverbs, demonstratives, and numerals.

The remaining four classes are devoid of morphology. Two of these contain proper names and interjections. Syntactically, these words behave as may be expected: the proper names behave like common nouns, while the interjections do not enter into syntactic relations at all.

The other two classes without morphology are: the **modal particles**; for instance *painare* 'perhaps', *ko:ro* 'please', and twenty others; and the **non-modal particles**; for instance *ra:pa* 'again', *manombo* 'not realized', and twenty-two others. Notice that the term 'particle' is being used here in its traditional sense of 'word without any morphology'. Even though the Carib elements show a few clitic-like features, these are not sufficient to deny them word status. However, the present article does not aim to contribute to the discussion on the general nature of words, clitics, and other grammatical elements (Reichling 1935, Zwicky 1986).

The modal particles (most of them markers of evidentiality, and a few of speaker's attitude or appeal to the hearer) function as sentential constituents. As such, they are confined to one fixed sentence position. For all but two of them this is the second position, the one after the first major constituent. Elsewhere (Hoff 1986) I have attempted to explain this rule as the grammaticalization of a natural tendency to place modal elements between theme and rheme because of their transitional role in information structure. For similar observations on other South American languages, see the work of Dooley (1982, and in the present volume).

The present paper will deal with the non-modal particles of Carib. Their defining characteristic syntactically is their placement after verbs, nouns, nominal phrases, postpositional phrases, and adverbs—being united with these in a constituency bond. They never occur as the first element of an utterance. 1-4 below serve to illustrate these points.

(1) kono:po [ki-n-o:-sa-n ra:pa]
     rain   S-3-come-t-I again
     'Again it is going to rain'

(2) [kono:po ra:pa] ki-n-o:-sa-n
     rain   again S-3-come-t-I
     'Rain again will fall'

(3) [[undi wiino] ra:pa]] kono:po ki-n-o:-sa-n
     south from   again rain   S-3-come-t-I
     'Again from the south rain is coming'

(4) [ti-pu:-ne   ra:pa] kono:po ki-n-o:-sa-n
     adj-flesh-adj again rain   S-3-come-t-I
     'Heavily again rain is coming'

The English renderings of 2-4 are only very loose approximations. In English, the special connections of 'again' with 'rain' in 2, with 'from the south' in 3, and with 'heavily' in 4, can only be established by means of accentuation. In Carib, on the other hand, the need for prosodic expression of these special connections is obviated by the existence of a constituency relation between *ra:pa* 'again' and the element preceding it, a relation which is expressed simply and clearly by their immediate succession in the specified order. Indeed, strong accents will only appear if strong contrasts have to be expressed, which in my tape-recordings occurs only infrequently. In the absence of such accentuation, the special relation of the particle to its co-constituent only confers a mild degree of salience on the referents of these elements (in the examples: *kino:san, kono:po, undi wiino*, and *tipu:ne*).

The present article is organized as follows. Section 3 will deal with syntactic matters, and provide specific arguments for the claim that particles form constituents with the elements preceding them. In this respect, Carib differs fundamentally from German (König 1987) and English (Quirk et al. 1972, 1985). The semantic effects of different placements of the particle will also be discussed here. Section 4 gives special consideration to prosody, which will prove to have a role to play after all, be it only a minor one. Section 5 is devoted to constituent order. The presence of a particle in a particular position will be shown to partly counteract and partly reinforce the general word order preferences of Carib. This dual effect will be explained on the basis of the syntactic and semantic observations in the two preceding sections. Finally, section 6 summarizes the argument and compares the Carib particles with their translation equivalents in German and English.

To pave the way for these discussions, section 2 presents a survey of the non-modal particles, and offers a description of both their individual meanings and their general semantic character. The latter will be found to be inherently dualistic. Thus, a meaning like 'again' not only serves to characterize an entity or an event as having the property of 'being recurrent', but at the same time requires access to supporting information concerning the actual nature of this recurrence. This semantic duality will be found to have its counterpart in a syntagmatic duality, which will be discussed in section 3.

2. SEMANTIC DESCRIPTION OF THE NON-MODAL PARTICLES

The non-modal particles of Carib do not give information on the reliability of the statement in which they occur, nor do they express the emotional involvement of the speaker or appeal to the hearer to act in accordance with the content of the utterance. Rather, they belong to the realm of Bühler's *Darstellung*: they contribute some specification to the description of the state of affairs the utterance is about.

This specification is generally characterized by a feature of duality which is common to the large majority of the particles, though it may be less clearly present in a few of them, and actually absent in one case: that of *hko* 'poor, poorly, small'. This duality resides in the fact that specifications like 'again', 'too', 'only', 'not', 'posterior', or 'same' cannot be understood autonomously, but have to be related to other information. Thus, in the following example:

(5) [[mo:ro are:pa] era:pa] ni-ʔma:tɨ-i
      the   bread   too   3-be.finished-r+E
      'The cassava-bread too is finished'

there is a primary semantic relation between *era:pa* 'too' and its syntactic co-constituent *mo:ro are:pa* 'the bread', and a secondary semantic relation of *moro are:pa era:pa* to the remainder of the utterance, which explains that the non-uniqueness of the bread resides in its belonging to a larger set of things that are finished. Such supplementary information is most often supplied, as in the above example, by other elements within the same utterance; but it may also be supplied by elements in neighbouring utterances, or by the non-linguistic context of the utterance. Indeed, for the particles *manombo* 'non-materialized' and *ya:non* 'recall', the relation to a completely separate state of affairs even is essential.

In the following semantic description of the non-modal particles, we will see that twenty turn out to belong to a single, tightly-knit, semantic field. They will be described in section 2.1, along with the particle *non* 'now', which is closely related to this field. Sections 2.2 and 2.3 will deal with *hko, manombo*, and *ya:non*, whose deviating semantics renders them outsiders to the field.

2.1 THE MAIN SEMANTIC FIELD. As shown in Table 1, the semantic field is built primarily on two oppositions: positive/negative and integrative/individuating.[2] The English glosses in the cells provide a first indication of the kind of meanings involved.

		positive		negative	
		integrative	individuating	integrative	individuating
1	A. CLASS positive: included negative: excluded, empty	pairo (1) *as well*	era:pa (2) *too*	wa:tɨ (3) *not*	ka:pɨn (4) *not*
	B. CONTINUITY positive: continuous negative: discontinuous	no:ron (5) *still*	ra:pa (6) *again*	rohkon (7) *only*	ro:ten (8) *just*
	C. QUANTITY positive: abundant negative: deficient	kopo:re (9) *more,* *excessive*	po:re (10) *more,* *effective*	ro:rɨpo (11) *deficient*	rɨ:po (12) *deficient,* *ineffective*
2	TIME positive: prior negative: posterior	naʔneng (13) *prior*	tera:pa (14) *(too) early,* *already*	po:ron (15) *posterior*	ko:u (16) *(too) late,* *at last*
3	IDENTITY positive: congruous negative: distinct	ko (17) *salient*	ro (18) *same*	ʔne (19) *no other,* *solely*	te (20) *different*

Table 1. Non-modal particles: the semantic field

For expository convenience, the discussion will start in 2.1.1 with the six positive particles in rows 1A, 1B, and 1C of Table 1. It will be continued in 2.1.2 with their negative antonyms. Section 2.1.3 will deal with the four temporal particles in row 2, as well as with the fifth temporal particle, *non* 'now', which neutralizes the two main oppositions shown in the columns of the table. Finally, 2.1.4 will deal with the four identificational particles in row 3.

2.1.1 POSITIVE PARTICLES OF CLASS, CONTINUITY, AND QUALITY.

(1A) The integrative particle *pairo*(1) 'as well' indicates that the referent of its co-constituent belongs to a previously existing group. Its individuating counterpart *era:pa*(2) 'too' indicates that the referent joins one or more other phenomena of its own kind, thereby establishing an open group to which further members may still be added. The following two examples illustrate the difference:

(6) mohko pɨ:yei   pairo(1) kɨ-ni:-kura:ma-non
    he   shaman as.well S-33-treat-t+I
    'The shaman treats her as well'

(7) mohko pɨ:yei   era:pa(2) kɨ-n-e:tawa:-non
    he   shaman too   S-33-visit-t+I
    'The shaman too visits her'

In the first example, the shaman was a member of a synchronously existing group of healers, together with a European doctor and a Black doctor; in the second example he joined, as an individual, an ad hoc assembly of visitors on some festive occasion.

(1B) The distinction integrative/individuating recurs with particles 5 and 6, where English for once provides adequate glosses: integrative *no:ron*(5) 'still' and individuating *ra:pa*(6) 'again'. The first indicates that the referent of its co-constituent belongs to some sort of coherent continuum, the second that it joins an open series, either by repetition or as a complement of some preceding event or thing. For instance:

(8) a:wu 0-ku:mɨ-ya-0   no:ron(5)
    I   1-be.hungry-t-E still
    'I am still hungry'

(9) o?wi:-no   me i-wo:-ko   ra:pa(6)
    one-nom as 23-strike-imp again
    'Knock once more'

(10) mo:se ra:pa(6) s-epo:rɨ-i
     him   again   13-find-r+E
     'I ran into **him** again'

(11) 0-wɨh-sa-0 ra:pa(**6**)

    1-go-t-E   again

    'I am leaving' (viz.: complementary to my coming; this is the standard formula
    for taking leave)

(12) a:wu ra:pa(**6**)

    I   again

    'And what about me?' (now that the interests of other people have received
    attention)

(1C) The integrative particle *kopo:re*(**9**) describes the referent of its co-
constituent as exceeding a certain level: either a contextually given level (as in
13), or the normal average (as in 14).

(13) t-oka:-ne   kopo:re(**9**) ka?ma

    adj-run-adj exceeding come.on

    'Come on, a bit faster'

(14) kusa:ri t-oka:-ne   kopo:re(**9**) m-a-0-n

    deer   adj-run-adj exceeding S+3-be-t-I

    'Deer run very fast'

The corresponding individuating particle *po:re*(**10**) indicates a specific
addition, which typically is decisive for the materialization of the event. For
instance:

(15) mohko y-e:pano:pɨ-i po:re(**10**)

    he   31-help-r+E more

    'He gave me some further help'

(16) mohko po:re(**10**) y-e:pano:pɨ-i

    he   effective 31-help-r+E

    'After others failed, he was the man to give me effective assistance'

(17) e:rome po:re(**10**) n-auhtɨ-na-0-:ton

    today   effective 3-house-vrb-r+E-P

    'Today they got a house (after having been on the list of the housing office for
    many days)'

2.1.2 NEGATIVE PARTICLES OF CLASS, CONTINUITY, AND QUANTITY. The six
particles discussed in the preceding section each have an antonym, as shown in
the rightmost columns of Table 1. This opposition, labeled positive/negative in
the table, is reminiscent of the distinction between additive and restrictive
subjuncts (such as *also* versus *only*) made for English in Quirk et al. (1985.604).
For expository convenience, the discussion of the negative particles will start
from the bottom of box 1 in Table 1.

(1C) The two negative quantifiers 11 and 12 both indicate a deficiency. With integrative *ro:ripo*(11), this deficiency permeates the whole state of affairs; with individuating *ri:po*(12), there is some specific frustrating factor or handicap. For instance:

(18) ti-wo?ni:-se   ro:ripo(11) mo:se iso?neng   m-a-0-n

    ptc-sleep-vn/a deficient   she   little.sister S+3-be-t-I

    'Sissy hasn't been sleeping very well (because of one or more permanent factors, like mosquitoes or insomnia)'

(19) ti-wo?ni:-se ri:po(12) mo:se iso?neng m-a-0-n

    'Sissy didn't sleep very well (because of a single, non-permanent factor, like a loud noise that woke her up)'

Integrative *ro:ripo* occurs in one of the conventional greeting formulas:

(20) yu?pa ro:ripo(11) m-a-0-n?

    good   deficient   2-be-t-I

    'Are you all right for the time being?'

Individuating *ri:po* would be inappropriate here, as it lacks the vagueness essential in a general-purpose formula. However, it could be used by a doctor in greeting one of his patients, if he is thinking of one particular ailment of the latter:

(21) yu?pa ri:po(12) m-a-0-n?

    'Are you tolerably well?'

Either particle used in the description of a finished event necessarily implies failure, as in 22 below. If, however, they are used in the description of an ongoing event, the activity may yet eventually succeed, as illustrated in 23.

(22) Utrecht po ri:po(12) wei-topo s-u:pi-0

           at deficient be-place 13-seek-r+E

    'In Utrecht I have tried in vain to find a house'

(23) Utrecht po ri:po(12) wei-topo s-upi:-ya-0

           at deficient be-place 13-seek-t-E

    'In Utrecht I am trying to find a house, as yet without success'

(1B) The negative continuity particles *rohkon*(7) and *ro:ten*(8) indicate: (i) discontinuity, a sequel being different from what preceded, (ii) absence of a further sequel, implying uniqueness. For instance:

(24) 0-ere:pa-ri   i?mati-ri   ke   am   ro:ten(8) ra:pa(6) s-aro:-take-0

    3-bread-cst   be.finished-cst because some   other   again   13-bring-f-E

    'Since his bread will be running out, I shall bring him some other (bread) in replenishment'

(25) o:ruwa   ro:ten(8) n-o:pɨ-i
     three   only   3-come-r+E

   'Only three have come' (of all the people that might have)

When modifying a verb, *ro:ten* permits the following interpretations (both falling under ii, above): 'to do nothing but this particular activity', and 'to act in a particular manner for want of enough sense to act in a more appropriate way':

(26) kɨ-n-e:mami:-na-non ro:ten(8)
     S-3-work-vrb-t+I   only
     'He is always working'

(27) mohko i-tu:rupo:-bɨ-ng   e:ne ʔne(19)   ro:ten(8) m-ɨh-sa-n?
     he   neg-heart-neg-nom see nothing else only   2-go-t-I
     'Don't you know better than to actually go and visit that scoundrel?'

Integrative *rohkon*(7) differs from individuating *ro:ten*(8) by imposing its restriction within the confines of a larger continuum; for instance:

(28) o:ruwa rohkon(7)!
     three only
     'Three (seats) only!' (viz.: in a canoe with a larger capacity than three, when the other seats have already been taken by other passengers)

In contexts which permit both particles to be used, *ro:ten*(8) will be found to express a more precise and more definite discontinuity than *rohkon*(7).

(1A) There are also two negatively classifying particles, integrative *wa:tɨ*(3) and individuating *ka:pɨn*(4). The first is used to negate a situation which in the positive case would be described by means of *pairo*(1): a referent being a member of a previously existing group. The following two examples illustrate this antonymic pair.

(29) datra pairo(1) m-a-0-n
     doctor as.well S+3-be-t-I
     'The doctor is present as well', or: 'there is a doctor as well' (besides nurses etc.), or: 'The doctor exists as a human being as well'

(30) datra wa:tɨ(3) m-a-0-n
     doctor not   S+3-be-t-I
     'Doctor is not there', or: 'there is no doctor (in this village)', or: 'doctors do not exist'

The individuating negative particle *ka:pɨn*(4) negates the constellation which in the positive case would be described by means of *era:pa*(2). The referent of the co-constituent of *era:pa* joins a class which is defined by some shared feature, but which doesn't have the status of a previously existing group. The negative counterpart of *era:pa* denies that the referent of its co-constituent joins such a class. For instance:

(31) datra   era:pa(2) mohko m-a-0-n
    doctor too   he   S+3-be-t-I
    'He too is a doctor'

(32) datra ka:pɨn(4)mohko m-a-0-n
    'He is not a doctor, he has not joined the medical profession'

The integrative feature of *wa:tɨ* (3) and the individuating feature of *ka:pɨn*(4) account for the fact that only the first can be used in a denial of existence, and that the second is especially suitable for the correction of a mistaken identification:

(33) pa:sito:ro kɨ-ng-ga:-non: "yo:rokan wa:tɨ(3) m-a-0-n"
    priest   S-3-say-t+I   evil spirit not   S+3-be-t-I
    'The missionary says: "evil spirits do not exist"'

(34) A: mo:ro   ahka-na:non   m-ene:-ya-n?
        that   shadow-nrel   2-see-t-I

    B: yo:rokan   ka:pɨn(4)   mo:ro m-a-0-n
        evil spirit   not   that   S+3-be-t-I

    A: 'Do you see that shadow?' B: 'It is not an evil spirit'

In other contexts the difference between the two particles is less clear, but it still can be shown to be there. In general, integrative *wa:tɨ* fits denials of a categorical kind, while individuating *ka:pɨn* may focus on a particular aspect and so produce a less complete denial. The following example corresponds to 32 above, but expresses a somewhat stronger denial as a result of *wa:tɨ* having replaced *ka:pɨn*:

(35) datra wa:tɨ(3) mohko m-a-0-n
    'He isn't a doctor at all'

The difference between the two negations can be illustrated further by their different potential for combination with *a:a* 'yes' and *uwa* 'no', as in the following examples. All four presuppose the question: 'is everything fine?'

(36) uwa, yuʔpa wa:tɨ(3)
    no   good   not
    'no, things are bad'

(37) *a:a, yuʔpa wa:tɨ(3)
    yes   good   not

(38) *uwa, yuʔpa ka:pɨn(4)

    no   good not

(39) a:a, yuʔpa kapɨn(4)

    yes good not

    'yes, but not quite good'

In 38-39, the individuating particle *ka:pɨn* resists combination with a straight 'no' while it accepts combination with 'yes'—apparently because it focuses its negating force on a particular detail or aspect and so leaves room for a partial affirmation. In 36-37, integrative *wa:tɨ* is seen to accept 'no' and reject 'yes', as normally would be expected with a categorical denial.

In the preceding examples, the negation particles were found to readily combine with nouns and adjectives. They also combine with postpositional groups, but they cannot, as a rule, be combined with a verb. The situation is complicated by the interaction of two further factors:

(i) The morphological paradigm of the verb already provides negative verb forms, as shown in 40-41.

(40) an-e:ne-hpa

    3-see-neg

    'Not seeing him'

(41) opɨ-hpa[3]

    come-neg

    'Not coming'

Because of competition from these morphological negatives, finite verbs are never negated by means of a particle. However, this doesn't mean that they are never found in construction with a negative particle. This is permitted in questions that ask for either an affirmation or a denial: 'hasn't he done this?, yes or no?', or that are turned rhetorically into an affirmation: 'hasn't he done this?, of course he has!'

(ii) Non-finite verbs, like nouns and adjectives, can always be negated with a particle; but in the process they may become more adjective-like, at the expense of their verbal character. To retain the latter, again morphological negation must be employed instead of a particle.

A few illustrations of these various points will be in order. To begin with, the morphological negation of an event:

(42) an-e:ne-hpa 0-we:i-0

    3-see-neg   1-become-r+E

    'I haven't seen him'

(43) datra   opɨ-hpa   m-a-0-n
     doctor come-neg S+3-be-t-I
     'The doctor isn't coming'

This type of negation is always used in by far the commonest situation, where the agent is thematic and the negative verb contributes the crucial new information. In cases where the need is felt to rhematize the agent, a negative particle will be added to the agent noun or pronoun, and a positive finite verb will be used:

(44) a:wu ka:pɨn(4) s-e:ne-i
     I   not   13-see-r+E
     'It wasn't me who saw him'

(45) datra   ka:pɨn(4) kɨ-n-o:-sa-n, i-poito-rɨ   te(20)   ?ne(19)   kɨ-n-o:-sa-n
     doctor not   S-3-come-t-I 3-assistant-cst different no other S-3-come-t-I
     'Not the doctor will come, but his assistant'

This ban on the combination of finite verbs with negative particles only affects their proper, negatory, employment. In questions and in rhetorical affirmations their combination is perfectly possible, as shown in 46-47.

(46) m-epe:katɨ-i ka:pɨn(4) kasu:ru
     23-buy-r+E   not   beads
     'You did buy beads, or didn't you?' or: 'Didn't you buy beads - of course you did'

(47) n-o:-sa-n   ka:pɨn(4) mohko tɨ-ka:-ke-ng
     3-come-t-I not   he   adj-fat-adj-nom
     'The governor does come, doesn't he?', or: 'Of course the governor will come'

Such non-negative uses of negative particles will also be found in combination with pronouns, nouns, and adjectives:

(48) mohko wa:tɨ(3) n-o:pɨ-i
     he   not   3-come-r+E
     'He did come after all'

(49) kari?na ka:pɨn(4) amo:ro
     Carib   not   you
     'Are you a Carib, or aren't you? or: 'You are a Carib, remember!'

Non-negative interpretations of overt negatives are evoked primarily by prosody: intonation contours are used that invite a reaction from the hearer. Furthermore, the negative particle is de-accented and may also be reduced phonologically (*ka:pɨn* losing its final nasal), or, on the contrary, be drawn out (*ka:piiin*). Non-prosodic cues evoking non-negative interpretations are: absence of the verbal prefix *ki-* 'strong evidentiality' (above, 47); omission of 'to be' (49); and emotional word order, with the verb being placed before the participant nominals instead of at its normal position behind them (46-47). Finally, individuating *ka:pin* is more easily used in semi-assertive questions and rhetorical affirmations than integrative *wa:ti*

Before we turn to a discussion of the temporal particles, an explanation should be given for the central point in the preceding discussion: if negation particles cannot negate finite verbs, why can they easily be added to finite verbs to produce a question or an indirect assertion? The answer is to be found in the fact that a negative verbal suffix is already available as a maximally efficient expression of negation. The use of a more elaborate means of expression, viz. of a separate negative particle, suggests special employments: those of rhetorical semi-assertion. These special employments demand special prosodic adaptations, which in turn require the presence of a separately accentable or de-accentable negative element (viz. a particle), rather than an affix (for a similar observation in a completely different context, see Labov 1970/1977.36).

With non-finite verbs, the situation is different. In principle, they accept negation by means of a particle, like the adjectives they resemble:

(50) t-o:ne   m-a-0-n
     ptc-see S+3-be-t-I
     'He has been seen, he is seen', or: 'He is popular'

(51) t-o:ne wa:ti(3) m-a-0-n
     'He is unpopular'

I suspect that, in general, negation by particle favours the more adjective-like interpretation of the non-finite verb, as in 51. When this is not intended, preference is given to morphological negation:

(52) ene-hpa ti-wei-ye   m-a-0-n
     see-neg ptc-become-vn/a S+3-be-t-I
     'He has not been seen'

2.1.3 TEMPORAL PARTICLES. Of the four temporal particles in row 2 of Table 1 (**13-16**), two indicate an earlier and two a later event. I suggest, without being able to supply specific arguments, that with these particles the distinction of 'early' versus 'late' is a manifestation of the general opposition positive/ negative.

Positive integrative *na?neng*(**13**) accords relative priority in time to persons, things, or events:

(53) mohko   naʔneng(**13**) n-o:pɨ-i
     he   prior   3-come-r+E
     'He has come first' (for instance in doctor's waiting room)

(54) a-wo:pɨ-rɨ   naʔneng(**13**) si-mo:mo:-sa-0
     2-come-cst prior   13-wait.for-t-E
     'I shall wait until you'll have come first'

The antonym *po:ron*(**15**) indicates relative posteriority:

(55) a:wu   po:ron(**15**)!
     I   posterior
     'And now, after this, it is my turn!'

The individuating particle *tera:pa*(**14**) differs from integrative *naʔneng*(**13**) by defining priority from a single point in time: the present. With *naʔneng*, the referent of its co-constituent travels in the full time dimension, preceding certain events but possibly being itself preceded by others still earlier, at distances that may vary from seconds to years. *Tera:pa*(**14**), however, only indicates 'prior to the present moment'. This meaning leaves room for the following special interpretations: 'earlier than expected', and 'coming as a (typically unpleasant) surprise'. For example:

(56) k-uku:tɨ-i   tera:pa(**14**)
     12-know-r+E already
     'I knew you already'

(57) ko:yo!   m-o:pɨ-i   tera:pa(**14**)
     interjection 2-come-r+E already
     'Dear me! there you are already!'

(58) yuʔpa rɨ:po(**12**) kɨ-n-e:mami:-na-non, indo-mbo tera:pa(**14**) 0-ani:kɨ-rɨ
     well   deficient S-3-work-vrb-t+I   that-past already 3-illness-cst
     n-aniʔma-i
     33-spoil-r-+E
     'It looked as if he was working fine, and then suddenly his illness upset it all'

In the rightmost column of Table 1, *ko:u*(**16**) forms the negative antonym of *tera:pa*(**14**). It indicates individuated posteriority, defined from the unique point of the present: 'late', 'at last', 'only after much delay':

(59) mohko   t-aki:ma-neng ko:u(**16**) 0-ɨ:wo-i
     him   3id-tease-nom at.last 3-hit-r+E
     'At last (after much provocation), he hit his tormentor'

A fifth temporal particle, *non*(21), does not partake in the two main oppositions that control Table 1, and therefore has not been included in it. Nevertheless, it is related to the other four precisely because it neutralizes the two oppositions of priority/posteriority and integration/individuation. It signals the suspension of any old or new activities to create room for something which has to be done 'now'. The suspension may take up any length of time between a few seconds and an entire day:

(60) ko:fi   non(21) kis-e?nɨ:-neng
      coffee now   1&2-drink-r+I
      'Let's have a coffee break'

(61) A: 'Let's go to the garden.'

     B: uwa, e:rome non(21) y-auhtɨ   s-amɨ:-ya-0
        no   today now   1-house 13-build-t-E
        'No, today is the time to set up my house'

2.1.4 IDENTIFICATIONAL PARTICLES. The four particles in the bottom row of table 1 (**17-20**) have in common that they all relate the referent of their co-constituent to knowledge which is present in the mind of the speaker without being part of the content of the uttered clause itself. Quite often, such extra-clausal knowledge has a verbal correlate, in a different part of the same utterance, or in a preceding utterance by the same speaker or by his speech partner. But the presence of a verbal correlate is not obligatory. As we shall be seeing presently (65 ff), the external knowledge may be either completely private or completely general; in either case it can remain without expression in words. This being so, notions like 'anaphora', 'old information', 'correction', or 'contrast', which might seem adequate in many instances, do not really provide an exhaustive characterization of the meanings of the four particles under consideration. I suggest that, actually, these meanings are best accounted for by the same two oppositions that control the other particles in Table 1.

The two positive particles *ko*(**17**) and *ro*(**18**) identify the referents of their co-constituents with something the speaker currently is aware of; the two negative particles *?ne*(**19**) and *te*(**20**) deny such an identity. The two individuating particles, positive *ro*(**18**) and negative *te*(**20**), relate the referent of their co-constituent to one specific, clearly delimited representation in the mind of the speaker; their integrative counterparts *ko*(**17**) and *?ne*(**19**) relate it to a larger, more complex set of representations.

Examples 62-64 are simple and straightforward. They contain individuating particles relating the referent of their co-constituent to a well-delimited piece of knowledge that has been introduced verbally.

(62) (old woman:) ta:mɨ   sa:no-rɨ 0-wo-ya-0, 0-pa:rɨ
               tobacco love-cst 31-kill-t-E 1-grandchild
               'I am dying for tobacco, my grandchild'

    (visitor:)   a:a pi:pi,   e:ro a-ta:mɨ-rɨ   ro(18)s-ene:pɨ-i
               right grandmother this 2-tobacco-cst same 13-bring-r+E
               'Right, grandmother, and tobacco it is that I have brought to you'

(63) e:rome e:ro nimo:ku si-tarangga-e,   koro:po te(20) s-ahpei-take-0
     today   this hammock 13-wind.warp-t+E tomorrow different 13-weave.woof-f-E
     'Today I shall wind the warp of this hammock, but tomorrow I shall weave its
     woof'

(64) mo:ro wa:ra wa:tɨ(3), e:ro wa:ra te(20)
     that   way not   this way different
     'Not in that way, but in this way'

The preceding examples illustrate the most frequent employment of *ro* and
te, where the relevant representation has been expressed before by verbal
means. Such verbal introduction, though, is not obligatory; the representation
may be present without having been mentioned explicitly:

(65) e:ro ro(18) s-upi:-ya-0
     this same   13-seek-t-E

     'This is what I had in mind while seeking' (uttered on finding the object the
     speaker had been looking for silently)

Moreover, *ro* and *te* may also be used to link the referent of their co-
constituent to general knowledge of the world, called to mind independently of
verbal context or immediate situation. In such cases, *ro* identifies the referent
of its co-constituent with a prototypical instance of what the co-constituent may
refer to; *te* indicates that it differs from the prototypical instance, and thus is of
a marginal or uncommon kind. This narrowing effect of both particles to the
positive (*ro*) or negative (*te*) prototypical instance, apparently is caused by their
shared feature of individuation. The following two examples illustrate:

(66) nu:ro ro(18) t-opo:-ye   ra:pa(6) m-a-0-n-don
     alive same ptc-find-vn/a again   S+3-be-t-I-P
     'They have been found back alive and kicking'

The next example shows the negative case, with *te.* It is the first line of a
traditional song:

(67) Ewa:rumɨ n-a:mokɨ:-rɨ te(20) ɨ-tɨ:mɨ-i   se
     Darkness pia-brew-cst distinct 31-inebriate-r+E interjection
     'Not normal beer, but the brew of the Spirit of Darkness made me drunk'

The integrative counterparts of *ro* and *te* are *ko*(17) and *ʔne*(19), respectively. They lack the strong tendency of the individuating particles to refer to elements within the verbal context - a difference which is intimately connected with the opposition individuating/integrative. The individuating particles relate to clear, well-defined representations, such as are evoked most effectively by verbal means. Their integrative conterparts relate the referents of their co-constituents to wider and less precisely defined amounts of knowledge, which for their evocation and delimitation are less dependent on the verbal context. Thus, in the free-of-context situation exemplified in 65 above, the effect of using integrative *ko* instead of individuating *ro* would be to chracterize the referent of *e:ro* 'this', not as 'the very thing' but as the 'the kind of thing' the speaker has been looking for; it adds the implication that the actual object found was not the only one that would have filled the bill:

(68) e:ro ko(17)   s-upi:-ya-0
     this about.same 13-seek-t-E
     'This is more or less what I had in mind while seeking'

In other cases, *ko* can be seen to identify the referent of its co-constituent with some mental object present in the mind of the speaker as part of a larger constellation of such objects. Within this larger cognitive context, the object in question is set apart by a positive feature: its greater salience.[4] For instance:

(69) pa:pa ko(17) an-u:kutɨ-hpa era:pa(2) m-a-0-n
     father salient 3-know-neg too   S+3-be-t-I
     'Even father doesn't know it'

Another example was produced when an informant explained the incorrectness of **wo:to ena:san* 'he eats fish' by pointing out that the eating of non-vegetable food is described by a different verb:

(70) are:pa m-ena:-sa-0, wo:to te(20)   ko(17) m-ono:-ya-0
     bread 23-ena:pɨ-t-E fish   different salient 23-o:no-t-E
     'You *ena:pɨ* bread, but fish - that you *o:no*'

This salience-conferring quality of *ko* also manifests itself in the fact that nominal co-constituents of *ko* tend to be agents (especially if animate), and tend to take up utterance-initial positions. When both *ko* and *ro* are present, as is the case in 71, *ko* is almost obligatorily combined with the animate agent and *ro* with the inanimate patient, the opposite collocation being unacceptable:

(71) Columbus ʔwa ko(17) Ame:rika ro(18) t-opo:-ye-mbo-me   m-a-0-n
              by   salient   same ptc-find-vn/a-distant-as S+3-be-t-I
     'It was Columbus by whom America was discovered, long ago'

A further demonstration of the natural connection between salience-conferring *ko* and the animate agent can be found in certain facts concerning a particular form of the finite verb which specifies both first and second person as participants, but is ambiguous with regard to their status as agent or patient. This ambiguity continues to exist when a personal pronoun is added (as in 72 below); but it vanishes when this pronoun becomes the co-constituent of *ko*, as in 73. *Ko* causes the pronoun to be interpreted as the agent.[5]

(72) a. k-uku:tɨ-i
   12/21-know-r+E

   b. amo:ro k-uku:tɨ-i
   you   12/21-know-r+E

   c. a:wu k-uku:tɨ-i
   I/me 12/21-know-r+E
   All: 'I have known you', and also 'You have known me'

(73) b. amo:ro ko(**17**) k-uku:tɨ-i
   you   salient 12/21-know-r+E
   'You are the one who has known me'

   c. a:wu   ko(**17**) k-uku:tɨ-i
   I   salient 12/21-know-r+E
   'I am the one who has known you'

If instead of *ko* its individuating counterpart *ro*(**18**) is added to the personal pronoun, the ambiguity remains.

The strong tendency of co-constituents of *ko* to take up sentence-initial positions is clearly demonstrated by the following examples. Normally, but not necessarily, thematic (scene-setting) temporal expressions come first, and personal pronouns second. However, when *ko* is added, arrangements other than those shown in 74 and 75 are virtually impossible:

(74) koiya:ro ko(**17**) aʔna   ni-tunda-i
   yesterday salient we(excl.) non.addressee-arrive-r+E
   'Yesterday was the day we arrived'

(75) aʔna   ko(**17**) koiya:ro ni-tunda-i
   we(excl.) salient yesterday non.addressee-arrive-r+E
   'We are the persons who arrived yesterday'

Again, this effect on the position of the co-constituent is peculiar to *ko*; it is not found with its individuating counterpart *ro*.

From these three observations (71-75) we may now conclude that the semantic effect of *ko*(**17**) can indeed be characterized in terms of the familiar notion of **salience**. In the present Carib context, this notion has turned out to be equivalent to 'positive identification' together with 'integration'—or, in a more elaborate paraphrase: 'identity of a referent with a representation present beforehand in the mind of the speaker, not in isolation but together with other knowledge, which however remains in the background and leaves the foreground to the single representation with which the referent is identified.'

Negatively identifying integrative *?ne*(**19**) is the negative counterpart of *ko*(**17**). Like *ko*, it identifies the referent of its co-constituent with a representation in the mind of the speaker, which representation is part of a larger constellation of mental objects. From this wider cognitive context it is set apart, however, not by the positive value of foregrounding, but by a negative value: viz. by the exclusion of all actual or potential alternatives present in the minds of speaker and hearer.

The first example is the utterance of a notoriously incompetent person, who suddenly and miraculously has become a good hunter. When his neighbours ask him: 'how did you learn it?', he replies:

(76) Kuru:pi   ?ne(**19**)   y-e:me:pa-i
     Kuru:pi (a spirit) no.other   31/teach-r+E
     'Nobody but Kuru:pi taught me'

If the referent of the co-constituent is a property, the elimination of its alternatives by *?ne* serves to delimit it more emphatically:

(77) nu:ro ?ne(**19**) t-opo:-ye   ra:pa(**6**) m-a-0-n-don
     alive no.other ptc-find-vn/a again   S+3-be-t-I-P
     'They have been found back alive - not dead, as might have been feared'

This contrastive assertion of the presence of a property may result in a sharpening of its definition which is rendered best as 'real, really':

(78) mo:se pita:ni n-awo:mɨ-i   ko:i :ne(**19**)[6]
     this   child   3-stand.up-r+E fast no.other
     'This child has begun to walk really early'

The same applies to activities:

(79) si-wo:-take-0 ?ne(**19**)   mo:se re:re
     13-kill-f-E   no.other this   blood.sucking.bat
     'I am really going to kill that bat - doing nothing less drastic'

Finally, *?ne* is able to evoke strong contrast, especially when combined with a suitable intonation contour. However, the particle is highly frequent (as are the other three identificational particles), and is certainly not restricted to such cases of strong contrast. Often, it only indicates uniqueness in some relatively minor aspect, as in 80; this was said when a small boy, upon seeing a white man for the first time in his life, asked his uncle: 'where is HE from?':

(80) mohko ʔne(19) Para:muru wïino m-a-0-n
　　 he　 no.other Paramaribo from S+3-be-t-I
　　 'He is the one from Paramaribo'.

Here the particle indicates that the white missionary in question is the only regular acquaintance of the Indians who doesn't live in the country district, but in town.

Finally, a note is in order on the role played by the identificational particles in both information structure and discourse structure—the former within the sentence, the latter beyond its limits. While other particles are relevant to these structures too (those meaning 'also', 'again', or 'only' providing clear cases, see Daneš 1981.88) the identificational particles are especially fit to serve in this area. The use of positive individuating *ro*, for instance, reminds one of the use of definite articles in other languages and shows similar complexities. In the present description, there is little room for further consideration of these syntagmatic aspects of the semantics of the particles; our major aim here is to establish, with as much exactitude as possible, their static semantic values within the paradigmatic field of which they appear to be members.[7]

2.2 ONE SEMANTICALLY AUTONOMOUS PARTICLE: *HKO*(22). As noted at the beginning of section 2, *hko* 'poor, poorly, small' differs from all other non-modal particles by attributing to the referent of its co-constituent an inherent property, i.e. a property that may be completely understood without supporting information. This autonomous character of *hko* comes out most clearly in combination with a noun:

(81) ay-e:remi:-rï　　　ro(18) ʔne(19) e:ro m-a-0-n,　wo:pï hko(22)
　　 2-ceremonial.song-cst same no.other this S+3-be-t-I aunt poor
　　 '(Even if you lost much,) you still have your musical talent, poor aunt'

There is a strong tendency to add *hko* to diminutives, and also to the sympathetic interjection *ce*:

(82) pïrï:wa ʔme hko(22) tï-ka:-se　　i-ʔwa m-a-0-n
　　 arrow small small ptc-make-vn/a 3-by S+3-be-t-I
　　 'A tiny little arrow has been made by him'

(83) ce　　hko(22)!
　　 oh dear poor
　　 'Poor soul!'

In 81 and 82, *hko* is used in combination with a noun, which it modifies in the same way as an adjective would do. When the complete event is to be described as occurring in a defective or a pitiful manner, the particle is placed behind the finite verb, as in 84b:

(84) a. mo:se I-pe:ti-mi-ng   hko(22) ki-n-o:-sa-n
         this   neg-thigh-neg-nom poor   S-3-come-t-I
         'Poor Thighless is coming'

     b. ki-n-o:-sa-n hko(22) mo:se I-pe:ti-mi-ng
         'Thighless is coming, in a stumbling manner'

A similar wide effect is produced when *hko*(22) combines with an adverbial:

(85) yuʔpa hko(22) ay-e:ne-ya-n?
     well   poor   32-see-t-I
     'Does he look after you well?' (this may be said to express either that the patient is in a poor condition, or that the nurse is well-meaning but not very competent, or both)

Hko may produce near-antonymic effects with adverbials:

(86) ka:wo hko(22) n-owa-hto-i
     high poor   3-hammock.rope-vrb-r+E
     'He (a little child) has tied his hammock low - since he couldn't reach very high'

Finally, it may be useful to summarize here the position of *hko* with reference both to the particles of the main field discussed in section 2.1 above, and to the modal particles discussed in Hoff 1986.98-99.

Syntactically, there is no difference between *hko* and a main field particle like *ri:po*(12) 'deficient'; in their syntactic mobility, they both differ from a modal particle like *su* 'expression of the feelings of the speaker'. The latter is restricted to one fixed position after the first constituent.

Semantically, *hko* differs from *ri:po* in its autonomous character: the pitifulness it ascribes to the referent of its nominal co-constituent exists independently of the event described by the utterance in which it occurs. *Hko* differs from modal *su* in pretending to give objective description—not expression of subjective feelings. Compare:

(87) mo:se Ipe:timing hko(22) kino:san
     'Poor Thighless is coming'

(88) mo:se Ipe:timing ri:po(12) kino:san
     'Thighless is coming, but all for nothing'

(89) mo:se Ipe:timing su (modal) kino-san

'There we have Thighless coming!'

2.3 Two particles relating separate states of affairs: *MANOMBO*(23) and *YA:NON*(24).

As noted at the beginning of section 2, *manombo* 'not materialized' and *ya:non* 'recall' differ from the majority of the particles in their even greater reliance on external information.

Manombo differs from the negations *wa:ti* (3) and *ka:pin*(4) in asserting that something which had been expected or had at least been possible has not materialized, due to the interference of some specific factor. This factor may be either mentioned explicitly or understood:

(90) m-uku:ti-ri   manombo(23)

    23-know-irr not.materialized

    'You might have known it'

(91) y-auran-imbo eta-hpo-mbo-to o-ʔwa m-uku:ti-ri   manombo(23)

    1-words-past hear-infp-past-if 2-by 23-know-irr not.materialized

    'If you had listened to me, you might have known it'

(92) fre:de ya:ko manombo(23)   i-wo:pi-ri   eka:riti-ri, monde   ya:ko

    Friday on   not.materialized 3-come-cst tell-cst   Monday on

       te(20)   kI-n-o:-sa-n

       different   S-3-come-t-I

    'His coming had been announced for Friday, but he came on Monday'

As all finite non-irrealis verbs depict a state of affairs as actually occurring in fact or fantasy, they do not collocate with *manombo*. Either the irrealis has to be used with *manombo*, as in 90-91 , or a non-finite verb form must be used, as in 92.[8]

Ya:non(24) indicates that the referent of its co-constituent, and through it the whole state of affairs described in the utterance, is connected with memories of the past which at that very moment are alive in the speaker's mind. The following example is the first sentence of a report of one of the informant's early childhood memories. *Ya:non* explicitly describes the mental return to *mo:ni* 'yonder, in former times':

(93) mo:ni ya:non(24) y-e:nu-ta-hpo-mbo i-seʔme   ot-u:ku:ti-hpa no:ron(5)

    yonder recall   1-eye-vrb-infp-past 3-though int-know-neg still

       ti-wei-ye-mbo-me   0-wa-0-0

       ptc-become-vn/a-past-as 1-be-t-E

    'I remember that in that remote time, (though) having become aware of my surroundings, yet I still had not become conscious of myself as a person'

This example provides the purest and simplest illustration of the meaning of *ya:non* as formulated above: 'return to the past'. More generally, though, this tacit reference to memories of the past is being used to characterize a current state of affairs—to wit, the one described in the utterance itself—as being consonant with past experience. The following examples illustrate this use.

(94) we:we ya:non(24) t-opɨ:rɨ-ke   ra!
     trees recall   adj-flower-adj interjection
     'Look, the trees are in bloom - as they always are, in this season!'

(95) s-uku:-sa-0 ya:non(24) mo:nɨ tansi-mi-nde   ʔwa 0-eka:rɨtɨ-hpo-mbo ɨ-ʔwa
     13-know-t-E recall   yonder grandfather-late-P by 3-tell-inf-past   1-to
     '(Of course) I know it, (because) as I remember, in those days it was told to me
     by my late grandfathers'

(96) na:re   su   ya:non(24) kɨt-o:rupa-n
     optative particle attitudinal particle recall   1&2-talk-r+I
     'Let's have a chat, as we were wont to'

3. SYNTAGMATIC RELATIONS AND LIMITS

In the preceding sections we have examined the different meanings that different particles contribute to the utterances they belong to. In the following sections, by contrast, we shall examine the different effects of joining one and the same particle to different constituents of otherwise identical utterances.

3.1 INTRODUCTION. It should be noticed at the outset that these syntagmatic side-effects are often fairly limited—mainly as a result of the inherent semantic duality of the particles in question, whose primary semantic characterization of their co-constituents cannot be assessed in full without regard to secondary information which in effect serves to substantiate the claim made with the particle itself. And because this substantiating information is generally provided by the remainder of the utterance in which the particle occurs, the mere presence of a syntactic link between a particle and one particular constituent will generally fail to stop other constituents from also playing their own part in the way the particle is understood. For example, the Carib equivalents of 97-98 below would both be understood as describing the non-unique event of John swimming:

(97) [John again] swims

(98) John [swims again]

They differ, however, in the way *ra:pa* 'again' would enter the interpretation process. In 97, 'again' primarily characterizes John as being non-unique, whilst 'swims' informs us in exactly what respect this characterization would be justified: John is non-unique qua swimmer. In 98, on the other hand, 'again' primarily characterizes a particular act of swimming as non-unique, with 'John' now adding that the non-uniqueness of this act lies in the fact that there have been other acts that also had John for their agent.

Now there may be situations, of course, in which these different perspectives on the non-uniqueness of John's swimming are not equally appropriate. But in the large majority of the cases, different placements of *ra:pa*, and of Carib non-modal particles in general, turn out to produce no more than slight differences in salience. We shall return to this issue in greater detail in section 3.3.

There are two further points requiring attention in this connection. The first of these concerns the upper limit of that part of an utterance which is available as a source of secondary information required to substantiate the primary claim made by the particle. In section 3.4 it will be argued that this domain is coextensive with the complete sentence, and not just with the clause containing the particle. In this regard, Carib is quite different from English. In English, a sentence like 99:

(99) the car that again had broken down was abandoned

is not ambiguous between 'broken down again' and 'abandoned again'. But precisely this ambiguity is characteristic of the Carib equivalent of 99. Of course, this difference between Carib and English is closely related to the fact that English *again*, unlike Carib *ra:pa*, is some kind of adverb.

The second point concerns the precise status of the link between a particle and the word or phrase immediately preceding it. So far, I simply have assumed that this link is codified syntactically as a constituency relation; in section 3.2 I give the evidence supporting this assumption. The claim that there is such a strong bond between a particle and its alleged co-constituent will play a crucial role in the discussions in sections 3.3 and 3.4.

3.2 PARTICLES AND CONSTITUENCY. As we have just seen, and shall see in more detail in section 3.3, the actual position of the particle does little to prevent the remainder of the sentence from playing a major part in the final interpretation of the particle; this fact casts some serious doubts on my claim that particles are linked to the word or phrase preceding them[9] in a syntactic constituency bond. In what follows, I shall try to dispel these doubts once and for all.

3.2.1 PATIENT NOMINAL AND FINITE VERB. Carib finite verbs of all personal categories (except one, which will be discussed presently) can be used as complete utterances. They may, however, also be complemented with one or two separate nominals to provide a more precise identification of the agent, the patient, or both. When such nominals are present, they generally precede the verb in the order agent-patient-verb; but they may freely follow the verb with only slight stylistic effects (see Hoff 1978, and below, section 5). Also, the nominals may be separated from the verb by an adverb like *ka:wo* 'high' (100), or by a sentential particle like the modal particle *hkuru* 'certainly' (101):

(100) y-auhti   ka:wo s-a:mi-i
         1-house high   13-build-r+E
         'I have built my house high'

(101) y-auhti   hkuru   s-a:mi-i
         1-house certainly 13-build-r+E
         'I certainly have built my house'

The exceptional situation is the one where both participants are third persons; in this case Carib verb morphology can no longer effectively distinguish between agent and patient. In this instance, a form of the finite verb is used that must be complemented with a patient nominal that **must** precede the verb and cannot be separated from it by adverbs or sentential particles. Apparently, nominal and verb are joined in a constituency bond which is so close as to be in fact impenetrable:

(102) *t-auhti   ka:wo 0-a:mi-i
         3id-house high   3-build-r+E

(103) ka:wo [t-auhti   0-a:mi-i]¹⁰
         [t-auhti 0-a:mi-i] ka:wo

         Both: 'He has built his house high'

Sentential particles like *hkuru* 'certainly' are restricted to the position after the first major constituent of the sentence (Hoff 1986). The unacceptability of 104 therefore provides an even stronger indication of the close bond between patient nominal and verb when both participants are third persons:

(104) *t-auhti   hkuru   0-a:mi-i
         3id-house certainly 3-build-r+E

(105) [t-auhti 0-a:mi-i] hkuru
         'He certainly has built his house'

The important point here is that this otherwise forbidden postition in 102 and 104 can readily be entered by non-modal particles—a freedom which can only be explained if it is asumed that non-modal particles become part of the preceding patient nominal in terms of constituency. This is indicated in 106:

(106) [t-auhti   na?neng(13)] 0-a:mi-i
         3id-house prior   3-build-r+E
         'The first thing he built was his house'

Non-modal particles also may be placed behind the verb, of course, as in 107. In such cases, verb and nominal are joined to the particle together.

(107) [t-auhti   0-a:mɨ-i]   naʔneng(13)
      3id-house 3-build-r+E prior
      'The first thing he did was to build his house'

On the relations between non-modal particles and freely mobile nominals and verbs, see section 5, below.

3.2.2 THE NOMINAL PHRASE. Nominal phrases that are more complex than one-word *t-auhti* 'his house' in 106, may also form a single constituent with a non-modal particle:

(108) [[a:mu ka:wo-non auhto] naʔneng(13)] 0-a:mɨ-i
        a   high-att house prior   3-build-r+E
      'He has built a high house first'

If a nominal phrase is not followed by a particle, there is in principle no fixed order of demonstrative (D), adjective (A), and noun (N). Presumably DAN is most frequent, but all the other arrangements are permitted too. However, when the scope of a particle encompasses the phrase in its entirety, as in 108, only DAN and NAD are possible. Direct linear contact between adjective and particle invites a direct connection between these two elements. Such arrangements were not always accepted by the informant:

(109) ?[a:mu auhto [ka:wo-non naʔneng(13)]] 0-a:mɨ-i
        a   house high-att   prior   3-build-r+E

Acceptance appeared to hinge on the semantic plausibility of a special relation between the particle and the immediately preceding adjective. Whenever such a relation made enough sense, the utterance proved to be fully acceptable:

(110) [a:mu auhto [ka:wo-non po:re(10)]] 0-a:mɨ-i
        a   house high-att   more   3-build-r+E
      'He has built a house that is much higher than the average'

The same is true for cases in which adjective and particle precede the noun. Again acceptability is guaranteed if the special connection between adjective and particle is plausible—as is the case with 'beautiful' and 'more' in the following example:

(111) [[[omi:ya po:re(10)] wo:rii] ri:po(12)] i-ʔwa t-apoi-ye
         beautiful more   woman deficient 3-by prt-take-vn/a
      'A most beautiful woman had been taken by him, in vain'

Three more examples show combinations of a negative particle with an adjective, and of *ro:ten* 'only' with *am/a:mu* 'something, somebody, a'; the latter word is syntactically equivalent to a demonstrative.

(112) [[e:rome:-non ka:pïn(4)] to:ri] iro-mbo   e:ro-kon m-a-0-n
      today-att   not   story this-passed this-P S+3-be-t-I
      'Furthermore, these are stories not of the present time'

(113) pe?ya   ?wa kï-n-ïx-sa-n, [[am ro:ten(8)]   pe?ya]   pa:to
      landing.place to S-3-go-t-I   a discontinuous landing.place at
      'She went to the landing place, a different landing place' (from the one
      mentioned earlier in the same story)

(114) [[[a:mu ro:ten(8)]   tï-me:-re-ng]   kami:sa]   s-upi:-ya-0
      a   discontinuous adj-painting-adj-att piece.of.cloth 13-seek-t-E
      'I am seeking a piece of cloth of a different colour'

The third example suggests a structure [[D A] N]. This possibility, however, has not been investigated any further.

A note should be added on prosody in the phonic realization of constructions like those exemplified in 110-114. In discussing such instances, my present informant generally uses accents and comma intonation to underline the special relation between the particle and a preceding adjective or demonstrative. Often, he covers both elements with a single intonation contour, in which prominence is given either to the adjective or to the particle, or to both, accompanied by the additional lengthening of one long vowel in each element (112, *e:romé::non kà::pïn*). At other occasions, he employs pauses and comma-intonation, either on both sides of the adjective-cum-particle constituent, or before and after the entire nominal phrase.

I believe that such prosodic underpinnings are not essential to the phonic expression of the constituency relation between a particle and a preceding adjective or demonstrative. This relation is expressed primarily, and sufficiently, by the order rule which always unites a particle to an immediately preceding word or phrase. In fact, in their original contexts in tape-recorded stories, 111-113 do not have any conspicuous prosodic markings of the special connection between particle and preceding element. In 112, only the adjective *e:romé:non* was accented; in 111 and 113 no clear accents could be observed at all—nor were these recordings found to be prosodically abnormal by the present informant (Hoff 1968.348, 342, 316).

His own preference for a more distinctly modulated articulation appeared to be motivated by the fact that *a:mu*, demonstratives, and nearly all attributive adjectives (*omï:ya* being one of the few exceptions) can function as nouns too: *am/a:mu* 'a thing or person', *e:rome:non* 'a thing of today'. Addition of a particle (*a:mu ro:ten, e:rome:non ka:pïn*) was felt by the informant to enhance the likelihood of this nominal interpretation, which would leave the rightful heads of the nominal phrases (*pe?ya* 'landing place' in 113, *to:ri* 'story' in 112) unconnected. His strong modulation apparently served to counteract this breaking-up of the nominal phrase.

3.2.3 OTHER CONSTRUCTIONS. For the sake of descriptive completeness, I shall add a few examples of combinations with postpositional phrases and with modifiers used adverbially or predicatively.

Particles may be related either to a postpositional phrase or to the nominal phrase inside a postpositional phrase:

(115) [[e:ro po:ko] ro:ten(8)] si-ka:-sa-0
      this according.to only 13-make-t-E
      'I am making it just according to this (model), which is the only way I can do it'

(116) [[e:ro ro:ten(8)] po:ko] si-ka:-sa-0
      this only according.to 13-make-t-E
      'I am making this according to just this (model), which is the only one I have'

In other cases, placing the particle inside or outside the postpositional phrase hardly affects its interpretation. The outside postion appears to be the favourite one:

(117) [[pira:ta po:re(10)] po:ko] s-epe:kati-i

      [[pira:ta po:ko] po:re(10)] s-epe:kati-i
      money with more 13-buy-r+E

      'I have bought it for a lot of money'

Modifiers belonging to the morphological category exemplified by *ka:wo* 'high' (see above, 3.2.1) cannot be used attributively. (On modifiers that **can** by used attributively, see 3.2.2 and also Hoff 1968.259ff). Instead, they are used adverbially, or predicatively with 'to be'. In either construction, they readily combine with particles.

(118) y-auhti [ka:wo po:re(10)] s-a:mi-i
      1-house high more 13-build-r+E
      'I have built my house very high, in a higher manner than normal'

(119) [ka:wo po:re(10)] m-a-0-n
      high more S+3-be-t-I
      'It is higher than normal'

3.3 INTERPRETIVE PRECEDENCE. Arguments have been presented above (3.2) for the existence of a constituency relation between the non-modal particles and the word or phrase preceding them. Such an immediate syntactic connection will be expected to manifest itself in an exclusive semantic relation between particle and preceding element. Although this special semantic relation can indeed be shown to exist in every single case, it is not exclusive, and therefore not always easy to recognize. This is a consequence of the semantic duality which we found to be a characteristic feature of the particles (sections 2 and 3). The semantic relation between a particle and its co-constituent is not so totally exclusive as the one between, say, an adjective and the noun it qualifies. In order to appreciate in what respect something or somebody is 'too', or 'only', or 'prior', or 'more', the hearer must depend on further information, which in most cases will be provided by other elements within the same utterance. Thus, in 106, the meaning of *tauhti na?neng* 'his house prior' can only be fully interpreted after the further relation has been established between this unit and the verb: the house is not just 'prior'—period; it is prior only in so far as he built it prior to certain other things he built.

I shall now try to show that this precedence in the process of interpretation (with the particle first being applied to its co-constituent, and the resulting product then being related to other constituents) is the truly constant factor in the different semantic effects of different particle placements.

Depending on the syntactic and semantic context, interpretive precedence may effect the content of the utterance in various degrees of magnitude. In its stronger manifestations, interpretive precedence may decide which participant is 'too':

(120) [mohko Kupi:risi era:pa(2)] mohko Tu:tiru:mɨ 0-sa:noma:-non
      he   Kupi:risi too   she   Tu:tiru:mɨ 3-love-t+I
      'Kupi:risi too loves Tu:tiru:mɨ'

(121) mohko Kupi:risi [mohko Tu:tiru:mɨ era:pa(2)] 0-sa:noma:-non
      'Kupi:risi loves Tu:tiru:mɨ too'

Such clear-cut differences are typically obtained with particles that tend to characterize individual entities or properties, rather than complete events or situations. In the same syntactic configuration, particles with less individualizing meanings produce less conspicuous differences:

(122) [mohko Kuru:pi rɨ:po(12)] mohko kari?na 0-eme:pa-i
      he   Kuru:pi deficient he   Carib 3-teach-r+E
      'Kuru:pi in vain taught the Carib'

(123) mohko Kuru:pi [mohko kari?na rɨ:po(12)] 0-eme:pa-i
      'The Carib was taught in vain by Kuru:pi'

The position of *ri:po*(12) 'deficient' cannot be used to specify which of the two participants was responsible for the failure indicated by this particle. From mythology, it is known that actually it was the pupil, but this does not prevent 122 from also being a true statement. The difference between the two utterances resides in the perspective from which the failure of the teaching-effort is presented. In 122, it is from the perspective of Kuru:pi, the teacher whose efforts ultimately proved to have been wasted; in 123, on the other hand, it is from the perspective of his pupil, who finds himself without the skills he was intended to possess.

Interpretive precedence, therefore, is a salience[11] factor when more than one participant is involved—the actual placement of the particle serves to direct the spotlight to the participant with which it is combined.

If the particle—and, with it, interpretive precedence—attaches to the finite verb, salience is conferred on the total event,[12] and neither of the two participants is particularly favored.

(124) mohko Kuru:pi mohko kari?na [0-eme:pa-i ri:po(12)]
      he   name   he   Carib   3-teach-r+E deficient
      'Kuru:pi taught the Carib, and it was all in vain'

In special cases, addition of the particle to the finite verb may result in much more conspicuous differences of interpretation. This happens with *no:ron*(5) 'continuous' because of the clear conceptual difference between continuity of process (verb + *no:ron*) and continuity of entities (noun + *no:ron*):

(125) mohko [ki-ni:-kumi:-ya-n no:ron(5)]
      he   S-3-be.hungry-t-I continuous
      'He is still hungry'

(126) [mohko no:ron(5)] ki-ni:-kumi:-ya-n
      he   continuous S-3-be.hungry-t-I
      'He is one more person that is hungry'

When the particle is added to an adjective, interpretive precedence again may produce a different result. Combinations of adjectives with *po:re*(10) differ from what is generally found with non-modal particles in that they can do without the adition of further information. In 111 above, 'most beautiful' is obviously interpretable on its own.

The second particle in 111, *ri:po* 'deficient', relates to the complete nominal group including *po:re*, and thereby confers the same kind of salience on its referent as was found in 122-124. In 111, the woman is salient, including her exceptional beauty, which yet did not suffice to make her husband stay with her. In a different position, *ri:po* would have indicated the same failure of the marriage but without implying that the fate of the husband was especially tragic because he had to leave his wife in spite of her beauty:

(111') [[omɨ:ya po:re(10)] wo:rɨi]] i-ʔwa t-apoi-ye   rɨ:po(12)
        beautiful more   woman 3-by prt-take-vn/a deficient

        'A most beautiful woman had in vain been taken by him'

Salience may also be conferred on a property directly by placing the particle
behind the adjective:

(127) [a:mu [tɨ-yaʔna-re-ng   rɨ:po(12)] we:we] s-ako:to-ya-0
       a   adj-hardness-adj-att deficient tree   13-cut.down-t-E

        'I am trying to cut down a hard tree, but its hardness defeats me'

An adjective plus particle construction may produce both the interpretatively
independent combination with *po:re* 'more, most' (111 above), and the
combination which for its ultimate interpretation depends on the remainder of
the sentence (127). In 111, *omɨ:ya po:re* 'most beautiful' can be understood on
its own, but *tɨyaʔnareng rɨ:po* 'hard plus deficient' cannot: the hardness of the
tree is only deficient in that it accounts for the failure of the cutter. The direct
syntactic relation between the adjective and *rɨ:po* 'deficient' only serves to
make the property of hardness salient; the unsuccessful attempt to cut down a
hard tree is presented with special atttention to the hardness of the tree.

3.4 THE MAXIMUM INTERPRETIVE DOMAIN OF THE PARTICLES. The conclusions
of the two preceding sections can be summarized as follows:

(i)   Non-modal particles form a constituent with a word of any class
      (and also with a nominal phrase or a postpositional phrase)
      when they immediately follow it (section 3.2).

(ii) The particles are not adverbs (implied by (i)).

(iii) Except for certain combinations with adjectives, a particle and its co-
      constituent cannot be interpreted autonomously, but depend on further
      information which, as a rule, is derived from the remainder of the
      utterance (section 3.3).

Together, (ii) and (iii) are responsible for some surprising cases of synonymy
and ambiguity that arise in sentences which contain both a finite verb and a non-
finite verb; the latter having syntactic properties which resemble those of nouns
and/or adjectives.

    Whenever a particle is added to one of the verbs in such a sentence, the
elements supplying 'further information' will include the other verb. This other
verb—finite or non-finite—may then have an overriding influence on the
ultimate interpretation of the particle, even masking that of the particle's
immediate verbal co-constituent. Compare, for instance, 129 and 130 below.
These two sentences occurred in a tape-recorded story in immediate succession

and express essentially the same message. After an earlier unsuccessful questioning, a girl demands to be told 'at last' by her prospective lover how he has managed to find her and her parents in the deep forest (Hoff 1968.308). In 130, *ko:u*(16) 'at last' is related to the finite verb 'you are going to tell it', where, in terms of ultimate interpretation, it belongs. In 129, it is related to the non-finite verb 'your having come', but still produces the same interpretation: 'at last you are going to tell it'.

(129) e:rome e:rome ro(18) [a-wo:pɨ-:po ko:u(16)] m-eka:ri:-sa-0 i-ʔwa
now now same 2-come-infp at.last 23-tell-t-E 1-to
'On this very moment, how you have come - at last you are going to tell it to me'

(130) a:a, e:rome :ne(19) a-wo:pɨ-:po [m-eka:ri:-sa-0 ko:u(16)] i-ʔwa
yes now no.other 2-come-infp 23-tell-t-E at.last 1-to
'Yes, now and at no other time, you are going to tell me at last how you have come'

In 129, 'your having come' is 'at last' in the sense that it refers to the story of the addressee's arrival that 'at last' will have to be told: 'your story at last—I demand to hear it'. The difference between 129 and 130 apparently boils down to the saliency-effect discussed in 3.3. It is impossible to render it in the English translations without introducing further differences (accentuation, marked word order) that are not found in the Carib originals.

Interviews with my present informant confirmed and amplified such observations from the recorded texts. Sentences that contain two verbs, one finite and one non-finite, are always ambiguous with respect to the particle that is attached to one of the two:

(131) [i-wo:pɨ-ri:-kon ra:pa(2)] 0-eka:no:-sa-n
3-come-cst-P again 3-expect-t-I

(132) i-wo:pɨ-ri:-kon [0-eka:no:-sa-n ra:pa(2)]

Both: 'He expected them to come again, to come back', and 'Again he expected them to come'

A similar, but more complicated, situation obtains when a full nominal is present which is an argument of the finite verb and is itself modified by a non-finite verb being used as an adjective:

(133) [[[mo:ro ka:reta] ra:pa(2)] uta:pɨ-hpo] s-epo:rɨ-i
that paper again lose-infp 13-find-r+E
'I found that lost paper again'

As shown by the translation, *ra:pa* 'again' cannot pertain to 'lost'—
apparently because *ra:pa* precedes the non-finite verb instead of immediately
following it; for when it does follow the non-finite verb, the same ambiguity is
found as in examples 131 and 132:

(134) [mo:ro ka:reta [uta:pɨ-hpo ra:pa(2)]] s-epo:rɨ-i

> s-epo:rɨ-i   [mo:ro ka:reta [uta:pɨ-hpo ra:pa(2)]]
> 13-find-r+E that   paper lose-infp   again

Both examples in 134 admit of either interpretation: 'I found the paper that
again had been lost', and 'Again I found the paper that had been lost, I found it
back'.

The interpretation 'found again', 'found back' may be blocked in two ways:
by separating *uta:pɨhpo ra:pa* and the finite verb by *ka:reta* 'paper' as in 135,
or by separating them with comma intonation as shown in 136.

(135) [mo:ro [uta:pɨ-hpo ra:pa(2)] ka:reta]] s-epo:rɨ-i
> that   lose-infp   again   paper   13-find-r+E
> Only: 'I found the paper that again had been lost'

(136) [mo:ro ka:reta [uta:pɨ-hpo ra:pa(2)]], s-epo:rɨ-i
> Only: 'I have found it, the paper that again had been lost'

Finally, exclusive scope of the particle may be guaranteed to both verbs
simply by repeating it after each verb:

(137) mo:ro ka:reta uta:pɨ-hpo ra:pa(2) s-epo:rɨ-i ra:pa(2)
> 'I found again that paper that again had been lost'.

All these observations confirm the findings of 3.2 and 3.3. The particles
bear a constituency relation to the element preceding them, which however
awards these elements no greater privilege than only some measure of salience;
their ultimate interpretation depends on further information drawn from the
sentence as a whole, and not just from the clause in which the particle occurs.
This maximum domain, coextensive with the sentence, can only be reduced by
typically ad-hoc devices: interposition of a noun, comma intonation, or
repetition of the particle.

4. THE CONTRIBUTION OF PROSODY

In the preceding section, placing the particle behind its co-constituent was
claimed to be a necessary and sufficient means for connecting the two
syntactically. Even where conspicuous accentuation plays a role in relating a
particle to a demonstrative or an adjective within a noun phrase, this role turns
out to be of an ancillary nature (3.2.2). In this respect, Carib differs fundamentally from languages like German and English, where 'focusing' expressed by

accentuation plays a central role in creating a special relation between particles like *only* and *auch* 'also', and a particular element or phrase elsewhere in the sentence (König 1987, Quirk et al. 1985.605).

For all that Carib differs from the other two languages in casting word order, not accentuation, in the leading role, it does not leave accentuation without any role at all. And even though this role is of a lesser status, it is of the same nature as found in English and German.

At least with some Carib particles, accentuation may be used to reinforce the relation between the particle and its syntactic co-constituent—a reinforcement which manifests itself semantically in narrowing-down the semantic reach of the particle: the meanings of the particle and the preceding element are integrated and interpreted semi-autonomously, with less dependence on substantiating information from the remainder of the sentence.

The effect is especially clear with *ʔne*(19) 'no other'. Other examples will be discussed later, in a wider context (5.2). With some particles the effect is so weak that I have been unable to get clear examples.

The highly frequent particle *ʔne* 'no other' is peculiar both semantically and phonologically. Semantically, it stands out by having the highest potential of all particles for contrastive employment. Because *ʔne* has the semantic feature of integration (section 2.1.4), such contrastive uses are of a highly global nature, pertaining to each and every conceivable alternative. This type of contrast permits semi-autonomous, adjective-like, interpretations, often trans-latable by 'the real one', 'really'.

Phonologiacally, *ʔne* is unique by the obligatory simplification of the initial cluster under accentuation. The glottal stop is deleted, or replaced by vowel length if the preceding word has its accent on the final vowel. The *e* of the particle itself is also lengthened and may furthermore carry a sustained high pitch level. For instance:

(138) [mo:ró :né:(19)] s-uku:-sa-0
        that   no.other 13-know-t-E
        'THAT, nothing else, is what I know'

Together, *ʔne*'s potential for contrast and its glottal stop deletion are responsible for an especially clear distinction between a narrower and a wider interpretation. When the double accentuation of 138 is absent and the particle thus retains its glottal stop, it becomes semantically dependent on 'substantiat-ing information' from the remainder of the sentence:

(139) [mo:ró ʔne(19)] s-uku:-sá-0
        that   no.other 13-know-t-E
        'That much do I know - nothing else is the case'

With double accentuation, as in 138, the domain of the particle is narrowed down to its co-constituent.[13]

Two idiomatic combinations produce even clearer examples of the narrowing effect of double accentuation. When the old tribal name *kari?na* 'Carib' came to include other Indians, and eventually even white and black people, *kari?na ?ne* obtained the special sense of 'true Carib'. In an analogous manner, *paru:ru ?ne* 'banana par excellence' became the name of the best-known kind of banana, *paru:ru* remaining the general name for all the many different plants of this type. In single-word utterances, for instance in citation, both idioms retain their glottal stops. In larger contexts, however, they can only keep their idiomatic meaning through double accentuation, which deletes their glottal stop.[14] Compare for instance:

(140) [kari?ná :né:(**19**)] ni-mondo-i!
      name   no.other 3-win-r+E
      'The Caribs have won!' (viz. the soccer game)

(141) [kari?ná ?ne(**19**)] ni-mondo-i
      name   no.other 3-win-r+E
      'The Indians really have won!'

The narrowing effect of double accentuation manifests itself in a special way when the particle follows a finite verb. Such verbs are semantically complex: in addition to a reference to some action, they also contain references to the participants involved. The former reference is expressed by the verbal lexeme as such, the latter by the personal prefix. When both the finite verb and the particle are accented, the semantic scope of the particle is narrowed down to the action expressed by the lexeme. When the particle has no accent, and so retains its glottal stop, it also encompasses the participant references, and so comes to qualify the entire event rather than the activity alone. Compare for instance:

(142) [si-nendo-yá-0 :né:(**19**)] mohko yopo:to
      13-respect-t-E solely   the   chief
      'I solely RESPECT the chief, my attitude towards the chief is: respect, nothing else'

(143) [si-nendo-yá-0 ?ne(**19**)] mohko yopo:to
      13-respect-t-E solely   the   chief
      'The plain and simple fact is that I respect the chief'

In cases like 143, finite verb and particle must precede the patient nominal; in cases like 142, they may either precede it or follow it. These facts will be discussed in 5.2 below.

5. EFFECTS ON CONSTITUENT ORDER

The normal constituent order in Carib is: (1) agent nominal, (2) patient nominal, (3) finite verb. When both agent and patient are third persons, the order patient nominal-verb is obligatory; otherwise, all deviating orders are permitted, producing only minor stylistic effects (Hoff 1978).

All this is only true when there is no particle. Though particles do not always affect the position of their co-constituents, they will do so under certain conditions. Such effects on constituent order have in common that they can always be characterized as anteposition: a **nominal** followed by a particle has to remain in its normal position before the verb and is no longer free to occupy the stylistically marked position behind it; a **finite verb** followed by a particle precedes the nominals, and thereby prefers an otherwise marked position to its normal position behind the nominals.[15]

Although particles appear to keep nominals in first position, and to bring verbs to first position, we are not dealing with a single phenomenon of anteposition. It will become clear that anteposition of nominals and anteposition of verbs are subject to quite different restrictions, which exclude the possibility of a unitary explanation:

(i)   With a nominal, the strength of the anteposition effect is the same for all particles. (It differs, however, for the different types of nominals: only the transitive agent is strongly affected).

(ii) With a verb, anteposition is restricted to particles that easily lend themselves to contrastive uses—the clearest cases being provided by *?ne*(19) 'no other'.

Nominal anteposition will be explained from an increase in the salience of the referent of the nominal, which is a consequence of the interpretive precedence which the particle bestows upon its co-constituent (cf. section 3.3). Verbal anteposition will be discussed in 5.2. It will be related to the earlier observations on the complex nature of the meaning of the finite verb and the narrowing effect of double, contrastive, accentuation (cf. section 4).

5.1 ANTEPOSITION OF NOMINALS BEFORE THE VERB. When a transitive agent nominal combines with a particle, it cannot be placed behind the verb but must be placed before it—which is the place normally taken by the agent nominal anyway. Sentences like 144, therefore, are not just stylistically marked, but are unacceptable.

(144) *we:we mi:ti 0-wo:-ya-n mohko Kuru:pi ra:pa(6)
      tree   root 3-hit-t-I   he   name   again

Acceptability can be restored either by omitting the particle or by placing the agent nominal together with the particle before the verb:

(145) mohko Kuru:pi ra:pa(6) we:we mi:ti 0-wo:-ya-n
      'Kuru:pi again was the one to hit the roots of the trees'

This avoidance of postposition is virtually obligatory with transitive agents only. With intransitive agents and with patients, there is at best a tendency to avoid postposition. On many occasions, it is true, the informant did feel that anteposition was desirable in order to improve utterances with post-verbal intrasitive agents or patients, but at other occasions he judged utterances like the following to be completely acceptable:

(146) n-e-pahka-i   mohko poinggo ra:pa(6)
      3-int-bring.out-r+I he   boar   again
      'The boar again has come out (of the bushes)'

(147) s-e:ta-i   ihpori:ri ke:ni po kaiku:si enggi ra:pa(6)
      13-hear-r+I creek   mouth at jaguar grunt again
      'At the mouth of the creek I heard the grunting of a jaguar again'

A tendency to prefer the position before the verb has also been observed with adverbs and postpositional groups when followed by a particle. Though acceptable in principle and occuring sporadically in texts, they too tended to provoke a correction from the informant when they were made to occur after the verb.

To explain anteposition of nominals before the verb, we should look for a factor that meets two conditions: (i) to some extent, it should influence all nonverbal constituents, not just agent and patient; (ii) only in the case of the transitive agent should it be fully effective.

The best candidate seems to be interpretive precedence. As discussed in section 3.3, the reference of an element directly related to a particle was found to possess interpretive precedence with regard to the synthesis of the semantic content of the utterance, including the specific contribution of the particle. In 145, for instance, the state of affairs is described as involving the **repeated** hitting of trees. This description is built up and presented from the perspective of the referent of the element before the particle: Kuru:pi, the constant factor in the repeated hittings.

The relation of an element to a particle thus results in a particular kind of salience for the referent of that element, namely that the state of affairs is described from this referent's perspective. Such salience may be conferred on animate and inanimate participants, and also on properties and circumstances.

The general tendency for any kind of constituent which contains a particle to avoid post-verbal positions, may now be seen as the natural consequence of the salience which particles confer upon the referents of their co-constituents. In and of itself, this salience effect is not strong enough to completely exclude post-verbal position. It does exclude this, however, in cases where it is joined by a second salience factor, viz. the natural predominance of transitive agents over patients and all other even less dynamic persons, entities, circumstances or properties. However, the natural salience of agents as originators of events only stands out in full relief when they are opposed to a less dynamic but otherwise similar counterpart: the patient (Kirsner 1979.150). And this explains why, in conjunction with interpretive precedence, only **transitive** agency really forces anteposition.

Forced anteposition because of the presence of a particle presupposes an undiminished semantic cohesion between agent and verb: in cases where the agent nominal is separated from patient and verb by means of comma intonation and added as a kind of afterthought, the utterance regains its full acceptability:

(144') we:we mi:ti 0-wo:-ya-n, mohko Kuru:pi ra:pa(**6**)

    tree   root   3-hit-t-I   he   name   again

    'He hits the roots of the trees - Kuru:pi again'

5.2 ANTEPOSITION OF THE VERB BEFORE THE NOMINALS. In stylistically unmarked utterances, the finite verb is generally found behind the participant nominals. When a particle is added to the verb, however, this otherwise normal order may produce unacceptable utterances. In such cases, the verb has to be placed before the nominals, in a position which otherwise is stylistically marked.

This anteposition effect of particles is subject to rather strong restrictions. In the first place, it is cancelled by comma intonation and also by double accentuation on both verb and particle. In the second place, it depends on the semantic character of the particle. With *?ne*(**19**) 'no other, nothing else' it is virtually categorical; with most other particles, in so far as they fit into contrastive contexts, it is at least a strong tendency. With two particles, *era:pa*(**2**) 'too' and *ra:pa*(**6**) 'again', which both have a very low potential for contrastive use, there is no forced anteposition at all.

The following examples illustrate the anteposition effect of *?ne*.

(148) *a:wu mohko yopo:to si-nendo-yá-0 *?ne*(**19**)

    I   the   chief   13-respect-t-E solely

(149) si-nendo-yá-0 *?ne*(**19**) a:wu mohko yopo:to

    13-respect-t-E solely   I   the   chief

    'The plain and simple fact is that I respect the chief'

As shown by the translation, here the particle encompasses both the activity and its participants. This wide semantic reach of unaccented *?ne* has already been discussed in section 4 (ex. 143).

The unacceptable constituent order in 148 can be made completely acceptable in either of two ways: by separating nominals and verb by comma intonation, as in 150; or by accentuating both the verb and the particle behind it, as shown in 151:

(150) a:wú,   mohko yopo:tó,   si-nendo-yá-0   ʔne(19)

     I   the   chief   13-respect-t-E   solely

     'I myself, I well and truly respect him, the chief'

(151) a:wu mohko yopo:to si-nendo-yá-0 :né:(19)
     I   the   chief   13-respect-t-E solely
     'I solely RESPECT the chief, my attitude towards the chief is: respect, nothing else'

The explanation for the remedial effect of comma intonation, I believe, lies in the same factor of weakened semantic cohesion that was invoked above to explain the acceptability of post-verbal agent nominals (section 5.1, ex. 144'). Explanations for the remedial effect of double accentuation, however, will have to take into account the special semantic effect of this accentuation, which consists in narrowing down the semantic scope of the particle to the verbal lexeme only (section 4, ex. 142). The relevance of this factor is confirmed by the fact that the anteposition effect itself is stronger in proportion to the potential of the particle for this kind of contrastive use.

For the sake of completeness, notice that a doubly accented verb-plus-:né: constituent is not confined to the position behind the nominals; as shown in 152 below, it can also appear before them. The difference between the two versions is of a stylistic nature: placement of the verb before the nominals adds a slight emotional colouring to the utterance (Hoff 1978). For ease of reference, I repeat the two other options and the unacceptable ordering:

(148) *a:wu mohko yopo:to si-nendo-yá-0 ʔne(19)
     I   the   chief   13-respect-t-E solely

(149) si-nendo-yá-0 ʔne(19) a:wu mohko yopo:to
     'The plain and simple fact is that I respect the chief'

(151) a:wu mohko yopo:to si-nendo-yá-0 :né:(19)

(152) si-nendo-yá-0 :né:(19) a:wu mohko yopo:to
     Both: 'I solely RESPECT the chief, my attitude towards the chief is: respect, nothing else'

The question remains: why is 148 unacceptable while the other three examples are fully acceptable? The answer, I believe, lies in the interaction of the following two factors: the different scopes of unaccented ʔne versus accented :né: and the general principle that the listener's full understanding of an utterance is partially determined by the things the speaker might have said instead, but did not actually say.

To begin with, notice that in 148 the agent pronominal a:wu 'I' and the patient nominal mohko yopo:to 'the chief' pass by without particles; these will be processed by the hearer before the verb and its accompanying particle present themselves. Now in keeping with the above principle, the very absence of a particle from the legitimate positions behind either agent or patient nominals strongly suggests that both participants are outside the semantic reach of any particle. Accordingly, when the verb finally appears together with a particle, a special relation is expected to obtain between the particle and the verbal lexeme, to the exclusion of the coreferential participant references encoded in the verbal prefix. But precisely this expectation is belied in 148, where the absence of double accentuation on the verb and the particle indicates that the particle encompasses participants and activity together. The resulting conflict, I suggest, explains the unacceptability of 148. Indeed, in 149, 151, and 152, all of which are perfectly acceptable, no such conflict arises. In 149, the reference to the activity and the participant references are firmly included together within the semantic scope of the particle, and the more precise identification of the participants by the following coreferent nominals comes too late to build up a bias towards the narrow interpretation. In both 151 and 152 there is no conflict either. If, in 151, the absence of a particle behind agent and patient suggests that both participants are outside the semantic reach of any particle, this suggestion turns out to be justified when the doubly accented combination of verb and particle appears - which demands precisely this interpretation. In 152, this same narrow interpretation agrees as well with the absence of a particle behind the participant nominals when the latter are placed behind the verb.

With most other particles, anteposition of the verb is a strong tendency rather than an obligation. The following examples with *po:ron*(15) 'posterior' parallel 148, 149, 151, and 152.

(153) ?*mo:se y-e:miiri   s-epa:nó:-sa-0 po:ron(15)
     this   1-daughter 13-help-t-E   posterior

(154) s-epa:nó:-sa-0 po:ron(15) mo:se y-e:miiri
     13-help-t-E   posterior   this   1-daughter
     'After having finished some other job, I am now helping my daughter'

(155) mo:se y-e:miiri s-epa:nó:-sa-0 po:ró::n(15)

(156) s-epa:nó:-sa-0 po:ró::n(15) mo:se y-e:miiri
     'After having carried out other activities on behalf of my daughter, I am now
     HELPING her'

Without accentuation, *po:ron* includes in its semantic scope the complete finite verb including both lexical meaning and participant references. It inspires the verb with the same dislike for its normal final position as *ʔne* does, though not so strongly: utterances without anteposition of the verb sometimes escaped condemnation by my informant (this never happened with *ʔne*).

In this respect, the majority of the particles behaves like *po:ron*. At the other extreme, there are two particles which never seem to require anteposition, viz. *era:pa*(2) 'too' and *ra:pa*(2) 'again'. These individuating particles, which indicate addition to an open group and to an open series respectively, hardly distinguish between narrower (only lexeme) and wider (the complete verb) interpretations. The fact that they were never found to influence the position of the verb can therefore be adduced in confirmation of the hypothesis that contrastive intonation, and the scope distinction related to it, are the crucial factors in the anteposition of the Carib verb.

6. CONCLUSION

Carib non-modal particles, like *era:pa* 'too' and *ro:ten* 'only', always form a constituent with the immediately preceding word or phrase (section 3.2). This syntactic relation is paralleled by a special semantic relation between the particle and its co-constituent, which manifests itself as a particular kind of interpretive primacy (3.3). This primacy falls far short of interpretive autonomy. The Carib equivalents of 'arrived too' or 'John only' differ from those of 'arrived late' or 'old John' by depending for their interpretation on additional information.   Such additional information is typically derived from the remainder of the sentence—not the clause—in which the particle occurs (3.4).

The non-modal particles, then, typically function in two dimensions. Syntactically and semantically, they have both a **special relation** to their co-constituent and a **wider relation** to the remainder of the sentence. I derived this notion of a syntagmatic duality from the flourishing West-German school of particle research, represented by Weydt, König, and many others inside and outside Germany. An evaluation of the present findings on the Carib particles, therefore cannot ignore the work done on the so-called degree particles of German. For many observations, moreover, parallels can be found in the English grammars by Quirk et al. (1972, 1985).

As the Carib non-modal particles and their German translations belong to the same semantic type, they are also subject to the same syntagmatic duality. In both languages, the 'special relation' is found side by side with the 'wider relation': the latter is indispensible because of the dependence of the particles on 'additional information'. Syntactically, however, the expression of this syntagmatic duality in the two languages is accomplished through highly different structures. In German, *auch* 'too', *nur* 'only', etc., are adverbs—just like their English equivalents.   From their high position in constituent hierarchy, adverbs have easy access to all other elements within the same clausal structure. Constituent structure therefore is the obvious channel for supplying the particles with 'additional information'. Indeed, the wider domain of the particles, called their Skopus in the German literature, is coextensive with the clause they belong to, whether main or dependent (König 1987).

The nature of the 'special relation' between the particles and one particular word or phrase—called their Fokus in the German literature—is less clear. The suggestion that the particles and their Fokus are simply joined in constituency has been rejected for both German and English on the basis of a number of arguments (cf. König 1987, Jacobs 1983.40-72, Quirk et al. 1972.431-432). Whatever the nature of the relation, its overt expression appears to be highly complex. Relative order of the particle and its Fokus apparently plays a role in German and English, but there is no single, simple order rule that is valid for each individual particle. Also, other words may separate the particle from the word or phrase it is especially related to, as shown in the following example (from Quirk et al. 1985.605):

(157) the girls *especially* objected to HIS MÀNNERS

Obviously, prosody is responsible here for indicating the special relation between *especially* and its Fokus *his manners*—a phrase which also is the focus of the utterance in terms of information structure (Quirk et al. 1985.605). It certainly is for good reasons that the German linguists use the term Fokus to refer to the element that the particle is related to, and that Quirk et al. call the English counterparts 'focusing subjuncts' (1985.604). However, focusing in this sense is not always a dependable instrument for marking the special relation between the particles and one particular word or phrase. As Daneš has pointed out, a German subject referring to a 'known' person and lacking any conspicuous accentuation is not 'focus' in the accepted sense, but can still be the element that has the special relation to the particle. In each of the following examples, *Peter* is related to *auch* 'too'; but only in the first two is *Peter* also the focus in the traditional sense (examples from Daneš (1981.92-93; I have added accent marks in accordance with the explanations on these pages).

(158) auch Pèter hat einen Wagen
    too   has a   car

(159) Pèter hat auch einen Wagen
    has too a   car

Both: 'Peter too has a car' (answers the question: 'are there any other car owners?')

(160) Peter hat aùch einen Wagen
    has too a   car
'As for Peter here, he ALSO has a car'

By way of a provisional conclusion, we may say that languages like English and German manage to indicate the special relation between non-modal adverbs and one particular word or phrase by a complex mixture of cues including word order and accentuation. In contrast, Carib primarily relies upon one simple syntactic rule to achieve the same purpose. Accentuation plays a supplementary role, at best, in narrowing down the semantic reach of the particles to the lexical morpheme inside the finite verb (section 4). Finally, if we compare the situation in Carib with that in the other two languages, we may observe that one and the same semantic task is carried out with highly similar overt means of expression (order, prosody), through highly dissimilar linguistic structures. The fact that Carib particles are not adverbs, but have their positions inside the major constituents, manifests itself indirectly in their influence on constituent order (section 5).

NOTES

* The research for this paper was part of the Leiden University research project 'Structural properties of language and language use,' financed by the Dutch Ministry of Education. It was also supported in part by NSF Grant No. BNS-8617854, NEH Grant No. RX-20870-87, and the University of Oregon Foundation. The paper was presented at the Working Conference on Amazonian Languages, held at the University of Oregon in August, 1987. I am grateful to my co-participants for critical comments, especially to Doris Payne, Daniel Everett, and two anonymous referees, who provided extensive written comments. For criticism at earlier and later stages, I owe thanks to Jan Kooij, my former teacher Bob Uhlenbeck, and Sjef Schoorl. The latter is entitled to a double share, as he not only helped me to improve the contents of the paper, but also went to great pains to improve its English expression.

Abbreviated interlinear morpheme glosses are: *J.* ambiguous segment, expressing either of two values; *.+.* fused segment, expressing two values; **1,2,3,1&2** first, second, third person, first and second person (inclusive dual 'we'); **3id** third person identical with agent; **12** etc. first person agent, second person patient, etc.; **adj** adjectivizer/adverbalizer; **att** affix for attributive form of adjective/adverb; **cst** constructed state; **E** extraspective evidentiality; **f** future tense; **I** introspective evidentiality; **inf** infinitive; **infp** perfective infinitive; **imp** imperative; **int** intransitivizer; **irr** irrealis mode; **neg** negative; **nom** nominalizer; **nrel** non-related; **p** past tense; **P** plural; **pia** the participant which is identified by a preceding prefix or nominal is the agent, not the patient; **ptc** participle; **r** realis mode; **S** strong evidentiality; **t** unmarked, present, tense; **vn/a** nominal or adjectival on a verbal base; **vrb** verbalizer.

[1] The Carib language (from which the name of the Cariban language family derives), is spoken by some 10,000 Indians in Venezuela, Guyana, Surinam, French Guiana, and north-eastern Brazil. The basis for the present paper was laid during a period of fieldwork in Surinam, in the late 1950's when I identified twenty-two of the twenty-four non-modal particles. I missed *kopo:re* 'excessive', and failed to distinguish *ko* 'salient' from a homonym. Also, at that time I had no opportunity for a serious semantic study. In the word index

of Hoff 1968 the English glosses of the particles provide just crude translation equivalents, such as seemed to fit their occurrences in the texts. When Robert Kiban, one of my informants in the fifties, later came to live in the Netherlands, we gave our undivided attention to the non-modal particles for more than two years (1984-1987). Starting from the texts I had collected in Surinam (most of them published in 1968), Mr. Kiban and I experimented substituting particles for each other and shifting their positions. While I attempted to test my hypotheses, Mr. Kiban increased the data with his own examples and recordings. He also was the first to sense the distinction integrative/individuating (section 2.1), when he characterized certain particles as being like an *ituhpo*, a pool with fishes in it, and others like a point.

Mr. Kiban was born in Bigi Poika, near Saramacca River in the central part of Surinam. His dialect differs phonologically from that of Western Surinam, which set the standard for my book of 1968. Here, I have modified my spelling in accordance with Mr. Kiban's pronunciation.

It will be obvious that the help of my informants—both in Surinam and later in The Netherlands—has been even more essential than that of my fellow-linguists. I once more express my gratitude to all of them, and especially to Mr. Kiban who is exceptionally able. There is now a small community of Caribs in The Netherlands. With characteristic confidence and determination, they have set up a society for keeping their language and culture alive—even in Europe. In this society, which is called 'Tukayana', Mr. Kiban plays a key role.

[2]   These terms will be explained presently. 'Integration' has some similarity to the notion of scalarity (Foolen 1983). It differs by being more general: because 'integration' lacks directionality, it can be a feature of both negative ('restrictive') and positive ('additive') particles.

[3]   In 40 and 41 these are from *e:ne* 'to see' and *wo:pɨ* 'to come'. The negating affix is *-hpa*. On the personal prefix *an-* and on *w*-deletion, see Hoff 1968(140,149).

[4]   Salience, a term borrowed from psycholinguistics, is used here in the sense of ad hoc mental prominence: in the mind of the speaker of a particular utterance, one of the referents involved is more prominently present than the others. Equivalents or near-equivalents for a salient referent in the linguistic literature are: foregrounded referent, referent in the centre or in the focus of speaker's attention or interest, referent the speaker empathizes with. See Ertel 1977.163-165, Zubin 1979.474,477,500, Kirsner 1976.390, idem 1979.92-99 and passim, Van Valin and Foley 1980.338-339, Kuno 1976.432.

In all these studies, salience is the proper semantic correlate of the nominative case (Zubin) or of the grammatical subject. As neither of the two is available in Carib, the role of indicating salience was free to be taken by a particle. Because of this different grammatical carrier, salience in Carib is not reserved for participants, but may incidentally also be conferred on attributes or activities. The essential identity of Carib salience with the subject-linked salience of other languages, however, is confirmed by its tendency to correlate with agency, coupled with a predilection for front position (this same section, below).

The freedom to relate not just *ko* but any particle to either one or the other participant provides a second source of salience, be it of a slightly different type; see sections 3.3 and 5.1.

[5] Note that the combination of *ko* with patient is not actually impossible. It may be found with all other finite verbs that lack the ambiguity exemplified in 72. For instance:

mohko ko(17) kɨs-uku:tɨ-i
he   salient 1&2/3-know-r+E
'He is the person we both know'

[6] On reduction of the glottal stop in *ʔne* under accent, see section 4.

[7] All four sequences of a positive and a negative individuating particle, or of a positive and a negative integrative particle, were categorically rejected by the informant: *ro te, *te ro, *ko ʔne, *ʔne ko. Apparently, they are too flatly contradictory. All four sequences of an individuating particle followed by an integrative one are fully acceptable and in fact occur frequently: *ro ʔne, ro ko, te ʔne,* and *te ko.* Such a sequence precisely identifies the referent of its co-constituent, and then relates it to a wider cognitive context. For instance: A: 'so Kurupi has been your teacher?' B: *a:a, Kuru:pi ró ʔne ye:me:pai* 'yes, this same Kurupi and no other taught me'.

On sequences in the opposite order (an integrative particle followed by an individuating one) I could not obtain conclusive data. While *ʔne te* tended to be accepted, *ko te* and *ko ro* did less well. Remarkably, the triplet *te ko ro* appeared to be fully acceptable, more so than *ko ro.* The pair *ʔne ro* appeared to have fused phonologically to produce a new particle *ne:ro* as in *para:nakɨ:rɨ ne:ro* 'a typical white person'.

[8] An apparent antonym of *manombo* is *seʔme* 'though, materialized in spite of some counteracting factor'. Because *seʔme* accepts a prefixed *i-* 'it', producing *iseʔme* 'in spite of it', it is better viewed as a morphologically defective postposition (compare *i-ta* 'in it'), than as a non-modal particle.

[9] There is always a preceding element, except in laconic rejoinders of the kind: 'So, he became angry?' 'Again!' Two further exceptions are of a different, more clearly idiomatic, kind. When one comes across something useful in abundance, it is appropriate to simply exclaim: *kopo:re!* The other expression is a standard comment on easy promises: *rɨ:po ra:pa!* '(it will turn

out to be) ineffective again!' Here we even have two particles, the second specifying the first.

[10] In this and the following examples, constituent structure is indicated only so far as it is relevant to the present discussion. It is neither possible nor necessary to present a full analysis here.

[11] Though completely different in origin, the present type of salience-by-precedence is virtually equivalent with the kind of salience produced by the particle *ko*(17). In the first part of the present paper (section 2.1.4, especially footnote 4 and examples 69 ff), we claimed that *ko* indicates that the referent of its co-constituent is in the centre of the speaker's attention. Salience in this sense of psychological centrality has been identified by several authors as the constant semantic correlate of either the nominative case or the grammatical subject. Remarkably, the semantic correlate of the subject has also been defined in terms that recall the present notion of salience-by-interpretive-precedence. According to Dik, subject function is assigned according to 'priority with respect to how the state of affairs is presented'. In this view, states of affairs are 'presented from the point of view or perspective of one of the participating entities', and subject function is assigned to the nominal which happens to refer to this entity (1978.71,143). Ertel actually mentions both views of salience, and explicitly relates them as two phases of the same process. First, he characterizes the referent of the subject nominal as the entity which is 'closer to the ego' than others within the 'cognitive field' of the speaker, and then goes on to say that the speaker creates this asymmetry 'to give his sentence a primary reference point' (1977.161). I therefore feel justified in subsuming both 'prominence by centrality' and 'prominence by priority' under the single name of salience.

It remains to specify relevant differences between Carib and those languages which use the grammatical subject for expression of salience. With the latter, the expression of salience is both obligatory and relative. Since most sentences contain a subject and one or even more objects, etc., salience may reduce to just relative topicality (Ertel 1977.165). In Carib, one is completely free to add *ko*(17) or not; therefore it will only be used when salience is clearly and positively present. Salience-by-precedence is somewhat more relative and less free, since the speaker must choose one particular scope element to which to attach any particle he wishes to use. Yet even here he may remain largely neutral by attaching the particle to the finite verb where it encompasses both participants together with the activity. Furthermore, Carib differs from the other languages by the fact that both *ko* and precedence may grant salience to other entities than just participant nominals.

Finally, I should like to stress that even though salience and topicality may often converge and even coincide for practical purposes, they are not the same. The first occupies an extreme position in a continuum of 'role prominence', the second in an essentially different continuum of 'referential prominence' (Riddle and Steintuch 1963). We have no room here for further discussion of this important issue.

[12] Under special conditions it may confer salience on the activity alone (sections 4 and 5.2).

[13] This is the real background of the marginal contrast between glottal stop and vowel length in *ʔne* and *:ne*, which I described in Hoff (1968.93, footnote 39) but could not explain at the time.

[14] Alternatively, retention of the glottal stop and idiomatic interpretation may be reconciled if *ʔne* is shielded from the effect of the accent by an added demonstrative, for instance *e:ro* 'this' in *paru:rú ʔne*(19) *e::ró sena:sa* 'I am eating this true banana'.

[15] For a second factor which imposes on verbs the otherwise marked position before the agent nominal, see Hoff 1986 (p.78-80). This factor is restricted to third person future extraspective verbs.

REFERENCES

Daneš, František. 1981. Eine Bemerkung zur Intonation im Textaufbau. *Satzsemantische Komponenten und Relationen im Text*. Ed. by František Daneš and Dieter Viehweger, 88-96. Praha: Ustav pro jazyk český.

Dik, Simon C. 1978. *Functional grammar*. Amsterdam: North Holland.

Dooley, Robert A. 1982. Options in the pragmatic structuring of Guarani sentences. *Language* 58.307-331.

Ertel, Suitbert. 1977. Where do the subjects of sentences come from? *Sentence production, developments in research and theory*. Ed. by Sheldon Rosenberg, 141-167. Hillsdale, N.J.: Erlbaum.

Foolen, Ad. 1983. Zur Semantik und Pragmatik der restriktiven Gradpartikeln: only, nur, und maar/alleen. *Partikeln und Interaktion*. Ed. by Harald Weydt (Reihe germanistische Linguistik 44). Tübingen: Max Niemeyer.

Hoff, Berend Jacob. 1968. *The Carib language* (Verhandelingen van het Koninklijk Instituut voor Taal-, Land-, en Volkenkunde 55) [The Hague: Nijhoff] Dordrecht/Providence: Foris.

Hoff, Berend Jacob. 1978. The relative order of the Carib finite verb and its nominal dependents. *Studies in fronting*. Ed. by Frank Jansen, 11-27. Dordrecht/Providence: Foris.

Hoff, Berend Jacob. 1986. Evidentiality in Carib. *Lingua* 69.49-103.

Jacobs, Joachim. 1983. *Fokus und Skalen: zur Syntax und Semantik der*

Gradpartikel im Deutschen (Linguistische Arbeiten 138). Tübingen: Max Niemeyer.

Kirsner, Robert S. 1976. On the subjectless 'pseudo-passive' in Standard Dutch and the semantics of background agents. *Subject and topic*. Ed. by Charles N. Li, 385-415. New York-London: Academic Press.

Kirsner, Robert S. 1979. *The problem of presentative sentences in Dutch*. Amsterdam: North Holland.

König, Ekkehard. 1987. Gradpartikeln. *Handbuch der Semantik*. Ed. by Arnim von Stechow and Dieter Wunderlich. Königstein: Athenäum.

Kuno, Susumo. 1976. Subject, theme, and the speaker's empathy. *Subject and topic*. Ed. by Charles N. Li, 417-444. New York-London: Academic Press.

Labov, William. 1970/1977. On the adequacy of natural languages: the development of tense. LAUT, series B 23. Trier.

Quirk, Randolph, Sidney Greenbaum, Geoffrey Leech, and Jan Svartvik. 1972. *A grammar of contemporary English*. London: Longman.

Quirk, Randolph, Sidney Greenbaum, Geoffrey Leech, and Jan Svartik. 1985. *A comprehensive grammar of the English language*. London-New York: Longman.

Reichling, A.J.B.N. 1935. *Het woord, een studie omtrent de grondslag van taal en taalgebruik*. (Reprint 1967.) Zwolle: Tjeenk Willink.

Riddle, Elisabeth, and Gloria Steintuch. 1983. A functional analysis of pseudo-passives. *Linguistics and Philosophy* 6.527-563.

Van Valin, Robert D. and William A. Foley. 1980. Role and Reference Grammar. *Syntax and semantics 13. Current approaches to syntax*. Ed. by Edith A. Moravcsik and Jessica R. Wirth, 329-352. New York-London: Academic Press.

Weydt, Harald (ed.). 1983. *Partikeln und Interaktion (Reihe germanistische Linguistik 44)*. Tübingen: Max Niemeyer.

Zubin, David A. 1979. Discourse function of morphology: the focus system in German. *Syntax and semantics 12. Discourse and syntax*. Ed. by Talmy Givón, 469-504. New York-London: Academic Press.

Zwicky, Arnold M. 1985. Clitics and particles. *Language* 61.283-305.

Cause and Reason
in Nambiquara

Ivan Lowe

INTRODUCTION

The object of this paper is to explore the concepts of cause and reason in the Nambiquara[1] language. Owing to limitations of space I am restricting myself to relationships between propositions realised by clauses, as even this involves looking at extensive data on four different morphemes and their discourse functions. These do, in fact, cover most of the instances where it is necessary to express the concept of cause or reason. I shall specifically omit any reference to constructions involving causative stems derived from verb roots by a causative affix. Although such causative stems can be elicited, one can go through hundreds of pages of Nambiquara text of various genres without finding a single instance of one. Evidentials are also related to causality; these have been dealt with in a previous paper (Lowe 1972).

The first step in the investigation is to attempt a definition of cause. This is not a simple task, as philosophers are by no means agreed as to what cause is and no linguist has, to my knowledge, defined it either. Following and adapting the ideas of Anscombe 1971, I present for the purposes of this paper the following definition:

A cause and effect relationship will be said to obtain between two phenomena if the second phenomenon (the effect) can be regarded, according to cultural norms, as being derived from the first (the cause).

Two things need to be noted here. The first is that effects derive from, arise out of, come out of their causes. (Anscombe's wording). The second is that cause and effect relationships are culturally oriented. Such relationships are not really 'out there' in the real world; rather they are something that the speaker introduces into his description of a situation through the medium of language; what he introduces will depend on his viewpoint—a culturally oriented viewpoint.

It is important to note that the effect is to be thought of as 'derived from' the cause rather than 'determined by' the cause. Anscombe has worded this very carefully and I adopt the wording quite deliberately here because even normal colloquial English is replete with data where the relationship between cause and effect is certainly not deterministic but could be appropriately described as being derivative. In the Nambiquara data which will be presented in this paper, almost all the examples show the weaker or derivative relationship between cause and effect; few show the stronger, deterministic relationship. The weaker relationship appears to be a much more realistic one to work with in describing natural language data; it seems that the deterministic relationship is too strong and best restricted to its use in the discussion of certain physical systems like Newtonian mechanics.

Clearly, the term 'derive' is still vague. The perceptive reader will ask, "By what principle or principles is the derivation done?" In other words, "How do we know when we have a derivative relationship and when we do not?" I shall endeavour to show that in Nambiquara the principle that needs to be invoked is that of cultural expectation, so that given a cause, there is a cultural expectation that a certain effect will follow.

Different from, but related to, the idea of cause and effect is that of reason. A reason is the speaker's way of justifying an action or attitude in terms of a set of beliefs, values or principles. In other words, a reason can be thought of as an interpretation of an action or a situation in terms of such beliefs, etc. (see Davidson, 1963). Reasons, like causes, are culturally oriented[2].

I will now give a brief outline of the argument of this paper. In Nambiquara, four morphemes[3], namely -*jau³*-, -*jut³*-, -*kxai³*-, -*kxe³*- figure centrally in expressing the interclausal relationship of cause/reason. Each one of these morphemes occurs in two-clause constructions which can be faithfully translated as expressing a cause or reason relationship. There is the added complication, however, that each one of these morphemes is used in other contexts where a causal relationship does NOT seem to be present.

The question I address that is central to the argument of this paper is 'What is the meaning of each of these morphemes?' Clearly, it will not do to gloss them all as 'cause' or 'reason' because such a description would not only distort the data where a causal relationship is not present, but would also neutralise any difference there might be between the meanings of the four morphemes. However, if one can find a separate, consistent unitary meaning for each of them, avoiding the terms 'cause' and 'reason' themselves as far as possible in the description, then these meanings should give valuable information on the Nambiquara view of cause/reason.

Two of the morphemes, namely -*jau³*- and -*jut³*- have well defined basic concrete meanings (which can be elicited from a good native informant), and their more abstract meanings, which are the ones used to express cause/reason, can be easily related to the more basic ones. Their analyses are given in sections 1 and 2. The morpheme -*kxe³*- dealt with in section 4, is a purely grammatical suffix whose function will be clearly defined there.

There remains the morpheme -*kxai³*- which is both the one that is found in the greatest variety of contexts and also the one that plays easily the greatest part in expressing the interclausal relation of cause/reason. Owing to its abstract nature, it is unfortunately not possible to elicit a basic concrete meaning for this morpheme from any native informant. In the analysis of -*kxai³*- given in section 3 of this paper, I look at its apparently different meanings in its different contexts of usage and from these I show that the idea of 'compatible' is present whenever the morpheme -*kxai³*- occurs. In particular, subsections 3.1 to 3.3 deal with the morpheme -*kxai³* occuring on nouns; here the compatibility means merely 'compatibility with the preceding linguistic context.' Subsections 3.4 and 3.5 deal with the morpheme sequence -*ha²kxai³*; here I show that it has the meaning 'extralinguistically or culturally compatible' and illustrate the function of this sequence in both clause and paragraph coordination. Such constructions in Nambiquara follow the principle that only culturally compatible activities can be expressed as coordinate. Finally, in subsection 3.6, I look at the morpheme sequence *xne³ha²kxai³*, showing that it has the meaning of 'compatible with cultural expectation' and illustrating its use in expressing the relationship of cause/reason in clause pairs.

Once one has arrived at the overall meaning of 'compatible' for -*kxai³*, the more specialised meanings of the sequence -*ha²kxai³* as 'culturally compatible' in coordination, and of the connective *xne³ha²kxai³* as 'compatible with cultural expectation' in cause/reason clause pairs are seen to be related to this overall meaning. Thus the motivation for the occurence of -*kxai³* in coordinate constructions and in the connective joining cause/reason pairs becomes transparent.

The analysis presented in this paper must start with the assumption that each of the morphemes above has a unitary meaning, even though the same morpheme may appear to have different meanings in different contexts. Such an assumption is justified provided it leads to consistent and insightful descriptions of the function of each morpheme. The danger of assigning disparate glosses for the same surface morpheme in different contexts is that each one of these disparate glosses will be assigned from an English speaker's point of view; until one struggles to find what, if anything, they have in common, the foreign viewpoint will be all that one has.

1. JAU³SXU² AND CAUSALITY

The morpheme -*jau³*- has the basic meaning of thought or 'idea', but has an extended sense which when used in the right morphosyntactic environment means 'mental motivation' for an action. It thus expresses one kind of causality.

1.1 *JAU³* EXPRESSING THOUGHT OR IDEA. First I give some examples of -*jau³*- expressing only its basic meaning of thought or idea. (There is no expression of causality here.)

(1) e^3-a^1-jau^3-xa^2

speak-I-words-specific=nom

'The words that I speak.'

(This is a very common way for a speaker to refer to what he has just spoken.)

In exs. 2 and 3, the nominalizer *na^1-jau^3-sxu^2* '1p-word-general=nom' means 'my thoughts' and is followed immediately by any suffix string which could be found on a finite verb. These suffix strings are *to^{3}ha^{1}tait^{1}tit^{2}tu^{3}wa^2* 'I have told you this repeatedly before', and *na^{1}hē^{2}ra^2* 'what was inside me (i.e. my thoughts)', respectively. Note that in these examples, there is no verb stem attached to the suffix string. In the morphosyntactic environment so described, *na^{1}jau^{3}sxu^2* serves simply to report the thoughts of the speaker.

(2) Context: A group of Nambiquara had been working, preparing an airstrip, but up to this point the speaker had done no work at all. He is speaking of his obligation to the rest of the group.

    1. xne^{3}ha^{2}kxai^3 kāi^2-xn^3-jut^{3}ta^{3}li^3 ī^{3}sa^{2}tā^3-kxain^1-nū^3-na^1-tū^{1}xā^1

      therefore   big -neg-work   throw-at them-also-I-intend

    2. kāun^{2}jen^{3}ta^3 ā^{3}wa^{2}su^1-ja^{1}xnēn^2-xn^3-nha^{2}khi^3

      airstrip   free-soon-neg-undesirable

    3. na^1-jau^{3}sxu^2 to^3-ha^1-tait^{1}ti^{2}tu^{3}wa^2

      my-THOUGHTS repeat-I-past.collective

Free translation: 'Therefore, *3.* my THOUGHTS ARE as follows: *1.* I intend to do a little bit of work for them. *2.* It is very undesirable for us not to be free from the (burden of) the airstrip soon'.

(3) *1.* hāun^{2}xwān^{3}ta^3 ha^{3}lo^{2}yut^{3}ta^2 e^3-a^1-jut^{3}txa^2-kxai^3

    later   the situation talk-I-situation-compatible

    2. ā^{3}nī^2-xna^{2}hxā^{3}nhi^2 *3.* na^1-jau^{3}sxu^2 na^1-hē^2-ra^2

    look at-deep want   my-THOUGHTS I-internal-comp asp

Free translation: '*1.* The things that I talked about, *2.* I want very much to take a good look at. *3.* These are my THOUGHTS'.

1.2 *JAU^{3}SXU^2* AS MENTAL MOTIVATION FOR AN ACTION. In exs. 4 to 7, the nominaliser *na^{1}jau^{3}sxu^2* still means 'my thoughts', but now it is followed by a main (finite) verb with its own stem and its own finite suffix string. In this morphosyntactic environment, the *na^{1}jau^{3}sxu^2* not only reports the thoughts of the speaker, but also tells us that these thoughts are the MENTAL MOTIVA-TION for the action (or lack of action) described by the main verb. There is thus a derivative relationship between the mental motivation and the action as the definition of causality in the introduction requires; the action derives from or arises from the mental motivation.

(4) *1.* xyãn¹ta¹ ha³lo²-ai²li² wẽ³-hai²li² xwã³-yu³ra²
    but   weather-this rain-this   come-signs.of

  2. xne³ha²kxai³ a³li³tat³-sa²-te³-lin²na¹
     therefore   cold.soak -me-about.to-deductive

  3. na¹jau³sxu²   ã³-sxã³ xĩ³xĩ²-na¹-ra²
     my-THOUGHTS leave-seq come back-I-comp=asp

Free translation: '*1.* But I saw the rain coming. *2.* Therefore I thought "It looks as if I'm going to get soaked." *3.* SO WITH THESE THOUGHTS, I left and came home'.

The *na¹jau³sxu²* is a quote margin for the thought 'It looks as if I'm going to get soaked', and this thought is the motivation for his leaving and coming home, expressed in the main verb *ã³sxã³ xĩ³-xĩ²-na¹-ra²* 'I left and came home'.

(5) Context: The speaker had been talking about plans to take a long journey on foot, but now he has second thoughts.

  1. kwxa² wẽ³ha³lxai²li² ã³-sxã³   xai³la³kxi²nha¹ha³tã¹
     random this.child   leave-seq walk.all.over.cautionary

  2. na¹-jau³sxu²   ã³la³kxi²-na¹-tait¹ti²nhe³
     my -THOUGHTS abandon-I-past.collective

Free translation: '*1.* I thought "I don't want to leave my child and go wandering all over the place." *2.* WITH THESE THOUGHTS, I gave up the plan (to take the journey on foot)'.

(His thoughts were his motivation for his abandoning the plan.)

(6) Context: The speaker had been talking about working and getting trade goods as pay. But there didn't seem to be any trade goods in evidence.

  1. kwxa² hxi²tha³-xnha²-na¹-hat³tã¹   *2.* na¹-jau³sxu²
     random tired-reflexive-I-cautionary   my-THOUGHTS

  wa³kon³-ye¹-xn²-si¹-xna³-wa²
  work -for-you-1pp-neg-incom=asp

Free translation: '*1.* I thought "I want to avoid tiring myself out for nothing." *2.* WITH THESE THOUGHTS, we are not working for you'.

(His fear of tiring themselves out for no pay was what made them desist from working.)

(7) *1.* na¹-kxai²nãn²txu² ĩ³ye³ha³txe²kxi²khaix³na¹xã¹
    I-if   I.really.clean.the.land

  2. hãun²xwãn³na¹te³nãu³a¹sa²kxai³lhu² sxa³-su³
     later   remain-shoots

  su¹-ai²nãn²ta³ wã²nãu²-li¹kxi²-na¹-ha²kxai³ na¹-tũ¹xã¹
  shoots-these break -bury -I -therefore   I-intend

3. na¹-jau³sxu²   ãu²-a¹-tait¹ti²tu³wa²
   my-THOUGHTS gather-I-past.collective

Free translation: '*1*. My thinking is: "I'll really clear the land. 2. Then later, I intend to plant these manioc shoots that are here." *3*. WITH THESE THOUGHTS, I gathered the manioc shoots'.

(His plan for clearing the land and gathering the manioc shoots was his mental motivation for his actually gathering them.)

2. JUT³SU² AND CASUALITY

The morpheme -*jut³*- 'situation' is also a morpheme that figures in signalling causal relationships in the appropriate contexts. Like -*jau³*-, it can be suffixed with a specific noun ending -*txa²* (an allomorph of the specific noun ending -*xa²*- used with -*jau³*- in the preceding section). The resulting sequence -*jut³txa²* always has the concrete meaning of either a specific time (ex. 8), or a specific location (exs. 9, 10), or a situation that has already been referred to in the preceding linguistic context (exs. 11, 12).

The same -*jut³*- can also be suffixed with a general noun ending -*su²* and prefixed with the substitute verb *xne³*- 'thus'. The resulting sequence *xne³jut³su²* comes between two main clauses, each with its own finite verb; in this morphosyntactic environment it has the meaning of the **general** situation reached at the point in the narrative where it was mentioned.

2.1 *JUT³* AS TIME AND LOCATION. In the examples of this subsection the -*jut³*-marking is specific and the noun so marked refers to either a time or a location.

(8) to³mĩn²kax³-ne³-jut³txa² ã³wi³-xi²-sĩn¹na¹-hẽ³-ra²
    Sunday -THAT-TIME   enter-again-1ppsubj-past-comp=asp
    Free translation: 'THAT SUNDAY we reentered the village'.

(9) ha³lo²a² ai³-ten³sa²te³-sxã³   kĩ³na² wi¹-jut³txa²
    land   go-look.round-sequ soil good-PLACE

    ã³ya³ti²-na¹-jut³txa² ã³xyau³-ya¹-xn²ta¹-i¹
    find-I-PLACE   stay-before-1pS.2pO-incomp=asp

    Free translation: 'I'll go round looking at the land, and the PLACES with good soil that I find, there I'll stay (before you)'.

Here, the *jut³txa²* refers to the PLACE where he finds good land and so has the idea of LOCATION. The idea of location also applies in the next example.

(10) ha³lo²a² ã²wi¹lhĩn¹khai¹xa² xwã³-sxã³-xyau³-ain¹-jut³txa²
     PLACE the.beginning   come-seq-live-they-PLACE

     ĩ²-te³-lai¹-na¹-hẽ³-ra²
     see-want-them-I-past-comp=asp

     Free translation: 'I wanted to see them at the PLACE where they came to live at the very beginning'.

The word *ha³lo²a²* is a lexical noun that means 'place' or 'time' or 'situation' or 'weather' in different contexts.

2.2 *JUT³* AS SITUATION NOMINALISER. In the examples of this subsection, *-jut³*-comes as a nominalizer on a lexical verb and it means 'situation' rather than 'time' or 'location'.

(11) *1.* xĩ³-ya³hin¹-kxa²-si³yo³na¹   *2.* xai³-la¹-jut³txa³la³
     go-you.two-of-back   walk-I-SITUATION

     ten³-sa²-xnãn³-nha²-wa²
     want-1pO-neg-internal-incompl=asp

Free translation: '*1.* While you (two) are gone, *2.* I don't want to go walking. (literally: You two being gone and I behind you, I don't want the SITUATION of my going walking)'.

(12) *1.* a²yen³kxa²   e³-kxi²-sa²hin¹-jut³txa²-kxai³la¹
          trade.goods talk-to-you.to.me-SITUATION-compatible

     2. wã²nũ¹hain³-nha¹-tu¹-wa²
          deliberate-I-future-incompl=asp

Free translation: '*1.* The SITUATION about trade goods, then, that you talked to me about, *2.* I will deliberate on'.

(For an explanation of the gloss of *-kxai³la¹* as 'compatible' see section 3.)

2.3 *JUT³* AS A NON CAUSAL SITUATION. In the examples of the two subsections 2.3 and 2.4, the morpheme *-jut³*- appears in the connective *xne³jut³-sxu²* 'thus-situation-general noun', or in its variant *jut³su²*. Here, *-xne³*- 'thus' is a proverb or substitute verb. The connective itself comes between two main clauses, each with its own finite verb. In this morphosyntactic environment, the *xne³jut³sxu²* means 'the general situation defined by the preceding linguistic context.' Such a situation can be thought of as a situational framework or a point of departure for the action or state described by the second main clause. Sometimes this situational framework has itself a causal relationship to the action or state but often there is no such relationship. Subsection 2.3 deals with situational frameworks which are noncausal, while subsection 2.4 deals with those that are causal.

In subsection 2.3 notice that the main verb in the second clause describes an action but that action is always a motion. No examples in which the action is not a motion have been found in the data. I have categorised the relationship between the constituent clauses in exs 13 and 14 as being non causal because there is no sense in which one can say that the action described by the second main clause is derived from or arises from the situation of the framework.

(13) *1.* xne^{3}hĩ^{1}nait^{3}ta^2 i^{3}hi^2-xwã^1-te^{3}nait^{1}ti^{2}tu^{3}wa^2
at.that.time escape-come.2p-past.deductive.collective

2. jut^{3}su^2 xĩ^{3}xĩ^2-ki̱^{3}-tait^{1}ti^{2}tu^{3}wa^2
SITUATION go.back-1p.inc-past.observation.collective.

Free translation: '*1.* At that time, you escaped and came to me. *2.* In that SITUATION, we went back home'.

The first clause expresses an enabling or necessary condition for the action of the second, but it is not a cause. In other words,'because of that we went back home' would not be an appropriate translation of the second clause.

(14) *1.* yen^{3}ki^{3}la^3 yũ^3-sa^2-xna^3-wa^2 xne^3-ai^1-na^1-hẽ^3-ra^2
goods have-1pO-neg-incom.=asp thus-3pO-1pS-past-comp=asp

2. xne^{3}jut^{3}su^2 yah^{3}lai^{2}na^2 pa^{3}rẽn^{2}jah^{3}lai^{2}na^2
SITUATION this.old.man Parente (man's name)

xwã^3-nhyain^1-to^3-nha^2-hẽ^3-ra^2
come-he.to.him-again-past-past-comp=asp.

Free translation: '*1.* I told them that I didn't have any goods. *2.* In that SITUATION, this old man called Parente arrived'.

(The old man arrived in a situation where the speaker had just told the people that he didn't have any goods, but his telling them that could not have been said to have caused the old man's arrival.)

2.4 *XNE^{3}JUT^{3}SU^2* AS A CAUSAL CONNECTIVE. When *xne^{3}jut^{3}su^2* is used as a causal connective, it joins pairs of clauses with a causal relationship between them. As a general cover description, we might say that the two clauses are in a circumstance⁀reaction relationship. A more fine grained description that covers all the data examined is:

adverse state⁀plan or intention of ameliorating action

adverse situation⁀adverse emotional state

favorable situation⁀favorable emotional state

difficulty in carrying out a plan⁀abandoning the plan with or without an adverse emotional state

In the above pairings, the term before the link is a pragmatic description of the content of the first clause while the term after describes the second clause. In each pair the situation of the second clause can be regarded as derived from or arising from that of the first, and thus according to the definition adopted in the introduction there is a causal relationship between the two situations.

The following examples illustrate these combinations. In the free translations of each, I have translated the *xne³jut³su²* as 'because of this'. In exs. 15 and 16, an adverse state gives rise to a plan or intention to do something that ameliorates that state.

(15) *1.* kxã³na³ha²ta²   to³nĩin²ku³   te²si³lxi³kj³ten¹tu³
       tomorrow   Sunday   it.appears.to.us.all

   2. yain³ti³ txa²-sa³-ha²kxai³   *3.* he³-sa³nha¹
       food   lack-me-therefore   hungry-me-internal

   4. xne³jut³su²   xai³-te²sĩ³lxi³-sa³-nha²wa²
       SITUATION   hunt-apparently-me-internal

Free translation: '*1.* Tomorrow is Sunday apparently. *2.* I am lacking food, so *3.* I am hungry. *4.* BECAUSE OF THIS I'm thinking of going hunting'.

(The situation of his hunger is causing him to think of going hunting.)

(16) *1.* yain³ti³ txa²-san³-su² *2.* xne³jut³su²   sxi²hye³nai²na²
       food   lack-me-nom   SITUATION   this.village

       ã³xnai³li² hxai²na¹kait³jã¹-na¹-tũ¹xã¹   na¹-hẽ²ra²
       walk   as.formerly-I-intend   I-internal

Free translation: '*1.* I am lacking food. *2.* BECAUSE OF THIS I intend to walk to the (other) village (where there might be food) as formerly'.

(Lack of food caused him to intend to visit the other village.)

In the next example, an adverse situation gives rise to an adverse emotional state.

(17) *1.* ro³to²fo³-ah³lo²su²   wa²lit¹ta³la³ kãi³-kxi²-sa²-to³-hin²ta²i¹
       Rodolfo(man's name) rubber   steal-from-me again-deductive

   2. jut³su²   an³tj³-sa³-nha¹i¹
       SITUATION angry -me -internal

Free translation: '*1.* Rodolfo must have been stealing my rubber. *2.* BECAUSE OF THIS, I am angry'.

Ex. 18 shows a favorable situation giving rise to a favorable emotional state.

(18) *1.* ka³li³-ki²lã²-khai¹-xnain¹-nĩn²ta²wa² *2.* xne³jut³su²
       happy-seems-very-they-deductive   SITUATION
       wi¹lon³kxi²-khai¹-xsa³-nha²wa²
       content-very-me-internal

Free translation: '*1.* They seem to be very happy. *2.* BECAUSE OF THIS I am very content'.

Finally, in ex. 19, difficulty in carrying out a plan leads to abandonment of the plan. (Note that this category overlaps with the corresponding category in *ha²kxai³*, ex 31.)

(19) Context: The speaker had been asked to thatch someone's house but the owner had insisted that a good kind of thatch be used, whereas the speaker had wanted to use an inferior kind and get the job done quickly.

    1. hãi¹xã²na¹-sa¹-hin¹-kxe³la³   *2.* he³la³nxãn³nxa²

    allow-me-you-if   buriti.leaves

    to³-na¹-tũ³xã¹   *3.* xyãn¹ta¹ sa¹-hxan³-tait¹ti²nhe³

    thatch-I-intend   but   me-you.neg-past.coll.verif

    4. xne³jut³su²   ha³lo²yut³ta³la³   ã³la³kxi²-sa²tẽ³-a¹-ti²nhe³

    SITUATION the.things   leave-continue-I-present.collective.verification.

Free Translation: '*1.* If you had allowed me to do it, *2.* I would have thatched the house with buriti leaves (the inferior kind of thatch). *3.* But as we know, you didn't let me, *4.* BECAUSE OF THIS I am just leaving things as they are'. (abandoning his plan)

In summary, this section has shown that *xne³jut³su²* sets up a situational framework which sometimes has causal properties and sometimes does not. When it does not have causal properties, what follows from the framework is an action and that action is always a motion (exs. 13, 14). When it does have causal properties, what is caused is either an emotional state, or a plan, or a decision to abandon a plan. In other words, the connective *xne³jut³su²* is associated with passive responses. The second clause does not describe an action that requires initiative, and often, as in ex. 15 to 18, it does not describe an action at all. In contrast, the responses associated with the connective *xne³ha²kxai³* are actions requiring initiative (see exs. 28 to 31 of subsection 3.6). So far I have not been able to ascertain whether the causal or noncausal nature of the *xne³jut³su²* framework is related to the kind of morphosyntactic environment, but certainly the pragmatic environment is well defined.

3. HA³KXAI³ AND CAUSALITY

Next, I deal with the suffix *-ha²kxai³* which does most of the work in signalling interclausal cause/reason relationships. Valuable insights into what this suffix is doing are found by first looking at the use of the form *-kxai³* by itself. This is found suffixed to temporal nouns, locational nouns and nouns referring to individuals.

The suffix *-ha²kxai³* itself, is always found suffixed to verbs, and verbs are never suffixed by *-kxai³* without the *-ha²* preceding it. It has been difficult to find a gloss for *-ha²* because it is always followed by *-kxai³*; the *-ha²-* never occurs word finally or followed by any morpheme other than *-kxai³*. However, in the course of this analysis, I shall propose a gloss for -*ha²*. (I should add here that no Nambiquara informant I have worked with has ever been able to give me any gloss for either -*kxai³* or -*ha²kxai³*.)

The morpheme -*ha²kxai³* is found typically in two contexts. First it is suffixed to each of a sequence of verbs describing coordinate activities (see subsection 3.4, exs. 24, 25). Second, it is found on the verb substitute -*xne³*- 'thus' and the resulting *xne³ha³kxai³* occurs between two main clauses and signals a cause/reason relationship between them (see subsection 3.6, exs 28 to 35). A rough translation of *xne³ha²kxai³* into English would be 'so.' It is clear that any serious analysis of the data will have to give an account of the similarity between the coordinate constructions and the cause/reason constructions, because -*ha²kxai³* appears in them both.

First, I give some examples of -*kxai³* suffixed to the various kinds of nouns. I deal successively in sections 3.1, 3.2, 3.3 with -*kxai³* on temporal nouns, locational nouns, and nouns referring to individuals, i.e. participants and props. Unlike -*jau³*- and -*jut³*-, -*kxai³* does not have a more 'basic' concrete meaning from which we can derive an extended meaning. Hence, to arrive at the meaning of -*kxai³* one needs to examine the words which carry this suffix in their discourse context. I shall endeavour to show in the next three sections that -*kxai³* has the following two essential properties:

(i) The identification of the referent of a -*kxai³* marked noun is always compatible with the preceding linguistic context. In some instances, this compatibility is simply a matter of anaphoric reference, while in others the referent identity can be inferred from the preceding context, even though that particular referent as such has never been mentioned before (see ex. 23).

(ii) -*kxai³* marks the noun as a framework for the next step in the story or argument. When the noun is a temporal or a locational, it becomes a time or locational framework for that next step. When the noun refers to an individual, it is the topic for the next step, often a resumptive topic.

3.1 -*KXAI³* SUFFIXED TO A TEMPORAL NOUN. Temporal nouns suffixed with -*kxai³* refer to a time that is inferrable from and thus compatible with the preceding linguistic context.

(20) Context: Two hunters have been in the forest unsuccessfully chasing an armadillo who escapes down a hole. So they decide to go back to their village and ask people to help. They said:

'Let's go home and talk to the people in the village and ask them to help us kill the armadillo. We have seen his footprints. When he's thirsty, he'll come out.' Having said that, we left the village. Then we spotted him.

na²ha¹te¹   kãx³na³ti³-kxai³lu²

change.of.direction night-COMPATIBLE

xu³-ka¹sain¹-na²-hẽ³-ra²

dig-we & they-ind=verif-past-comp=asp

Free translation: 'During that very night THEREFORE, we dug with them (for the armadillo)'.

(following context: But we dug and dug, finally we got to his tail, and he went off and we dug and dug in the middle and at dawn, we killed him.)

The *kxã³na³ti³kxai³lu²* has been glossed 'that very night therefore'. It is the night which is inferrable from the context, which is compatible with the context. Moreover, the story tells us that the hunters had been chasing the armadillo for several days, and that that night was the turning point in the chase; it was, in fact, then that they cornered him and finally killed him. Thus the -*kxai³* on the night marks it as the point when the story definitely moved forward.

3.2 *KXAI³* SUFFIXED TO A LOCATIONAL NOUN. Similarly, locational nouns suffixed with -*kxai³* refer to a location inferrable from and thus compatible with the preceding linguistic context.

(21) Context: A man is discussing his plans for working in his slash and burn fields. He has told of the land he has already cleared and what he has planted and plans to plant there. He now goes on to tell of what he plans to do with the land that is still overgrown with brush and not yet cleared.

1. ha³lo²a² au³-tãu³-ai²na²su²   *2.* ya³la³na² tẽ³-nũ²la²

land   overgrown-location-this   scythe   take-seq

ĩ³wait³-sxã³ ĩ³tãu³-a¹-kait³jã¹-xna¹-tũ¹xã¹

hit-seq   cut-I-of old-I-intend

na¹-hẽ²ra² *3.* na¹-jut³ta²sa²-kxai³lu²   te²yã¹xne²

I-intend   my-place-COMPATIBLE   as.before

ĩ³ya³nat³-sxã³ ĩ³ya²lut¹-ta³na¹   na¹-ka³tu³

dry.out-seq   die-pres.internal I -seq

4. te²yã¹xne² sa²li¹-na¹-kxa²yã¹-xna¹-tũ¹xã¹ na¹-hẽ²ra²

as.before   hoe-I-as.usual-I-intend   I-internal

Free translation: '*1.*The place which is overgrown, *2.*I plan to cut down with a scythe like I used to. *3.*My place THEREFORE, when it dries out and (the vegetation) dies as usual, *4.*I plan to hoe it like I've done before'.

The speaker here has decided to work the overgrown part of his fields in two steps. The first step, described in clauses 1 and 2, consists in cutting down the underbrush with a scythe. Then, when the underbrush has fully dried out, he will clear the weeds with a hoe. The *-kxai³* marked locational noun *na¹jut³ta²sa²kxai³lu²* 'my place THEREFORE' that begins clause 3, refers to the land that he will have been working on. It marks the end of the first step and is the locational framework for describing the second and final step of his program.

3.3 *-KXAI³* ON NOUNS REFERRING TO INDIVIDUALS. Nouns suffixed with *-kxai³* refer to either participants or props and these become topical at the point of the text where the marked noun is found. The identification of the referent of the marked noun can be inferred from the preceding linguistic context.

(22) Context: The speaker is a young Nambiquara talking to two foreign linguists who have been living in his village but who are about to leave on a long journey and want to know that he will not also leave but stay behind in the village to look after things. He reassures them by saying:

1. na¹-jut³su²   dxai²nãn²tu³ ã³xnai³-lha²-xnã³-nha¹
my-situation I   walk-me-negative-internal

2. na¹-kxai²nãn²tu³   xĩ³-ya³hin¹-kxai²nãn²tu³
I-if   go-you.two-if

hxi²kau³kau³-nha²-sxã³ xai³-la³-txa³hẽ²
confused-reflexive-seq walk-dual-prohibitive

3. xĩ³-ya³hin¹-tãu³la³ ya³hin¹-xna²ha¹te¹
go-you.two-when you.two-change.topic

dxai²na²sa²-kxai³lu² hãi¹-sxã³ sxa³-na¹tũ¹
I-COMPATIBLE   only-seq stay-intend

4. ãn³six³ken³ti³-sxã³ xai³-lha²-lhun¹-nũn³-nha¹
branch.off-manner walk-me-desire-also-internal

5. xyãn¹ta¹ xai³-lha³-xnãn³-nha¹
but   walk-me-negative-internal

Free translation: '*1.* My situation (is that) I will not go. *2.* If I am like that, and you two go, then don't be all worried as you go. *3.* When you go (change topic),I THEREFORE will do nothing but stay. *4.* I want to go off on a journey in another direction, *5.* but I will not go'.

Note that in sentence 22.2, the speaker talks about his hearers, telling them that when they go away they shouldn't be all worried. In sentence *3*, however, there is first a topic changing signal *ya³hin¹xna²ha¹te¹* 'you.two-topic change' followed immediately by *dxai²na²sa²KXAI³LU²* 'I-then'. This *-kxai³* marked pronoun is thus a resumptive topic, it serves to reintroduce the speaker (already introduced in the first sentence); the next step in his argument is a report of what he intends to do.

(23) *1.* yã²na¹la² ha¹li¹ a³-nain¹te³nait¹ti²tu³wa²

    jaguar   two   shoot-they-deductive.past.coll.verification

  2. ãu³-ain¹-kxe³su² yo³li²-hxat³-tain¹-tait¹ti²tu³wa²

    hungry-they-rel divide.up-all-they-observe.past.coll.verif.

  3. xyãn¹ta¹ dxai²li² ĩ²-a¹-ha²kxai³

    but   I   eat-I-CONSEQUENTLY

    ĩ³ton³-sa³-hẽ²ra² *4.* xne³-sxã³ o²-nha²-sxã³

    sick-me-past   thus-seq scare-refl-seq

    ã²wãn³-kxe³-kxai³   ũ³-ai¹-na¹-ha²kxai³

    remain-rel-COMPAT give-them-I-CONSEQUENTLY

  5. wa³ya³lxa² yait¹-thxat³-tain¹-na²hẽ³ra²

    dog   eat-all-they-past.ind.verification

Free translation: '*1.* They shot two jaguars, *2.* being hungry, they divided all (the meat) up. *3.* But, I, I ate some and I got sick. *4.* So I got scared, and WHAT WAS LEFT OVER CONSEQUENTLY (of the meat) I gave to them, *5.* and the dogs ate it all up'.

Here the *-kxai³* 'COMPATIBLE' in *ã³wãn³KXE³KXAI³* 'what was left over CONSEQUENTLY (or compatibly) of the meat' marks its referent as compatible with, that is to say inferrable from, the previous context. The *-kxai³* also marks this referent as the topic (here a prop) that is under attention, and consideration of which is the next step (in fact the final step, here) in the story.

It should be carefully noted that although the *-kxai³* marked nominal is compatible with the preceding context in the senses explained above, the *-kxai³* does not JUST mark anaphoric reference, rather the marked item becomes topical as well. When a Nambiquara speaker wishes to mark anaphoric reference and nothing more, he merely uses a proform that is either zero or a noun classifier corresponding to the class of the noun being substituted for.

In the last three subsections, I have dealt with all the usages of *-kxai³* on nouns. Now I pass on to consider *-ha²kxai³* which is suffixed to verbs.

3.4 *-HA²KXAI³* IN CLAUSE COORDINATION. First, I give some essential details of the morphosyntax. In the constructions dealt with in this subsection, each coordinate clause has its non-verbal constituents, such as subject, object, etc. which are followed by the verbal constituent consisting of a verb stem, a person suffix, and the suffix *-ha²kxai³*, in that order. The verbs in the coordinate clauses are not separately suffixed for tense, aspect, orientation and verification as a normal finite verb in Nambiquara would be; however, the whole construction is terminated by a finite verb suffix string expressing the four inflexional categories above, but with a zero lexical verb head. In both the examples about to be presented, this finite suffix string is *na¹tū¹xã¹ na¹hẽ²ra²*.

In the constructions of this subsection, the gloss 'compatible' for -*kxai³* is still valid, subject to conditions which will be discussed after the examples have been presented.

(24) Context: the speaker is talking about his plans for hoeing and planting his garden.

1. hã³nãu³kxa² ĩ³li¹-na¹-jut³tan²tu³   *2.* wa³li³fa³ri²
separately hoe-I-where   flour.manioc

su³-ai²nãn²ta³ ĩ³-a¹-ha²kxai³,   *3.* hã³nãu³kxa²
shoots-these plant-I-COMPAT   separately

ĩ³li¹-nũn³-na¹-jut³tan²tu³ *4.* wa̱³ya³ka̱³la²su³ai²nãn²ta³
hoe-also-I-where   sweet.manioc.shoots

ĩ³-a¹-ha²kxai³   *5.* jut¹tai²na² a²li¹-na¹-jut³tai²nãn²tu³
plant-I-COMPAT   right.here hoe-I-where

6. wa³lin³sa³te̱³ta²su³ai²nan²ta³ ĩ³-a¹-ha²-kxai³
yellow.manioc.shoots   plant-I-COMPAT

7. na¹-tũ¹xã¹ na¹-hẽ²ra²
I-intend   I-internal

Free translation: '*1.* In one place where I hoed, *2.* I'll plant shoots of manioc for flour, *3.* Separately in another place where I also hoed, *4.* I'll plant sweet manioc, *5.* **and** right here where I hoed, *6.* I'll plant yellow manioc, *7.* that's what I intend to do'.

Here the three plantings of different kinds of manioc in three different plots in the garden are activities that are commonly accepted as good practice among the Nambiquara. In this sense, the activities are compatible with each other in Nambiquara culture, and the clauses that describe these activities are parallel and coordinate. Note that there is no time sequence implied between the three coordinate activities, and this is generally true in this kind of coordination.

(25) *1.* na¹-kxai²nãn²txu̱³ ne³kax³kax³tũ²la²
I-if   at.midday

ã³nã̄¹a¹ka³txu̱³ *2.* ho³xi²-na¹-ha²kxai³   *3.* tu³ha²
leave-I-sequence bathe-I-COMPATIBLE   red.grease.paint

wã²hũ²kxi²-nha¹-ha²kxai³   *4.* na¹-tũ¹xã¹ na¹-hẽ²ra²
redden-myself-COMPATIBLE   I-intend   I-internal

Free translation: '*1.* As for me, I'll leave at midday, *2.* and I'll take a bath *3.* and I'll redden myself with grease paint. *4.* That's what I'm intending to do'.

Taking a bath and reddening oneself with grease paint are regarded as coordinate activities. In fact, a Nambiquara who has taken a bath normally rubs himself with the red grease paint from the Urucum plant to strengthen himself against the evil sprits. The two coordinate activities here happen to be in time sequence as well, but the time sequence is not essential to this kind of coodination.

Looking at the examples in the present subsection 3.4 where the -*kxai³* is always preceded by -*ha²*, and comparing them with the examples in subsections 3.1 to 3.3 where the -*kxai³* is never so preceded, it is possible to advance a hypothesis for the meaning of -*ha²*. Taking the gloss for -*kxai³* as 'compatible', we see that the times, locations, and individuals referred to by the -*kxai³* marked nominals of those subsections have identifications which are compatible with the preceding linguistic context, or inferrable from that context alone. In contrast, the coordination examples of the present subsection do show compatiblity between the coordinate activities marked by -*ha²kxai³* (within each example) but that compatibility can be seen only if we invoke extralinguistic criteria. Specifically, here we need cultural criteria, i.e, what things do the Nambiquara plant in adjacent garden plots? It is not possible to see any compatibility by looking merely at the preceding linguistic context. Therefore, I propose the gloss of -*ha²*- to be 'extralinguistically evoked' and it follows that -*ha²kxai³* will be glossed 'extralinguistically compatible', that is to say that the compatibililty will be seen by invoking non-linguistic, i.e.cultural, criteria. And finally, in the coordinate clause construction using -*ha²kxai³* as illustrated in exs. 24 and 25 of this subsection, the activities marked by -*ha²kxai³* are extralinguistically compatible but with no necessary time sequence between them.

3.5 *NA¹HA²KXAI³* IN PARAGRAPH COORDINATION. In the last subsection, 3.4, examples were given of the use of -*ha²kxai³* in clause coordination. In the present, I consider the use of *na¹*-*ha²kxai³* 'I-extralinguistically compatible' in what I call paragraph coordination, in which both the antecedent and the consequent of the connective are sequences of clauses. All such coordinated paragraphs have the following characteristics: the first sequence of clauses before the connective gives one description of a situation, while the second sequence of clauses after the connective give another description of the SAME situation. The two descriptions have the same space-time framework and the same participants, but the attention is on two different sets of events.

I give two examples. In these I have given just the English translation and omitted the vernacular, as the morphological details are not germane to the discussion at this level.

(26) Today I worked in the garden. But the rain drenched me and I came home.

   na¹-ha²kxai³ 'I-extralinguistically compatible'

   I transplanted a few papaya plants into the sugarcane patch.

Here the two sequences of clauses separated by *na¹ha²kxai³* describe two sets of events which cover the same time span and occur in the same situation. The second run through is a replay of the first but with a different focus.

(27) Today I planted those manioc shoots you saw. But a few shoots got left and I came home. These shoots, then, I'll plant tomorrow just like I did today.

na¹-ha²kxai³ 'I extralinguistically compatible'

The patch that I hoed and cleaned is getting filled up nicely (with plants). So being short of water, I was thirsty. I couldn't drink the water (from the stream) as it was too far away. So I drank up all the water (that was in my gourd) and came home.

Here the clauses before the connective talk about his planting, while those after talk about his struggles with thirst. Both clause sequences cover the same time span and the same situation. Both end up reporting that he left and came home.

Again the gloss of *-ha²kxai³* as 'extralinguistically compatible' is confirmed. The two clause sequences, one before and one after the connective, are compatible in that they describe the same situation but one needs to go outside the text and into the real world in order to see this compatibility.

3.6 *XNE³HA²KXAI³* EXPRESSING CAUSE/REASON RELATIONSHIPS BETWEEN TWO MAIN CLAUSES. First, I give the essential details of the morphosyntax of these constructions. There are two main clauses, each having its own finite verb with full suffixation for tense, aspect, orientation and verification. Between these clauses is the connective *xne³-ha²kxai³* 'thus-extralinguistically compatible'. The *xne³-*, glossed as 'thus', is a substitute verb which can be replaced by the verb stem of the first clause without essential change of meaning (but with a change of information focus); in fact, occasionally speakers will indeed make such a replacement in speech.

The main aim of this subsection is to examine a representative set from the corpus of clause pairs connected by *xne³ha²kxai³*. These data will test whether the gloss I have proposed for *xne³ha²kxai³* is an insightful one or not, and thence give some idea of what causality as signalled by this connective means. The clause pairs in the data fall into the following three broad pragmatic categories:

problem⁻response,

circumstance⁻conclusion,

reason⁻assertion,

where in the above descriptions, the word before the link is a pragmatic characterization of the content of the first clause, and the word after of the second clause[4].

In the problem⁻response clause pair, the first clause reports a problem and the second reports a participant's response to that problem. Similarly, in the circumstance⁻conclusion pair, the second clause reports a conclusion which has been arrived at by observing the circumstance reported in the first clause. Finally in the reason⁻assertion pair, the second clause is an assertion and the first clause is a reason or justification for that assertion. Further subcategories of these types will be given when the examples are presented.

It will be noticed that in the first two pair types, the second clause (response or conclusion) describes the way the participant reacts or responds to the phenomenon that the first clause describes (problem or circumstance). In this sense, the phenomenon of the second clause can be regarded as derived from that of the first, thus satisfying the working definition of cause-effect given in the introduction.

The first, and by far most numerous, of the above types is the problem⁻response. There are various kinds of problems that can be described by the first clause, and the response will depend on the kind of problem that has been raised.

In exs. 28 and 29, the problem is an undesirable personal state and the response is an attempt to ameliorate that state. The undesirable state motivates the response action.

(28) *1*. sa²tã³-yux³-kĩ³tot³-sa³-hẽ²ra²   2. xne³-ha²kxai³

stub-foot-sick-me-recent.int   THUS-EXT.COMPAT

hĩ³ne³ka² ĩ³ye³-kxi¹-xna²-ha¹-ten¹tu³wa²

medicine speak-to-you-I-recent.coll=verif.

Free translation: '*1*. I stubbed and hurt my foot. *2*. So I spoke to you about medicine'.

(Or more literally: 'I stubbed and hurt my foot. COMPATIBLE WITH CULTURAL EXPECTATIONS in such a situation, I spoke to you about medicine.')

(29) ãu³-sa³-hẽ²ra²   xne³-ha²kxai³

hungry-me-recent.internal   thus-EXT.COMPAT

xai³-na¹-te¹ni²tu³wa²

hunt-I-recent.coll=verification

Free translation: 'I was hungry. So I went hunting'.

(More literally: 'I was hungry. Compatible with cultural expectations in such a situation, I went hunting.')

In the above two examples, the first clause describes an undesirable personal state which is a problem, i.e. having a hurt foot and being hungry respectively. The second clause describes the speaker's response which in both cases is an attempted solution, respectively asking someone for medicine and going hunting to get some food. It should be noted that both the responses are according to expected patterns of behaviour.

In ex. 30, the problem is an adverse circumstance that has prevented a course of action. The response is a compromise course of action. The problem has caused the compromise to be adopted.

(30) Context: The speaker had gone hunting and shot a wild pig, but he brought home only a leg. Here is his explanation.

1. he^3-sa^{2}sĩn^1-ka^{2}ka^{3}ya^{3}lhu^2 ĩ^2-hxat^3-si^1-na^{1}hẽ^{3}ra^2

hungry-we-being   eat-all-we-past.indiv=verification

2. xne^3-ha^{2}kxai^3 ã^{2}nxẽ^{2}ka^{3}nũ^{1}ta^2 so^{3}lxi^3

THUS-EXT.COMP the.leg   only

wi^{1}so^1-na^{1}ra^2

bring-I.recent

Free translation: '*1.* Being hungry we ate it (the pig) all up. *2.* So I brought only the leg home'.

The first clause describes the speaker's problem. Having eaten up the whole pig, he was faced with the problem of having nothing to bring home. His response was a compromise solution, i.e. to just bring home a leg, and this again is quite common practice among the Nambiquara.

In ex. 31, the response to the problem is to abandon the original plan.

(31) Context: a hunter is chasing an armadillo who has hidden himself down a hole. Thus:

1. sa^{3}nãi^{3}a^2 sxa^3-na^2-hẽ^{3}ra^2 *2.* te^{2}a^2 o^{2}la^{3}kxi^2-na^1-ta^1

armadillo stay-3p-past   this work.at-I-but

3. a^{2}ẽn^{1}su^2 a^{3}li^{3}kxi^2-xna^3-hẽ^{2}ra^2 *4.* xne^3-ha^{2}kxai^3

hole   come.out-neg-past   thus-EXT.COMP

ã^3-sxã^3 xĩ^3-ye^1-xna^2-ha^1-ra^2

leave-sequence come.home-to-you-I-comp=aspect

Free translation: '*1.* The armadillo stayed (down the hole). *2.* I worked at (getting him out) but *3.* he didn't come out. *4.* So I left and came home to you'.

The problem was that the armadillo would not come out of the hole, despite the hunter's efforts. His response was to abandon the hunt, regarding it as hopeless. Again, the Nambiquara do this quite often.

It is important to note that although there is time sequence between the situations reported by the first and second clauses when such clauses are separated by the connective *xne³ha²kxai³*, time sequence as such is not in focus. In many instances when this kind of construction is used, the second situation does not have to take place immediately after the first—specifically, in both the last two examples there was a considerable time lag between the antecedent and consequent situations. What the connective really expresses is compatibility with cultural expectation rather than time sequence. Thus in each of exs. 28 to 31, the response described by the second clause is a culturally expected one. This response can be seen as derived from or arising from the problem situation, given the cultural expectations.

In a narration of a number of events in time sequence, a different connective *-ka³tu³* is used. Thus for example:

(32) ĩ³ha²no¹-na¹-ka³tu³   a³-na¹-hẽ³ra²

approach-I-time=sequence shoot-I-past

Free translation: 'I approached (the wild pig), and I shot it'.

Here, the two events, 'approach' and 'shoot' are in rapid immediate time sequence, but there is no sense in which the first is the cause of the second.

In the circumstance‾conclusion type of clause pair, the first clause reports a set of circumstances and the second reports the participant's reaction to these circumstances. This reaction is in the form of a thought with propositional content; I have called it a conclusion. Sometimes, as in ex. 33, the conclusion leads to an overt action. However, it does not always do so, as ex. 34 shows.

(33) *1*. ha³lo²ai²li²   wẽ³-hai²li²   xwãn³-yu²ra²
weather.this rain-this   come-evidence

2. xne³-ha²kxai   a³lxi³tat³-sa²-te³-lin²nha¹
THUS-EXT.COMP. soak-me-immediate-deduction

na¹-jau³sxu² *3*. ã³-sxã³   xĩ³xĩ²-na¹ra²
my-thought   leave-sequence come.home-I-comp=asp

Free translation: '*1*. About the weather, I saw signs that rain was coming. *2*. So I thought to myself, "I'm going to get soaked," *3*. So thinking, I abandoned things and came home'.

The first clause describes circumstances (approaching black clouds) that were evidence that rain was likely to come. The second clause describes the inference or conclusion that the speaker reached, that he was about to get soaked. Any good Nambiquara seing approaching black clouds would, from his knowledge of his world, conclude that he was about to be soaked. Thus his conclusion is compatible with patterns of cultural expectation. In this sense, the conclusion is derivable from the circumstances and thus satisfies the cause-effect definition.

(34) *1.* xyãn¹ta¹ dxai²na¹xai²na² wa³lin³ta³ yũ³-sa²-xna³wa²

     but   I   manioc   have-me-neg

  2. xne³-ha²kxai³   wa³li³xna²   a³-ain¹te²a² *3.* nũt³-sxã³

    THUS-EXT.COMP manioc   grate-those   share-seq

    wi¹so¹-ya³sain¹-hi³xn²-na³na¹   na¹-hẽ²ra²

    gather-3p.with.1p-should-thought I-internal

Free translation: '*1.* But I have no manioc. *2.* So I am thinking that those who are grating manioc, *3.* would share and I could gather some from them'.

Here the circumstance that the speaker has no manioc gives rise to his thought that others who were grating some would share with him. His thought that others would share with him is in fact very much according to patterns of expectation in Nambiquara, because in that culture those who have are obliged to share with those who do not. In this sense his conclusion is indeed derivable from the circumstances and the cause-effect definition is satisfied. However, this example would not seem to show a cause and effect relationship from a Western scientific standpoint. Using a unitary gloss and looking at the culture has clearly given a more insightful solution in this case.

Finally there is the reason‾assertion type of clause pair. In this, the second constituent is an assertion and the first constituent is the speaker's reason or justification for his assertion.

(35) Context: An Indian chief is involved in a dispute as to who has the right to live on his land. He says:

  1. kxã³nãu³u¹tai²na² a²nũ²a² so³lxi³

    long.ago   Indians only

    xyau³-ta³kox³-sin²ta²wa² *2.* hai³ti³   kat³ja³la²

    live-land-deductive   negative white.man

    kxã³nãu³u¹tai²na² yũ³-txi³he²-xne³ta³-ko³-sxa³wa²

    long.ago   exist-never-relation-land-neg

  3. xne³ha²kxa³   a²nũ²a² so¹lxi³ xyau³-ta³kox³ ai²la¹wa²

    thus.EXT.COMP Indians only   live-land   it.is

Free translation: '*1.* A long time ago, our land was where only Indians lived. *2.* There were absolutely no white men around a long time ago. *3.* Therefore it is now land only for Indians to live on'.

This example illustrates reason rather than cause-effect. What the speaker asserts in the third clause is that the land he is living on is Indian land only (and that white men should keep off it.) The reason he gives to support or justify his assertion is that historically, only Indians used to live there. But note again that it is a culturally oriented reason.

The three pragmatic pairings of problem ⌐ response, circumstance ⌐ conclusion and reason⌐assertion do correspond to pairings that an English speaker would think of as showing a cause/reason type of interclausal relationship. We can get further insights, however, by looking more carefully at the relationships within the language. The $xne^3ha^2kxai^3$, having a (substitute) verb stem but no finite verb suffixation, is best regarded as a reduced kind of subordinate clause whose accompanying main clause is in fact the immediately following clause. In addition, the -$kxai^3$, marks the situation referred to by the xne^3- as a framework for what follows (in the same way that the -$kxai^3$ marking the nouns of subsections 3.1 to 3.3 made them frameworks for what followed).

Moreover, the -ha^2- ensures that this framework situation is culturally compatible with the situation described by the clause that follows, (compatibility with what precedes being trivially assured by the substitute verb xne^3-). This relationship between the framework and the following clause is both culturally compatible and sequential, and it remains to discuss the nature of the sequentiality. A sequence in time is not always involved, and is never at issue even when it is involved. Thus in the reason⌐assertion relationship, time sequence is completely absent (see ex. 35). And in the problem⌐response and circumstance⌐conclusion relationships, the situation of the first constituent certainly precedes that of the second but there can be a long time interval between the two situations.

The issue becomes clearer, however, if we look again at what cultural compatibility means for this kind of construction. Given a $xne^3ha^2kxai^3$ and the framework or antecedent situation that it sets up, there are certain culturally acceptable ways of following on from there. Specifically, given a certain problem, there is a set of culturally expected responses to it; given a set of circumstances, there is a set of culturally expected conclusions you can draw from it, etc. Similarly, having made a statement, a speaker can use that statement as a reason to support a following assertion provided the reason and the assertion are related according to the culturally accepted patterns of inference. So there is relation of cultural expectation between the first and second situation in each case, and this is what is meant by the kind of causality that $xne^3ha^2kxai^3$ marks in Nambiquara.

Actually this definition of cause-reason isn't as far fetched or as weak as might first appear. In English, for instance, we associate cause largely with cause and effect relationships, and, in fact, given a cause there is a high expectation that the effect will follow; that expectation is grounded on scientific beliefs which are, of course, culturally conditioned. But even in English, there are also expectations based on more general cultural norms. Similarly, a reason is regarded as a good reason if it is according to the socially accepted patterns of reasoning or inference—otherwise it is a poor reason or an excuse.

The Nambiquara data show expectations based on their cultural norms but with virtually no bias towards scientific beliefs. Similarly, good reasons and justifications are based on cultural values and cultural patterns of inference. It is poignantly true in the context of example 35 that while the Indian chief felt that the Indians had a right to live on their land because historically they had always done so, the white man who was disputing his claim at this point did not accept his reason as valid at all.

Thus the description of the function of $xne^3ha^2kxai^3$ in terms of cultural compatibility is more consistent with the data and thus more likely to be a faithful description of native reaction. However, if we want terms that we are more familiar with, we can consider the connective to mean 'cause' in the problem⌐response and circumstance⌐conclusion pairs, and 'reason' in the reason⌐assertion pairs, provided that we recognize the limitations of such a characterisation.

3.7 A STOCKTAKE. Let us now draw together the conclusions of the various subsections of section 3, and see how the suffixes $-kxai^3$ and $-ha^2kxai^3$ relate to each other in their various usages, and how this builds up for us a picture of this aspect of causality in Nambiquara.

When $-kxai^3$ is suffixed to a noun we know two things. First, the identification of the referent of that noun is compatible with the preceding linguistic context. Second, the noun so marked is a temporal, locational or individual framework for a sequence of predications that follow it; together the framework and the associated sequence form the next step in the story or argument.

When $-ha^2kxai^3$ is used in clause coordination the various actions described by $-ha^2kxai^3$ marked verbs are compatible with each other, but that compatibility is determined by cultural, i.e. extralinguistic, criteria rather than from the preceding linguistic context. The compatibility holds between all the marked verbs within the linguistic unit bounded by the finite verb suffix strings (which in exs. 24 and 25 are both $na^1tu\bar{u}^1x\bar{a}^1 na^1h\bar{e}^2ra^2$).

When the connective $xne^3ha^2kxai^3$ occurs between two main clauses, the substitute verb xne^3- stands for the verb of the first clause and the whole connective functions as a subordinate clause and therefore as a framework for the second main clause that immediately follows it. There is both a relationship of cultural compatibility and one of sequentiality between the two situations described by the clauses. Putting these two relationships together, it means that there is a relation of cultural expectation between the two situations; given the first as antecedent there is a set of culturally expected consequent situations that can follow from it. Specifically, with the data that has been examined, this relation narrows down to mean 'compatible with cultural expectation' in the problem ⌐response and circumstance ⌐conclusion pairings and to mean 'compatible with accepted patterns of inference' in the reason⌐assertion pairings.

Note here that the relationships between the clauses in the -*ha²kxai³* coordinate construction, and the relationships between the first and second clauses in the *xne³ha²kxai³* cause/reason construction, are partly similar and partly different. In the coordinate construction, there is cultural compatibility between the situations described by the coordinate clauses but NO sequentiality. That is to say, it is culturally acceptable for the situations to occur together but there is no sense in which any one situation can be regarded as derived from any of the others. In the cause/reason construction, on the other hand, there is both cultural compatibility AND sequentiality, and the two together lead to the relationship of cultural expectation between the first and second clauses of this construction; once the situation described by the first clause is realised, there is an expectation that the situation of the second clause will realised as well. Because of the sequentiality, the relationship between the clauses of the *xne³ha²kxai³* construction is an assymetric one, whereas the relationship between the clauses of the coordinate construction is symmetric. Finally, in the *xne³ha²kxai³* or cause/reason construction, the relationship of cultural expectation gives us the derivative component of the relationship between cause and effect that the original definition in the introduction requires.

Thus the conclusion is that the relationship of compatability is signalled whenever the morpheme -*kxai³* is present. As a subset of all compatability relationships, whenever the morpheme sequence -*ha²kxai³* is present, there is extralinguistic or cultural compatibility. Further, as yet a subset of the -*ha²kxai³* relationships, there are the *xne³ha²kxai³* relationships in which sequentiality as well as cultural compatibility is involved and these are the relationships which satisfy the definition of cause.

4. KXE³SU² AND CAUSALITY

The last morpheme that I will deal with that figures in cause/reason relationships between clauses is the verb suffix -*kxe³*-. This relativizes the object of a transitive verb and the subject of an intransitive verb, as illustrated in exs. 36 to 38.

(36) tu²ta³la²   su²-la¹-kxe³-su²
     armadillo kill-I-relativizer-gen=noun

     'The armadillo which I killed'

(37) a³hũ³lyau³-xai²li²   xu²-kxe³-su²
     water-this   far-rel-gen=noun

     'The water which was far away'

Sometimes the relative clause is headless, as in ex 38:

(38) a³hũ³ne³ka²   hãu¹-ye²-kxe³-su²   an³-to³-nha²i¹
     headwaters   bathe-at-rel-gen=noun shoot-repeat-internal

     'He shot again at what was bathing at the headwaters'.

The -kxe³su² relative clause, like relative clauses in English and some other languages, can have either a restrictive (i.e., identificational) or a non-restrictive (i.e., attributive function). Thus, examining the preceding context in the story of ex. 38 confirms that the relative there does have an identificational function; the animal that was shot at had never been previously mentioned in the story. And in this example, there is no causal relationship between the content of the relative clause and that of the main clause.

However, the majority of -kxe³sxu² relativizations have a NON-restrictive function; in all such cases that have been examined, the content of the relative clause has a cause-effect relation of the problem⁻response kind to the content of the main clause. Exs. 39 to 42 illustrate this. In ex. 39 I present data to show that if both the cause and effect had been encoded in main clauses, the connective xne³ha²kxai³ would have come interclausally.

(39) *1.* yã²na¹la² ha¹li¹ a³-nain¹-te³nait¹ti²tu³wa²

jaguar   two   shoot-they-collective.deduct.past

2. ã²xne³te³nait¹ta²   ãu³-ain¹-kxe³su²

these   hungry-they-rel

ĩ²-hxat³-tain¹-tait¹ti²tu³wa²

eat-finish-they-collect.past.obs

Literal translation: '*1.* They killed two jaguars. *2.* These (jaguars), they who were hungry ate them right up'.

However, there is a causal relationship between the people being hungry and their eating up the jaguars. A free translation might run: 'They killed two jaguars. Because they were hungry, they ate them right up'.

Note that the 'they' of the relative clause is coreferential with the subject of the verb 'shoot' of the first clause, and so has already been identified. Thus the relative has a non-restrictive function.

It is also possible in Nambiquara to describe the part of the above situation that involves the causal relation in the following way:

ãu³-ain¹-na²hẽ³ra²   xne³ha²kxai³   i²hxat³tain¹tait¹ti²tu³wa²
hungry-they-indiv.   THUS.EXT.COMP   they.ate.them.right.up

'They were hungry. So they ate them right up'.

Thus, pragmatically, there is a cause and effect relationship between the hunger and the eating up which could be expressed with xne³ha²kxai³ if main clauses were used to encode both cause and effect. The same applies to all the examples of this subsection. Note, however, that a restatement in the form of two main clauses results in a radical redistribution of information.

(40) Context: the speaker was sound asleep, and suddenly there was a loud noise above.

    1. xne^{3}ha^{2}kxai^3 ãu^{3}xi^2-sa^2-kxe^{3}su^2 *2.* ain^{3}kxi^2-sxã^3

    and.so   sleepy-me-rel   hear-seq

    3. ã^3-ain^1-sxa^3 *4.* ĩ^{3}yãu^{3}xi^2-xi^2-na^1-hẽ^3-ra^2

    leave-them-seq   fall.asleep-again-I-past-comp=asp

Literal translation: '*1.* And so, I who was sleepy, *2.* heard (the noise) *3.* ignored them and *4.* went back to sleep again'.

But a free translation could run: 'And so, because I was sleepy I heard (the noise), ignored them and went back to sleep again'.

(41) *1.* a̱^{3}li^3-sa^2-kxe^{3}su^2 kax^{3}tax^{3}tax^3-sa^2-kxe^{3}su^2

    cold-me-rel   shivering-me-rel

    2. hai^{3}tı̱^{3} ĩ^{3}yĩ^1-te^{2}sĩ^{3}lxi^2-xna^{3}i^1

    negative firmly-appears-neg.I

Literal translation: '*1.* I, who am cold and shivering, *2.* am apparently not able to say anything clearly (firmly)'.

A free translation might go: 'Because of my cold and shivering, it appears I am not able to say anything clearly'.

Clearly, in exs. 40, 41 the relative clause does not serve any identificational function.

(42) Context: The speaker is complaining that there are insufficient tools, i.e. hoes and scythes for him to work properly in his fields. He says:

    1. yen^{3}kxai^{2}nãn^{2}txu^3 ka^{3}lxa^2-xna^3-kxe^{3}su^2

    tools   many-neg-rel

    2. hxi^{2}kan^{1}tı̱^{3} wa^{3}kon^3-tai^1-xna^3-wa^2

    able.to   work-for them-I.neg-incomp=aspect.

Literal translation: '*1.* The tools which are few, *2.* I am not able to work for them'.

A free translation could go: 'For lack of tools, I am not able to work for them'. Examination of the text shows that the tools have been identified and talked about repeatedly in the preceding linguistic context. Nor is there any question of there being any contrast between two sets of tools. So again the function of the relative is non-restrictive.

In 42 the nominal constituent *yen³kxai²nãn²tu³ ka³lxa²xna³kxe³su²* 'the tools which are not many' has a relationship of 'cause' to the verbal predicate, identical to the relationship of the first constituent 'medicine' to the verbal predicate in:

(43) hĩ³ne³ki³su² xwã³-na¹wa²

    medicine   come-I-incompl=aspect

    'I am coming because of medicine' (or more freely: 'I am coming because I want medicine.')

The conclusion of this section then, is that the content of any -*kxe³su²* marked relative clause has a causal relationship to its main clause, provided the relative is non-restrictive.

5. CONCLUSIONS

The surface devices used to express interclausal relationships of cause/reason in Nambiquara and the meanings of these relationships are as follows:

(i)   -*jau³*- in -*jau³su²* marks a mental motivation as the cause of an action,

(ii)   -*jut³*- in -*jut³su²* marks a situational framework as the cause of a mental or emotional state,

(iii)   -*kxai³* in *xne³ha²kxai³* marks an event as being in a causal relationship with another event or a proposition as being in a reason relationship with another proposition in that there is a relationship of 'compatibility of cultural expectation' between the two events or propositions.

(iv)   -*kxe³*- in -*kxe³su²* marks the content of a non-restrictive relative clause to be in the same kind of cause-effect relationship with the content of the main clause as would be signalled by *xne³ha²kxai³* if main clauses had been used to encode both situations.

First, mental motivations are easily understood. A thought or idea arising in an individual's mind motivates that individual to take on a course of action. The morphosyntax is also unambiguous. A subordinate clause encodes the motivating thought and is identified as having this function by two suffixes forming the sequence *jau³sxu²*. The main clause which follows then encodes the action which the idea motivates. The -*sxu²* 'general nominal' ending is very important. If the specific nominal ending -*xa²* replaces it, the subordinate clause no longer expresses a motivating idea but describes speech.

Second, a situational framework can at times have a causal relationsip to what follows. The essential morpheme here is -*jut³*- which has the basic meaning of 'time' or 'place' when it is suffixed with a specific noun ending *ta²*, but which can be extended to mean 'situation' when suffixed with the general noun ending -*su²* and thus set up a situational framework. When such a situational framework is non-causal, the main verb is always a motion verb. When the situational framework does have a causal relationship to the main verb, that verb reports either an emotional state or an act of abandoning a course of action. In such causal relationships, the main verb describes a passive response to the situation; it never describes an action that requires any initiative.

The main surface device for expressing a cause/reason relationship between clauses is the connective $xne^3ha^2kxai^3$. The $-kxai^3$ in this connective has the meaning of 'compatible' and is also found suffixed to nouns with temporal, locational and individual reference. Nouns so marked have referent identification compatible with the preceding linguistic context, and are the temporal, locational or individual framework for the next sequence of predications. The framework and the predications that arise from it together form the next step in the story or argument.

When $xne^3-ha^2kxai^3$ comes between two main clauses, the pair of clauses come under one of the following three pragmatic descriptions: problem ⌐ response, circumstance ⌐ conclusion, or reason ⌐ assertion. The connective then means 'compatible with cultural expectation' in problem⌐response and circumstance⌐conclusion pairs, and 'compatible with accepted patterns of inference' in reason⌐assertion pairs. Thus the overall concept in Nambiquara is one of compatibility and from this we get causality as a more restricted concept within the overall one in that cause means 'compatibility with cultural expectation', while reason means 'compatibility with accepted patterns of inference'

This description of causality in Nambiquara may look somewhat strange to someone with a Western orientation. Such an analyst is probably used to thinking of causal relationships from a scientific and essentially deterministic viewpoint. Thus Talmy 1985 has given an interesting and ingenious account of certain causal relationships in English in terms of a force dynamics model. Such a model, however, seems strongly deterministic and would need extensive reformulation before it could account for all of the Nambiquara data. To the best of my knowledge, the Nambiquara do not even have a word for 'force', and they rarely talk about physical phenomena as causing other phenomena to happen.

We are faced with a large body of data in Nambiquara and a good deal of it does not fit the Western concept of cause and effect. Typical of the data that would be distorted by such a model are exs. 34 and 35, and there is always the similarity of the marking of clause coordination (section 3.4) and the $xne^3ha^2kxai^3$ cause/reason constructions (section 3.6) which is so baffling from a Western viewpoint. However, the description which uses 'compatibility' as the overall concept, can describe clause coordination as the coordination of activities which are compatible because they commonly occur together in Nambiquara culture, and the clause/reason constructions as those situation pairs which are compatible according to cultural expectation and in which there is sequentiality. This is a simple description which fits the data.

NOTES

[1]   Nambiquara was classified by McQuown and Greenberg 1960 as in the Ge-Pano-Carib phylum. Further details of dialects are given in Price 1978. The data of this paper are from Southern Nambiquara as defined by Price. There are approximately 200 speakers of the dialect studied and they live in the villages of Serra Azul and Campos Novos in the north western part of the state of Mato Grosso, Brazil.

The present study is based on a corpus of some 2500 pages of transcribed oral Nambiquara text of various genres gathered in the course of field trips on various occasions during the years 1960-77 and representing a total time of residence of about seven years in the villages of Serra Azul, Camarare and Campos Novos. The author wishes to thank the inhabitants of these villages for their hospitality and their patience in teaching him the language. The work was made possible by contracts between the Summer Institute of Linguistics and the Museu Nacional do Rio de Janeiro and more recently between the Institute and the Fundacao Nacional do Indio.

[2]   There are times in an analysis of this kind when we find ourselves in the fuzzy area between cause and reason. Concerning this, Anscombe 1957 remarks that in cases of doubt, if an action is described as a mere response to something, then that something is a cause. However, if an action is described as a response to something that is thought upon or dwelt upon by the actor then that something is a reason.

[3]   The consonant phonemes of Nambiquara are /p/, /t/, /k/, /d/ (implosive alveolar stop), /x/ (glottal stop), /j/ (alveopalatal affricate), /n/ with six allophones: [m] syllable finally, following the nasalized vowel glide /ău/, [bm] syllable finally, following the oral vowel glide /au/, [ŋ] syllable finally, preceding a velar stop and following a nasalized vowel other than the glide /ău/, [gŋ] syllable finally, preceding a velar stop and following an oral vowel other than the glide /au/, [dn] syllable finally following an oral vowel other than /au/, [n] syllable finally following a nasalized vowel other than /au/, and always syllable initially, /r/, /l/, /s/, /h/, and semivowels /w/, /y/. The vowels are /i/, /e/, /a/, /u/, /o/, all of which except /o/ can be contrastively nasalized, as can the vowel glides /ai/ and /au/. All vowels can also be contrastively laryngealized, this being symbolised by underlining the vowel. There are three contrastive tones indicated by the superscripts [1, 2, 3.] at the end of each syllable; [1] is a downglide, [2] is an upglide, and [3] is a low level tone.

The verb morphology of Nambiquara is complex and in this note here I can give just the bare essentials of the categories of suffixation on finite verbs in order to facilitate understanding of the data to be cited.

Finite verbs are obligatorily inflected for person, tense, aspect, verification, orientation and world.

Person can be first, second or third; singular, dual or plural, with two first plural inclusives, viz first plus second, or first plus third, as well as the first dual and first plural exclusive.

Tense can be past, recent, present or future. Aspect can be complete or incomplete.

Verification has to do with whether the speaker assumes that the information he is giving in the verb is already known to the addressee, or whether he assumes that it is known only to the speaker himself. I call the former collective verification and the latter individual verification.

Orientation has to do with how the speaker obtained the information that he is reporting. I call it observational orientation when the speaker reports an action that he actually observed, deductive orientation when the speaker reports his deduction that an action must have taken place because he came across associated circumstances or actions which served as evidence, narration orientation when the speaker reports information that has been transmitted to him by word of mouth. Unfortunately, it is not the case that each of the orientations is marked by its own affix morpheme. Rather, what happens is that the two verifications and the three orientations together yield $2 \times 3 = 6$ combinations, and each such combination has its own paradigm. Thus the combination collective verification and observational orientation has its own paradigm, etc, etc.

In the actual glossing of verb forms in the examples, it is important to avoid long, unwieldy and unnecessarily repetitive glosses. Therefore, any verb form which is left unmarked for orientation will be understood to have observational orientation. Any verb form which is left unmarked for both orientation and verification will be understood to have observational orientation and individual verification.

World has to do with whether the speaker is reporting a state of affairs in the outside world external to himself, or his own mental, emotional or psychological state which is internal to himself. Thus the two values of the variable here are external and internal. However, in the actual glossing of verb forms, only the internal world forms will be explicitly marked. Any verb form that refers to an external world will be left unmarked. This is necessary to avoid excessively long, unwieldy glosses.

[4]   Hoey 1983 proposes a problem solution description for certain clause pairs in English.

REFERENCES

Anscombe, G. E. M. 1957. Intention. *Proceedings of the Aristotelian Society.* 57.321-32.

Anscombe, G. E. M. 1971. *Causality and determination.* Cambridge: CUP.

Davidson, Donald. 1963. Actions, reasons and causes. *Journal of Philosophy* 60.685-700.

Kroeker, Barbara J. 1972. Morphophonemics of Nambiquara. *Anthropological Linguistics* 14(1).19-22.

Kroeker, Menno H. 1975. Thematic linkeage in Nambiquara discourse. *The thread of discourse.* Ed. by Joseph E. Grimes, 361-8. The Hague: Mouton.

Hoey, Michael. 1983. *On the surface of discourse.* London: Allen and Unwin.

Lowe, Ivan. 1972. On the relation of formal and sememic matrices with illustrations from Nambiquara. *Foundations of Language* 8(3).360-90.

Lowe, Ivan. 1986. Topicalization in Nambiquara. *Sentence initial devices.* Ed. by Joseph E. Grimes, 131-47. Dallas: Summer Institute of Linguistics and University of Texas at Arlington.

Lowe, Margaret. 1986. Participants in Nambiquara myths and folktales. *Sentence initial devices.* Ed. by Joseph E. Grimes, 187-98. Dallas: Summer Institute of Linguistics and University of Texas at Arlington.

McQuown, Norman and Joseph Greenberg. 1960. Aboriginal languages of Latin America. *Current Anthropology* 1.431-6.

Price, P David. 1976. Southern Nambiquara phonology. *International Journal of American Linguistics* 42.338-48.

Price, P David. 1978. The Nambiquara linguistic family. *Anthropological Linguistics* 20.14-37.

Talmy, Leonard. 1985. Force dynamics in language and thought. *Papers from the Parasession on Causatives and Agentivity.* Ed. by William H. Eilfort, Paul D. Kroeber, and Karen L. Peterson, 293-337. Chicago: Chicago Linguistic Society.